TWO ANSWERS

TO

CARDINAL PERRON,

AND

OTHER MISCELLANEOUS WORKS

OF

LANCELOT ANDREWES,

SOMETIME LORD BISHOP OF WINCHESTER.

WIPF & STOCK · Eugene, Oregon

Wipf and Stock Publishers
199 W 8th Ave, Suite 3
Eugene, OR 97401

Two Answers to Cardinal Perron, and Other Miscellaneous Works
of Lancelot Andrewes
By Andrewes, Lancelot and Bliss, James
ISBN 13: 978-1-55635-047-4
Publication date 3/5/2009
Previously published by Oxford, 1854

PREFACE.

THIS volume completes the collections of Bishop Andrewes' works; and it is believed that the Edition now finished contains all that is known to have been written by him, with the exception of Latin notes on several books of Holy Scripture, apparently made for his own use. These notes are contained in five small volumes in the Library of the British Museum.[a]

As it was desired to bring together in this volume all that remained unprinted of Bishop Andrewes' English works, and, also, a full collection of memorials and notices of his life, the contents are necessarily of a very miscellaneous character.

A few remarks must be added to introduce them to the notice of the reader.

It has been considered desirable to reprint the Life of Bishop Andrewes by his amanuensis, Henry Isaacson, as being the most authentic account, and which, though meagre in itself, has formed the groundwork of all subsequent Biographies; as, *e.g.*, of that in the Biographia Britannica, which is in many parts a mere transcript of Isaacson, and of

---

[a] MS. Harl. No. 6616. Libellus in 8vo. scriptus, A.D. 1602, et continens Expositionem Evangelii S. Lucæ a cap. nono. Ab Episc. Andrewes, et propria manu descriptus, ut videtur.
6617—6619. In 8vo. Tres Tomi eadem manu scripti, in Annis 1608, 1612, et 1619.
1620. Libellus eadem manu scriptus et continens, 1. Fragmentum notarum in Psalmos, novem foliis. 2. Notas in Epistolam ad Hebræos, inceptus A.D. 1586, Apr. 10.

Mr. Teale's Life of the Bishop, published in 1840, among the Lives of several other eminent English Divines.

To this has been subjoined Sir John Harington's Memoir of the Bishop, from his " Briefe View of the State of the Church of England ; " written during the Bishop's life, though only for private use : and such Letters of the Bishop as have been discovered.

In order in some measure to supply still further the deficiencies of Isaacson's Biography, a large body of notes has been added, illustrative of his statements, and also, in many cases, furnishing additional and very interesting matter. Such notices of the Bishop, from contemporary and other authentic sources, as could not be conveniently inserted in notes, will be found arranged in the Appendices subjoined to the Life. In one of these Appendices there is given a chronological arrangement of the Bishop's Sermons, with notices of them from contemporaries; and a detailed account, as far as the Editor was able to ascertain them, of the Editions of the Sermons, whether single or collected, as well as of the Bishop's other works. These notices will, it is hoped, be found of interest to the Bibliographer, as well as to the Theologian. The other Appendices contain further notices of the Bishop in connexion with some of his most distinguished contemporaries, as Casaubon, Grotius, and Archbishop Laud. It is believed that a larger amount of information respecting Bishop Andrewes has been here brought together, than had previously been collected by any of his Biographers; though it is possible that some, already accessible, may have escaped the researches of the Editor, and that further notices may remain to be gathered from unpublished documents bearing on the history of those times.

To these are added the Bishop's Will, which is now printed at full length for the first time.

It must be borne in mind, that these Appendices must be read and compared together in order to form a full understanding of the events of the Bishop's life in their regular order.

The Bishop's writings contained in this volume are:—

I. Two Answers to Cardinal Perron, and two Speeches made in the Star-Chamber. These are reprinted from the Opuscula Posthuma, printed in 1629, of which volume they formed the concluding part. The Latin treatises which preceded them, have already been printed separately.

II. A Discourse against Second Marriage after Divorce. This tract, as is stated in the Preliminary Notice, is now printed for the first time from MS. Birch, 4149, Art. 38.

III. Articles of Visitation for the Diocese of Winchester, in 1619, and 1625. The Bishop's Articles for the Diocese of Chichester in 1606, for Ely in 1609, and for Winchester in 1622, have unfortunately not been met with; though the two former are referred to in a copy of Visitation Articles for the Diocese of Norwich in 1636, with MS. notes, by Bishop Wren, (Tanner MSS. vol. lxviii. fol. 63); and those of the latter date were no doubt issued, though no mention has been found of them.

IV. Notes on the Book of Common Prayer. These are reprinted from Nicholls's Commentary on the Book of Common Prayer, Lond. 1710, with collations of MSS. in the British Museum, Lambeth, and Durham University Libraries.

V. Form for Consecrating Church Plate. This is now printed for the first time from MS. Lamb. 577, pp. 113—115, with a collation of MS. Harl. 3795, Art. 8.

VI. A Form of Induction. This is printed for the first time from the same MS.

VII. A Manual of Directions for the Sick.

PREFACE.

VIII. A Manual of Private Devotions and Meditations.

These two works are sufficiently noticed in Appendix B, and in the Preliminary Notices prefixed to them respectively.

IX. Index of Texts to Sermons.

X. General Index to Sermons, and to the Minor Works contained in this volume.

These Indices have been prepared by the present Editor.

The Editor begs, in conclusion, to express his thanks to the Rev. J. Barrow, the Superintending Editor, for his many valuable services during the progress of this and other volumes through the press.

JAMES BLISS.

Ogbourne St. Andrew,
June 16, 1854.

ERRATUM.

P. lxiii.—The Sermon before two Kings was first included in the Fourth Edition of Sermons, in 1641.

CONTENTS.

		PAGE
I.	Isaacson's Life of Bishop Andrewes	i
II.	Harington's Memoir	xxxv
III.	Letters	xxxix
IV.	Appendix A. (Miscellaneous Notices)	li
V.	,, B. (Notices of Works)	lx
VI.	,, C. (Andrewes and Casaubon)	lxxviii
VII.	,, D. (,, Grotius)	lxxxvii
VIII.	,, E. (,, Laud)	xcv
IX.	,, F. (Plan of Chapel)	xcvii
X.	,, G. (Will and Codicil)	c
XI.	,, H. (List of Portraits)	cxx
XII.	,, I. (Pedigree)	cxxiii
XIII.	Two Answers to Cardinal Perron, &c.	1
XIV.	A Discourse against Second Marriage	106
XV.	Visitation Articles	111
XVI.	Notes on the Book of Common Prayer	141
XVII.	Form for Consecrating Church Plate	159
XVIII.	Form of Induction	164
XIX.	Manual for the Sick	165
XX.	Manual of Devotions	223
XXI.	Index to Texts of Sermons	339
XXII.	General Index to Sermons	391

An exact Narration

OF THE

LIFE and DEATH

OF THE

Late reverend and learned Prelate,

and painfull DIVINE,

LANCELOT ANDREWES,

Late Bishop of WINCHESTER,

Which may ferve as a Pattern of Piety

and Charity to all godly difpofed

CHRISTIANS.

Faithfully Collected by

HENRY ISAACSON.

[HENRY ISAACSON, the writer of this Memoir, son of Richard Isaacson, was born in the parish of St. Catherine, Coleman-street, Sept. 1581. He is said to have been brought up at Pembroke College, Cambridge; on leaving which, he became an inmate of Andrewes' house, and remained with him as his amanuensis, in which capacity he attended him several times at Court. (See the Dedic. to Saturni Ephemerides.) He was buried in the Church of his native parish, Dec. 4, 1654, to the poor of which he had previously been a considerable benefactor.

This Memoir of Bishop Andrewes was published, as the title indicates, in 1650. It was not reprinted, as is usually stated, in Fuller's Abel Redivivus. Copies only of the edition of 1650 were inserted in that volume between pp. 440, 441, with this direction on p. 440, " Place here Bishop Androwes his life, marked with this signature * * *, having no folioes."

It appears, however, that the copies of this edition differ from each other in several points; some, *e.g.*, having, and others omitting, the name of the author on the title-page; besides the very important variation noticed below, p. vii. But the occurrence of the same misprints, and the correspondence of the pages, lead to the conclusion that only one edition was put forth, and that the variations which appear, were made during its progress through the press.

In the present reprint pains have been taken to introduce additional illustrative matter, from various sources.]

THE LIFE AND DEATH

OF THE LATE

REVEREND AND WORTHY PRELATE,

LANCELOT ANDREWES,

LATE BISHOP OF WINCHESTER.

THIS grave and honourable prelate was born in the city of London [a], in the parish of All-Saints, Barking [b], of honest and religious parents; his father [c] (having most part of his life used the seas) in his latter time became one of the Society, and Master of the Holy Trinity, commonly called the Trinity House: and was descended from the ancient family of the Andrewes, in Suffolk [d].

From his tender years he was totally addicted to the study of good letters; and in his youth, there appeared in him such

---

[a] [In 1555. The day is not known. The account of his life in Tanner MSS. vol. clvii., states that it was Sept. 25: but this may arise from a misunderstanding of Buckeridge's language in his funeral sermon, who observes, " Yea, then his life did begin, when his mortality made an end; that was *natalis*, his birth-day, September the twenty-fifth."—Funeral Sermon, Works, vol. v. p. 297.]

[b] [In the Register of this parish are several entries relating to the family of Andrewes, which will be found below, appended to the Bishop's Will.]

[c] [His father's name was Thomas Andrewes; his mother's name is not known.]

[d] [Bp. Buckeridge (Funeral Sermon, Works, vol. v. p. 288) states that his parents, "besides his breeding in learning, left him a sufficient patrimony and inheritance, which is descended to his heir at Rawreth, in Essex."

Morant professes that he was unable to discover what this property was. (Morant's Essex, vol. i. p. 286.) But he informs us that the manors of Malgreffs or Malgraves, in the parish of Horndon, and of Goldsmiths, in the parish of Langdon, Essex, were in this family. " Anne, daughter of Mr. Thomas Andrews, citizen of London, brought it to her husband, Thomas Cotton of Conington, in Cambridgeshire." This Anne must have been the Bishop's niece. Her only daughter, Frances, married Dingley Ascham, Esq. (Ibid. pp. 218, 247.]

aptness to learn, answerable to his endeavours, that his first two schoolmasters, Master Ward and Master Mulcaster [e], (conceiving, or foreseeing that he would prove a rare scholar,) contended who should have the honour of his breeding [f]. From Master Ward, Master of the Coopers' Free School in Radcliffe [g], he was sent to Master Mulcaster, Master of the Merchant-Tailors' Free School [h] in London, where he answered the former opinion conceived of him; for by his extraordinary industry, and admirable capacity, he soon outstripped all the scholars under Master Mulcaster's tuition, being become an excellent Grecian and Hebrician: insomuch as Thomas Wattes [i], Doctor of Divinity, Prebend and Residentiary of Saint Paul's, and Archdeacon of Middlesex, who had newly founded some scholarships in Pembroke Hall, in Cambridge [k],

[e] [Richard Mulcaster was educated at Eton, elected Scholar of King's, 1548, Student of Christ Church, 1555, Head Master of Merchant Tailors' School, September 24, 1561, Vicar of Cranbrooke in Kent, April 1, 1590, Prebendary of Sarum, April 29, 1594, Master of S. Paul's School, 1596, (Wilson incorrectly says 1586.) Rector of Stamford Rivers, 1598. He died April 15, 1611, and was buried at Stamford. (Wood, Ath. Ox. vol. ii. pp. 93—95.) The account of his Mastership at Merchant Tailors' School is given by Wilson in his History of that School, pp. 21—85.]

[f] ["In his tenderest years he showed such readiness and sharpness of wit and capacity, that his teachers and masters saw in him that he would prove *lumen literarum et literatorum*, 'the burning and shining candle of all learning and learned men.' And therefore, those two first masters that had the care of the first elements of his learning—Master Ward, of Ratcliffe, and Master Mulcaster, of the Merchant Tailors' School—contended for him, who should have the care of his breeding, that after became the honour of their schools and all learning. Master Ward first obtained of his parents that he should not be a prentice, and at length Master Mulcaster got him to his school; and from this time, *perit omne tempus quod studiis non impenditur;* he accounted all that time lost that he spent not in his studies, wherein in learning he outstripped all his equals, and his indefatigable industry had almost outstripped himself. He studied so hard when others played, that if his parents and masters had not forced him to play with them also, all the play had been marred. His late studying by candle, and early rising at four in the morning, procured him envy among his equals, yea, with his ushers also, because he called them up too soon."—Buckeridge's Sermon, p. 289.]

[g] [A school and almshouses at Ratcliff were founded by Nicholas Gibson, citizen and grocer, sheriff, A.D. 1538, who by his will, dated 23d September, 1540, left to his wife, Avice, all his property, on condition she should assure the same for their maintenance and support for ever. She subsequently married Sir Anthony Knyvett, and made a surrender of the property to the Coopers' Company in 1552, pursuant to the terms of Mr. Gibson's will.]

[h] [Merchant Tailors' School had just been founded, and Mulcaster elected its first Head Master.]

[i] [Thomas Watts was collated to the Preb. of Totenhale in 1559, and succeeded Nowell in the Archdeaconry of Middlesex, Jan. 31, 1560. He had the Rectory of Bocking conferred on him by the Archbishop of Canterbury, August 1570, and was commissioned to the deanery there, April 5, 1571, being D.D. He died before May 28, 1577. (Newcourt, Rep. vol. i. p. 82.) He is mentioned repeatedly in Strype.]

[k] [Dr. Watts founded six scholarships in 1571.]

sent him thither[1], and bestowed the first of his said scholarships upon him; which places are since commonly called the Greek Scholarships.

As soon as he was a Bachelor of Arts[m], and so capable of a Fellowship, there being then but one place void in the said College, and Thomas Dove[n], late Lord Bishop of Peterborough, being then a Scholar also in the said college, and very well approved of by many of the society; the Master and Fellows put these two young men to a trial before them, by some scholastical exercises: upon performance whereof they preferred Sir Andrewes, and chose him into the fellowship then void, though they liked Sir Dove so well also, that, being loth to lose him, they made him some allowance for his present maintenance, under the title of a *Tanquam Socius*.

In the meanwhile, Hugh Price[o], having built Jesus College in Oxford, had heard so much of this young man, Sir Andrewes, that, without his privity, he named him, in his foundation of that college, to be one of his first Fellows there[p].

His custom was, after he had been three years in the University, to come up to London once a year to visit his parents, and that, ever about a fortnight before Easter, staying till a fortnight after: and against the time he should come up, his father, directed by letters from his son, before he came, prepared one that should read to him, and be his guide in the attaining of some language or art, which he had not attained before. So, that within few years, he had laid the foundations of all arts and sciences, and had gotten skill in most of the modern languages. And it is to be observed, that in his jour-

---

[1] [He was admitted into the College in 1571.]

[m] [He was B.A. Jan. 1, 157$\frac{3}{4}$, but was not chosen Fellow till October 1576.]

[n] [Thomas Dove was educated at Merchant Tailors' School, and admitted Scholar of Pembroke College in the same year as Bishop Andrewes. Dove, as well as Andrewes, was appointed on the new foundation of Jesus College, Oxford: on June 16, 1589, he was installed Dean of Norwich; in 1600, was appointed Bishop of Peterborough; and died August 30, 1630.]

[o] [Hugh Price, or Ap Rice, was born at Brecknock, probably before the year 1500. He graduated as LL.D. as early as 1525. It is said that he was educated at Oseney Abbey, by an uncle, who was one of the Canons. He was one of the first Canons of Rochester Cathedral, and about the same time Treasurer of S. David's. On the foundation of Jesus College in 1571, the Fellows and Scholars, whose names are given by Wood (Hist. of Colleges, p. 569), were nominated by the Queen on the recommendation of Hugh Price.]

[p] [He was incorporated M.A. of Oxford, July 11, 1581, (Wood's F. O, vol. i. p. 219,) by which it appears probable that he did not visit Oxford on his nomination as Scholar (not Fellow, as stated in the text,) of Jesus College.]

neys betwixt London and Cambridge, to and fro, he ever used to walk on foot [q], till he was a Bachelor of Divinity; and professed that he would not then have ridden on horseback, but that divers friends began to find fault with him, and misinterpret him, as if he had forborne riding only to save charges.

What he did, when he was a child, and a schoolboy, is not now known, but he hath been sometimes heard to say, that when he was a young scholar in the University, and so all his time onward, he never loved or used any games or ordinary recreations, either within doors, as cards, dice, tables, chess, or the like; or abroad, as buts, quoits, bowls, or any such: but his ordinary exercise and recreation was walking either alone by himself, or with some other selected companion, with whom he might confer and argue, and recount their studies; and he would often profess that to observe the grass, herbs, corn, trees, cattle, earth, waters, heavens, any of the creatures, and to contemplate their natures, orders, qualities, virtues, uses, &c., was ever to him the greatest mirth, content, and recreation that could be: and this he held to his dying day.

After he had been some while a Master of Arts [r] in the University, he applied himself to the study of divinity, wherein he so profited, that his fame began to be spread far and near. Insomuch, as being chosen Catechist [s] in the college, and purposing to read upon the Ten Commandments every Saturday and Sunday, at three o'clock after noon, which was the hour of catechising; not only out of other colleges in the University, but divers also out of the country, did duly resort unto the college chapel, as a public divinity lecture [t].

Before I proceed to his life after he left the University, let me add what the general opinion of him was while he remained there. That, as he was an excellent catechist for

---

[q] [This seems to have been the usual practice with students in those days. See Walton's Life of Hooker.]

[r] [He was admitted M.A. 1578, and ordained Deacon, 1580. In the latter of these years he was Junior Treasurer of the College; and in 1581, Senior Treasurer. He took his degree of B.D. in 1585. The "Thesis de Usuris" was read by him on April 22 in that year, as his exercise for that degree. See Opusc. Posthuma, p. 119.]

[s] [The result of his labours as Catechist remains to us in his "Pattern of Catechistical Doctrine," of which see more below.]

[t] [It seems probable that his Sermons on "the Temptation of Christ in the Wilderness," and on "the Lord's Prayer," originally published respectively in 1592, and 1611, were taken from the notes of his hearers on these occasions.]

his profoundness in the fundamental points of religion, and eminent in all other kind of learning, as being skilful in the Oriental tongues; so especially that which made him no less admired than his catechising was, that he was a man deeply seen in all cases of conscience[u], and in that respect was much sought unto by many, who ever received great satisfaction from him in clearing those doubts which did much perplex them. To proceed: his general worth made him so famous[x], that Henry Earl of Huntingdon[y], hearing of it, sent for him, and thought himself much honoured by his accompanying him into the north, whereof he was President[z]; and where God so blessed his painful preachings, and moderate private conference, that he converted recusants, priests, and others, to the Protestant religion.

Sir Francis Walsingham[a], Secretary of State to Queen Elizabeth, took also especial notice of his abilities, and highly affected him; and, being loth that he should not be better known to the world, wrought means to make him Vicar of S. Giles without Cripplegate, London[b]; then Prebend and Residentiary of S. Paul's[c]; and afterwards Prebend of the Collegiate Church of Southwell[d].

[u] [See Harington's life, printed below.]

[x] [This passage in another copy of the Life stands as follows:—

"Before I proceed to his life after he left the University, give me leave to relate a story of him while he yet remained there, and that as near as I can from his own mouth, and in his own words.

"Upon his first showing himself at Cambridge in his divinity studies, especial notice was soon taken of him, among his abilities and eminences, as a man deeply seen in all cases of conscience, and he was much sought to in that respect. To proceed with his own particular: his worth made him so famous," . . .]

[y] [Henry Hastings, third Earl of Huntingdon, Lord Lieutenant of Leicester and Rutland, was one of the peers who had charge of Mary, Queen of Scots. He was President of the North, 1572—1595.]

[z] [There are several letters from him in this capacity to Bishop Chaderton, in Peck, Desid. Cur. lib. iv.]

[a] [Buckeridge states that Walsingham "obtained him of the Earl, intending his preferment, in which he would never permit him to take any country benefice, lest he and his great learning should be buried in a country church. His intent was to make him a Reader of Controversies in Cambridge; and for his maintenance, he assigned to him, as I am informed, the lease of the Parsonage of Alton, in Hampshire, which, after his death, he returned to his Lady, which she never knew or thought of."—Funeral Sermon, p. 290.]

[b] [The date of his institution is not known.]

[c] [He was admitted to the Stall of S. Pancras, May 29, 1589, at which time he was only B.D. It appears from Newcourt (Repert. vol. i. p. 193) that Thomas Kempe, Bishop of London, founded a chantry in 5 Edw. IV. for one priest who should be Confessor to the Bishop of London, and that from the time of the endowment of this chantry, and its annexation to the Stall of S. Pancras, the Prebendary, on admission to his stall, was admitted also to the office of Penitentiary.]

[d] [His stall is not known.]

Being thus preferred to his own contentment, he lived not idly, but continued a painful labourer in the Lord's vineyard; witness S. Giles' pulpit, and that in S. Paul's Church, where he read the lecture[e] thrice a-week in the term time. And indeed, what by his often preaching at S. Giles, and his no less often reading in S. Paul's, he became so infirm, that his friends despaired of his life[f].

Upon the death of Dr. Fulke[g], he was elected to the Mastership of Pembroke Hall[h], whereof he had been a Scholar and Fellow; a place of credit, but of little benefit, for he ever spent more upon it than he received by it.

Afterwards he was made Chaplain in ordinary attendance, of which kind there were then but twelve, to Queen Elizabeth, who took such delight in his preaching and grave deportment, that first she bestowed a Prebend at Westminster[i] upon him, and not long after, the Deanery[k] of that place; and what she intended further to him, her death prevented[l].

---

[e] [The Divinity Lecture, in S. Paul's Cathedral, was founded by Richard de Gravesend, Bishop of London. The Chancellor is required to be Lecturer, but he may appoint a deputy.]

[f] See the title of "'Ἀποσπασμάτια sacra," mentioned below in List of Works.]

[g] [William Fulke, originally Fellow of S. John's, Cambridge. He began by studying the law; but on taking orders was suspected of Puritanism, and expelled the college. In 1578 he was admitted Master of Pembroke College. Wood states that he was Margaret Professor; but his name is not given in Le Neve's list. His principal work is his "Comment on the Rhemish Testament."]

[h] [This was in A.D. 1589. He may be presumed to have taken his degree of D.D. about this time. There is no date to the "Concio ad Clerum," he preached for that degree. See Opusc. Posth. p. 1. Bishop Buckeridge (Sermon, p. 291) states that his "Determinatio de Decimis" was delivered by him at this time, but no date is given in the title-page.

As an evidence of the line he had taken against the Puritans, it may be observed that he was denied that degree on his first application for it, by Dr. Preston (Master of Trinity Hall), then Vice-Chancellor. (Strype's Whitgift, vol. i. pp. 613, 614.) He was at this time Archbishop Whitgift's chaplain.

Walsingham at this time writes to Burleigh (MSS. Harl. Numb. 6994. p. 103):—

"Aug. 28, 1589.

"And for the Mastership of Pembroke Hall, If I did not think that Mr. Andrewes shall do more good by the retaining of him in these parts than there, I had sought to prefer him therein, and therefore have been a mean to excuse the recommendation for the other, so as your Lordship do judge him fit for the same."]

[i] [He was appointed to the 11th Stall in 1597. (Newcourt, Repert. vol. i. p. 927.)]

[k] [On the death of Gab. Goodman, in 1601. He held this Deanery, with the Stall of St. Pancras, and the Vicarage of S. Giles, Cripplegate, till his promotion to the See of Chichester. See Newcourt, Repert. vol. i. pp. 197, 357, 719.]

[l] [The following notices of Andrewes in Elizabeth's reign may be here inserted:—

After the condemnation of John Udal, Lancelot Andrewes, and Nowell, the Dean of St. Paul's, were appointed by Archbishop Whitgift (at the direction of the Lords of the Council) to hold conference with them. (Strype's Whit-

He soon grew into far greater esteem with her successor, the most learned King James, who, to say but truth, admired him beyond all other divines, not only for his transcendent gift in preaching, but for his excellency and solidity in all kinds of learning [m]; selecting him, as his choicest piece, to vindicate his regality against his foulmouthed adversaries [n].

gift, book iv. chap. vii. vol. ii. p. 97.) They presented him a form of submission, to which he gave his consent. "A few days afterwards," as Udal relates in his own narrative, "Mr. Doctor Andrewes returned unto me, signifying that all that was done was mistaken; for that was not the submission that was meant of me, but another. Which when I had perused, I found it the same (only the last clause left out) which was offered me by the Judges at the Assizes. And he said, the clerk to whom the sealing of the letter to Mr. Nowell was committed put in one for another. And because I utterly refused to consult of it, as having yielded before to so much as I might, he prayed me to understand what I took exceptions against, and for what reasons. So we entered into many discourses; as first, how the discipline could be said to be against the Queen's prerogative royal, seeing it was (as I said I did believe) expressed in the Scripture, whereby all lawful privileges of princes are warranted. Then we debated whether the supremacy of a Christian prince be the same with an heathen, or diverse from it. After that, whether the authority of princes in making Church-laws be *de jure*, or *de facto* only : and lastly, of the most points of discipline. Thus we continued five or six hours, and at last he would have no answer of me then, but he prayed me to advise of it, for he would come again. I answered, that the oftener he came, the welcomer he should be; but I told him I would not accept of it. Yet he came twice after ; and took my reasons of my refusal to yield thereunto ; and, promising me all the favour he could procure me, he departed." — (State Trials, vol. i. col. 187.)

And in 1593, after sentence had been passed on Henry Barrow, the notorious Puritan, he was deputed, with other divines, to confer with him, in the hope of his recantation. (See Heylin's History of the Presbyterians, lib. ix. § 30, p. 324.)

In 1594, he was appointed by Whitgift one of the Commissioners for inquiring into the state of the Ecclesiastical Courts in the Diocese of London (Strype's Whitgift, book iv. chap. xii. vol. ii. p. 194); and he was also proposed, in 1603, to be put into a Commission for perusing and suppressing all books published without authority, or brought into the realm. (See Strype's Whitgift, book iv. chap. xxxii. vol. ii. p. 504.)]

[m] [" His excellency and solidity in all kinds of learning," justly entitled him to a place in the Hampton Court Conference; and he was also, as is well known, employed as one of the translators of the Bible.]

[n] [This was in reply to Bellarmine, who, under the name of Matthew Tortus, had attacked the King's Defence of the Oath of Supremacy. (See Preface to Tortura Torti, and the Resp. ad Apol. Card. Bellarmini.) Chamberlain writes to Sir D. Carleton, Oct. 21,1608: "They say that the Bishop of Chichester is appointed to answer Bellarmine about the Oath of Allegiance, which task I doubt how he will undertake and perform, being so contrary to his disposition and course to meddle with controversies." — Birch's Court of James I., vol. i. p. 77. And again, Nov. 11 : "I thank you for your remonstrance of the French Clergy, which will give me occasion perhaps to visit the good Bishop of Chichester, though I doubt he be not at leisure for any bye matters; the King doth so hasten and spur him on in this business of Bellarmine's, which he were likely to perform very well (as I hear by them that can judge) if he might take his own time, and not be troubled nor entangled by arguments obtruded to him continually by the King."—Ibid. p. 81.

On the publication of the volume, (Tortura Torti,) Dudley Carleton thus writes to Sir Thomas Edmondes, June 9, 1609 : "The Bishop of Chichester's book is now in the press, whereof I have seen part, and it is a worthy

His Majesty, not long after his happy entrance to this crown, bestowed upon him the Bishopric of Chichester [o], which he held about four years [p], and withal made him Lord Almoner [q] : and because of the exility of that Bishopric, soon after added the Parsonage of Cheam, in Surrey [r], to his commendam.

Upon the vacancy of the Bishopric of Ely [s], his Majesty made him Bishop thereof ; and there he sat about nine years [t] : in which time he was made a Privy Councillor, first

work ; only the brevity breeds obscurity, and puts the reader to some of that pains which was taken by the writer."—Ibid. p. 99.

Respecting the 'Responsio ad Apologiam Card. Bellarmini,' Chamberlain thus writes to Sir Ralph Winwood : "The Bishop of Ely is set to work in reply to Cardinal Bellarmine's Answer to the King's Book, whereof I perceive he makes no great account; but thinks that either the man is much crazed from what he was, or else that he did it with a contemptuous negligence." — (Winwood's Memorials, vol. iii. p. 117.]

[o] [Up to this time he had retained the Mastership of Pembroke College. The last act in which he took a part in College, was the election of Matthew Wren into a Fellowship, Nov. 5, 1605. He probably resigned his Mastership on that day, as his successor Harsnett was elected Nov. 9.]

[p] [" Lancelotus Andrewes, S. T. P. ex DecanoWestmon. in Ep'um Cicestr. electus 16 Oct. 1605 ; confirmatus 31 Octob.; consecratus Lambethæ ab Archiep., assistentibus Ep'is London., Norwich, Glocestr. et Roffen., 3 Nov. 1605."—Kennett, (e Reg. Bancroft.) MSS. Lands. 984, p. 81.

The probability of his promotion was thus noticed by a writer of the time : "The Bishop of Chichester dead, rich for so mean a living, and bestowed the greatest part of his wealth upon his kindred and servants. Dr. Andrews is like to be Bishop and Almoner in his place, and his Deanery of Westminster goes to one Dr. Neal, a man of no great note, more than that he is the Earl of Salisbury's Chaplain; and his Parsonage of St. Giles's to Dr. Buckeridge ; and his other parcels to meaner men." — Mr. John Chamberlain to Mr. Winwood, Oct. 12, 1605. Winwood's Memorials, vol. ii. p. 141.]

[q] [The King, on appointing Andrewes to this office, granted, in augmentation of the King's alms, the goods, chattels, and debts of all who were *felones de se*, as well as all deodands in England and Wales, exempting him moreover from rendering an account of his receipts from these sources. (Rymer, Fœd. VII. ii. 143.)]

[r] [" Ecclesiam de Cheyham, sive Cheam in agro Surrien. simul cum Ep'atu tenuit, ad quam admissus est 25 Jul. 1609 ; eam vero ad Ep'atum Eliensem translatus dereliquit." — Kennett.]

[s] [Vacant by the death of Martin Heton.]

[t] [It seems to have been the general expectation that, on the death of Bancroft, Andrewes would have been raised to the primacy. The interest of the Earl of Dunbar, in the absence of Andrewes's friends, succeeded in obtaining that important post for Abbot, who, within less than two years, had held in succession the two Sees of Lichfield and London.

George Calvert (afterwards Lord Baltimore) thus writes to Sir Th. Edmonds, March 10, 16$\frac{10}{11}$: " For our news here, your Lordship will not look for so long an inventory as that of John de Garres [author of ' Inventoire Général de l'Histoire Général de France.' Paris. 1608] from me, that have had no time to gather. Yet, since my coming, I understand these few,—that the Bishop of London, by a strong *north* wind, coming out of Scotland, is blown over the Thames to Lambeth ; the King having professed to the Bishop himself, as also to all the Lords of his Council, that it is neither the respect of his learning, his wisdom, nor his sincerity, (although he is well persuaded there is not any one of them wanting in him,) that hath made him to prefer him above the rest of his fellows, but merely the recommendation of his faithful servant, Dunbar, that is dead, whose suit on behalf of this Bishop he cannot forget, nor will suffer to

of England [u], and then of Scotland, in his attendance of the King thither [x]. He was afterwards preferred to the Bishopric of Winchester [y], and the Deanery of the King's Chapel [z],

lose his intention."—Birch's Court of James I. vol. i. p. 110.

The regret expressed by Clarendon at this unhappy appointment (Hist. Rebell. vol. i. p. 157) need only be alluded to; as well as Heylin's confident opinion that, "if Andrewes had succeeded Bancroft, and Laud followed Andrewes, the Church would have been settled on so sure a foundation that it could not easily have been shaken."—Cypr. Ang. p. 59.]

[u] [Sept. 29, 1616. "This honour was done the Bishop," says Chamberlain, "to put him in heart upon the distaste he had in missing the Bishopric of Winchester; but for aught I hear he is yet as silent as Mr. Wake's nuncio, the new Cardinal."—Chamberlain to Sir Dudley Carleton, Oct. 12, 1616. Birch's Court of James I. vol. i. p. 429.

Buckeridge states of him, (Fun. Serm. p. 292,) that in this capacity "he spake and meddled little in civil and temporal affairs, being out of his profession and element; but in causes that in any way concerned the Church and his calling, he spake fully and home to the purpose, that he made all know that he understood and could speak when it concerned him." Lloyd (State Worthies, p. 1024) says, "He did not concern himself much with civil politics. He would say, when he came to the Council Table, 'Is there anything to be done to-day for the Church?' If they answered, 'Yea,' then he said, 'I will stay:' if 'No,' then he said, 'I will be gone.'"]

[x] [Andrewes naturally felt an interest in Scotch Ecclesiastical affairs, having been one of the Bishops who consecrated the Scotch Prelates on Oct. 21, 1610, and thus restored to that country the blessings of the Episcopate.

Two different accounts of his conduct, on this occasion, are given by Spotswood and Heylin.

Spotswood's account is as follows:—
"A question in the meantime was raised by Dr. Andrewes, Bishop of Ely, touching the consecration of the Scotch Bishops, who, as he said, must first be ordained Presbyters, as having received no ordination from a Bishop. The Archbishop of Canterbury, who was by, maintained, that thereof there was no necessity, seeing when Bishops could not be had, the ordination given by the Presbyters must be esteemed lawful; otherwise that it might be doubted, if there were any lawful vocation in most of the Reformed Churches. This applauded to by the other Bishops, Ely acquiesced, and in the day and place appointed, the three Bishops were consecrated." — Spotswood's History of the Church of Scotland, p. 514.

The following is Heylin's statement:—

"And that this character might be indelibly imprinted on them, his Majesty issues a Commission under the Great Seal of England, to the Bishops of London, Ely, Wells, and Rochester, whereby they were required to proceed to the consecration of the said three Bishops, according to the rules of the English Ordination; which was by them performed with all due solemnity, in the chapel of the Bishop of London's house, near the Church of St. Paul's, Octob. 21, 1610. But first, a scruple had been moved by the Bishop of Ely, concerning the capacity of the persons nominated, for receiving the Episcopal consecration, in regard that none of them had formerly been ordained priests: which scruple was removed by Archbishop Bancroft, alleging, that there was no such necessity of receiving the order of Priesthood, but that Episcopal consecrations might be given without it; as might have been exemplified in the cases of Ambrose and Nectarius; of which, the first was made Archbishop of Millain; and the other Patriarch of Constantinople, without receiving any intermediate orders, whether of Priest, Deacon, or any other (if there were any other) at that time in the Church." —Heylin's Hist. of Presbyt. lib. xi. § 24, pp. 387, 388.]

[y] [The Congé d'élire is dated June 29, 1618 (Rymer, Fœd. VII. iii. 67); the election took place Aug. 3, 1618 (Kennett); the order to confirm his election, Feb. 9, 161⅞ (ibid. pp. 92, 93); the restitution of the temporalities, March 19, 161⅞ (ibid. p. 100).]

[z] [1618. 1 Jan. — Lancelotus Andrews electus Winton. a Camerario in

which two last preferments he held to his death, which happened about eight years after, in the third year of the reign of our late King Charles, with whom he held no less reputation than he had done with his father before him [a].

It is worth the observation, that, having been preferred to many, and those no small dignities, yet he never used any means to obtain the least of them, but they were all conferred upon him, without the least suit on his part [b]; for he was so far from ambition or covetousness, as that when the Bishoprics of Salisbury and Ely were at several times tendered unto him, upon some propositions prejudicial to the state of those churches, he utterly refused them [c].

The virtues and good parts of this honourable prelate were so many, and those so transcendent, that to do him right, a large volume would be but sufficient, which I shall leave to some of better abilities to perform, which I shall, by way of an epitome, only point a finger at, in these heads which follow.

His first and principal virtue was his singular zeal and

Decanum Capellæ juratus in vestiario.—Kennett.]

[a] ["He (K. James) desired, when death was near him, to have received the communion at the hands of the Bishop of Winchester; but he was so sick when he was sent for that he could not come."—Joseph Mede to Sir Martin Stuteville. Birch's Charles I. vol. i. p. 5.

And yet he had never wrongly flattered the King, as may appear by the following anecdote, recorded in Waller's Life, and which, though well known, must be here repeated. It is stated that, "on the day of the dissolution of the Parliament," (he means the "prorogation" in 1623. See Nichols, vol. iii. p. 976,) "he went to see the King at dinner, with whom were Dr. Andrews, Bishop of Winchester, and Dr. Neile, Bishop of Durham, standing behind His Majesty's chair. There happened something very extraordinary in the conversation these prelates had with the King, on which Mr. Waller did often reflect. His Majesty asked the Bishops, 'My Lords, cannot I take my subjects' money, when I want it, without all this formality in Parliament?' The Bishop of Durham readily answered, 'God forbid, Sir, but you should; you are the breath of our nostrils.' Whereupon the King turned, and said to the Bishop of Winchester, 'Well, my Lord, what say you?' 'Sir,' replied the Bishop, 'I have no skill to judge of Parliamentary cases.' The King answered, 'No put offs, my Lord, auswer me presently.' 'Then, Sir,' said he, 'I think it's lawful for you to take my brother Neile's money, for he offers it.' Mr. Waller said the company was pleased with this answer, and the wit of it seemed to affect the King.... The truth of this conversation is not to be doubted, it having been often told Dr. Birch by Mr. Waller himself, one of whose daughters he had married, and the Doctor communicated it to us with several other passages concerning our author."

Fuller states that "his gravity in a manner awed King James, who refrained from that mirth and liberty in the presence of this prelate, which otherwise he assumed to himself."—(Church Hist. book xi. sect. i. § 46.]

[b] [See Buckeridge's Funeral Sermon, p. 291.]

[c] [This must have been at the time when Coldwell was appointed to the See of Salisbury, and Heton to that of Ely.]

piety, which showed itself, not only in his private and secret devotions between God and himself, in which, they that were about him well perceived that he daily spent many hours, yea, and the greatest part of his life in holy prayers, and abundant tears, the signs whereof they often discovered [d],—but also in his exemplary public prayers with his family in his chapel; wherein he behaved himself so humbly, devoutly, and reverently, that it could not but move others to follow his example [e]. His chapel, in which he had monthly communions, was so decently and reverently adorned, and God served there with so holy and reverend behaviour of himself and his family, by his pattern, that the souls of many, that *obiter* came thither in time of divine service, were very much elevated, and they stirred up to the like reverend deportment; yea, some that had been there were so taken with it, that they desired to end their days in the Bishop of Ely's chapel.

The next is his charity and compassion, which he practised even before he came to great preferments; for, while he was yet in private estate, he extended his charity in liberal manner to the relief of poor parishioners, prisons, and prisoners, besides his constant Sundays' alms at his parish of Saint Giles [f]. But when his means became greater, his charity increased to a large proportion; releasing many prisoners of all sorts, that were detained either for petty debts, or keeper's fees. And one thing in his charity is remarkable; that whereas he sent much money at several times to the relief of poor parishes,

---

[d] [See Humphry Mosely's and Drake's Prefaces to his Private Devotions, below, pp. 225, 226, 233.]

[e] [Bishop Buckeridge remarks, "After he came to have an episcopal house with a chapel, he kept monthly communions inviolably, yea though himself had received at the Court the same month. In which his carriage was not only decent and religious, but also exemplary; he ever offered twice at the altar, and so did every one of his servants, to which purpose he gave them money, lest it should be burdensome to them."—Fun. Serm. p. 296.

A description of his chapel will be found in the Appendix.]

[f] ["Neither did he stay to do good and distribute till his death, that is, then gave his goods to the poor, when he could keep them no longer. The first place he lived on was St. Giles': there, I speak my knowledge, I do not say he began, sure I am he continued his charity; his certain alms there was ten pounds per annum, which was paid quarterly by equal portions, and twelve pence every Sunday he came to church, and five shillings at every communion; and for many years, since he left that cure, he sent five pounds about Christmas, besides the number of gowns given to the poor of that parish when he was Almoner. And I have reason to presume the like of those other parishes mentioned in his will."—Buckeridge's Funeral Sermon, p. 294.]

prisons, prisoners, and the like, he gave strict charge to his servants whom he entrusted therewith, that they should not acknowledge whence this relief came [g] : but directed that the acquittances, which they, to make the discharge of their trust appear to him, desired from them that received such relief, should be taken in the name of a benefactor unknown. Other large sums he bestowed yearly, and oftener, in clothing the poor and naked, in relieving the sick and needy, in succouring families in time of infection, besides his alms to poor housekeepers at his gate; insomuch that his private alms in his last six years, besides those public, amounted to the sum of 1,300*l.* and upwards. Lastly, though it might well have been supposed by that which is said already, that he had been in his lifetime his own almoner, yet, as he lived a pattern of compassion and work of mercy, so he died also; for it appeareth by his will, that his chief care was, to provide that his pious works should never have end, leaving 4,000*l.* to purchase 200*l.* land *per annum* for ever, to be distributed by 50*l.* quarterly, thus :—To aged poor men and decayed, with an especial eye to seafaring men, wherein he reflected upon his father's profession, 50*l.* ; to poor widows, the wives of one husband, fifty pounds ; to the binding of poor orphans apprentices, fifty pounds; and to the relief of poor prisoners, fifty pounds. Besides among other, too many to be comprehended in an epitome, he left to be distributed, presently after his decease, among maid-servants of honest report, and who had served one master or mistress seven years, the sum of two hundred pounds. Lastly, a great part of his estate, which remained after his funeral and legacies discharged, he left to be distributed among his poor servants.

[g] [Bp. Buckeridge writes : "And lest his left hand should know what his right hand did, he sent great alms to many poor places, under other men's names; and he stayed not till the poor sought him, for he first sought them, as his servants employed on that service can witness—as appeareth at Farnham, at Waltham, and Winchester; and in the last year of great sickness, he gave in this parish of St. Saviour an hundred marks."—Fun. Serm. p. 295.
 This caused him, during his lifetime, to lie under the charge of illiberality, as appears by what Joseph Mede writes to Sir Martin Stuteville, October 3, 1626 :—" My Lord of Winchester, they say, died not worth 12,000*l.* ; which makes many change their uncharitable conceit they had formerly of him, finding that he gave much to the poor and prisons in London, and other good uses, the author not being known till now he is dead. And no doubt but that he hath received a reward openly of God of what he did in secret."—Birch's Charles I. vol. i. p. 153.]

The third is his fidelity and integrity; faithful, upright, and just he ever was, whether you respect him in his ordinary transactions, in which no man could ever justly tax him with the least aspersion of injustice; or whether you look upon him as entrusted with those great offices and places which he did undergo, and they were either his spiritual preferments or temporal office, besides some other matters committed to his fidelity [h]. In the first of which he declared evidently to the world, that he reputed himself but God's steward, and that he must give an account to his Lord and Master for them. To begin then with the lowest account: he was ever faithful, provident, and careful to keep in good repair the houses of all his spiritual preferments, and spent much money that way; as upon the Vicarage-house of Saint Giles, the Prebend's and Dean's houses of Westminster, and the Residentiary's house of Saint Paul's [i]. Upon the house belonging to the bishopric of Chichester, he expended above 420*l.* [j]; of Ely, above 2,440*l.* [k]; of Winchester, besides a pension of 400*l. per annum*, from which he freed his see at his own charge [l], he spent two thousand pounds [m].

But in that part of the account which concerned him more nearly to perfect, which was his pastoral and episcopal charge, the cure of souls, and the well ordering of the several dioceses committed to his trust, never any made a more just and exact account.

Some particulars of this account was the promoting of sufficient able and good men to livings and preferments which fell within his own gift [n]. To the better discharge of

[h] [He was appointed one of the first Governors of the Charter-House, and one of the overseers of the Founder's will, in which capacity he attended his funeral, May 28, 1612. He also addressed a letter to Sutton's executors, directing them to pay the sum of 10,000*l.* for the repair of Berwick Bridge, in fulfilment of the provisions of his will, which directed a certain sum to be applied to charitable uses. (See Bearcroft's Hist. of the Charter-House, pp. 46, 102, 118—120.)]

[i] [This house he not only built, but recovered to the Church. (Buckeridge, Funeral Sermon, p. 293.)]

[j] ["1605, die 14 Martii, Arch'e'pus concessit Lanceloto Ep'o Cicestr. licen-tiam demoliendi plura ruinosa, deformia et inutilia ædificia in palatiis Ep'alibus de Cicestr. et Aldingbourn." —Kennett, e Reg. Bancroft.]

[k] [He repaired Ely House in Holborn, Ely Palace at Downham, and Wisbech Castle.]

[l] [This probably was a charge put on the see in the time of either Bp. Ponet, or Bp. Horne.]

[m] [He repaired the episcopal residences at Farnham and Waltham, and Wolvesey Palace at Winchester.]

[n] [The following instances may be mentioned:—

1. Samuel Harsnet to the Vicarage of Chigwell, June 14, 1597 (see Kennett's note in Wood's Fast. Ox. vol. i.

this part of the account he took order still beforehand, by continual search and inquiry to know what hopeful young

p. 219, and Newc. vol. ii. p. 143). He was afterwards Bishop of Chichester and Norwich, and Abp. of York.

2. William Bedwell, presented by him, as one of the Residentiaries of S. Paul's, to the Rectory of Tottenham, Oct. 8, 1607. Bedwell, who was almost the only Arabic scholar in England at this time, was employed as one of the translators of the Bible. His reputation was well known to Isaac Casaubon, who addressed to him in 1603 the letter, which now stands cccxliv. in his collected Epistles, p. 183, Roter. 1709; Casaubon, on coming to England, became personally acquainted with him, and afterwards, on his going abroad, introduced him to Daniel Heinsius in the following terms:— "Vir clarissime, qui tibi has reddidit, amicus meus est; (*Wilhelmus Bedwellus, de quo nos alibi*, Colomes. in marg.) amicus de meliore nota, et D. Episcopi Eliensis a multis annis οἱονεὶ πελάτης. Is quum multos annos in illustranda lingua Arabica consumpserit, optavit, priusquam sua ederet, posse inspicere τὰ τοῦ μακαρίου Herois (Josephi Scaligeri). Ea sola illi fuit causa suscipiendi hujus itineris, hortatio τοῦ πάνυ Eliensis, qui nullis parcere cupit sumptibus, ut studiis literarum consulatur. Ille vir magnus, a quo scis te amari et æstimari κατὰ τὴν ἀξίαν, petiit a me, ut huic communi amico aditum patefacerem per literas ad tuam amicitiam. Speramus per te posse ipsi fieri copiam inspiciendi, quem servas, thesaurum. Quia vir simplex est, probus, et pius, putamus non eum indignum tua benevolentia et gratia."— Is. Casauboni Epist. dcccxxi. Danieli Heinsio, Lond. Cal. Aug. 1612, p. 478. He gave him introductions, at the same time, to Grotius and Erpenius; (vide Epist. dcccxxii. dcccxxiii. pp. 478, 479;) and in a subsequent letter to Stephen Hubert, spoke of him in terms the most complimentary. (Epist. dcxxxi. p. 484.)]

3. Nicholas Fuller to the Rectory of Bishop's Waltham (it is said). Wood, Ath. Ox. ii. col. 327, where see an account of Fuller's writings. Fuller (Church Hist. book xi. sect. i. § 50) says that "a living of great value was sent by Bishop Andrewes on the welcome errand to find out Mr. Fuller to accept the same."

4. John Bois, one of the translators of the Bible, to be Prebendary of the second Stall at Ely, which he afterwards exchanged for the first Stall. (Bentham's Ely, i. 245.)

"When he had given him, as we commonly say, joy of it, (which was his first salutation at his coming to him,) he told him, that he did bestow it freely on him, without any one moving him thereto, though, said he, some pickthanks will be saying, they stood your friends therein."—Peck's Desid. Curiosa, book viii. p. 335. Lond. 1779. Bois prepared under Andrewes' direction a volume entitled, "Veteris Interpretis cum Beza Collatio." It was published in 1655, and appears to be the same book as that which is mentioned in the Biogr. Britann. in Sancroft's Life, as Bp. Andrewes's Defence of the Vulgar Version. If this conjecture is correct, Sancroft is the author of the Preface, in which Andrewes is termed, *in linguis Mithridates, in artibus Aristoteles*.

5. Meric Casaubon to the Rectory of Bleadon, in Somersetshire.

6. Matthew Wren to Teversham in Cambridge, and to the first Stall in Winchester Cathedral (installed Nov. 10, 1623). Wren was also one of Andrewes's chaplains. He was afterwards the celebrated Bishop of Hereford, Norwich, and Ely.

7. Roger Andrews, (brother of the Bishop,) formerly Fellow of Pembroke Hall, Vicar of Chigwell, (Dec. 20, 1605, per resign. Harsnett (Newcourt, Repert. vol. ii. p. 143), Prebendary, Archdeacon, and Chancellor of Chichester, Vicar of Cowfold, Sussex; Rector of Emnet, Norfolk; Prebendary of fourth Stall in Ely, 1617; Prebendary of Winchester, 1625; Master of Jesus Coll. Cambridge, 1618. These preferments were all conferred on him by his brother.

8. Paul Clapham, his chaplain, Vicar of Farnham, and Rector of Martyr Worthy. (Rymer, Fœd. VIII. ii. 37.)

9. Hierom Beale, sometime Fellow of Pembroke Hall, Rector of Nuthurst, Sussex, and Preb. of Chichester, collated to third Stall in Ely Cathedral, before December 21, 1616; Master of Pembroke Hall, Feb. 21, 161⅝; Vice-Chancellor in 1622; Chaplain and Sub-almoner to King James I. (Bentham's Ely, vol. i. p. 248.)

10. Samuel

men were in the University; his chaplains and friends receiving a charge from him to certify him what hopeful and towardly young wit they met with at any time; and these, till he could better provide for them, were sure to taste of his bounty and goodness for their better encouragement.

Divers eminent men in learning that wanted preferment, when anything fell in his gift convenient for them, though otherwise they had no dependence at all upon him, nor interest in him, he would send for before they knew why, and entertain them in his own house, and confer the preferment upon them, and also defray the very charges incident for a dispensation, or a faculty, yea, of their very journey; and all this, that he might have his diocese in general, and his preferments in particular, the better fitted: so that that may fitly be applied to him, which was sometimes to St. Chrysostom: *In administratione episcopatus, præbuit se fidelem, constantem, et vigilantem ministrum Christi.*

And if you look upon him in those temporals wherewith he was entrusted, you shall find him no less faithful and just; as first, divers sums, and many of them of good value, were sent to him to be distributed among poor scholars and others, at his discretion; all which he disposed with great care and fidelity, even according to the donors' minds and intents.

For his faithfulness in managing those places, wherein he was intrusted for others jointly with himself, let Pembroke Hall and Westminster College speak for him; for when he became Master of the first, he found it in debt, being of a very small endowment, then especially; but, by his faithful providence, he left above eleven hundred pounds in the

10. Samuel Collins, collated by Bishop Andrewes to the sixth Stall in Ely Cathedral, Feb. 19, 1617. (Bentham's Ely, vol. i. p. 261.) Collins took a part in the controversy with Bellarmine.

11. Roger Fenton, Nov. 14, 1606, to the Vicarage of Chigwell, (Kennett, apud Wood, F. O. vol. i. p. 259, and Newc. vol. ii. p. 143.) He was the author of several sermons, &c.

12. Christopher Wren, Rector of Fonthill Bishops, 1620, and of East Knoyle, 1623. He was the brother of the Bishop, and was afterwards Dean of Windsor.

13. John Browning, Rector of Buttermere, 1624. The author of six Sermons concerning Public Prayer and the Fasts of the Church. Lond. 1636.

14. Christopher Green, Rector of Stockton, 1625.

15. Thomas Woods, Rector of Buttermere, 1625.

The last four instances are taken from Sir T. Phillipps's Wiltshire Institutions.

16. Cosin, when a young man, was invited to be his librarian; but he declined the offer, and took service with Bishop Overal.]

treasury of that college, towards the bettering of the estate thereof[o]. And when he was made Dean of the other, it is not unknown to some yet living, who will testify, that he left it for all orders, as well of the church as of the college and school, a place then truly exemplarily collegiate in all respects, both within and without, free from debts and arrearages, from encroachments and evil customs; the schoolboys, in the four years he stayed there, being much improved, not by his care and oversight only, but by his own personal and often labours also with them [p].

To these may be added, that whereas, by virtue of his Deanery of Westminster, his Mastership at Pembroke Hall, and his Bishopric of Ely, the election of scholars into the School of Westminster, and from thence to the two Universities [q], as also of many Scholars and Fellows in Pembroke

[o] [He obtained for the College a licence of mortmain for 80*l.* a-year from Queen Elizabeth, and for 200*l.* a-year from K. James. (Parker's σκελ. Cantab.)]

[p] ["In this school he (Hacket) first became known to the incomparable Bishop Andrewes, who, being then Dean of Westminster, in the necessary absence of the Master, would sometimes come into the school, and teach the boys. There that learned and pious Bishop first took notice of this young scholar, for his great diligence, modesty, pregnancy of parts, strong inclinations to learning and virtue, which he afterwards constantly cherished, both at school and university, to his death. On the other side, our young scholar ever revered this great person *in loco parentum*, often retired to him for advice in his studies, and ever honoured him, as St. Cyprian did Tertullian, *tanquam magistrum.*" — Plume's Life of Hacket.

Among the scholars of Westminster School at this time were Brian Duppa, afterwards Bishop of Chichester, who learned Hebrew from Andrewes; and also Dr. David Stokes, who speaks of Andrewes as the chiefest guide and encourager of his studies, and as having put him into the happiest method and order of them. (Verus Christianus, Append. p. 2.) Stokes was the first publisher of portions of the Bishop's Devotions in Greek and Latin.]

[q] [Bishop Hacket, in his Life of Abp. Williams, par. i. p. 45, thus speaks of the interest Andrewes took when Dean in the studies of the Westminster scholars:—"I told him" (Williams) "how strict that excellent man was to charge our masters that they should give us lessons out of none but the most classical authors; that he did often supply the place both of head schoolmaster and usher, for the space of an whole week together, and gave us not an hour of loitering time from morning to night; how he caused our exercises in prose and verse to be brought to him, to examine our style and proficiency. That he never walked to Chiswick for his recreation without a brace of this young fry, and in that wayfaring leisure had a singular dexterity to fill those narrow vessels with a funnel. And, which was the greatest burden of his toil, sometimes thrice in a week, sometimes oftener, he sent for the uppermost scholars to his lodgings at night, and kept them with him from eight till eleven, unfolding to them the best rudiments of the Greek tongue, and the elements of the Hebrew grammar; and all this he did to boys without any compulsion of correction; nay, I never heard him utter so much as a word of austerity among us." Hacket adds, "He was the first that planted me in my tender studies, and watered them continually with his bounty."]

Hall[r], some in Saint Peter's College[s], and some in Jesus College[t], were in his power and disposal; he was ever so faithful and just, that he waived all letters from great personages for unsufficient scholars, and cast aside all favour and affection, and chose only such as in his judgment were fittest. And lastly, which is not the least in this kind, being many times desired to assist at the election of scholars from the free schools of the Merchant-Tailors[u], and from that at Saint Paul's of the Mercers; and perceiving favour and affection, and other by-respects, sometimes to oversway merit with those to whom the choice belonged; and that divers good scholars were omitted, and others of less desert preferred; he, of his own goodness, divers times took care for such as were so neglected, and sent them to the University, where he bestowed preferment upon them.

To conclude this account of him, take a view of his fidelity in that great place of trust, the Almonership; which was sufficiently evident, especially to those who attended him nearly. First, in that he would never suffer one penny of that which accrued to him by that place to be put or mingled with any of his own rents or revenues; and wherein he kept a more exact account than of his own private estate; and secondly, being so separated, he was as faithful in the disposing of it; not only in the general trust of his sovereign, in the daily charges incident to that place, expended by the sub-almoner, and other yearly ordinary charges; but when he perceived that he had a surplusage, those charges defrayed, he would not suffer it to lie by him; but some of it he dis-

[r] [The concurrence of the Master is requisite for the election of a Fellow of Pembroke College.]

[s] [It appears that in the election of the Master of S. Peter's College, two candidates are presented to the Bishop of Ely, who selects and institutes one of them; and that if, after a third scrutiny, no two candidates have a majority, the appointment is vested absolutely in the Bishop of Ely. The Fellows also are instituted by the Bishop after a year of probation.]

[t] [In Jesus College, the Mastership, to which Bishop Andrewes appointed his brother Roger in 1618, and Bishop Stanley's Fellowship, are in the exclusive gift of the Bishop of Ely: in the case of the other Fellowships, the College nominates two candidates, of whom the Bishop chooses one. There is also a Stanley Fellowship in St. John's College, to which the Bishop of Ely nominates.]

[u] [In Wilson's History of Merchant Tailors' School there is repeated mention made of Bishop Andrewes' presence at the annual examinations; and in page 73 he is especially spoken of as trying the scholars in the Hebrew Psalter. It was from his knowledge of Wren at these examinations that he obtained for him a scholarship at Pembroke, and afterwards took him under his patronage.]

posed to the relief of poor housekeepers, some in releasing of poor prisoners, and comforting them which lay in misery and iron; and some in furnishing poor people with gowns, hose, shoes, and the like: for all which, many, so bestowed by him, had he reserved to his own use, (his patent being *sine computo*[x],) no man could have questioned him: but he was a faithful steward in this, as in the rest, and expected that joyful *Euge*, "Well done, thou good and faithful servant; thou hast been faithful, &c.: enter thou into the joy of thy Lord;" which, no doubt, but he possesseth.

The next is his gratitude or thankfulness to all from whom he had received any benefit. Of this virtue of his there are and were lately divers witnesses: as Dr. Ward, son to his first schoolmaster, upon whom he bestowed the living of Waltham, in Hampshire [y]: and Master Mulcaster, his other schoolmaster, whom he ever reverently respected during his life in all companies, and placed him ever at the upper end of his table; and, after his death, caused his picture, having but few other in his house, to be set over his study door. And not only showed he this outward thankfulness to him, but supplied his wants many times also, privately, in a liberal and plentiful manner; and at his own death, the father being dead, he bequeathed a legacy to his son of good value. Concerning the kindred of Doctor Wattes, who, as is said before, bestowed a full scholarship on him in Pembroke Hall, after much inquiry, he found only one, upon whom, being a scholar, he bestowed preferments in Pembroke Hall; and, he dying there, his Lordship much grieved that he could hear of no more of that kindred, to whom he might express his further thankfulness. And yet, he forgat not his patron, Dr. Wattes, at his end; for by his will he took order, that out of the Scholarships of that foundation, the two Fellowships which he himself founded, as you shall see by-and-by, in Pembroke Hall, should be supplied, if they should be found fit for them.

Lastly, to Pembroke Hall, omitting the legacies by him bequeathed to the parishes of Saint Giles, Saint Martin Ludgate, where he had dwelt, Saint Andrew's in Holborn,

---

[x] [See above, p. x. note q.]
[y] [Buckeridge states that the preferment was bestowed on Ward the father. (Funeral Sermon, p. 289.)]

Saint Saviour's in Southwark, All Saints, Barking, where he was born, and others; to that college, I say, where he had been a Scholar, Fellow, and Master, he gave one thousand pounds, to purchase land for two Fellowships, and for other uses in that college expressed in his will; besides three hundred such folio books of his own to the increase of that college library, as were not there before. Together with a gilt cup, and a bason and ewer, in all points, as weight, fashion, inscription, &c., so like to the cup, bason, and ewer given about 300 years since to that college, by the religious foundress thereof, as that not *ovum ovo similius;* and these, he professed, he caused to be made and given, not for the continuance of his own memory, but for fear that those which she had given so long since might miscarry, and so her remembrance might decay [z].

The fifth is his munificence and bounty. To prove which, little need be said more than that which has been touched in his bountiful charity. But besides that, the two famous Universities, and they which then were poor scholars in them, will witness for him in this point; he never coming near either of them, after he was Bishop, but that he sent to be distributed among poor scholars sometimes one hundred pounds, and ever fifty pounds, at the least. One thing I cannot pass over in silence; that when King James was pleased to grace the University of Cambridge with his presence, in 1617[a], this reverend father being present also at the

[z] [This plate was probably sent by the College to King Charles I. The Foundress's original cup still remains; but Bishop Andrewes' gifts had passed from the College at the restoration of Charles II.]

[a] [This visit was paid by the King in March, 161¾ (not in 1617, as mentioned in the text). A full account of it is given in Nichols's Royal Progresses, vol. ii. pp. 48—65, as well as of the second visit the King paid that University in the following May. Chamberlain writes to Sir Dudley Carleton: "The Divinity Act was performed reasonably well, but not answerable to the expectation; the Law and Physic Acts stark naught; but the Philosophy Act made amends, and, indeed, was very excellent, insomuch that the same day the Bishop of Ely sent the Moderator, the Answerer, the Varier, or Prevaricator, and one of the Repliers, that were all of his house, twenty angels a-piece." A long account of the Philosophy Act is given in Ball's Life of Preston, (quoted by Nichols,) from which it appears that " Mr. Wren, of Pembroke Hall (afterwards Bishop of Ely), was Answerer, or Respondent, in it; Dr. Preston, of Queens' College, First Opponent; and Dr. Meade, of Pembroke Hall, Moderator; and the question in it was, whether dogs could make syllogisms,—a question very well suited to the King's love for hunting, and perhaps suggested, either by a passage from Chrysippus, in Sir Walter Raleigh's 'Sceptic,' in which the position is affirmed, or by Montaigne's 'Apology for Raimond de Sebonde,' where he takes occasion to mention

Philosophy Act, he sent at his departure to four of the disputants forty pieces of gold, of two-and-twenty shillings a-piece, to be equally divided among them.

But what speak I of these? Was ever prince better entertained, and in more magnificent but orderly manner, than was his said Majesty at Farnham Castle, one of the houses belonging to the Bishopric of Winchester, where in the space of three days he spent three thousand pounds, to the extraordinary contentment of his Majesty, and the admiration of all his followers [b].

The next is his hospitality; from the first time of his preferment to means of any considerable value, even to his dying day, he was ever hospitable, and free in entertainment to all people of quality and worthy of respect, especially to scholars and strangers; his table being ever bountifully and neatly furnished with provisions, and attendants answerable; to whom he committed the care of providing and expending in a plentiful yet orderly way; himself seldom knowing what meat he had, till he came from his study to dinner, at which he would show himself so noble in his entertainment, and so

---

this passage in Chrysippus." "Dr. Wren," says Fuller, in his "Worthies," (vol. ii. p. 67, London, 1811,) "kept this Philosophy Act with no less praise to himself than pleasure to the King; where, if men should forget, even dogs would remember his seasonable distinction what the King's hounds could perform above others, by virtue of their prerogative." (Nichols's Royal Progresses of King James, vol. iii. pp. 57, 58.) In the Appendix to vol. iii. (p. 1093), Nichols adds (on the authority of Gauden), that the Prevaricator on this occasion was Ralph Brownrig, afterwards Bishop of Exeter. Gauden describes the part of Prevaricator as "joco-serious, a mixture of philosophy with wit and oratory." See Gauden's Life of Brownrig, subjoined to his Funeral Sermon, p. 154. Lond. 1660.

Walton writes, that King James I., on his visiting Cambridge, " was attended by Sir Francis Bacon (Lord Verulam), and by the ever memorable and learned Dr. Andrewes, Bishop of Winchester, both which did at that time begin a desired friendship with our Orator. . . . For the learned Bishop, it is observable, that at that time there fell to be a modest debate betwixt them two about predestination, and sanctity of life: of both which the Orator did, not long after, send the Bishop some safe and useful aphorisms, in a long letter, written in Greek; which letter was so remarkable for the language and reason of it, that, after the reading it, the Bishop put it into his bosom, and did often show it to many scholars, both of this and foreign nations; but did always return it back to the place where he first lodged it, and continued it so near his heart till the last day of his life."—Walton's Life of Herbert, in Wordsworth's Eccl. Biogr. vol. iv. p. 15.]

[b] [King James visited Farnham Aug. 31, 1620, on his return from his Western Progress. Chamberlain writes to Sir Dudley Carleton, on July 27: "The King is in progress by this time as far as Salisbury, and makes his return by Farnham Castle, where the Bishop of Winchester entertains him, and makes account it will cost him 1,000*l*."—Birch's Court of James I. vol. ii. p. 207.

Andrewes also entertained the King for six days in 1622. See ibid. p. 326. This was perhaps the occasion when the 3,000*l*. were expended.]

gravely facetious, that his guests would often profess, they never came to any man's table where they received better satisfaction in all points, and that his Lordship kept Christmas all the year, in respect of the plenty they ever found there. And yet, by the way, take this, that he ever strictly observed in his provisions of diet, the time of Lent, Embers, and other fasting days, according to the laws of this kingdom, and the orders of the Church.

I shall not need to speak of the extraordinary great hospitality he kept, and the large expense he was at, in entertainment of all sorts of people in Scotland, at what time he attended King James thither [c]; the nobility, clergy, gentry, and others of both nations there present, will, as they often already have, speak of it for me, to his exceeding great honour. So that I know not whether I have fitly couched it under this head of hospitality, or whether it had more properly belonged to that of his munificence and bounty.

The seventh is, his humanity and affability, not only to the last mentioned, his guests, but to every one that did converse with him; for which, not only divers famous scholars and others of this kingdom, but others of foreign parts, as they had just cause, have admired him. As, not to mention natives, Master Casaubon [d], Master Cluverius [e], Master Vossius [f], Master Grotius [g], Master Moulin [h], Master Barclay [i], and, besides many others, Master Erpenius [k], to whom he

[c] [Bishop Andrewes attended King James to Scotland, in 1617, together with Bishops Montagu and Neile, the latter of whom Laud accompanied as Chaplain. Andrewes preached on Easter-day (April 20) at Durham Cathedral, and again on Whit-Sunday (June 8) at Holyrood House.]

[d] [The intimacy between Casaubon and Bishop Andrewes will be noticed at length in the Appendix.]

[e] [Philip Cluverius, the celebrated geographer and linguist.]

[f] [Gerard John Vossius, Professor of Divinity at Leyden, the intimate friend and correspondent of Laud, who obtained for him a Stall in Canterbury Cathedral.]

[g] [The opinion which Grotius entertained of Andrewes, will be found in the extracts from his letters to Overall, given in the Appendix.]

[h] [Peter Du Moulin, or Molinæus, a French Protestant. King James presented him, in 1615, with a Prebendal Stall at Canterbury. His correspondence with Andrewes on Episcopacy, is printed in the Opusc. Posthuma, pp. 173—216.]

[i] [John Barclay, the author of the "Argenis." He resided in England for six years, and assisted King James in the composition of his "Apologia pro Juramento Fidelitatis." His father, William Barclay, a Scotchman by birth, had already written against the ultramontane claims in his treatise "De Potestate Papæ;" to which Bellarmine published a reply.]

[k] [Thomas Erpenius, or Van Erpe, the Professor of Oriental Literature at Leyden; one of the great revivers of Oriental learning.]

tendered an annual stipend, to have read and taught here the Oriental tongues, wherein, long before his death, he himself had been well versed, as may appear by his Commencement verses; the experienced professors whereof he much delighted in, and did much for them; as Master Bedwell, to whom he gave the Vicarage of Tottenham in Middlesex [1], if living, among others would testify. And the reason for this a late reverend father of this Church hath given, *Omnes quid in se amant, in aliis venerantur;* 'loving and honouring those gifts in others, which he had in himself [m];' for among the other parts of his profound learning, he by his industry had attained to the knowledge of fifteen tongues, if not more [n].

To these former may be added his modesty, which was ever such, that although the whole Christian world took especial notice of his profound and deep learning, yet was he so far from acknowledging it in himself, that he would often complain of his defects, even to the extenuating, yea vilifying of his own worth and abilities; professing many times, that he was but *inutilis servus,* nay, *inutile pondus;* insomuch that being preferred by King James to the Bishopric of Chichester, and pretending his own imperfections and insufficiency to undergo such a charge, as also that he might have not only his Clergy, but all others to take notice thereof, he caused to be engraven about the seal of his Bishopric, those words of St. Paul, *Et ad hæc quis idoneus?* "And who is sufficient for these things?" 2 Cor. ii. 16.

One note of his modesty, mixed with his last virtue of humanity, may be added, that after his chaplains had preached in his chapel before him, he would sometimes privately request them, that he might have a sight of their notes, with very good words and full of encouragement; insomuch that they would profess of him, that they would never desire a more candid auditor. So that what was said of Beda, may as fitly be said of him, *A pietate, modestia, et castitate, nomen Venerabilis adeptus est.*

---

[1] [See above, p. xvi.]
[m] [Buckeridge's Funeral Sermon, p. 292.]
[n] [Fuller (Ch. Hist. book xi. sect. i. § 46) thus writes of him: "The world wanted learning to know how learned this man was, so skilled in all (especially Oriental) languages, that some conceive he might, if then living, almost have served as an interpreter-general at the confusion of tongues."]

His indefatigability in study cannot be paralleled, if we consider him from his childhood to his old age. Never any man took such pains, or at least spent so much time in study, as this Reverend Prelate; for even in those days, when it might have been supposed he would have taken some ease for his former pains, then also from the hour he arose, his private devotions finished, to the time he was called to dinner, which, by his own order, was not till twelve at noon at the soonest [o], he kept close at his book, and would not be interrupted by any that came to speak with him, or upon any occasion, public prayer excepted. Insomuch, that he would be so displeased with scholars that attempted to speak with him in a morning, that he would say, "he doubted they were no true scholars, that came to speak with him before noon."

After dinner, for two or three hours space, he would willingly pass the time, either in discourse with his guests or other friends, or in despatch of his own temporal affairs, or of those, who, by reason of his Episcopal jurisdiction, attended him; and being quit of these and the like occasions, he would return to his study, where he spent the rest of the afternoon even till bed-time, except some friend took him off to supper, and then did he eat but sparingly.

Of the fruit of this his seed-time, the world, especially this land, hath reaped a plentiful harvest in his sermons and writings: never went any beyond him in the first of these, his preaching, wherein he had such a dexterity, that some would say of him, that he was quick again as soon as delivered; and in this faculty he hath left a pattern unimitable [p]. So

[o] [See the anecdote told by Bishop Wren, quoted below, in Appendix.]

[p] ["He was always a diligent and painful preacher. Most of his solemn sermons he was most careful of, and exact. I dare say, few of them but they passed his hand, and were thrice revised, before they were preached; and he ever misliked often and loose preaching without study of antiquity, and he would be bold with himself, and say, when he preached twice a day at St. Giles's, he prated once; and when his weakness grew on him, and that by infirmity of his body he grew unable to preach, he began to go little to court, not so much for weakness, as for inability to preach."—Buckeridge's Funeral Sermon, pp. 295, 296.

Fuller (Worthies, vol. ii. p. 66) thus writes: "He was an unimitable preacher in his way; and such plagiaries who have stolen his sermons could never steal his preaching; and could make nothing of that, of which he made all things as he desired. Pious and pleasant Bishop Felton (his contemporary and colleague) endeavoured in vain in his sermons to assimilate his style; and therefore said merrily of himself, 'I had almost marred my own natural trot, by endeavouring to imitate his artificial

that he was truly styled, *Stella prædicantium,* and " an angel in the pulpit." And his late Majesty took especial care in causing that volume of his sermons to be divulged q, though but a handful of those which he preached, by enjoying whereof this kingdom hath an inestimable treasure.

And for his acuteness and profundity in writing against the adversary, he so excelled all others of his time, that neither Bellarmine, champion to the Romanists, nor any other of them, was ever able to answer what he wrote; so that as his sermons were unimitable, his writings were unanswerable.

To draw to an end of deciphering his virtues, and endowments; it may truly be said of him, that he had those gifts and graces, both of art and nature, so fixed in him, as that this age cannot parallel him; for his profundity and abyss of learning was accompanied with wit, memory, judgment, languages, gravity, and humility; insomuch, that if he had been contemporary with the ancient fathers of the primitive Church, he would have been, and that worthily, reputed not inferior to the chiefest among them.

He generally hated all vices: but three, which he ever reputed sins, were most especially odious unto him. First, usury, from which he was so far himself[r], that when his friends had need of such money as he could spare, he lent it to them freely, without expectance of aught back but the principal. Secondly. The second was simony, which was so detestable to him, as that for refusing to admit divers men to livings, whom he suspected to be simoniacally preferred, he suffered much by suits of law; choosing rather to be compelled against his will to admit them by law, than voluntarily to do that which his conscience made scruple of. And for the livings and other preferments which fell in his own gift, he ever bestowed them freely, as you have seen before, upon deserving men, without suit[s]: so that we may say of him,

amble.'" Fuller further observes, in his Church History (book xi. sect. i. § 48), "As for such who causelessly have charged his sermons as 'affected and surcharged with verbal allusion,' when they themselves have set forth the like, it will be then time enough to make this Bishop's first defence against their calumniations."]

q [It was published, at the King's command, by Bishops Buckeridge and Laud.]

r [See his "Determinatio de Usuris," in Opusc. Posthuma.]

s [Hyde writes thus to Dr. John Barwick, Nov. 28, 1659: "I have always been of the opinion, that the method you say was observed by

as was said long since concerning Robert Winchelsey, Archbishop of Canterbury, *Beneficia Ecclesiastica nunquam nisi doctis contulit: precibus ac gratia nobilium fretos, et ambientes semper repulit*[t]. Thirdly. The last was sacrilege, which he did so much abhor, that when the Bishopric of Sarum, and that of Ely, before it was so much deplumed [u], were offered to him upon terms savouring that way, he utterly rejected them. Concerning that of Salisbury [x], give me leave to add a particular passage of his, which happened many years after his said refusal of it, which was this: At a Parliament under King James, when an Act was to pass, concerning Sherbourne Castle, it was observed, that only Bishop Andrewes and another gave their votes against the same; that the other

Bishop Andrewes, and the Bishop of Ely [Wren], is the right; and if the King were at Whitehall to-morrow, he should never prefer any man in the Church, who sought it."—(Vita J. Barwick, p. 371. Lond. 1721.)]

[t] [Godwin de Præsul. Ang. pp. 102, 103. Cant. 1743.]

[u] [Hatton obtained of Bishop Cox, a lease of the best part of Ely House, Holborn, and the garden and closes belonging to it, for a lease of twenty-one years, at little or no rent. He afterwards endeavoured to obtain a perpetual alienation of this property, to which Cox would not accede. (Strype's Annals, vol. ii. p. 533.) Subsequently it was arranged that the Bishop should, by way of mortgage, convey to the Queen, and the Queen to Mr. Hatton, the house and gardens, &c., at that time in lease to him; but withal to be redeemable upon the payment of 1,800*l.*; the sum which Hatton affirmed he had laid out on it. Nothing was done towards paying off this mortgage till Bishop Andrewes's time, who resolved to pay it, lest the Church should suffer at the long run; but this was prevented by the removal of him to Winchester. See Bentham's Ely, vol. i. p. 206, note 3, where the subsequent history of the property is detailed.

After Cox's death, (the see which had been vacant for eighteen years, having been refused by Andrewes,) Sir John Harington states that Heton "was compelled in a sort to take it (for *potentes cum rogant jubent*), and as long as there was not *quid dabis*, but *hæc auferam*, the more public it was, and by authority then lawful, he may be thought the more free from blame." —State of Church of England, p. 79. Lond. 1653.]

[x] [The manor and castle of Sherborne, after having been recovered from Sir John Horsley by Bishop Capon, were again alienated by Bishop Coldwell to Sir Walter Raleigh. On this business, Harington (pp. 88, 89) writes in the following strain:— "How Dr. John Coldwell, of a physician became a bishop, I have heard by more than a good many, and I will briefly handle it, and as tenderly as I can, bearing myself equal between the living (Sir Walter Raleigh) and the dead (Bishop Coldwell). I touched before how this Church of Salisbury surfeited of a Capon; which laying heavy in her stomach, it may be thought she had some need of a physician. But this man proved no good Church physician. Had she been sick of a plurisy, (too much abounding with blood, as in ages past,) then such bleeding physic perhaps might have done her no harm. But now inclining rather to a consumption, to let her bleed afresh at so large a vein, was almost enough to draw out the very life-blood," &c.

Upon Sir Walter Raleigh's attainder, these lands came, by the King's gift, to Prince Henry, after his death to Carr, the Earl of Somerset, and then to Digby, Earl of Bristol. See "An Account of the Strange Curse belonging to Shireburne Castle." from a MS. of the late Bishop of Ely, Dr. John More, in Peck's Desid. Curiosa, lib. xiv. pp. 518—520.]

should so do was not much marvelled at, but that Bishop Andrewes should do it, when none but that other Lord did so, was so remarkable, as that he was demanded by a great person, what his reason was for it. To which he most worthily replied, that it could not be well wondered, why he should now vote against that, which if he would have yielded unto many years before, in the days of Queen Elizabeth, he might have had this Bishopric of Sarum; which reason of his, when his late Majesty, being then Prince and present at the passing of the Act, heard, he beshrewed him, that when he denied his consent, he did not declare the reason of his denial also; professing that had he been made acquainted with the state of that case, as now he was, he would, with the King his father's good leave, have laboured against the passing of the said Act. To close up this point, this Reverend Prelate went yet a degree further, in refusing, when he was Bishop of Winchester, divers large and considerable sums to renew some leases, because he conceived that the renewing of them might be prejudicial to succession.

Now let us lay all these together: his zeal and piety; his charity and compassion; his fidelity and integrity; his gratitude and thankfulness; his munificence and bounty; hospitality, humanity, affability, and modesty; and to these, his indefatigability in study, and the fruits of his labours in his sermons and writings, together with his profundity in all kind of learning; his wit, memory, judgment, gravity, and humility. His detestation of all vices and sin, but especially of three. All which, by couching them only in this compend, we have seen in him, as *ex ungue leonem,* or by Hercules' foot his whole body; and consider, whether the Church of God in general, and this in particular, did not suffer an irreparable loss by his death y.

y [Hacket's eulogy of him may be here introduced: "This is that Andrewes, the ointment of whose name is sweeter than all spices. (Cant. iv. 10.) This is that celebrated Bishop of Winton, whose learning King James admired above all his chaplains; and that King, being of most excellent parts himself, could the better discover what was eminent in another. Indeed, he was the most apostolical and primitive-like divine, in my opinion, that wore a rochet in his age; of a most venerable gravity, and yet most sweet in all commerce, the most devout that ever I saw, when he appeared before God; of such a growth in all kind of learning, that very able clerks were of a low stature to him; *colossus inter icumculas;* full of alms and charity, of which none knew but his Father in secret; a certain patron to scholars of fame and ability, and chiefly to those that never expected it.

In

Having taken a short survey of his life, let us now see him dying. He was not often sick, and but once till his last sickness in thirty years before the time he died; which was at Downham, in the Isle of Ely [z]; the air of that place not agreeing with the constitution of his body. But there he seemed to be prepared for his dissolution, saying oftentimes in that sickness, " It must come once, and why not here?" And at other times before and since he would say, " The days must come, when, whether we will or nill, we shall say with the Preacher, ' I have no pleasure in them [a].' "

Of his death he seemed to presage himself a year before he died [b], and therefore prepared his oil, that he might be admitted in due time into the bride-chamber [c]. That of *qualis vita,* &c. was truly verified in him; for as he lived, so died he. As his fidelity in his health was great, so increased the strength of his faith in his sickness; his gratitude to men was now changed into his thankfulness to God; his affability, to incessant and devout prayers and speech with his Creator, Redeemer, and Sanctifier. His laborious studies, to his restless groans, sighs, cries, and tears; his hands labouring, his

In the pulpit, a Homer among preachers, and may fitly be set forth in Quinctilian's judgment of Homer: *Nonne humani ingenii modum excessit ? Ut magni sit viri, virtutes ejus non æmulatione, quod fieri non potest, sed intellectu sequi.* I am transported, even as in a rapture, to make this digression; for who could come near the shrine of such a saint, and not offer up a few grains of glory upon it?"—Hacket's Life of Williams, par. i. p. 45.]

[z] [See his letter to Isaac Casaubon, printed below. It will also be remembered that he was prevented by illness from attending King James's death-bed.]

[a] Eccles. xii. 1.

[b] [Mede writes to Sir Martin Stuteville, May 27, 1626 : " The Bishop of Winchester is also very ill, and hath long been sick."]

[c] [" Of this reverend Prelate I may say, *Vita ejus vita orationis,* ' his life was a life of prayer;' a great part of five hours every day did he spend in prayer and devotion to God. After the death of his brother, Master Thomas Andrewes, in the sickness time, whom he loved dearly, he began to foretell his own death before the end of summer, or before the beginning of winter; and when his brother, Master Nicholas Andrewes, died, he took that as a certain sign and prognostic and warning of his own death; and from that time till the hour of his dissolution, he spent all his time in prayer; and his Prayer-book, when he was private, was seldom seen out of his hands; and in the time of his fever and last sickness, besides the often prayers which were read to him, in which he repeated all the parts of the Confession, and other petitions, with an audible voice, as long as his strength endured, he did—as was well observed by certain tokens in him—continually pray to himself, though he seemed otherwise to rest or slumber; and when he could pray no longer *voce*—with his voice, yet, *oculis et manibus*—by lifting up his eyes and hands, he prayed still; and when, *nec manus nec vox officium faciunt*—both voice and eyes and hands failed in their office, then *corde*—with his heart, he still prayed, until it pleased God to receive his blessed soul to Himself."—Buckeridge's Fun. Serm. pp. 296, 297.]

eyes lifted up, and his heart beating and panting to see the living God, even to the last of his breath. And Him, no doubt, he sees face to face, his works preceding and following him, and he now following the Lamb, crowned with that immortality which is reserved for every one who lives such a life as he lived.

He departed this life September 25, 1626, in the seventy-first year of his age [d]; and lieth buried in the upper aisle of the parish church of St. Saviour's in Southwark [e]. His execu-

---

[d] [Selden thus notices his death in a letter to Sir Robert Cotton:—"Since I wrote this, I hear of the loss of my Lord of Winchester. His lingering sickness hath, together with his age, made his best friends the easier take it. I doubt not it was rather nature than death that took him away, if they might be divided in him. I heartily wish his library may be kept together, at least till we may see it. Something I have in it that I value much, and something else of slight moment. That which I would take care of is an Armenian dictionary. I never saw another copy, and my Lord borrowed it of me two years since. A (sic) he hath also of mine, which I must render to Mr. Boswell. These two I would not willingly lose. What else his library hath of mine, is of no great moment; but I shall know it when I come to mine own, where I have something also that was his."—Birch's Charles I. vol. i. pp. 152, 153.

Among other tributes to his memory, his death was lamented in a Latin elegy by Milton, then a student at Christ's College, Cambridge.]

[e] [The following account of his funeral is copied by Thomas W. King, Esq., York Herald, from a MS. in the Heralds' College:—

"The Right reuerend father in God Launcelot Andrews late Bishop of Winchester, Deane of his Ma[ts] Chappell, prelate of y[e] moste noble Order of y[e] Garter, and one of his Ma[ts] most honourable priuie Councell, Departed this mortall life at Winchester house in Southwark on fryday being y[e] 26th of September 1626 whose funerall was most honourably solempnized according to his degree on Satterday y[e] 11th of November following, and proceeded from his house aforesaid to the parrish Church of S[t] Saviours in Southwark, where his body lieth interred. This most reuerend father in God having spent his whole course of life piously and Religiously, and attayned to y[e] age of 71 yeares and moneths all y[t] tyme living a single life, died, most charitably disposing of a great part of his estate to his kindred, servants, and friends, but y[e] greatest parte to Charitable vses partly appoynted by himselfe and partly lefte to y[e] discreation of Mr. John Parker Esquior (sometyme elected Alderman of London, and payed his fyne) whom he made his sole Executor, he being a man of whose integrity he had a great confidence y[t] all things should be accomplished and according to his owne desire, And who hath not fayled in any thing either in doing him honor or fulfilling y[t] great trust and charge committed vnto him by his last will. This funerall was ordered and directed by S[r] William Segar Garter principall King, Henry S[t]. George Richmond Herauld, and George Owen Rouge-crosse. The Bishop of Duresme[1] chiefe mourner assisted by Docter Andrews [2], brother of y[e] Defunct, Mr. Burrell [3], Mr. Salmon [4], Mr. Roger Andrews [5], and Mr. Rooke [6]. The great Banner borne by Mr. William Andrews [7], The 4 bannerolls borne by Mr.

---

[1] [Richard Neile.]
[2] [See above, p. xvi.]
[3] [The husband of his sister Mary.]
[4] [The husband of his sister Martha.]
[5] [The son of his brother Thomas.]
[6] [The husband of his niece, Mary, daughter of Mary Burrill.]
[7] [The son of his brother Nicholas.]

tors have erected to him a very fair monument of marble and alabaster[f]. And one that formerly had been his household chaplain, whom this honourable and reverend Prelate loved most tenderly from his childhood, rather like a father than a lord or patron, but since his death has been a successor to him in some of his places in the Church[g]; for the duty and reverence which he ever bare to him while he lived, hath most gratefully and cordially in his everlasting honourable

Princeps[8], Mr. Samuel Burwell[9], Mr. Peter Salmon[10], and Mr. Thomas Andrews[11]. The Corps assisted by Docter Collyns[12], Docter Beale[13], Docter Wrenne[14], and Docter Greene[15]. This Certificate was taken by Henry St. George Richmond, and is testified by ye subscription of Mr. John Parker aforesaid his Executor.
From the Book of Funeral Certificates marked 'I. 8,' (*fol.* 31,) *in the College of Arms, London.*"
It is stated in Manning and Bray's Survey, that in 1626, on the funeral of Lancelot Andrewes, Bishop of Winchester, who had been a benefactor to the parish, the inhabitants honoured the solemnity of his funeral, by hanging the church and chancel with 165 yards of black bays. The house mourners made an offering, and Mr. Archer, one of the Chaplains, received 11*l.* 17*s.* 7*d.*, which he paid to the Wardens as their due, but they handsomely returned it to him and Mr. Micklethwaite (the other Chaplain)."]

[f] [It is thus described in Manning and Bray's Survey (vol. iii. p. 575): " In the middle is an altar tomb, with the figure of Bishop Andrewes, recumbent in his scarlet robes, as Prelate of the Order of the Garter; he has a black cap, and small ruff, his right hand with a book rests on his breast, the left arm is extended on a tablet supported by Justice, and Fortitude or Faith ; at his feet are his arms, the See of Winchester impaling Arg. on a band engrailed between two cotices Sable, three mullets Or, encircled by the Garter. At his head is inscribed : 'Sept. 25, die Lunæ, horâ matutinâ ferè quartâ, Lancelotus Andrews Episcopus Wintoniensis, meritissimum lumen orbis Christianum, mortuus est,' (Ephemeris Laudiana anno Domini 1626,) ' ætatis suæ 71.' Over this tomb there was originally a fair canopy supported by black marble pillars ; but the roof falling in, and the chapel being much defaced by the fire in 1676, the canopy was broken, and was not repaired ; and the following inscription was also lost and not restored." (Here follows a Latin inscription as in the text.) At the west end of the tomb is inscribed, 'Monumentum quoad hoc restitutum 1703, 1764. Iterum restitutum 1810.'"

This monument was situated in the easternmost chapel, now entirely destroyed. We are informed, that, " Upon removing the tomb, about July 1830, when the Bishop's chapel was taken down, the inside was found closely bricked up, and upon opening it, a very large leaden coffin was discovered, inscribed, " L. A." on the lid ; excepting the iron rings at each end, it was in excellent preservation. This coffin and monument are now deposited at the western end of the Lady Chapel, in the centre, against the back of the altar screen."—Wilkinson's Londina Illustrata.]

[g] [Bishop Wren.]

---

[8] [The son of his sister, Martha Salmon, by her first husband.]
[9] [Third son of his sister, Mary Burrill.]
[10] [Eldest son of Martha Salmon, by her second husband.]
[11] [The eldest son of his brother Thomas.]
[12] [See above, p. xvii.]   [13] [See above, p. xvi.]
[14] [See above, p. xvi.]
[15] [Christopher Green, of C. C. C. Oxford. (See Wood, F. O. vol. i. p. 407.) He was Rector of Stockton, Wilts. See above, p. xvii.]

memory, added to it a most excellent, significant, and speaking epitaph, which followeth[h]:—

LECTOR.

SI CHRISTIANUS ES, SISTE:
MORÆ PRETIUM ERIT,
NON NESCIRE TE, QUI VIR HIC SITUS SIT
EJUSDEM TECUM CATHOLICÆ ECCLESIÆ MEMBRUM,
SUB EADEM FELICIS RESURRECTIONIS SPE,
EANDEM D. JESU PRÆSTOLANS EPIPHANIAM,
SACRATISSIMUS ANTISTES, LANCELOTUS ANDREWES,
LONDINI ORIUNDUS, EDUCATUS CANTABRIGIÆ
AULÆ PEMBROCH: ALUMNORUM, SOCIORUM, PRÆFECTORUM
UNUS, ET NEMINI SECUNDUS.
LINGUARUM, ARTIUM, SCIENTIARUM,
HUMANORUM, DIVINORUM OMNIUM
INFINITUS THESAURUS, STUPENDUM ORACULUM;
ORTHODOXÆ CHRISTI ECCLESIÆ
DICTIS, SCRIPTIS, PRECIBUS, EXEMPLO,
INCOMPARABILE PROPUGNACULUM:
REGINÆ ELIZABETHÆ A SACRIS,
D. PAULI LONDON. RESIDENTIARIUS,
D. PETRI WESTMONAST. DECANUS,
EPISCOPUS CICESTRENSIS, ELIENSIS, WINTONIENSIS,
REGIQUE JACOBO TUM AB ELEEMOSYNIS,
TUM AB UTRIUSQUE REGNI CONSILIIS,
DECANUS DENIQUE SACELLI REGII.
IDEM EX
INDEFESSA OPERA IN STUDIIS,
SUMMA SAPIENTIA IN REBUS,
ASSIDUA PIETATE IN DEUM,
PROFUSA LARGITATE IN EGENOS,
RARA AMŒNITATE IN SUOS,
SPECTATA PROBITATE IN OMNES,
ÆTERNUM ADMIRANDUS:
ANNORUM PARITER, ET PUBLICÆ FAMÆ SATUR,

---

[h] [Mr. Hallam (Const. Hist. chap. viii.) sneers in his usual manner at one expression in this epitaph. He thus writes: "Andrewes' epitaph in Winchester Cathedral (!) speaks of him as having received a superior reward in heaven, on account of his celibacy; *cœlebs migravit ad aureolam cœlestem.* 'Aureola,' a word of no classical authority, means, in the style of popish divinity which the author of this epitaph thought fit to employ, the crown of virginity." The word is used by S. Th. Aquin.]

SED BONORUM PASSIM OMNIUM CUM LUCTU DENATUS,
CŒLEBS HINC MIGRAVIT AD AUREOLAM CŒLESTEM
ANNO
REGIS CAROLI II°. ÆTATIS SUÆ LXXI°.
CHRISTI MDCXXVI°.
TANTUM EST, LECTOR, QUOD TE MŒRENTES POSTERI
NUNC VOLEBANT, ATQUE UT EX VOTO TUO VALEAS, DICTO

SIT DEO GLORIA.

HIS WORKS[i].

In the volume of his Sermons, there are seventeen sermons of the Nativity, preached upon Christmas-day. Eight sermons upon Repentance and Fasting, preached upon Ash-Wednesday. Six sermons preached in Lent. Three sermons of the Passion, preached upon Good Friday. Eighteen sermons of the Resurrection, preached upon Easter-day. Fifteen sermons of the sending of the Holy Ghost, preached upon Whitsunday. Eight sermons preached upon the fifth of August. Ten sermons preached upon the fifth of November. Eleven sermons preached upon several occasions [k].

A Manual of Private Devotions and Meditations, for every day in the week.

A Manual of Directions for the Visitation of the Sick.

His Opera Posthuma. Concio ad Clerum pro Gradu Doctoris. Ad Clerum in Synodo Provinciali. Coram Rege habita V°. August, 1606. In discessu Palatini XIII°. April, 1613. Theologica Determinatio de Jurejurando. De Usuris. De Decimis.

Responsiones ad 3 Epistolas Petri Molinæi. An Answer to the 18 and 20 cc. of Cardinal Perron's Reply. A Speech in the Star Chamber against Master Thraske. Another there concerning Vows, in the Countess of Shrewsbury's Case.

Responsio ad Torti librum. Ad Apologiam Cardinalis Bellarmini.

---

[i] These will be noticed more fully in the Appendix.

[k] [This does not include the Sermon "preached before two Kings," which was first printed among the collected Sermons, in the folio of 1661. See below in List of Sermons, Aug. 5, 1606.]

Reader, be serious, let thy thoughts reflect
On this grave Father with a large respect;
Peruse his well-spent life, and thou shalt finde
He had a rare and heav'n-enamell'd minde.
He was our kingdome's Star, and shin'd most bright
In sad affliction's darke and cloudyst night;
Let his example teach us how to live
In love and charity; that we may give
To those, whose wants inforce them to implore
Our ayde, and charity makes no man poore.
ANDREWES was fill'd with goodnesse, all his dayes
Were crown'd and guilded with resounding praise.
The world shall be his Herald to proclaime
The ample glories of his spreading fame.

A MEMOIR

OF

BISHOP ANDREWES.

From Sir John Harington's tract, " A Supply or Addition to the Catalogue of Bishops, to the year 1608;" published under the title of, " A Briefe View of the State of the Church of England. Lond. 1653." pp. 141—147. (Reprinted, with corrections, from the original MS., in Harington's Nugæ Antiquæ, vol. ii. p. 189. Lond. 1804.)

His Majesty having a great desire to prefer Doctor Andrews, then Dean of Westminster, made special choice of him to succeed him [a], as well in the Bishopric as the Almonership, and I suppose if Henry the Third his Chaplain [b] had been so good a scholar, he had not been refused for his learning. This Bishop your Highness [c] knoweth so well, and have heard him so oft, as it may be you think it needless to hear more of him. But I will be bold to say your Highness doth but half know him, for the virtues that are not seen in him are more and greater than those that are seen. I will therefore play the blab so far, that your Highness may know him better. He was born in London, and trained up in the school of that famous Mulcaster, and for the special towardness that was found in him in very young years, he was not only favoured, but had liberal exhibition given him by a great councillor of those times [d], as I shall note hereafter. The course of his study was not, as most men's are in these times, to get a little superficial sight in divinity, by reading two or three of the new writers, and straight take Orders, and up into the pulpit. Of which kind of men a reverend bishop

[a] [Anthony Watson.]
[b] [Robert Paslew, mentioned by Harington in the previous page.]
[c] [Harington's work was written for the use of Prince Henry. See Nugæ Antiquæ, vol. i. pp. 9, 10.]
[d] [Sir F. Walsingham.]

yet living said as properly as pleasantly, when one told of a young man that preached twice every Lord's-day, besides some exercising in the week-days, 'It may be,' saith he, 'he doth talk so often, but I doubt he doth not preach.' And to the like effect the late Queen said to the same Bishop, when she had on the Friday heard one of those talking preachers much commended to her by somebody, and the Sunday after heard a well laboured sermon, which some disgraced as a bosom-sermon, that smelt of the candle, 'I pray,' said she, 'let me have your bosom-sermons, rather than your lip-sermons; for when the preacher takes pains, the auditor takes profit.'

But to come to Dr. Andrews, that gathered before he did spend, reading both new writers and old writers, not as tasting, but as digesting them, and finding according to our Saviour's saying, ὁ παλαιὸς χρηστότερος, the old to be more profitable; at last his sufficiency could be no longer concealed. But as an industrious merchant, that secretly and diligently follows his trade with small show, till his wealth being grown so great, it can be no longer hidden, is then called on for subsidies and loans, and public services: so did this man's excellency suddenly break forth. His patron (that studied projects of policy as much as precepts of piety) hearing of his fame, and meaning to make use thereof, sent for him (as I have credibly heard), and dealt earnestly with him, to hold up a side that was even then falling, and to maintain certain state points of Puritanism. But he that had too much of the ἄνδρος [ἀνδρεῖος?] in him to be scared with a councillor's frown, or blown aside with his breath, answered him plainly, they were not only against his learning, but his conscience. The councillor seeing this man would be no Friar Pinkie (to be taught in a closet what he should say at Paul's), dismissed him with some disdain for the time; but afterward did the more reverence his integrity and honesty, and became no hinderer to his ensuing preferments. Of these, one was a Prebend in Paul's, belonging to him they call the Confessor or Confessioner, a place notoriously abused in time of Popery by their tyranny and superstition, but now of late, by a contrary extreme, too much forgotten and neglected. While he held this place, his manner was, especially in Lent time, to walk duly at certain hours in one of the aisles of the church, that if any came to him for spiritual advice and comfort, (as some did, though not many,) he might impart it to them. This custom being agreeable to the Scripture and Fathers, expressed and required in a sort in the Communion Book, not repugning the XXXIX. Articles, and no less approved by Calvin in his Institutions, yet was quarrelled with by divers (upon occasion of some sermons of his[e]) as a point of Popery. The like scandal was taken of some, though not given by him, for his reverent speaking of the highest mystery of our faith and heavenly food, the Lord's Supper, which some are so stiff in their knees, or rather in their hearts, that they hold it idolatry to receive it kneeling. But whatsoever such barked at, he ever kept one tenor of life and doctrine, exemplar[y] and unreprovable.

Two special things I have observed in his preaching, that I may not omit to speak of. One, to raise a joint reverence to God and the Prince, to the spiritual and civil Magistrate, by uniting and not severing them. The other, to lead to amendment of life, and good works, the fruits of true repentance. Of the first kind, he made a sermon before the Queen long since, which was the most famous, of this text: 'Thou leddest Thy people like sheep by the hands of Moses and Aaron[f].' Which sermon, (though courtiers' ears are commonly so open, as it goes in at one ear, and out at the other,) yet it left an *aculeus* behind in many of all sorts. And Henry Noell, one of the greatest gallants of those times, sware as he was a gentleman, he never heard man speak with such a spirit. And the like to this was his sermon before the King, of two silver trumpets to be made of one piece[g]. Of the second kind I might say all his sermons are, but I will mention but his last, that I heard the fifth of the last November, which sermon I could wish ever to read upon that day. 'When the Lord turned the captivity of Sion[h],' &c. And I never saw his Majesty more sweetly affected with any sermon than with that.

But to conclude; I persuade myself, that whensoever it shall please God to give the King means, with consent of

[e] [See below, List of Sermons, March 30, 1600.]
[f] [Sermon ii. in Lent.]
[g] [Sermons on several Occasions, serm. vii.]
[h] [Sermon ii. on Gunpowder Treason, preached in 1607.]

his confederate princes, to make that great peace which His blessed word, *Beati pacifici*, seemeth to promise,—I mean the ending of this great schism in the Church of God, procured as much by ambition as superstition,—this reverend prelate will be found one of the ablest, not of England only, but of Europe, to set the course for composing the controversies; which I speak not to add reputation to his sufficiency by my judgment; but rather to win credit to my judgment by his sufficiency. And whereas I know some that have not known him so long as I have, yet have heard and believe no less of his learning than I speak, find fault that he is not so apt to deliver his resolution upon every question moved, as they could wish, who if they be not quickly resolved of that they ask, will quickly resolve not to care for it: I say this cunctation is the mean between precipitation and procrastination, and is specially commended by the Apostle St. James, as I have heard him allege it, *Sit omnis homo βραδὺς εἰς τὸ λαλῆσαι, tardus ad loquendum, tardus ad iram.*

LETTERS OF BISHOP ANDREWES.

LETTER I.

TO SIR FRANCIS WALSINGHAM.

[Teale's Lives of English Divines, pp. 12, 13 [a].]

I DO in humble manner crave pardon of your honour, in that I have not myself attended in the re-delivery of the enclosed, to render to your honour my bounden duty of thanks for the contents thereof. Being, besides mine exercise to-morrow, on Monday morning, at the feast of my father's Company, to preach at Deptford[b], I promised myself from your honour a favourable dispensation for the forbearing of my presence till then, what time I shall wait on your honour, to present unto the same my unfeigned humble thanks, and not my thanks only, but my service and myself too, to be ordered and employed by your honour every way. The same of my right and duty belonging to your honour, as well in regard of your honour's great bounty to me these years past, which while I live I am bound to acknowledge, as now for the instant procurement of these two Prebends [c], the one of them no sooner ended, than the other of them straight begun. They are to me both sufficient witnesses of your honour's care for my well-doing, and mindfulness of me upon any occasion. My prayer to God is that I may not live unworthy of these so honourable dealings, but that in some sort, as His holy wisdom shall appoint, I may prove serviceable to your honour, and to your honour's chief care, this Church of ours.

[a] [From MSS. Harl. Numb. 6996. 96.]
[b] [The Corporation of the Trinity House holds its annual meeting on Trinity Monday, when they attend service at Deptford Church.]
[c] [At Southwell, and S. Paul's.]

What your honour hath and further shall vouchsafe to promise in my name, in this or aught else, shall be, I trust, so satisfied as shall stand with your honour's liking every way. So recommending to your honour the perfecting of your honour's own benefit, with my very humble duty, I end.

The Lord Jesus, of His great goodness, grant unto this realm long to enjoy your honour. Amen. May 24, [1589.]

Your honour's in all humble duty and service, so most bound,

L. ANDREWES.

LETTER II.

TO DR. HENRY PARRY.

[Hooker's Works, vol. i. p. 115. Oxf. 1836[d].]

Salutem in Christo.

I cannot choose but write though you do not: I never failed since I last saw you, but daily prayed for him till this very instant you sent this heavy news[e]. I have hitherto prayed, *Serva nobis hunc:* now must I, *Da nobis alium.* Alas, for our great loss! and when I say ours, though I mean yours and mine, yet much more the common: with [which?] the less sense they have of so great a damage, the more sad we need to bewail them and ourselves, who know his works and his worth to be such as behind him he hath not (that I know) left any near him. And whether I shall live to know any near him, I am in great doubt, that I care not how many and myself had redeemed his longer life to have done good in a better subject than he had in hand, though that were very good. Good brother, have a care to deal with his executrix or executor[f], or (him that is like to have a great stroke in it) his father-in-law, that there be special care and regard for preserving such papers as he left, besides the three last books expected. By preserving I mean, that

---

[d] [Mr. Keble states that he has not been able to trace the original of this letter, which appeared first in the edition of Hooker published at Oxford, 1793.]

[e] [Of the death of Hooker, which had taken place Nov. 2.]

[f] [His widow was left his sole executrix.]

not only they be not embezzled, and come to nothing[g], but that they come not into great hands, who will only have use of them *quatenus et quousque*, and suppress the rest, or unhappily all: but rather into the hands of some of them that unfeignedly wished him well, though of the meaner sort; who may upon good assurance (very good assurance) be trusted with them; for it is pity they should admit any limitation. Do this, and do it *mature*: it had been more than time long since to have been about it, if I had sooner known it. If my word or letter would do any good to Mr. Churchman[h] it should not want. But what cannot yourself or Mr. Sandys[i] do therein? For Mr. Cranmer is away[k], happy in that he shall gain a week or two before he know of it. Almighty God comfort us over him! whose taking away I trust I shall no longer live, than with grief I remember; therefore with grief, because with inward and most just honour I ever honoured him since I knew him.

Your assured
Poor loving Friend,
L. ANDREWES.

At the Court, 7 Nov. 1600.

LETTER III.

TO MR. HARTWELL.

[Archæologia, vol. i. Introduction, p. xv.]

SIR,—I have received the enclosed (as it was said) by direction from you: but the party I know not: it was not your hand: it had no mention of my name; and I talked with Mr. Clarentieux[l], and he would not certify me that I was made of your number[m], and yet he was at your last meeting, where

---

[g] [The reader need hardly be reminded that Hooker's papers were destroyed by Charke and another Puritan minister.]

[h] [Hooker's father-in-law.]

[i] [Edwin Sandys, his friend and former pupil. He was appointed with Churchman overseer of his Will.]

[k] [George Cranmer was then absent in Ireland with Lord Mountjoy, where he was killed in a battle with the rebels.]

[l] [William Camden, the celebrated antiquarian.]

[m] [Andrewes was admitted member of the Society of Antiquaries, of which Hartwell was Secretary.]

such things (as he said) used to be agreed on before any came in, whereby I thought it likely the party might be mistaken that brought his note. But if I may have notice from yourself or Mr. Clarentieux that you have vouchsafed me the favour, then you shall perceive well that I will not fail in obedience, though unless it be that I dare not promise, because I cannot perform aught else, for I learn every day more and more gladly. But that this afternoon is our translation time, and most of our company are negligent[n], I would have seen you; but no translation shall hinder me, if once I may understand I shall commit no error in coming. And so, commending me to you in mine ambition and every way beside, I take my leave, this last of November, 1604.

Your very assured poor Friend,
L. ANDREWES.

To the Right Worshipful my very
good Friend Mr. Hartwell, at his
House at Lambeth.

LETTER IV.

TO ISAAC CASAUBON.

[Casauboni Ephemerides, pp. 1203, 1204 [o].]

Factum astu famuli mei, ut cum alio scilicet iter faceret, Londinum excurrerit (ubi uxor illi et liberi) atque id facturum se me clam haberet. Fecissem alioqui, clarissime vir quod nunc facio, ac libens. Nam quem ego mortalium saluto libentius? Quod si autem sic apud vos canis sæviit, præterquam quod non simul æstus (cum Dna) cætera multo hic te mitius habuisses. Nam Dunamiæ mira caloris $ἀδυναμία$, nec æstus, quod sciam, ullus æstate hac tota. Sed tot in urbe parietum reflexio in aërem ex fumo carbonum fossilium et reliqua illuvie spissiorem facit, ut qui nobis vix canicula, vobis molossus fuerit. Ex me argumentum sumito, quem non ex æstu sed

---

[n] [He refers to the translation of the Bible, which had just commenced. The members of his company were Dr. John Overal, Dr. Adrian Saravia, Dr. Clarke, one of the six preachers at Canterbury, Dr. Layfield, Dr. Leigh, Mr. Burleigh, Mr. King, Mr. Thompson, and Mr. Bedwell. They met at Westminster.]

[o] [From Burney MSS. Numb. 363. 15.]

vespertino frigore, cui diutius quam par inhæsi, occupavit febris, cujus adhuc exitum exspecto, quem voluerit, bonus, quem habemus, Dnus. Tu, quæso, sic urge opus, ut tu illud ad finem, non illud tuæ ad detrimentum aliquod sanitatis. Magno stabit Christianæ reipublicæ vel levissima ejus in te jactura. Sed valetudinem et vires sufficiet tibi Deus votis multorum, meisque inter multos affectu certe non ultimis. Etsi autem cum Patre Paulo[p] non sentio esse opus illud Annalium non magni momenti; at id tamen omnes scimus, parem te oneri, satis jam tibi superque virium esse atque verborum ad hoc duellum[q]. Tantum, amabo, in minutiis illis chronologicis ne nimium diu hæreas, ad illa majora cito te confer, Ecclesiastica te digna, ad quæ te vocat exspectatio literatorum omnium. De Puteano[r] memini me in aliquo non ita pridem catalogo legere nomen illud in fronte libri cum literis S. J.; nec librum inspexi, nec opus. Oportet infelici sidere natum esse hominem, si te lacessat. Verum annon percommode accidit? Tu Puteanum exspectas, ego Flaminum. Committamus, si placet, Puteum cum Flammis, nisi Puteus illi inanis sit, huic Flamma stuppea, frigeat vero ille, hic abeat in fumos. Sed extra jocum; agnosce, quæso te, in hoc facto astu Jesuiticum. Multorum, sat scio, jam in te stylos excitabant, non alio id autem animo, quam ut abducant a præclaro instituto, ne Baronium egregie vexes, ne veram lucem afferas historiæ sacræ. At tu ne te sinas avocari, quæso, obtestorque, vel ad momentum: quasi catulos allatrantes proculca atque præteri: urge iter, quod ingressus es, cœlo hominibusque faventibus. Molinæus me non fallit[s], si bene novi illius ingenium, vult ἀριστεύειν καὶ ὑπείροχος ἔμμεναι ἄλλων, et (est ut dicis) Sirenem habet, qua mirifice delinivit Regem, ut omnia de illo bona sæpe dici, nihil unquam sinistri audiri sustineat. Litem ipsam quod attinet, desipiam, si quid in ea videam nisi καινοφωνίας. At ego ex antiquitate mallem vel tres lineas, quam tot istorum chartas, quæ nihil redolent nisi τὸ φιλόκαινον.

[p] [Father Paul, the celebrated Venetian controversialist.]

[q] [Casaubon was preparing for the press his 'Exercitationes in Baronium.']

[r] [Erycius Puteanus had just published his 'Stricturæ in Casaubonum.']

[s] [This was Peter Du Moulin the elder. He had not at this time come to England, though he had been in correspondence with the King. Casaubon in several passages of his letters speaks of him very unfavourably. (See Epistt. dccxliii. dccxliv. p. 433. Roter. 1709.)]

Servet autem Regi nostro optimo mentem Deus, quam jam ante dedit, ne se velit et nos his litibus immiscere. Sat enim nobis litium, nec opus sic indies serere novas. Quod si autem Numen non intercedat, res mihi eruptura videtur in morbum. Tu vero, qui superiori anno discessisti hinc D. Augustino (si meministi) infenso (dies enim discessus tui dies in Fastis notatus illius nomine[t]) qui pluviis testatus abitum sibi hinc tuum minus placuisse, redi hoc anno, si placet propitio eodem Scto. Patre. Redi et vide nundinas tota Anglia celeberrimas[u]; vel si minus nundinæ te capiunt, vide manuscriptum illud S. Matthæi exemplar Hebraicum, quod hic asservatur in Bibliotheca Corp. Christi. Sine te exorem ut redeas. Viso te, convalescam illico. Pauculos tantum hic dies laxabis animum nobiscum. Figes damam, et trimestres tuos labores paullisper intermittes. Reverteris ubi voles. Hæc memento a febricitante esse. At te Deus nobis valentem atque incolumem servet magnum rei literariæ ornamentum. Vigilia D. Bartholomæi; Dunamiæ. Omni studio atque officio semper tuus Eliensis. [1612.]

Clarissimo Viro Dno. ac amico mihi
plurimum servando Dno. Isaaco Casaubono, Londinum.

LETTER V.

TO ISAAC CASAUBON.

[Casauboni Ephemerides, pp. 1204, 1205[x].]

Vix tandem eluctatus sum, nec plane tamen. Sed signa sunt salutaria. Dei autem unius beneficio, nam medicorum opera usus non sum. Quis est ille igitur Puteanus? Non Prior alicujus societatis, sed hic a Lovanio orator novus; quare tanto magis præteribis. Exsiccabis, ubi voles, uno radio tuo totum hunc puteum vocularum et fæcularum plane inanem. Item autem sentio unica tibi præfatione et hunc, et reliquos qui prorepserint obterendos simul. Ab instituto autem, quæso, ne te dimoveant, quod ʻqui dedit ut primam manum, dabit ut et ultimam imponas, a et ω. Ego vero de

[t] [See Casaub. Ephem. p. 877.]
[u] [Sturbridge fair.]
[x] [From Burney MSS. Numb. 365. 16.]

ἀπροσδιονύσοις nec cogitavi. Absit id tantum, quia video Chronologorum nodos illos vix explicabiles, nolim te in illos induas valde. In illis materia litis satis ampla, si libeat post campum illum ingredi. Te premere scio, quæ rei Ecclesiasticæ ingenti usui atque emolumento futura sunt. Ad illa ergo accinge te, illa excute, illic effunde quicquid habes ex multa lectione et diligenti observatione reconditi. Liceat vero, libere liceat semper, adeoque liberrime, quæ meditata habes de doctrinæ capitibus, in medium proferre. Ego incredibilem, scio, voluptatem ex eorum lectione capiam; discam multa senex, debebo tibi multorum vel memoriam quæ exciderunt, vel notitiam quæ non advertentem præterierunt. Quod jam ut te hic videam, rebus tuis minus commodum sit, vicem meam doleo: tanto magis approximabo ut tu me illic. Debebo Londino, quod nequeo Dunamiæ. Thompsonus[y] valet, et novum magistratum meditatur, in eoque totus est. Ego Deum veneror, ut Dnæ facilem et felicem partum concedat, et Anglo Casaubono augeat familiam tuam[z]. Deus te servet, Cl. Vir. Dunamiæ, Nativitate B. Virginis 1612. (Sept. 8.) Omni studio omnique officio tuus semper, Eliensis.

Clarissō. Viro Dno. ac amico mihi
  plurimum observando Dno. Isaaco
  Casaubono, Londinum.

LETTER VI.

TO DANIEL HEINSIUS [a].

[Is. Casauboni MSS. Coll. vol. ix. p. 419.]

Serius rescribo, clar. Heinsi; aberam enim ab urbe procul in diœcesi mea, cum redditæ mihi sunt a te posteriores hæ. Nam et priores illas accepisse non dissimulo, utrasque erudi-

[y] [Richard Thompson, to whom Casaubon addressed many of his letters, and who is repeatedly mentioned in them with respect. He was an Oriental scholar, and one of the translators of the Bible. Prynne speaks of him in very scurrilous terms. (Wood, F. O. i. 273.)]

[z] [His son James was born the following October.]

[a] [To this letter the following remarks are prefixed by the transcriber: "Reverend. et Illustris. viri Dñi Ep'i Winton. [Lancelot] Andrææ Epist. ad Dan. Heinsiū de (sic) morte Isaaci Casauboni Descripta e lituraria ejus charta, ubi multa inducta, superscripta, eadem verbis aliis atque aliis expressa ad delectum; ut valde difficile fuerit aliquid certum excerpere. Erant præterea et lacunæ multæ."]

tione, humanitate, elegantia, Heinsio plenas; sane fateor tardis nominibus annumerandum me, quod tamdiu tibi debitor sum istius officii ἀμοιβαῖον. Nec est quod pro me afferam, nisi bona sæpe nomina non appellando fieri mala. Qui mihi tuas tum dedit, quisque fuit non appellavit, . . . et appellet opus, imo vero interpellet . . . arescente jam stylo sequior sum . . . nec assuevi ad vos literas dare heroas literarios. Verum enim a calamo mihi mens vel charta non pendet. Scito me vel in alto silentio omni studio atque officio tuam indolem et egregios illos animi dotes quæ in scriptis lucent . . . Fuit, ut dicis, fuit magni illius viri et memoriæ omni mihi vita venerandæ et suis, et nobis, quod et nos habebat pro suis, et bonis omnibus obitus immaturus. Ac in reliquis quidem cedo tibi; at in eo, quem et illius morte percepi dolore, nemini, ne tibi quidem cedo. Cujus ego convictu, alloquio quoties frui datum, mirifice recreabar. Patere vero te exorem ne consilium mutes de itinere huc instituendo. Etsi ille sublatus, quem tu, qui te, libentissime, in vitam meliorem, erant qui te videre velint, ego imprimis ædes meas beatas habiturus sum tali hospite. Quod si quid in illius obitum meditaris, facis quod te dignum est, atque in ea, quam Deus tibi mentem, uti pergas magnopere te rogatum volo.

Quod de excessu quæris summi viri, obiit ille Kal. Julii Stylo veteri. Dies erat Veneris. Eo mane suscepit Eucharistiam sacram de manu mea, quod ut faceret, triduo ante a me petierat. Sumpta Eucharistia recitari voluit Simeonis canticum, *Nunc dimittis servum tuum, Domine.* Præeuntes, ut erat tum languida voce, sed non sine contentione, subsecutus est. Nihil in toto mundo nisi religiosum, pium, Christiano homine, Casaubono dignum, ne tum quidem cum propter totius bidui ἰσχουρίαν in summo esset cruciatu. Post liberis ac toti familiæ benedixit. Dein se composuit ad quietem, nec multa post id tempus nec libenter locutus.

δ. Horas post circiter quinque spiritum Deo reddidit non dubito quin gratum, (quia) veritatis pacisque semper studiosum.

Compescite vero putidum illum Jesuitam[b], cui nec de

---

[b] [This refers to the book of Heribert Rosweyd, the Jesuit, published shortly before Casaubon's death, entitled, " Lex Talionis duodecim Tabularum." It was intended as a reply to his " Exercitationes ;" and contained, also, a large collection of stories and floating rumours respecting him. The

mortuo mentiri religio est, quasi nutasset in religione. Ille vero haud unquam nutavit, et sequius mihi multo rem narravit de Perronio: qua in fide natus est et educatus, in eadem jam ἐπὶ γήραος οὐδῷ mori se professus est. Prius autem totos x̄. dies quam obiit plane valedixerat rebus humanis, et testamento signato, totum se Deo, totum cœlo tradidit; et in terris cœlum præoccupavit. Senserat ipse intra se lethale quid. Medici calculum prægrandem hallucinati sunt, at is in dissecto corpore nullus comparuit; tantum vesiculare apostema, quo interiit, præmio vitæ sedentariæ. . . .

Dominum Chabanæum [c] nec salutare licuit, nec complecti. Cui ego et sua et vero avunculi sui causa honestissime cupio et, si res feret, testatum dabo. . . . . . .

. . . .

Exuviæ ejus in templo Westmonasteriensi repositæ sunt, præ foribus Sacrarii illius, in quo Regum nostrorum monumenta visuntur.

Funus sequuti sumus 6 Episcopi, 2 Decani, ac Clerus pæne urbis universus. Pro funere laudavit et concionem habuit Lichfeld.[d] qui hospes illi ad menses aliquot fuerat, cum primum huc in Angliam venisset [e]. [1614.]

LETTER VII.

TO DR. WILLIAM GAGER.

[Wood, Ath. Ox. ii. 259.]

'Right Reverend Father in God, my very good Lord and Brother, I have received letters from the King's Majesty, the tenour whereof here followeth:—

" Right trusty and well-beloved Counsellor, we greet you well. Whereas the enemies of the Gospel have ever been

particular charge here referred to was, that he had promised Card. Perron to join the Romish Church at Whitsuntide, 1610. See Rosweyd, Præf. ad Leg. Talionis, and Mer. Casauboni Pietas, p. 85. Roter. 1609.]

[c] [Chabanæus was the son of Casaubon's sister.]

[d] [John Overal.]

[e] [This note is subjoined by the transcriber:—

" In eadem Schedula, quæ tota scripta erat manu ipsius Rev[i]. Ep'i erant et hæc. 'Et meo καὶ τοιούτων δέκα qualis ego sum, funeribus redimendum.' Item, 'Viri et bono Literarum nati, et non nisi detrimento mortui, qui merito inter sæculi sui decora numerandus.'"]

forward to write and publish books for confirming their erroneous doctrine, and impugning the truth; and now of late seem more careful than before to send daily into our realm such their writings, whereby our loving subjects, though otherwise disposed, might be seduced, unless some remedy thereof should be provided: We, by the advice of our Council, have lately granted a corporation, and given our allowance for erecting a College at Chelsey for learned divines to be employed to write, as occasion shall require, for maintaining the religion professed in our kingdoms, and confuting the impugners thereof[f]. Whereupon Dr. Sutcliffe, designed Provost of the said College, hath now humbly signified unto us, that upon divers promises of help and assistance towards the erecting and endowing the said College, he hath at his own charge, begun and well proceeded in the building, as doth sufficiently appear by a good part hereof already set up in the place appointed for the same; we therefore, being willing to favour and further so religious a work, will and require you to write your letters to the Bishops of your province, signifying unto them, in our name, that our pleasure is, they deal with the clergy and other of their dioceses, to give their charitable benevolence for the perfecting of this good work so well begun; and for the better performance of this our desire, we have given order to the said Provost and his associates to attend you and others unto whom it may appertain, and to certify us from time to time of their proceeding. And thus, nothing doubting of your care herein, we bid you farewell. Thetford, the fifth of May, 1616."

Now, because this so pious and religious a work, conducing both to God's glory and the saving of many a soul, within this kingdom, I cannot but wish that all devout and well-affected persons should, both by yourself and by the preachers in your diocese, as well publicly as otherwise, be excited to contribute in some measure to so holy an intendment now well begun. And although these and the like motives have been frequent in these latter times, yet let not those whom

---

[f] [See a full account of Chelsea College in Fuller's Ch. Hist. book x. sect. iii. §§ 19—27, where these letters of the King and Archbishop are also printed.]

God hath blessed with any wealth be weary of well doing, that it may not be said, that the idolatrous and superstitious Papists be more forward to advance their falsehoods than we are to maintain God's truth. Whatsoever is collected I pray your Lordship may be carefully brought unto me, partly that it pass not through any defrauding hands, and partly that his Majesty may be acquainted what is done in this behalf. And so forbearing to be further troublesome, I leave your Lordship to the Almighty. From Lambeth, December 20, 1617.

Your loving Brother,
G Cant. [Abbot.]"

This letter and the briefs pertaining to it, I have kept by me till Easter was past, and St. Mark's day, and May day, to the end the collection may be less grievous. Have all due care, I pray, of that which is raised, that we may take good account of our trust, and let me be advertised what success it hath. And I recommend you to God's blessed keeping. Ely House, 17° Maii, 1618.

Your very loving Friend,
L. Elien.

To the right wor^{ll}. my verye loving frend, Mr. Do^r. Gager, Chanceler of ye dioces of Ely, at his house at Cambridge, ad.

LETTER VIII.

TO HIS ARCHDEACON.

[Cabala, p. 112. Lond. 1663.]

Salutem in Christo.

I have received letters from the Most Reverend Father in God, the Lord Archbishop of Canterbury, the tenour whereof followeth :—

" Right Reverend Father in God, my very good Lord and Brother, I have received from the King's most excellent Majesty a letter, the tenour whereof here ensueth :—

" ' Most Reverend Father in God, right trusty, and right entirely beloved Counsellor, We greet you well. Forasmuch as the abuses and extravagances of preachers in the pulpit have been, &c.' "

According to the tenour of these letters, you are to see that these limitations and cautions herewith sent unto you be duly and strictly from henceforth observed and put in practice, and that several copies of those directions be speedily communicated to every one of those whom they shall concern, and that you may employ your uttermost endeavours in the performance of so important a business, considering that his Majesty will have a special eye over you and me, and expect a strict account at both our hands, whereof praying you to have all possible care, I commend your endeavours therein to the blessing of God.

Your very loving Friend,
LAN. WINTON.

From Farnham, Aug. 15, 1622.

APPENDIX A.

TABLE OF THE PRINCIPAL DATES OF BISHOP ANDREWES'S LIFE,

WITH FURTHER NOTICES[a].

1555. Born.
c. 1563. At the Coopers' School.
c. 1565. At Merchant Tailors' School.
1571. Scholar of Pembroke Hall.
   Scholar of Jesus College, Oxford.
157$\frac{4}{5}$, Feb. 4. B.A. (See Add. MSS. Brit. Mus. 5885.)
1576, Oct. Fellow of Pembroke Hall.
1578. M.A.
1580. Ordained Deacon.
   Junior Treasurer of Pembroke Hall.
1581. Senior Treasurer.
   July 11. Incorporated M.A., Oxford.
1585. B.D.
1586. Chaplain to Henry Earl of Huntingdon.
c. 1586. ———— Archbishop Whitgift.
c. 1586. ———— Queen Elizabeth.
1589. Vicar of S. Giles', Cripplegate.
   Preb. of Southwell.
   May 29. Preb. of S. Paul's.
   Master of Pembroke Hall.
1590. D.D.
1593. Conference with Udal.
   ———————— Barrow.
1594. On a Commission for inquiring into Ecclesiastical Courts in the Diocese of London.
1597. Preb. of Westminster.

[a] Where no authority is here given, the reader is requested to refer to the previous Memoir. It will be understood that this and the following Appendices must be read in connexion with each other.

1601. Dean of Westminster.
1603, July 25. Assisted at King James's coronation. (Nichols's Progresses, vol. i. p. 233.)
Aug. 26. On the High Commission. (Rymer, Fœd. VII. ii. 93.)
160¾, Jan. 14—16. At Hampton Court Conference. He here specially defended the use of the cross in baptism. (Barlow's Sum of the Conference.)
1604, July 22. Appointed one of the Translators of the Bible. The part entrusted to him and his company was the translation of the Pentateuch, and the History from the Book of Joshua to the First Book of Chronicles exclusive. (Collier, Eccl. Hist. vol. ii. p. 693.)
1605, Nov. 3. Consecrated Bishop of Chichester, by Richard Bancroft, Archbishop of Canterbury; Richard Vaughan, Bishop of London; John Jegon, Bishop of Norwich; Thomas Ravis, Bishop of Gloucester; and William Barlow, Bishop of Rochester. (Percival on Apostolical Succession, p. 181.)
Lord High Almoner.
Nov. 5. Resigned Mastership of Pembroke Hall.
1607, July 12. Assisted at the consecration of Henry Parry, Bishop of Gloucester. (Percival, p. 181.)
1608, April 17. Assisted at the consecration of James Montagu, Bishop of Bath and Wells. (Percival, p. 181.)
Oct. 9. Assisted at the consecration of Richard Neile, Bishop of Rochester. (Percival, p. 181.)
1609. Published TORTURA TORTI.
July 25. Rector of Cheam.
Sept. 22. Translated to Ely. In Cole's MSS. vol. xxvii. pp. 69—71, is an account of his election and enthronization.
Dec. 3. Assisted at the consecration of George Abbot, Bishop of Lichfield, and Samuel Harsnet, Bishop of Chichester. (Percival, p. 181.)
1610, June 4. Present at the creation of Henry Prince of Wales. (Rymer, Fœd. VII. ii. 169.)
Oct. 21. Took part in the consecration of Scotch Bishops. The Commission was issued Oct. 15. (Rymer, Fœd. VII. ii. 176.)
Published RESPONSIO AD. APOLOGIAM CARDINALIS BELLARMINI.
1611, June 9. Assisted at the consecration of Giles Thompson, Bishop of Gloucester, and John Buckeridge, Bishop of Rochester. (Percival, p. 182.)
1612, Dec. 7. At Prince Henry's funeral. (Nichols's Progresses, vol. ii. p. 498.)
1613. On a Commission to inquire into the validity of the marriage of the Earl of Essex and the Lady Frances Howard. On this subject the following contemporary notices may be quoted:—
"Before the King's parting from Windsor, he sent for the Commissioners employed in the divorce of the Earl of Essex

and his lady; and being desirous to see it at an end, and to
know their opinions, he found that the Bishops of Ely [An-
drewes], Coventry and Lichfield [Neile], the two Chancellors
of the Duchy and Exchequer [Sir Th. Parry and Sir Julius
Cæsar], with Sir David Donne, were directly for it, and to
pronounce it a nullity. But the Archbishop of Canterbury
[Abbot], the Bishop of London [King], Sir John Bennet, and
Dr. Edwards, Chancellor of London, were as directly against it.
Whereupon the King hath added two Bishops more, Winchester [Bilson] and Rochester [Buckeridge], and two Deans,
Westminster [Montaigne] and St. Paul's [Overal], who, together with the rest, must labour in it 'twixt this and Michaelmas,
and then give their resolutions, which, *computatis computandis*,
and considering the King's inclination, is like to be for the
dissolution. At my last being with the Bishop of Ely not long
before my coming out of town, I found which way he leant, for
he made no dainty to tell me his opinion; which I could wish
were otherwise, if there be no more reason in it than I see or
conceive."—John Chamberlain to Sir Dudley Carleton, Aug. 1,
1613. Birch's Court of James I. vol. i. pp. 261, 262.

" Of the nullity [of this marriage] I see you know as much
as I can write, by which you may discern the power of a king
with judges; for of those which are now for it, I knew some of
them, when I was in England, were vehemently against it, as
the Bishops of Ely [Andrewes] and Coventry [Neile]. For
the business itself, I protest I shall be glad, if it may lawfully,
that it shall go forward; though of late I have been fearful of
the consequence, and have had my fears increased by the last
letters which came to me; but, howsoever, the way of inter-
posing gives me no contentment."—Earl of Southampton to
Sir Ralph Winwood, Aug. 6, 1613, quoted in Nichols's Royal
Progresses, vol. ii. p. 672. The marriage was declared null by
a majority of only seven to five; the Bishops of Winchester
and Rochester being of the former number. Bishop Bilson's
son was shortly afterwards created a Baronet, it is supposed
for his father's share in this business, and was entitled by the
courtiers, Sir Nullity Bilson.

A full account of this case will be found in the State Trials,
and in Archbishop Abbot's " Memorials touching the Nullity
between the Earl of Essex and his Lady," &c.

1614, April 5. Attended the King on the opening of Parliament.
(Nichols's Progresses, vol. iii. p. 1092.)

June. "At the breaking up of the Parliament, the Bishops
agreed among themselves to give their best piece of plate, or
the value of it in present of money, as a speedy benevolence
to supply the King's want. The Archbishop of Canterbury
began with a basin and ewer, and redeemed it with 140*l*. The

Bishop of Winchester, as much; Ely [Andrewes], 120*l*."—John Chamberlain to Sir Dudley Carleton, June 30, 1614.—Nichols's Progresses, vol. iii. p. 7.

1614¾, March. Attended the King to Cambridge. (Nichols's Progresses, vol. iii. p. 56.)

1615, July 9. Assisted at the consecration of Rich. Melbourne, Bishop of S. David's. (Percival, p. 182.)

Dec. 3. Assisted at the consecration of Rob. Abbot, Bishop of Salisbury. (Percival, p. 182.)

1616, Sept. 29. Privy Councillor of England. (Nichols's Progresses, vol. iii. p. 190.)

Nov. 4. Present at the creation of Charles Prince of Wales. (Rymer, Fœd. VII. ii. 217.)

To this year may be referred the following anecdote recorded by Bacon (Apophthegms, numb. 158): " The Lord Bishop Andrewes was asked at the first coming over of the Archbishop of Spalato, whether he were a Protestant or no? He answered: ' Truly, I know not; but I think he is a detestant:' that was, of most of the opinions of Rome [b].

Dec. 8. Assisted at the consecration of Arthur Lake, Bishop of Bath and Wells, and Lewis Bayly, Bishop of Bangor. (Percival, p. 183.)

1617, April 5. On a Commission for releasing certain persons imprisoned for not taking the oath of allegiance. (Rymer, Fœd. VII. iii. 4.)

March 15—Sept. 16. Attended the King to Scotland.

Privy Councillor of Scotland.

Dec. 5. Joined in a letter to the King respecting the retrenchment of his expenses. (Bacon's Letters, numb. cxciv. Works, vol. iii. p. 357. Lond. 1778.)

Dec. 14. Assisted at the consecration of Nicholas Felton, Bishop

---

[b] These references to Bacon naturally suggest some notice of the intimacy between these distinguished persons. Bacon, it appears, sent Andrewes the MS. of his " Cogitata et visa," requesting his criticisms on it, referring at the same time to his former services of this kind. Bacon thus writes :—

" If your Lordship be so good now as when you were the good Dean of Westminster, my request to you is, that not by pricks, but by notes, you would mark unto me whatsoever shall seem unto you either not current in the style, or harsh to credit and opinion, or inconvenient for the person of the writer, for no man can be judge and party; and when our minds judge by reflection on ourselves, they are more subject to error," &c. (Letter xcvi. Works, vol. iii. p. 241.)

In another letter addressed to King James, dated Oct. 12, 1620, (ibid. p. 584,) Bacon mentions that the Bishop was acquainted for nearly thirty years with his intention of writing the Novum Organon.

After his retirement he also dedicated to Bishop Andrewes his Advertisement touching a Holy War; concluding his Dedication in these words: " This work . . . I have dedicated to your Lordship, in respect of our ancient and private acquaintance; and because amongst the men of our times I hold you in special reverence." (Works, vol. ii. p. 282.)

of Bristol, and George Montaigne, Bishop of Lincoln. The Archbishop of Spalato also assisted. (Percival, p. 183.)

161$\frac{7}{8}$. On a Commission respecting the tithes of the London Clergy. (Bacon's Letter to Sir Henry Yelverton, Jan. 19, 1617; Works, vol. iii. p. 544.)

1618, June 23. On a Commission for banishing Jesuits, seminary priests, &c. (Rymer, Fœd. VII. iii. 65.)

Aug. 3. Translated to Winchester.

Correspondence with Du Moulin. (Works, vol. ix. p. 173.)

161$\frac{8}{9}$, Jan. 1. Dean of Chapel Royal.

1619, March and April. Attended the King at Royston, during his illness. (Nichols's Progresses, vol. iii. p. 533.)

May 13. Present at funeral of the Queen. (Ibid. p. 538.)

1620, March 26. Attended the King to St. Paul's, to give encouragement to its repair. (Ibid. p. 600.)

April 27. On a Commission for selling some of the crown jewels. (Rymer, Fœd. VII. iii. 131.)

April 29. On the High Commission. (Rymer, Fœd. VII. iii. 134.)

Aug. 31. Entertains the King at Farnham.

Sept. 17. Consecrated Jesus Chapel, near Southampton. His Chaplains on this occasion were Matthew and Christopher Wren. Matthew Wren preached at the evening service. (Works, vol. vi. p. 309.)

162$\frac{0}{1}$, March. At the rising of the Convocation, the Bishops of Winchester [Andrewes] and Lincoln [Montaigne], in the name of all the rest, presented to the King at Hampton Court a grant of subsidies passed by the Clergy of the Province of Canterbury. (Nicholls' Royal Progresses, vol. iii. p. 658.)

1621, April 30. Attended with other peers on Lord Bacon, to ascertain from him whether he acknowledged as his own the petition and confession made in his name to the House. (Biog. Brit. pp. 403, 404.)

June 10. Present at the delivery of the Great Seal to John Williams, Dean of Westminster. (Rymer, Fœd. VII. iii. 199.)

July 12. On a Commission for examining Lewis Bayly, the Bishop of Bangor. (Birch's Court of James I. vol. ii. p. 266.)

Oct. 3. On a Commission to inquire whether Archbishop Abbot had incurred any irregularity by casual homicide. (Cabala, p. 279, and Collier, Eccl. Hist. vol. ii. p. 721.)

The Commissioners gave their unanimous opinion in the Archbishop's favour. (Ibid. p. 722.) Fuller (Ch. Hist. book x. sect. v. § 16) remarks thus on Andrewes's connexion with this affair: " The party whom the Archbishop suspected his greatest foe, proved his most firm and effectual friend; even Lancelot Andrewes, Bishop of Winchester. For when several Bishops inveighed against the irregularity of the Archbishop, laying as much (if not more) guilt on the act than it would bear, he mildly checked them. 'Brethren,' said he, 'be not too busy to condemn any for uncanonicals according to the strictness thereof, lest we render ourselves in the same condition. Besides, we all know, *Canones, qui dicunt lapsos, post actam pœnitentiam ad clericatum non esse restituendos, de rigore loquuntur disciplinæ, non injiciunt desperationem indulgentiæ.*'"

Heylin (Cypr. Angl. pp. 81, 82, Edit. 1671), having stated that it was through the exertions of Andrewes and Sir Henry Martin that the rest of the Commissioners adopted the milder course, and having referred to the Bishop's speech which Fuller has given, gratuitously ascribes his forbearance to a fear that if Abbot were removed, Williams, who was then in high favour at court, would succeed to the primacy.

1621, Nov. 22. On a Commission for dispensing with the Archbishop for any irregularities. (Rymer, Fœd. VII. iii. 220.)

Dec. 12. Joined in a letter with other Bishops, granting a dispensation to the Archbishop. (Collier, vol. ii. Append. numb. cviii.)

1622, April 20. On a Commission for banishing Jesuits and others. (Rymer, Fœd. VII. iii. 236, 238.)

May 31. Joins the Lords of the Council in an order to the Vice-Chancellor of Oxford to burn Paræus's Works. (Wood's Annals, vol. ii. p. 344.)

July 4. On a Commission for defective titles. (Rymer, Fœd. VII. iii. 247.)

Aug. 10—15. Entertained the King at Farnham. (Birch's Court of James I. vol. ii. p. 326, and Nichols, vol. iii. p. 775.)

162⅔, Feb. 14. On a Commission of grievances. (Rymer, Fœd.VII.iv. 43.)

1623, March 30. On a Commission with Archbishop Abbot, Bishops of Lincoln (Williams), London (Montaigne), and Durham (Neile), respecting the case of the Archbishop of Spalato, who was ordered by them to depart the realm within twenty days. (Heylin's Cypr. Angl. p. 103.)

July 20, Sunday. Present at the ceremony of the King swearing to the articles of the Spanish match.

In the account given by Nichols (Progresses, vol. iii. p. 882), from Lansd. MSS. numb. 225, it is stated that during the reading of the Articles, "his Majesty and the Ambassadors sat uncovered, and, those finished, the Ambassadors took his Majesty's oath in the name of their master, which was administered by the Bishop of Winton, and taken by his Majesty kneeling. Then the *testes* of the nobility then present were added to the instrument, and read; after which a hymn was sung, made on purpose for the time.

Nov. Read over, and approved of, Dean White's Reply to Jesuit Fisher.

"The same Saturday, as also on Monday, the Dean was again with the King about his book which he is to set forth; the Bishop of St. David's [Laud] being present, who, as also the Bishop of Winchester, had perused it over, and not altered one word. But the King, as he was turning over the leaves, by chance espied the word 'idolatry,' which he by all means wanted to have put out, but the Dean would not. The King said it should; the Dean still persisted; until the Bishop of St. David's humbly besought his Majesty it might stand; and so it doth."—From a letter to Joseph Mede—Birch's Court of James I. vol. ii. p. 435.

1623, Sept. 29. Chief Commissioner on an appeal in a matrimonial cause between Abraham Sunderland and Milicent Conyers. (Rymer, Fœd. VII. iv. 83.)

Approved a Book of Canons for the Isle of Jersey. (Collier, Eccl. Hist. ii. 706.)

There may be here inserted the following anecdote from Hearne's edition of Langtoft's Chronicle, vol. i. App. to Preface, pp. ccviii.—ccxiii. Oxf. 1725. It was printed from a MS. of Dugdale, in the Ashmolean Museum, entitled, "A Transcript of a certain Narrative written by the late Bishop of Ely, (Dr. Matthew Wren,) with his own hand, of that remarkable Conference, which, after his return from Spain, with Prince Charles, (anno 1623,) he had with Dr. Neale, then Bp. of Durham, Dr. Andrews, Bp. of Winchester, and Dr. Laud, Bp. of St. David's, touching the said Prince; whereat something prophetical was then said by that Reverend Bishop of Winchester."

"After our return from Spain, my Lord of Winchester (among other great expressions of his respects to me) made me promise to him, that, upon all occasions of my coming to London, (for I abode still at Cambridge,) I would lodge with him. To which end he caused three rooms near the garden to be fitted and reserved for me; and twice or thrice I had lodged there.

"And at another time, coming suddenly to London and late, I lodged at my sister's in Friday-street; and the next day, (being Friday,) I went to Winchester House to dinner, and craved his Lordship's pardon, that I lodged not there. . . .

"But, on Saturday, going to do my duty to my Lords of Durham and St. David's, and telling them of my sudden return, they would needs overrule me, and made me promise them, tho' I had taken my leave of my Lord of Winchester, yet to meet them next day at Whitehall, at my Lord's chamber at dinner. I did so; and there we sat after dinner above an hour . . . On Monday morne by break of the day . . . there was a great knocking at the door where I lay. And at last an apprentice (who lay in the shop) came up to my bedside, and told me, there was a messenger from Winchester House to speak with me. The business was to let me know, that my Lord, when he came from Court last night, had given his steward charge to order it so, that I might be spoken with, and be required as from him without fail to dine with him on Monday; but to be at Winchester House by ten of the clock, which I wondered the more at; his Lp. not using to come from his study till near twelve. My business would hardly permit this; yet because of his Lordship's importunity, I got up presently, and into Holborn I went, and there used such despatch, that soon after ten of the clock I took a boat, and went to Winchester House, where I found the steward at the Water-gate waiting to let me in the nearest way; who telling me, that my Lord had called twice to know if I were come, I asked where his Lordship was? He answered, In his great gallery (a place where I knew his Lp. scarce came once in a year). And thither I going, the door was lockt: but upon my lifting the latch, my Lord of St. David's opened the door, and letting me in, lock'd it again.

" There I found but those three Lords, who causing me to sit down by them, my Lord of Durham began to me : ' Doctor, your Lord here will have it so, I that am the unfittest person, must be the speaker. But thus it is. After you left us yesterday at Whitehall, we entering into further discourses of those things, which we foresee and conceive will ere long come to pass, resolved again to speak to you before you went hence.

" ' We must know of you, what your thoughts are concerning your master the Prince. You have now been his servant above two years, and you were with him in Spain. We know he respects you well; and we know you are no fool, but can observe how things are like to go.' 'What things, my Lord?' (quoth I.) 'In brief,' said he, ' how the Prince's heart stands to the Church of England, that when God brings him to the crown, we may know what to hope for?'

" My reply was to this effect, that, however I was the most unfit of any to give my opinion herein, attending but two months in the year, and then at a great distance, only in the closet and at meals; yet, seeing they so pressed me, I would speak my mind freely. So I said, ' I know my master's learning is not equal to his father's, yet I know his judgment to be very right; and as for his affection in these particulars, which your Lordships have pointed at, for upholding the doctrine and discipline, and the right estate of the Church, I have more confidence of him than of his father, in whom they say (better than I can) is so much inconstancy in some particular cases.'

"Hereupon my Lords of Durham and St. David's began to argue it with me, and required me to let them know, upon what ground I came to think thus of the Prince. I gave them my reasons at large; and after many replyings, (above an hour together,) then my Lord of Winchester (who had said nothing all the while) bespake me these words:—

"'Well, Doctor, God send you may be a good prophet concerning your master's inclinations in these particulars, which we are glad to hear from you. I am sure I shall be a true prophet: I shall be in my grave, and so shall you, my Lord of Durham; but my Lord of David's, and you, Doctor, will live to see that day, that your master will be put to it, upon his head, and his crown, without he will forsake the support of the Church.'

"Of these predictions made by that holy father, I have now no witness but mine own conscience, and the Eternal God, who knows I lie not; nobody else being present when this was spoken, but these three Lords."

Nichols, (Progresses of King James, vol. iii. p. 1117,) in recording this anecdote, disingenuously assumes that the "hopes" of the three Bishops, related only to their own personal interests, and not, as the narrative itself implies, to the general welfare of the Church. He uncharitably observes, that they "were the three principal courtiers among the Clergy of the æra, and were, like other courtiers, watchful over their own interests."

1624, Dec. 24. On a Commission for banishing Jesuits and seminary priests. (Rymer, Fœd. VII. iv. 168.)

162$\frac{4}{5}$, Jan. 1. On the High Commission. (Rymer, Fœd. VII. iv. 172.) In consequence of illness, unable to attend King James in his last sickness.

1625, May 9. He appears to have resigned his Almonership before this time, as Montaigne, Bishop of London, is then mentioned as holding the office. (Rymer, Fœd. VIII. i. 58.)

June 7. On a Commission for mortgaging some of the crown lands to Edward Allen and others. (Rymer, Fœd. VIII. i. 73.)

Sept. 8. On a Commission for charitable uses, to inquire into the disposition of the property of Andrew Windsor, Esq., who had bequeathed property for the support of eight poor persons in an almshouse, founded by himself at Farnham. The gift was declared good. (Manning and Bray's Surrey, vol. iii. p. 157.)

162$\frac{5}{6}$, Feb. 15. On the High Commission. (Rymer, Fœd. VIII. i. 204.)

March 6. On a Commission for banishing Jesuits. (Rymer, Fœd. VIII. i. 219.)

March 8. On a Commission for reprieve of persons condemned to death. (Ibid. p. 223.)

APPENDIX B.

LIST OF WORKS, WITH BIOGRAPHICAL AND OTHER NOTICES.

I.

SERMONS, ETC. IN CHRONOLOGICAL ORDER.

1585. April 22. Theologica Determinatio de Usuris, pro assequendo Baccalaureatus in SS. Theologiæ Gradu.—Opusc. Posth. pp. 113—150.

1588. April 10. Spital Sermon, on 1 Tim. v. 17—19.—Works, vol. v. pp. 3—53.

    Maunsell, Book Catalogue, p. 96, states that this Sermon was printed without the author's consent by Widow Butter, 1589. Herbert (Edition of Ames's Typograph. Antiq. p. 1348) says that she had licence, 24 Aug. 1590, for "a Sermon of M. Andrewes, called the 'Rich-man's Scripture,' licensed by the Bishop of London."

1589. Concio pro Gradu Doctoris in Prov. xx. 25.—Opusc. Posth. pp. 7—28.

    This appeared in 1646, under the following title: "Sacrilege a snare. A Sermon preached ad Clerum, in the University of Cambridg, by the R. Reverend Father in God, Lancelot Andrews; late L. Bishop of Winchester, when he proceeded Doctor in Divinity. Translated for the benefit of the Publike. London. Printed 1646."

Theologica Determinatio de Decimis.—Ibid. pp. 151—171.

    This appeared in 1647, under the following title: "Of the Right of Tithes. A Divinity Determination in the Publike Divinity Schools of the University of Cambridg, by the Right Reverend Father in God Lancelot Andrews; late Lord Bishop of Winchester, when he proceeded Doctor in Divinity, &c. London . . . 1647."

15$\frac{89}{90}$. March 4, Ash-Wednesday, at Whitehall.—Vol. i. pp. 305—320.

The date of this Sermon is incorrectly given as 1598.

March 11, at Greenwich, on Psal. lxxv. 3.—Vol. ii. pp. 3—15.

159$\frac{0}{1}$. Feb. 24, at Greenwich, on Psal. lxxvii. 20.—Ibid. pp. 16—36.

1591. July. Theologica Determinatio de Jurejurando ἐπακτῷ. —Opusc. Posth. pp. 95—115.

This was first printed at the end of " An Apologie for Sundry Proceedings by Jurisdiction Ecclesiasticall, &c. London. 1593."

159$\frac{1}{2}$. Jan. 9, at S. Giles's, Cripplegate, on Acts ii. 42.— Vol. v. pp. 54—70.

1592. June 11, at St. Giles's, Cripplegate, on Jer. iv. 2.— Ibid. pp. 71—81.

Seven Sermons on the Temptation.—Vol. v. pp. 477—558.

These Sermons are here inserted, because there appeared this year a small volume, with the following title: "The wonderfull Combate (for God's glorie and man's salvation) betweene Christ and Satan, opened in seven most excellent, learned and zealous Sermons, upon the Temptations of Christ in the wilderness, &c. Seene and allowed. London. Printed by John Charlewood, for Richard Smith; and are to be sold at his shop, at the West doore of Paules, 1592."

In Herbert's Ames, p. 1324, there is the following note respecting this volume:—" This book seems to have occasioned him (the Publisher) some trouble; however it gave the Stationers' Company some; for in the Warden's account of expenses from 15 July, 1592, to 15 July, 1593, are the following articles, viz.: 'John Wolf, 23 Nov. when he rode to Croydon about Dr. Andrew's Sermons, printed for Mr. Smythe, 4 sh.' 'John Wolf, to and fro Lambeth, about Dr. Andrews's Sermons for Rich. Smythe, who appeared 25 Nov. 10d.' 'A link for the Mr. and Warden the same night going to search for Mr. Andrewes's bookes.' What the result of this was does not appear among the decrees and ordinances of the Company."

These Sermons appeared again in 1627, under the title of " Seven Sermons on the wonderfull Combate, &c. Delivered by the Reverend Father in God, Doct. Andrewes, Bishop of Winchester, lately deceased, &c. London... 1627:" and were reprinted in 1642 at the end of "The Moral Law expounded." Lond. printed by Rich. Cotes. 1642.

159⅔. Feb. 20. Concio ad Clerum in Synodo Provinciali, Act. xx. 28.—Opusc. Posth. pp. 29—51.

Some notes of this Sermon, taken down at the time, are preserved in Strype's Whitgift, Records, book iv. [numb. xiv.]

1593. March 30, at S. James's, on Mark xiv. 4—6.—Vol. ii. pp. 37—60.

159¾. March 6, at Hampton Court, on Luke xvii. 32.—Ibid. pp. 61—77.

159⅘. March 5, at Richmond, on Luke xvi. 25.—Ibid. pp. 78—97.

1596. April 4, at Greenwich, on 2 Cor. xii. 15.—Ibid. pp. 98—116.

1597. March 25, Good Friday, on Zech. xii. 10.—Ibid. pp. 119—137.

159⁸⁄₉. Feb. 21, Ash-Wednesday, at Richmond, on Deut. xxiii. 9.—Vol. i. pp. 321—335.

1600. March 30, at Whitehall, on John xx. 23.—Vol. v. pp. 82—103.

Rowland White thus writes to Sir Robert Sydney on this sermon:—" Dr. Andrews made a strange sermon at court on Sunday; his text was the xx. chapter of the Gospel St. John, the 23d verse, touching the forgiveness of sins upon earth. That contrition without confession and absolution, and deeds worthy of repentance, was not sufficient. That the ministers had the two keys of power and knowledge delivered unto them; that whose sins soever they remitted upon earth, should be remitted in heaven. The court is full of it, for such doctrine was not usually taught there. I hear he was with Mr. Secretary about it, it may be to satisfy him."—Sydney Letters, vol. ii. p. 185.

Nov. 23, at Whitehall, on Jer. xxiii. 6.—Vol. v. pp. 104—126.

There is a MS. copy of this sermon among the Lambeth MSS. numb. 374, Art. 3.

1601. Nov. 15, at Whitehall, on Matt. xxii. 21.—Ibid. pp. 127—140.

160½. Feb. 17, Ash-Wednesday, on Jer. viii. 4—7.—Vol. i. pp. 336—355.

1603. Aug. 21, at Chiswick, on Ps. cvi. 29, 30.—Vol. v. pp. 223—234.

This sermon was reprinted separately in 1636.

1604. April 6, Good Friday, on Lam. i. 12.—Vol. ii. pp. 138—157.

This was originally published under the following title: "The Copie of the Sermon preached on Good Friday before the Kings Maiestie. By D. Andrewes, Deane of Westminster, vi. April 1604. ¶Imprinted at London by Robert Barker, Printer to the King's most excellent Maiestie."

1605. March 29, Good Friday, at Greenwich, on Heb. xii. 2. —Ibid. pp. 158—184.

Nichols places this erroneously under the following year, (see Royal Progresses of K. James, vol. ii. p. 47.) The King was at Greenwich on Good Friday, 1605, (see Nichols, vol. i. p. 505.)

Christmas-day, at Whitehall, on Heb. ii. 16.—Vol. i. pp. 1—17.

1606. April 20, Easter-day, at Whitehall, on Rom. vi. 9—11. —Vol. ii. pp. 187—205.

The date is given erroneously in the Sermons, and in Nichols, as April 6.

June 8, Whitsunday, at Greenwich, on Acts ii. 1—4. —Vol. iii. pp. 107—129.

Aug. 5, Gowrie Conspiracy, at Greenwich, on Ps. cxliv. 10.—Vol. v. pp. 235—256, and Opusc. Posth. pp. 53—74.

This sermon was preached in Latin, and printed at London in 1610 by Robert Barker, under the title, "Concio latine habita, &c." (as in Opusc. Posth.) It was printed also the same year in English, with one preached on the same occasion in 1610. The title of the two is as follows: "Two Sermons preached before the King's Majestie, the one at Greenwich, the fifth of August, 1606, the King of Denmark then being there; the other at Holdenby the fifth of August last, 1610, by the Bishop of Chichester, his Majestie's Almoner," (thus given by Nichols, vol. ii. p. 80.) It was first included among the collected Sermons in 1661.

Sept. 28, at Hampton Court, on Numb. x. 1, 2.— Vol. v. pp. 141—168.

This sermon was preached "for the reduction of the two Melvilles, and other Presbyterian Scots, to a right understanding of the Church of England," (Wood, Ath. Ox. ii. 507.) It was printed the same year, under the following title: "A Sermon preached before the Kings Maiestie at Hampton Court, concerning the right and power of calling assemblies, on Sunday the 28 of September, Anno 1606. By the Bishop of Chichester. ¶Imprinted at London by Robert Barker, Printer to the King's most excellent Maiestie. 1606." It was reprinted by Barker in 1618, with other Sermons of Andrewes, which will be noted in their places. There is also a copy of another edition in Cambridge Univ. Library. (E. 12. 9.)

It was afterwards translated into Latin, and appeared as " Concio habita coram serenissimo Jacobo, Angliæ, Scotiæ, Franciæ et Hiberniæ Rege, fidei defensore, &c. apud curiam Hamptonensem de jure ac potestate convocandorum cœtuum, Die Dominico 28 Septemb. Anno 1606, per D. Doctorem Andrews, Episcopum Chicbestrensem latinitate donata. Londini, MDCVIII." It was also translated into Dutch, and printed at Leyden in 1610. (Brit. Mus. Cat.)

1606.   Nov. 5, at Whitehall, on Ps. cxviii. 23, 24.—Vol. iv. pp. 203—222.

Christmas-day, at Whitehall, on Is. ix. 6.—Vol. i. pp. 18—31.

160⁶⁄₇.   March 5.

Nichols states that Bishop Andrewes preached before the court at Richmond, Tuesday, March 5, in this year. (Progresses, vol. ii. p. 123.) This is obviously a mistake; for in this year March 5 fell on Thursday. The sermon to which he refers, (the fifth in Lent,) is said, in the Sermons, to have been preached Tuesday, March 5, 1596. This is also clearly erroneous: for in that year March 5 was on Friday. But as the sermon is placed between one preached in 1594 and another preached in 1596, its date should probably be *Wednesday*, March 5, 159¾, (which was the Ash-Wednesday of that year,) as it is placed above.

March 24, at Whitehall, on Judges xvii. 6.—Vol. v. pp. 169—187.

1607.   April 5, Easter-day, at Whitehall, on 1 Cor. xv. 20.—Vol. ii. pp. 206—220.

May 24, Whitsunday, at Greenwich, on Acts ii. 4.—Vol. iii. pp. 130—144.

Not in 1608, as stated in Sermons and Nichols.

Aug. 5, at Romsey, on 2 Sam. xviii. 32.—Vol. iv. pp. 3—23.

Nov. 5, at Whitehall, on Psal. cxxvi. 1—4.—Ibid. pp. 223—240.

See Harington's notice of this Sermon, above, p. xxxvii.

1607. Christmas-day, at Whitehall, on 1 Tim. iii. 16.—Vol. i. pp. 32—44.

Christmas-day was on Friday, not Thursday, as stated in Sermons and Nichols.

(No day mentioned,) at Greenwich, on James i. 22.—Vol. v. pp. 186—202.

1608. March 27, Easter-day, at Whitehall, on Mark xvi. 1—7.—Vol. ii. pp. 221—237.

Whitsunday.

The sermon stated to be preached on Whitsunday this year, is to be referred to 1607. See above.

Aug. 5, at Holdenby, on 1 Sam. xxvi. 8, 9.—Vol. iv. pp. 24—45.

1609. April 16, Easter-day, at Whitehall, on John xx. 19.—Vol. ii. pp. 238—251.

Nov. 5, at Whitehall, on Luke ix. 54—56.—Vol. iv. pp. 241—260.

Christmas-day (Monday), at Whitehall, on Gal. iii. 4, 5.—Vol. i. pp. 45—63.

Respecting this sermon Chamberlain writes to Sir D. Carleton, Dec. 13, 1609: "The Bishop of Ely preached at court on Christmas-day, with great applause, being not only *sui similis*, but more than himself, by the report of the King and all his auditors." (Birch's Court of James I. vol. i. p. 102.) And on the following Feb. 13, 16$\frac{09}{10}$, he thus writes to Sir Ralph Winwood respecting the same sermon: "I hope we shall have his sermon (upon the third to the Galatians, and 4th verse), preached on Christmas-day with great applause. The King (with much importunity) had the copy delivered to him on Tuesday last, before his going toward Roiston, and says 'he will lay it still under his pillow.'" (Winwood's Memorials, vol. iii. p. 117.) The sermon was published under the following title: "A Sermon preached before the King's Maiestie at Whitehall, on Monday the 25 of December, being Christmas-day, anno 1609, by the Bishop of Elie, his Maiestie's Almoner. Imprinted at London by Robert Barker, Printer to the King's most excellent Maiestie." It was also reprinted in 1610, with the Christmas-day Sermon of that year, and with other Sermons in 1618.

1610. April 8, Easter-day, at Whitehall, on Job xix. 23—27.—Vol. ii. pp. 252—269.

May 27, Whitsunday, at Whitehall, on John xiv. 15, 16.—Vol. iii. pp. 145—162.

1610. Aug. 5, at Holdenby, on 1 Chron. xvi. 22.—Vol. iv. pp. 46—75.

This sermon was printed separately under the following title: " A Sermon Preached before His Maiestie, on Sunday the fifth of August last at Holdenbie, By the Bishop of Elie, His Maiesties Almoner. ¶ Imprinted at London by Robert Barker, Printer to the Kings most Excellent Maiestie. Anno Dom. 1610." It was also reprinted in 1618. See likewise the notice at Aug. 5, 1606.

Christmas-day, at Whitehall, on Luke ii. 9, 10.— Vol. i. pp. 64—84.

This sermon was printed separately under the title, "A Sermon preached Before His Maiestie at White-Hall, on Tuesday the 25. of December, Being Christmas day, ¶ By the Bishop of Elie, his Maiesties Almoner. Anno 1610. ¶ Imprinted at London by Robert Barker, Printer to the Kings most excellent Maiestie." This sermon, and that for the previous Christmas, likewise appeared together under the title, " Two Sermons preached before the King's Majestie at Whitehall; of the Birth of Christ; the one on Christmas-day, anno 1609, the other on Christmas-day last, anno 1610. By the Bishop of Elie, His Majesties Almoner," &c. It was also reprinted in 1618.

161$\frac{1}{0}$. March 24, Easter-day, at Whitehall, on Ps. cxviii. 22 —24.—Vol. ii. pp. 270—289.

This sermon first appeared under the following title : " A Sermon Preached Before his Maiestie at Whitehall, on the 24. of March last, being Easter-day, and being also the day of the Beginning of His Maiesties most Gracious Reigne. ¶ By the Bishop of Elie, His Maiesties Almoner. ¶ Imprinted at London by Robert Barker, Printer to the King's most Excellent Maiestie. Anno 1611." It was also reprinted in 1618.

1611. May 12, Whitsunday, at Windsor, on John xvi. 7.— Vol. iii. pp. 163—179.

Christmas-day, at Whitehall, on John i. 14.— Vol. i. pp. 85—101.

Nineteen Sermons concerning Prayer, &c.—Vol. v. pp. 299—476.

These Sermons first appeared under the following title: " Scala Cœli. Nineteene Sermons concerning Prayer. The first sixe guiding to the true Doore. The residue teaching how to knocke thereat that wee may enter. The former part containing a preparation to prayer; the latter an Exposition upon the severall petitions of the Lord's Prayer. James iv. 3. 'Yee ask and receive not, because yee aske amisse; that ye may spend it upon your lustes.' London. Printed by N. O. for Francis Burton, dwelling in Paul's Churchyard, at the signe of the Greene Dragon. 1611." They appeared again in 1641, under this title: "Nineteen Sermons concerning Prayer. The first six shewing the nature of Prayer as a preparative thereunto; the residue a large and full exposition upon the Lord's Prayer. By that learned Divine, Lancelot Andrews, Doctour of Divinitie, and late Bishop of Winchester. James iv. 3: 'Ye aske,' &c. Cambridge: Printed by Roger Daniel, Printer to the Universitie. 1641." They were also published in 1642, at the end of "The Moral Law expounded."

1612.   April 12, Easter-day, at Whitehall, on Col. iii. 12.—Vol. ii. pp. 290—308.

May 31, Whitsunday, at Whitehall, on Acts xix. 1—3.—Vol. iii. pp. 180—220.

Nov. 5, at Whitehall, on Lam. iii. 22. —Vol. iv. pp. 261—276.

The King and Queen were not present, in consequence of the illness of Prince Henry, who died the following day. Chamberlain writes to Sir Dudley Carleton: " Going the next morning, the 5th of November, to hear the Bishop of Ely preach at court upon the 22d verse of the third chapter of Lamentations, I found by the King and Queen's absence from the sermon, and by his manner of praying for him, how the case stood, and that he was *plane deploratus.*" See Nichols's Royal Progresses of King James, vol. ii. p. 467, and Birch's James I. vol. i. p. 203. The Bishop attended at the Prince's funeral, Monday, Dec. 7, following. Nichols, vol. ii. p. 498.

Christmas-day, at Whitehall, on Heb. i. 1—3.—Vol. i. pp. 102—117.

1613.   April 13, at Greenwich, on Is. lxii. 5.—Opusc. Posth. pp. 75—93.

This sermon first appeared under the title: "Concio Latine habita coram Regia Majestate," &c. (as in Opusc. Posth.) This Sermon is not noticed by Nichols.

April 18, Easter-day, at Whitehall, on Col. iii. 12.—Vol. ii. pp. 309—322.

May 23, Whitsunday, at Whitehall, on Eph. iv. 30.—Vol. iii. pp. 201—220.

Nov. 5, at Whitehall, on Prov. viii. 15.—Vol. iv. pp. 277—295.

1613. Christmas-day, at Whitehall, on John viii. 56.—Vol. i. pp. 118—134.

1614. April 24, Easter-day, at Whitehall, on Phil. ii. 8—11.—Vol. ii. pp. 323—343.

This Sermon first appeared under the following title: "A Sermon preached Before his Maiestie, At Whitehall, on Easter day last, 1614. ¶ By the Bishop of Elie, His Maiesties Almoner. ¶ Imprinted at London by Robert Barker, &c. 1614." It was also reprinted in 1618.

June 12, Whitsunday, at Greenwich, on Psal. lxviii. 18.—Vol. iii. pp. 221—240.

Aug. 5, at Burleigh, near Okeham, on Psal. lxxxix. 20—23.—Vol. iv. pp. 76—100.

Nov. 5, at Whitehall, on Prov. xxiv. 21—23.—Ibid. pp. 296—317.

This Sermon is not noticed by Nichols.

Christmas-day at Whitehall, on Isaiah viii. 14.—Vol. i. pp. 135—152.

1615. April 9, Easter-day, at Whitehall, on John ii. 19.—Vol. ii. pp. 344—363.

May 28, Whitsunday, at Greenwich, on Luke iii. 21, 22.—Vol. iii. pp. 240—261.

Not on May 29, as stated in Sermons.

Aug. 5, at Salisbury cathedral, on Psal. v. 1—4.—Vol. iv. pp. 101—125.

Nov. 5, at Whitehall, on Psal. cxlv. 9.—Ibid. pp. 318—340.

Christmas-day, at Whitehall, on Micah v. 2.—Vol. i. pp. 153—174.

Camden states that "the King being sorely troubled with the gout, was not able to go to Divine Service, but heard a sermon in private, and took the Sacrament." See Nichols, vol. iii. p. 123.

1616. March 31, Easter-day, at Whitehall, on 1 Pet. i. 3, 4.—Vol. ii. pp. 364—382.

May 19, Whitsunday at Greenwich, on John xx. 22.—Vol. iii. pp. 261—279.

Aug. 5, at Burleigh, near Okeham, on Esther ii. 21.—Vol. iv. pp. 126—152.

1616. Nov. 5, at Whitehall, on Isa. xxxvii. 3.—Vol. iv. pp. 341—361.

Nichols (vol. iii. p. 215) gives the text erroneously as Ps. xxvii. 3, and repeats the error (p. 225), though he adds the following anecdote from Chamberlain's letter to Sir Dudley Carleton : " The memory of the last prince runs still so much in some men's minds, that on Tuesday [Nov. 5] I heard the Bishop of Ely, preaching at court upon the third verse of the 37th of Isaiah, *Venerunt filii ad partum, et non erant vires parienti*, pray solemnly for Prince Henry without recalling himself." Chamberlain's letter is given in full in Birch's Court and Times of James I. vol. i. pp. 434—436.

Christmas-day, at Whitehall, on Ps. lxxxv. 10, 11.— Vol. i. pp. 175—195.

Chamberlain writes to Sir Dudley Carleton, Jan. 4, 161$\frac{5}{6}$: " The Earl of Arundel [who had recently left the Church of Rome] received the Communion on Christmas-day in the King's Chapel, where there were two excellent sermons made that day by the Bishop of Winchester [Montagu] and the Bishop of Ely [Andrewes], and a third that afternoon in Paul's by the Bishop of London [King], and I heard the Bishop of Rochester [Buckeridge] as much commended at his parish of S. Giles without Cripplegate." The Editor of Birch's Court and Times of James I. (vol. i. p. 385) incorrectly places this letter at the beginning of 1616. A passage from it is quoted at its proper date by Nichols (vol. iii. p. 232).

1617. April 20, Easter-day, at Durham Cathedral, on Matt. xx. 39, 40.—Vol. ii. pp. 383—403.

The King was then on progress to Scotland, having in his retinue the Bishops of Winchester, Ely, and Lincoln, (Montagu, Andrewes, and Neile,) on the latter of whom Laud was attendant as Chaplain.

June 8, Whitsunday at Holyrood House, on Luke iv. 18, 19.—Vol. iii. pp. 280—300.

The following anecdote recorded by Aubrey may possibly apply to this sermon, the only one preached in Scotland :—" A Scottish Lord, when King James asked him how he liked Bishop Andrewes's sermon, said, that he was learned, but he did play with his text as a jackanapes does, who takes up a thing, and tosses and plays with it, and then takes up another, and plays a little with it. Here's a pretty thing, and there's a pretty thing."—Aubrey's Lives of Eminent Men, as quoted in Nichols's Progresses, vol. ii. p. 47.

1617. Nov. 5, at Whitehall, on Luke i. 74, 75.—Vol. iv. pp. 361—384.

" The Bishop of Ely's text that day at court was, ' That we being delivered out of the hand of our enemies, might serve him without fear,' and they say he handled it excellently."—Birch's James I. vol. ii. p. 50. The sermon was printed originally under the following title: " A Sermon preached before His Maiestie, at Whitehall, the fifth of November last, 1617. By the Bishop of Elie, His Maiesties Almoner. London, Printed by John Bill. M.DC.XVIII."

Christmas-day.

He did not preach this Christmas, being laid up by illness. See Chamberlain's Letter to Sir Dudley Carleton (Birch's Court and Times of James I. vol. i. p. 456). The letter as it stands is misplaced a whole twelvemonth, having been written Jan. 10, 161$\frac{7}{8}$.

1618. April 5, Easter-day, at Whitehall, on 1 Cor. xi. 16.— Vol. ii. pp. 404—428.

This sermon was first published separately under this title, " A Sermon preached before His Maiestie at Whitehall, on Easter day last, 1618. By the Bishop of Elie, His Maiesties Almoner. London, Printed by John Bill. M.DC.XVIII."

May 24, Whitsunday, at Greenwich, on Acts ii. 16— 21.—Vol. iii. pp. 301—322.

Camden mentions that on this day the King put forth his permission to use sports on the Lord's day. See Nichols's Progresses, vol. iii. p. 481.

Nov. 5, at Whitehall, on Esther ix. 31.—Vol. iv. pp. 385—405.

Chamberlain writes to Sir Dudley Carleton, " The Bishop of Winchester made an excellent sermon at court." — Birch's James I. vol. ii. p. 105.

Christmas-day, at Whitehall, on Luke ii. 12, 13.— Vol. i. pp. 196—214.

16$\frac{18}{19}$. Feb. 10, Ash-Wednesday, at Whitehall, on Joel ii. 12, 13.—Ibid. pp. 356—374.

Nichols refers this erroneously to the following year. See Progresses, vol. iii. p. 586.

March 28, Easter-day, at Royston.

Chamberlain mentions the Bishop's preaching, but the sermon is not extant. The King was then lying at Royston under severe illness, just after the Queen's death. See Nichols's Progresses, vol. iii. p. 533.

1619. May 16, Whitsunday, at Greenwich, on Acts x. 34, 35.
—Vol. iii. pp. 323—343.

Christmas-day, at Whitehall, on Luke ii. 14.—Vol. i. pp. 215—232.

1620. April 16, Easter-day, at Whitehall, on John xx. 11—17.—Vol. iii. pp. 3—22.

This sermon was printed the same year, under the following title: "A Sermon preached at Whitehall, on Easter Day, the 16 of April, 1620, By the Bishop of Winchester. London, Printed by Robert Barker and John Bill, Printers to the King's most Excellent Maiestie. M.DC.XX."

June 4, Whitsunday, at Whitehall, on 1 John v. 6.—Ibid. pp. 344—360.

This is the date given in the Sermons, but Camden states that the King kept his Whitsuntide at Greenwich. He also mentions that the King took the sacrament, which was administered by Bishop Andrewes, and that Mountaine, Bishop of Lincoln, preached his first sermon before the King. See Nichols's Progresses, vol. iii. p. 609.

Christmas-day, at Whitehall, on Matt. ii. 1, 2.—Vol. i. pp. 233—248.

1621. Jan. 30, on Ps. lxxii. 1.—Vol. v. pp. 203—222.

This sermon was preached in Westminster church before the King, Prince, and Lords spiritual and temporal, at the opening of the Parliament. (Nichols's Progresses, vol. iii. p. 650.)

Feb. 14, Ash-Wednesday, at Whitehall, on Matt. vi. 16.—Vol. i. pp. 375—397.

This sermon is not mentioned by Nichols.

April 1, Easter-day, at Whitehall, on John xx. 17.—Vol. iii. pp. 23—38.

May 20, Whitsunday, at Greenwich, on James i. 16, 17.—Ibid. pp. 361—376.

$16\frac{21}{22}$. March 6, Ash-Wednesday, at Whitehall, on Matt. vi. 16.—Vol. i. pp. 398—416.

Nichols speaks of this sermon as having been preached Feb. 13, evidently confusing it with that of the previous year (which he omitted to notice), the texts of both being the same. See Nichols's Progresses, vol. iii. p. 752.

1622. April 21, Easter-day, at Whitehall, on John xx. 17.—Vol. iii. pp. 39—59.

1622. June 9, Whitsunday, on 1 Cor. xii. 4—7.—Vol. iii. pp. 377—401.

> This sermon was only prepared to be preached.

Aug. 5, at Windsor, on 1 Sam. xxiv. 5—8.—Vol. iv. pp. 153—182.

> Chamberlain writes to Sir Dudley Carleton on this sermon: " His voice grows very low, but otherwise he did extraordinary well, and like himself. I dined with him that day, and could not leave him till half an hour after five o'clock. The weather was so very hot, and he so faint and wet, that he was fain to go to bed for some little time, after he came out of the pulpit."—Birch's James I, vol. ii. p. 325.

Christmas-day, at Whitehall, on Matt. ii. 1, 2.—Vol. i. pp. 249—264.

1623. Feb. 26, Ash-Wednesday, at Whitehall, on Matt. iii. 7, 8.—Ibid. pp. 417—434.

> Nichols gives both date and text of this year's Ash-Wednesday sermon erroneously, confusing them with those of former years. See Nichols's Progresses, vol. iii. p. 815.

April 13, Easter-Sunday, at Whitehall, on Isaiah lxiii. 1—3.—Vol. iii. pp. 60—79.

Aug. 5, (place not stated,) on Gen. xlix. 57.—Vol. iv. pp. 183—200.

> This sermon was only prepared to be preached.

Christmas-day, at Whitehall, on Eph. i. 10.—Vol. i. pp. 265—283.

1624. Feb. 11, Ash-Wednesday, at Whitehall, on Matt. iii. 8. —Ibid. pp. 435—454.

> Nichols is in error again, making Ash-Wednesday fall on Feb. 26. (See Nichols's Progresses, vol. iii. p. 966.)

March 28, Easter-day, on Heb. xiii. 20, 21.—Vol. iii. pp. 80—103.

Christmas-day, at Whitehall, on Ps. ii. 7.—Vol. i. pp. 284—302.

The Sermons first appeared in a collected form in 1629, and were reprinted in 1632, 1635, 1641, 1661.

II.

PRIVATE DEVOTIONS.

A VERY imperfect edition of these Devotions was first published in 1647, by Humphrey Moseley (the title of which is given below, p. 225). In the year following there appeared a more complete edition, being a translation of the Greek Devotions, by the Rev. Richard Drake, formerly Fellow of Pembroke Hall, from a MS. copy by Samuel Wright, the Bishop's amanuensis, which will be more fully described below.

The edition thus put forth by Drake, was reprinted in the years 1670, 1674, 1692.

But previous to the publication of the first of these reprints, a volume had appeared with the following title : " Holy Devotions, with Directions to pray, &c., by the Right Reverend Father in God, Lancelot Andrews, late Bishop of Winchester. The fourth edition, printed for Henry Seile, &c. 1655."

The publisher in his preface states that " the true father and primary author of these Devotions, was the great and eminent Andrews." And adds, that " the parentage of this book, comes now to be vindicated to its true nativity."

The first edition of this book had appeared in 1630 under a different title : "Institutiones Piæ; or Directions to pray ;" and the initials of the author, or compiler, are given as H. I. This was retained in the next two editions.

There is no question that H.I. was Henry Isaacson, who died in 1654; which accords with Henry Seile's statement in the preface to the fourth edition, already referred to, that "the three previous editions had been dressed up by a kind foster-father, who now sleeps in the Lord."

It is most likely that the volume was compiled by Isaacson from some of the Bishop's papers. The earlier portion appears to be notes of sermons, either made by Andrewes himself, to assist in composition, or else taken down by some of his hearers. Other passages agree exactly with portions of his Latin Devotions, especially with some now published in this edition for the first time, and which will be mentioned below. The volume can in no other and stricter sense be regarded as Andrewes's. The original editor states that he had originally compiled the devotions for his own use; and though not professing to be anything more than a compiler, does not specify the sources from which the compilation was made. Under this uncertainty, and with the suspicion naturally attaching to a book, whose title was altered in its fourth edition, after the death of the original compiler, we cannot venture to include the " Holy Devotions " in the number of the Bishop's works.

We now pass on to the edition of the " Preces Privatæ," in Greek and Latin, which was first published in 1675. They were issued from the Oxford press, with a short preface, but without either the name or the initials of the editor [a].

He mentions the two main sources from which his materials were obtained. The Greek, which forms the first part, and a large portion of the Latin, which appears in the second, were supplied by Richard Drake, mentioned above, and the remainder was taken from the Appendix to the " Verus Christianus," published at Oxford in 1668, by Dr. David Stokes, Fellow of Eton College [b].

The transcript of the Greek Devotions, furnished by Drake, is still preserved in Pembroke College, Cambridge. It is most valuable as having been made by Samuel Wright, the Bishop's amanuensis, from the original autograph. It is a small volume, 12mo. size, most beautifully and carefully written, and consists of 168 pages, one or two here and there being left blank, and contains the whole of the Greek Devotions, without any Latin translation, down to the " Meditation on the Day of Judgment," at p. 252 of the present edition.

Drake has added, on the first page, the following notice : " Amicissimus meus Samuel Wright, Lanceloto Wintoniensi Ep'o olim a chartis, nunc autem Matthæo Eliensi a Registris, pretiosum hoc κειμήλιον sua manu accurate descriptum dono dedit mihi Richardo Drake." It had probably been in Drake's possession for many years, as he speaks of it in his preface to the translation of the Devotions, published in 1648. Some various readings and other corrections have been taken from this interesting MS. in the Appendix to the present edition of the Greek Devotions; the Editor not having been aware of its existence till the earlier part of the volume was printed.

The two meditations " On the last Judgment," and " On human Frailty," were taken from the Appendix to Dr. Stokes's " Verus Christianus," as well as many passages in the Latin Devotions, which in the present edition have been arranged as they were first printed by Stokes.

The " Preces," as thus edited, have been reprinted in 1828, and 1848.

There appears in the present edition, for the first time, a third part, printed from MSS. Harleian. Num. 6614.

This is a small book, neatly bound, clasped, and gilt edged. On the back is a rose, surmounted by an earl's coronet, between the letters V. M. On the first leaf is the following notice, in the handwriting of J. Cole : " Ex manu propria Lancelloti Andrews Wintoniensis olim

---

[a] Antony Wood, however, informs us (F. O. ii. 235) that he was John Lamphire, and adds that he afterwards obtained a more perfect copy of these prayers, which he was about to publish, but was hindered by other affairs.

[b] He is termed, by mistake, in the preface, " Guilielmus Stoke."

Episcopi, sicut a fide dignis accepi." And on the second leaf are the arms of the See of Winchester impaling Andrewes's. The volume consists of forty-two written leaves, and thirty-five blank.

There seems to be no question that this is not in the Bishop's handwriting, both from the great dissimilarity to his writing at an earlier period, and what is more, from the numerous errata with which it abounds.

It appears as if it were written out fair for the Bishop, and that it was left incomplete in consequence of his death. It will be observed that the prayers, as far as they extend, are regular and systematic; but, as the volume contains no intercessions and no prayers for each day of the week, it bears about it marks of incompleteness.

III.

MANUAL OF DIRECTIONS FOR THE VISITATION OF THE SICK.

See the notice of this volume below, p. 167.

IV.

OPERA POSTHUMA.

The dates of Sermons and Theological Dissertations contained in this volume are noticed among the English Sermons in their chronological order.

The Correspondence with Du Moulin, Answer to Perron, &c., are noticed below in this volume in their respective places. They formed the latter part of the Opuscula Posthuma.

V.

RESPONSIO AD TORTI LIBRUM.

The correct title of this work is "Tortura Torti." The circumstances relating to its publication are noticed in the preface to the volume itself.

VI.

RESPONSIO AD APOLOGIAM CARD. BELLARMINI.

See the preface to the volume itself.

The above are all the works of Bishop Andrewes noticed by his biographer, and are here placed in the order in which he mentioned them. The following volumes, however, still remain to be noticed:—

VII.

A Pattern of Catechistical Doctrine,

AND

The Moral Law Expounded.

These are placed under the same head, as being in fact the same work, cast into different forms.

The first edition of the "Catechistical Doctrine" appeared in 1630, under the following title: "A Patterne of Catechisticall Doctrine, Wherein many profitable Questions touching Christian Religion are handled, and the whole Decalogue succinctly and judiciously expounded. London, Printed for William Garrett. 1630."

The editor of the new edition of that volume considered that probably this may have been the manual used for catechising by Andrewes himself. But from there being no mention made of it by Isaacson, we may consider that it stands only in the same position as the other editions of the "Catechistical Doctrine," and "The Moral Law," and is formed out of notes made by the hearers of the lectures.

In 1641 there appeared another edition under the same title, with the words "with additions" only inserted.

This was followed, in 1642, by the following work: "The Moral Law Expounded: 1. learnedly; 2. largely; 3. orthodoxly. That is the long and much desired work of Bishop Andrewes, upon the Ten Commandments, &c."

In 1650 was published an enlarged edition of "The Pattern of Catechistical Doctrine," under the title, "The Pattern of Catechistical Doctrine at large; or a learned and pious Exposition of the Ten Commandments, &c. By Lancelot Andrewes, &c." And in 1675, the same work was reprinted, under the same title.

VIII.

In 1641 there appeared, "A Summarie View of the Government both of the Old and New Testament, whereby the Episcopall Government of Christ's Church is Vindicated, out of the rude draughts of Lancelot Andrewes, late Bishop of Winchester. . . . Oxford. . . . 1641." It formed part of a volume, the general title of which was, "Certain briefe Treatises, written by diverse learned men, concerning the Ancient and Modern Government of the Church, &c."

This treatise was reprinted by Dr. Nicholas Bernard, in his "Clavi Trabales," A.D. 1661, and is there stated to be both confirmed and enlarged by Archbishop Ussher.

Milton remarks on these fragments: "Others better advised, are content to receive their beginning from Aaron and his sons, among whom, Bishop Andrewes of late years, and in these times, the Primate of Armagh, for their learning, are reputed the best able to say what may be done in this opinion."—Milton, The Reason of Church Government urged against Prelates, book i. chap. iii. Works, p. 47. Lond. 1753. And again, "It follows here now to attend to certain objections in a little treatise, lately printed among others of like sort at Oxford, and in the title said to be out of the rude draughts of Bishop Andrews. And surely they be rude draughts indeed, insomuch that it is a marvel to think, what his friends meant, to let come abroad such shallow reasonings with the name of a man so much bruited for learning."—Chap. v. p. 49.

IX.

A learned Discourse of Ceremonies retained and used in Christian Churches, &c. Lond. 1653.

See the introductory note in this edition, vol. vi. p. 365.

X.

Ἀποσπασμάτια SACRA; or a collection of Posthumous and Orphan Lectures, delivered at St. Paul's and St. Giles his Church. Lond. 1657.

This volume contains Sermons on the first four chapters of Genesis, which occupy more than 500 pages. The rest of the volume comprises "Sermons on several choice texts." There does not appear to be sufficient evidence to justify one in ascribing these sermons, at least in their present form, to Bishop Andrewes. Accordingly, they are not reprinted in this edition.

XI.

FORM FOR THE CONSECRATION OF A CHURCH OR CHAPEL.

This was first published in 32mo in 1659, with a Preface dated May 29 of that year. The only copy of this Edition which the Editor knows is now in the Bodleian Library. It was afterwards reprinted in 4to, and appended to Sparrow's Collection of Articles.

XII.

JUDGMENT OF THE LAMBETH ARTICLES, AND CENSURE ON BARRETT.

These were published in the Appendix to Elis's Articulorum xxxix. Eccl. Angl. Defensio, which came out in 1660; but the Editor has not seen any edition earlier than 1696.

APPENDIX C.

ANDREWES AND CASAUBON.

It was in the month of October, 1610, that Isaac Casaubon came to England. His patron, Henry IV. of France, had, a few months before, fallen by the hand of an assassin; and he was glad to avail himself of the opportunity afforded him of seeking a refuge in England, and of gaining a closer knowledge of the English Church, of whose peculiar character he had hitherto been acquainted only by hearsay, and which seemed likely to furnish a solution of the doubts and difficulties which he felt, and which could not be satisfied by the claims of either of the religious communions in his own country.

His reputation had already preceded him; and both the King, and the principal English Bishops, were ready to give him a hearty reception.

It was a time of active theological controversy: Andrewes had just published his "Tortura Torti," and was on the eve of publishing his "Responsio ad Apologiam Card. Bellarmini;" and being the most prominent controversialist of the time, and in constant attendance on the King, he was, almost as a matter of course, brought into immediate communication with Casaubon.

Their acquaintance soon ripened into the closest intimacy. And it will be seen, by the extracts which will be given from the letters and Diary of Casaubon, that he and Andrewes were frequently in almost daily communication.

Casaubon was present, shortly after his arrival in London, at the consecration of the Scottish Bishops, on Oct. 21. (prid. Kal. Nov. according to his reckoning [a].) (Ephem. p. 789. Oxon. 1850.)

On the following Friday, Oct. 26, (al. Non. Nov.,) there is this entry in his Diary: "Cum sapientissimo et doctissimo viro D. Eliensi aliquot horas posui, et miram illius erga me humanitatem et benevolentiam agnovi." (Ephem. pp. 790, 791.)

The next entry records their employment on the 14th of November: "viii. Kal. Dec. A prandio accitus sum ab Episcopo Eliensi cum hospite meo viro doctissimo [b], ut ille nobis librum a se scriptum et mox edendum

---

[a] Casaubon's dates are according to the New Style.   [b] J. Overallo.

recitaret^c. Mirati sumus viri eruditionem et acumen." And again, Nov. 15: "vii. Kal. Dec. Totus fere dies in studiis Dei beneficio actus, inter doctos certe, et maxime apud Episcopum Eliensem longe doctissimum." (Ephem. pp. 790, 791.) It appears from the next entries in his Diary, that he was with the Bishop on the 17th, "v. Kal. Dec. Apud Episcopum Eliensem hodie fui, et magnum fructum ex ejus doctrina et pietate cepi," (ibid. p. 791,) and again on the 19th and 20th, on the former of which days he suggested some corrections in the Bishop's work, which were favourably received: " Meas notulas non neglexit, imo pluris fecit, quam merebantur." (Ephem. p. 792.)

The next day, Nov. 21, (Kal. Dec.) he writes thus to the Bishop of Bath and Wells[d], on these several interviews: "Jussus ... fueram legere, quæ a viro præstantissimo, D. Eliensi, adversus Bellarminum sunt scripta, ut quid mihi de ea scriptione videretur, serenissimæ Majestati exponerem. Ego vero adfui D. Eliensi, sua legenti D. Decano, hospiti meo doctissimo, mihique; et postea domum allatas easdem chartas legi ipse, et, quanta maxima poteram attentione, singula expendi. Ac licet non ita insaniam, ut de tanti viri scriptis judicare me posse existimem; quia tamen jussus eram, optavi sententiam meam apud sapientissimi καὶ εὐσεβεστάτου Regis Majestatem exponere. Cujus voti quoniam facultas non contigit, ad te, Vir Reverendissime [scribo]; ut per te, nisi grave est, Rex cognoscat, me quod fueram jussus, incredibili quadam cum voluptate animi partim esse executum, partim quotidie exequi. Legi enim, et lego quotidie opus, in quo pietas sincera cum eruditione varia, et suavissima quadam elegantia sic certant, ut quid prius laudes, aut mireris, non facile scias. Miserum vero Cardinalem, qui in hac effœta sua ætate Antagonistam sortitus sit, ingenii copia, doctrina exquisita, et dicendi facultate cum maxime florentem, et omnibus plane rebus ad hujusmodi certamen necessariis longe superiorem. Quod si quid pudoris in fronte Cardinalis salvi superest, non puto ipsum cum hoc Adversario in arenam unquam descensurum; certe enim 'impar congressus Achilli.' Sciat vero per te, obsecro, Regia Majestas, ita me in hoc negotio esse versatum, ut hominem φιλαλήθη et candidum decebat; nam qui omnia tribuam D. Eliensi, atque ipsum admirer summopere, sic ejus legi scripta, atque omnia expendi, quasi Auctori nihil tribuerem. Quare etiam dubitationes meas, si quid forte incidebat, de quo dubitarem, chartæ illevi, et ad ipsum retuli. Sed nihil fuit ejusmodi, in quo non inter nos conveniret; neque hoc, quia auctoritati viri tanti modeste cederem; sed quia ex animo penitus cum illo sentio: nam et ipse cum antiquis Patribus consentit; quorum doctrinam, ubi consentire ipsos inter se video, probare et religione quadam me colere, adeo me non diffiteor, ut præ me feram. Utinam, Reverendissime Domine, iterum utinam, qui in nostra Gallia Theologica tractant, D. Eliensem vellent imitari! Ausim affirmare, uberrimos fructus suæ moderationis eos fore

[c] That is; the Responsio ad Apol. Card. Bellarmini.
[d] In the edition of Casaubon's Letters which is here followed, the Bishop is called by mistake "Richardus," not "Jacobus" Montagu.

percepturos: nunc utique cum bonorum omnium animi a manifesta tyrannide Romani Pontificis abalienati, defensores illius cane et angue pejus oderunt, et perditos cupiunt."—Epist. dcxcviii. Jacobo Montacuto. Lond. Kal. Dec. 1610. Epist. p. 366. Roterod. 1709.

A few days after there occurs the following entry in his Diary relating to the same subject:—" Prid. Non. Dec. Mane aliquid egi in studiis: a prandio apud D. Eliensem fui, et legentem illum audivi caput libri sui octavum. Mira elegantia vir doctissimus quisquilias, nænias et ineptias, imo aliquando impias blasphemias Bellarmini confutat: ut quod negaverat ille Catholicos appellare B. Virginem, vel *Divam*, vel *Deam:* nam profert Eliensis multa Lipsii loca, in quibus ita illam appellat, Lipsii veteris amici mei, qui hac in parte satis vituperari non potest. Tantine nominis virum tantam ausum esse impietatem? Proh facinus! Ego frivolum putavi utrumque scriptum illius, tamen impium non putavi. Sit beata, sit sancta, sit venerationi omnibus mortalibus mater Jesu Christi Maria; sit denique evecta in quantum maximum ἡ κτίσις capere et consequi potest honorem, certe Deam se dici non pateretur, neque tot anilibus fabulis immisceri, quas narrat Eliensis." (Ephem. pp. 793, 794.)

The next entry relating to Andrewes must be introduced somewhat out of its proper order:—"iv. Non, Jan. Ad aulam hodie profectus .. regem conveni. Prandenti affui, et toto prandio, quam longum illud fuit, audivi examinantem notas appositas Versioni Anglicæ S. Bibliorum, quæ nuper Duaco prodiit. Legebat Episcopus Bathoniensis, Rex censebat. Censuras approbabant qui aderant Episcopus Eliensis, Episcopus Coventrensis, et ego cum illis." (Ephem. p. 809.)

Casaubon was soon after employed, at the King's wish, in compiling a tract of his own, which occupied him during the early part of the next year. This was his celebrated letter to Fronto Ducæus, which was published separately at the time, and which is numbered dccxxx. in his collected Epistles. In this letter he enters into the history of the Gunpowder Plot, and the part taken in it by the Jesuits.

From the following notices, it appears that he was assisted by Andrewes in obtaining materials, as well as in other ways, during the progress of the work:—

" viii. Eid. Dec. Mane pensum a Rege impositum me habuit: deinde a prandio eandem ob causam apud D. Episcopum Eliensem fuimus." (Ephem. p. 795.)

" Eid. Dec. Apud Episcopum Eliensem pransus, totum fere diem cum illo egi. O doctum, O humanum virum." (Ibid. p. 798.)

"xviii. Kal. Jan. Τὰ ἐγκύκλια in penso quotidiano, cum Episcopo Eliensi, et privatis studiis." (Ibid.)

"xii. Kal. Jan. ... pensum apud D. Eliensem absolvi." (Ibid. p. 801.)

" Accepi a Domino Eliensi ... chartas simul nonnullas ad meum propositum spectantes. Eæ quum sint scriptæ Anglice, danda mihi opera est, ut aliena opera adjutus, ipsas perlegam et intelligam. Non est futurum in eo parum ponderis, quod liquido et sancte potero affirmare, ipsas me Garneti literas legisse." (Lond. a. d. viii. Eid. Mart. MDCXI. Epist. dccxii. Jacobo Montacuto, p. 376.) " xi. Kal. Jul. Hodie libelli quem nondum absolvi, partem dedi D. Episcopi Eliensis amanuensi, ut exscriberet." (Ephem. p. 845.)

From the following extracts from the letter itself, it appears that he regarded it as a vindication of Andrewes's integrity, which had been assailed by the Romanists [e]:—

"Poteramus quidem hoc labore supersedere, quum ex iis literis [f] τὰ καιριώτατα dudum descripserit et publicaverit integerrimus reverendissimusque vir Dominus Episcopus Eliensis; de cujus alta doctrina in omni genere disciplinarum quidquid dixero, minus erit." (Epist. dccxxx. Frontoni Ducæo, p. 408.) And again, "Omitto alia ejus rei indicia . . . ab Episcopo Eliensi ita perspicuis argumentis demonstrata, ut ne ipsi quidem hostes veritatis possint jam de eo dubitare." (Ibid.)

"Nam qui rationibus viri sine controversia maximi, integerrimi, et undequaque doctissimi, respondere non magis posset, quam Pygmæus aliquis aut Thiodamas Lydius Herculi clavam extorquere, ne ad libri conspectum factus esse repente mutus suis ἐργοδιώκταις videretur, rationibus calumnias opposuit, argumentis convicia, doctrinæ stupendæ detestandam maledicentiam. Accusat gravissimum Præsulem, quod Terentium et Plautum legerit juvenis in Academiis; nam ex eo tempore, hoc est, ab annis triginta, Plautum vix in manus aliquando meminit sumpsisse; Terentium ne semel quidem attigit. Si qua igitur veteris lectionis vestigia in scriptis senis venerandi apparent, accuset felicem ejus memoriam, et cum Deo, ejus beneficii auctore, expostulet." (Epist. dccxxx. p. 423.) "Accusat Præsulem, quod non alienus sit a doctrina Catholicæ Ecclesiæ in non paucis; et homo amens persuasurum se Regi Serenissimo putat, melius se, qui Romæ est, quam Majestatem ipsius Episcopum nosse, cujus intimi sensus ex quotidiano usu Regi omnes patent. Nos vero hoc scimus et affirmamus; si cætera Ecclesiæ vestræ omnia illa probarentur (quid autem probet, quid improbet, scripta faciunt fidem) vel unicum tamen de Papæ omnipotentia et tyrannide in Reges dogma ita ipsum abominari, ut Ecclesiam, in qua ea doctrina vigeat, pro vera et incorrupta nunquam sit habiturus. Desinat vero Andreas Regi sapientissimo palpum obtrudere, quamdiu Episcopo obtrectabit, cujus innocentiam, integritatem et παντοίην ἀρετήν, nemo novit melius, nemo prædicat libentius, quam serenissimus Rex Jacobus." (Ibid. p. 423.)

This letter was completed by the beginning of July, (Ephem. pp. 847, 848,) but was not forwarded to Ducæus till nearly the end of October. (See Epist. dccxlvi. pp. 434, 435.)

Shortly after its completion, Casaubon accompanied Andrewes into

---

[e] The person especially alluded to was the Jesuit L'Heureux, who wrote under the assumed name of Andreas Eudæmon-Johannes. The title of his book was, "Parallelus Torti et Tortoris."

[f] It is mentioned by Mr. Jardine, (Criminal Trials, vol. ii. Pref. p. x.) that many of the letters quoted by Casaubon are no longer extant; so that the greatest value now attaches to these extracts.

the country, and again on a more lengthened visit to his Episcopal palaces at Downham and Ely, to Cambridge, and other parts of his diocese, where he remained during July and August.

The following entries in his Diary, mention the commencement of the journey, and the incidents most worthy of notice:—

"iii. Kal. Jul. Quod Deus bene vertat, hodie rus proficiscimur cum Domino Episcopo Eliensi."—(Ephem. p. 847.)

"Prid. Kal. Jul. O Domine, quantæ doctrinæ, quantæ humanitatis hospitem sum nactus! Cui tu, Christe, pro beneficiis in me hic alterum jam diem rusticantem omnia bona perpende." (Ibid.)

"v. Non. Jul. Κυριακὴ dies ad Regem vocat et D. Episcopum in cujus sum comitatu, et me. Imus igitur." (p. 848.)

"iii. Eid. Jul. Hodie apud Prætorem Londinensem cum D. Eliensi, D. Decano Paulino, et aliis sum pransus." (p. 850.)

"vii. Kal. Aug. Quod Dominus Jesus velit esse faustum, ad solatium meæ tam diuturnæ solitudinis Londino relicto, cum reverendo viro D. Episcopo Eliensi Cantabrigiam et Eliam iter institui." (p. 854.)

"vi. Kal. Aug. Cantabrigiam hodie appulimus, . . . et in collegio Petri, quod primum occurrit, regiturque a Domino Richardson, mansimus. Et nos quidem humanitate cum Domini Episcopi tum D. Richardson mirifice recreamur." (p. 855.)

"v. Kal. Aug. Apud hospitem nostrum . . . pransi, Eliam venimus, et postquam ibi D. Episcopus Decanum senio et morbo confectum invisisset, ad hanc D. Episcopi domum pervenimus. Deus benedicat illi, qui nobis hæc otia fecit, viro maximo." (Ibid.)

"Prid. Kal. Aug. Diem Κυριακὴν, ut et reliquos omnes dies, ex quo sumus cum magno hoc Episcopo, ex parte in templo egimus, beati hoc genere vitæ et consuetudine tanti viri." (p. 856.)

"iv. Non. Aug. Reficior . . . suavissima admirandi Præsulis doctrina et humanitate incredibili . . . Hodie Eliam invisi. Templum ibi magnificum plane spectavi, sed Laternam imprimis sum admiratus." (p. 857.)

"v. Eid. Aug. Etiam hodie summo mane profectus cum Domino Episcopo Laternam quam vocant accuratius spectavi, opus plane dignissimum spectatu." (p. 861.)

"xix. Kal. Sept. Hodie sacrosanctæ Domini cœnæ participavimus Deum venerati, ut hujus tanti mysterii daret nobis intelligentiam." (p. 863.)

"xviii. Kal. Sept [g] Hodie comitati sumus D. Episcopum Eliam proficiscentem, ut diem festum ob liberationem Regis a Comitum Gowriorum insidiis celebraret in sua Ecclesia. Erat Decanus in primo aditu templi, ubi excepit D. Episcopum, et inde præeuntibus et canentibus ψαλμοὺς Canonicis processio facta est intra ædem illam sacram. Postea preces matutinæ habitæ. Tum autem concionatus est D. Episcopus pie et graviter. Postremo celebrata est inter paucos S. Eucharistia." (pp. 863, 864.)

---

[g] The difference between Old and New Style must be kept in mind.

" xvii. Kal. Sept. Hodie cum D. Episcopo Wisbicum urbem petimus." (p. 864.)

" xvi. Kal. Sept. Quum superiorem noctem mansissemus Duninch-choniæ sive Dunintoniæ, hodie Wisbicum pervenimus . . . Tandem Wisbicum appulimus, prodieruntque obviam D. Episcopo Judex oppidi, item decem primi, et caterva ingens equitum, ut videantur fuisse in comitatu D. Episcopi, cum urbem est ingressus, ad CL. equites." (pp. 864, 865.)

"xv. Kal. Sept. Concioni hodie interfui in templo satis elegantis structuræ. Inde loca in arce invisimus, ubi servati sunt sub extrema tempora Elizabethæ quidam Jesuitæ et alii Pontificii." (pp. 865, 866.)

" xiv. Kal. Sept. A prandio conscensis equis inspeximus canales hujus agri. Progressus est igitur D. Episcopus cum paucis comitibus in adversam urbis et terrarum partem illi unde venimus. Confecimus quatuor aut quinque millia . . . Ambulabamus toto fere hoc itinere post unum aut alterum a Wisbeco milliare in aggeribus quos vocant 'sea-bancs,' . . . In reditu aliam viam ingressus est Episcopus, cujus exitum quum non inveniret, quæsitus est dux qui nos inde educeret. Erat ibi $\dot{a}\nu\epsilon\mu o\lambda\acute{\epsilon}\tau\eta s$, et in eo puer qui indicinam vadi promisit, atque adeo viam præire statim cœpit. Non confeceramus ducentos passus, cum pervenimus ad vadum, quod nisi Deus adfuisset D. Episcopo fatale illi fuerat futurum: qui, animadverso præeuntes non sine ingenti periculo trajicere, ut pedem referat flectit equum. Ille in collem se erigere incipit, ac sessorem dejicit; qui neque in $\pi\tau\acute{\omega}\sigma\epsilon\iota$, neque dum est humi intra pedes equi, damnum ullum accepit." (pp. 866, 867.)

" xiii. Kal. Sept. De more lectis aliquot psalmis ad perspiciendam urbem prodiimus. . . . Sunt etiam ea die absoluta judicia solennia, uti vocant, quæ præsidente D. Episcopo fuerunt celebrata. . . . Hoc die domum reversi sumus Dunamiam itinere per Norfolciam instituto . . . Simul Episcopus ad canales quosdam inspiciendos est deductus $\delta\delta o\hat{v}$ $\pi\acute{a}\rho\epsilon\rho\gamma o\nu$." (pp. 867, 868.)

"ix. Kal. Sept. Ad uxorem literas dedi, postquam rediissemus a lapidicina Eliensi, quam cum D. Episcopo spectavimus." (p. 874.)

" iv. Kal. Sept. A prandio partem magnam circumjacentis agri circa et ultra Eliam in equo lustravi cum reverendissimo Episcopo." (p. 875.)

" Prid. Kal. Sept. Magnus hodie nobilitatis Eliensis concursus ad D. Episcopum, qui, ut semper, eos excepit epulis dapsilibus et adjicialibus." (p. 875.)

" viii. Eid. Sept. Adhuc tenet me captivum, sed aureis vinculis suæ humanitatis, $\dot{o}$ $\pi\acute{a}\nu\nu$ D. Episcopus . . . Sed discedendum tamen $\sigma\grave{v}\nu$ $\Theta\epsilon\hat{\omega}$ ad summum die crastina." (p. 877.)

" vii. Eid. Sept. Quod Deus bene vertat, hodie domum redeo, hoc est Londinum: discedens a viro æternum mihi admirando; cui $\dot{a}\nu\tau\grave{\iota}$ $\phi\iota\lambda o$-$\xi\epsilon\nu\acute{\iota}\eta s$ det Deus $\mu\nu\rho\acute{\iota}a$ $\dot{a}\gamma a\theta\acute{a}$. (Ibid.)

His general impressions of this visit, may be gathered from the following passages in his letters to Thuanus:—

"Est in hoc regno admirandæ vir pietatis et doctrinæ, Episcopus

Eliensis ... Hic Præsul optimus et mei amantissimus in hæc loca sui Episcopatus me deduxit, ubi sermonibus cum ipso, et librorum, quos hic nancisci possum, lectione me sustento. ... Ad Eliam, in ædibus Domini Episcopi .... a.d. vi. Eid. Aug. MDCXI." (Epist. dccxl. p. 431.) " Heri Londinum redii ab Elia et Episcopo Eliensi, qui ipsos dies quadraginta et octo me tenuit, et vix tandem discedendi a se copiam fecit. Est omnino vir ille ejusmodi, quem si notum haberes, vehementer adamares. Dies totos cum illo de Literis, præsertim Sacris, sæpe disserui; neque possum verbis exprimere, quantum probitatis et veræ pietatis in eo Præsule observaverim. Utinam et vestri, et Protestantes ejus ingenii et doctrinæ plures haberent Episcopos! Sperarem ad concordiam viam fore planam et facilem, quæ nunc culpa hominum non dicam difficilis, sed plane jam patet nulla. Τὸ κατ' ἀνθρώπους λέγω· Θεῷ γὰρ πᾶν ἄπορον πόριμον. Dum eram Eliæ, ne sederem semper otiosus, regionem lustravi, multaque observavi, quæ cogito, si Deus animum aliquando dederit ad studia tranquillum, integra Epistola tibi exponere. Londini, Kal. Sept. MDCXI." (Ibid.)

From the following entries in the Diary, it appears that Andrewes shortly afterwards returned to London, and that repeated communications took place between him and Casaubon :—

" iv. Kal. Nov. Quum Waræ noctem egissemus, mane Roistonum ivimus. Regem vidimus, allocuti sumus." (Ephem. p. 895.)

" iii. Kal. Nov. Κυριακὴν apud Regem et cum Rege egimus." (Ibid.)

" Prid. Kal. Nov. Cum Rege de negotio egimus, cujus causa ego et vir magnus D. Eliensis fueramus acciti." (p. 896.)

" xviii. Kal. Dec. Apud D. Eliensem fui, et de penso cum eo communicavi." (p. 897.)

" viii. Kal. Dec. Roistonum hodie cum reverendissimo Episcopo Eliensi sum profectus." (p. 897.)

" vii. Kal. Dec. Totum diem Rex optimus nobis tribuit, fuimusque ego et D. Episcopus Eliensis a prandio et ante prandium cum ejus Majestate plurimas horas. Ita negotium transactum, cujus caussa veneramus: ac statim itineri nos accinximus. Θεῷ χάρις." (p. 899.)

" Non. Dec. Magnam diei partem cum D. Eliensi egi, et D. Legato, non meliori cupiditate literas expectans e Gallia de nuperi libelli acceptione." (p. 901.)

" Prid. Eid. Dec. Roistonum hodie perveni cum Domino Eliensi, viro magno, et cujus humanitati ipse plurimum debeo. Reddat illi Deus suam erga me φιλανθρωπίαν." (p. 902.)

" Eid. Dec. Hodie perfecimus cum serenissimo Rege, quod heri non potueramus." (Ibid.)

" xvi. Kal. Jan. Ad D. Eliensem adii ob literas D. Bathoniensis, qui etiam ad me scripsit Regis jussu repetens chartas quas nuper retuleramus." (p. 903.)

These extracts (the latter of which are placed out of their chronological order) refer to the letter to Cardinal Perron, which Casaubon was then preparing under the King's direction.

On the 26th of November, he thus writes to Daniel Heinsius:—
" Mihi cum illo Præsule quotidiana consuetudo intercedit, atque ille vir mihi in hoc loco magni Thuani desiderium cum oppido paucis aliis lenit : nam et profunda hominis doctrina capior, et comitas incredibilis in summa dignitate mirifice illum mihi commendavit." (Epist. dcliv. p. 438.)

From this time the notices of Andrewes become less frequent, both in Casaubon's Diary and Letters. Towards the close of this year (1611), we find him, in a letter to Samuel Collins, confirming the truth of some statements made by Andrewes in the Tortura Torti, which had been questioned by his opponents, and addressing Andrewes himself on the subject of the letter to Cardinal Perron, which, as stated above, was then in preparation. (See Epistt. dccliii. dcclxvii. pp. 443, 444. 446.)

The following notices occur during the next year :—
" Eid. Feb. Apud amicos fui hodie D. Decanum [Overal] et D. Eliensem, quos solos Anglorum familiares habeo." (Ephem. p. 916.)

"xiii. Kal. Maii. Hodie pransus apud D. Eliensem, a prandio cum uxore interfui lotioni pedum pauperum, quæ fit in hac Ecclesia egregie [h]." (p 926.)

And again, in 1613 :—
" Excipieris a Domino Eliensi sane quam amicissime. Nuper eram apud illum, quando amicus tuus et ipsi et mihi tuas reddidit. Excepit prolixa humanitate tuum amicum, quem neque ipse, neque ego postea vidimus. Dixit etiam mihi Dominus Episcopus, se tibi statim responsurum. Utinam omnes docti viri, quos habet hoc regnum non paucos, (etsi pares Eliensi oppido paucos,) pari candore cum ipso essent præditi. Londini, A.D. iv. Non. Januar. Stil. Lil. 1613." (Epist. dcccxlix. Danieli Heinsio, pp. 512, 513.)

In this letter he compares Andrewes's conduct, with some suspected unfairness on the part of Rich. Montagu and Sir H. Savile, in publishing Montagu's Origines Ecclesiasticæ, at the time when Casaubon was preparing his " Exercitationes in Baronium " for the press. In the following extract from the Diary, Andrewes's name is not mentioned; but it will be seen, on reference to the List of Sermons, that he was the preacher on the occasion :—

" Prid. Non. Jan. Hoc die celebravimus in aula Regis εὐσεβεστάτου Natalem Domini et S. Cœnæ participes sumus facti." (Ephem. p. 963.)

The next reference to Andrewes in the Epistles is in a letter addressed to Heinsius :—

" D. quoque Eliensis te posse aliquando in ædibus suis complecti vehementer cupit. Quod si hujus Insulæ invisendæ cupiditas te unquam

---

[h] This, according to the English computation, was April 9, which this year was Maundy Thursday. In Drake's Eboracum, p. 137, as quoted in Hierurgia Angl. p. 334, it is stated that, in 1639, King Charles " kept his Maundy at York, where the Bishop of Ely [Dr. Wren] washed the feet of thirty-nine poor aged men in warm water, and dried them with a linen cloth. Afterwards, the Bishop of Winchester [Curle] washed them over again in white wine, wiped and kissed them."

invadat, debes illos menses omnino evitare, quibus urbe abest ὁ πάνυ Eliensis; sunt autem fere hi, Julius, Augustus, September; solet ille per hoc trimestre spatium in Episcopatu suo manere, digna sane regione, quam semel videas: ille autem dignissimus, quem docti invisant, ubicunque tandem locorum fuerit."—Londini, prid. Eid. April. 1613. (Epist. dccclxxxi. Danieli Heinsio, p. 529.)

The two following notices in the Epistles have no date :—

"'Ο πάνυ Eliensis heri quæsivit a me, quando te esset visurus."— (Epist. dccclxxxvii. Hug. Grotio, p. 533.)

" Dominus Eliensis ægrotabat heri, nec fuit in Aula." (Epist. dccclxxxviii. Eidem. Ibid.)

There are also the following brief notices from the Diary :—

"[April] 12. Jeudi. Non multum hodie scripsi. Occurrit enim gravis materia, et magna diei parte fui apud D. Eliensem." (Ephem. p. 975.)

"19 Jeudi. Apud D. Eliensem fui cum D. Grotio." (p. 976 [h].)

" xvii. Kal. Nov. Interfui sacris apud D. Eliensem." (p. 1017.)

The following are the only entries relating to Andrewes in the succeeding year (1614 [i]):—

" Kal. Mai. Volui igitur servari in eo (filio, sc. Merico [k]) ritum Anglicanum, ut, priusquam admitteretur ad κοινωνίαν, examinaretur, et ab Episcopo confirmaretur. Is Episcopus fuit Eliensis ὁ πάνυ. Ego actioni interfui, et post preces, post concionem, post confirmationem ego cum filio sacram μερίδα a manu D. Eliensis accepimus, multum mirati in illo excellente Præsule exactam vetustatis imitationem quantum fieri potest." (Ephem. p. 1054.)

"ix. Kal. Jun. Pransus deinde sum cum D. Eliensi, unde reversus... incidi in febrem, &c." (p. 1059.)

[h] This interview with Grotius will be noticed more at length in the next Appendix.
[i] These entries are according to the English computation. See Ephem. p. 985.
[k] See a notice of Meric Casaubon above, p. xvi.]

APPENDIX D.

ANDREWES AND GROTIUS.

SOME of the later extracts from Casaubon's Diary have already introduced Grotius to our notice, who visited England in 1613. His mission appears to have been partly political, partly religious, and it is evident that much alarm was felt by the Calvinistic party at the influence he would be likely to gain over King James.

The following extract from a letter written at that time by Archbishop Abbot, giving an account of the visit of Grotius and Casaubon to Bishop Andrewes, April 19 (Old Style), 1613 (see above, p. lxxxvi), shows in a striking manner the prejudices which were entertained against him, and the very unjust estimate formed of his abilities.

After complaining of Grotius's habit of attracting the whole conversation to himself, the Archbishop proceeds: "Afterwards he fell to it again, as was especially observed one night at supper at the Lord Bishop of Ely's, whither being brought by Mr. Casaubon (as I think), they had entreated him to stay to supper, which he did. There was present Dr. Steward, and another civilian, unto whom he flings out some question of that profession, and was so full of words, that Dr. Steward afterwards told my Lord, that he did perceive by him, that, like a smatterer, he had studied some two or three questions, whereof when he came in company he must be talking to vindicate his skill; but if he were put from those, he would show himself but a simple fellow. There was present also Dr. Richardson, the King's Professor of Divinity in Cambridge, and another doctor in that faculty, with whom he falleth in also about some of those questions which are now controverted among the ministers in Holland. And being matters wherein he was studied, he uttered all his skill concerning them; my Lord of Ely sitting still at the supper all the while, and wondering what a man he had there, who never being in the place or company before, could overwhelm them so with talk for so long a time. I write thus unto you so largely, that you may know the disposition of the man, and how kindly he used my

Lord of Ely for his good entertainment."—Archbishop Abbot to Sir Ralph Winwood, June 1, 1613.—Winwood's Memorials, vol. iii. p. 459.

The acquaintance which thus commenced between Grotius and Andrewes brought on the Bishop very grave suspicions from those of the Dutch who were opposed to the views of Grotius and his friends.

John Chamberlain writes thus to Sir Dudley Carleton, Oct. 31, 1617:—

"Upon the receipt of your letter of the 19th of this month, I went to the Bishop of Ely, whom I had not seen long before his going into Scotland, nor since he was counsellor. I was very welcome to him, and he used me with extraordinary kindness, though he expostulated with me very much for my long absence. I delivered him your proposition, and withal, upon long conference, something you had written touching the Arminians countenancing themselves with some of his letters. Whereupon he fell into long speech of a writing that the Archbishop Whitgift had got from him in some parts of that argument, and that he knows not what became of it, for he never gave a copy of it, but only one to Mr. Hooker, who promised to return it, but never did [a]. But he expressed not all the while which opinion he inclined to, but still insisted, if they had any writing of his, they should show it, concluding that I should assure you that they have no letter of his, and with that vehemency, that he would give me leave to send you his head in a platter, if they could show any letter of his. He told me further that Grotius, when he was here, dined once with him, and supped another time; but other communication than passed at table he had none with him, though he understands since that he gave out and fathered many things upon him that were neither so nor so. Surely he hath a wonderful memory, for he not only calls to mind any matter that passed at any time, but the very time, place, persons, and all other circumstances, which seemed strange to me in a discourse of almost two hours." (Birch's James I. vol. ii. p. 47.) And again, Feb. 14, 16$\frac{17}{18}$: "I made an errand to Ely House, to have shown the Bishop the Pope's determination 'twixt the Franciscans and Jacobins, if he had not seen it; as likewise what you wrote concerning Grotius, to make him at least more wary hereafter, though, for aught I ever heard, he hath used caution enough that way; but he was at Lambeth." (Ibid. pp. 63, 64.)

Chamberlain obtained an interview with him a few days after, and writes thus, Feb. 21:—

"I went again this week to my Lord of Ely, and had some speech with him concerning Grotius, from whom he confesses he had letters lately, and that before Christmas one came to him for an answer; but, being presently to preach at court, and not finding himself well at ease, he made his excuse. But I perceived by this that he holds him for a very learned and able man: yet I doubt not, but this little conference will serve him for a caveat hereafter. I lent him the Pope's determina-

---

[a] This appears to be the Judgment on the Lambeth Articles, and on the Censure of Barrett. See Works, vol. vi. pp. 287—305.

tion 'twixt the Franciscans and Jacobins, and the censure of the Sorbonists upon the Archbishop of Spalato's books, which I met with all by chance, none of which he had, or had seen." (Ibid. p. 66.)

It was during the course of this latter year that the following letters passed between Overal and Grotius. The object which Grotius had in view was to obtain Andrewes's opinion on his treatise, "De Imperio Summarum Potestatum in Sacra," which was not then published. They are taken from the "Epistolæ Præstantium et Eruditorum Virorum." Amst. 1684.

(1.)

Joannes Overallus Hugoni Grotio, S. P.

Clarissime Domine: Redditæ mihi sunt literæ tuæ, cum libro de Imperio summarum potestatum in sacra, et exemplari libri Thomsoniani; de quibus singulis tibi gratias ago; de libro tuo potissimum, quem statim raptim percurri, non minore delectatione quam aviditate. . . . . Quam brevi remitti tibi librum velis cupio cognoscere. Episcopus Eliensis in Scotia est cum serenissimo Rege reversurus ad Michaelis, sive mense Septembri. Deum precor ut turbas vestras sedet, et laboribus tuis benedicat. Londini, Junii 20, 1617.

Tui studiosissimus,
J. OVERALLUS,
Coventrensis et Litchfeldensis.

(Epist. cclxxxviii. p. 484.)

(2.)

Joanni Overallo, Episcopo Coventrensi et Litchfeldensi.

Reverendissime Domine ac Pater: Exosculatus sum aliquoties literas, ex quibus et te vivere, et mei memorem esse intelligo. . . . . Meam de Imperio summarum potestatum diatribam velim et legas diligenter, et iis, quorum judicio aliquid tribuis, tradas legendum, servesque donec redibit Eliensis . . . . ac deinde collecta omnium judicia, si impetrari id potest, cum libro ad me redeant. . . . . Vale, mi Pater. ix. Julii, 1617, juxta calendarium novum. Roterodami.

Tuæ pietatis reverentissimus,
H. GROTIUS.

(Epist. cclxxxix. pp. 484, 485.)

(3.)

Joannes Overallus Hugoni Grotio.

Salutem in Christo.

. . . Ego hodie diœcesim meam peto, in occursum Serenissimi Regis, per eam e Scotia redeuntis; qui abiens in mandatis mihi dedit, ut illi reduci ad Coventriam adessem, zelotarum quorundam causa, qui in illa urbe morem Ecclesiæ nostræ, sacramentum corporis et sanguinis Christi de geniculis accipiendi, oppugnant; aut eum saltem colere et custodire recusant. Ubi, si Eliensis in comitatu regio fuerit, tradam illi librum tuum de Imperio summarum potestatum circa sacra, uti rogas; sin prius a Regis comitatu in suam diœcesim diverterit, remittam Londinum ad ædes ejus, quam primum illuc redierit. Tu recte feceris, si literas ad eum eo nomine perscripseris; interea dum ad urbem rediero, quod ineunte Octobri, Deo volente, facturus sum, et te præstantissime Groti, et causam vestram Deo Opt. Max. commendabo precibus meis, nec alias verbis factisque defuturus sum, si eam quocunque modo promovere potuero. Vale. Idibus Augusti, 1617.

Tui studiosissimus,
J. OVERALLUS,
Coventrensis et Litchfeldensis.

(Epist. ccxc. p. 485.)

(4.)
Joannes Overallus Hugoni Grotio.

Clarissime Domine : Tradidi librum tuum, de Imperio summarum potestatum circa sacra, legendum D. Episcopo Eliensi, calendis hujus mensis Septembris, Coventriæ, ubi, Rege eo veniente, convenimus. Respondit ille, se non posse pro eo, quo apud Regem est, loco, librum hujusce argumenti legere, quin eundem Serenissimo Regi ostendat; id an tu probare velis aut permittere, cupere se prius, quam lectionem aggrediatur, a te certiorem fieri : cum dixissem, me non nosse quidem, sed tamen probabiliter putare, te isthoc si ita sibi visum fuerit, non improbaturum ; subjunxit se literas tuas hac de re velle exspectare; ne si forte Rex, quod in quodam Joannis Wtenbogarti libro fecerat, editionem non probaret, sibi hoc vitio verteretur : cum adderem, me non dubitare quin facile Serenissimo Regi probaretur, quod pro imperio summarum potestatum tam docte præsertim scriptum esset; subjecit, Serenissimum Regem, nec sibi sumere, nec in aliis potestatibus laicis probare, ut ipsi per se de rebus sacris aut divinis, præcipue Catholicæ fidei, judicium ferant; id eos potius delectis ad hoc certis eruditis Theologis aliisque doctis in his rebus viris debere committere, quorum sententiam exploratam probatamque sola sua demum auctoritate confirment. Adjeci denique, librum tuum hac de re non multo secus disputare, aut si quid discriminis esset, gratum tibi fore id ab eo intelligere, quod ipsi aut Serenissimo Regi minus probaretur : hoc enim fine tuum te librum illi legendum misisse. Hæc summa est illius sermonis qui cum Eliensi tum mihi intercessit : nec plus licuit Rege abitum accelerante, Eliensi Regem comitante, me ad visitandam diœcesim meam divertente ; quod nunc quam primum Londinum reversus sum tibi significandum putavi, ut hac in re mentem tuam eidem literis scriptis aperias, ne forte ejusdem ignoratio lectionem prædictam longius moretur. Mentio supra facta per Eliensem scripti Wtenbogarti me monet te rogare, quia nihil illius nisi commune scriptum Remonstrantium videre contigit, ut si quid aliud ipse Latine scripserit, certiorem me velis facere. Credo pauca esse in libro tuo, quæ Eliensi aliisque ex doctoribus nostrum non probentur, nisi forte in illis hæreant, quæ judicium de rebus fidei definitivum laicis potestatibus tribuere, et potestatem ac jurisdictionem veram pastorum Ecclesiæ negare, et Episcopatum in non necessariis ponere videntur. Tenent enim nostri, judicium de rebus fidei definiendi, synodis Episcoporum aliorumque doctorum ministrorum Ecclesiæ, ad hoc delectorum et convocatorum, deferendum esse secundum consuetudinem veteris Ecclesiæ, ex Sacris Literis per consensum veteris Ecclesiæ, non privatum spiritum Neotericorum explicatis, terminandum. Tenent, presbyteros Ecclesiæ veram habere potestatem, etsi ministerialem, solvendi et retinendi peccata, (clave non errante,) non tantum declarandi soluta aut retenta esse; ut et veteres ex majore parte judicarunt, et potestatem ecclesiasticam excommunicandi veram jurisdictionem esse, licet solo verbo non pœna corporali exercitam: tenent Episcopatum esse juris divini, sicut presbyteratum et diaconatum, nec posse ministeria ecclesiastica sine προστασίᾳ (præminentia) et certo regiminis ordine, quod res est episcopalis officii, unitatem ecclesiasticam conservare; de re enim Episcopatus moderni loquuntur, ubi Episcopus per se aut suos officiales, sine consensu aut consilio presbyterii sui, omnes partes ecclesiasticæ jurisdictionis exercet expeditque. Notum est enim antiquitus nihil majoris momenti aut Episcopum sine consilio sui presbyterii, aut presbyteros sine Episcopo fecisse; donec multitudo canonum et legum minorem locum reliquit consilio sacerdotum, et ad rem facti magis explorandi, quam juris consulendi dicendique nostram jurisdictionem redegit; sed habent etiam presbyteria recentia suos quoque προεστῶτας (præsides seu præfectos) aut superintendentes, id est, aliquam, etsi temporariam, veteris Ecclesiæ imaginem. Cum charta desino, te tuosque et vestra divinæ benedictioni in Christo Jesu precibus commendo. Vale.

Londini, prope Ecclesiam
Belgarum, (Fratrum quo-
rundam Augustiniorum,)
Septemb. 25, 1617.

Tuus totus,
J. OVERALLUS,
Coventrensis et Litchfeldensis.

(Epist. ccxcii. p. 486.)

(5.)

Joanni Overallo, Episcopo Coventrensi et Litchfeldensi, Hugo Grotius, S. P.

Reverendissime Domine: ... Ad Reverendum Episcopum Eliensem scribo: rogo ut librum de jure imperii legat et emendet, conscio etiam Rege. Sane multæ sunt causæ cur id argumentum tractari debeat, tum ne sententia mea sequius quam se habet accipiatur, tum ut seditiosis hominibus occurratur, quorum magna apud nos est seges, qui tumultui ac violentiæ religionis nomen imponunt. Commendavi et Spalatensi et Eliensi statum Ecclesiæ et reipublicæ nostræ, cui ad cætera mala accessit, quod oratione nuper habita a Regio Legato, atque ita ipsius etiam Regis auctoritate, premitur hic melior de gratia ac arbitrio sententia, simulque promovetur schisma exempli pessimi. Obsecro vos omnes, quantum fieri potest, veritati tuendæ et unitati sarciendæ detis operam; quam ad rem usui vobis esse poterit qui has fert literas, vir clarissimus Petrus Hoofdius optimo natus genere, literis supra modum excultus, testis oculatus eorum quæ apud nos sub pietatis titulo prave atque perniciose geruntur. Quod de Utenbogardo quæris, nihil ille Latine unquam edidit, Belgice nonnulla, in quibus est liber haud magnus ejusdem, quod a me tractatum est, argumenti. Ejus libri interpretationem Latinam Rev. Episcopo Eliensi transmissam memini: cæterum Remonstrantium sententiæ si quis argumenta ac rationes propius nosse desideret, ei legenda sunt examen Perkinsianum Arminii, ejusdem collatio cum Francisco Junio, Johannis Arnoldi Corvini responsio ad libellum Tileni, item adnotata Bogermanni, deinde Nicolai Grevinchovii dissertatio adversus Amesium. Si qua horum ad manus tuas non pervenerunt, ut habeas curabo. Ad eas partes libri nostri de summarum potestatum jure quod attinet, in quibus hæsitaturum existimas Rev. Eliensem, aliosque in Anglia viros eruditos, paratus sum audire eorum sententias, et meliora docentibus cedere. Cæterum judicia synodica, aut etiam quæ extra synodos a viris piis atque eruditis petuntur, in libro nostro ostenduntur maximi facienda. Neque certiorem esse viam ullam discendi dogmatum veritatem. Sed sicut post judicium Ecclesiæ singuli de fide sua judicant, (ut enim Rex ait, unusquisque super propria scientia fidei fundamentum debet collocare,) ita et Reges ad ea agenda quæ non possunt agere nisi Reges. Hoc judicium $\dot{\epsilon}\pi\iota\kappa\rho\iota\sigma\iota\nu$ (ultimum judicium) non incommode in scripto quodam vocavit $\dot{o}$ $\mu\alpha\kappa\alpha\rho\iota\tau\eta s$ (beatæ memoriæ) Casaubonus. Optime Episcopus Eliensis, non debere Regem ita ab alieno ore pendere, ut ipse a se nihil dijudicet. Et Bilsonus non minus recte requirit, ut judicium præcedat usum gladii. Similia apud Paræum aliosque leguntur plurima. Et apud nos, qui maxime jactant nomen Ecclesiæ, consensum ferocissime repudiant. Presbyteros remittere peccata, id est, remissa declarare, cum Magistro sententiarum exposui, cum quo consentire video Protestantium plerosque. Neque tamen negem, alio etiam modo ministerialiter remittere, quatenus actione sacerdotali ac pastorali aut Deum movent ad remittendum, aut hominem ad accipiendam remissionem disponunt. Recte etiam a Lombardo adjectum remitti insuper a pastore peccata, quoad pœnas satisfactorias, et quoad excommunicationem. Si quid his superaddendum sit in honorem presbyteralis muneris, de eo monitus libenter supplebo quod deerit: ita tamen, ut si fieri potest, libenter mansurus sim intra ea de quibus protestantes consentiunt. Jurisdictionis vocem usurpavi ex juris civilis consuetudine, ita ut includat $\tau\grave{o}$ $\dot{\alpha}\nu\alpha\gamma\kappa\alpha\sigma\tau\iota\kappa\grave{o}\nu$, (potestatem cogendi,) quam ob rationem etiam eam notionem quæ Episcopis jure positivo attributa est, maluerunt imperatores audientiam quam jurisdictionem appellare. Neque tamen inficias eo, in potestate excommunicandi esse aliquid jurisdictioni $\dot{\alpha}\nu\dot{\alpha}\lambda o\gamma o\nu$ (proportione respondens) quod eadem etiam voce, latius paulo et extra usum veteris Romani sermonis sumpta, recte indicetur. Episcopatus vocem sumpsi eo significatu ut προστασίαν (præfecturam) indicet, non temporariam, sed perpetuam: hanc defendo, juris esse divini approbantis et suadentis, non tamen universaliter imperantis : cæterum προστασίαν (præfecturam) sumptam abstracte, citra considerationem durationis, esse juris divini, etiam imperantis, ostendi ab ipso Beza agnosci. Hæc si recte expendantur, spero haud multum fore controversi, et si quid est tale, parebo meliora monstrantibus. Domino Jesu, summo pastori, R. T. D. unice commendo. Idem nostras tempestates serenet. Hagæ Comitatensi, 1617.

T. R. D. addictissimus
H. GROTIUS.

(Epist. ccxciii. p. 487.)

(6.)

Joannes Overallus Hugoni Grotio, S. P.

Clarissime Domine . . . Nondum recipere aut recuperare doctissimam tuam dissertationem de jure summarum potestatum in sacra a Reverendo Eliensi potui, non satis otii ad hoc, ut videtur, ad singula perlegenda, et æstimanda nacto. Significavit tantum se putare te nimium politicæ potestati in sacris et ecclesiasticis rebus deferre, quæ per ecclesiasticas personas episcopos et presbyteros transigi solent et debent. Sed forte latius se posthac explicabit. Ego appellabo, ut occasio dabitur, atque interea te tuaque ac vestrorum studia Deo Optimo Maximo et in Christo Patri, pro Ecclesiis commendabo. Vale.

Tuus totus in Christo,
J. OVERALLUS,
Coventrensis et Lichfeldensis.

(Epist. ccxcv. pp. 488, 489.)

After Overal's death, and Grotius's escape from confinement, Cosin wrote to Grotius a letter, of which the following is a part:—

Hugoni Grotio Joannes Cosin, S. P.

Moriens vero secretissimæ fidei et curæ meæ missum ad eum a te librum, illum quem de Imperio summarum potestatum circa sacra inscripseras, commisit; simul imperans, ut, si quando benignus Deus te a solitudine illa et periculis imminentibus liberaret, eum ad dominationem tuam quam secretissime et tutissime mittendum curarem. Tandem beavit nos, quam avide expectabamus, fama, liberatum te scilicet ab ingrata illa custodia, et non sine divina providentia Lutetiam evasisse. Ego, dum literas tibi mittendas meditabar, et de fidissimo nuntio solicitus eram, ecce a Reverendissimo Patre Domino Wintoniensi Episcopo audivi missum huc a te intimum et fidelissimum amicum, ut per eum liber ille ad dominationem tuam rediret. Gratulabar illico opportunitatem tam feliciter oblatam, et statim ad illustrissimum Præsulem librum tuum una cum hisce literis tibi tradendum mittebam.

J. COSIN.

Cantab. e Collegio de Goneville et Cajus; Junii 20, 1621.

(Epist. cccxcv. pp. 659, 660, and Bp. Cosin's Works, vol. iv. pp. 487, 488, Angl. Cath. Ed.)

Cosin urges strongly the publication of the work, and says it was what Overal wished. Overal died in 1619. Grotius escaped March 22, 1621. The book was not published till 1647, two years after the author's death. The States in Holland had assumed power in religious matters on behalf of the Arminians. The book was written to maintain the power of the civil governors in ecclesiastical affairs, and is extremely Erastian.

APPENDIX E.

ANDREWES AND LAUD.

The following extracts from Archbishop Laud's Diary not only explain the connexion between these two great divines, but the importance which, at that trying period in the Church's history, was attached to the opinions of Bishop Andrewes :—

1625.

April 9. In mandatis accepi, ut Reverendum Episcopum Winton. adirem, et quid velit in causa Ecclesiæ sciscitarer, responsumque referrem, præcipue in Quinque Articulis, &c.

April 10. Die Solis post concionem finitam adii Episcopum, qui tum in camera sua in aula regia erat. Protuli quæ accepi in mandatis. Responsum dedit. Simul inde invisi (leg. ivimus), ut preces in Domo Somersetensi audituri. Audimus. Postea ibi invisimus corpus nuperrimi Regis Jacobi, quod ibi expectabat adhuc diem funeris.

April 13. Die Mercurii, retuli ad Ducem Buck. quid responderit Episcopus Winton.

Junii 6. Episcopus venerabilis L. Winton. et ego simul proficiscimur ad ædes Tusculanas, quas juxta Bromlye possidet Joh. Roffensis [Buckeridge].

Junii 24. Rex jussit Archiep. Cant. cum sex aliis quos nominavit Episcopis consilium inire de jejunio publico et precibus publicis, ut Deus misereatur nostri, dum grassari inciperet pestilentia, et cœlum supra modum nubilum minabatur famem : et simul ut bearet classem jam mare petituram. Episcopi erant Londinens., Dunelmensis, *Winton.*, Norwicensis, Roffen., *Menevensis.*

Jan. 16. Consultum est jussu Regis, quid in causa Rich. Montacutii agendum. Aderant Episcopi Lond., Dunelm., *Winton.*, Roffens., *Meneven.*

Jan. 17. Responsum per literas dedimus[a].

[a] This letter is as follows (Harl. MSS. 7000. num. 104) :—
 "To my most gracious Lord the Duke of Buckingham. These.
 " May it please your Grace,
 " Upon your last letters directed to the Bp. of Winchester, signifying his Ma[ties] pleasure, that taking to him the Bps. of London, Durham, Rochester, Oxford, and St. David's, or some of them, he and they should take into consideration the business con-

Jan. 18. Jussu Regis Archiep. Cant. cum Lond., Dunelm., *Winton.*, Roffens., *Meneven.* consulebant de Precum Formula, ut gratias agamus pro peste remissa.

1626.

April 12. Die Mercurii, hor. 9 ante meridiem, convenimus Arch. Cant. Episcopi *Winton.*, Dunelm. et *Meneven.* jussi a Rege consulere de concione, quam habuit coram Majestate Regia Episcopus Glocestrensis, Dr. Goodman, Dom. 5 Quadrag. ultimo elapsa. Consulemus; et responsum damus Regi; Quædam minus caute dicta, falso nihil; nec innovatum quidquam ab eo in Ecclesia Anglicana, &c.

Laud, in numerous passages of his History, refers to Bishop Andrewes, as furnishing him with a model for the arrangement of his chapel, and for the consecration of churches and church vessels.

cerning Mr. Montagu's late book; and deliver their opinions touching the same, for the preservation of the truth and the peace of the Church of England, together with the safety of Mr. Montagu's person. We have met and considered, and for our particulars do think, that Mr. Montagu in his book hath not affirmed anything to be the doctrine of the Church of England but that which in our opinions is the doctrine of the Church of England, or agreeable thereunto. And for the preservation of the peace of the Church, we in humility do conceive, that his Matie shall do most graciously to prohite all parties members of the Church of England any further controverting of these questions by public preaching or writing, or any other way to the disturbance of the peace of this Church, for the time to come. And for anything that may further concern Mr. Montagu's person in that business, we humbly commend him to his Maties gracious favour and pardon. And so we humbly recommend your Grace to the protection of the Almighty. Resting

"Your Grace's faithful and
    humble Servants,
      "GEO. LONDON.
      R. DUNELM.
      LA. WINTON. D.C.
      JO. ROFFENS.
      GUIL. MENEVE.
"*From Winchester House,
    January* 16, 1625."

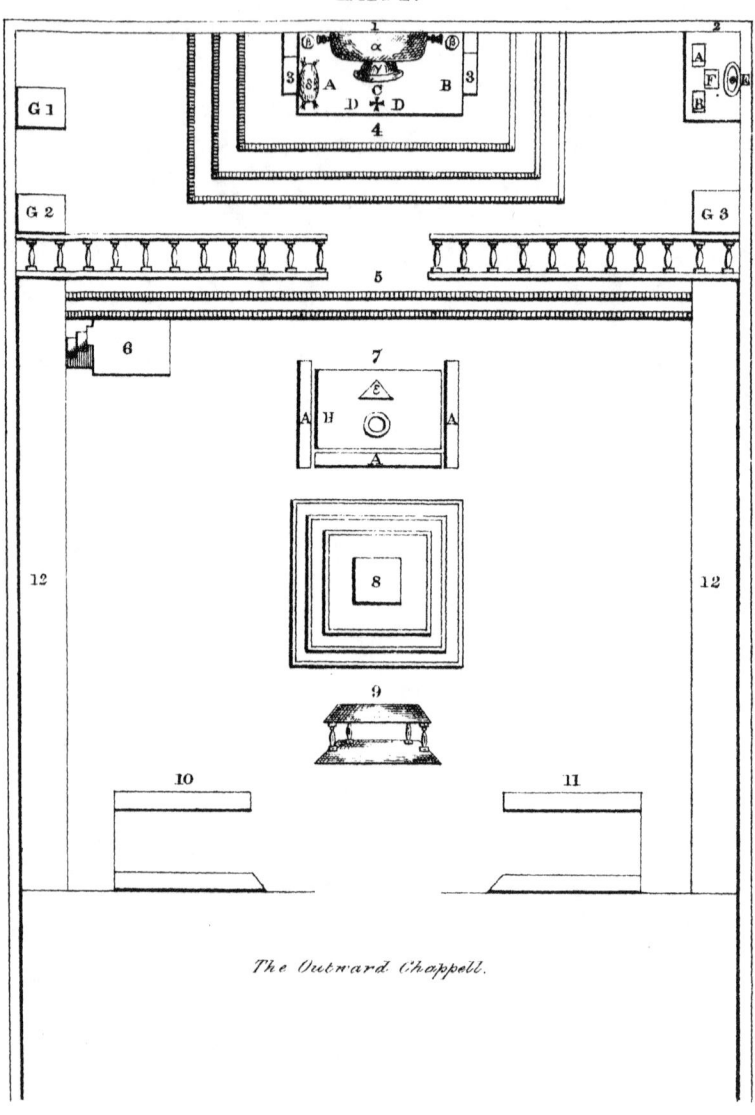

PLAN OF BISHOP ANDREWES' CHAPEL.

APPENDIX F.

BISHOP ANDREWES'S CHAPEL[a].

THE following description of Bishop Andrewes's chapel is taken from Prynne's Cant. Doom, pp. 121—124. The paper containing it was found by Prynne among Laud's papers, and is now preserved in the British Museum, MS. Harl. 3793. Art. 7, endorsed in the Archbishop's own hand.

1. The altar, 1 yard ¼ high, 1 yard ¾ long, 1 yard broad.
  a. A cushion.
  β.β. Two candlesticks, with tapers.
  γ. The basin for oblations.
  δ. A cushion for the service-book.
  } The daily furniture for the altar.

A. The silver and gilt canister for the wafers, like a wicker basket, and lined with cambric laced. B. The tonne, upon a cradle. C. The chalice, having on the outside of the bowl Christ with the lost sheep on His shoulders; on the top of the cover, the wise men's star; both engraven: it is covered with a linen napkin, (called the aire,) embroidered with coloured silks. D.D. Two patens. ✠. The tricanale, being a round ball with a screw cover, whereout issued 3 pipes, and is for the water of mixture.

2. A sier [side?] table, on which, before the communion, stand A and

---

[a] [Dr. Twiss, the notorious Puritan, thus writes to Joseph Mede, March 20, 1636:—
"In like sort concerning bowing towards the altar... I profess unto you I have hitherto received no satisfaction... By Mr. B. I heard, as from yourself, the practice of Bishop Andrewes's chapel was that which first cast you upon such a way, so as from thence to observe the course and practice of antiquity."—Mede's Works, pp. 1037, 1038. Lond. 1664.
Worthington, in his Life of Mede, (pp. iv. v.) informs us that at a very early period of his life he had attracted the attention of the Bishop. "His first showing himself abroad was by an address he made to that great patron and example of learning, Dr. Andrewes... in a Latin tract, 'De Sanctitate relativa,' &c.... This early specimen of his theological studies gained the approbation of so great a judgment as his was to whom it was presented, insomuch that shortly after he having need of the King's favour, concerning his election to a fellowship, that worthy Bishop stood his firm friend, and not only maintained his right then, but afterward desired him for his Household-Chaplain. Which place notwithstanding he civilly refused, as valuing the liberty of his studies above any hopes of preferment."]

B upon two napkins. E. A basin and ewer, to wash before consecration. F. The towel appertaining.

3.3. The kneeling-stools, covered and stuffed.

4. The foot-pace, with three ascents, covered with a Turkey carpet, of fir boards. G.G.G. Three chairs used at ordinations, or (by) prelates communicant.

5. The septum, with two ascents.

6. The pulpit.

7. The music-table, with (A.A.A.) three forms. E. A triquertral censer, wherein the clerk putteth frankincense at the reading of the first lesson. H. The navicula, like the keel of a boat, with a half-cover, and a foot, out of which the frankincense is poured.

8. A foot-pace with three ascents, on which the lectern standeth covered, and thereon the great Bible.

9. The faldstory, whereat they kneel to read the Litany.

10. Is the Chaplain's seat, where he readeth the service.

11. A seat, with a canopy over it, for the Bishop; but at the communion time he sits on G. 3.

12.12. Two long forms for the family.

Furniture belonging to the Chapel.

Behind the altar: a piece of hanging, 11 feet deep, and 5 yards $\frac{3}{4}$ long. Another piece of hangings: The story of Abraham and Melchisedec; part of the story of David.

A table, with a frame of deal, used for the altar, 1 yard $\frac{1}{4}$ high, 1 yard $\frac{3}{4}$ long, 1 yard broad. A back-piece of crimson and violet damask paned, 1 yard $\frac{1}{3}$ deep, 3 yards long.

A front-piece of the like, 1 yard $\frac{1}{4}$ deep, 3 yards long.

A pall of violet damask, 1 yard $\frac{1}{4}$ broad, 3 yards $\frac{1}{4}$ long.

A cushion of violet and crimson damask, $\frac{1}{2}$ yard broad, 1 yard long.

A rail of wainscot banisters before the altar.

Two traverses of taffeta crimson and velvet paned, 3 yards $\frac{1}{4}$ deep, 4 yards $\frac{3}{4}$ broad.

A foot-pace, with two ascents of deal, underneath the altar, 3 yards $\frac{3}{4}$ long, 1 yard $\frac{31}{48}$ broad.

A Turkey carpet to it, 4 yards $\frac{3}{4}$ long, 2 yards $\frac{11}{48}$ wide.

Two low stools to kneel on at each end of the altar, stuffed, and covered with purple baise.

A square pulpit of wainscot, 1 yard $\frac{3}{4}$ high, 1 yard square.

A pulpit cloth of crimson and violet damask paned, 1 yard $\frac{1}{4}$ deep, 3 yards long.

A music-table of deal.

Three forms to it, covered with purple baise.

A carpet of purple broad-cloth, 3 yards long.

A carpet of purple baise, 3 yards long, and $\frac{3}{4}$ broad.

A foot-pace of three ascents, 2 yards $\frac{1}{2}$ square, and thereupon a lectern with the great Bible.

A cloth to the lectern of purple broad-cloth, 3 yards long.
Another of purple baise, 3 yards long, 1 yard $\frac{3}{4}$ broad.
A faldstory of wainscot, 1 yard 1 nail high, 1 yard lacking a nail broad at top, 1 yard lacking two nails breadth below.
A cloth to it of purple broad-cloth, 2 yards $\frac{3}{4}$ long, 1 yard $\frac{1}{2}$ broad.
Another of purple baise, 2 yards $\frac{3}{4}$ long, 1 yard $\frac{1}{4}$ broad.

Over the Bishop's seat.

A canopy of crimson and violet damask paned, 2 yards $\frac{11}{48}$ long, 2 breadth.
The valence to it, 3 yards compass, $\frac{11}{48}$ deep.
A cushion to it of violet damask, 1 yard long, $\frac{11}{28}$ yards broad.
A folding table of wainscot near the altar.
A carpet of baise on it, 1 yard $\frac{1}{2}$ wide, 1 yard $\frac{1}{2}$ long.
Four folding chairs of leather.

Plate for the Chapel.

Two candlesticks, gilt, for tapers . . 60 oz. at 5s. 6d. the ounce.			
A round basin for offerings, gilt and chased . . . . . . 31½ oz.	6	8	—
A round basin for alms, gilt and chased 30 oz.	6	0	—
An oval basin and ewer, gilt and chased 51 oz.	6	0	—
Two patens, gilt . . . . . 36 oz.	10	0	—
Ditto, for cutting the figure, 13s. 4d.			
A chalice and cover, gilt . . . 43 oz.	10	0	—
For making the star on the chalice, 3s.			
A tun, gilt . . . . 47 oz. 3 dwt.	6	11	—
A cradle to it, gilt . . . . 18¾ oz.	6	11	—
A funnel to it, gilt . . . . 3 oz.	6	11	—
A canister, gilt . . . . . 5¾ oz.	10	0	—
A triquertral censer . . 85 lack 6 dwt.	7	0	—
Ditto, for gilding it, at 16d. the ounce.			
A laten pan for it, 5s.			
For making the knob of it, 2s.			
A cruet, gilt, with 3 spouts . . 10 oz. $\frac{11}{21}$	7	9	—
Another, gilt, with a bird's bill . 4 less 5 dwt.	6	8	—

Linen.

Five copes.
Five surplices.
Two altar-cloths.
Two towels thereto.
A cloth to lay over the chalice, wrought with coloured silk, called the aire.

APPENDIX G.

BISHOP ANDREWES'S WILL [a].

IN THE NAME OF GOD, AMEN. I LANCELOT ANDREWES (vnworthie of the name or place) BISHOP OF WINCHESTER, being at this present acrased in my health but sound in mind and memory (I praise God for it), onely haueing before myne eyes my yeares and my infermities, wth the manifold uncertainties of this lief, doe make, ordaine and declare this my last Will and Testament, revokeinge all former Wills by mee made whatsoever. First and aboue all, wth all due humilitie and in most devout manner, I yeeld vpp into the hands of Allmightie God that wch he hath created, that wch he hath redeemed, that wch he hath regenerated (that is my Soule and body), most humbly beseeching him to make mee (a most wretched and vnworthie Sinner) partaker by the mercies of the Father and through the meritts of his Sonne, of the forgiveness of my Sinnes, and all the comforts of his Holy Spirit pertāying to his covenant made wth mankind in the death of his Sonne. Whomsoever I haue offended any waies I do on my knees desire to be forgiven of them, and who hath any waies offended mee, I freely and fully forgive them, as I wish to haue my Sinnes which are manie, great and greivous, forgiven mee at the handes of God. As my Spirit I commend to God that gave it, soe my bodye to the earth whence it is, to be buried in such place as I shall signifie, or (if I faile to do it) by the discrecōn of my Executo^r or Executo^rs, Administrato^r or Administrators. To the bearing of my funeralls, if it be thought requisite I bee in any solemn manner buried, I allowe six hundred pounds if my estate will beare it; if noe such solemnitie be required or expected, then wth a lesse chargeable and only wth an honest decent funerall. And what soever is saved of the said sume the same to bee bestowed in workes of charitie & noe otherwise, and that vppon accompt to be made and given. Alwaies my will is that accordinge to the number of the yeares of my lief (wch are at this present three score and ten) and soe as it shall please God I live a yeare or more there bee soe many poore men clad (not as the manner is each

---

[a] [This Will is here printed from the original in the Registry of the Prerogative Court of Canterbury. Some extracts from it have already appeared in Gutch's Collectanea Curiosa, vol. ii. pp. 22—24.]

a gown) but each a good warme cassocke, a paire of breeches of the same, a paire of nether stockes, a paire of shoes and a hatt, the said poore men (if my funeralls shalbe in London) to bee taken out of the Parishes of Alhallowes Barkinge, where I was borne, St Giles Without Cripplegate, where I was Vicar, St Martins wth in Ludgate, St Andrews in Holborne, and St Saviours in Southwarke, where I haue beene an Inhabitant, yet not exceptinge any that shall have more need, of what Parish soever. My funeralls borne, Next my will is that my iust and true debts whatsoever bee discharged and paid all. The residue of the porcōn of the goods or good blessings of God pteyninge to this lief, wherewith it hath pleased him to indewe mee, I thus dispose and my will is: I give and bequeath to the Master, Fellowes and Schollers of the Colledge or Hall of Mary Valence, commonly called Pembrooke Hall, in Cambridge, the some of one thousand poundes, to the end to purchase therewith landes and tenements to the cleare yerely value of fiftie poundes ouer and above all reprises to the founding of two Fellowships therein for euer and to other vses specified more at large in a Codicill to this my Will annexed; if I shall not in my lifetime assure them lands of such value, wch I much desire. I further give and bequeath to the said Master, Fellowes and Schollers and their Successors for ever, the perpetual advowson, donacōn, nominacōn, free disposicōn and right of patronage of the Rectory or Parish Church of Rawreth in the Countie of Essex, wth all the writings, evidences and muniments therevnto belonging, one only grant of the first or next advowson thereof excepted, wch my will is should first take place. And that for ever after ye disposeinge thereof to bee in the free election of the said Master, Fellowes, and Schollars. Yet wth this condicōn, that if either of ye two Fellowes of my foundacōn shall at the tyme of any vacancy of the said Parsonage falling void bee a person capable thereof, then he the said Fellowe of my foundacōn, or the Senior of them if both be capable, to haue the preferment therevnto for his sake that gave it. Item, I further give and bequeath to the said Master, Fellowes and Scolars and to theire Successor^s the Basin and Ewre of Silver parcell guilt wch I caused to bee made in imitacōn as neere as could bee to the Foundresse Basin and Ewre wth her Armes in the midst of the basin. And alsoe I give and bequeath to them the Cupp of silver guilt wch I likewise caused to bee made in imitacōn as neere as could be to the Foundress Cupp, commonly called my Ladies Cupp, as a poore memoriall of my dutie and thankfull remembrance of that good Lady by whose bountie I was soe longe maintayned at my booke there. I give and bequeath the some of two thousand pounds to bee laid out and bestowed in the purchase of one hundred pounds land by the yeare over and aboue all reprises to bee imployed for ever to the reliefe of poore aged impotent persons past theire labour, of poore Widowes, of orphants and of poore prisoners, by such persons and wth such condicōns as are conteyned in a Codicill to this my Will annexed, specifying my mynde more at large. I further give and bequeath the some of two thousand pounds to the redemeing or buying in of such or so many impropriacōns as by the said sume will or maie bee bought in and redeemed, the same to bee ordered and disposed in such manner as I haue likewise expressed and sett downe in a Codicill concerning it to this my Will annexed. To my Brothers and Sisters Children I give and bequeath in manner followinge. To William Andrewes, the Sonne of my Brother Nicholas deceased, one hundred pounds. To the Children of my Brother Thomas deceased: to his eldest Sonne Thomas two hundred pounds. To his second Son Nicholas one hundred pounds. To his youngest Son Roger one hundred pounds; to his eldest Daughter Ann (now married to Arthur Wollaston) one hundred pounds. To his youngest Daughter Mary two hundred pounds. To the Children of my Sister Marie Burrell: to her eldest son Andrew one hundred pounds. To her Sonne John one hundred pounds; to her Sonne Samuell one hundred pounds. To her Sonne Joseph one hundred pounds; to her Sonn James one hundred pounds; to her Sonn Lancelot two hundred pounds. To her Daughter Mary Rooke one hundred pounds; to her Daughter Martha one hundred pounds. To the Children of my Sister Martha Salmon : To her Sonne Thomas Princep by her former Husband Robert Princep one hundred pounds. To her Sonne Peter Salmon one hundred pounds. To her Son Thomas Salmon one hundred pounds. And to my Sister Martha Salmon, wch she shall deliver over in whole or in part to such persons as her Daughter Ann Best shall nominate and appointe, one hundred pounds. To my kindred removed I give and bequeath as followeth. To my Cousin Ann Hockett ten pounds, and to her five Children, viz. two Sonnes and three Daughters, each of them ten pounds, in all the some of three score pounds. To my Cosin   Sandbrooke ten pounds. To my Cosin Robert Andrewes and to his two Children, to each of them ten pounds; in all the sume of thirtie pounds : to my Cosin Rebecca ten pounds. I give and bequeath to my Fathers half Sister Johan (her first husbands name was Bousie) twentie pounds, And to each of her two Children ten pounds apiece ; in all the some of fortie pounds : and more kindred I know not. I give and bequeath to Peter Muncaster the Sonne of Mr Richard Muncaster my Schoolmaster, twentie pounds. I give and bequeath to Mr Robert Barker (latelie the Kings Printer) the some of one hundred pounds, and I freely forgive him those several somes wherein he stands bound to my Brother Thomas deceased to my vse as good and true debt to mee. And I give and bequeath to his two Sonnes Robert and Charles my Godsonnes, to either of them ten pounds. And I give and bequeath unto my Godsonne Lancelot Lake^b, noe otherwise than as a remembrance for a ring, the some of ten pounds. And I beseech God that his blessing may be vppon them all their daies. To those of my household I give and bequeath as followeth. First my will is that all and every of those that serve me for wages shall haue the quarters wages wherein it shall please God to call mee out of this life, paid them duly, as if I had lived out to the end of the quarter, allthough it happen me to die at the beginning of it, the several somes are well knowne

^b [Son of Sir Thomas Lake.]

what they are. I give and bequeath to Ralph Hendre^c the some of
two hundred pounds, to William Greene fortie pounds. To Thomas
Cotton fortie pounds, to Roger Nicholson twentie pounds, to Thomas
Walker twentie pounds. To Thomas Eddie twentie pounds, To Frede-
rick Porter ten pounds. To John Helme ten pounds, to John Weale ten
pounds, to Robert Rogers twentie pounds, to Anthony Bull at the Court
ten pounds. To Charitable vses I give and bequeath as followeth: to
the several Prisons of the Kings Bench twentie pounds, of The White
Lion twenty pounds, of the Marshalseas ten pounds, of the Clincke five
pounds, of the Compter in Southwark five pounds : to the several Prisons
in London, of Newgate twentie pounds, of the Compter in the Poultry
twentie pounds, of the Compter in Wood Street twentie pounds, of
Ludgate ten pounds, of the Fleete ten pounds, of the Gate house five
pounds. To the Common Goale in Winchester ten pounds, to Winchester Prison five pounds, to the Prison there belonginge to the Cheney
Court five pounds. To the Hospitals: to that of Saint Bartholomews
twenty pounds, to that of Saint Thomas in Southwarke twenty pounds,
to that of Bedlam without Bishopsgate ten pounds. To the poor of several
Parishes I give and bequeath, to the parson and Churchwardens or to
the Vicar and Church Wardens respectively of these Parishes following,
of St Giles Without Cripplegate to the poor of the Parish there one
hundred pounds, of All Saints Barking by the Tower of London to the
vse of the poore there twentie pounds, of Horndon on the Hill in Essex
to the vse of the poor there ten pounds, of the Towne and Parish of
Rawreth in the same Countie to the vse of the poore there five pounds,
to the Parish of St Saviours in Southwarke to the vse of the poore
there twentie pounds, of Saint Andrews in Holborne to the vse of the
poore there ten pounds, of St Martins wthin Ludgate to the vse of the
poor there five pounds, to the poore of the Cittie of Chichester ten
pounds, of the Cittie of Ely twentie pounds, of the Cittie of Winchester
twentie pounds, of the Soke there twenty pounds, of the Town of Farne-
ham in Surry ten pounds, of the Town of Bishops Waltham in Ham-
shire ten pounds. And I do further give and bequeath as followeth.
To the bringing vp and bindinge apprentises of poore orphans, especially
such as goe about the Streets, two hundred pounds. To the relief of
poore Widowes aboue the age of fiftie, and wherof each hath been the
Wife of one husband, one hundred pounds. To the relief of such persons
as by age or impotencie are not hable to labour, but did labour while
they were able, one hundred pounds. To the marriage of poor maidens,
such as haue continued in service wth one Master or Mistress by the
space of seven years, one hundred pounds : to the setting up of young
beginners in trades or handicrafts to bee lent them freely vpon good
assurance by the discretion of my feoffes in trust mentioned in the
second Codicill to my Will annexed, so that it exceed not the some of
ten pounds to any one man, nor above the term of three yeares, two
hundred pounds. To the amendinge of the high waies, such as are in

^c [This person died shortly after the Bishop, and was buried on the same day.]

great need in any of the Dioceses where I haue been Bishop, one hundred pounds; and to the repaire of Brydges wch are in decaye, and neede it in any of the said three Dioceses, fiftie pounds. And for the severall bequeasts and legacies to the Children of my Brothers and Sisters and kindred, or any other person, my will is that yf the severall parties be either married or haue accomplished the age of one and twentie yeares, payment be made vnto them of their severall somes bequeathed w^thin three months after my decease; or in case they bee not married or vnder the age before specified, securitie be given to them or their friends of the due payment of the severall somes at the tyme of their marriage, or one and twentie yeares accomplished, whether shall come first. And my will is that if any of them shall dye before the legacies grow due, the porcōn or legacy of such person soe dying shall accrue to the residue of the Brethren and Sisters of such partie soe dyinge and bee equallie devided among them. I give and bequeath the sume of one hundred pounds to bee bestowed in Rings of gold vpon such my good friends as I am bound in all thankfullness to remember, whose names I will set down in pticular in a list to my Will annexed. I reserve power to myselfe to add yet one or more Codicills vnto this my Will, and to add to it or alter things in it as I shall see cause. Of this my Will and Testament I make and ordaine Executo^r Mr John Parker, Cittizen and Merchant Taylor of London, reposing my trust in him that he will see duly performed what I have herein bequeathed, or shall hereafter in any Codicill or Codicills bequeath and order to be done, as to God and me he will answer when accompt shall be taken of all just and vnjust dealings, and especiallie of deceaveing trust reposed, and yet more specially of deceaveing the trust of the last Will of the dead. And I do very earnestly desire my good friends Sr Thomas Lake [d], Sr Henry Martin [e], and Dr Nicholas Styward [f] to be Overseers of this my Will, and to advise and direct my Executo^r or Executo^rs by their Councell; and my express will is that my Executo^r bee directed by them. And that if any doubt arise concerning the meaninge of any clause or clauses therein, that the interpretinge thereof bee to them referred, and being by them made bee stood to finally. And I give and bequeath to either of them for theire paines one hundred ounces of plate. Soe I take my leave of the world, and most humbly desire God of his goodnesse to receive my Spirit when it shalbe his good pleasure to appoint the tyme of my dissolution. LA. WINTON.

September 22, 1626. Regis Caroli 2do.

Published and declared this to bee the last Will and Testament of the foresaid Reverend Father Lancelot Bp. of Winton in the presence of vs,

ROB. BOSTOCKE [g].   JOHN BROWNINGE [h].
JOSEPH FENTON.   T. EDDIE.   W^M. GREENE.

[d] [Secretary of State to King James, and brother of Dr. Arthur Lake, Bishop of Bath and Wells.]
[e] [Judge of the Court of Arches.]
[f] [A distinguished Civilian. See Collier, Eccl. Hist. vol. ii. p. 721.]
[g] [Canon of Chichester.]
[h] [See above, p. xvii.]

THIS IS THE FIRST CODICIL

MENTIONED IN MY WILL. LA. WINTON. MANU PROPRIA.

THE FIRST CODICIL.

UPON hope trust & confidence and wth this intent and meaninge and vpon condicōn that they the said Master, Fellowes and Scollars aforesaid wth the said some of one thousand pounds shall and will acquire obtayne and purchase to them and theire Successors the inheritance in fee simple of mannor^s, lands, tenements or hereditaments holden in free and comōn socage to the clear yearly value of fiftie pounds or more of good and lawful money of England over and aboue all charges, deductions and reprises: And yet netheretheless wth and vppon this condicōn alsoe and meaninge that from and after such purchase soe had and made and the first halfe yeares payment thereof receaved, they shall from tyme to tyme for ever nominate, elect, finde and maintaine two ffellowes over and over the ordinary number of eightene fellowes that now are in the said Colledge or Hall. The said two Fellowes to bee and soe to bee accompted, deemed and taken in every respect as other the Fellowes of the Foundacōn, and to have their Chambers, wages, all manner of dividends and other emoluments as the Fellowes of the Foundacōn now have or ought to have and receive, and they to bee governed likewise in all respects by the locall Statutes of the house, only that these two or either of them bee from tyme to tyme, at every vacation by death or departure, chosen out of the number of those Schollars of that house wch are called Dr Watts or the Archdeacon of Middlesex his Scholars, and they to be preferred *Ceteris paribus* before all others. But if at any tyme of the elecōn there shall stand or be found any of eminent desert either in that Colledge or Hall or any other within the said Vniversitye of Cambridge, that then in such case chiefe regard be had of the worthines of the partie. This restraint or any other matter or thinge therein to ye contrarie notwithstandinge. To and towardes the maintenance of wch two Fellowes allowance to bee made of thirtie pounds by the yeare out of the said fiftie pounds p annum so to bee purchased. And the other twentie pounds or more remayninge to bee thus disposed of, viz. five pounds yearely to the Master of the Colledge or Hall for the tyme being and his Successor^s in augmentacōn of his and theire stipend or wages, to bee paid half yearly at the taking down of wages at those two tearmes when the other some of five pounds *Ex nova concessione* is not paid. Other ten pounds yearely to the Fellowes and their Successors in augmentacōn likewise of their Stipend or wages, to be paid halfe yearely by equal porcōns at the feaste of the annunciacōn and at the takeing downe of wages before Sturbridge faire as the manner hath beene. Provided that if any Fellow or Fellowes not beinge let by sickness or otherwise vpon great and urgent necessitie shall not keepe his or theire Problemes or common places in theire owne person, but neglect the same wholy, then he or they to haue noe porcōn of the said ten pounds, but his or theire part to goe and to be devided among the residue of the Fellows that shall performe their exercise themselves as all should do. The five pounds remaininge to bee thus disposed, viz. thirtie shillings thereof yearely to those three fellowes that shall performe the three commendations at the end of the three tearms, to every of the three ten shillings apeece over and above the two shillings by Statute allowed them, that soe they maie bee the more incouraged wth diligence to performe the same; and one other thirtie shillings to bee disposed on a refection or in increase of theire commons from yeare to yeare on that daie wherein it shall please God to call mee out of this life; and fortie shillings, the remainder of this last five pounds, to bee paid to the fower Senior Schollars of those wch are called Do^r Watts or the Archdeacon of Middlesex his Scholars, to every of them yearely ten shillings apeece, to bee paid them by even and equal porcōns at the feast of the annunciacōn and at the takeing downe of wages at Sturbridge for ever. The foresaid some of one thousand pounds wherwith to make the said purchase to bee paid to the said Master, Fellowes and Scholars, or theire lawful Atturney, vpon notice given, as soone as they shall have found a fitt purchase to bestowe it on and are agreed vpon a price for the same. And I doe further give and bequeath to the said Master, Fellowes and Scholars the some of twenty pounds more of like good and lawfull money of England towardes their charges and expences in vsing and reteyning of Counsell to bee had in the conveighance and sure makeinge of the said purchase to the said Colledge or Hall. Published and Declared this to bee the first Codicill in my Will menconed and subscribed by mee 1° May, 1626, Regis Caroli 2do.

LA. WINTON.

DANIELL WIGMORE[1].   ROB. BOSTOCKE.
JOHN BROWNINGE.   W^M. GREENE.

THE THIRD CODICILL.

CONCERNING the redeeming, obteyneinge, getting or purchaseing of certaine impropriacōns of benefices: my will and meaninge is that mine Executor or Executors, administrator or administrato^{rs}, doe and shall before the proveing of this my Will enter into bond and bee sufficiently bound vnto the Most Reverend Father in God The Lord Archbishop of Canterbury or his Successors for the time being, in some convenient some or sommes of good and lawful money of England as to them shall seeme reasonable, or (the See being void) to the Judge or Master of the Court of the Prerogative for the tyme being, and therein and thereby shall stand bound well and trulye to pay or cause to bee paid the some of two thousand poundes of like good and lawfull money of England

---

[1] [Prebendary of Ely, and Archdeacon of Suffolk.]

into the handes of the Master, Warden and Fellowship of the Company
of Marchant Tailors of the Cittie of London for the tyme beinge; or if
the said Company of Merchant Taylor^{rs} shall refuse to accept thereof,
then vpon the refusall to the Master and Warden of the Fellowship of
the Company of Drapers of the same Cittie. And if the said Company
of Drapers shall allso refuse to accept thereof, then to the Master,
Warden and Fellowship of the Company of Mercers of the same Cittie,
wthin three monthes (accompting eight and twenty daies to every
moneth) next after my decease, and to bring and deliver or cause to be
brought or delivered vnto the said Most Reverend Father in God, or
(the See being void) to the Judge of the Prerogative for the tyme beinge,
a testimony of the receipt thereof in writing vnder the seale of the
Company soe receaving it. And further my will and meaning is that
the said some of two thousand pounds shall remaine and bee in the
Custodie of the said Company as a sume in trust deposited wth them
and noe otherwise, freely and without any vse, interest or consideration
at all in any manner wise to be paid or rendered by them for the same
for all or any part of the time that it, or any part thereof, hath or shall
continew in the hands, custody or possession of the said Company.
And my will and meaninge allso is, that when and as soone as the Master
Fellowes and Scholars of the Colledge or Hall of Mary Valence, commonly called Pembrooke Hall, in Cambridge, for the tyme being and
their Successors shalbe ready with a purchase of some impropriacōn,
one or more, wch hath thereunto annexed the advouzon and perpetuall
Patronage of the Vicarage (unlesse it be in case that there is not, nor
ought to be any Vicar), and shall have gone through and agreed for the
price thereof, that then immediately or within fourteen daies after this
demand by themselves or their lawfull Attorney the said Company
what received the said two thousand pounds shall out of the said some
pay such (and so much) money as the said purchase by the said agreement or goeing through with shall come vnto, at one whole and entire
payment wthout further delaye. The said Impropriacōn or Impropriacōns so to bee purchased, obteyned or had to bee and remayn to the
only use and behoof of the said Master, Fellowes and Scholars and
their Successors for ever, and they the said Master, Fellowes and Scholars of the said Colledge or Hall to have the whole estate and possession
thereof to the vse and with the condicōn following, that is to saie, The
one moiety of the cleare yearely rent of every and each of the said
impropriacōns shalbe for and towards the findinge and maintaÿinge of
a Divine hable and lycensed to preach and to bee residing at the Parish
Church of the said impropriacōns, The said Divine being one of theire
Societie and not provided for of any other Livinge; and if none of that
Society will accept it, then the same to goe and bee for the maintaÿing
of a Divine of any other Societye, he being qualified as aforesaid.
Provided alwaies, and it is yet nevertheless condicioned by theese
p̄ntes, that the said Divine or another Divine that shall enjoy any
benefitt by this intended redeeming of any impropriacōns at or before

his nominacōn, presentacōn or other appointment thereto, shall enter bound and bee sufficiently bound to the said Master, Fellowes and Scollars of the Colledge or Hall abouenamed for the tyme being in some convenient some or somes of good and lawful money of England, and therein and thereby shall and will stand firmely bound well and truly to reside at or vpon the saied Livinge (fowerscore daies in the yeare only excepted, and in them dureing that time to leave the Cure of that Impropriacōn well and sufficiently officiated by a lawfull and able Preacher), vpon payne of forfeiture of his said Bond. And in case he refuse to enter the said Bond, then he to bee vncapable of the said Liveing or maintenance, and some other to be appointed in his place that doth and will agree soe to bee bound; and the said Divine or Preacher to hold himselfe contented with that moietie, wthout requiring any more out of the said impropriacōn then the moicty till the tyme hereafter specified or lymitted. Provided allwaies and it is expressly condicioned and my further intent and meaning is, that the said Master, Fellowes and Schollars and their Successors, before ever they receive from the said Company the money to discharge and paie for the said purchase, shall and will sufficientlye bind themselves to the said Company in an Obligacōn or writing obligatory of a convenient some or somes of like good and lawful money of England, not to medle or make title to the other moiety or any part or parcell thereof at any tyme or tymes hereafter, but to suffer the said Company quietlye to receave the same. And further my intent and meaninge is, that yearlye and from yeare to yeare the said Company shall have and receave the said second or other moiety for soe many yeares as the several yearlye receipts shall or maie without fraud or covin make vp and amount to the whole some that was before defrayed and paid for the said purchase. And that then and from thenceforth the foresaid Divine or Preacher for the tyme being that ontill that tyme had received but one moietye, shall for ever after by himself and his Successors have and receave yearely the whole rent, soe long as he and they shall reside, bee and continue Divines or Preachers there, and noe longer. And if it shall happen y^t any of the said impropriations so to be bought, obtained or gotten, bee in lease att the tyme of such their buying in of the same, then the rent reserved vpon the lease to bee (for and during the said lease) devided into two moieties or halfes, one moietie or halfe whereof to goe and remaine to and for the incumbent nominated, and the other moietie or half to bee reserved as aforesaid; and when it shall growe out of the lease, the whole revenue, issues and profitts thereof to bee and remaine to his and theire only behoof, for soe long tyme only as he or they do preache and performe other eccl'ical duties at the place of his or their Incumbency or abode at the Church or Parish aforesaid. The choice and appointment of the said Divine or Preacher and the presentation of the said Vicarage (if any Vicarage bee) successivelie to bee solie and intirely in the said Master, Fellowes and Scholars and in their Successors for ever. And my will and meaning is that the some soe to bee raised out of the aforesaid yearlie moietie or moieties being now growne, to make vpp the originall some which was imployed paid or laid out for the said purchase, shall in like manner be for the purchase of another new impropriacōn or impropriacōns. The said impropriacōn and impropriacōns to bee in all and every respect ordered, guided and imployed as the first two thousand pounds were, and this very course to bee holden, observed and kept from tyme to tyme perpetually. Published and declared this to bee the third Codicill in my Will mencōned and subscribed by me 1º May, 1626, Rj. Caroli 2º.

LA. WINTON.

DAN. WIGMORE.   ROB. BOSTOCKE.
JOHN BROWNINGE.   W^{M.} GREENE.

THE SECOND CODICILL.

AND touching the subscripcōn and reliefe of the poore wch I intend to and for them perpetuallie, my will and meaning is that mine Execut^r or Executo^{rs}, Administrato^r or Administrato^{rs}, do and shall in like sort enter into and become bound vnto the Most Reverend Father in God the Lord Archbishop of Canterbury or his Successors for the tyme beinge, or (the See being void) to the Judge of the Court of the Prerogative for the tyme being, in and by an obligacōn or obligacōns of some convenient sume or sumes of good and lawful money of England as to them shall seeme reasonable, wth condicōn or condicōns to the same to bee annexed, that he or they the said Executo^r or Executors, Administrator or Administrators, shall and will wthin convenient time next after the said obligacōn or obligacōns entered into, and the same tyme by his grace or the said Judge to bee lymitted or appointed (the wch I wish might bee as short as maie bee), disburse and defraye the some of two thousand pounds of like good and lawful money of England in and for the purchasing of lands and hereditaments holden in free and comōn Socage of the cleare yearlye value of one hundred pounds or more aboue all charges, deducōns and reprizes. And hauing so purchased them shall forthwth and immediately infeoff such persons as I shall hereafter name as feoffes in trust, or as many of them as shalbe then living, to imploy the same to the vses and intents following; that is to say, 1º, to the relief of poor aged or impotent persons; 2º, and of poore Fatherlesse Children; 3º, and of poore aged Widowes; 4º, and of poore prisoners : each of these four sorts yearely respectively five and twentie pounds apeece, in manner and forme following: (that is to saye), 1º, yearely on the Eve of the Nativity of St John Baptiste, commonly called Midsomer Eve, the some of twenty five pounds, to the reliefe and sustentation of psons that be past their labour for age, or otherwise vnhable thereto, by reason of impotencie, some disease or maime any waies bereaveing them of the vse of such limmes as are necessarilie required to worke withall. And among them speciall regard to be had of such as while they were hable, for their yeares, healthe of bodye, or soundnesse of limmes, did trulye labor for theire liveinge; 2º, and yearlye other five and twentie pounds, on the Vigil or Eve of S[t] Michael the Archangell, to the reliefe of poore fatherlesse Children, In w[ch] number I comprehend such as goe vp and downe in the Streets from doore to doore begging, to binde and place them forth apprentices to some honest occupacōn, trade or handicraft. To the end that thereby they may be brought vpp in the feare of God and in labour, and prove honest men and women in their vocations another daie. 3. And yearly also a third five and twentie pounds, on the third daie of Januarie, to and for the reliefe of poore and aged Widdowes of fiftie yeares old at the leaste, and such as have beene the Wives of one husband, and as have been allwaies of honest conversacōn and report, and that have noe kindred, Children or friends to yeeld them succour or maintenance. 4. And yearly for the fourth five and twenty pounds remayning, the same to bee paid or disbursed in the weeke next before Easter, for and towards the reliefe and succour of poore prisoners, either in quite freeing them out of prison (if theire debt bee small), or otherwise to the Common reliefe of those as are in no likelihood to bee freed: Wherein my meaning is that the prisoners in the prisons of Southwarke bee respected before those of London, where there are a great number of more wealthie persons hable to relieve. Noe person that hath had reliefe one yeare to haue it again till they [that] have had none have had their course and turne. That as neere as maie bee all in their proporcōn maie bee equallie partakers of the Charitie intended. And my will is and I do name for the first feoffes of the said landes and hereditaments to be purchased these persons following, that is to say, Mr. John Parker, Cittizen and Merchant Tayl[r] of London, Mr. Joseph Fenton, Mr. Roger Cole on the Bankside, one of the Proctors of the Arches and Registrar to the Archdeacon of Surry, Thomas Andrewes, Sonne of my Brother Thomas deceased, Thomas Princep my nephew, Sonne of my Sister Martha by her former husband, and Arthur Wollaston, Citizen and Draper of London. And my will and meaning is that any of these or any other hereafter chosen or to be chosen as feoffee or feoffees in trust, dying or otherwise removeing theire dwelling from the Cittie or Suburbes of London, or leaving such his place of feoffee, the other five, or so many of them as do or shall remaine in full life, shall make choice of one or so many as there shall be places void within the space of three months from and after the daie of such avoydance; or in case they shall faile, then it shalbe in the Vicar of S[t] Giles without Criplegate in London and his Successors Vicars there for the tyme beinge to nominate himself (if he shall so thinke good,) or if not himselfe, some other, into the place or places then void, *toties quoties*, yet so as he the said Vicar, together with those w[ch] he shall name besides himself, exceed not the number of three at any time. And further my will and meaning is that every of the aforesaid five and twenty pounds shall extend itselfe to the yearlye reliefe of seaven persons; that is, to two of the most aged and needy of the old men and Widowes five pounds apeece, and to the other five three pounds apeece; to two of the least aged and most needy of the fatherlesse Children five pounds apeece, and to the other five three pounds apeece; and amongst the prisioners, to two of the most needy and that have longest lyen in prison five pounds apeece, but if they thinke good to dispose it not to the prisoners, but to the prisons, then to the greatest prisons most surcharged wth poore prisoners five pounds apeece, and to the rest three pounds apeece; or by the discrecōn of the said feoffees, not to all the rest alike, but according to the number and proporcōn of the prisoners in them. Yet it is not my will and meaning soe to restraine the said feoffees to the said severall set somes formerly mencōned, but that upon some speciall occasion if they shall comiserate the estate of some one or more, they maie by common consent encrease the same. But soe allwaies as that it be not above the some of five poundes to any, nor to any pson twise unless it shall come in order to theire turne againe, but that they bee carefull soe to husband theire almes as that the benefitt thereof maie extend to as many as convenientlie it can. And if it shalbe in the power of the said feoffees or the greater number of them, to deliver the said somes either at once in whole or by partes at several tymes, in ready money or otherwise, in providing them apparell or other necessaries, as they shall hold itt most fitt and convenient for the benefit of the parties to bee relieved. And my will and meaning is that there be a book made and kept as well of the severall yeares, moneths and daies of the choice and succession of the feoffees, as of the several persons or prisons y^t were and of the several somes wherewith they were relieved, that soe there may bee an accompt given at anye tyme, as is provided by the Statute for the employment of lands to charitable vsses: and it is further my will purpose and desire, that in the distribucōn of any some or somes in any of the aforesaid branches specified there be respect had of the poore of St Giles wthout Cripplegate aforesaid, of St Saviours in Southwark, of Alhallowes Barking, nere the Tower of London, and of the Poore of Trinity house in Deptford, that is, Old and impotent mariners and their Widowes and Orphans, and of such mariners as shalbe in prison, soe that it be not for piracie or felonie, but lye in for debt or for some other small accōn or accōns of trespasse. And my will and meaninge is that if the landes purchased or to bee purchased wth the said two thousand pounds shall exceed the value of one hundred poundes by the yeare, there bee allowed five pounds yearly foorth of the same surplusage to be spent at the meeting of the said feoffees. And whatsoever it shall come to aboue it bee faithfullye and rateably added to the increase of the aforesaid Almes, either to all or to some one or more of the former quarterlie allowances, wch they shall thinke meete, requisite and needfull: and my will and meaninge is that as soon as a first halfe yeares rent is or may bee receaved, had or taken, imeadiatly, the first of the foure daies wch shall then next follow ye distribucōn bee given to those parties that to the said daie are lymitted, and soe from thencefoorth successively in order from quarter to quarter. And that the feoffees shall from among themselves choose one of them to receave the rent for y^t yeare, and soe from yeare to yeare. No feoffee to be receavor two yeares togeather vnless it be the ioynt desire of them all. But if (wch God forbid) it should fall out that the feoffees should not bee orderly continued and chosen, or the said quarterly distribucōn not duly made as is before provided, then after such cessacōn by the space of one whole yeare, my will is that my next heire or heires at the common lawe then liveing shall enter vpon the said landes, and now as then, and then as now, I give and bequeath them to him and his heires for ever. And yett wth and vnder this trust also, that seeing what my will and meaning is, he wilbe careful and have a conscience to performe or see the same p̄formed accordingly. And I do further give and bequeath to the said feoffees the some of fortie pounds more of like good and lawfull money of England towards theire charges and expences in vseing and reteyning of Counsell to bee had in the conveiance and sure makeing of the said purchase for the releife of the poore aforesaid. Published and declared this to bee the second Codicill in my Will mencōned and subscribed by mee 1º May, 1626, Regis Caroli 2do.

LA. WINTON.

DANIEL WIGMORE.   ROB. BOSTOCKE.
JOHN BROWNINGE.   W^M. GREENE.

AND whereas I was once purposed to laie out two thousand pounds to the redeeming of certaine Impropriacōns, according to the purport of a former Codicill, yet now vppon more mature delibācōn and better advisement I have thought good vtterly the said former purpose and resolucōn to annihilate, frustrate and make void. Soe as there shall come noe manner of effect thereof or question concerning the same to any such intent or purpose whatsoever. And yet because there should nothing be gotten or gayned by defeating of a thing so well intended, I am absolutely of purpose and mind that the said two thousand pounds shall purchase an other hundred pounds per annum to the vse of the poore, to be paid, given or distributed at such tymes and termes, and in such manner and form every waie, as the former are and were in theire Codicill limited. And whereas in the making of my Will at Waltham in October 1625, I then vndervalued my estate, and doe now find that I might and may have made a farr better allowance and benefitt vnto the Children of my Brothers and Sisters, I doe therefore now supply what then was therein wanting, that is to saie, that if it were one hundred pounds then, it shall be two hundred pounds now, and if two hundred pounds then, it shall be four hundred pounds now, and soe *pro rata portione*, professing that nothing shalbe lost, but shall grow to a better proporcōn then before. And further my will is that my said Executo^r for his paynes in execucōn of my Will shall have the some of five hundred pounds, and the remainder of my goods vnbequeathed shall be divided among my kindred and Servants by the discrecōn of my said Executo[r] and within one yeare after my decease.

A List of those persons to whom I intend rings as in my Will is mencōned: My Lord of Canterbury [m], My Lord of Durham [n], My Lord of Rochester [o], My Lord of Bath and Wells [p], Sir Thomas Edmunds [q], S[r] Julius Cæsar [r], S[r] Thomas Lake [s] and his Lady [t], S[r] Henry Martin [u], The Deane of Winchester [x], D[r] Steward [y], D[r] Collins, Provost of King's Colledge [z], D[r] Ward of Waltham [a], D[r] Beale of Pembroke Hall [b], D[r] Wren of Peterhouse [c], M[r] Man of Westm. [d], M[r] Roger Cole [e], M[r] Edward Greene of Bristoll [f], M[r] W[m] Johnson, M[r] Joseph Fenton.

PROBATUM fuit testamentum suprascriptum vna cum Codicillis etiam annex. apud London. coram Magistro Gulielmo James legum Doctore Surrogato venerabilis viri Domini Henrici Martin Militis legum etiam Doctoris Curiæ Prerogativæ Cantuariensis mag͞ri Custodis sive commissarii l͞tme constituti vicesimo sexto die mensis Septembris anno Domini millesimo sexcentesimo vicesimo sexto Juramento Johannis Parker Executoris in hujusmodi Testo. nominat. cui commissa fuit administratio omnium et singulorum bonorum iurum et creditorum dicti defuncti de bene et fideliter administrando eadem ad Sancta Dei Evangelia jurat.

[m] [George Abbot.]
[n] [Rich. Neile.]
[o] [John Buckeridge.]
[p] [It seems doubtful whether this was Bp. Lake or Bp. Laud. If this list is of the same date as the Codicils it is the former, if of the same as the Will it is the latter. Bp. Lake died May 4, 1626. It appears most probable that it was Bp. Laud.]
[q] [Comptroller of the Household, &c. See an account of his diplomatic services in Lodge's Illustrations of English Hist. vol. iii. p. 94.]
[r] [Master of the Rolls.]
[s] [Secretary of State in the reign of King James.]
[t] [Mary, daughter of Sir William Rither.]

[u] [Judge of the Prerogative Court.]
[x] [John Young. He was brother to the celebrated Patrick Young.]
[y] [A distinguished civilian. See above, p. civ.]
[z] [See above, p. xvii.]
[a] [The son of his old schoolmaster. See above, p. cii.]
[b] [See above, p. xvi.]
[c] [See ibid.]
[d] [Probably Thomas Man, a bookseller.]
[e] [A Proctor in the Arches Court.]
[f] [Probably the person mentioned above, p. xxxi. note [e], who was also a Prebendary of Bristol. There seems, however, to be a mistake in his Christian name.]

CODICILLUS EPISCOPI WINTON.

Biblia interlinearia.
Biblia Græca, Basil. 1545.
Biblia Græca, Francof. 1597.
Biblia Græca, Venetijs, 1518.
5 Testamentū Vetus interp. 72.
  Rom. 1587.
Biblia Vulgar. Froben.
English, Tindall.
English Byble, in 4 vol.
  Geneve. 1607.
10   Thom. M^t.
  [*i.e.* Thomas Matthew.]
Wallica.
Germanica.
Hispanica.
Gallica.
15 Italica.
Sclavonica.
Hungarica.
Novum Testamentū Gre. R.
  Steph.
      Græcolatinū, Bezæ.
20   Irish.
Psalterium quadrilingue, Jo.
  Potkin.
      Nebien.
Concordantie Hebra.
Supplemen. Henri. Stepha. ad
  Concord.
25 Pagnini Isagoge.
Ariæ Montani Apparatus, &c.
Concilia Nicolini.
Photii Nomocanon.
Concil. Nicen. & Ephes., per
  Ab. Scult.

30 Joverii Sanctiones.
Concil. Colon.
Maximus, Melissa, &c.
Athanasius, Latin.
Joh. Cassian. cum notis, Dion.
  Carth. &c.
35 Cyrillus Alexan. in Isaiam,
  Lat.
Idem in 12 Prophetas, Græco-
  Lat.
Theodoret, Lat.
Procopius in Octateu. Lat.
      in Isaiam, Græco-
  Lat.
40 Græcorū Patrum Catena in
  50 Psalm.
Clementis Recognitiones cū
  Ēpis diversis.
Tertullianus Pamelij.
Eucherius.
45 Lanspergius in Epiās cū
  Chrysolo.
Eugyppius Abbas, &c.
Homilie Patrum.
Antidot. coñ^t Hereses.
Haymo in Psalmos.
Rabanus in Epiās. Ms.
50 Idem de Cruce.
Druthmar in Math. cū Pau.
  Diacono de gestis Longo-
  bard.
Oecumenius, 2 volu. Gre.
Euthymius, &c.
Rupertus, in 3 volu.
55 Petrus Blesensis.

Hugo de S^{to} Victore.
Ivonis decretum.
Corpus Juris Canon.
60 Antiquæ collectiones Decretal.
   cum emendat. Ant. Augustin.
   Hostiensis Summa.
   Durandi Speculum.
   Navarrus, in 2 volu.
   Turrecremata super partem Decret.
65 Eiusd. Summa de Ecclesia.
   Mediavilla, in 3 volu.
   Gab. Biel, in 2 volu.
   Diony. Carthus. in Senten.
   Adrianus Sextus.
70 Io. Maior.
   Marsilius in Senten.
   Io. de Bassolis in 4 Sent.
   Paulus Cortesius in Senten. cū Hiero. Savanaro. Opus. de fide.
   Altisiodorensis.
75 Aquinas, in 11 volu. 53.
   Summa Theolog. Aquina.
   Opuscula.
   Henricus de Gandav.
   Tho. Waldensis, in 3 vo.
80 Turrecremata in Decretal.
   Caietanus in 2^{am} 2^{æ} Th. Aqui.
   Bart. Medina in 1^{am} 2^{æ}⎱ Tho.
   Idem in 3^{am} ⎰ Aqui.
   Aquinas in Novum Testamentū.
85 Nicola. Cusanus.
   Gerson, in 3 volu.
   Æneas Silvius.
   Fasciculus rerū expetendar.
   Almain.
90 Steuchus.
   Hosius.
   Driedo.
   Stapleton.
   Gul. de Ocham, 2 vo.
95 Sanders de visib. Monar. et de Clave David.
   Suarez, opuscula.

Lindani Panoplia.
Polus de Primatu cū alijs.
Catharinus in 5 pri. Cap. Genes. et Epias.
100 Lippomanni catena in Genes.
    Oleastro in Pentateuchum.
    Caietanus in Psalmos.
    Arboreus in Ecclēn. et Cantica cū Pighij contro.
    Forerius in Esaiam.
105 Ribera in 12 Prophetas.
    Toletus in Lucam.
           Johannem.
           & ad Roman.
    Discipuli Sermones.
110 Merspurgensis Catechismus.
    Canisij Catechism.
    Plesis de la Messe.
        verification.
    Zeiglerus in Genesin.
115 Zuinglij et Oecolampadij Epiæ.
    Mercerus in Genesin.
    Zanchius de Operibus Dei.
    Mercerus in Job.
    Bucerus de Regno Christi. Ms.
120 Postel de Orbis Concordia.
    Alphonsus a Castro.
    Onus Ecclesiæ.
    Alvarus de Planctu.
    Budæus de Transitu.
125 Catalogus Gloriæ Mundi.
    Liturgie prim. Græ.
    Missale Rom.
    — vetus Eboracen.
    Rituale Eboracense. Ms.
130 Albertus de Officio Missæ.
    De divinis Officijs.
    Service Book Edward 6, English.
    Irish.
135 A book of ordeyninge Ministers.
    Tauler & Rushbroch.
    Abbas Blosius.
    Soto de Jure et Justitiâ.
    Fagij Targum.
140 Talmud Hierosoly.

Cabal. Aucthores.
Mechiltha.
R. Solomon.
Porchetti Victoria, &c.
Altercatio Eccliæ & Synago.
Beda de Temporis Raōne.
145 Galatin. et Jo. Reuchlin.
D. Kimchi in Psalmos.
Mason, of the Consecration of Bishopps.
Leges Romuli et 12 Tabulæ.
Ansegisus.
150 Topica legal.
Pandect. 3 volu.
Thesaurus Accursian.
Justiniani Constitu. Novellæ.
Covarruvias, 2 volu.
155 Jus Græco-Roma.
Constitutiones Impīales, 3 volu.
Marta de Jurisdictione.
Partidas, 3 volu.
Bertechini repertorium, 3 volu.
160 Calvini Lexicon Juridicum.
Codex Theodosian.
Statutes, 2 volu.
Rastalls Abridgement.
Collection of Statutes.
165 Sʳ Edw. Cookes Reportes, 4 volu.
Lawes of Scotland.
The Customers Reply.
Alphabet.
Statutes of K. James.
170 Bodinus de Repub.
Jo. Ferr. Mont. de Rep. bene institut.
Choppin de sacra Politia.
Directoriū Inquisi.
Suetonius cum alijs.
175 Cassiodori varia.
de Anima.
Rosini Antiquitates cum Freig.
Ora. de Ant.
Hospinian. de Templis.
Hospinian. de Monachatu.
Bucer in Epiām ad Ephes.

Streinnij Stemmata.
Zonaras cū Nicep. Chalco. &c.
180 Idem cū Niceta, &c.
Turpinus cum Rheg. Sigeb. &c.
Zosimus cum Procopio, Jornand. &c.
Marianus Scotus cum Dode. et M. Polo.
Otho Frisingensis cum Gunth. Argentin. &c.
185 Abbas Vrspergensis cum Jo. Maria. &c.
Blondus.
Antoninus, in 3 volu.
Scriptores Britannici.
Gule. Malmesbur. cum Hunt. Hove. &c.
190 Walsingham cū alijs.
The Booke of Martirs.
Camdeni Britannia.
Jo. Temporarius.
Chronica Chronich.
195 Baronij Martyrologiū.
Pontanus.
Notitia Imperij.
Notitia vtr. Dignitatum.
Knolles Turkishe Historie.
203 Cæsaris Comment. cum Scholijs Hotoma. &c.
Froissard.
Cuspinianus.
Onuphri. Panv. cum alijs.
Aretini Histor. Florent.
205 The Historie of Florence, in English.
Trithemij opera.
Eiusdem Chron. Hirsaugiense.
Hieron. Rom. de la Rep. del Mundo.
210 Philostratus de Vita Apollonij, Græco-lat. Paris. 1608.
Atriū Heroicum.
Crusij Turco-Græcia.
Witichindi Annales.
Comineus Engli.

Nauclerus.
215 Annales Boioru.
Rerum Alemannicarum.
Laziardus.
Jo. Mariana.
220 Bergomens.
Volateranus.
Freculfi Chron. cum alijs.
Saxogrammaticus.
Speculū exemplor.
225 Monarch. Roma. Imper.
Notitia Episcopatuum.
Sigonius de Jure Roman.
Historia Francorum et Bibliot. Pithœi.
Dithmari Chron.
Origines Palatinatus.
230 Thevet. de Viris illustrib. Gallo.
Calvini Epītæ.
Scaligeri Thesaur. Tempo.
Eusebij Chron. cū supplement. &c.
Scaliger de Emendatione Temporis.
235 Beroaldus.
Bucholcerus.
Genebrard.
Mercatoris Tabula Geogr. Gall.
Adrichom. de Terra Sancta.
240 Hackluits b. of Voyages, in 2 volu.
Linschoten's Voyages to the E. Indies.
Novus Orbis, &c.
Fr. Irenicü Exegesis German.
Dictionariū Hebr. Jo. Reuchlyn.
Ant. Reuchlyn.
245 Forsteri Lexicon.
David de Pomis.
Meursij Glossarium Græco-barb.
Arias. [Montanus?]
250 Methurgeman.
Ciceronis Opera, 4 vol.
Hermes Trismegistus.

Agricola de Metallis.
Jd. de Ponderibus.
255 Budæus de Asse.
Gilberti Philoso. Magneti.
Dion Chrisostom, Græcolat.
Casaubon in Atheneum.
Stuckij Antiquitates Conviviales.
260 Ari. Montani Hist^a Naturæ.
Copernicus.
Schoneri Opera Mathemat.
An oulde Herball.
Plessis Misteriū Iniquitat.
265 Sir Thomas Moores workes.
Id. ag^t Tyndall.
Raynolds & Hart, Lat.
The crafte to live and dye well.
Hookers Ecclesiasticall Politie, 2 volu.
270 Mortons Protestants Apologie.
Willet on the Romanes.
Ortelius.
A booke of Mappes of the Shyres.
Thesaurus Linguæ Lat. in 3 volu.
275 Barretts Dictionarie.
The Legend.
Chaucer.
Benedicti Regulæ.
280 Possevini Apparatus sacer. 2 volu.
Bibliothe. select.
Gesneri Bibliotheca.
Defensor Pacis.
De Jurisdict. Imper. & P P.
Hus & Prage, in 2 vol.
285 Catalogus Testium Veritatis, Argent.
Dialogus Creaturarum.
Pausanias, Græ.
Dio Cassius, Græco-Lat.
Sigonius de Regno Italiæ.
290 Jo. Arculani Opera Medica.
Fasciculus Temporum.

Raphelengij Lexicon Arab.
L. Guicciardini Descript. Belg.
Theatro de l'Antichrist. Vignier.
295 Maffei Historia Rerum Indica.
Freymonij Symphonia Juris.
Panormitan. super 3, 4, 5 Decretal.
Casauboni Exercitati. in Baronium.
Caietanus in Pentateuchum.
300 Martins Chronicle.
Babingtons Workes.
S^r Ph. Sydneys Arcadia.
Pontificale.
Alciati Comment. Juris.
305 Alcuini Opera.
Paulinus Aquileiensis.
G. Cassandri Opera.
Topographia Romæ per Boissardum.
Cluverius de Germania.
Τριώδιον και πεντεκοστάριον.
310 Μηνάριον, Græ. 5 volu.
Turnebi adversaria.
Franc. de Mayronis in 1^a Senten.
Dubravij Histo^a Boiemica.
Ænei Silvij Hist^a Boie'.

Gaguini Annales RerumGallic.
315 G. August. Curionis Hist^a Sarracen.
Lindwoods Provinciale.
Constit^{es} Othonis et Ottoboni.
Sandes travales.
Camdens Elizabeth.
320 Hospinianus de Festis.
Nicephori Chronolog. Lat. p. Joach. Camera.
Hist^a Synodi Nicen.
Penitentiale.
Antonini Confessionale.
Dialogus de Sacramentis.
Morisons Travailes.
Perons Replye to the Kinges Aunswere.
325 Spalatensis Archie. de Rep. Ecclie, pars secunda.
Cartwrights confutacon of the Rhemish translation of the New Testament.
Petri Suavis Hist^a Concilij Trident.
Homilies newe printed.
Camden Hist^a Selden.
Sclatiers Historie of Brittaine.
330 Cluverij Italia.
Sicilia.
332 Dr White ag^t Fisher.

This paper is endorsed,

'The Catalogue of ye Librarie in Pembroke Hall,
and
A Note of the Bookes in fol° in my Lords Librarie, which are not in ye Catalogue. By Eleaz. Duncon.'

Lecta lata et promulgata fuit hec sententia diffinitiva per dominum Henricum Marten, militem, legum Dc̄orem, Curiæ Prerogatiuæ Cant. Mr̄um Custodem sive Commissarium lt̄ime constitutū secundo die Juridico post festum sive diem Sti Valentini Epi, die Veneris decimo sexto vizt die mensis Februarij, Anno Dno juxta cursum et computacoem Ecclesiæ Anglicanæ millīmo sexcentesimo vicesimo sexto, in loco consistoriali infra Eccliam Cathedralem Divi Pauli London. judicialiter et pro Tribunali seden. ad peticoēm Georgij Cole No^{rij} publici procūris dcōr. magri Socior. et Scholarium Aulæ sive Collegij beatæ Mariæ de Valentia als̄ Pembrooke Hall pred. ac in p̄ntia Jacob Ireland, No$^{rl}{}_j$ pub^{ci}, procuris dcōr. Johis Parker, Rogeri Andrewes sacræ Theologiæ Professoris, Marie Burrell als̄ Andrewes et Marthe Salmon als Andrewes, super cujus sententiæ prolacōne dnus Cole requisivit me Robertum Erswell No^{rium} Publicū tunc p̄ntem ad conficiend. sibi v^{um} vel plura instrumenta pub^{ca} ac testes &^{c}, p̄ntibus tunc et ibm̄ Magris Thoma Ryves, Thoma Talbott, Thoma Gwyñ et Thoma Benet, legum Doctoribus, Augustino Rawe, Nicholao Hunt, Willm̄o Backhowse et Johanne Fishe, No^{rijs} Publicis, dictæ Curiæ procurībus testibus.

[This last has been compared with the Catalogue of Bishop Andrewes's Books in Pembroke College Library, drawn up by Bishop Wren, and several inaccuracies in the office copy have been corrected.]

APPENDIX H.

PORTRAITS OF BISHOP ANDREWES.

The following is a more complete list of the Portraits of Bishop Andrewes than is elsewhere to be found. The information is gathered from Granger and Bromley, and other incidental sources.

PAINTINGS.

The following paintings are preserved at—
1. Pembroke College, Cambridge.
2. Trinity Hall, Cambridge.
3. Picture Gallery, Oxford.
4. Picture Gallery, Oxford.
5. Durham Castle.

ENGRAVINGS.

1. 1618. As Bishop of Ely. By Simon Pass.
   Motto to Arms: " Et aratro et aræ."

   Under the Portrait are the following lines by George Wither:—

   " Those lineaments of art have well set forth
   Some outward features (though no inward worth),
   But to these lines his writings added can
   Make up the fair resemblance of a man.
   For as the bodies form is figured here,
   So there the beauties of his soul appear.
   Which I had praised; but that in this place
   To praise them were to praise him to his face."

   GE. WI.

2. 1618. As Bishop of Winchester. By Simon Pass.
   Motto to arms: " Et altaræ (sic) et aræ."
   The same lines are subjoined.
3. 1629. Prefixed to Sermons. John Payne fecit.
   Under the Portrait are the following lines—

" See heer a shadow from that setting sunne,
Whose glorious course through this horizon runn
Left the dimm face of our dull Hemisphære,
All one great Eye all drown'd in one great Teare,
Whose rare industrious Soule led his free thought
Through Learning's Universe, and (vainly) sought
Room for her spacious Self; untill at length
She found ye way home: with an holy strength
Snatch't herself hence to heav'n; fill'd a bright place
Midst those immortal Fires, and on the face
Of her Great Maker fix't a glancing eye,
Where still she reads true, pure Divinitie.
And now y^t grave Aspect hath deign'd to shrink
Into this less appearance. If you think
'Tis but a dead face Art doth heer bequeath,
Look on the following leaves and see him breath."

   This Portrait is prefixed to the subsequent editions of Sermons in 1632, 1635, 1641, 1661, and also to Pattern of Catech. Doctrine, in 1650 and 1675.
4. 1642. Prefixed to " Moral Law Expounded."
5. 1643. Prefixed to Sparrow's Rationale. W. Hollar fecit.
6. 1648. Prefixed to Manual of Devotions.
   Under the Portrait are the following lines :—

" If ever any merited to be
The Universal Bishop, this was he,
Great Andrewes, who ye whole vast sea did drain,
Of learning, and distilled it in his brain.
These pious dropps are of the purest kind,
Which trickled from the limbeck of his mind."

   This Portrait was also prefixed to the editions of his Devotions in 1674, 1692.
7. 1650. Prefixed to Isaacson's Life.
8. 1653. Prefixed to Discourse of Ceremonies.
9. 1657. Prefixed to Orphan Lectures. Vaughan sculp.
10. 1671. Prefixed to Sparrow's Collection of Articles.
11. 1675. Prefixed to Preces Privatæ. D. Loggan sculp.
12. 1684. Prefixed to Sparrow's Rationale.
13. 1721. Prefixed to Spinckes's " True Church of England man's Companion." Van der Gucht sculp.
    This Portrait is repeated in subsequent editions.

14. 1730. Prefixed to Stanhope's edition of Devotions.
15. 1822. From Picture in Bodleian. Engraved by J. Tuck.
16. 1828. Prefixed to Isaacson's Life.
17. 1830. Prefixed to Stanhope's Devotions.
18. 1830. Prefixed to Private Devotions, by Peter Hall. And also to edit. 1839.
19. 1846. Prefixed to Teale's Eminent English Divines.

The following notices of BISHOP ANDREWES's family are based on These authorities are distinguished respectively by the letters W. and R.

TH

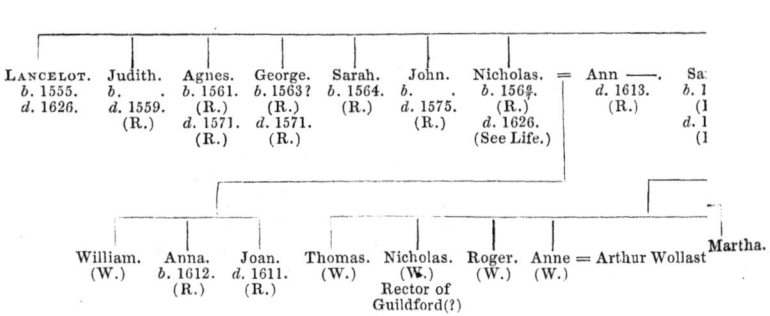

LANCELOT.	Judith.	Agnes.	George.	Sarah.	John.	Nicholas.	=	Ann ——.	Sa:
b. 1555.	b.	b. 1561.	b. 1563?	b. 1564.	b.	b. 156?.		d. 1613.	b. 1
d. 1626.	d. 1559.	(R.)	(R.)	(R.)	d. 1575.	(R.)		(R.)	(1
	(R.)	d. 1571.	d. 1571.		(R.)	d. 1626.			d. 1
		(R.)	(R.)			(See Life.)			(1

William.	Anna.	Joan.	Thomas.	Nicholas.	Roger.	Anne	=	Arthur Wollast	Martha.
(W.)	b. 1612.	d. 1611.	(W.)	(W.)	(W.)	(W.)			
	(R.)	(R.)		Rector of					
				Guildford(?)					

*** The Bishop mentions several other distant relations in his Will; Villiam and Richard Andrewes, as well as of other persons of the same name;

^a This Register contains a record of the following
1593. Mr. Tho
1594. Mrs. Joa
1626. Lancelot
1644. Mr. Joh1

TWO ANSWERS TO CARDINALL PERRON,

AND TWO SPEECHES IN THE STARR-CHAMBER:

BY
THE RIGHT REVEREND FATHER
IN GOD, Lancelot, LATE
Bishop of *VVinchester*.

STRICTVRÆ:

OR,

A BRIEFE
ANSWER TO THE

XVIII. Chapter of the firſt Booke of CARDINALL PERRON's *Reply* written *in French, to* KING IAMES--*his Answer* written by Mr. CASAVBON in Latine.

PREFACE.

ISAAC CASAUBON, on coming to England in 1610, was deputed by Cardinal Perron, to open a communication between King James and himself.

Casaubon, in fulfilment of this engagement, presented to the King some pieces of the Cardinal's poetry, which he had given him for the purpose; and received in return a complimentary message, which he duly transmitted.

The Cardinal, in acknowledging the favourable terms in which the King had spoken of him, felt himself obliged to state, that the King needed only the title and name of Catholic, to make him a perfect and accomplished prince [a].

Casaubon, in reply, vindicated the King's claim to this appellation.

Perron, in his second letter, (dated July 5th, 1611,) maintained at great length his former proposition; which elicited from Casaubon an answer written in the King's name and at his dictation [b], dated Nov. 9th, 1611 [c], and transmitted to him Dec. 29th, the same year [d].

---

[a] See the notice 'Au Lecteur' prefixed to Perron's 'Replique à la Response,' &c.

[b] "Le Roy s'est servy de moi pour Secretaire, mais la piece est de Sa Majesté. . . . . Il a exactement medité cette sienne Reponse; et j'ay fait maints voyages en Cour pour cette cause, ayant eu cet honneur d'y aller toujours en la compagnie de Mr. l'Evêque de Ely, personnage très-docte, très-moderé, et d'une singuliere humanité."—Is. Casaub. Epist. DCCCXXXIX. pp. 505, 506. Roterod. 1709.

[c] The date given at the end of the Letter, (as published by Casaubon himself (Lond. 1612,) and reprinted in King James's Works, p. 408, and Casaubon. Epist. DCCCXXXVIII. p. 505,) is a. d. V. Eid. Nov. 1612. But this is evidently a mistake, as the Preface to the printed letter, which refers to its previous publication in France, is dated IV. Eid. April. 1612. In his Ephemerides, (p. 897, Oxon. 1850,) he gives V. Eid. Nov. 1611, as the date of his beginning the letter; and says, in the letter itself, that it was written little more than a year after he came to England. (Epist. p. 489.)

[d] See Casaub. Ephem. IV. Kal. Jan. 1611. p. 904.

PREFACE.

After the lapse of more than eight years appeared Perron's voluminous and elaborate reply, entitled " Replique à la Response du serenissime Roy de la Grand Bretagne, à Paris, 1620." The delay in its publication was occasioned by the death of the Author, which took place Sept. 5th, 1618, though he had previously carried a part of it through the press [e].

To two small portions of this work the following treatises contain what may be considered the outline of an answer.

For convenience of reference, the whole of the xviii[th]. Chapter of the First Book is here subjoined, and numbers added in the margin corresponding with the several sections of Andrewes's reply. Portions, also, of the xx[th]. Chapter of the Fifth Book, (which specially relates to the Controversy between Bellarmine and Andrewes on the Invocation of Saints,) will be found inserted in the places in which they are referred to.

Those who may wish to examine this subject more in detail, will find Perron's second letter (as above mentioned) prefixed to the ' Replique à la Response ; ' and Casaubon's Reply in the Collection of his Letters, (Epist. DCCCXXXVIII. pp. 489—505); as also in King James's Works, pp. 380—408. Lond. 1619. There is a detailed account of this Controversy, with some additional information, in Dupin's Eccl. Hist., Cent. xvii. Book v. under the head, Card. Perron.

[e] The Book, as it now stands, is evidently incomplete, containing no reference to the closing remarks of the King's letter; and it differs materially in arrangement, from what the author seems to have intended, as may be seen by comparing the references in the chapter here extracted, and the divisions of books and chapters in the latter part of the printed volume.

PERRON
REPLIQUE
A LA
RESPONSE DU ROY.

[p. 82] *De la conference de l'ancienne Eglise Catholique avec la moderne.*

Chap. XVIII.

SUITTE DE LA RESPONSE DU ROY.

Et icy, Cardinal Illustrissime, sa Majesté requiert de vous, que vous veüilliez vous representer combien grande difference il y a entre les temps de Sainct Augustin & les nostres: combien la face & toute la forme exterieure de l'Eglise, afin que nous ne disions rien maintenant de l'interieure, est changée.

REPLIQUE.

ET c'est dequoy je supplie moy-mesme tres humblement sa Majesté, asçavoir, de se remettre devant les yeux quel estoit l'estat de l'Eglise Catholique au temps de S. Augustin, & des quatre premiers Conciles. Une Eglise qui croyoit[a] la vraye & reelle presence & manducation orale du corps de Christ au sacrement, sous les especes, & dans les especes sacramentales, comme Zuingle le principal Patriarche des Sacramentaires le recognoist luy-mesme en ces mots, [b] *Dés le temps de Sainct Augustin* (c'est à dire, il y a douze cents ans) *l'opinion de la chair corporelle avoit déja gaigné le dessus.* Une Eglise qui en ceste qualité [c] adoroit l'Eucharistie, non seulement avec pensées & devotions internes, mais avec gestes & adorations externes, comme contenant actuellement, reellement & substantiellement le vray & propre corps de Christ. Car je ne veux point parler pour ceste heure de la Transsubstantiation, à laquelle je reserve un traicté à part. Une Eglise qui croyoit que le corps de Christ estoit au sacrement, [d] mesme hors l'usage, & à ceste occasion le gardoit apres

[i.]

[ii.]

[iii.]

---

[a] Voyez cy dessous, l. 7. chap. 10. & suivans.
[b] Zuingl. tom. 2. l. de ver. & fals. relig. capit. de Euch.
[c] Cyrill. Hier. Catech. Myst. 5. Chrys. in 1 Cor. Hom. 24. Aug. in Psal. 96. Theod. dial. 2. & autres. Voiez cy dessous, l. 7. c. 8.
[d] Cyril. Alex. Ep. ad Calosyr. Basil. Ep. ad Cæsar. Patric. & autres. Voyez cy dessous, l. 7. c. 9.

[iv.] la consecration ᵉ pour les communions domestiques, ᶠ pour le donner aux malades, ᵍ pour le porter sur mer, ʰ pour l'envoyer aux provinces éloignées. Une Eglise qui croyoit ⁱ que la communion sous les deux especes n'estoit pas necessaire pour l'integrité de la participation, mais que tout le corps & tout la sang se prenoit en chacune des especes : Et à ces causes ᵏ aux communions domestiques, aux communions des [83] enfans, aux communions des malades, aux communions sur mer, aux communions des penitens en l'article de la mort, aux communions envoyées aux
[v.] provinces éloignées, le distribuoit sous une espece. Une Eglise qui croyoit que l'Eucharistie estoit ˡ un vray, plein & entier sacrifice, ᵐ succedant seul à tous les sacrifices de la loy : ⁿ la nouvelle oblation du nouveau testament, ᵒ le culte externe de latrie des Chrestiens : et non seulement sacrifice Eucharistique, mais aussi ᵖ sacrifice propitiatoire par application de celuy de la Croix : & en ceste qualité l'offroit tant pour les absents que pour les presents, tant pour les communians que pour les non communians, tant pour les vivants ᑫ que pour les morts.
[vi.] Une Eglise qui pour l'oblation de ce sacrifice usoit d'autels & de bois & ʳ de pierre, ˢ erigez & dediez à Dieu en memoire des Martyrs, & les consacroit par certaines formules de paroles & ceremonies, & entre
[vii.] autres par l'enchassement de leurs reliques. Une Eglise en laquelle les fideles faisoient des voyages & pelerinages ᵗ aux corps des mesmes Martyrs, pour estre ᵘ associez à leurs merites, & aidez par leurs intercessions : prioient les saincts Martyrs ˣ de prier Dieu pour eux, ʸ celebroient leurs festes, ᶻ veneroient leurs reliques, ᵃ s'en servoient pour exorciser les malins esprits, ᵇ les baisoient, ᶜ y faisoient toucher des fleurs, ᵈ les portoient dans les linges de soye & des vaisseaux d'or, ᵉ se prosternoient devant leur chasses, ᶠ offroient des sacrifices à Dieu sur leur tombeaux, ᵍ touchoient les treillis des lieux où leurs reliques estoient conservées, ʰ prenoient & cherissoient la poudre de dessus leurs reliquaires, y alloient prier les Martyrs, non seulement pour le salut spirituel, ⁱ mais aussi pour la santé & prosperité temporelle de leurs familles, ᵏ y portoient leurs enfans, voire mesme leurs animaux malades pour obtenir guerison. Et quand ils avoient receu quelque secours de Dieu par l'intercession des mesmes Martyrs, ˡ appendoient aux temples

ᵉ Tert. ad Ux. l. 2. Cypr. de Laps.
ᶠ Euseb. Hist. l. 7.
ᵍ Ambros. de Obit. Satyr.
ʰ Euseb. Hist. Eccles. l. 5.
ⁱ Voyez cy dessous, l. 12. chap. De la Commun. sous une espece.
ᵏ Voiez les lieux sus-alleguez.
ˡ Cypr. ad Cæcil. ep. 63.
ᵐ Aug. de Civit. l. 17. c. 20.
ⁿ Iren. l. 4. c. 32.
ᵒ Aug. contr. Faust. l. 20. c. 21.
ᵖ Euseb. de Vit. Const. l. 4. Cyrill. Hieros. & autres sous l. 8.
ᑫ Chrysost. in 1. Cor. Hom. 41.
ʳ Greg. Nyss. de Baptis.
ˢ Aug. ubi supr.
ᵗ Basil. in 40 Martyr.

ᵘ Aug. supra.
ˣ Ambr. de Vid. Greg. Naz. in Cypr. & autres sous l. 10.
ʸ Aug. ps. 63. & 88.
ᶻ Hieronym. ad Marcell. Ep. 17.
ᵃ Idem contr. Vigil.
ᵇ Ibid.
ᶜ Aug. de Civit. l. 22. c. 8.
ᵈ Hier. contr. Vigil.
ᵉ Ruff. Histor. Eccl. l. 2. cap. 33. Chrys. 2 Cor. Hom. 26.
ᶠ Hier. contr. Vigil.
ᵍ Aug. ubi sup.
ʰ Greg. Nyss. in Theod.
ⁱ Theodoret. de Græc. aff. l. 8.
ᵏ Paul. Nol. in Fœl. nat. 6.
ˡ Theod. supr.

& aux autels erigez en leur memoire, pour tribut & signal de l'impetration de leurs vœux, des images d'or & d'argent des parties de leurs corps qui avoient esté gueries : & cela les doctes & pieux Evesques de l'antiquité le recitans, le celebrans & l'exaltans, comme autant de rayons, d'éclairs & de triomphes de la gloire de Christ. Une Eglise qui tenoit [viii.] les [m] Traditions Apostoliques non écrites, mais consignées de vive voix, & par la visible & oculaire prattique des Apostres à leurs successeurs, pour égales aux écrits Apostoliques : & tenoit pour Traditions Apostoliques toutes les mesmes choses [84] que nous recognoissons & embrassons en qualité de Traditions Apostoliques. Une Eglise qui faisoit des [ix.] prieres, & privées, & publiques [n] pour les morts, afin de leur acquerir rafrechissement & repos, & pour obtenir que Dieu les traittast plus misericordieusement que leur pechez n'avoient merité ; & tenoit ceste coustume pour chose [o] necessaire à l'allegement de leurs ames, [p] & pour Doctrine de Tradition Apostolique, & mettoit [q] ceux qui ne l'observoient point au catalogue des heretiques. Une Eglise qui tenoit le jeusne de quarante jour de Caresme pour coustume [r] non libre & volontaire, mais necessaire & de Tradition Apostolique, [s] & contoit entre les heretiques ceux qui ne l'observoient point ; & durant le cours du Caresme, comme en un dueil public des Chrestiens, [t] interdisoit la celebration des nopces, & la solemnization des mariages. Une Eglise qui hors la Pentecoste, tenoit [xi.] le jeusne de tous les Vendredis de l'an, en memoire de la mort de Christ, excepté celuy où se recontroit le jour de Noël, [u] lequel elle en exceptoit nommément, pour Tradition Apostolique. Car je ne parle point des Mecredis suppléez en Occident par les Samedis. Une Eglise [xii.] qui tenoit [x] l'interdiction faitte aux Evesques, Prestres & Diacres, de se marier depuis leur promotion, pour chose necessaire & de Tradition Apostolique. Une Eglise qui tenoit [y] le mariage apres le vœu de virginité, pour peché, & cela de Tradition Apostolique ; [z] & reputoit les religieux & religieuses qui se marioient apres le vœu solemnel du cœlibat, non seulement adulteres, mais incestes. Une Eglise qui [xiv.] tenoit [a] le meslange de l'eau avec le vin au sacrifice de l'Eucharistie, pour chose necessaire & de Tradition divine & Apostolique. Une [xv.] Eglise qui tenoit les [b] exorcismes, exsufflations, & abrenunciations qui se faisoient au Baptesme, pour ceremonies sacrées & de Tradition Apostolique. Une Eglise qui outre le Baptesme & l'Eucharistie qui [xvi.] estoient les deux sacrements initiatifs de la religion Chrestienne, tenoit [c] la Confirmation faitte avec le chresme & le signe de la Croix, pour vray

[m] Basil. de S. Sp. & autres, sous l. 6.
[n] Tert. de Mon. Aug. de Verb. Apost. & autres sous l. 9.
[o] Aug. de Cur.
[p] Chrys. Phil. Hom. 3.
[q] Epiph. Hær. 75. Aug. de Hæres. c. 53.
[r] Hieron. ad Marcel. Ep. 54.
[s] Epiph. in Compend. & in Anaceph.
[t] Concil. Laod. cap. 52.
[u] Epiph. in Compend.
[x] Conc. Neoc. c. 1. Euseb. de Demonstr. Evang. l. 1. c. 9. Conc. Car. 2. c. 2. Epiph. Hæres. 59. & autres.
[y] Epiph. contr. Apostolic. Hæres. 61.
[z] Chrys. ad Theod. Or. 2. Ambr. ad Virg. Laps. Hier. contra Jovin. l. 1.
[a] Cypr. ad Cæcil. Ep. 63. Conc. Carth. 3. c. 24.
[b] Aug. de Pec. Orig. c. 40.
[c] Aug. contr. Petil. l. 3. c. 4.

& propre sacrement, & deferoit ᵈ aux seuls Evesques le pouvoir de le conferer : ᵉ le Mariage pour vray & propre sacrement : ᶠ la Penitence, pour vray & propre sacrement : & ᵍ la Confession vocale aux Pasteurs de l'Eglise, pour une des conditions necessaires à ce sacrement : ʰ l'Ordre, pour vray & propre sacrement : ⁱ & l'Extreme Onction, pour vray & propre sacrement : qui sont avec le Baptesme & l'Eucharistie, les sept Sacrements que l'Eglise Romaine recognoist, & ᵏque la com[85]munion Grecque fait aussi profession d'embrasser avec nous. Une Eglise qui

[xvii.] aux ceremonies du Baptesme usoit ˡd'huile, ᵐ de sel, ⁿ de luminaire, ᵒ d'exorcismes, ᵖ du signe de la Croix, ᵠ du mot, *Epheta*, & autres semblables accompagnemens : pour témoigner par l'huile, qu'au Baptesme nous estions faits Chrestiens, c'est à dire, participans de l'onction de Christ : par le sel, que Dieu contractoit avec nous au Baptesme une alliance d'eternité, suivant le style de l'Escriture qui appelle les alliances eternelles, alliances de sel : par le luminaire, que Christ est la lumiere qui illumine tout homme venant au monde : ʳ par les exorcismes, que le baptesme nous mettoit hors de la possession du Diable : ˢ par le signe de la Croix, que c'est la mort de Christ qui donne force à tous les Sacrements : ᵗ par le mot, *Epheta*, que Dieu accomplit spirituellement en nous au Baptesme, ce qu'il opera corporellement en l'homme sourd & muet.

[xviii.] Une Eglise qui estimoit le Baptesme aux personnes d'age, necessaire de necessité conditionée : ᵘ & aux enfans, necessaire de necessité absoluë :
[xix.] & a ceste occasion permettoit ˣ aux Laïques en peril de mort, de les baptiser. Une Eglise qui usoit d'eau beniste & consacrée par certaines paroles & ceremonies, & s'en servoit, ʸ & pour le Baptesme, ᶻ & pour dissiper les enchantements, ᵃ & pour faire les exorcismes & conjurations des malins esprits. Dont est que ᵇ sainct Gregoire le Grand, bien que posterieur aux quatre premiers Conciles, neantmoins irrecusable aux Anglois, qui ont pris l'origine de leur mission de luy, ordonna quand l'Angleterre revint du Paganisme à la religion Chrestienne, que l'on n'y demolist point les temples des Payens, mais qu'on les expiast par l'as-
[xx.] persion de l'eau benite. Une Eglise qui en l'œconomie du ministere Ecclesiastique tenoit divers degrez, ᶜl'Evesque, le Prestre, le Diacre, l'Acolyte, l'Exorciste, le Lecteur & l'Huissier, & les consacroit & benissoit par diverses formules & ceremonies ; Et en l'ordre Episcopale recognoissoit divers sieges de jurisdiction de droict positif, asçavoir,

ᵈ Hier. contra Lucif.
ᵉ Aug. de Nupt. & Conc. l. 1. c. 17.
ᶠ Ambr. de Pœnit. c. 7. Aug. de Baptis. contr. Don. l. 5. c. 20.
ᵍ Leo 1. Ep. 91, & autres. Voyez cy dessous, l. 2.
ʰ Aug. contr. Parm. l. 2. c. 13.
ⁱ Innoc. I. ad Decent. c. 8.
ᵏ Censur. Orient. Eccl. c. 7.
ˡ Cypr. Ep. 70.
ᵐ Conc. Carth. 3. c. 5.
ⁿ Gregor. Naz. de Bapt.
ᵒ Aug. Ep. 101.
ᵖ Aug. contr. Jul. l. 6. c. 8.
ᵠ Ambr. de Sacr. l. 1.

ʳ Aug. Ep. 105.
ˢ Aug. in Joan. tract. 118.
ᵗ Ambr. de Sacr. l. 1.
ᵘ Aug. de an. & ejus orig. l. 3. c. 15.
ˣ Tertull. de bapt. Hier. contr. Lucif.
ʸ Basil. de S. Sp. c. 27.
ᶻ Epiph. hær. 30.
ᵃ Theod. hist. Eccl. l. 5. c. 23.
ᵇ Lib. 9. Epist. 71.
ᶜ Concil. Laod. c. 24. Conc. Carth. 4. c. 2, & suivans. Imper. Valent. Valens & Grat. cod. l. 1. ti. 3. l. 6. Hier. Ep. ad Tit. l. 3. & autres.

les Archevesques, les Primats & les Patriarches, & ᵈ un superéminent de droict divin, qui estoit le Pape, ᵉ sans lequel rien ne se pouvoit decider des choses qui appartenoient à l'Eglise universelle, & le defaut de la presence duquel, ou par soy, ou par ses Legats, ou par sa confirmation, rendoit tous les Conciles pretendus universels, illicites. Une Eglise qui tenoit ᶠ la succession non interrompuë de l'Episcopat depuis la mission originale des Apostres, pour condition essentielle de l'Eglise, & reputoit ceux qui ne l'avoient point, ou qui communiquoient avec ceux qui ne l'avoient point, pour [86] schismatiques & coulpables de la mesme malediction que Coré, Dathan & Abiron. Une Eglise qui tenoit la distinction de l'Evesque & du Prestre, & nommément au fait de l'ordination, pour chose de droict divin, ᵍ & de Tradition Apostolique ; ʰ & condamnoit comme heretiques ceux qui ne la tenoient point. Une Eglise ⁱ qui tenoit le liberal arbitre pour doctrine de foy & revelée en la saincte Escriture ; ᵏ qui tenoit que la foy seule sans les œuvres Evangeliques, ne suffisoit pas à salut, ˡ que les méchants perseverans jusques à la fin estoient reprouvez, mais non predestinez à mal ; ᵐ que la certitude que les particuliers presument avoir de leur predestination, estoit chose temeraire. Une Eglise en laquelle le service se faisoit par tout l'Orient en la langue Grecque, & par tout l'Occident, tant en Afrique qu'en l'Europe, ⁿ en la langue Latine ; encore qu'en nulle des provinces, ny de l'Europe ny de l'Afrique, excepté en Italie & aux villes où residoient les Colonies Romaines, la langue Latine ne fust entenduë du simple peuple, mais seulement des hommes doctes. Et bref une Eglise qui usoit ou en genre, ou en espece, ou en forme, ou en analogie, de toutes les mesmes ceremonies, qui sont les paroles des yeux, dont use aujourd'huy universellement l'Eglise Catholique : ᵒ Observoit la distinction des festes & jours ordinaires, la distinction des habits Laïques & ᵖ Ecclesiastiques, ᵠ la distinction & veneration des vases sacrez, l'usage ʳ des tonsures & ˢ onctions pour la collation des ordres, la ceremonie ᵗ du lavement des mains à l'Autel avant la consecration des mysteres, ᵘ donnoit le baiser de paix avant la communion, ˣ prononçoit une partie du service de l'Autel a basse voix & non ouyë,

[xxi.]

[xxii.]

[xxiii.]

[xxiv.]

[xxv.]

ᵈ Hier. ad Damas. Ep. 57. Aug. de duab. ep. Pelag. l. 1. c. 1. Idem Ep. 92. Concil. Chalc. Ep. ad Leon. & autres, sous ch. 25.
ᵉ Socr. hist. Eccles. l. 2. c. 8. Sozom. l. 3. c. 10.
ᶠ Cyprian. ad Magn. Epist. 76. & de unit. Eccl. Chrys. ad Eph. hom. 11.
ᵍ Hier. ad Evag. Ep. 85. in fin.
ʰ Epiph. de hær. 75. Aug. de hær. c. 53.
ⁱ Aug. de grat. & lib. arb. c. 2. & ep. 46. Cyrill. in Joann. l. 4. c. 7.
ᵏ Aug. de grat. & lib. arb. c. 8. & l. 83. quæst. q. 76.
ˡ Prosp. ad artic. sibi impos.
ᵐ Aug. de corrept. & grat. c. 13. & ailleurs.

ⁿ Sous liv. 12. ch. de la langue du service.
ᵒ Aug. Ep. 118. Id. Ps. 63. & 88.
ᵖ Concil. Laod. c. 22 & 23. Hier. ad Helio. ep. 3. Theod. Histor. Eccl. l. 2. c. 27. Cod. tit. 2. l. 21.
ᵠ Hier. præf. in ep. Theophil. Opt. l. 1.
ʳ Theod. hist. l. 5. c. 8. Victor. Turon. in Zenon. Isid. de div. off. l. 2. c. 4. & Conc. in Trull. c. 33. ambo ex veteri usu Ecclesiæ.
ˢ Greg. Naz. de pac. or. 1. Idem in Basil. Author de unct. Chrism. Greg. in Reg. l. 4. c. 5.
ᵗ Cyrill. Hier. Catech. Myst. 5.
ᵘ Conc. Laod. c. 19.
ˣ Conc. Laod. ibid.

ʸ faisoit les processions avec les reliques des Martyrs, accompagnoit les morts au sepulchre avec ᶻ cierges et luminaires en signe de la joye & certitude future de leur resurrection, avoit les peintures de Christ & de ses Saincts, & ᵃ hors les Eglises, & ᵇ dedans les Eglises, & ᶜ sur les Autels mesmes des Martyrs, non pour les adorer, entant qu'adoration signifie culte divin, mais pour venerer par elles les athletes & champions de Christ : ᵈ usoit du signe de la Croix en toutes ses conversations, ᵉ l'imprimoit sur le front des Catechumenes, ᶠ le peignoit sur le portail de toutes les maisons des fideles, ᵍ donnoit la benediction au people avec la main par le signe de la Croix, ʰ l'employoit pour chasser les malins esprits, ⁱ proposoit en Hierusalem la vraye Croix à adorer le jour du Vendredy sainct, [87] se servoit ᵏ d'encens en ses Synaxes, non particulierement d'encens d'Arabie, mais indifferemment de gommes odorantes : Car elle ne tenoit plus lors l'encensement pour sacrifice, comme au temps de la loy, mais pour une simple ceremonie destinée à representer l'effect des prieres, décrit par ces paroles de David, *Que mon oraison monte comme l'encens en ta presence :* Et par celles-cy de l'Apocalypse, *La fumée des encens des oraisons des Saincts, monta de la main de l'Ange devant Dieu.* Et finalement une Eglise qui tenoit que l'Eglise Catholique avoit la promesse infaillible de devoir estre ˡ perpetuellement visible & eminente en sa communion, perpetuellement pure & incorrompuë en sa doctrine & en ses sacrements, & perpetuellement liée & continuée en la succession de son ministere, ᵐ & qu'à elle seule appartenoit la garde des Traditions Apostoliques, l'authorité de l'interpretation de l'Escriture, & la decision des controverses de la foy : & que hors de la succession ⁿ de sa communion, ᵒ de sa doctrine & ᵖ de son ministere, il n'y avoit ny Eglise ny salut. Voila ce que le serenissime Roy, quand il luy plaira d'y penser avec loisir suffisant, trouvera qu'estoit l'Eglise Catholique au temps de sainct Augustin & de quatre premiers Conciles. Que sa Majesté voye si à ces traicts de visage elle recognoistra celle de Calvin ou la nostre.

ʸ Aug. de civit. Dei. l. 22. c. 8.
ᶻ Greg. Naz. in Jul. or. 2.
ᵃ Euseb. de vit. Const. l. 3.
ᵇ Paulin. ep. 12. Basil. in martyr. Barlaam. Greg. Nyss. in S. Theod.
ᶜ Prudent. in S. Cassian.
ᵈ Tert. de cor. milit.
ᵉ Aug. de Symb. ad Catech. l. 2.
ᶠ Cyrill. contr. Jul. l. 6.
ᵍ Hier. in vit. Hilar.
ʰ Ath. contr. idol.
ⁱ Paulin. ep. 11.
ᵏ Chrys. in Matt. hom. 89. Evag. Hist. Eccl. l. 4. c. 7.

ˡ Sus chap. 3.
ᵐ Tert. de præsc. Iren. l. 3. c. 3. & l. 4. c. 32. & autres. Voyez sous l. 6.
ⁿ Cypr. de unit. Eccles. Concil. Carth. 4. c. 1. Aug. de symb. ad Catech. l. 4. & autres sus ch. 2. & 16.
ᵒ Hier. contra Lucif. Aug. Psalm. 57. Id. de util. cred. c. 8. Id. contr. Cresc. l. 1. c. 33.
ᵖ Cypr. ad Pup. epist. 69. & ad Magn. ep. 76. Chrys. ad Eph. hom. 11. Hier. ad Tit. c. 3. & autres, sous chap. 37.

I. *The Belief of Christ in the Sacrament* sub speciebus. 1.¹

¹ [That is, one authority is quoted by Perron on this subject; and so elsewhere.]

1. To represent to us the outward face and form of the Church in Saint Augustine's time, the Cardinal beginneth with *Qui Croyoit*, with a point of belief; and with *l'opinion avoit gaignée*, with matter of opinion. This is to stumble at the threshold. Points of faith or opinion (what men think or hold) seem rather to pertain to the inward parts, than to the *face* or exterior form of the Church. The *face*, the outward form of the Church is to be seen, as subject to the eye. Belief or opinions are not; they are within the breast, *Corde creditur*ᵃ: or within the brain, where opinions are bred. Sometime they happen to be accompanied with some outward act; but then, in that case, that outward act is to be recounted, and not they. It is the Agend of the Church he should have held him to. In that is the *Face* of the Church; in outward acts, not in inward conceits. His *Croyoits, Tenoits, Estimoits* are not, nor cannot be rightly termed *Traicts de visage*; they are not visible, as the visage is.

And in this manner doth the Cardinal forget himself, in a third part of his points, viz. this first, the viii. xiii. xvi. xviii. xxi. xxiii. xxvi. for which he allegeth forty-two places, all of them beside the purpose: they being *Tenets* only (as he termeth them), and no exterior acts at all, which only lie open to the view, and come under the term of the *face* or *visage* of the Church.

2. To tell us out of Zuinglius, what was done in Saint Augustine's time, is somewhat suspiciousᵇ. Saint Augustine

ᵃ [Rom. x. 10.]
ᵇ †Unde facile adducimur, Augustinum præ aliis acuto perspicacique ingenio virum, sua tempestate, non fuisse ausum diserte veritatem proloqui, quæ jam casum magna parte de-

† [The notes marked thus † are removed from the end of the chapter, where they were printed in the original edition, and for the sake of convenience placed under the text.]

hath written, no man more plenteously. Why hear we not out of himself, what was holden in his time? But the terms of *Sous les especes*, or *dans les especes Sacramentales*, it would pose the Cardinal and all the whole College to find they were ever heard or dreamt of in Saint Augustine's time, or many hundred years after.

3. For Zuinglius, the Cardinal well knoweth that in the very same place he citeth, Saint Augustine is three several times alleged by him against the carnal presence, viz. his Preface upon the iii. Psalm [c], his xxvi.[d] and his xxvii.[e] Homily upon John. And if Saint Augustine were against it, what he held might very well go for the *Tenet* of his time.

4. If Saint Augustine were so judicious, and withal so godly a man, and (as Zuinglius affirmeth) knew the truth, is it credible that he durst not plainly utter the truth, who so plainly both spake and defended the truth against the Manichees, Pelagians, Donatists, or whatsoever error else prevailed in his age?

The truth is, Zuinglius was more afraid than hurt. It is well known whither he leaned; that, to make this point straight, he bowed it too far the other way. To avoid *Est* in the Church of Rome's sense, he fell to be all for *Significat*, and nothing for *Est* at all. And whatsoever went further than *significat* he took to savour of the *carnal presence*. For which, if the Cardinal mislike him, so do we. And so he doth not well (against his own knowledge) to charge his opinion upon us. But what Saint Augustine believed and held in this point will appear after in the third Allegation of the next head following.

---

derat. Vidit omnino pius homo, quid hoc Sacramentum esset, et in quem usum esset institutum; verum invaluerat opinio de *corporea carne*.—[Huld. Zuing. de vera et falsa Religione. § De Eucharistia. Op., tom. ii. fol. 213. b. Tiguri, 1545.]

[c] ["Et in historia Novi Testamenti Ipsius Domini nostri tanta et tam miranda patientia, quod eum, Judam videlicet, tam diu pertulit tanquam bonum, cum ejus cogitationes non ignoraret, cum adhibuit ad convivium, in quo corporis et sanguinis sui figuram discipulis commendavit et tradidit."—S. Aug. in Ps. iii. Op., tom. iv.

col. 9. C. D., quoted by Zuinglius, Op., tom. ii. fol. 213. a.]

[d] [S. Aug. Tract. xxvii. in S. Joan. Evang. ad init. 'Exposuit . . . adversos.' Op., tom. iii. coll. 1988. D. 1989. B., quoted by Zuinglius, Op., tom. ii. fol. 213. b.]

[e] ["Si per carnem nobis multum profuit Christus, quomodo caro nihil prodest? Sed per carnem Spiritus aliquid pro salute nostra egit. Caro vas fuit; quod habebat attende, non quod erat."—S. Aug. Tract. xxvii. in S. Joan. Evang. § 5. Op., tom. iii. col. 1991. B., quoted by Zuinglius, ibid.]

II. *The external Adoration of the Sacrament.* 4.

2. This second indeed is an act, *avec gestes et adorations externes.* Four places are alleged for it [f].

[i.] We will not question the Author, as well we might[g]. Be it Cyril (or whosoever it was), he in that place teacheth the people how they should *receive the Cup.* And this is indeed a principal point, pertaining to the outward *face* of the Church. Now let the world judge ; that which Cyril teacheth the people to do is *at the taking the Cup :* and in the *face* of the Roman Church there is by them no *Cup* taken at all. What gaineth the Cardinal by this place ? This is indeed a pregnant place to prove that in the *face* and outward practice of the Church in Cyril's time *the People received the Cup;* which the Cardinal will grant, I trust, is changed since, and no such matter to be seen in the *Traicts de visage* of the Church of Rome. So in an evil time was Cyril alleged.

And that of the *gesture* toucheth not us at all: for he would have the party that receiveth it, κύπτειν, that is, to *bow himself,* and cast his eyes to the ground; that is, in humble and reverent manner to do it. And so do we. And τρόπῳ προσκυνήσεως, *after the manner of adoring,* amounteth not to *adoring :* for *after the manner,* or *as men use to do, that adore,* is a term qualified, and restrained to the outward manner. In which manner our Church enjoineth it to be received.

Cyrill.
Hieros.
Cat.
Myst. V.

---

[f] †Accedens autem ad Communionem, non expansis manuum volis accede, neque cum disjunctis digitis, sed sinistram veluti sedem quandam subjicias dextræ, quæ tantum Regem susceptura est : et concava manu suscipe corpus Christi, dicens, Amen. Sanctificatis ergo diligenter oculis, tam sancti corporis contactu, communica. *Et paulo post.* Tum vero, post communionem corporis Christi, accede, et ad calicem sanguinis Illius, non extendens manus, sed *pronus* (κύπτων) *adorationis in modum et venerationis,* dicens, *Amen.* Sanctificeris eo sanguine Christi quem assumis : et cum adhuc est humiditas in labiis tuis, manibus attingens, et oculos et frontem et reliqua sensuum organa consecra.

[Καὶ προσιὼν οὖν μὴ τεταμένοις τοῖς τῶν χειρῶν καρποῖς προσέρχου, μηδὲ διῃρημένοις τοῖς δακτύλοις· ἀλλὰ τὴν ἀριστερὰν θρόνον ποιήσας τῇ δεξιᾷ, ὡς μελλούσῃ βασιλέα ὑποδέχεσθαι, καὶ κοιλάνας τὴν παλάμην, δέχου τὸ σῶμα τοῦ Χριστοῦ, ἐπιλέγων τό, ʼΑΜΗʼΝ. μετ᾽ ἀσφαλείας οὖν ἁγιάσας τοὺς ὀφθαλμοὺς τῇ ἐπαφῇ τοῦ ἁγίου σώματος, μεταλάμβ αε ... Εἶτα μετὰ τὸ κοινωνῆσαί σε τοῦ σώματος Χριστοῦ, προσέρχου καὶ τῷ ποτηρίῳ τοῦ αἵματος· μὴ ἀνατείνων τὰς χεῖρας, ἀλλὰ κύπτων, καὶ τρόπῳ προσκυνήσεως καὶ σεβάσματος λέγων τό, ʼΑΜΗʼΝ, ἁγιάζου, καὶ ἐκ τοῦ αἵματος μεταλαμβάνων Χριστοῦ. Ἔτι δὲ τῆς νοτίδος ἐνούσης τοῖς χείλεσί σου, χερσὶν ἐπαφώμενος, καὶ ὀφθαλμοὺς, καὶ μέτωπον, καὶ τὰ λοιπὰ ἁγίαζε αἰσθητήρια. — S. Cyr. Hier. Catech. xxiii. (Myst. v.) §§ 21, 22. Op., pp. 331. C.D. 332. A. B.

[g] [On the supposed spuriousness of these discourses of S. Cyril, see Cave, Hist. Lit. tom. i. p. 212, who maintains their genuineness. See also Resp. ad Bell. p. 42. Lond. 1610; p. 55. Oxon. 1851.]

And for the term of *adoring* itself, the Cardinal confesseth after in the xxv[th]. that *adoring* doth not alway import, or signify, *Cultum divinum*, but only *venerationem* [h]. And we (by the grace of God) hold the Sacrament to be *venerable*, and with all due respect to be handled and received.

Chrysostom in 1 ad Cor. Hom. xxiv. 4

[ii.] Chrysostom can best tell us his own meaning. Thus concludeth he the place cited[i], and showeth plainly whereto all tendeth that he there urgeth, of the *wise men's coming to Christ, This I say, not that we should not come to the Sacrament, but that we should not come to it at a venture, carelessly, or in homely manner*[j]*:* Not so; but (as he had said before) *With much fear and reverence* [k].

August. in Psa. 96.

[iii.] Augustine's place is mis-cited: where it is truly cited, it showeth, the Cardinal hath very ill success in his citations. Upon the 96. Psalm there is nothing to that purpose. But upon the 98. Psalm these words are, which (I dare say) he means: *Nemo autem carnem illam manducat, nisi prius*

[h] "Non pour les adorer, entant q'*adoration* signifie *culte divine*, mais pour venerer."—[Vide supra, p. 12. num. xxv.] See Resp. ad Apol. Bell. p. 49. [p. 65. Edit. Oxon. 1851.]

[i] †Τοῦτο τὸ σῶμα καὶ ἐπὶ φάτνης κείμενον ᾐδέσθησαν μάγοι· καὶ ἄνδρες ἀσεβεῖς καὶ βάρβαροι τὴν πατρίδα καὶ τὴν οἰκίαν ἀφέντες, καὶ ὁδὸν ἐστείλαντο μακρὰν, καὶ ἐλθόντες μετὰ φόβου καὶ τρόμου πολλοῦ προσεκύνησαν. Μιμησώμεθα τοίνυν κἂν τοὺς βαρβάρους ἡμεῖς οἱ τῶν οὐρανῶν πολῖται. Ἐκεῖνοι μὲν γὰρ καὶ ἐπὶ φάτνης ἰδόντες, καὶ ἐν καλύβῃ, καὶ οὐδὲν τοιοῦτον ἰδόντες, οἷον σὺ νῦν, μετὰ πολλῆς τῆς φρίκης προσῄεσαν. σὺ δὲ οὐκ ἐν φάτνῃ ὁρᾷς, ἀλλὰ ἐν θυσιαστηρίῳ, οὐ γυναῖκα κατέχουσαν, ἀλλὰ ἱερέα παρεστῶτα, καὶ πνεῦμα μετὰ πολλῆς τῆς δαψιλείας τοῖς προκειμένοις ἐφιπτάμενον. Οὐχ ἁπλῶς αὐτὸ τοῦτο τὸ σῶμα ὁρᾷς ὥσπερ ἐκεῖνοι, ἀλλ᾽ οἶσθα αὐτοῦ καὶ τὴν δύναμιν καὶ τὴν οἰκονομίαν ἅπασαν, καὶ οὐδὲν ἀγνοεῖς τῶν δι᾽ αὐτοῦ τελεσθέντων, μετὰ ἀκριβείας μυσταγωγηθεὶς ἅπαντα. Διαναστήσωμεν τοίνυν ἑαυτοὺς καὶ φρίξωμεν, καὶ πολλῷ τῶν βαρβάρων ἐκείνων πλείονα ἐπιδειξώμεθα τὴν εὐλάβειαν, ἵνα μὴ ἁπλῶς, μηδὲ ὡς ἔτυχε προσελθόντες, πῦρ ἐπὶ τὴν ἑαυτῶν σωρεύσωμεν κεφαλήν. Ταῦτα δὲ λέγω, οὐχ ἵνα μὴ προσίωμεν, ἀλλ᾽ ἵνα μὴ ἁπλῶς προσίωμεν.—Chrysost. in 1 ad Cor. Hom. xxiv. [Op., tom. iii. pp. 400. 401.]

Hoc corpus, etiam jacens in præsepi, reveriti sunt Magi: et viri impii et barbari patria et domo relicta, et longam viam confecerunt, et quum venissent, cum multo metu et tremore adorarunt. Imitemur ergo vel barbaros nos cœlorum cives. Nam illi quidem quum et in præsepi vidissent et in tugurio; neque tale quidpiam vidissent, quale tu nunc, cum magna accesserunt reverentia. Tu autem non in præsepi vides, sed in altari; non fœminam eum tenentem, sed sacerdotem adstantem, et spiritum cum magna copia ea quæ sunt proposita supervolantem. Non solummodo hoc ipsum corpus vides, sicut illi, sed nosti ejus et virtutem et dispensationem, et nihil ignoras ex iis quæ per ipsum effecta sunt, ut qui in omnibus mysteriis sis exacte et accurate initiatus. Nos ergo ipsos excitemus, et formidemus, et longe majorem quam illi barbari ostendamus reverentiam; ne si temere et inconsiderate accesserimus, in nostrum caput ignem congeramus. Hæc autem dico, non ut non accedamus, sed ne temere et inconsiderate accedamus.

[j] Ταῦτα δὲ λέγω οὐχ ἵνα μὴ προσίωμεν, ἀλλ᾽ ἵνα μὴ ἁπλῶς μηδὲ ὡς ἔτυχε προσίωμεν. [See note [i].]

[k] Ἀλλὰ μετὰ πολλῆς φρίκης καὶ εὐλαβείας. [Implied in passage quoted note [i].]

adoraverit[1], which, I trust, no Christian man will ever refuse to do; that is, *to adore the flesh of Christ*. Wherein yet, lest any might mistake it with the Cardinal, with a wrong *Croyoit, comme contenant le vray et propre corps de Christ*, Saint Augustine presently is careful to warn his auditors, that the word *manducat* there is to be spiritually understood, and he bringeth in Christ thus speaking; *Non hoc corpus, quod videtis, manducaturi estis, et bibituri illum sanguinem, quem fusuri sunt, qui me crucifigent. Sacramentum aliquod vobis commendavi; spiritualiter intellectum vivificavit vos. Etsi necesse est illud visibiliter celebrari, oportet tamen invisibiliter intelligi.* Which show that Saint Augustine was not of the Cardinal's *Croyoit* touching the Sacrament.

[iv.] This place serves the Cardinal's purpose worst of all. [Theodor. Dial. II.] For, therein Theodoret affirms, that the *Sacramental Symbols, after the consecration, go not from their own nature, but abide in their former substance, shape, and kind*[m]. And he gains nothing by it; for προσκυνεῖται in the Cardinal's sense, may be taken *pour venerer*, (that is, *to honour and reverence*;) and is to be taken in that sense, and cannot, here, be taken in any other. For the *Symbols so abiding*, it is easily known no *divine adoration* can be used to them, nor any other than hath been said.

III. *Reservation of the Sacrament.* 7.

Of seven places cited there is not any that relieveth the Cardinal, or toucheth us. It cannot be denied but *reserving*

---

[1] †" Nemo autem illam carnem manducat, nisi prius adoraverit."—[S.] August. in Psal. xcviii. [§ 9. Op., tom. iv. col. 1521. A.] *Sed postea:* "Ille autem instruxit eos, et ait illis; ' Spiritus est qui vivificat, caro autem nihil prodest. Verba quæ locutus sum vobis, Spiritus sunt et vita.' Spiritualiter intelligite quod locutus sum. Non hoc corpus, quod videtis, manducaturi estis; nec bibituri illum sanguinem, quem fusuri sunt, qui me crucifigent. Sacramentum aliquod vobis commendavi, spiritualiter intellectum vivificabit vos. Etsi necesse est illud visibiliter celebrari, oportet tamen invisibiliter intelligi."—[Ibid. D. et col. 1522. A.]

[m] †Οὐδὲ γὰρ μετὰ τὸν ἁγιασμὸν τὰ μυστικὰ σύμβολα τῆς οἰκείας ἐξίσταται φύσεως. μένει γὰρ ἐπὶ τῆς προτέρας οὐσίας καὶ τοῦ σχήματος καὶ τοῦ εἴδους, καὶ ὁρατά ἐστι καὶ ἁπτά, οἷα καὶ πρότερον ἦν. νοεῖται δὲ ἅπερ ἐγένετο, καὶ πιστεύεται, καὶ προσκυνεῖται, ὡς ἐκεῖνα ὄντα ἅπερ πιστεύεται.—Theodor. Dial. II. [Op., tom. iv. p. 126.]

Neque enim signa mystica post sanctificationem recedunt a sua natura. Manent enim in priore substantia, et figura et forma, et videri et tangi possunt, sicut et prius: intelliguntur autem ea esse, quæ facta sunt, et creduntur, et adorantur, ut quæ illa sint, quæ creduntur.

the Sacrament was suffered a long time in the Primitive Church.

1. In time of Persecution they were permitted to carry away how great a part they would, and to keep it by them, and to take it at times to comfort them.[n] Because they knew not when they should, or whether ever they should, meet at the Sacrament again.

2. And those that lived as Anchorites and Hermits[o], in remote desert places, were likewise permitted to carry away with them how much they thought good, to take at times; because a long time together they were not to come back to places where any Churches were.

Having it then with them in their own hands and power, they might, and did *keep it in their chests, eat it at home, carry it about with them in their journey.*

For, as for *sending it into far Countries,* Eusebius hath no word of *far Countries :* but that, such as held not their Fasts, or keep not their Easter, as the Church of Rome did, notwithstanding, when they came to Rome, had it sent them by the Deacon, as others there had [p].

But all this is from the matter. For, it is well known, this is not now the face or fashion of the Church of Rome. For no man, there, may carry the Sacrament home, and eat it to Breakfast, or carry it to Sea, or tie it up in his *orarium*[q]. For, this of *carrying it home,* and there *reserving* it, was long since taken away; and order taken, that every man, what was delivered him, he should receive and take it down in the church. And it is to be noted that this was done, Saint Augustine living, both by the Council of Saragossa, Can. III. in the year 381, upon pain of Anathema[r]: and by the first

---

[n] [See Tertull. ad Uxor., and S. Cyprian de Lapsis, as quoted in Resp. ad Apol. Bellarm. p. 259. note[k], Oxon. 1851.]

[o] [Πάντες γὰρ οἱ κατὰ τὰς ἐρήμους μονάζοντες, ἔνθα μή ἐστιν ἱερεὺς, κοινωνίαν οἴκοι κατέχοντες, ἀφ' ἑαυτῶν μεταλαμβάνουσιν. . . "Απαξ γὰρ τὴν θυσίαν τοῦ ἱερέως τελειώσαντος καὶ δεδωκότος, ὁ λαβὼν αὐτὴν ὡς ὅλην ὁμοῦ, καθ' ἑκάστην μεταλαμβάνων, παρὰ τοῦ δεδωκότος εἰκότως μεταλαμβάνειν καὶ ὑποδέχεσθαι πιστεύειν ὀφείλει. — S. Basil. Ep. xciii. (al. cclxxxix.) ad Cæsar. Patric., Op., tom. iii. p. 189.

A.B. Compare also S. Cyril. Alex., Epist. ad Calosyrium in præf. libri contra Anthropomorph. (Op., tom. vi. p. 365.) as referred to by Perron.]

[p] ['Αλλ' αὐτοὶ μὴ τηροῦντες οἱ πρό σου πρεσβύτεροι, τοῖς ἀπὸ τῶν παροικιῶν τηροῦσιν ἔπεμπον εὐχαριστίαν. — S. Iren. apud Euseb. Hist. Eccl.] lib. v. cap. 25. [p. 248.]

[q] [See S. Ambr. de Excessu Fratris Satyri, § 43. Op., tom. i. col. 1125.]

[r] ["Item legit (Lucius sc.) Eucharistiæ gratiam si quis probatur acceptam non sumpsisse, [*in marg.* consumpsisse,] anathema sit in perpe-

Council of Toledo, Can. XIV. in the year 405, upon pain of *being cast out as a sacrilegious person* [s]. Which was so ordered, because of divers and sundry evil practices, whereto the Priscillianists and other heretics and bad persons were known to abuse it. So that this pertaineth nothing to the *face* of the *Church* now, either as it is with them, or as it is with us.

But for the *Sick*, it was always sent them home, were the distance never so great. And against the time of extremity it was thought not amiss to have it *reserved;* that, if the priest should not then be in state to go to the sick party, and there to consecrate it, for him; yet at least it might be sent him, as in the case of Serapion [t]. For it is sure they made far greater account of the receiving it as their *viaticum*, than some do now.

But neither doth this touch us, who at the desire of any that is in that case, may not refuse but go to him, and minister it him. So that *Reservation* needeth not; the intent is had without it.

IV. *The Communion under one kind.*

For this there is no authority at all alleged, but the Cardinal puts us off to another place [u].

V. *The Eucharist a Sacrifice.* 6.

1. The *Eucharist* ever was, and by us is considered, both as a *Sacrament,* and as a *Sacrifice*[v]. 2. A *Sacrifice* is proper and appliable only *to divine worship*[w]. 3. The *Sacrifice of*

---

tuum. Ab universis Episcopis dictum est, Placet." — Conc. Cæsar-August. Can. iii.—Conc. tom. ii. col. 1010. A.]

[s] [" Si quis autem acceptam a sacerdote Eucharistiam non sumpserit, velut sacrilegus propellatur."— Conc. Tolet. I. A.D. 400.—Conc. tom. ii. col. 1225. D.]

[t] Euseb. [Hist. Eccl.] lib. vi. cap. 44. [pp. 316—318.]

[u] [Perron, Replique à la Response du Roy, liv. vi. 'Seconde Instance,' p. 1107. seq. It is referred to by Perron as liv. xii., see above p. 8. not. [i].]

[v] [He refers to S. Cypr. ad Cœcil. Ep. lxiii. as quoted by Perron, "Ille sacerdos vice Christi vere fungitur, qui id quod Christus fecit, imitatur: et sacrificium verum et plenum tunc offert in Ecclesia Deo Patri, si sic incipiat offerre secundum quod ipsum Christum videat obtulisse."—S. Cypr. Op., p. 155. ed. Fell. But the word *sacramentum* as well as *sacrificium* is applied to the Eucharist throughout this Epistle.]

[w] [This alludes to the words in S. Aug. contra Faustum. lib. xx. cap. xxi. (Op., tom. viii. col. 545. B.) "At illo cultu, quæ Græce λατρεία dicitur, ... cum sit quædam proprie Divini-

Christ's death did succeed to the Sacrifices of the Old Testament[x]. 4. The *Sacrifice* of *Christ's death is available* for *present, absent, living, dead*[y], (yea, for them that are yet *unborn*[z].) 5. When we say the *dead,* we mean it is available for *the Apostles, Martyrs,* and *Confessors,* and all (because we are all members of one body :) these no man will deny.

6. In a word, we hold with Saint Augustine in the very same chapter which the Cardinal citeth, *quod Hujus Sacrificii Caro et Sanguis, ante adventum Christi, per victimas similitudinum promittebatur; in passione Christi, per ipsam veritatem reddebatur; post adventum* [leg. *ascensum*] *Christi, per Sacramentum memoriæ celebratur* [a].

VI. *Altars.* 2.

If we agree about the matter of *Sacrifice,* there will be no difference about the *Altar.* The holy Eucharist being considered as a *Sacrifice,* (in the representation of the breaking the bread, and pouring forth the cup,) the same is fitly called an *Altar;* which again is as fitly called a *Table,* the *Eucharist* being considered as a *Sacrament,* which is nothing else but a distribution and an application of the *Sacrifice* to the several receivers. The same Saint Augustine that, in the place alleged, doth term it an *Altar*[b]; saith in another place, *Christus quotidie pascit. Mensa Ipsius est illa in medio constituta. Quid causæ est, o audientes, ut* mensam videatis, et

---

tati debita servitus, nec colimus, nec colendum docemus, nisi unum Deum. Cum autem ad hunc cultum pertineat oblatio sacrificii," &c. St. Augustine's argument is, that Christians did not worship the martyrs, because they did not offer the sacrifice (of the Eucharist) to them, but to God only.]

[x] [" Id enim sacrificium successit omnibus illis sacrificiis veteris Testamenti."—S.] Aug. de Civitate [Dei], lib. xvii. cap. 20. [Op., tom. vii. col. 767. B. Compare also, S. Iren. contra Hær. "Novi Testamenti novam docuit oblationem." (Lib. iv. cap. xvii. § 5. p. 249. ed. Bened.) The whole chapter is to the same effect.]

[y] [S. Chrys. in 1 Cor. Hom. xli., Op., tom. iii. p. 524. Οὐδὲ μάτην ὁ παρεστὼς τῷ θυσιαστηρίῳ τῶν φρικτῶν μυστηρίων τελουμένων βοᾷ· ὑπὲρ πάντων τῶν ἐν Χριστῷ κεκοιμημένων. See the whole passage. See also Euseb. de Vit. Const.,

lib. iv. capp. 45 and 71, on offering for the absent and the departed, and S. Cyril. Hieros. Catech. Myst. V. §§ 9, 10. Μεγίστην ὄνησιν πιστεύοντες ἔσεσθαι ταῖς ψυχαῖς, ὑπὲρ ὧν ἡ δέησις ἀναφέρεται, τῆς ἁγίας καὶ φρικωδεστάτης προκειμένης θυσίας . . . Χριστὸν ἐσφαγιασμένον ὑπὲρ τῶν ἡμετέρων ἁμαρτημάτων προσφέρομεν, ἐξιλεουμένοι ὑπὲρ αὐτῶν τε καὶ ἡμῶν τὸν φιλάνθρωπον Θεόν.—Op., p. 328. B.C.]

[z] [Bp. Andrewes probably refers to the words of Chrys. in Matt. Hom. xxv. Διὸ δὴ καὶ ὁ ἱερεὺς ὑπὲρ τῆς οἰκουμένης, ὑπὲρ τῶν προτέρων, ὑπὲρ τῶν νῦν, ὑπὲρ τῶν γεννηθέντων ἔμπροσθεν, ὑπὲρ τῶν μετὰ ταῦτα ἐσομένων εἰς ἡμᾶς εὐχαριστεῖν κελεύει, τῆς θυσίας προκειμένης ἐκείνης. — S. Chrysost. Op., tom. iii. p. 179.]

[a] [S. Aug. contra Faustum. lib. xx. cap. 21. Op., tom. viii. col. 546. B.C.]

[b] [See below, p. 21, not. ⁸.]

ad epulas non accedatis^c? The same Nyssen in the place cited, with one breath calleth it θυσιαστήριον, that is, an *Altar,* and ἱερὰ τράπεζα, that is, the holy *Table*^d.

Which is agreeable also to the Scriptures; for the *Altar,* in the Old Testament, is by Malachi^e called *Mensa Domini.* And of the *Table,* in the New Testament, by the Apostle it is said, *Habemus Altare*^f. Which, of what matter it be, whether of *stone,* as Nyssen^g, or of wood, as Optatus^h, it skills not. So that the matter of *Altars,* makes no difference in the *face* of our Church.

VII. *Worship of Martyrs and their Relics.*

This point hath been dealt in heretofore; seven of the places answered, in the *Answer to* Bellarmine's Apology, viz. the place,

Of Basil, page 40 [i].

Of Ambrose *de Viduis,* page 45 [k].

Of Nazianzen *upon Cyprian,* page 42 [l].

Of Ruffin, (touching Theodosius,) page 45 [m].

Of Chrysostom, page 42 [n].

Of Hierome, page 49 [o].

Of Nyssen *in Theodorum,* page 48 [p].

Saint Augustine we agree with, we *celebrate the memories* [q], we *hold the Feast of the blessed Martyrs* [r]; *as of Saint Stephen,* and the *Blessed Innocents*: as well for *imitation,* as that *we may be partakers of their* intercession, *and attain to the society of that which they have obtained* [s].

---

[c] [S. Aug.] Hom. xlvi. de Verbis Domini secundum Joannem. [al. Serm. cxxxii. cap. 1. Op., tom. v. col. 931. A.]

[d] ['Ἐπεὶ καὶ τὸ θυσιαστήριον τοῦτο τὸ ἅγιον, ᾧ παρεστήκαμεν, λίθος ἐστὶ κατὰ τὴν φύσιν κοινός.... ἐπειδὰν δὲ καθιερώθη τῇ τοῦ Θεοῦ θεραπείᾳ, καὶ τὴν εὐλογίαν ἐδέξατο, ἔστι τράπεζα ἁγία, θυσιαστήριον ἄχραντον.—S. Greg. Nyss. de Baptismo Christi. Op., tom. iii. pp. 369. D. 370. A. Paris. 1638.]

[e] Mal. i. 7.

[f] Heb. xiii. 10.

[g] [S. Greg.] Nyssen. de Bapt. [See above, not. [d].]

[h] [" Sed, ut æstimo, alio loco copia lignorum frangi jussit, aliis vero ut altaria raderent, lignorum inopia imperavit."—S. Opt. de Schism. Donat. lib. vi. cap. 1. p. 90.]

[i] [Resp. ad Apol. Card. Bell. pp. 50, 51. Oxon. 1851.]

[k] [Ibid. pp. 58, 59.]

[l] [Ibid. p. 54.]

[m] [Ibid. p. 59.]

[n] [Ibid. p. 53.]

[o] [Resp. ad Apol. Card. Bell. p. 65. Oxon. 1851.]

[p] [Ibid. pp. 62, 63.]

[q] [" Dixerunt ista martyres, quorum natalitia celebramus." S. Aug. in Ps.] lxxxviii. [§ 11. Op., tom. iv. col. 1360. D.]

[r] [" Passionis Sanctorum martyrum diem hodie festum habentes, in eorum recordatione gaudeamus." S.] Aug. in Ps. lxiii. [§ 1. Op., tom. iv. col. 881. B.]

[s] [" Populus autem Christianus memorias martyrum religiosa solemni-

For their *Relics* (were we sure they were true and uncounterfeit) we would carry to them the regard that becometh us. But the Cardinal himself will not say that Saint Hierome ever meant *to adore the ashes of* Saint John Baptist[t]; for Hierome himself will say the contrary, *Nos autem, non dico Martyrum Reliquias, sed ne Solem quidem et Lunam, non Angelos, non Archangelos, non Cherubin, non Seraphin, et omne nomen quod nominatur in præsenti sæculo et in futuro, colimus et adoramus; ne serviamus creaturæ potius quam Creatori, qui est benedictus in sæcula. Honoramus [autem] reliquias Martyrum, ut Eum, cujus sunt Martyres, adoremus. Honoramus Servos, ut honor Servorum redundet ad Dominum*[u]. Saint Hierome opposed to Vigilantius, that used reproachful terms, to the *ashes and relics* of *Martyrs*, (then) calling them *vilem pulvisculum*, and *vilissimum pulverem*, and *illud nescio quid*[x]: for which he was, and was to be, justly censured at any time, but specially at that time, while there lived so many heathen men. It was rashly and undiscreetly done of him, so to abase his terms.

And had [they] the power of doing miracles, as those of Saint Stephen had (reported by Saint Augustine [y]) and those of Felix (by Paulinus [z]), we would esteem them so much the rather; but yet in their degree, and nothing so high as the Cardinal would seem to set them. And yet, the *carrying them about in linen clothes, and kissing them*, which Vigilantius doth object, if he did it truly, we would rather bear with it, and excuse it, as proceeding from popular and private devotion, which will many times overshoot itself, than commend it: for if it had been *solum honorare*[a], it seems Vigilantius would not have found fault with it.

tate concelebrat, et ad excitandam incitationem, et ut meritis eorum consocietur, atque orationibus adjuvetur; ita tamen ut nulli martyrum, sed ipsi Deo martyrum, quamvis in memoriis martyrum, constituamus altaria."—S. Aug.] cont. Faustum, lib. xx. cap. 21. [Op., tom. viii. coll. 544. D. 545. A.]

[t] [" Quando nobis liceat . . . Samariam pergere, et Joannis Baptistæ, Elisæi quoque et Abdiæ pariter cineres adorare."—Ep. S.] Hieron. [sub nom. Paulæ et Eustoch.] ad Marcellam [sect. 12. apud S. Hier. Ep. xlvi. Vall.

(al. xvii.) Op., tom. i. col. 207. A.B.]
[u] [S. Hier.] Ep. [cix. Vall. (al. liii.)] ad Ripar. con. Vigil. [sect. 1. Op., tom. i. col. 720. A.B.]
[x] [See below, note. [a].]
[y] [See S. Aug. de Civit. Dei, lib. xxii. cap. viii. § 15, sq., Op., tom. vii. coll. 1067, seq.]
[z] [S. Paulin. in S. Felic. Nat. vi.— Bibl. Max. Patrum, tom. vi. p. 270, seq.]
[a] [" Quid necesse est (ait Vigilantius) te tanto honore, non solum honorare, sed etiam adorare illud nescio

To that book *de curandis Græcorum affectibus*[b], questioned whether it be Theodoret's[c], or no, we oppose that which is Theodoret's out of question upon the 2d and 3d Chap. to the Colossians; where he expressly says, (and that by the authority of the Council of Laodicæa [d],) *Angels are not to be prayed to*[e]. And if not *Angels*, not *Martyrs*.

VIII. *Traditions.* 1.[f]

This is matter of opinion, not of practice; and so toucheth not the *face* of *the Church*.

Exceptions have been made by Erasmus [g], and other learned men, to this book : we oppose to it, out of Basil's treatise *de Fide*, which never was questioned till now, or late by the Cardinal [h], these words; *Haud dubie manifestissimum hoc infidelitatis argumentum fuerit, et signum superbiæ certissi-*

quid, quod in modico vasculo transferendo colis? Quid pulverem linteamine circumdatum adorando oscularis?" S.] Hier. con. Vigil. [sect. 4. Op., tom. ii. col. 390. D. To whom S. Jerome replies, "Male facit ergo Romanus Episcopus, qui super mortuorum hominum Petri et Pauli, secundum nos ossa veneranda, secundum te vilem pulvisculum, offert Domino sacrificia, et tumulos eorum Christi arbitratur altaria ; et non solum unius Urbis, sed totius orbis errant Episcopi, qui cauponem Vigilantium contemnentes, ingrediuntur basilicas mortuorum, in quibus pulvis vilissimus, et favilla, nescio quæ, jacet linteamine convoluta, ut polluta omnia polluat."—Ibid. sect. 9. col. 395. A.B.]

[b] [Εἰς δὲ τούτους οὐχ ἅπαξ ἢ δίς γε τοῦ ἔτους ἢ πεντάκις φοιτῶμεν· ἀλλὰ πολλάκις μὲν πανηγύρεις ἐπιτελοῦμεν, πολλάκις δὲ καὶ ἡμέρας ἑκάστης τῷ τούτων Δεσπότῃ τοὺς ὕμνους προσφέρομεν . . . . οὐχ ὡς θεοῖς αὐτοῖς προσιόντες, ἀλλ' ὡς θείους ἀνθρώπους ἀντιβολοῦντες.] Theodoret. de Gr. Aff. cur. lib. viii. [Op., tom. iv. p. 921.]

[c] [See below, p. 56. in marg.]

[d] ["Ὅτι οὐ δεῖ χριστιανοὺς . . . ἐγκαταλείπειν τὴν ἐκκλησίαν τοῦ Θεοῦ, καὶ ἀπιέναι, καὶ ἀγγέλους ὀνομάζειν, καὶ συνάξεις ποιεῖν· ἅπερ ἀπηγόρευται· εἴ τις οὖν εὑρεθῇ ταύτῃ τῇ κεκρυμμένῃ εἰδωλολατρείᾳ σχολάζων, ἔστω ἀνάθεμα, ὅτι ἐγκατέλιπε τὸν Κύριον ἡμῶν Ἰησοῦν Χριστὸν, τὸν Υἱὸν τοῦ Θεοῦ, καὶ εἰδωλο- λατρείᾳ προσῆλθεν.—Conc. Laod. Can. xxxv. Conc. tom. i. col. 1504. A.]

[e] [Οἱ τῷ νόμῳ συνηγοροῦντες, καὶ τοὺς ἀγγέλους σέβειν αὐτοῖς εἰσηγοῦντο, διὰ τούτων λέγοντες δεδόσθαι τὸν νόμον· ἔμεινε δὲ τοῦτο τὸ πάθος ἐν τῇ Φρυγίᾳ καὶ Πισιδίᾳ μέχρι πολλοῦ. Οὗ δὴ χάριν καὶ συνελθοῦσα σύνοδος ἐν Λαοδικείᾳ τῆς Φρυγίας νόμῳ κεκώλυκε τὸ τοῖς ἀγγέλοις προσεύχεσθαι, καὶ μέχρι δὲ τοῦ νῦν εὐκτήρια τοῦ ἁγίου Μιχαὴλ παρ' ἐκείνοις καὶ τοῖς ὁμόροις ἐκείνων ἐστὶν ἰδεῖν, τοῦτο τοίνυν συνεβούλευον ἐκεῖνοι γίνεσθαι, ταπεινοφροσύνῃ δῆθεν κεχρημένοι, καὶ λέγοντες, Ὡς ἀόρατος ὁ τῶν ὅλων Θεὸς, ἀνέφικτός τε καὶ ἀκατάληπτος, καὶ προσήκει διὰ τῶν ἀγγέλων τὴν θείαν εὐμένειαν πραγματεύεσθαι. — Theod. in Col. ii. 18. Op., tom. iii. p. 490.]

[f] [Τῶν ἐν ἐκκλησίᾳ πεφυλαγμένων δογμάτων καὶ κηρυγμάτων, τὰ μὲν ἐκ τῆς ἐγγράφου διδασκαλίας ἔχομεν, τὰ δὲ ἐκ τῆς τῶν ἀποστόλων παραδόσεως διαδοθέντα ἡμῖν ἐν μυστηρίῳ παρεδεξάμεθα· ἅπερ ἀμφότερα τὴν αὐτὴν ἰσχὺν ἔχει πρὸς τὴν εὐσέβειαν.—S.] Basil. de Spir. S[ancto] ad Amph. cap. 6. [*leg.* sect. 66. Op., tom. iii. p. 54. D.]

[g] [See Desid. Erasmi Epist. dedic. ad init. S. Basil. de Sp. Sancto, Basil. 1532. And Erasmi Op., tom. viii. coll. 491, 492.]

[h] [See Perron Repl. liv. ii. Observ. v. chap. vii. p. 757. The question is discussed by Garnier, Præf. in S. Basil., Op., tom. ii. § xi. num. 30. 31.]

mum, si quis eorum quæ scripta sunt, aliquid velit rejicere, aut eorum quæ non scripta introducere [i].

IX. *Prayer for the Dead.* 6.

For *offering* and *prayer for the dead*, there is little to be said against it; it cannot be denied, but that it is ancient.

X. *Lent.* 3.

It is in the *face* of our Church, as well as theirs. Neither is it a *time of marriage* [k], with us, but by special dispensation [l].

XI. *No Fast on Christmas-Day, though it be a Friday.* 1.

We *fast not on Christmas-Day*, though it fall upon *a Friday* or *Saturday*.

XII. *Priests' Marriage.* 4.

The restraint of *Priests from marrying*, neither is, nor ever was, conceived to be, but *positivi juris*; which being restrained upon good reason, it might upon as good reason be released. And Pius II. was of opinion, that there was better reason to release them, than to restrain them [m]. And so were divers other at the Council of Trent, if there had been fair play [n].

The Canons that seem to restrain it, were not general [o]: when they were urged as general, they were opposed by the VI. General Council, Can. 13 [p]; where the Church of Rome is in express terms taxed for urging them. Nor in those places where such Canons were, were they generally observed, as appeareth by Epiphanius, in the place alleged [q].

---

[i] Φανερὰ ἔκπτωσις πίστεως καὶ ὑπερηφανίας κατηγορία ἢ ἀθετεῖν τι τῶν γεγραμμένων, ἢ ὑπεισάγειν τῶν μὴ γεγραμμένων.—[S. Basil. de Fide, cap. 1. Op., tom. ii. p. 224. D.]

[k] [Perron refers to Conc. Laod. Can. lii. Ὅτι οὐ δεῖ ἐν τεσσαρακοστῇ γάμους ἢ γενέθλια ἐπιτελεῖν. — Conc. tom. i. col. 1505. C.]

[l] [On Dispensations for marriages in Lent, see Hooker, Ecc. Pol. lib. v. chap. lxxiii. sect. 4, notes 99 and 4. Keble's Edition, Oxford, 1836; and Johnson's Vade Mecum. vol. i. chap. xxi.]

[m] ["Sacerdotibus magna ratione sublatas nuptias, majori restituendas videri."]—Platina in Vita ejus, [in Vitis Pontif. p. 329.]

[n] [See Father Paul's History of the Council of Trent, book viii. p. 698. Lond. 1676.]

[o] [As the 1st Canon of the Council of Neocæsarea, and the 2d Canon of the 2d Council of Carthage, referred to by Perron.]

[p] [Ἐπειδὴ ἐν τῇ Ῥωμαίων ἐκκλησίᾳ ἐν τάξει κανόνος παραδεδόσθαι διέγνωμεν, τοὺς μέλλοντας διακόνου ἢ πρεσβυτέρου ἀξιοῦσθαι χειροτονίας καθομολογεῖν, ὡς οὐκέτι ταῖς αὐτῶν συνάπτονται γαμεταῖς· ἡμεῖς τῷ ἀρχαίῳ ἐξακολουθοῦντες κανόνι τῆς ἀποστολικῆς ἀκριβείας καὶ τάξεως, τὰ τῶν ἱερῶν ἀνδρῶν κατὰ νόμους συνοικέσια καὶ ἀπὸ τοῦ νῦν ἔρρωσθαι βουλόμεθα.—Conc. Trull. seu Quinisext. Can. xiii.—Conc. tom. vi. col. 1147. B.C.]

[q] [Καὶ ταῦτα ἀσφαλῶς ἡ ἁγία τοῦ Θεοῦ ἐκκλησία μετὰ ἀκριβείας παραφυ-

But that an *Apostolic Tradition* or *Canon* it could not be[r], but quite beside them, it is plain, by the 5. Canon of the Apostles; where it is taken as granted that they had wives, and ordered that *they should not put them away under pretence of religion* [s]. And that doth the VI. General Council [t] affirm to have been the ancient and Apostolic Tradition [u], Can. 13.

XIII. *Marrying after Vow of Single Life.* 4.

We hold such vows as be orderly and duly made, are to be kept, and cannot be broken without offence. All the question is about the undue and disorderly making of them.

XIV. *Mingling of Wine with Water in the Eucharist.* 2.

Saint Chrysostom against the *Hydroparastatæ*, or *Aquarii*, seemeth to oppose it [v]. We hold it a matter not worth the standing on: so all else were agreed, we would not stick with them to put as much *water* in as the Priests use to do.

XV. *Exorcisms and Exufflations.* 1.

It cometh in here, out of place; it is afterwards repeated again at the XVII.

XVI. *The Five Sacraments.* 9.

We deny not but that the title of *Sacrament* hath sometimes been given by the Fathers unto all these five, in a

---

λάττεται, ἀλλὰ καὶ τὸν ἔτι βιοῦντα καὶ τεκνογονοῦντα, μιᾶς γυναικὸς ὄντα ἄνδρα, οὐ δέχεται, ἀλλ' ἀπὸ μιᾶς ἐγκρατευσάμενον, ἢ χηρεύσαντα, Διάκονόν τε καὶ Πρεσβύτερον, καὶ Ἐπίσκοπον, καὶ Ὑποδιάκονον, μάλιστα ὅπου ἀκριβεῖς κανόνες οἱ Ἐκκλησιαστικοί.—S. Epiph.] Hæres. lix. [Cathar. cap. iv. Op., tom. i. p. 496. B.]

[r] [So Perron asserted it to be. See above, p. 9. num. xii. The remaining passage quoted by Perron, Euseb. Demonst. Evan. i. 9. (p. 33. D. Colon. 1688.) simply asserts the fact.]

[s] Τὴν ἑαυτοῦ γυναῖκα μὴ ἐκβαλλέτω προφάσει εὐλαβείας. — [Can. Ap. v. Conc. tom. i. col. 25. D.]

[t] Ἡμεῖς τῷ ἀρχαίῳ διακολουθοῦντες κανόνι τῆς ἀποστολικῆς ἀκριβείας καὶ τάξεως, &c. [See above, note [p].]

[u] [Εἴ τις οὖν τολμήσοι] παρὰ τοὺς ἀποστολικοὺς κανόνας, [κινούμενος, τινὰ τῶν ἱερωμένων, πρεσβυτέρων φαμὲν ἢ διακόνων, ἢ ὑποδιακόνων, ἀποστερεῖν τῆς πρὸς νόμιμον γυναῖκα συναφείας τε καὶ κοινωνίας, καθαιρείσθω.— Conc. Trull. seu Quinisext. Can. xiii. ad fin.—Conc. coll. 1147. E. 1149. A.]

[v] [Καὶ τίνος ἕνεκεν οὐχ ὕδωρ ἔπιεν ἀναστὰς, ἀλλ' οἶνον; Ἄλλην αἵρεσιν πονηρὰν πρόρριζον ἀνασπῶν· ἐπειδὴ γάρ εἰσί τινες ἐν τοῖς μυστηρίοις ὕδατι κεχρημένοι, δεικνὺς ὅτι καὶ ἡνίκα τὰ μυστήρια παρέδωκεν, οἶνον παρέδωκε, καὶ ἡνίκα ἀναστὰς χωρὶς μυστηρίων ψιλὴν τράπεζαν παρετίθετο, οἴνῳ ἐκέχρητο, Ἐκ τοῦ γεννήματός, φησι, τῆς ἀμπέλου. Ἡ ἄμπελος δὲ οἶνον, οὐχ ὕδωρ γεννᾷ.—S. Chrys.] Hom. lxxxiii. in cap. 26. Mat. aut lxxxii. secundum Græcam Editionem. [Op., tom. ii. p. 511. lin. 12. The use of water instead of wine seems only to be condemned in this passage.]

larger *signification*ˣ. But so is it also to many things more: and, namely, (as it is alleged after by the Cardinal, in the XVII. Head,) *salt* is called a *Sacrament: Sacramentum Catechumenis non detur, nisi solitum Sal*ʸ. But *pour vray et propre Sacrament,* there is not any of the Fathers so affirms any of the five. The whole matter is a mere λογομαχία. If the thing were agreed upon, we should not strive for the name.

XVII. *The Ceremonies of Baptism. Chrism, Salt, Candles, Exorcisms, Sign of the Cross, Ephata, and the Consecration of the Water.* 10.

These being all matter of Ceremony, are therefore in the Church's power, upon good reason, either to retain, or to alter. As appeareth by the Cardinal's own allegation of *not fasting the Fridays between Easter and Whitsuntide*ᶻ, which notwithstanding, the Church of Rome now fasteth, as well as other Fridays before and after it. And by the ceremony of *not kneeling all that time,* nor *all the Sundays in the year:*ᵃ which, though it were *Apostolic* (as were also the *Agape*ᵇ, and the *maintaining of widows*ᶜ), yet are all left, as well by them, as by us; and so, plainly show the Church's power over Ceremonies. Wherein our Church useth her liberty.

*Chrism*ᵈ, indeed, is very ancient, yet never but as a ceremony, which though we retain not, yet the invocation of the grace of the Holy Ghost we do.

Exorcisms though we retain not, yet the substance of them, the *forsaking the Devil and all his works,* we do.

The *Sign of the Cross* we do retain.

So do we the *Consecration of the Water by Prayer.*

Salt, Candles, and *Ephata,* we do not, as having nothing in them proper to the Sacrament. And his reasons are but

---

ˣ [The number of the Sacraments was first expressly defined by Peter Lombard, Lib. Sent. iv. Dist. ii. § 1. See Bramhall's Answer to De La Millétière. Works, vol. i. p. 55. Oxf. 1842. and Bellarm. de Sacr. lib. ii. cap. xxv. Op., tom. iii. p. 51. E.F.]

ʸ Con. Carthag. III. cap. 5. [Conc. tom. ii. col. 1167. E.]

ᶻ [See Epiphanius, Hæres. lxxv. Aërian. cap. vi. Op., tom. i. p. 910. B. and Exposit. Fid. cap. xxii. ibid. pp. 1104. D. 1105. A.]

ᵃ [See Conc. Nic. Can. xx., Conc. tom. ii. col. 245 B.C.; and S. Basil. de Sp. Sancto, cap. xxvii. Op., tom. iii. p. 56. C.D.]

ᵇ [Jud. ver. 12.]

ᶜ [1 Tim. v. 3. seq.]

ᵈ ["Ungi quoque necesse est eum, qui baptizatus sit, ut accepto chrismate, id est unctione, esse unctus Dei, et habere in se gratiam Christi possit," &c.—S.Cyp. Ep. lxx. Op., pp. 190, 191.]

poor ones : for *salt* may with as good reason be used in *Orders*, which are *perpetual*, and not to be iterated[e]; and the rather for that they which are ordained, are, *in the Scriptures' style*, said to be the *salt of the earth*. And *lights*, by as good reason, may be used in all the rest; for Christ *is the Light of the World*[f], no more in one than in another. As for *Ephata*, it is no more to be said to the ears to open them (which was one miracle), than *clay* to be put on the eyes of the child, to *lighten* them (which was another). The Cardinal's very reasons show they may with reason be taken away.

XVIII. *Necessity of Baptism.* 3.

We hold the same *necessity of Baptism* that the Fathers did hold, which is, *Via ordinaria:* yet, *non alligando gratiam Dei ad media*[g], no more than the Schoolmen do.

XIX. *Holy Water.* 3.

For *Holy Water* there are alleged only two Miracles, of Joseph the Convert Jew, in Epiphanius[h]; and Marcellus the Bishop of Apamea[i] in Theodoret: which, if they were so done, were done rather by virtue of the faith in Christ, than of the *Water* or *Sign*, which is known, many times since, to have had no such effect. Two Miracles[k], without any Canon to enjoin it, will not conclude any rule for the practice of it in the Church.

XX. *The five Orders.* 10.

A Point not worth the standing on. While the revenues of the Church were able to maintain so many degrees, it cannot be denied but that there were so many, but by the

---

[e] [Perron's words, see above, p. 10.]
[f] [As Perron here speaks of Him.]
[g] [S. Thom. Aquin. Sum. Theol. par. Quæst. lxxxiii.]
[h] [Λαβὼν τὸ αὐτὸ ἄγγος τοῦ ὕδατος ἐνώπιον πάντων ... μεγάλῃ τῇ φωνῇ ὁ ἀνὴρ σταυροῦ σφραγῖδα ἐπιθεὶς τῷ ἄγγει διὰ τοῦ ἰδίου δακτύλου, καὶ ἐπικαλεσάμενος τὸ ὄνομα 'Ιησοῦ, εἶπεν οὕτως· Ἐν ὀνόματι 'Ιησοῦ τοῦ Ναζωραίου, ὃν ἐσταύρωσαν οἱ πατέρες μου καὶ τούτων πάντων τῶν περιεστώτων, γένηται δύναμις ἐν τούτῳ τῷ ὕδατι, εἰς ἀθέτησιν πάσης φαρμακείας καὶ μαγείας, ἧς οὗτοι ἔπραξαν, καὶ εἰς ἐνέργειαν δυνάμεως τῷ πυρὶ εἰς τὸ ἐπιτελεσθῆναι τὸν οἶκον Κυρίου. καὶ οὕτως λαμβάνει τὸ ὕδωρ ἐν τῇ χειρί, καὶ ῥαίνει ἑκάστῳ φόρακι ἐκ τοῦ ὕδατος. καὶ ἀνέλυετο μὲν τὰ φάρμακα, τὸ πῦρ δὲ ἐνώπιον πάντων ἀνεβλύστανεν.— S.] Epiph. Hær. xxx. [cap. xii. Op., tom. i. pp. 136. D. 137. A.]
[i] [Marcellus is said to have caused the destruction of the temple of Jupiter at Apamea by the use of holy water.]—Theod. Hist. Eccl. v. 21. [p. 222.]
[k] [S. Greg. the Great, the other authority quoted by Perron, is not noticed, as being beyond the period (the first four centuries) specified by Casaubon.]

Church's own order, neither by commandment nor example of Scripture. But, what is this to the present estate of the Church, scarce able to maintain two? And, it is well known, that in the Church of Rome they do take these five, and with them the Order of Deacon, all in one day; and that the five are rather for matter of form and of fees, than for anything else. So that this is nothing but a σκιαμαχία.

And as for the great mystery, that the degrees among Bishops, of Archbishops, Primates, and Patriarchs, should be *de jure positivo*, but that the Pope should be *de jure divino*; it is so gross (that in one uniform ascent or scale of four degrees, one degree only should be *de jure divino*, and all the other three *de jure positivo*) that it deserves rather to be scorned than answered.

We know that Saint Hierome, when he was vexed in the East, by the Bishop and Clergy of Hierusalem, had recourse to Damasus Bishop of Rome [1], whom he had served in sorting his papers. But, we say withal, when he was angry with the priests of Rome, he set as light again by them, and the See itself, and said, *Quid mihi profers unius urbis (Romæ) consuetudinem? major est Orbis urbe. Episcopus sive Romæ, sive Eugubii, ejusdem meriti, ejusdem est et Sacerdotii* [m].

Saint Augustine [n] and the Council of Milevitum did truly acknowledge the Bishopric of Rome was a See of higher place and account than any in Africa, as being the See of the Imperial City [o]. But when Apiarius appealed to Rome, it is

---

[1] [" Quoniam vetusto Oriens inter se populorum furore collisus indiscissam Domini tunicam, et desuper textam, minutatim per frustra discerpit ... ideo mihi Cathedram Petri et fidem Apostolico ore laudatam censui consulendam."—S.] Hieron. ad Dam. Ep. [xv. Vall. (al.)] lvii. [sect. 1. Op., tom. i. col. 37. A.B. "Quanquam igitur tui me terreat magnitudo, invitat tamen humanitas. A Sacerdote victima salutem, a Pastore præsidium ovis flagito. Facessat invidia; Romani culminis recedat ambitio, cum successore Piscatoris et discipulo crucis loquor. Ego nullum primum nisi Christum sequens, Beatitudini tuæ, id est, Cathedræ Petri communione consocior. Super illam Petram ædificatam Ecclesiam scio. Quiquumque extra hanc domum agnum comederit, prophanus est. Si quis in Noe arca non fuerit, peribit regnante diluvio. . . . Quiquumque tecum non colligit, spargit: hoc est, qui Christi non est, Antichristi est."—Ibid. sect. 2. coll. 37. D. 38 A. B.]

[m] [" Si auctoritas quæritur, orbis major est urbe. Ubiquunque fuerit Episcopus, sive Romæ, sive Eugubii, sive Constantinopoli, sive Rhegii, sive Alexandriæ, sive Tanis, ejusdem meriti, ejusdem est et sacerdotii."—S.] Hieron. [Ep. xlvi. Vall. (al. lxxxv.)] ad [Evang. al.] Evagrium, [sect. 1. Op., tom. i. coll. 1076. D. 1077. A.]

[n] [S. Aug. contra duas Epistt. Pelag. lib. i. cap. i. Op., tom. x. col. 797. A.]

[o] [Ep. Conc. Milev. ad Innoc. Pap. Conc. tom. ii. col. 1545. A. et S. Aug. Ep. clxxvi. (al. xcii.) Op., tom. ii. col. 927. B.]

well known what the Council and Saint Augustine writ and did in that case [p].

The Council of Chalcedon's Epistle to Leo is answered, Respons. ad Apol. p. 170 [q], that, for all that term, yet in that Council a Canon was made by the *members*, which Leo, the *head*, took in very evil part [r], but could not amend it, nor by default of his consent make the Council unlawful.

Last, for the complaint of Julius in Socrates and Sozomen. It is true that no General Council (whose Canons only did bind the whole Church) was to be holden without the presence of the Bishops of the four chief Sees, by themselves or their deputies. But what is this more to Rome, than to Constantinople, Alexandria, or Antioch? All is but *Sacerdotalis lex* [s], *Canon Ecclesiasticus* [t], as they are there termed.

XXI. *Succession without interruption.* 3.

We plead there is no *interruption* in the *Succession of our Church.* And so this Article fights with a shadow.

XXII. *Distinction of Bishop and Priest.* 3.

Our Church doth hold, there is a *distinction* between *Bishop* and *Priest,* and that, *de jure divino.* So this toucheth not us.

XXIII. *Points of Opinion.* 7.

Neither are these to the point, or touch the outward *Face* of the Church; neither do we hold them.

1. We hold *Freewill* as Saint Augustine held it [u].

2. We hold *good works necessary to Salvation:* and that *faith without them saveth not* [x].

---

[p] [Vide Conc. Afric. capp. ci. cv. Conc. tom. ii. coll. 1670. seq. et 1674. seq.]

[q] [Resp. ad Apol. Card. Bell. pp. 229, 230. Oxon. 1851.]

[r] [See Resp. ad Apol. p. 230. notes p–u. Oxon. 1851.]

[s] [Εἶναι γὰρ νόμον ἱερατικὸν, ὡς ἄκυρα ἀποφαίνειν τὰ παρὰ γνώμην πραττόμενα τοῦ 'Ρωμαίων ἐπισκόπου.] — Sozom. [Hist. Eccl.] lib. iii. cap. 10. [p. 105.]

[t] [Καίτοι κανόνος ἐκκλησιαστικοῦ κελεύοντος, μὴ δεῖν παρὰ τὴν γνώμην τοῦ ἐπισκόπου 'Ρώμης τὰς ἐκκλησίας κανονίζειν.]—Socr. [Hist.Eccl.] lib. ii. cap. 8. [p. 85.]

[u] [" Revelavit autem nobis per scripturas suas sanctas, esse in homine liberum voluntatis arbitrium," &c.—S. Aug. de Grat. et lib. Arb. cap. ii. Op., tom. x. col. 1231. A. " Si igitur non est Dei gratia, quomodo salvat mundum ? et si non est liberum arbitrium, quomodo judicat mundum?"—S. Aug. Epist. ccxiv. (al. xlvi.) § 2. Op., tom. ii. col. 1200. A.]

[x] [" Vidit utique putare posse homines hoc ita dictum, quasi necessaria

3. We hold, that *no man is predestinate to do evil*^y.

4. We think it not safe, for any man, *peremptorily to presume himself predestinate*^z.

XXIV. *Service in Latin or in Greek.*

There is no authority cited for this, but we are referred to another place ^a.

XXV. *Certain Ceremonies of the Church at large.* 35.

1. *Distinction of Holy days*, 3. We hold it.

2. *Distinction of Habit between Clergy and laymen*, 4. We hold it.

3. *Distinction of vessels*, 2. Our Church holds it.

4. *Use of Shaving*, 4. The Church of Rome holds it not; witness the book *Pro Verbis Sacerdotum*. One place only is alleged, of Timothy that cut off Maximus *his beard* ^b; but if he had come to cut off Perron's, he would have had his scissors taken from him. Perron that is painted with a beard, can but evil speak for *shaving*. All the *censures* else come too late, without the compass of Saint Augustine's time, every one.

5. *Anointing at the giving of Orders*, 4, as a ceremony, might be used, but was not necessary so to be, as nothing pertaining to the essence of Orders. There is no ceremony, in Scripture, but *imposition of hands*. This was taken up

---

non sint opera bona credentibus, sed eis fides sola sufficiat; et rursus posse homines de bonis operibus extolli, velut ad ea facienda sibi ipsi sufficiant; mox itaque addidit, *Ipsius enim sumus figmentum, creati in Christo Jesu in operibus bonis.*"—S. Aug. de Grat. et lib. Arb. cap. viii. Op., tom. x. col. 1244. A. And compare S. Aug. Lib. de Quæst. lxxxiii. Quæst. lxxvi. " De eo quod Apostolus Jacobus dicit; *Vis autem scire, O homo inanis, quia fides sine operibus otiosa est?*"—S. Aug. Op., tom. vi. col. 122. B.]

^y [" Quisquis igitur ex prædestinatione Dei, veluti fatali necessitate homines in peccata compulsos cogi dicit in mortem, non est Catholicus. Nullo enim modo prædestinatio Dei iniquos facit, neque cujusquam omnino est causa peccati." — S. Prosp. Aquit. Resp. ad Capit. Gall. Sent. i. Op., p. 126. col. 1. Venet. 1744.]

^z [" Quis enim ex multitudine fidelium, quamdiu in hac mortalitate vivitur, in numero prædestinatorum se esse præsumat? Quia id occultari opus est in hoc loco, ubi sic cavenda est elatio, ut etiam per Satanæ angelum, ne extolleretur, tantus colaphizaretur Apostolus." — S. Aug. de Corrept. et Grat. cap. xiii. Op., tom. x. coll. 1311. D. 1312. A.]

^a [See Perron Repl. liv. vi. Prem. Instance. chap. i. p. 1073. It is referred to by Perron as liv. xii. See above, p. 11. note ⁿ.]

^b [Μάξιμόν τινα κεχειροτόνηκε Κυνικὸν, εὐθὺς αὐτοῦ τὰς Κυνικὰς ἀποκείρας τρίχας.]—Theod. Hist. [Eccl.] lib. v. cap. 8. [p. 202.]

by the Church's power, and by the same may be laid down again.

6. *Washing of the Priest's hands before his going to the Eucharist*, 1. A very high point, a thing which in civility might be used, but not made a *Tenoit* written in the forehead of the Church.

7. The *Pax*, 1. Only one place (of the Council of Laodicæa) is quoted for *Osculum Pacis*[c], which the Communicants used to give one to another, before the Sacrament. But for the Cardinal's *Pax*, it were strange to find it in the Council of Laodicæa, or many hundred years after.

8. *Pronouncing some part of the Service in a low voice not to be heard.* 1. It appears by the Council [d], that there were three prayers before the Communion. One of which was left, to every particular receiver, to pour out of his heart privately in silence to God; which kind of prayer, in some cases, our Church also useth. But this was no *low voice;* it was no voice at all; which maketh nothing to the Cardinal's purpose.

9. *Processions*, 1. We find *occursum et concursum*[e], a great concourse of people; but that makes not a *procession.* Yet *Processions* also our Church useth, in some cases [f].

10. *Torches at the burying of the dead*, 1. And great reason, seeing they were buried in the night, as appeareth by that which is added, *nocturnis cantionibus* [g].

11. *Painting images*, [5.] Eusebius saith nothing [h]. Paulinus saith, Saint Martin was painted only *in loco refectionis* [i],

---

[c] [See following note.]

[d] [Περὶ τοῦ δεῖν ἰδίᾳ πρῶτον μετὰ τὰς ὁμιλίας τῶν ἐπισκόπων, καὶ τῶν κατηχουμένων εὐχὴν ἐπιτελεῖσθαι· καὶ μετὰ τὸ ἐξελθεῖν τοὺς κατηχουμένους, τῶν ἐν μετανοίᾳ τὴν εὐχὴν γίνεσθαι· καὶ τούτων προσελθόντων ὑπὸ χεῖρα, καὶ ὑποχωρησάντων, οὕτως τῶν πιστῶν τὰς εὐχὰς γίνεσθαι τρεῖς· μίαν μὲν τὴν πρώτην διὰ σιωπῆς, τὴν δὲ δευτέραν καὶ τρίτην διὰ προσφωνήσεως πληροῦσθαι, εἶθ᾽ οὕτως τὴν εἰρήνην δίδοσθαι. Καὶ μετὰ τὸ πρεσβυτέρους δοῦναι τῷ ἐπισκόπῳ τὴν εἰρήνην, τότε τοὺς λαϊκοὺς τὴν εἰρήνην διδόναι· καὶ οὕτω τὴν ἁγίαν προσφορὰν ἐπιτελεῖσθαι.]—Concil. Laod. Can. xix. [Conc. tom. i. col. 1500. C. D.]

[e] [" Ad Aquas-Tibilitanas episcopo afferente Præjecto reliquias martyris gloriosissimi Stephani; ad ejus memoriam veniebat magnæ multitudinis concursus et occursus."—S.] Aug. de Civitate [Dei], lib. xxii. cap. viii. [sect. 10. Op., tom. vii. col. 1065. C.]

[f] [As *e.g.* in the Burial Service. See also numerous other instances in Hierurgia Anglicana.]

[g] ['Ο μὲν γὰρ (Κωνστάντιος) παραπέμπεται πανδήμοις εὐφημίαις τε καὶ πομπαῖς, καὶ τούτοις δὴ τοῖς ἡμετέροις σεμνοῖς, ᾠδαῖς παννυχίοις καὶ δᾳδουχίαις, αἷς Χριστιανοὶ τιμᾶν μετάστασιν εὐσεβῆ νομίζομεν.—S. Greg.] Nazian. [Orat. iv.] in Julian. Orat. ii. [Op., tom. i. p. 118. D.]

[h] Euseb. in Vita Constan. lib. iii. [cap. 49. p. 605.]

[i] [" Recte enim in loco refectionis humanæ Martinus pingitur, qui cœlestis hominis effigiem perfecta Christi imitatione portavit."]—Paulin. Ep. xii. [ad Severum, Bibl. Max. Patr. tom. vi. p. 191. C.] But the 'locus refectionis' was a Baptistery; for he says just be-

that is, in a dining-room. Basil's is a piece of oratory, for disabling his own discourse of Barlaam's martyrdom, he wisheth that some skilful painter would draw it more lively than he had or could set it forth: but when all is done, where it should be bestowed, he says never a word [k]. Nyssen speaks as well of *painting flowers and beasts*, as of the *martyrdom* of Theodorus [1]: *for the adjoining of the Church, all.* Prudentius speaks of no *painting, upon the Altar;* but, whatsoever it was, upon the ground it was, for he saith, *Stratus humi tumulo advolvebar*——[m]. To have a story painted, for memory's sake, we hold it not unlawful, but that it might well enough be done, if the Church found it not *inconvenient* for her Children [n].

12. *Crossing themselves.* [6.] For the sign of the *Cross* we are no enemies to it, we use it in *Baptism* [o].

fore: "Tu vero etiam baptisterium basilicis duabus interpositum condidisti;" and Paulinus remonstrates with him for introducing his portrait with that of St. Martin. "Sed in eo metuo, ne operibus tuis ... salebram offensionis immisceas, quod splendidos devotionis in Christo tuæ titulos nostris nominibus infuscas: et justis laboribus hanc iniquitatem inseris, ut locum sanctum etiam vultibus iniquorum polluas." By the "locus refectionis humanæ" he means the place of man's new birth; according to the literal meaning of the word, 'new making,' See his lines on the Font:—

"Hic reparandarum generator fons
    animarum
Vivum divino lumine flumen agit,
Sanctus in hunc cœlo descendit Spiritus amnem,
Cœlestique sacras fonte maritat
    aquas.
Concipit unda Deum; sanctamque
    liquoribus almis
Edit ab æterno semine progeniem.
Mira Dei pietas! Peccator mergitur undis,
    Mox eadem assurgit justificatus
    aqua.
Sic homo et occasu felici functus et
    ortu,
Terrenis moritur, perpetuis oritur.
Culpa perit, sed vita redit, vetus
    interit Adam,
Et novus æternis nascitur imperiis."
—Bib. Patr. Max. tom. vi. p.191. G.H.]
[k] ['Ανάστητέ μοι νῦν, ὦ λαμπροὶ τῶν ἀθλητικῶν κατορθωμάτων ζωγράφοι· τὴν τοῦ στρατηγοῦ κολοβωθεῖσαν εἰκόνα ταῖς ὑμετέραις μεγαλύνατε τέχναις. Ἀμαυρότερον παρ' ἐμοῦ τὸν στεφανίτην γραφέντα τοῖς τῆς ὑμετέρας σοφίας περιλάμψατε χρώμασιν, κ.τ.ἑ.—S.] Basil. [Hom. xvii.] in Barlaam [Martyr., cap. 3. Op., tom. ii. p. 141. B.]

[1] [Οἶκον ἐμβλέπων ὡς Θεοῦ ναὸν ἐξησκημένον λαμπρῶς τῷ μεγέθει τῆς οἰκοδομῆς, καὶ τῷ τῆς ἐπικοσμήσεως κάλλει, ἔνθα καὶ τέκτων εἰς ζῴων φαντασίαν τὸ ξύλον ἐμόρφωσεν, καὶ λιθοξόος εἰς ἀργύρου λειότητα τὰς πλάκας ἀπέξεσεν. ἐπέχρωσε δὲ καὶ ζωγράφος τὰ ἄνθη τῆς τέχνης ἐν εἰκόνι διαγραψάμενος, τὰς ἀριστείας τοῦ μάρτυρος, τὰς ἐνστάσεις, τὰς ἀλγηδόνας, τὰς θηριώδεις τῶν τυράννων μορφὰς, τὰς ἐπηρείας, τὴν φλογυτρόφον ἐκείνην κάμινον, τὴν μακαριωτάτην τελείωσιν τοῦ ἀθλητοῦ, τοῦ ἀγωνοθέτου Χριστοῦ τῆς ἀνθρωπίνης μορφῆς τὸ ἐκτύπωμα, πάντα ἡμῖν ὡς ἐν βιβλίῳ τινὶ γλωττοφόρῳ διὰ γραμμάτων τεχνουργησάμενος.—S. Greg.] Nyssen. in S. Theodor. [Op., tom. iii. p. 578. C.D. The word "flowers" seems to be used metaphorically.]

[m] ["Stratus humi tumulo advolvebar, quem sacer ornat
    Martyr, dicato Cassianus corpore."]
—Prud. [Περὶ Στεφ. Hymn. ix.] in S. Cassian. [Gall. Bib. Pat. tom. viii. p. 452. col. 1. E.]

[n] [See what is said on this point in the second part of the Homily against Peril of Idolatry.]

[o] [See S. Aug. de Symbol. Serm. ad Catech. cap. i. Op., tom. vi. col. 930. B.]

Tertullian's authority is too rank[p], for no Papist, now, makes a *Cross* every time he *puts on his shoes,* nor *at every step he goes,* nor *upon his stool* every time he sits down.

In the time of persecution, and after, in the time of peace, so long as the Christians dwelt mingled with the heathen, they showed plainly by making and using the Cross, that they were not ashamed of that sign, wherewith the Heathen men did use to deride them [q].

In Hilarion's life[r], there is no *blessing of the people with it.*

That not the *Sign of the Cross*[s], but the faith of him that made it, might scatter enchantments, it might well be: but, the faith of working miracles being gone, that effect now ceasing, it is to small purpose to keep the sign on foot.

This concerneth not any now: there is no *Cross* at *Hierusalem*, in the *face of the Church, to be shown on Good Friday.* And so Paulinus[t] might have been spared.

13. For *burning of incense,* 2. The place of Chrysostom is cited amiss[u]. And Evagrius[v] is out of the compass of Saint Augustine's time, which is the time in question. And yet he is too rank too: for, his *incense* was a *Sacrifice*, which the Cardinal will by no means admit of, but have it only a bare ceremony.

14. There were *Lights,* there was *Incense* used by the Primitive Church, in their service. Not for any mystical

---

[p] ["Ad omnem progressum atque promotum, ad omnem aditum et exitum, ad vestitum, ad calciatum, ad lavacra, ad mensas, ad lumina, ad cubilia, ad sedilia, quacunque nos conversatio exercet, frontem signaculo crucis terimus."—Tert.] de Coron. Mil. cap. iii. [Op., p. 102. A. B.]

[q] [See Resp. ad Apol. pp. 270. 271. Oxon. 1851.]

[r] [The following miracle is recorded of St. Hilar. by St. Jerome. (Is this the passage referred to by Perron?)
"Qui quum tria crucis signa pinxisset in sabulo, manusque contra tenderet, incredibile dictu est in quantam altitudinem intumescens mare ante eum steterit; ac diu fremens, et quasi ad obicem indignans, paulatim in semetipsum relapsum est." — S.] Hieron. in Vita ejusd. [sect. 40. Op., tom. ii. col. 36. C.]

[s] [Εἰ γὰρ τοῦ σταυροῦ γενομένου, πᾶσα μὲν εἰδωλολατρεία καθῃρέθη, πᾶσα δὲ δαιμόνων φαντασία τῷ σημείῳ τούτῳ ἀπελαύνεται, καὶ μόνος ὁ Χριστὸς προσκυνεῖται ... πῶς ... ἔτι ἀνθρώπινόν ἐστιν ἐπινοεῖν τὸ πρᾶγμα, καὶ οὐ μᾶλλον ὁμολογεῖν Θεοῦ Λόγον καὶ Σωτῆρα εἶναι τοῦ παντὸς τὸν ἐπὶ τοῦ σταυροῦ ἀναβάντα.—S.] Athanas. con. idola, [al. Cont. Gentes, sect. 1. Op., tom. i. p. 2. A.B.]

[t] ["Quam Episcopus urbis ejus, quotannis cum Pascha Domini agitur, adorandum populo, princeps ipse venerantium proponit."—S.] Paul. Ep. xi. [Bibl. Max. Pat. tom. vi. p. 190. F.]

[u] [See S. Chrysost. Hom. lxxxviii. (al. lxxxix.) in S. Matth. Op , tom. ii. p. 544.]

[v] [Θυμιατήριον ἐξῃτήσατο, καὶ πάντα τὸν χόρον ἐν ᾧ καθειστήκεισαν ἐπιθυμιάσας. ἐπὶ γῆς ἑαυτὸν ῥίπτει, προσευχαῖς τε καὶ λιταῖς τὸν Θεὸν ἱλεούμενος. — Evagr. Hist. Eccl.] lib. iv. cap. 7. [p. 389.]

meaning, but (as it is thought) for this cause: that where the Christians in time of persecution had their meetings most commonly *in cryptis,* in caves and grots under-ground, places dark and so needing *light,* and dampish and so needing good *savours,* they were enforced to provide *lights*[x] against the one, and *incense* against the other. After, when peace came, though they had churches then above-ground, with light and air enough, yet retained they both the *lights* and the *incense,* to show themselves to be the sons and successors of those ancient Christians which in former times had used them, (though upon other occasion,) showing their communion in the former faith, by the communion of the former usages. Whereto the after ages devised meanings and significations of their own, which from the beginning were not so.

19 XXVI. *Of the Church's visibleness, incorruptness, perpetuity of succession, &c.* 14.

This is a *qui tenoit,* matter of opinion, and not pertaining to the *Face* of *the Church.* For whether the *Church* be *visible,* whether always *incorrupt in doctrine and sacraments, &c.* are points doctrinal; there is no *traicts de visage,* or external form of the Church to be noted in them: and there is not any of them but we shall willingly subscribe unto.

---

20 *A Brief of the Twenty-six Heads in the Chapter.*

THERE are in the *Chapter* twenty-six *Heads,* every one beginning with *Une Eglise qui.*

Of these twenty-six, two have no authority quoted for them, but we are put off to another place.

Those two are, the fourth, of the *Communion under one kind.*

The twenty-fourth, of the *Church Service in Greek or Latin only.*

Of the twenty-four left, eight are dogmatical; matters of opinion; and pertain not to the outward practice or face of the Church.

---

[x] ["Cereos autem non clara luce accendimus, sicut frustra calumniaris; sed ut noctis tenebras hoc solatio temperemus, et vigilemus ad lumen, ne cæci tecum dormiamus in tenebris."— S. Hier. contra Vigil. sect. 8. Op., tom. ii. col. 394. A. B.]

These eight are the
- 1. Of believing *Christ's body to be* sub speciebus.   1.
- 8. Of holding *Traditions equal to the Scriptures.*   1.
- 13. ... *Marriage after a vow unlawful.*   4.
- 16. ... *Five Sacraments of the seven.*   9.
- 18. ... *Baptism to be necessary.*   3.
- 21. ... *Succession without interruption.*   3.
- 23. ... *Free-will: Good works necessary, &c.*   7.
- 26. ... *The Church visible, Succession of doctrine, no Salvation out of it.*   14.

Of which eight, we differ not in five of them.   21

We hold it *After a lawful vow unlawful to marry.*
We hold *Baptism to be necessary.*
.. *Succession not to be interrupted.*
.. *That there is Free-will: that good works are necessary, &c.*
.. *That the Church is visible, &c.*

The other three are answered.
Of *Christ's body* sub speciebus.
.. *Traditions.*
.. *The five Sacraments of the seven.*

Of the sixteen left, which are matter of outward practice.
In six we differ not.
- 2. *We receive the Sacrament with due reverence.*   4.
- 5. *We grant the Eucharist a Sacrifice.*   6.
- 6. *We are not against Altars, we have them.*   2.
- 10. *We observe Lent.*   3.
- 11. *We fast Fridays and Saturdays, yet not Christmas Day if it fall on them.*   1.
- 22. *We maintain the difference between a Bishop and a Priest.*   3.

And in some points of the other, we agree.
- 7. As in holding *Feasts, in memory of the Saints and Martyrs.*   2.
- 17. ... *The Cross in Baptism.*   2.
- 25. ... *The Feasts of Christ's Birth, &c.*   3.   22
  Distinction of Habit between Priests and Laymen.   4.
  Of Vessels holy from common.   2.

Of the ten left, wherein we vary.

7.	...	*Worship of Martyrs and their Relics.*	19.
12.	...	*The Marriage of Priests.*	4.
20.	...	*Five inferior Orders.*	10.

Matter of Ceremonies.

17.	⎧ Either of *Baptism.*		10.	(6.)
15.	⎨ To which we refer *Exorcisms.*			1.
25.	⎩ Or at large.		35.	(13.)
14.	To which we refer *Mixture of water with the wine.*			2.
19.	...	*Holy water.*		3.

Two remain.

3.	...	*The Reservation of the Eucharist.*	7.
9.	...	*Prayer for the dead.*	6.

23   *A Brief of the* 158 *places quoted in the Chapter.*

Of the places quoted, in number 158,
- 5 we find not.
- 8 are twice cited, or with *ut supra.*
- 14 are after St. Augustine's time.
- 10 have been answered of late. *Respon. ad Apolog.*
- 39 are spent in points dogmatical, five of which may be agreed.
- 30 in points we differ not in, besides those five.
- 39 in matter of Ceremonies.
- 13 in the points of *Reservation* of the *Eucharist,* and *Prayer for the dead.*

158

AN ANSWER
TO THE XX. CHAP-
TER OF THE FIFTH

Booke of CARDINALL PERRON's
Reply, written in French, to KING IAMES-
his Anſwer written by M^r. CA-
SAVBON to the CARDINALL
in Latine.

An Answer to the XX. Chapter of the Fifth Book of Cardinal Perron's Reply.

[The heading of Card. Perron's Chapter is, " Des difficultez apportées par Monsieur d'Ely, contre les passages des Peres, touchant l'invocation des Saincts."—Perron, Repl. p. 1010.]

THERE are seven places of Cardinal Bellarmine's answered by the Bishop of Ely[a]. To five of which, Cardinal Perron makes not any reply at all; nor once toucheth any of them. But deals only with the rest, besides those seven: which are such, as he hath himself likewise alleged: (as, indeed, they be the best of his allegations.)

["Car je ne veux point toucher icy les lieux qu'il accuse, comme citez a faux, d'autant que cela ne touche pas un de ceux que j'ay employez; seulement diray-je, que des deux allegations qu'il accuse de faux, la faute s'en doit remettre sur les Traducteurs, ou Imprimeurs, & non sur les allegateurs, qui s'estants fiez, pour le regard d'Eusebe, sur l'edition Latine tournée par Trapezunce, homme Grec, & possible fourny d'un autre exemplaire Grec que Robert Estienne, & sur la revision de Gryneus, Ministre de Basle, qu'il a conferée avec le manuscrit Grec de Basle, & l'a fait imprimée avec ceste mesme lecture à Basle; Et pour le regard de Sainct Chrysostome, sur l'impression de Basle."—Card. Perron, Repl.] p. 1012.

Only, to two of those seven of Cardinal Bellarmine's allegations, which are manifestly false, he is fain to use a poor defence: 1. *That it might be, Bellarmine had not Eusebius, or Chrysostom, in Greek;* 2. *That* he *did rely himself, upon the Latin translation, of the Basil edition revised by Grynæus:* which defence, how seely[1] it is, let the world judge.   [1 silly.]

The Place of Chrysostom.

["Il dit donc, pour le regard du passage de sainct Chrysostome, que ceste Homilie au peuple d'Antioche, a esté suspecte dés il y a long temps à Erasme, de n'estre point de sainct Chrysostome. Et que toutes les

---

[a] [See Andrewes's Resp. ad Apol. pp. 38—42, Lond. 1610; pp. 48—55, Oxon. 1851.]

soixante & tant d'Homilies, qui portent le tiltre d'Homilies au peuple d'Antioche, n'ont pas esté faittes au peuple d'Antioche, voire non pas mesme vingt-six, entre lesquelles celle-là n'est point."—Card. Perron, Repl., p. 1013.]

Cardinal Bellarmine alleged the sixty-sixth Homily *ad Populum Antiochenum* [b].

The Bishop. It is certain, Chrysostom made but twenty-two Homilies (at the most) *ad Populum Antiochenum.* Therefore, to allege the sixty-six Homilies, was somewhat wide.

Since which, Bellarmine himself confesseth as much. These are his words [c]: *In quinto Tomo omnia fere sunt certa, et indubitata,* exceptis Homiliis ad Populum Antiochenum, *ex quibus xxi. tantum reperiri dicuntur in Manuscriptis* [leg. *Manuscriptæ*] *in antiquis Bibliothecis.*

So Possevine [d], who allegeth Fronto Ducæus [e]; and he holdeth, there are but twenty-one, and that all the rest are but *Centones,* or *fragmenta consarcinata,* at the best.

Yea Perron himself confesseth as much: that all, besides the twenty-two, *ne sont tissuës que de pieces . . recueillies des autres homilies de cest autheur* [f].

So is it also set down in the last edition of all at Paris.

And even in the old edition, of Frobenius, anno 1517, and of Cratander, anno 1521, to sever those twenty-one from the rest that followed, and to show, that they were at an end, and that a new sort of Homilies began after the twenty-one, there is a new title, as an Introduction to the rest.

["Mais veut-on voir toutes les difficultez levées conjoinctement? Qu'on lise la vingt-sixiéme Homilie de Sainct Chrysostome, sur la seconde Epistre aux Corinthiens, & on y trouvera ces mesmes paroles expresses & formelles, imprimées, non seulement en l'edition Grecque de Veronne, mais aussi en celle de Heidelberg, & conservées en toutes les editions Grecques, manuscrittes des Bibliotheques d'Orient & d'Occident; comme les autres Homilies, qu'on a pensé avoir esté prononcées au peuple d'Antioche,

---

[b] ["Nam et ipse qui purpuram indutus est, accedit ista complexurus sepulcra, et fastu deposito stat Sanctis supplicaturus, ut pro se apud Deum intercedant."—S. Chrysos. Hom. lxvi. ad Pop. Antioch., quoted by Bellarm. Apol. pro Resp. cap. i. Op., tom. vii. col. 712. D.]

[c] Bellar. de Scriptor. Eccl. p. 178. [Op., tom. vii. col. 79. B.]

[d] [See Ant. Possevini Apparat. Sacr. sub voc. Joann. Chrysost. tom. ii. p. 155. Venet. 1606.]

[e] [See S. Joan. Chrysost. Op. by Fronto Ducæus, tom. i. p. 276; and the notes of Fronto Ducæus at the end of the same vol., p. 61. Paris, 1621.]

[f] [Perron, Repl. p. 1014.]

depuis la vingt & deuxiéme, jusques à la LXXX. & derniere, ne sont tissuës que des pieces rapportées & recueillies des autres Homelies de cest Autheur."—Card. Perron, Repl.] p. 1014.

But Cardinal Perron hath since found it, in the twenty-sixth Hom. on the second to the Corinthians; and sets it down, (Greek and all [g].)

The Bishop. But the Cardinal knoweth well, and was told by the Bishop; Erasmus smelt [h], that those Homilies, upon the second to the Corinthians, were not, as they should be : which made him, when he came to the seventh Homily [i], that he would translate no further.

Which made him also, in his preface before his Latin translation of Basil de Spiritu Sancto ad Amphilochium, (a book likewise corrupted,) to say : *Quædam rursus ejusmodi, ut indole referant parentem suum, viz. eum, qui doctissimis Athanasii libellis de Spiritu Sancto suas loquaces sed elumbes attexuit nænias ; quique* in Epistola [*leg.* Epistolam] ad Corinthios posteriore [*leg.* posteriorem], *et in Actis Apostolorum,* [leg. *Apostolorum Acta,*] Chrysostomus haberi studuit. *Porro, sceleratissimum contaminandi genus est, egregiorum virorum clarissimis purpuris suos pannos intertexere : aut (ut melius dicam) generosa illorum vina suis vasis* [leg. *vapis* (i. e. *vappis*)] *corrumpere*[k].

Cardinal Perron saith, that these words are to be found, in all editions, and all *Libraries, both of the East, and of the West.*

The Bishop. It should seem the Cardinal talks of more editions than he hath seen. For in the Latin edition by Stelsius at Antwerp, 1556, set forth by Joannes Afinius, there is no such matter to be found. And Afinius directly sets it down, in the margin, that the *Verona copy* did *there vary from his :* so that all copies then had it not.

---

[g] [The passage is, Καὶ γὰρ αὐτὸς ὁ τὴν ἁλουργίδα περικείμενος ἀπέρχεται τὰ σήματα ἐκεῖνα περιπτυξόμενος, καὶ τὸν τῦφον ἀποθέμενος ἕστηκε δεόμενος τῶν ἁγίων, ὥστε αὐτοῦ προστῆναι παρὰ τῷ Θεῷ. — Op., tom. iii. p. 687. S. Chrysost. in S. Pauli Epist. tom. iii. fol. 81. b. Veronæ, 1529; and tom. iii. p. 687. Edit. Sav. The Verona Edition rested on the authority of only one MS. But other MSS. have since been found, containing these Homilies. See Mr. Field's Preface to the Homilies, on the Epist. to Rom. and 2 Corinth.]

[h] [See Erasmus's Epistle to Tonstal, Ep. MXCII. Op., tom. iii. col 1264.]

[i] [See Erasmi Op., tom. viii. col. 266.]

[k] [Des. Erasmi Epist. Dedic. ad init. S. Basil. de Spir. Sancto. Basil. 1532. and Erasmi Op., tom. viii. coll. 491, 492.]

1. There being then nothing near sixty-six Homilies ad Pop. Antiochenum; and so no such place there to be found: 2. And, this place new found, in the second to the Corinthians, smelling so rank in Erasmus's nose: when we could not find it in them, we found it by good hap, in Garetius, *De Sanctorum Invocatione*, page 96, cited under the name of Theodorus Daphnopatus[1]: and so, we could take him, and no other, to be the father of it.

> ["Quant à Garetius, il ne nous apprend point, que ceste Homilie soit de Theodorus Daphnopathus, qu'il appelle ainsi par corruption; Car Cedrenus a nous apprend, que son nom estoit Theodorus Daphnopates; ains allegue disertement ceste Homilie, sous le tiltre d'Homilie soixante & sixiesme de Sainct Chrysostome au peuple d'Antioche; Et celle qu'il cite de Theodorus Daphnopathus, ou pour mieux dire, Daphnopates, il le cite sous le tiltre d'Homilie des loüanges de Sainct Paul, & adjouste que ses paroles sont prises par ce Theodore de Sainct Chrysostome, tant s'en faut qu'il revoque en doute, que l'Homilie soixante & sixiesme, au peuple d'Antioche, de laquelle ce Theodore Daphnopates, qui estoit un Pedant & Maistre d'Eschole . . . avoit pris ces parolles, fust vrayement de Sainct Chrysostome."—Card. Perron, Repl. p. 1013.]

Cardinal Perron here falls upon petty points: 1. In quarrelling Garetius, who styles him Daphnopatus; for that it should be Daphnopates.

The Bishop. Yet (by the Cardinal's leave) Daphnopatus is more agreeable to the analogy of the Greek idiom, than the other. 2. It will not easily be proved, that Daphnopates Theodorus, in Cedrenus, is the same that Garetius doth allege: but, that they may be two several men. For Cedrenus (who ended his story in the beginning of Isacius Comnenus' reign, about 1060) citeth many authors; and among them, Daphnopates is the very first[m], as a writer of more antiquity than the rest. Whereas Daphnopatus is, by Garetius, ranked in order immediately before Hildebert, Bishop of Tours[n], who lived anno 1120, which is 60 years after Cedrenus's time, and so seemeth to be later than Cedrenus himself was.

Cardinal Perron affirmeth Daphnopates to have been a *Pedant*.

---

[1] [See Garetius de Invoc. Sanct. sub nomine "Theodorus Daphnopatus," fol. 96. a. Gandavi. 1570. Where it is added in the margin, "Oratione de laudibus S. Pauli Apostoli ex Chrysostom. sunt hæc desumpta." But in fol. 56. b, the words are cited by Garetius from Hom. lxxvi. ad Pop. Antioch.]

[m] [Vide Georg. Cedren. Hist. Comp. p. 1. Basil. 1566.]

[n] [Garetius, fol. 96.]

The Bishop. How he will prove that, no man knows. If it be but for the word μάγιστρος, it is well known μάγιστρος was a higher style than *magister* is[o]. But Cedrenus cites him as an historiographer, or writer of lives: as there is the life of Theodorus Studita, written by him in Greek, in the Catalogue of Auspurg Library[p].

[" Gesnerus cotte un certain maistre Theodore, qui avoit fait trente six Eclogues, ou recueils des Homilies de sainct Chrysostome. Au moyen dequoy, si ce Pedant Grec Theodore, qui a fait ces recueils des Homelies de sainct Chrysostome, est ce mesme Theodorus Daphnopates, qui cite Garetius, tant s'en faut que de là on puisse inferer, que ce passage ne soit point de sainct Chrysostome, qu'au contraire, c'est un argument pour prouver qu'il est de sainct Chrysostome, puis qu'il se trouve dans le compilateur de sainct Chrysostome."—Card. Perron, Repl. p. 1013.]

Cardinal Perron hath found in Gesner[q] one Theodorus, that made collections out of Chrysostom.

Now, if that Theodorus should happen to prove this Daphnopatus, (for all goes by hap,) then, the Cardinal thinks, he hath said somewhat. But if he fall out to be some other, (as there is no proof he is the same; at leastwise, he makes no proof,) then what shall become of the Cardinal and of his poor conjecture?

But (here) if this Theodorus would write an oration, in the praise of St. Paul, and take it out of Chrysostom, what need he go to the Second of the Corinthians, to furnish himself thence, when Saint Chrysostom had written nine several Homilies in the praise of Saint Paul (yet extant), from whence, by all likelihood, he might better have made his collection?

[" Car quant à ce que Monsieur d'Ely adjouste, que ses paroles de Sainct Chrysostome racontent un faict, & non un precepte ; C'est un faict qui presuppose un droict, & encore un droict de foy, asçavoir, que les Saincts morts estoient protecteurs des Empereurs de la terre, recevoient leurs prieres, les presentoient à Dieu, & les accompagnoient de leurs intercessions envers luy."—Card. Perron, Repl.] p. 1015.

And yet, *posito, sed non concesso,* that these words were Chrysostom's indeed : they are but the relation of an act proceeding from the Emperor's own private devotion, which reacheth not home: because his Majesty denies not, but

[o] [See Du Cange, Glossar. ad Script. med. et inf. Græcit.ad voc. Μάγιστρος.]
[p] [See Catalog. Græc. Codd., qui sunt in Bibliotheca Reip. August. Vindel., num. lxvi. 6. p. 38. Aug. Vindel. 1595.]
[q] [" Magistri Theodori Eclogæ ex diversis sermonibus Chrysostomi." Conr. Gesn. Bibl. fol. 611. A. Tigur. 1545.]

that there might be some example found; but that there was no rule of the Church for it. For, what one or two shall do, carried away with their own devout affection, is not straightway a rule of the Church.

Nor yet, granting the holy Apostles to be intercessors for us, will their intercession for us infer our invocation of them; as issue was joined with Cardinal Bellarmine, and now is with him.

The Place of Nazianzen [r].

["Il dit en second lieu, que la foy de l'oraison de sainct Gregoire de Nazianze, en la loüange de sainct Cyprian, n'est pas assez claire, d'autant qu'il est incertain, si ce sainct Cyprian-là est le sainct Cyprian de Carthage, ou le sainct Cyprian d'Antioche, ou l'un & l'autre, ou ny l'un, ny l'autre; comme s'il estoit question là de la foy historique, en laquelle saincte Gregoire de Nazianze a peu confondre, à cause de la similitude des noms, quelque chose de l'histoire de sainct Cyprian d'Antioche, avec celle de sainct Cyprian de Carthage."— Card. Perron, Repl.] p. 1015.

The Bishop is content to refer it to any indifferent reader, whether it be credible that Nazianzen (one of so great learning, judgment, and memory) could be so grossly mistaken as to commit these errors following;—Saint Cyprian being, 1. a Bishop, 2. at Carthage, 3. in Africa, 4. never in his life any sorcerer, but always of honest profession, 5. converted by Cæcilius, 6. martyred under Valerian and Gallien, 7. and that near unto Carthage, 8. there beheaded, 9. and buried *in Area Candidi Procuratoris;* 10. his Feast, the fourteenth of September.

The other Cyprian, of the same name, being a, 1. Deacon, 2. at Antioch, 3. in Asia, under Anthimus, (Bishop there) 4. a professed sorcerer, at first; 5. in love with a maid, and converted by her; 6. after martyred under Diocletian; 7. at Nicomedia, in Asia, by the river Gallus, 8. and there fried to death; 9. buried with Ruffina; 10. his day being the second of October [s]: whether, I say, he could be so strangely mistaken, as that he should take one of these for the other, and make a mingle-mangle of them both; making Saint Cyprian, Bishop of Carthage, a sorcerer, which he never was;

---

[r] [Σὺ δὲ ἡμᾶς ἐποπτεύοις ἄνωθεν ἵλεως, καὶ τὸν ἡμέτερον διεξάγοις λόγον καὶ βίον, καὶ τὸ ἱερὸν τοῦτο ποίμνιον ποιμαίνοις.—S. Greg. Naz. Orat. xviii. in laud. S. Cyprian. Op., tom. i. p. 286. B.]

[s] [See Acta Sanctorum, tom. i. Mens. Maii. p. xlv.]

and in love with a maid at Antioch, where he never was; and in all this to be mistaken. Saint Cyprian, the Bishop, having yearly a public holiday to keep the remembrance of him, and this being within less than 100 years of his very martyrdom. Whether, I say, it can seem probable to any man, *tam fœdo errore prolapsum esse* (to use Billius's own words [t]), that he was so foully overseen, as in a set oration, upon a set feast, within so short a time, not to be able to distinguish one of these from the other; but to ascribe that unto Saint Cyprian, Bishop of Carthage, in Africa, that (if it were at all) was done by Cyprian, the Deacon of Antioch, in Asia. That story of Saint Cyprian being clear, and of undoubted credit; this other not so. For, where it is said in this oration that Cyprian himself was in love with the maid, the legend saith that it was one Aglaides that was in love with her, who used Cyprian's sorcery as a means to win her. And the legend sets down his martyrdom doubtfully, *either under* Decius, or under Claudius (Decius *his successor*); whereas Claudius was not his successor, there being at the least three years between them. For his part, the Bishop inclineth to believe the oration to be none of Nazianzen's, rather than he would lay upon Nazianzen the imputation of this so senseless an error.

[" Car quant à ce que Monsieur d'Ely maintient, que ceste histoire-là est le faict d'une fille, & non le statut de l'Eglise, & que ce n'est pas des actions des filles qu'il faut prescire la reigle de la Foy, nous répondons, qu'aussi n'est-ce pas du faict d'une fille, mais de l'usage universel de l'Eglise, du temps des quatre premiers Conciles."—Card. Perron, Repl.] p. 1016.

But yet, say it were Nazianzen's own report [u]; it being but a private act, out of the devout affection in a maid, it cannot be drawn to a rule of faith. Neither is it proposed as any example to be followed, but only by way of bare narration, what she did. And this answer may stand till the Cardinal can show it to have been the *general use* of *the universal Church during the time of the four first Councils.*

[t] [See Billius's note on this oration. S. Greg. Naz. Op., tom. ii. col. 687. B.]
[u] [Ταῦτα καὶ πλείω τούτων ἐπιφημίζουσα, καὶ τὴν παρθένον Μαρίαν ἱκετεύουσα βοηθῆσαι παρθένῳ κινδυνευούσῃ, τὸ τῆς νηστείας καὶ χαμευνίας προβάλλεται φάρμακον.—S. Greg. Naz. Orat. xviii. in laud. S. Cypr. Op., tom. i. p. 279. D.]

The Place of Epiphanius [v].

["Il n'y a rien de commune entre le faict de sainte Iustine, que sainct Gregoire de Nazianze celebre ... & le faict des Prestresses des Collyridiens que reprend S. Epiphane, car S. Epiphane ne censure nulle part les Collyridiens, pour aucune priere qu'ils fissent à la Vierge, d'interceder envers Dieu pour eux, mais pource qu'ils offroient des sacrifices faits de toutes de fleur de farine à la Vierge, & les luy effroient en qualité de vrais sacrifices, & culte de Latrie, à l'imitation de ceux dont parle Hieremie ... Contre ceste heresie donc sainct Epiphane crie, & monstre ... que le sacrifice qui est le culte de Latrie, le culte souverain, le culte qui infere Deïte en celuy à qui il est offert, ne pouvoit estre offert qu'à Dieu seul."— Card. Perron, Repl.] pp. 1016, 1017.

The Bishop. That fact of Nazianzen's maid, and that of the Collyridians, which Epiphanius condemneth, are of the same kind. For, whether is greater, to offer a cake, or to offer a prayer, in the Virgin's name? And, so again, to offer a cake, or to offer a wax candle, (which is yearly done in the Church of Rome,) what odds is between these two?

But, in a cold chance doth Cardinal Perron insert the mention of the forty-fourth of Jeremiah, and the name of the Queen of Heaven there [x]. For he knoweth in what Church there are yearly offered matters of as great moment as cakes, expressly in the Prophet's words, and the name of *Regina cœli*.

Invocation (offering a prayer) is *culte de latrie, culte Soveraine, culte qui infere Deïte,* no less than to offer a cake. Epiphanius saith plainly, that this cake they offered, *either as adoring the Virgin Mary, to her, or for her;* both which alike he condemneth. *The adoring* it is that makes the heresy; and that Epiphanius finds fault with, and bendeth all his force against that point of *adoring,* no less than in six several places, *Mariam nemo adoret* [y]. Now, *adoration* being con-

---

[v] [Χλεύης γάρ ἐστι τὸ πᾶν, καὶ γραῶν ὁ μῦθος, ὡς εἰπεῖν, τῆς αἱρέσεως τὸ διήγημα· ποία δέ τις γραφὴ διηγήσατο περὶ τούτου; ποῖος Προφητῶν ἐπέτρεψεν ἄνθρωπον προσκυνεῖσθαι, οὐ μὴν γυναῖκα λέγειν; ἐξαίρετον μὲν γάρ ἐστι τὸ σκεῦος, ἀλλὰ γυνὴ, καὶ οὐδὲν τὴν φύσιν παρηλλαγμένη, τὴν δὲ γνώμην, καὶ τὴν αἴσθησιν ἐν τιμῇ τετιμημένη.—S. Epiph. Hær. lxxix. (Collyrid.) cap. v. Op., tom. i. p. 1062. A. Referred to by Bishop Andrewes, Resp. ad Apol. p. 42. Lond. 1610; p. 54. note ꝗ. Oxon. 1851.]

[x] [S. Epiphanius quotes this very passage in condemnation of the Collyridians. Φιμούσθωσαν ὑπὸ Ἱερεμίου αἱ τοιαῦται γυναῖκες, καὶ μὴ θορυβείτωσαν τὴν οἰκουμένην. μὴ λεγέτωσαν, Τιμῶμεν τὴν βασίλισσαν τοῦ οὐρανοῦ.—S. Epiph. Hær. lxxix. (Collyrid.) cap. viii. Op., tom. i. p. 1065. B. C.]

[y] [Ναὶ μὴν ἅγιον ἦν τὸ σῶμα τῆς Μαρίας· οὐ μὴν Θεός. ναὶ δὴ παρθένος ἦν ἡ Παρθένος, καὶ τετιμημένη, ἀλλ' οὐκ εἰς προσκύνησιν ἡμῖν δοθεῖσα.—S. Epiph. Hær. lxxix. (Collyrid.) cap. iv. Op., tom. i. p. 1061. C. D. Ποῖος προφητῶν ἐπέτρεψεν ἄνθρωπον προσκυνεῖσθαι, οὐ

demned, it cannot be conceived that adoring her, and offering to her, they prayed not also to her, and required of her somewhat again. So that Nazianzen's Maid praying, and the Collyridians' adoring, differ not so much as the Cardinal gladly would have them to seem.

The Place of Nazianzen again [z].

["Et comme s'il n'avoit pas toujours esté aussi bien licite à sainct Gregoire de Nazianze de faire mention de l'Ache, qui estoit une des herbes dont on courronnoit ceux qui disputoient, le prix aux jeux de la Grece, appellez Nemées; comme à S. Paul d'appeller la retribution, *Couronne de Justice*."—Card. Perron, Repl.] pp. 1017, 1018.

For the *apples, and olives*, and *smallage*, whereof that Oration of Nazianzen's speaks to Cyprian, then dead, rather in trifling than in serious manner, Cardinal Perron is wonderfully mistaken in telling us (and that in good earnest) that, by a *garden of pleasures, wherein are apples*, is meant the joys of Heaven; and citing a great number of Scriptures to that purpose. For the Oration can mean no such matter, seeing it calls his *apples, Delphicas nugas*, which, I trust, the Cardinal will not apply to the joys and felicity of Heaven. And so his answer to this point is little better itself than *Delphicæ nugæ* indeed.

The Place of Cyril Hierosolymitanus [a].

["Car ce n'est pas de la Bibliotheque d'Ausbourg qui le tire, laquelle il n'a point veuë, mais de Gesnerus, Ministre de Zurich. ... Combien que quand ces Catecheses seroient de Iean Evesque de Hierusalem, l'authorité n'en seroit pas gueres moindre pour le regard de l'antiquité, que celle de sainct

μὴν γυναῖκα λέγειν ... εἰ γὰρ 'Αγγέλους προσκυνεῖσθαι οὐ θέλει, πόσῳ μᾶλλον τὴν ἀπὸ "Αννης γεγεννημένῃ, τῇ ἐκ τοῦ 'Ιωακεὶμ τῇ "Αννῃ δεδωρημένην.—Ibid. cap. v. p. 1062. A. C. 'Εν τιμῇ ἔστω Μαρία, ὁ δὲ Πατὴρ, καὶ Υἱὸς, καὶ "Αγιον Πνεῦμα προσκυνείσθω, τὴν Μαρίαν μηδεὶς προσκυνείτω. Καὶ εἰ καλλίστη ἡ Μαρία, καὶ ἁγία, καὶ τετιμημένη, ἀλλ' οὐκ εἰς τὸ προσκυνεῖσθαι.—Ibid. cap. vii. pp. 1064. D. 1065. B. "Ητοι γὰρ ὡς αὐτὴν προσκυνοῦντες τὴν Μαρίαν, αὐτῇ προσφέρουσι τὴν κολλυρίδα αἱ ἀργαὶ αὗται γυναῖκες· ἤτοι ὑπὲρ αὐτῆς προσφέρειν ἐπιχειροῦσι τὴν προειρημένην ταύτην σαθρὰν κάρπωσιν, τὸ πᾶν ἐστιν ἠλίθιον, καὶ ἀλλότριον, καὶ ἐκ δαιμόνων κινήσεως, φρύαγμά τε, καὶ ἀπάτη ... 'Η Μαρία ἐν τιμῇ, ὁ Κύριος προσκυνείσθω.—Ibid. cap. ix. p. 1066. C. D.]

[z] [Αὗταί σοι τῶν ἐμῶν λόγων αἱ ἀπαρχαὶ, ὦ θεία καὶ ἱερὰ κεφαλή. τοῦτό σοι καὶ τῶν λόγων γέρας, καὶ τῆς ἀθλήσεως, οὐ κότινος 'Ολυμπικὸς, οὔτε μῆλα Δελφικὰ παίγνια, οὐδὲ 'Ισθμικὴ πίτυς, οὐδὲ Νεμαίας σέλινα, δι' ὧν ἔφηβοι δυστυχεῖς ἐτιμήθησαν.—S. Greg. Naz. Orat. xviii. in laud. S. Cypr. Op., tom. i. p. 286. A.]

[a] [Εἶτα μνημονεύομεν καὶ τῶν προκεκοιμημένων, πρῶτον πατριαρχῶν, προφητῶν, ἀποστόλων, μαρτύρων· ὅπως ὁ Θεὸς ταῖς εὐχαῖς αὐτῶν καὶ πρεσβείαις προσδέξηται ἡμῶν τὴν δέησιν.—S. Cyril. Hier. Catech. xxiii. (Myst. v.) § 9. Op., p. 328. A.]

Cyrille. . . . Le style de cest autheur respire la vraye & pure antiquité."—Card. Perron, Repl.] pp. 1018, 1819.

The question here is, whether those Catechisms were Saint Cyril's (whose name they bear) or no. Cardinal Perron saith, that the Bishop hath not seen the Library of Auspurg, but took it upon trust on Gesner's report.

36 The Bishop saith, that Gesner he never yet saw, but the Library of Auspurg he hath seen, and had ever since 1595, the year it first came forth.

In the place quoted in the margin by the Cardinal, it is thus: *Catecheticæ Institutiones Episcopi Hierosolymitani, quem Cyrillum esse puto* [b]. But what needed Hœschelius, or (as Possevine citeth him [c]) Velserus say, *Quem Cyrillum esse puto*, if his name had been put to them? So that there is not Cyril's name to them *in all Libraries in the East and West, as the Cardinal* pretends. For, in this library, they are the Catechisms of one whom Hœschelius, or Velser, thought to be Cyril, but not Cyril's by name.

But that which followeth puts the matter clean out of question; which the Cardinal begins to allege, but leaves off where the point is made most clear. For, there Hœschelius, or Velser, saith, *Ejusdem autem Auctoris, et has, et quæ sequuntur, existimo* Μυσταγωγικαὶ κατηχήσεις πέντε Ἰωάννου ἐπισκόπου Ἱεροσολύμων [d]; which could not, but even wilfully, be so left out by the Cardinal. For, by this it plainly appeareth, that John, Bishop of Hierusalem, was author of these five, and not Cyril [e]. Now, Velser, or Hœschelius, think that the former, and these, were all of one man's, and so unthink that which they thought before; *quem Cyrillum esse puto*. For, if these be John's, and the former and these all one man's, then are those other not Cyril's neither.

Now, it is altogether needless to answer the Cardinal's

[b] [See Catalog. Græc. Codicum qui sunt in Biblioth. Reip. August. Vindel. num. xxiii. p. 20. Aug. Vindel. 1595.]

[c] [See August. Vindel. Reip. Biblioth. in the Catal. MSS. Græc. p. 83. apud Possevini Appar. Sacr. tom. ii. ad fin. Velser appears to have entrusted the execution of the Catalogue to Hœschelius. See Hœschelii Epist. Dedic. ad init. Catal. Bibl. Reip. Aug.]

[d] [Catal. Græc. Cod. &c. (as above, note [b].) p. 21.]

[e] [This and other arguments against the genuineness of these last five Catechetical Discourses are answered by the Benedictine Editor, Dissert. ii. cap. 3. coll. civ–cx. Even if any value is to be set on the authority of this one MS., they were written by John, S. Cyril's immediate successor; and thus are of almost equal antiquity as if they had been written by S. Cyril himself.]

conjectures that they are Cyril's, and not John's, when we have the name of John expressly set to them.

As for the character, all men scent not alike; that which, to the Cardinal, seemeth to savour of true and pure antiquity, to others seems not so.

That *mentionem facimus*[f] in Cyril is not all one with *invocamus*, there is no man but seeth. As for the mention of the saints made, or the end for which it was made, we see no reason to deny either.

The Place of Saint Augustine [f].

["Et ce que le mesme sieur d'Ely dit, qu'ils fondent ceste negation sur la foy de S. Augustin, qui afferme, que les Saincts sont là nommez à l'Autel, mais nie disertement qu'ils y soient invoquez ; il abuse de l'intention de Sainct Augustin, qui parle de la seule invocation directe faitte en l'acte du sacrifice, laquelle ne se faisoit en l'ancienne Eglise, ny ne se fait encore maintenant qu'à Dieu le Pere seul, & non aux Saincts, voire non pas à Jesus Christ mesme, d'autant que l'invocation directe, qui accompagne le sacrifice, estant faitte pour diriger, addresser, & dédier le sacrifice, elle ne le peut diriger qu'à Dieu le Pere seul . . . Et pourtant, ce que Monsieur d'Ely replique, pourquoy ce qui n'est point licite au sacrifice, est licite hors du sacrifice ? pourquoy ce qui n'est point licite en l'oblation de la messe, est licite aux Matines ? se pourroit demander de nostre Seigneur mesme, auquel il est defendu d'addresser aucune priere directe en l'acte de l'oblation, pour monstre que c'est au Pere, & non à luy que le sacrifice s'offre precisement & directment. Ce que Sainct Augustin donc a dit, *Qu'au sacrifice les Martyrs, comme hommes de Dieu, qui ont vaincu le monde par la confession d'iceluy, sont nommez en leur lieu & en leur ordre, mais ne sont pas invoquez par le Prestre qui sacrifie,* (Aug. de Civ. l. 22. c. 10.) se doit entendre de l'invocation directoire du sacrifice, & faitte en la priere ou invocation sacrificale, & non pas de l'invocation relative & subalterne."—Card. Perron, Repl.] pp. 1020, 1021.

Cyril's *mentionem facimus*, and Augustine's *nominamus*, seem not to differ. But, if Cyril's *mentionem facimus* be an invocation (as to that end is alleged before), the Bishop would be glad to know why Saint Augustine's *nominamus* should not be so too? But Saint Augustine flatly opposeth *invocamus* to *nominamus* (*nominantur, sed non invocantur*[g]), and by the same reason it is likewise opposed to *mentionem facimus*. And so Cyril's place alleged to no purpose.

[f] [See p. 47. not. ª.]
[g] ["Ad quod sacrificium (Martyres), sicut homines Dei, qui mundum in Ejus confessione vicerunt, suo loco et ordine nominantur, non autem a Sacerdote, qui sacrificat, invocantur."—S. Aug. de Civ. Dei, lib. xxii. cap. 10. Op., tom. vii. col. 1073. D.]

The Cardinal's division of, 1. *Invocation direct and indirect,* or *oblique;* 2. as also of Invocation *absolute* and *relative;* 3. *Sovereign* and *Subaltern;* they be three new devices of the Cardinal's, and yet help him not. For though the Invocation of them be not a *direct, absolute,* and *sovereign invocation;* yet if it be an *indirect, relative,* or *subaltern invocation,* an *invocation* it is: (and such a one is the invocation at the altar in the Mass: for thus it is, *Libera nos, intercedente pro nobis Beata Virgine, &c. Beatis Apostolis, &c. cum omnibus Sanctis*[h]:) and so what shall become of Saint Augustine's *non invocantur,* who knew none of these distinctions of the Cardinal's, which in that age, and many ages after, were never heard of?

Neither can the Cardinal allege any reason, why, if the Saints may be prayed unto, they may not be so as well by the priest as by the people; as well at Mass as at Matins; as well in the body of the church as at the altar?

But if *we might ask Christ himself*[i], *and he tell us,* (as the Cardinal seems to say,) Christ's answer were enough. But he allegeth not any place where Christ saith any thing that ways: whereas, *Venite ad me omnes* seems to say the contrary.

As for the Cardinal's new distinction of *sacrificial* and *unsacrificial invocation;* and his conceit that the *Sacrifice is offered unto God the Father alone;* it is refuted by the Canon itself of the Mass: the conclusion whereof is, *Placeat Tibi, Sancta Trinitas obsequium servitutis meæ, et præsta, ut hoc Sacrificium, quod oculis Tuæ Majestatis indignus obtuli, sit Tibi acceptabile.* So that the sacrifice is offered to the whole Trinity.

The twenty-third Canon of the Third Council of Carthage, *Ut cum altari assistitur, semper ad Patrem dirigatur oratio*[j], that Canon is not held in the Church of Rome neither, where both the foresaid prayer to the Trinity is said *in medio altaris;* and besides there are three Collects more, directed unto Christ himself; viz. the Collect, 1. *Domine Jesu Christe, qui dixisti,* &c.[k]; 2. and again, *Domine Jesu Christe, Fili Dei vivi,* &c.[l];

---

[h] [In the Canon of the Mass.]
[i] "Se pourroit demander de nostre Seigneur mesme." — [Card. Perron, Repl. p. 1020.]
[j] [Conc. Carth. III. can. xxiii. Conc. tom. ii. col. 1170. D.]
[k] [In the Canon of the Mass.]
[l] [Ibid.]

3. and the Collect, *Perceptio corporis*, &c. [m]; all of them said *dum assistitur altari*.

The Place of Gaudentius [n].

["Sieur d'Ely dit en un autre lieu, & sur un autre propos, parlant de Gaudentius Evesque de Bresse, qu'il est par dessous l'exception, &c."—Card. Perron, Repl.] p. 1021.

Seeing we vary not concerning that which is brought out of Gaudentius, it is not worth the standing on, what exception may be laid against him. This exception may, that he is an author new crept out; and so not to be received so readily being a stranger, as those with whom the Church hath long been acquainted. For, as for the Cardinal's scent, it is not so above exception as we dare rely on it alone for the discerning the character of authors newly set forth, of late, and by parties suspected.

The Place of Saint Ambrose [o].

["Le sieur d'Ely ... s'est aidé de trois autres exceptions: La première, que S. Ambroise en ce lieu-là rend le sang de Christ superflu, par ce qu'il dit, que les Martyrs ont lavé leurs pechez dedans leur propre sang."—Card. Perron, Repl.] p. 1022.

The first point is, whether in these words, *Possunt pro peccatis nostris rogare, qui proprio sanguine etiam (sua), si qua habuerunt peccata, laverunt:* First, his *si qua habuerunt*, that it may be called in doubt whether the Martyrs *had any sins* or no: the second is, whether it may properly be said, *Lavantur peccata Martyris, etiam sanguine Martyris ipsius proprio.* Whether either of these be not inconveniently spoken? 1. Either to call in doubt whether they *have any sin;* 2. Or, to say, the *sins that they had they did themselves wash away with their own blood?* The third is, if their own blood did wash them away, whether the blood of Christ might not be

---

[m] [In the Canon of the Mass.]
[n] ["Ut venerandas ... Sanctorum reliquas haberemus, Deus noster tribuit; deinde ut hanc honori earum Basilicam fundare valeremus, Ipse largitus est."—Gaudent. Tractat. xvii. Die Dedic. Basil. Sanct. xl. Martyrum; Bibl. Max. Patr. tom. v. p. 968. G. quoted by Bellarm., Apol. pro Resp. cap. i. Op., tom. vii. col. 714. C.]

[o] ["Obsecrandi sunt Angeli pro nobis, qui nobis ad præsidium dati sunt, Martyres obsecrandi, quorum videmur nobis quoddam corporis pignore patrocinium vindicare. Possunt &c." as in the text.—S. Ambr. de Viduis, cap. ix. (sect. 55.) Op., tom. ii. col. 200. F. quoted by Bell., Apol. pro Resp. cap. i. Op., tom. vii. col. 713. C. D.]

spared? For what needs Christ's blood do that which was done already? For either the Martyrs so washed away their sins before, and then Christ's blood comes too late: or else, Christ's blood having first washed their sin, that which his blood first had done, theirs could not after do.

[" Il y a trois sortes de Baptesme, par lesquelles, comme par les causes instrumentales & applicatives du merite du sang de Christ, nos pechez sont lavez ... asçavoir le Baptesme de l'eau ... le Baptesme de l'Esprit ... et le Baptesme du sang."—Card. Perron, Repl.] p. 1023.

1. So that the Cardinal is forced to have recourse to his distinction of *subaltern* and *instrumental;* for the places alleged relieve him not. For *in the baptism of blood, blood* may supply the place of water; but it cannot supply the place of *Christ's blood,* which is it that *purgeth us from all our sins.*

[" Et si l'Escriture a dit, *Que la charité couvre la multitude des pechez,* & *Que l'ausmosne ... esteint le peché comme l'eau esteint le feu,* d'autant que ce sont causes subalternes & instrumentales, qui nous appliquent le merite du sang de Christ."—Card. Perron, Repl. p. 1023.]

2. The place of Saint Peter, of *Charitas operit multitudinem peccatorum* [p], is confessed to be taken out of the Proverbs [q], where the sense is far otherwise than as the Cardinal takes it. For Solomon saith there, that men being in hatred will disclose one another's faults, but being in love and charity, they will cover them. Which is not to be alleged as any way pertaining to the taking away of sins before God: but to the living peaceably of one man with another. I hold it then as unproperly laid by him, that the love or charity of Martyrs wash away their sins, as the other of Saint Ambrose.

[" Comment est-ce que la charité du martyr ... & que ceste mort soufferte pour Christ, de laquelle il dit; *Que qui perd son ame pour luy, la trouvera,* ne pourra estre ditte cause subalterne & applicative du sang de Christ?"—Card. Perron, Repl. p. 1023.]

3. For that which Christ saith, *He that loseth his life shall find it,* doth only show what shall follow, or be the consequent, and not what is the cause. For though of the *losing of our life for Christ* this shall follow, that *we shall find it:* yet our *losing* is not the cause of our *finding;* but the merit and death of Christ only.

[p] 1 Pet. vi. 8.   [q] Prov. x. 12.

["Et si l'eau elementaire trop plus vile en soy, que le sang des Martyrs ... est appellée le lavement de regeneration ... Comment est ce que le sang, la passion & la charité du martyre considerée ... comme cause subalterne, instrumentale & applicative du merite de son sang, ne pourra estre ditte laver les pechez des Martyrs, sans faire tort à son sang?"—Card. Perron, Repl. pp. 1023, 1024.]

4. Neither doth the Cardinal's argument hold *a minore ad majus*, from the *water of Baptism* to the *blood of Martyrs*. For the *water of Baptism* is not less. For though the *death of his Saints be precious in his sight,* yet the Sacrament being God's own divine institution must needs be allowed to be greater than it. To speak safely and properly therefore: *The blood of Christ purgeth us from our sins*[r]*:* and it is He who *washeth us from our sins in his blood*[s]. *Laverunt stolas suas in sanguine Agni.* The blood of *Martyrs* is not the *blood of Christ:* and therefore that speech was neither so safely nor properly set down.

The Bishop giveth as high honour to Saint Ambrose, as doth the Cardinal. Yet the Cardinals both are pleased sometimes to say as well of him as of other the Fathers, *Quod minus caute locuti sunt* [t].

["La seconde exception est, que ce livre a esté écrit par S. Ambroise encore Neophyte, &c."—Card. Perron, Repl.] p. 1024.

The next point is, when it was that Saint Ambrose wrote this book *De Viduis,* and whether he were a young divine at the time of the writing it. We will take no other judge than Cardinal Baronius, who, at the commandment of Pope Sixtus, wrote Saint Ambrose his life with all diligence [u]. It is plain that Saint Ambrose, before he was bishop, was a secular judge and no divine; nay, no Christian at all: but that his Christianity and divinity began both together, after he was chosen Bishop of Milan; for he was fain to be christened before he could be consecrated. Now the very next year after that he wrote his Commentaries upon Luke, as Baronius proveth by Saint Ambrose's own words, in his ninth book

---

[r] [1 S. John i. 7.]
[s] [Rev. i. 5.]
[t] [Bellarmine uses these particular words of Nicolas de Lyra. Vide Bell. de Rom. Pont. lib. ii. cap. 10. § 'Porro.' Op., tom. i. p. 165. E. There are several similar expressions respecting the Fathers quoted from Bellarmine in Tortura Torti, p. 338. Lond. 1609; pp. 410, 411. Oxon. 1851.]
[u] [See the Life of S. Ambrose by Baronius, apud S. Ambros. Op., tom. vi. Romæ, 1579—1585.]

upon the twentieth chapter[v]. In which Commentaries he citeth his book *De Viduis*[x]: which therefore must needs be written before those Commentaries, and so consequently in the first year of his divinity and Christianity both. Saint Augustine saith: *Ambrosius, vix Christianus, de rebus Ecclesiæ scribit.* But Ambrose's own confession of himself is best in the beginning of his first book *De Officiis.* *Homines autem discunt, prius quam* [*quod*, Ben.] *doceant, et ab alio* [*illo*, Ben.] *accipiunt, quod aliis tradant. Quod ne ipsum quidem mihi accidit. Ego enim, raptus de tribunalibus atque administrationis infulis ad Sacerdotium, docere vos cœpi, quod ipse non didici. Itaque factum est, ut prius docere incipiam, quam discere. Discendum igitur mihi simul et docendum est, quoniam non vacavi* [*vacavit*, Ben.] *ante discere*[y]. For, as he saith in another place, *Quantus enim adolescere usus poterit* [*potuit*, Ben.] *in tam parva initiatæ Religionis ætate*[z]: at what time he saith of himself he was *nondum triennalis sacerdos*[a], and, as Baronius reckoneth, he had been but two years and six weeks Bishop[b].

["La troisiéme exception est, que S. Ambroise en un autre lieu déja plus aagé, & mieux appris, tient une autre opinion.... Tous les doctes de l'un & d'autre party sçavent, qui est que ce commentaire de S. Ambroise, sur l'Epistre aux Romains, non seulement n'est point de S. Ambroise, mais ne ressent rien ny de son style, ny de ses conceptions."—Card. Perron, Repl.] p. 1025.

The third point is, the place out of the *Epistle to the Romans*[c]; where he tells us, that these Commentaries upon the Epistles are not Saint Ambrose's; and that all *learned men know it*[d].

[v] [Baron. Ann. Eccl. ad ann. 376. num. ix.] Tom. iv. 324. [col. 465. Mogunt. 1601. See also, ad ann. 377. num. x.] 327. [col. 469. where he quotes the passages from S. Ambr. de Viduis, given below. Baronius argues from the following passage that the commentaries on S. Luke were written A.D. 376, just after the persecution of Justina had ceased: "Ecce tempus acceptabile, quo non hyemalibus perfidiæ caligantis primus annus riget, nec altis nubibus informis crusta blasphemiæ, gelu durante, concrescit, etc."— S. Ambr. Expos. Evang. S. Luc. lib. ix. (sect. 32.) But the Benedictine Editors fix their date just before A.D. 386, and that of the treatise De Viduis, after A.D. 377.]

[x] [S. Ambr. Exp. in Luc. lib. ii. sect. 62. Op., tom. i. col. 1301. E.]

[y] [S. Ambr. de Off. Ministr. lib. i. cap. 1. sect. 3. 4. Op., tom. ii. col. 3. A.B.]

[z] [S. Amb. de Virg. lib. ii. cap. 6. (sect. 39.) Op., tom. ii. col. 172. D.]

[a] [Ibid.]

[b] [Baron. Ann. Eccl. ad ann. 377. num. x. tom. iv. col. 469.]

[c] ["Ad Deum autem... suffragatore non est opus."—Hilar. Diac. in Ep. ad Rom. cap. i. apud S. Ambros. Op., tom. ii. Append. col. 33. A. B.]

[d] [These Commentaries on the Epistles are now commonly ascribed

Yet he knoweth well that Pope Sixtus V. knew not so much. For he, in his edition of Saint Ambrose, hath set them there as Saint Ambrose's, without any censure at all[e]; and therefore let him look how he refuseth them.

Further, he knoweth that they go usually, and are cited continually, under Saint Ambrose's name by all learned writers; namely, by Sixtus Senensis, lib. iv.[f]; by Cardinal Bellarmine, in five sundry places, *De Christo*, iv. 14[g], *De summo Pontifice*, i. 25[h], *et* ii. 16[i], *et* 35[k]; *De Clericis*, i. 19[l]; by Cardinal Alan, in his defence of Purgatory, cap. 7[m], (who yet know as much of this matter as the Cardinal doth:) So that the Cardinal may, if it so please him, lament that *such clear and goodly spirits* as Pope Sixtus V., Cardinal Alan, and Cardinal Bellarmine, with Sixtus Senensis, and divers others, suffered the same eclipse, and *knew not that which all learned men both of the one* and *other side* do *know, that these Commentaries are not indeed* Saint Ambrose's; thereby inferring, in effect, that these were no learned men.

As for us, we are not so straitened, that we need make any great reckoning whether those Commentaries be questioned or no; for we after allege a place of Saint Ambrose, out of his works, of which there is no question[n]. Only this would be marked, that when they cite these Commentaries, for *cujus hodie Rector est Damasus*[o], to prove the Pope to be ruler of the whole Church; then, they can find none of these same *choses cy ineptes et impertinentes, et interpretations ridi-*

---

to Hilary, a Deacon of the Roman Church, and contemporary with Pope Damasus. See the prefatory notice of the Benedictine Editors. S. Amb. Op., tom. ii. Append. coll. 21. sqq.]

[e] [Vide S. Ambr. Op., tom. iv. p. 184. Romæ, 1579, seq.]

[f] [In omnes Pauli Epistolas lib. xiv. breves quidem in verbis sed sententiarum pondere graves.—Sixt. Senens. Bibl. Sanct. lib. iv. sub voc. 'Ambrosius, Episc. Mediol.' tom. i. p. 222. col. 1. A. Lugd. 1575.]

[g] [Bell. de Christo, lib. iv. cap. 14. Op., tom. i. p. 121. A.]

[h] [Bell. de Rom. Pont. lib. i. cap. 25. Op., tom. i. p. 153. B.]

[i] [Bell. de Rom. Pont. lib. ii. cap. 16. Op., tom. i. p. 169. A.]

[k] [Bell. de Rom. Pont. lib. ii. cap. 31. Op., tom. i. p. 183. B.]

[l] [Bell. de Clericis, lib. i. cap. 19. Op., tom. ii. p. 316. F.]

[m] [A Defense and Declaration of the Catholike Churches Doctrine touching Purgatory and Prayers for the Soules departed, by William Allen, cap. 7. fol. 65. b. Antwerp. 1565.]

[n] [" Neque adorandum quicquam præter Deum legimus."—S. Ambr. de Spiritu, lib. iii. cap. xi. (sect. 78.) Op., tom. ii. col. 680.F. quoted by Andrewes, Resp. ad Apol. cap. i. p. 47. Lond. 1610; p. 61. Oxon. 1851.]

[o] [" Ut cum totus mundus Dei sit, Ecclesia tamen domus Ejus dicatur, cujus hodie rector est Damasus."— Hilar. Diac. Comment in 1 Tim. iii., apud S. Amb. Op., tom. ii. Append. col. 296. A.]

culeux[p]. Nor then they be no *escrits supposes ou apocryphes*, and *qui n'ont rien ny du stile, ny du sense de Saint Ambroise*[q].

Be it as it will, we can be content to give them good leave to except to this place, if we may be allowed to lay the same exception against *cujus hodie Rector est Damasus*, which stands them in more stead than this place doth us. And so, let the *Commentaries* be quit on both sides, and go for none of Saint Ambrose's, in God's name.

Or at least, I trust, we may be allowed to cite them as the Cardinal doth himself, and say, as he saith[r], *Saint Ambroise ou l'autheur contemporain à luy, du Commentaire qui luy est attribué sur la première epistre à Timothée:* and then all shall be well, and we shall escape these *ridiculous impertinent interpretations* as well as he.

["Combien qu'encore au fonds, quand ce commentaire seroit vrayment de S. Ambroise, & non comme pensent quelques uns d'Hilaire Diacre Luciferien.... il ne se trouveroit pas pour cela, que S. Ambroise die rien de contraire en ce passage, à ce qu'il a écrit aux autres lieux de la priere relative des Saincts."—Card. Perron, Repl.] p. 1026.

But whereas the Cardinal would father these Commentaries upon Hilary, a Deacon, and a Luciferian Heretic, or on some other uncertain and unknown author, that we may not yield him. For, albeit it might well be guessed that the author of them might be one Hilarius, (inasmuch as Saint Augustine, under that name, citeth a passage to be found in them, for the understanding of that text, in the Epistle to the Romans, *in quo omnes peccaverunt*,) yet he citeth it under the name of Sanctus Hilarius; which title Saint Augustine[s] would never have given to a Luciferian Heretic, we may be sure. Therefore, were it Ambrose, or were it Hilary, we may be bold to say, an *holy man* he was; and one of good authority worth the citing, and therein we shall say and do no more than Saint Augustine hath said and done.

["L'autheur de cét écrit. ne veut pas dire par ces paroles, *A Dieu il n'est point besoin de suffragateur*, que les hommes n'ayent besoin de personnes pour les favoriser de prieres & intercessions envers Dieu.... Mais il veut dire, que Dieu pour cognoistre dequoy nous sommes dignes, & apprendre,

---

p [Card. Perron, Repl. p. 1025.]
q [Card. Perron, Repl. p. 1026.]
r P. 115. hujus libri.

s [S.] Aug. ad Ep. Pelag. [lib.] iv. [cap.] 4. [Op., tom. x. coll. 878. D. 879. A.]

l'estat des affaires particulieres des hommes, n'a point besoin de donner d'avis & d'avertisseur ...... Car c'est ce que signifie là le mot suffragateur.... Et en ce sens l'employe non seulement Tertullian," &c.—Card. Perron, Repl.] pp. 1026, 1027.

Then falleth the Cardinal to yield, it may be Saint Ambrose's, and to run into a long discourse of *suffragatur* and *suffragari;* telling us how they be taken in heathen authors, (in which sense, I deny not, but these words may still be used,) *to give a voice.* But, in the style of the Church, he knoweth that *Suffrages* are taken for *prayers.* Witness his Portuise[t], where, in the Litany and Suffrages, *Suffrages* are taken for *ora pro nobis,* which we now are about. And those prayers, which we pray the Saints to make for us, are nothing but their *Suffrages,* in the language of the Massbook.

O Brigitta mater bona, Dulcis ductrix et matrona,
  Nobis fer Suffragia[u].
Katharinæ collaudemus Virtutum insignia
Ut spe certa respiremus Per ejus Suffragia[v].

And the Master of the Sentences, when he saith, *Oramus ergo, ut Sancti intercedant pro nobis, id est, merita eorum nobis suffragentur*[x], did not mean, they should *give their voices with us.* Nor Alexander Hales, when he said, *Per eorum Suffragia, quod petimus, impetramus*[y]. Nor Thomas, when he said, *Merita Sanctorum exsistentia coram Deo, sunt nobis Suffragia, id est, mediantibus Sanctorum Suffragiis, Dei beneficia in nos diffunduntur*[z].

[" C'est en ce sens que l'autheur dont il s'agist nie qu'il soit besoin de donner à Dieu des suffragateurs, c'est à dire des Referendaires & donneurs d'advis, comme les Payens donnoient à Dieu les Astres & les Elements, pour l'advertir & informer du merite des hommes."—Card. Perron, Repl. p. 1027.]

And when all is done, it would be known why God should have no need of some (be it *Elements, Stars, Angels,* or *Saints*) to interpose between God and men, *pour l'informer,*

---

[t] [Portiforium or Breviary.]
[u] [See Chemnitz, Examen Conc. Trident. par. iii. p. 154. Francof. ad Mœn. 1574, from whom Bp. Andrewes appears to have borrowed all his citations on this subject.]
[v] [Ibid. p. 162.]
[x] [Pet. Lomb. in Lib. Sent. lib. iv. Distinct. xlv. cap. v. fol. 208. col. 1. Col. 1513.]
[y] [These words appear to have been taken by Bp. Andrewes from Chemnitz, Examen Conc. Trident. par. iii. p. 147. Chemnitz refers to De Causis orandi Sanctos. (Caus. ii.) Alensis discusses this question in Sum. Theol. p. iv. Quæst. xcii. Memb. i. Art. iv. § fol. ccclxv. col. 3. Lugd. 1515. seq. But the words do not there occur.]
[z] [S. Thom. Aquin. Sum. Theol. Suppl. in par. iii. Quæst. lxxii. Art. iii. § 'Respondeo dicendum.']

and should have need of some to interpose between God and men, *pour les favoriser*. As He needs no referendary to give Him intelligence, nor no counsellor to give Him advice; so, neither needeth He any solicitor to incline Him to hear the prayers of a devout spirit, but the Great Mediator of all, which is Christ our Saviour.

["Le Roy a besoin de l'interposition des Gouverneurs ... pour l'informer du merite et de la suffisance de ceux qui sont sous leurs charges .... pour obtenir des faveurs de Dieu, il n'est point besoin de suffragateur; c'est à dire, de donner d'advis."—Card. Perron, Repl.] pp. 1028, [1029.]

Now, the answer which the Cardinal makes here, is there, by way of objection, made by the author of the Commentaries, under Saint Ambrose's name[a], in the very same terms that the *Church of Rome* useth it; that is, that by others we may go to God, as men do by the courtiers come to the King. But he in the same place takes it away, as we do; that they go to the King by courtiers, because he is a man, and knoweth not many things; but God, who is ignorant of nothing, *il n'est point besoin pour l'avoir propice de suffragateur*[b]; and again, *pour obtenir des faveurs de Dieu il n'est point besoin de suffragateur.*

Now, in the Cardinal's sense it is never taken. For his interpretation of *suffragateur* is, to be a referendary, or adviser, which serves properly to give notice, and to make things known; and not to make God propitious to persons, which is properly the part of an intercessor, by suffrages, according to the very style of the Church.

["Non en niant, qu'il soit necessaire à nostre infirmité d'estre aidée par les prieres d'autruy envers Dieu, mais en niant qu'il soit besoin à Dieu, d'estre aidé de l'information d'autruy pour avoir la cognoissance de nos merites ou demerites."—Card. Perron, Repl.] p. 1029.

---

[a] ["Solent tamen pudorem passi, neglecti Dei misera uti excusatione, dicentes per istos posse ire ad Deum, sicut per comites pervenitur ad regem. Age, numquid tam demens est aliquis, aut salutis suæ immemor, ut honorificentiam regis vindicet comiti; cum de hac re si qui etiam tractare fuerint inventi, jure ut rei damnentur majestatis? Et isti se non putant reos, qui honorem nominis Dei deferunt creaturæ, et, relicto Domino, conservos adorant; quasi sit aliquid plus quod reservetur Deo. Nam et ideo ad regem per tribunos aut comites itur; quia homo utique est rex, et nescit quibus debeat rempublicam credere. Ad Deum autem, Quem utique nihil latet (omnium enim merita novit) promerendum, suffragatore non opus est, sed mente devota. Ubicunque enim talis loquutus fuerit Ei, respondebit illi."—Hilar. Diac. Comment. in Ep. ad Rom. cap. i. apud S. Ambr. Op., tom. ii. Append. col. 33. A. B.]

[b] [S. Ambr. as translated by Perron, Repl. p. 1029.]

The Cardinal saith, *Non est opus suffragatore* is not said on our part, but on God's. It would be asked of him, when it is said, *Ad Deum suffragatore non est opus*, whether *non est opus* shall be *non est opus nobis*, or *non est opus Deo*. To say, *Non est opus Deo* were absurd; so it must be, *Non est opus nobis;* and so the *opus est* must needs lie on our parts.

[" Ce qui neantmoins est tres-vray de l'invocation absoluë & souveraine; mais pour faire que Dieu remplaceast la perte de Theodose en la personne de ses enfants, &c. il falloit recourir non aux autres remedes," &c.—Card. Perron, Repl.] p. 1030.

The fourth point is out of Ambrose, *in Obitum Theodosii, Tu solus, Domine, invocandus es.* Which, saith the Cardinal, is very true of *invocation absolute* and *sovereign:* as much as we desire. For, as for his *relative* and *subaltern*, we know them not. For, *to recompense the loss of Theodosius in the person of his children, and to make their government like his, so that there need be no lamenting for the death of the father, they had no recourse to any other remedy but to God alone, as to Him who turneth the hearts of kings*[c]. All which we take to make for us. As to that,—whether saints have particular knowledge of things below, and are set in particular as presidents over them[d],—we meddle not with it; nor the author of the Commentaries neither: but in *Tu solus, Domine, invocandus es* we have our purpose.

And we will hope well that Theodosius might intercede with God for his children; we see no cause to the contrary. But that Theodosius should be called on by his children, that is the question. And that will not stand with *Tu, Domine, solus invocandus es.*

[" Car de dire, comme fait Mr. d'Ely, que sainct Ambroise a composé un livre exprez de l'oraison, où toutefois il ne fait aucune mention des Saincts: Qui ne sçait que les consequences tirées de l'authorité negativement sont vitieuses," &c.—Card. Perron, Repl.] p. 1031.

45

The last point is, divers of the Fathers having expressly written Books of Prayer, and none of them ever mentioning this *oblique, subaltern, relative, transitory prayer* of the Cardinal's; but telling us only of what is *direct, absolute, sovereign,* and *final,* this is no argument, *ab auctoritate nega-*

---

[c] [" Conteror corde; quia ereptus est vir, quem vix possumus invenire; sed tamen tu solus, Domine, invocandus es, tu rogandus, ut eum in filiis repræsentes."—S. Ambr. de Obit. Theodos. sect. 36. Op., tom. ii. col. 1207. D.]

[d] [Vide Card. Perron, Repl. p. 1030.]

tive, but a great probability that they knew none of those obliquities or transitory passages. For if they had, so many, so divers Fathers, in so many treatises, must somewhere have mentioned them.

And Saint Ambrose, in his book (be it *de Oratione*, or *de Interpellatione*[c]), after his complaint made of the miseries of mankind, would have had recourse to some of these *relative, subaltern prayers;* which, because he never goes about, it is likely he knew them not. For (say the Cardinal what he will) it concerneth men to know, not only what they pray for, but whom they pray to, and by whom. For *quibus auxiliis* is a necessary circumstance, which it behoved them not to leave out, nor to leave their people ignorant of that point. Which yet they do, never telling them word (in all their treatises of prayer) of these *oblique* and *transitory means*, to help them in their devotion.

[" Pour le regard de Prudentius & de Paulinus, il en reproche les écrits, non comme faussement attribuez à leurs autheurs, mais comme de Poëtes, avec ceste sentence d'Horace; *Que les Poëtes et les Peintres ont toutjours eu pareille license de tout oser*[f]," &c.—Card. Perron, Repl.] pp. 1031—1034.

For Prudentius and Paulinus, there was nothing said of them, but in Bellarmine's own words, *Nihil aliud respondeo, nisi, more poetico, lusisse Prudentium*[g]; and so much the Cardinal had no reason to be offended with.

In rhetorical amplifications, it is well known, men take great liberty; but in poetry much more. Besides, their words serve them not at will, as they do in prose; but they must often take such to make up their verse, as were otherwise inconvenient to be used. Moreover, the fervour of their invention carrieth them further oftentimes than, in a temperate speech, they would be carried. And when all is said that can be, it is not a piece of poetry that must carry this point. Let poets, in the name of God, when they make hymns in praise of God, be as poetical as they can; there is no fear of flattering God, or extolling him too much. But, in all other matters, that divine art must come to the touch of divinity, and not divinity to the touch of it.

[c] [S. Ambr. de Interpellatione Job. et David. lib. iv. Op., tom. i. col. 625. seq.]
[f] [See Andrewes, Resp. ad Apol.
cap. i. p. 46, Lond. 1610; p. 61, Oxon. 1851.]
[g] [Bell. de Purg. lib. ii. cap. 18. § 'Ad quintum.' Op., tom. ii. p. 415. G.]

For the Place of Ruffin, of Theodosius[h].

["Il dit que Theodose ne demandoit pas l'ayde aux Saincts, mais demandoit l'ayde à Dieu par l'intercession des Saincts, c'est à dire, ne demandoit pas aux saincts qu'ils intercedassent pour luy, mais demandoit à Dieu que l'intercession que le Saincts faisoient de leur propre mouvement, & sans en estre priez pour luy, fust exaucée." — Card. Perron, Repl.] p. 1035. [1033. bis.]

All that is said is, that Theodosius would not have lain prostrate before the tombs of the Apostles, unless he had meant that *by so doing they would hear him.* What the Emperor meant, is hard to say. But Ruffin shows what he did, and all he did he might do without any such meaning.

For the Place of Origen.

["Car quant à ce que Monsieur d'Ely dit, que les Saincts prient de leur propre mouvement pour nous, sans en estre priez, le mot, *ultro*, ne veux pas dire dans Origene, d'où il l'a pris, sans en estre priez, mais sans estre marchandez & achettez par fumées," &c.—Card. Perron, Repl.] p.1034. [bis.]

Be it referred to the indifferency of any reader, whether, when Origen saith, *The Saints pray for us ultro,* his meaning be not, that they pray for *us, de leur propre gré et volontairement*[i]; but that they pray for us *ultro,* that is, *sans estre marchandez et achettez*[i]; all the merchandise being but *nidor Sacrificii,* a little smoke.

---

[h] ["Circuibat ... omnia orationum loca, ante Martyrum et Apostolorum thecas jacebat cilicio prostratus, et auxilia sibi fida sanctorum intercessione poscebat." — Ruffin. Hist. Eccl. lib. ii. (al. xi. ad calc. Euseb. Hist. Eccl.) cap. 33. p. 259.]

[i] Pp.1045. 1048.[This brief reference needs a fuller statement; Cardinal Perron, in the places referred to, is commenting first on the following passage of Origen against Celsus, lib. viii. cap. 64.(tom. i. col. 789.A.):—Ἀλλὰ καὶ συμπράττουσι τοῖς βουλομένοις τὸν ἐπὶ πᾶσι θεὸν θεραπεύειν, καὶ ἐξευμενίζονται, καὶ συνεύχονται, καὶ συναξιοῦσιν· ὥστε τολμᾶν ἡμᾶς λέγειν, ὅτι ἀνθρώποις, μετὰ προαιρέσεως προτιθεμένοις τὰ κρείττονα, εὐχομένοις τῷ θεῷ, μυρίαι ὅσαι ἄκλητι συνεύχονται δυνάμεις ἱεραὶ συμπαρεχοῦσαι τῷ ἐπικήρῳ ἡμῶν γένει, καὶ, ἵν' οὕτως εἴπω, συναγωνιῶσαι. Of this work the Latin translation only was then known, in which the passage runs thus :—" Sentiunt enim qui sunt digni favore cœlestis numinis, quibus non solum ipsi bene volunt, verum etiam dant operam ut Deum ei servire volentibus concilient, et una nobiscum precantur; ut quotquot eum colimus audeamus dicere, hominibus bonæ voluntatis precantibus *ultro* se adjungere innumera sanctorum angelorum millia, et (ut ita loquar) laborare nobiscum in hoc certamine," &c.—Orig. Op., Latine, tom. ii. p. 530. H. ed. Par. 1619. On this Cardinal Perron remarks : "*Et ce qu'il dit, qu'ils le font volontairement et gratuitement (ultro), n'est pas pour exclurre la necessite de les prier, mais pour exclurre la necessité de leur sacrifier,*" &c. He recurs to the subject in p. 1048, where he is meeting Andrewes' argument; he first quotes part of his words from Responsio ad Bellarm. p. 37. (Lond. 1610), wherein the margin the references were only from Orig. in Cantic. Hom. iii. and in

Responses generales.

["Reste, de l'expedition de ces responses particulieres, passer aux responses generales, qui sont trois; la première, que les exemples que nous apportons de la priere des Saincts, sont pris des Sermons faicts aux peuples, & non pas des decrets des disputes de la Foy, & que ces choses Demegoriques ne nous doivent pas suffire à decider la Foy."—Card. Perron, Repl.] p. 1034.

The Bishop saith not, that all the examples brought are taken out of *Demegorica*, or Homilies of the Fathers to the people. For he hath answered that of Saint Ambrose and others that are not thence taken; but that some places in those Homilies are not *litis decretoria*. Οὐ γὰρ κανὼν δογμάτων τὰ πανηγυρικῶς ἐν ταῖς ἐκκλησίαις λεγόμενα[k], That things panegyrically uttered in churches are no rules of opinion, as it is in the third Dialogue of Theodoret. Specially when they run forth into figures of rhetoric, and keep not themselves close to points of doctrine, as in the place alleged. As Cardinal Bellarmine himself saith of Chrysostome. Sometime, *dico Chrysostomum, per excessum, ita esse locutum, ut et quædam alia:* and again, *et alia id genus, quæ certum est dicta esse, amplificandi gratia*[1].

And as Sixtus Senensis saith of him: *Multa enim concionatores* [leg. *declamatores*] *per hyperbolen crebro enunciant, et inculcant, vel occasione temporum, locorum,* [*ac*] *personarum adducti, vel affectuum impetu et orationis cursu rapti quod* [leg. *rapti. Hoc*] *interdum Chrysostomo contingit*[m]. And Saint Hierome saith of himself, *Rhetoricati (ibi) sumus et in modum declamatorium* [leg. *morem declamatorum paululum*] *lusimus*[n].

Rom. ii. (see p. 47. notes [j], [k], Oxford ed. 1851), which references belonged to the words following those which Perron cites. The point of Andrewes' argument, however, he rightly states; viz. that invocation is not necessary, because the saints pray for us *ultro*, not being excited by our prayers, *mais de leur propre grē et volontairement*. He then observes that the word *ultro* which Andrewes had used is not found in the Homily on Canticles, but in the 8th book against Celsus (quoted above), which he had before explained (and from which, possibly, Andrewes had taken the word, though he did not note the reference), adding further, that it does not there signify, "without being prayed to, but *sans estre marchandé, & acheté par le commerce et traffic de la graisse et du sang des victimes, comme estoient les Demons des Payens*." The point at issue between them being this, whether the statement that the saints or angels pray for us *ultro* means, that they do it without being addressed by us in prayer, or without being gained by sacrifices. It may be observed that the discovery of the Greek ἄκλητι decides in a remarkable way the correctness of Bp. Andrewes' interpretation.]

[k] [Eranistes apud Theod. Dial. iii. Op., tom. iv. p. 202.]

[1] [Bell.] de Missa, lib. ii. c. 10. [Op., tom. iii. p. 227. E.F.]

[m] [Sixt. Senens. Bibl. Sanct.] lib. vi. Annot. clii. [tom. ii. p. 174. col. 2. A.]

[n] [S. Hier.] Adv. Helvidium, [sect. 22. Op., tom. ii. col. 230. C.]

Neither was it ever the Father's mind, by using those flowers of oratory, to teach the people idolatry. For who is there that when he heareth an apostrophe to a thing without sense, or to a party dead, but knoweth it is a figure of rhetoric, and not any serious invocation? Let the point here be truly spoken to, whether in funeral orations, any figure be more usual than apostrophe: and if there be not, what needs any more to be said in that point? For even among us in England they are daily used, who yet intend no invocation thereby.

["Les paroles que Sainct Gregoire de Nazianze addresse à la Pasque, ne sont point addressées à la feste de Pasque, ... mais sont addressées à Christ, qui est nostre vray Pasque."—Card. Perron, Repl.] p. 1038.

Where he saith, that Nazianzen's *Apostrophe* to *Easter*[o] *is not to the Feast itself, but to Christ, who is our true Passover.* The very words themselves show he is mistaken. For Nazianzen adds immediately, Ὡς γὰρ ἐμψύχῳ σοι διαλέξομαι: that is, *For I will speak to thee as to one that hath life.* Which by no means can be applied to Christ, but to the Feast only. He would never say to Christ, *I speak to thee as to one having life.*

["Et pour le regard de l'eau du Baptesme, ce n'est point à elle en particulier, que sainct Ambroise parle, mais en general, à tout l'element."—Card. Perron, Repl.] p. 1039.

And whether Saint Ambrose make his apostrophe, or speak to the *water* of *Baptism*, or to *water* in general, it is not much material. For either is sufficient to show, that in apostrophe we speak to things we never think can hear us. And yet when he saith, *O aqua, quæ Sacramentum Christi esse meruisti, quæ lavas omnia nec lavaris, tu incipis prima, tu comples perfecta mysteria, A te principium, in te finis, vel potius tu facis ut finem nesciamus*[p]. And the words wherewith he concludes all, *Regenerationis nostræ de tribus una es testibus. Tres enim testes sunt, Aqua, Sanguis, et Spiritus: Aqua, ad lavacrum; Sanguis, ad pretium; Spiritus, ad resurrectionem*[q], can hardly be understood but of the water of *Baptism*.

[o] [Ὦ πάσχα τὸ μέγα καὶ ἱερὸν, καὶ παντὸς τοῦ κόσμου καθάρσιον· ὡς γὰρ ἐμψύχῳ σοι διαλέξομαι.—S. Greg. Naz. Orat. xlii. (in Pasch. ii.) Op., tom. i. p. 696. D.]

[p] [S. Ambr. Expos. in Luc. lib. x. sect. 48. Op., tom. i. col. 1514. B.]

[q] [Ibid. D.]

[" Il dit, que ces mesmes Peres ne permettent pas qu'on les interprete autrement, parce qu'ailleurs ils advoüent, qu'ils ne sçavent si ceux, à qui ils parlent ainsi, les entendent, d'autant que Sainct Gregoire de Nazianze escrivant contre Julien l'Apostat, dit," &c.—Card. Perron, Repl.] p. 1039.

Touching the doubt that the Fathers had, whether those they spake to, being dead, did hear them or no (to Constantius, *si quis sensus*[r]), he grants Constantius had none. So it seems Martyrs only had sense, and none else.

[" Et quant à Gorgonia, que le verbe Grec, συνεπαισθάνεσθαι, ne signifie pas simplement *sentir* . . . mais . . . estre touché & passionné de joye ou de douleur en sentant," &c.—Card. Perron, Repl.] pp. 1039, 1040.

To that of Gorgonia[s] (yet she was no martyr neither) he makes another answer; wherein he cannot well get out, but by putting to ἐπαισθάνεσθαι, Nazianzen's word, the preposition συν, and so making it συνεπαισθάνεσθαι. And then lo! if this may be allowed him, he finds in Budee's Dictionary that συνεπαισθάνεσθαι is, not only to have sense of a thing, but to be affected with it[t]. And Gorgonia (he grants), though she knew, yet she was not any ways *affected with her knowledge*. But the truth is, the word is but ἐπαισθάνεσθαι: and then that will not serve his turn. Billius turneth it (no otherwise than the Bishop did), *Si hoc præmii sanctis animabus a Deo confertur, ut ista persentiscant, suscipe hanc nostram orationem funeream*[u].

[" Qui ne sçait que c'est chose coustumiere aux autheurs, d'employer souvent l'adverbe, *si*, non pour une note de doute, mais pour une note de redoublement d'affirmation."—Card. Perron, Repl.] p. 1040.

But trusting to neither of these, he tells us, that *si* is not *une note de doute, mais une note de redoublement de affirmation*, and is sometime taken for *for;* as in, *If I be God, where is mine honour?* and in, *Si Deus est animus*, &c. And so Nazianzen must say to Constantius, *Hear me, for thou hast sense;* and to Gorgonia, *Hear me, for thou hast not only sense, but art affected*. Yet even very now he confessed, that neither

[r] ["Ακουε καὶ ἡ τοῦ μεγάλου Κωνσταντίου ψυχὴ, εἴ τις αἴσθησις, ὅσαι τε πρὸ αὐτοῦ βασιλέων φιλόχριστοι.—S. Greg. Naz. Orat. iii. (in Julian. i.) Op., tom. i. p. 50. A.]

[s] [Εἰ δέ τις σοὶ καὶ τῶν ἡμετέρων ἐστι λόγος, καὶ τοῦτο ταῖς ὁσίαις ψυχαῖς ἐκ Θεοῦ γέρας τῶν τοιούτων ἐπαισθάνεσθαι, δέχοιο καὶ τὸν ἡμέτερον λόγον. —S. Greg. Naz. Orat. xi. in laudem sororis suæ Gorgoniæ. Op., tom. i. pp. 189. D. 190. A.]

[t] [See Budæi Comm. Ling. Græc. p. 528. Paris. 1548.]

[u] [Billius' translation is, "Si—hoc præmii sanctis animabus divinitus contingit, ut ista sentiant, nostram quoque orationem pro multis ac præ multis funebribus donis accipias velim."—S. Greg. Naz. Op., tom. i. pp. 189. D. 190. A.]

Constantius had sense, nor Gorgonia was affected. And so one of his answers overthrows the other.

But there is no man, but if he read these places unpartially, 1. *Hear, if there be any sense;* 2. *Hear, if God grant it as a privilege to souls deceased to have sense of these things,* but he will conceive that '*si*' is no *double affirming,* but is a note of some doubt, in them at least.

[" Mais il n'y a rien de flottant, pour le regard de l'estat de l'ame du Martyr Theodore, laquelle il est tres-asseuré d'estre en Paradis, & jouïr de la felicité eternelle, & de la vision de Dieu. Car ces alternatives sont seulement, s'il reside, ou en la suprême region du Ciel, ou en quelqu'un des orbes celestes, ou s'il est assistant à Dieu entre les Anges Ministres, & Appariteurs de la Deïté, ou adorant la Deïté comme serviteur fidèle, entre les principautez & les puissances."—Card. Perron, Repl.] pp. 1040, 1041.

Now for Nyssen's speech concerning Theodorus, *ubicunque tandem fueris*[x]. He tells us that Nyssen was very sure that he was in Paradise, but not in which corner of it. That he could not tell whether he were (1) in the upper region of heaven, or whether (2) in one of the celestial orbs; or whether he were (3) assisting, as one of God's apparitors with the angels; or whether he were (4) adoring the Deity with the principalities and powers. So he knew that there he was, but yet he knew not where he was. As if *ubicunque* did not refer to the place itself, but to some part or corner of it. Or as if Nyssen should not have said, *ubicunque tandem in paradiso fueris,* if such had been his meaning.

[" Conclud, que sainct Hieróme n'a peu parler avec les Saincts, ny donc les prier; comme s'il n'avoit pas difference entre parler avec quelqu'un, qui presuppose une forme de colloque & de devis, & une alteration reciproque de parolles; & parler à quelqu'un."—Card. Perron, Repl.] p. 1042.

After the same sort doth he answer the place of Saint Hierome, of Nepotian: *Cum quo loqui non possumus*[y], with *parler avec,* speaking with; and *parler,* a speaking to. That Saint Hierome might speak *to* Nepotian, being dead; but not with him, because Nepotian did not talk to him again. (And yet he was near enough to have answered, if *he laid his*

---

[x] [Σὺ δὲ δεῦρο δὴ πρὸς ἡμᾶς, ὅπου ποτ' ἂν ᾖς, τῆς ἑορτῆς ἔφορος, καλέσαντα γάρ σε ἀντικαλοῦμεν.—S. Greg. Nyss. de S. Theodoro. Op., tom. iii. p. 585. B.]

[y] [" Quem corpore non valemus, recordatione teneamus. Et cum quo loqui non possumus, de eo loqui nunquam desinamus."—S. Hier. Ep. lx. Vall. (al. iii.) ad Heliod. Epitaph. Nepot. sect. 19. Op., tom. i. col. 345.]

hands over his shoulders and embraced him[z], as it follows there.) But neither doth *parler avec* necessarily infer an answer; no, not with the Cardinal himself. For immediately after (forgetting himself), of Constantia to Hilarion (that was likewise dead), he saith that Constantia did *parler avec luy*, (and not *parler à luy*,) and yet Hilarion answered her not. Neither did she anything more than the Cardinal would have us do, *quasi cum præsente, ad adjuvandas orationes suas sermocinari*[a].

And where it is said, *Nepotianus hæc non audit*[b], that is, *Nepotian heard them not*, (not the invasions and barbarous massacres of the Goths,) he tells us, *Nepotian heard them*, though, but *not with the ears of his head*. Now, Saint Hierome saith, *He was happy, because he heard them not:* and if he heard them, with his ears or without his ears, howsoever he heard them, he was *not happy*; for he was *happy in his not hearing*; and the very *hearing* made him not *happy:* and so the Cardinal falls foul upon Saint Hierome here.

["Il est vray, Tertullian, sainct Cyprian, sainct Gregoire de Nysse, ont fait des livres d'oraison, c'est à dire, de l'oraison Dominicale . . . . Comme il ne se parle en ces lieux-là, que des chefs generaux de la priere, aussi ne s'y parle t'il que de la priere absoluë & souveraine, & de l'object final, auquel elle se termine, & non de la priere relative, c'est à dire, de la priere de prier, de laquelle les Peres ne parlent non plus en ces lieux-là, pour le regard de Christ que pour le regard des Saincts."—Card. Perron, Repl.] p. 1042.

The Bishop thought he had spoken to the purpose, when he advised that those points were best resolved by the books of the Fathers written *dogmatically* or *didactically;* that is, those books of theirs touching prayer. The Cardinal confesseth that Tertullian, Cyprian, Nyssen, have made books of prayer, (and of divers others he might have confessed the like,) but saith withal, their books were only of *prayer absolute* and *sovereign*, and not of *prayer relative*, of which he confesseth they speak nothing: and so in this point the

---

[z] ["Hæc (caritas) semper vivit in pectore; ob hanc Nepotianus noster absens, præsens est, et per tanta terrarum spatia divisos utraque complectitur manu."—Ibid. supra.]

[a] ["Erat enim solita pervigiles in sepulcro ejus noctes ducere, et quasi cum præsente ad adjuvandas orationes suas sermocinari."— S. Hier. Vit. S. Hilar. sect. 47. Op., tom. ii. col 40. C.]

[b] ["Felix Nepotianus, qui hæc non videt; felix qui ista non audit."— S. Hier. Ep. lx. Vall. (al. iii.) ad Heliod., Epitaph. Nepot. sect. 17. Op tom. i. col. 343. C.]

cause is gained. For if divers of them, writing divers books of *Prayer,* none of them had the grace once to remember *Prayer Relative,* it is a sign they made cold account of it.

And as to that of Christ's *Intercession,* the people hearing daily, *Per Christum Dominum nostrum* to conclude every prayer, they needed not to be put in mind of it, as no more should they have needed, if they had heard their prayers concluded, *Per Sanctum Dionysium,* or *Per S. Genovefam,* &c. And this is the chief reason, that the Fathers in their treatises *dogmatical* (*au quelles,* saith he, *les Peres escrivent ingenuement ce qu'elles tenent*[c],) and namely, in those which were purposely and expressly written touching *prayer* itself, and no invocation of Saints so much as once mentioned or pointed at, that the ancient Fathers, for the four hundred years after Christ, had nothing so great conceit of it as the Cardinal would fain have them seem to have had.

[" Il dit, que pour le moins, il falloit tirer ces preuves des écrits polemiques des Peres, c'est à dire, des écrits qu'ils ont faits, ou pour disputer contre les heretiques, comme sainct Athanase contre les Arriens .... ou contre les Payens, comme Origene contra Celsus, ou sainct Cyrille contre Julian."—Card. Perron, Repl.] p. 1043 [*leg.* 1042].

Next to the dogmatical writings of the Fathers, the Bishop wisheth something might have been brought for the Invocation of *Saints* out of their writings *Polemic.* Not *Polemic* simply, or generally, but such as wherein this question came properly to be handled; as it did in Origen against Celsus[d], and Cyril against Julian[e]. Where Celsus and Julian did object, that the *Christians* did yield like worship, and did in each respect their service to their *martyrs,* as the heathen men did to their *heroes* or *semidei,* which Origen and Cyril do expressly deny.

[" Comme s'il n'estoit pas beaucoup meilleur d'alleguer des écrits pacifiques des Peres de l'Eglise, que des écrits polemiques, ausquels l'ardeur de la dispute emporte quelquefois les disputants plus loin qu'ils ne se laisseroient emporter, s'ils parloient ou escrivoient de sens froid."—Card. Perron, Repl.] p. 1042.

Here the Cardinal tells us that their writings *Pacific* are

[c] [Perron, Repl.] p. 1043.
[d] [See Orig. contra Cels. lib. v. sect. 4. Op., tom. i. pp. 579. F. 580. A.; and lib. viii. sect. 64. ibid. p. 789. D—F.]
[e] [See S. Cyril. Alex. contra Julian. lib. vi. Op., tom. vi. B. p. 203. D. E.]

rather to be alleged than the writings *Polemic*. To what purpose, seeing that was done by the Bishop already? For he did first allege the writings *Pacific, Dogmatic, Didascalic*, before he came to these writings *Polemic, Gymnastic,* or *Agonistic*. Those to be first: but then these to be second in their place.

It is true that in their *Polemics* concerning some one point, while they follow it eagerly, the Fathers do forget themselves concerning some other; and so is Saint Basil's saying to be understood [f]. But never touching that very question which they have in hand. For therein always they hold themselves close to the point, and their *tenets* are ever most sound and direct.

[" En ces lieux-là sainct Athanase parle de la seule invocation absoluë, c'est à dire, qui se termine en celuy auquel elle est addressée, &c."—Card. Perron, Repl.] p. 1043.

The like may be said concerning Athanasius against the Arians: where Athanasius proves that Christ is God, because *he is prayed to* [g]. The Major of which argument must be, *None but God can be prayed to*. Which the Cardinal cannot tell [how] to avoid, but by *his prayer relative* and *subaltern*, which neither Athanasius nor the Arians ever heard of, else Athanasius' argument had been answered straight, that is, None but God *can be prayed to*, unless it be by *prayer relative* and *subaltern;* but so might the *Saints* be prayed to as well as Christ.

But where the Cardinal saith that Origen and the other Fathers, writing against the Heathen, *Sont quelques fois de dire non ce qu'ils croyent, mais le dissimuler & dire ce qui sert*

[f] [This refers to the following passage of S. Basil quoted by Perron, in which S. Basil apologizes for the language used by S. Greg. Thaumaturg. Καθῆκον δέ τινα πεῖραν δι' ἐπιστολῆς καὶ πρὸς τὸν ὁμόψυχον ἡμῶν Ἄνθιμον τὸν Τυάνων ἐπίσκοπον· ὡς ἄρα Γρηγορίου εἰπόντος ἐν ἐκθέσει πίστεως, Πατέρα καὶ Τἱὸν ἐπινοίᾳ μὲν εἶναι δύο, ὑποστάσει δὲ ἕν· Τοῦτο δὲ ὅτι οὐ δογματικῶς εἴρηται, ἀλλ' ἀγωνιστικῶς ἐν τῇ πρὸς Αἰλιανὸν διαλέξει, οὐκ ἠδυνήθησαν συνιδεῖν, οἱ ἐπὶ λεπτότητι τῶν φρενῶν ἑαυτοὺς μακαρίζοντες.—S. Basil. Epist. ccx. (al. lxiv.) ad Neocæsarienses, § 5. Op., tom. iii. p. 316. C. D.]

[g] [Διὸ καὶ διηκόνουν αὐτῷ οἱ ἄγγελοι, ὡς ἄλλῳ παρ' αὐτοὺς ὄντι· καὶ προσκυνεῖται παρ' αὐτῶν, οὐχ ὡς τῇ δόξῃ μείζων, ἀλλ' ὡς ἄλλος παρὰ πάντα τὰ κτίσματα, καὶ παρ' ἐκείνους ὤν, μόνος καὶ τοῦ Πατρὸς ἴδιος ὢν κατ' οὐσίαν Υἱός ... οὐκοῦν Θεοῦ ἐστι μόνου τὸ προσκυνεῖσθαι, καὶ τοῦτο ἴσασι καὶ αὐτοὶ οἱ ἄγγελοι, ὅτι κἂν ἄλλων ταῖς δόξαις ὑπερέχωσιν, ἀλλὰ κτίσματα πάντες εἰσί, καὶ οὐκ εἰσὶ τῶν προσκυνουμένων, ἀλλὰ τῶν προσκυνούντων τὸν Δεσπότην.— S. Athan. Orat. ii. contra Arian. sect. 23. Op., tom. i. p. 491. A. C.]

à leur cause, pour la defendre des objections de Gentiles [h] ;
and so, that *ils leur celassent* [&] *dissimulassent & déguisassent
beaucoup de choses* [i], Origen and the Fathers are much beholden to him that makes them dissemble and disguise many
things in *Christian religion;* as if without dissembling and
disguising many things they could not have maintained it.

But (though there were never any such thing indeed) this
is well feigned and devised of him, that the Fathers *fuyoient
& declinoyent le plus qu'ils pouvoient les occasions de parler ...
des prieres que l'eglise faisoit aux Saints, de peur qu'il ne semblast aux Gentils, qu'il y'eust quelque superficielle apparence
de conformité (bien que fausse & equivoque) entre ce que l'eglise
faisoit à l'endroit des Saints ... & ce que les Payens deferoyent
à leurs faux Dieux; Et que les Payens ne prinssent occasion de
là de retorquer contre eux (bien qu'à fausses enseignes) l'usage
de l'eglise* [j]. (Did shun and avoid as much as they could all
occasions to speak of the prayers of the Church to the Saints,
lest the Gentiles might think that there was some superficial
appearance of conformity (though but false and *equivocal*)
betwixt that which was practised by the Church in this matter,
and that which the heathen did perform to their idols, and
so might take occasion (though upon no just ground) to retort
upon them their own practice). And this showeth well where
the Cardinal is pinched.

["Sainct Cyrille ne nie pas ceste conformité, pource que l'Eglise ne priast
pas les Saincts ... mais pource que l'Eglise ne sacrifioit pas aux Martyrs
comme les Gentils faisoient à leurs Heros."—Card. Perron, Repl.] p. 1046.

Now for Cyril against Julian, Julian objecting that the
Christians *honoroyent de pareille culte les martyrs que les
Payens leurs Heröes*, all that the Cardinal hath to answer
is that the *pareille culte* was only in *Sacrifice done to them,
and nothing else.* Where it is well known, that the heathen
prayed as well as sacrificed to Hercules and the other *heroes*
after their manner, in like sort as they did to their higher
gods. And where he fleeth to Theodoret [k], to help out Saint

---

[h] [Perron, Repl. p. 1043.]
[i] [Ibid.] p. 1044.
[j] [Ibid.] pp. 1044, 1045.
[k] [The following are the passages of Theodoret referred to by Perron: Τί δήποτε τοίνυν ... νεμεσᾶτε ἡμῖν, οὐ θεο-

ποιοῦσιν, ἀλλὰ τιμῶσι τοὺς μάρτυρας, ὡς Θεοῦ γε μάρτυρας καὶ εὔνους θεράποντας; —Theod. de cur. Græc. Affect. lib. viii. (de Martyribus) Op., tom. iv. p. 908. Ἡμεῖς δὲ, ὦ ἄνδρες, οὔτε θυσίας, οὔτε μὴν χοὰς τοῖς μάρτυσιν ἀπονέμομεν,

Cyril, the reader doth well understand that there is great difference between Julian's time, against whom Saint Cyril wrote, and the later times, in which Theodoret wrote his book (if it were Theodoret which wrote the book, for that is not agreed upon by all).

Objections.

["S. Paul parle là de l'invocation absoluë, dont il venoit de dire, *Quiconque invoquera le nom du Seigneur, sera sauvé* ... Sainct Hieróme mesme nous apprend, que nous croyons, selon quelque degré de proportion & analogie, aux Saincts .... car .. les habitants de Hierusalem ... croyoient, selon quelque sorte, en S. Pierre."—Card. Perron, Repl.] p. 1047.

With the objection out of the Rom. chap. 10, the Cardinal is hard beset : so that he is fain to say, *Que nous croyons selon quelque degree de proportion & analogie aux Saints.* And that those in Act. chap. 5, *croyoient selon quelque sorte en Saint Pierre.* So that rather than he will not pray to saints he is content to believe in saints, and to defend his prayer *relative* he is fain to set up a *faith relative ;* and so consequently a faith in *obliquity* and a *faith transitory ;* terms and things never heard of in the Church before, for any man relatively to believe in Saint Peter or in any of the Saints.

And yet further to establish this new *Creed* or *Belief*, he is fain to destroy the old received difference in *Christ's Church*, of *believing one*, and *believing in one*[1]. So that if one *believe* an honest man he must also *believe* in him ; or, as the Cardinal's words are : A Christian man doth believe *aussi bien en l'article de l'eglise, comme à ceux de la Trinité.* As well in the Church (he should say, if he durst), as in the *Trinity :* otherwise he speaks unproperly. For, we believe the Articles, we *believe* not in the Articles. We *believe* the *Articles* both of the *Trinity* and the *Church* true : but so as we *believe* in the *Trinity*, which is the object of some Articles, and *believe* not in the *Church*, which is the object of some other.

ἀλλ' ὡς θείους καὶ θεοφιλεῖς γεραίρομεν ἄνδρας.—Ibid. p. 911. Καὶ ὡς πολιούχους τιμῶσι καὶ φύλακας· καὶ χρώμενοι πρεσβευταῖς πρὸς τὸν τῶν ὅλων δεσπότην, διὰ τούτων τὰς θείας κομίζονται δωρεάς. —Ibid. p. 902. Οἰχ ὡς θεοῖς αὐτοῖς προσιόντες, ἀλλ' ὡς θείους ἀνθρώπους ἀντιβολοῦντες, καὶ γενέσθαι πρεσβευτὰς ὑπὲρ σφῶν παρακαλοῦντες.—Ibid. p. 921.]

[1] Croyre en quelqu'un, croyre à quelqu'un.

Des Peres.

["Obmettant l'examen plus ample de ceste objection, nous viendrons à celle qu'il fait des écrits des Peres, qui sont trois.

"La première est tirée des écrits d'Origene, sur le Cantique des Cantiques, & sur l'Epistre aux Romains," &c.—Card. Perron, Repl.] pp. 1048, 1049.

For Origen upon the Canticles and the Romans, we shall not need to stand much. We grant the words as the Cardinal sets them down: *Que cy aussi tous les Saints qui sont decedez de ceste vie ayants encore la charité envers ceux qui sont en ce monde, sont dits avoir soin de leurs salut & les ayder par leurs prieres & leur intercession envers Dieu, cela ne sera point mal convenable* [m]. And in the other upon the Romans, *Si etiam extra corpus positi vel Sancti qui cum Christo sunt, agunt aliquid et laborant pro nobis* [n] (*laborant pro nobis* or *orant pro nobis*) we agree to either.

For, as for the other two places of Origen, 1. The one where he saith, *Ego sic arbitror* [o], that is but a faint affirmation neither. 2. The other is taken from an allegory [p], which kind of divinity (as the Cardinal knows well) *non est argumentativa*, arguments cannot be drawn from it; although, for the matter, we doubt not of it at all.

["S'ensuit l'autre objection, qui est un canon du Concile de Laodicée ... De ce mot, *religion des Anges*, auquel consiste tout le nerf de l'objection, pource qui est de la part de Sainct Paul, les interpretations des Peres ne sont pas uniformes : Car aucuns, comme Sainct Hierôme, entendent par les Anges dont il est là parlé, les mauvais Anges."—Card. Perron, Repl.] p. 1050. [1051.]

We come now [1,] to the place in the second chapter to the

---

[m] ["Sed et omnes sancti, qui de hac vita decesserunt, habentes adhuc charitatem erga eos qui in hoc mundo sunt, si dicantur curam gerere salutis eorum, et juvare eos precibus suis, atque interventu suo apud Deum, non erit inconveniens."—Orig. in Cant. Hom. lib. iii. (Rufino interprete.) Op., tom. iii. p. 75. d. col. 1.]

[n] ["Jam vero si etiam extra corpus positi vel sancti, qui cum Christo sunt, agunt aliquid, et laborant pro nobis ad similitudinem angelorum, qui salutis nostræ ministeria procurant ... habeatur et hoc quoque inter occulta Dei nec chartulæ committenda mysteria."—Orig. in Epist. ad Rom. lib. ii. (Rufino interprete.) Op., tom. iv. p.479. col. 2. B. C.]

[o] [' Ego sic arbitror, quod omnes illi qui dormierunt ante nos patres, pugnent nobiscum, et adjuvent nos orationibus suis."—Orig. in Jos. Hom. xvi. cap. 13. Op., tom. ii. p. 437. col. 1. E. Both this and the following passage refer to the Old Testament saints.]

[p] [" Quis enim dubitat, quod sancti quique patrum et orationibus nos juvent, et gestorum suorum confirment atque hortentur exemplis."—Orig. in Numer. Hom. xxvi. Op., tom. ii. p. 373. col. 2. B. Origen is here comparing the two tribes and a half, who assisted their brethren in gaining the land over the Jordan, in which they themselves were not to have their inheritance, to the fathers of the Old Testament, who themselves received not the promises (Heb. xi. ult.), yet aid us in obtaining them.]

Colossians; 2, the Canon of the Council of Laodicea; 3, and Theodoret upon them both: for these three depend one upon another. 1. The place to the Colossians he cannot deny but that it is truly alleged, as it is set down by Theodoret. But then he tells us, that concerning the angels, there S. Hierome will have them to be ill angels [q], and Theodoret good.

Now here it cometh to our course, to take up the same lamentation over the Cardinal and his fine spirit in this his citation of Hierome upon the Epistles, that he doth take up over the Bishop (and so might over Pope Sixtus V., Bellarmine and Alan likewise) for citing S. Ambrose on the Epistles; and tell him we might, with a great process and long circumstance, that all learned men know that those Commentaries were written by Pelagius the heretic, (and not by S. Hierome,) and are every where stuffed with Pelagianism. But so will we not do, but spare the Cardinal. Others have done it besides him, while they follow the common tract of those who have usually heretofore alleged them, and then stand critically scanning how they may take the least advantage that may be. But then let him also be spare in finding fault with the Bishop, for that if these be cited under S. Hierome's name by many, those other be cited under S. Ambrose's name by as many, and more.

[" Et moy, s'il m'est permis comme à Ruth de glaner encore quelque espy dedans le champ des Escritures.... j'y ajousteray une troisiéme interpretation... Ne veut point signifier par ce mot, *religion des Anges*, la religion exhibée aux Anges, mais la religion reçevée des Anges ... c'est à dire, la religion Judaïque ... *par Philosophie, & vaine tromperie*, c'est à dire, par les specieux & fallacieux discours des Docteurs des Juifs... *Tradition des hommes* ... c'est à dire, selon les preceptes & ceremonies de la Loy Judaïque, lesquels il appelle Elements ... *Elements du monde*, entendant par le monde, la religion Judaïque ... *Et la bassesse du sens*, ... c'est à dire, en la bassesse du sens litteral de la Loy ... *Comme vivants au monde*, c'est à dire, comme vivants sous le joug de la Loy Judaïque ... Car c'est ce que signifie là le mot ἀπόχρησις, asçavoir un usage prolongé par delà son terme .. *en une culte à plaisir*, c'est à dire, auquel nous ne sommes plus assujettis .. *& en l'inquietude du corps sans intermission*, c'est à dire, en l'occupation perpetuelle, qui attache l'esprit à avoir soin perpetuellement des choses, qui concernent le corps ... Le mot Grec, τιμή, signifie souvent autant que le mot Latin, *mulcta* ... Que l'on ne prenne point occasion de l'affranchisement du joug de la Loy touchant l'abstinence des viandes, pour en abuser contre l'austerité des vrayes macerations & morti-

---

[q] [S. Hier. Epist. cxxi. (al. cli.) Quæst. x. Op., tom. i. col. 875. D.]

fications de la chair : comme sont les abstinences Chrestiennes."—Card. Perron, Repl.] pp. 1051—1055.

As to the Cardinal's gleanings, they are none of Ruth's gleanings, nor ever gathered in Boaz' fields. Indeed of those gleans he hath made a strange piece of work upon the second to the Colossians, as will appear by these twelve *c'est à dires* following. 1. The *Religion of Angels* ; that is, *the Religion of the Jews.* 2. *Philosophy* ; that is, *the discourses of the doctors of the Jews.* 3. *Traditions of men ;* that is, *the precepts of the Law.* 4. *The elements of the world ;* that is, *the commandments and ceremonies of the Law.* 5. *The world ;* that is, *the religion of the Jews.* 6. *Humility of mind ;* that is, *the literal sense of the Law.* 7. *Living in the world ; in the world,* that is, *under the yoke of the Law.* 8. *Ipso usu,* or ἀποχρήσει· that is, *the use of the ceremonies prolonged beyond their time.* 9. *Voluntary worship ;* that is, *the Law, because we are no longer subject now to the observation of the Law.* 10. *Not sparing the body ;* that is, *having continual care of the things concerning the body.* 11. Τιμὴ, (ever hitherto translated *honour ;*) that is, *punishment.* 12. *Saturitatem carnis ;* that is, *to abuse the freedom of abstinence from Jewish meats, against the austerity of true Christian mortification.* All which *c'est à dires* are so uncouth and unheard of, and even one of them contrary to another, that sure a rueful gleaning he hath made : for instead of good corn he hath gleaned nothing but straw all the while. To rehearse them is to confute them.

[" Mais en somme . . . il est certain, qu'il parle de ceux qui nommoient les Anges à l'exclusion de Christ, nommoient les Anges au lieu de Christ."—Card. Perron, Repl.] p. 1055.

For the Canon of the Council[r] he giveth divers senses to carry the reader about ; but in the end he resolveth it must needs be the *worship of Angels, excluding Christ :* of which *excluding of Christ* neither the Council nor Theodoret make any mention, but count the worship of Angels an excluding of Christ.

[" Reste Theodoret, lequel alleguant ce Canon sur le propos des parolles de S. Paul dit ainsi, *Ceux qui,* &c. . . . Il y a dans le Grec εὐκτήρια, qui signifie proprement Oratoire, pour prier avec sacrifice . . . Il parle de ceux qui prioient les Anges à l'exclusion de Christ, & en le laissant ; c'est à dire,

---

[r] [Of Laodicea. See above, p. 23.]

prioient les Anges, comme le dernier object de la Religion. Lesquelles parolles (Theod. de Martyr. lib. viii.ˢ) sont si claires & expresses pour la priere que l'Eglise fait aux Saincts decedez, de prier pour les fidèles vivants, que les adversaires de ceste doctrine . . . sont contraints de fuïr à la recusation de l'auther, & dire, que ce livre n'est point de Theodoret."
—Card. Perron, Repl.] pp. 1056—1058.

Now for Theodoret, who saith expressly, the Council by that Canon doth forbid *that we should pray unto angels, under pretence of humility, saying that we cannot come to God, but it behoveth us by the angels to procure ourselves his favour and good-will*: he is put to a pitiful shift, first, to trifle that εὐκτήρια are places to pray in with sacrifice, contrary to the nature and use of the word, as all men know. And further, to say that those against whom the Canon was made, made the *angels* the uttermost object of religion, and contented themselves to adore them, without passing any further. Which he speaketh *gratis*: for Theodoret is plain that we should *offer up our prayers and thanks unto God by Christ himself, and not by the angels*ᵗ. And so, as the Bishop said before, so he saith again, that there is the same reason of *saints* that there is of the *angels*; and therefore we are to offer up our prayers and thanks to God by Christ himself, and *not by the saints*.

For the books *De Martyribus* (which is the eighth book *De Curat. Græc. Affect.*) and the *Religiosa* or *SS. Patrum Historia*, whether they be Theodoret's true works or no, the Bishop meddled not, and so leaveth him to try that with Monsieur Rivet and others that have dealt in that matter ᵘ. Always the Bishop thinketh he hath the better here, in that Theodoret upon the Epistles was never questioned by any man; but those two, which the Cardinal citeth, have long been,

ˢ [Καὶ αἱ μὲν γενναῖαι τῶν νικηφόρων ψυχαὶ περιπολοῦσι τὸν οὐρανὸν τοῖς ἀσωμάτοις χοροῖς συγχορεύουσαι· τὰ δὲ σώματα οὐχ εἷς ἑνὸς κατακρύπτει τάφος ἑκάστου. ἀλλὰ πόλεις καὶ κῶμαι ταῦτα διανειμάμεναι σωτῆρας καὶ ψυχῶν καὶ σωμάτων ἰατροὺς ὀνομάζουσι, καὶ ὡς πολιούχους τιμῶσι καὶ φύλακας· καὶ χρώμενοι πρεσβευταῖς πρὸς τὸν τῶν ὅλων δεσπότην, διὰ τούτων τὰς θείας κομίζονται δωρεάς.—Theod. de curand. Græc. Affect. lib. viii. (de Martyr.) Op., tom. iv. p. 902.]

ᵗ [Ἐπειδὴ γὰρ ἐκεῖνοι τοὺς ἀγγέλους σέβειν ἐκέλευον, αὐτὸς τὸ ἐνάντιον παρεγγυᾷ, ὥστε καὶ τοὺς λόγους καὶ τὰ ἔργα κοσμῆσαι τῇ μνήμῃ τοῦ Δεσπότου Χριστοῦ· καὶ τῷ Θεῷ δὲ καὶ Πατρὶ τὴν εὐχαριστίαν δι' Αὐτοῦ, φησίν, ἀναπέμπετε, μὴ διὰ τῶν ἀγγέλων.—Theod. in Col. iii. 17. Op., tom. iii. p. 496.]

ᵘ [" Libris de Græcorum Affectionibus curandis ejusmodi nonnulla addita esse, malim dicere, quam de auctore dubitare."—Andr. Riveti Crit. Sacr. lib. iv. cap. 21. Op., tom. ii. p. 1143. Roterod. 1652; and Conf. Coci Censur. quorund. Script. p. 195. Lond. 1614.]

and still are by learned men called in doubt, whether he were the true author or no. And that upon good reason, seeing Theodoret is by their great author, Sixtus Senensis, reckoned up among those that held the saints departed did not enjoy the presence of God till after the general resurrection [x]. Which if he held that they did not, then would he not hold that they were to be prayed to, they being secluded from God's presence; and so not hearing, seeing, nor knowing whether prayer were made to them at all, or no. And then *prier pour prier* were to small purpose.

["Pource que Monsieur d'Ely semble revoquer en doute ceste Oraison-là, encore qu'il n'en cotte nulle cause, neantmoins d'autant que d'autres avant luy l'ont recusée avec specification des causes de leur recusation, il est necessaire de les destruire."—Card. Perron, Repl.] p. 1064.

And for Nyssen *in Theodorum Martyrem,* seeing we disagree not about that which is alleged out of him, we shall not need for this time to controvert that Oration, till something shall happen to be alleged out of it wherein we disagree, and that may give occasion to speak further; what time they may perhaps know what can reasonably be objected against it. In the meantime it maketh the matter somewhat suspicious, that the Cardinal mistrusteth his own author, in that (no word being spoken by the Bishop to impugn him) he, before any occasion given, enters into a needless defence of him of his own accord; which plainly showeth all is not well with his Nyssen, but that he laboureth of somewhat, somewhere, wherever it is.

This one point is needful to be observed throughout all the Cardinal's answer, that he hath framed to himself five distinctions: 1. Prayer *direct,* and Prayer *oblique,* or *indirect.* 2. Prayer *absolute,* and Prayer *relative.* 3. Prayer *sovereign,* and Prayer *subaltern.* 4. Prayer *final,* and Prayer *transitory.* 5. Prayer *sacrifical,* and Prayer *out of,* or *from the sacrifice.* Prayer *direct, absolute, final, sovereign, sacrifical,* that must not be made to the Saints, but to God only. But as for *Prayer oblique, relative, transitory, subaltern, from*

---

[x] [Vide Sixti Senens. Bibl. Sanct. lib. vi. Annot. cccxlv. tom. ii. p. 257. col. 1. D. The passage in Theodoret, on which this opinion is grounded, is Οἱ μὲν οὖν τούτων ἀγῶνες τοσοῦτοι καὶ τηλικοῦτοι, ἀλλ' ὅμως οὐδέπω τῶν στε- φάνων ἀπήλαυσαν· ἀναμένει γὰρ ὁ τῶν ὅλων Θεὸς τοὺς τῶν ἄλλων ἀγῶνας, ἵνα, τοῦ σταδίου λυθέντος, κοινῇ πάντας τῶν ἀναρρήσεων ἀξιώσῃ τοὺς νικηφόρους.—Theod. in Heb. xi. Op., tom. iii. pp. 623. 624.]

or *out of the Sacrifice,* that, saith he, we may make to the Saints.

For all the world, like the question in Scotland, which was made some fifty years since ʸ; whether the *Pater noster* might not be said to *Saints.* For, then they in like sort devised the distinction of 1. *Ultimate, et non ultimate;* 2. *Principaliter, et minus principaliter;* 3. *Primarie, et secundarie;* 4. *Capiendo stricte, et capiendo large;* and, as for *ultimate, principaliter, primarie, et capiendo stricte,* they concluded it must go to God; but *non ultimate, minus principaliter, secundarie, et capiendo large,* it might be allowed Saints.

Yet it is sure, that in these distinctions is the whole substance of his answer. And whensoever he is pressed, he flees straight to his *prayer relative,* and *prayer transitory;* as if *prier pour prier* were all the Church of Rome did hold; and that they made no prayers to the Saints, but only to pray for them. The Bishop well remembers, that Master Casaubon, more than once, told him, that reasoning with the Cardinal touching the invocation of Saints, the Cardinal freely confessed to him, that he had never prayed to Saint, in all his life, save only when he happened to follow the procession; and that then he sung *ora pro nobis* with the clerks, indeed, but else not.

Which cometh much to this opinion he now seemeth to defend; but wherein others of the Church of Rome will surely give him over. So that it is to be feared, that the Cardinal will be shent for this, and some censure come out against him by the Sorbone. For the world cannot believe, that *oblique relative* Prayer is all that is sought; seeing it is most evident, by their Breviaries, Hours, and Rosaries, that they pray *directly, absolutely,* and *finally* to Saints, and make no mention at all of *prier pour prier,* to pray to God forgive them; but to the Saints, to give it themselves. So that all that he saith, comes to nothing. They say to the Blessed Virgin, *Sancta Maria,* not only *ora pro nobis;* but, *Succurre miseris, juva pusillanimes, refove flebiles, accipe quod offerimus, dona quod rogamus, excusa quod timemus* ᶻ.

ʸ [See Foxe's Acts and Monuments, A.D. 1551. tom. ii. pp. 528. 529. Lond. 1684.]

ᶻ [These and the following passages appear to have been extracted from Chemnitz, Exam. Conc. Trid. p. iii. p. 150. Francof. 1574. Chemnitz professes to have quoted most of them

"O Regina Poli, mater gratissima proli,
  Spernere me noli, me commendo tibi soli [a]."

And not only,
"O Maria generosa,
  Super omnes speciosa,
    Impetra nobis veniam [b];"

But also,
"O Maria gratiosa,
  Dulcis, mitis, et formosa,
    Applica nobis gratiam [c];"

And likewise,
"O Maria gloriosa,
  In deliciis deliciosa,
    Præpara nobis gloriam [d]."

"Reparatrix et Salvatrix
  Desperantis animæ,
Irroratrix et largitrix,
  Spiritualis gratiæ,
Quod requiro, quod suspiro,
  Mea *sana* vulnera:
Et *da* menti te poscenti
  Gratiarum munera:
Ut sim . . . .
  Corde prudens, ore studens
    Veritatem dicere;
  Malum nolens, Deum volens,
    Pio semper opere [e]."

Tibi Domina gloriosa commendo hodie et quotidie animam meam; ut me, in tuam custodiam *commendatum, ab omnibus malis et fraudibus Diaboli* custodias; *atque in hora mortis constanter mihi* assistas, *ac animum ad æterna gaudia . . . perducas* [f].

Dona *mihi de præteritis emendationem, de præsentibus custodiam, de futuris cautelam* [g].

To St. George:—
"Hic nos solvat a peccatis,
  Ut in cœlo cum beatis,
    Possimus requiescere [h]."

---

from the Hours of the Virgin used in the Church of Hildensheim, and other German office books, to which access has not been obtained. Several of them (as noted below) are given by Cassander, which is so far a confirmation of Chemnitz's fairness in quotation. And numerous hymns of a similar kind are found in acknowledged Romish Books of Devotion.]

[a] [Chemnitz, ibid. p. 163.]
[b] [Ibid. p. 150.]
[c] [Ibid.]
[d] [Ibid.]
[e] [Ibid. p. 151.]
[f] [Ibid.]
[g] [Ibid.]
[h] [Ibid. p. 152.]

To St. Erasmus :—

> "Sit Erasmus præparatus
> Nostros tergat ut reatus [i]."

To St. Christopher :—

> "Sis memor nostri ... omni hora
> Et tuere, sine mora,
> Corpus, sensum et honorem,
> *Conserva*(*tu*), qui cœli florem
> Meruisti hic portare
> Inter ulnas, ultra mare.
> Nos per tantam dignitatem
> *Fac* vitare pravitatem ;
> Et amare, corde toto,
> Deum verum, laude, voto,
> Præ cunctis mundanis istis ;
> Ut, post mundi hujus tristis
> Blandimenta, te præsente,
> Perducamur ad cœli regna [k]."

To St. Godard :—

> "Opem nobis, Præsul bone,
>   Fer, in nostris angustiis ;
> Et nos solve, in agone,
>   Ab æternis suppliciis [l]."

To St. Augustine :—

> "Canemus totis viribus,
> Jungamus preces precibus,
> Ut, Augustini meritis,
> Cœli fruamur gaudiis."

To St. Ambrose :—

> "O Præsul beatissime,
>   Ambrosi Doctor inclyte,
> Vitæ meæ *rege* cursum ;
>   Post hanc vitam, *trahe* sursum
>   Animam, ad gaudia ;
> Ubi, Deum contemplari,
> Justis piis sociari,
>   Merear, in gloria [m]."

To St. Brigitt :—

> "Naufragantes, in hoc mare,
>   *Tuo ductu* salutare
>   Duc ad vitæ bravia [n]."

---

[i] [Chemnitz, ibid. p. 152.]
[k] [Ibid. pp. 152. 153.]
[l] [Ibid. p. 153.]
[m] [Ibid.]
[n] [Ibid. p. 154.]

To the 11,000 Virgins :—

> "O præclaræ vos puellæ,
> Nunc *implete* meum velle;
> Et dum mortis venerit hora,
> *Subvenite* sine mora.
> In tam gravi tempestate
> Me precantem *defensate*,
>   A Dæmonum instantia [o]."

To all Saints :—

> "Omnes quos Dei Gratia
> Exemit ab hac patria,
> Bona *donantes* cœlestia
> Nostra *laxate crimina* [p]."

To St. Martin :—

> "Martinus autem prævius
> Fac ut sit, horis omnibus,
> Ne, dæmonum fallacia,
> Pes noster impactus ruat;
> *Hic* arma nobis *cœlica*
> Instante pugna *conferat;*
> *Hoc* præliante cominus,
> Hostis *fugetur* noxius;
> *Hic* nos, per undas sæculi,
> Clavo *gubernat* prospero,
> Ne forte nostram spumea
> Puppim Charybdis sorbeat;
> *Hic* nos, triumpho nobili,
> Et laureatos mystice,
> *Aptet* tuis conspectibus
> Junctos supernis civibus [q]."

To St. Nicolaus :—

> "Ergo pie nos exaudi
> Assistentes tuæ laudi,
> Ne subdamur hostis fraudi,
>   Nobis *fer* auxilia :
> Nos, ab omni *malo ducas*
> Via recta nos *conducas,*
> Post hanc vitam nos *inducas,*
>   Ad æterna gaudia [r]."

To him again :—

> "O venerande Pontifex,
> Pius nec tardus opifex,
> Cunctis, qui corde credulo
> *Te quærunt* in periculo,

---

[o] [Chemnitz, ibid. p. 154.]
[p] [Ibid. p. 161.]
[q] [Ibid. p. 162. et G. Cassand. Op., p. 277.]
[r] [Ibid.]

Aufer mortis dispendia,
Confer vitæ stipendia,
Quo, post carnis exilia,
Tecum simus in gloriaˢ."

To Thomas Beckett.

*Deus, pro cujus Ecclesia, gloriosus Pontifex Thomas gladiis impiorum occubuit: præsta quæsumus, ut omnes, qui ejus implorant auxilium, petitionis suæ salutarem consequantur effectum*ᵗ.

62. All which, and many more, show plainly that the practice of the Church of Rome, in this point of invocation of Saints, is far otherwise than Cardinal Perron would bear the world in hand. And that *prier pour prier* is not all; but that *Tu dona cœlum, Tu laxa, Tu sana, Tu solve crimina, Tu duc, conduc, induc, perduc ad gloriam; Tu serva, Tu fer opem, Tu aufer, Tu confer vitam,* are said to them *totidem verbis*: more than which cannot be said to God himself. And again, *Hic nos solvat a peccatis, Hic nostros tergat reatus, Hic arma conferat, Hic hostem fuget, Hic gubernet, Hic aptet tuo conspectui;* which, if they be not *direct* and *absolute*, it would be asked of them, what is *absolute* or *direct*?

ˢ [Chemnitz, ibid. p. 162. et G. Cassand. Op., p. 252.]

ᵗ [Oratio in die S. Thomæ Mart., Miss. Sarum, fol. xvi. a. Paris. 1555.]

A SPEECH

DELIVERED IN THE

STARR-CHAMBER AGAINST

THE TWO IVDAICALL

OPINIONS OF

Mr. TRASKE.

BY THE R. HONORABLE AND

R. FATHER IN God, Lancelot,

late Bishop of *Winchester*,

deceased.

A Speech delivered in the Star-chamber *against the two Judaical opinions of* M. TRASKE.

[John Traske was a native of Somersetshire, and a schoolmaster in the same county. On applying for ordination to James Montague, Bishop of Bath and Wells, he was rejected by Dr. Samuel Ward, the Bishop's chaplain, for insufficiency. Fuller (Church History, book x. cent. xvii. § 61,) asserts that he was subsequently ordained, but it seems doubtful whether he were ever in Holy Orders. He came to London about 1617, where he gained many followers, and went so far as to presume to give the Holy Ghost by laying on of his hands, and to confer the power of curing diseases by anointing with oil. One of his disciples, Hamlet Jackson, persuaded himself that the seventh, and not the first day was to be observed as the day of Rest; and Traske was not unwilling to adopt the same view, having already taught the Jewish distinction of meats, and that the Lord's day was to be observed with the same strictness as the Jewish Sabbath. Jackson afterwards went to Amsterdam, where he apostatized from the faith, and not only became a Jew himself, but perverted many others. Traske was cited before the Star-Chamber[a], and sentenced to be placed in the pillory at Westminster, to be whipped from thence to the Fleet, and there to be imprisoned. He afterwards made his recantation in the Star-Chamber, December 1, 1619[b], and the next year published "A Treatise of Liberty from Judaism." But his wife, whom he had perverted, still continued to hold the same opinions, and remained in prison fifteen or sixteen years, till her death. A full account of Traske and his doctrines is to be found in Pagett's Heresiography, sixth edit. Lond. 1661, pp. 161. *seq.* It contains, (1.) A Letter to Mistriss Trask, who lay prisoner in the Gatehouse many years, for keeping the Jewish Sabbath, and for Working on our Lord's Day. (2.) A Relation of the Life and Proceedings of Master Trask. (3.) A Letter of Mary Chester, imprisoned for the same opinions, written to Master Christopher Sands, renouncing her former Errors, with a Relation of her relapsing afterwards into the same opinions again. (4.) Also a brief Relation of Mistris Trask her Life and Death. (5.) The following Speech of Bishop Andrewes.

---

[a] [Traske's Case is thus given in Hobart's Reports, p. 236: "John Traske, a Minister that held opinion that the Jewish Sabbath ought to be observed, and not ours, and that we ought to abstain from all manner of swine's flesh; being examined upon these things, he confessed that he had divulged these opinions, and had laboured to bring as many to his opinion as he could. And had also written a letter to the King, wherein he did seeme to tax his Majesty of Hypocrisie, and did expressly inveigh against the Bishops high Commissioners, as bloudy and cruel in their proceedings against him, and a papall Clergy.

"Now he being called *ore tenus*, was sentenced to fine and imprisonment, not for holding those opinions, (for those were examinable in the Ecclesiasticall Courts, and not here,) but for making of conventicles and factions by that means, which may tend to sedition and commotion, and for scandalizing the King, the Bishops, and the Clergy."]

[b] [See Lord Bacon's Letter to the Marquis of Buckingham. Works, vol. iii. p. 572. Lond. 1778.]

Traske wrote the following works:—
A Pearle for a Prince, or a Princely Pearle. Lond. 1615.
A Treatise of Liberty from Judaisme; or an Acknowledgement of True Christian Libertie. Lond. 1620.
The Power of Preaching; or the Powerfull Effects of the Word truely preached and rightly applyed. Lond. 1623.]

IT is a good work to make a Jew a Christian: but to make Christian men Jews, hath ever been holden a foul act, and severely to be punished.

When a great Apostle did but by his example only, by *shifting company a little* [c], seem but to induce the Gentiles to Judaize, we know who it was that thought it his duty *to withstand him to his face* [d], *and to ask him, Quomodo?* how, or why, he made the Gentiles to Judaize [e]?

The reason he gives is strong: *That which I have destroyed, if I build it anew;* that which is buried, if I take it up again, *prævaricatorem me constituo* [f], it is plain *prevarication*, that, for a Christian so to do. The word is παραβάτην, which was Julian's surname, and doth indeed signify plain apostasy.

Now if he were so zealous, for offering it but to a few Gentiles lately converted, what ought we to be, when it is sought upon Christians, of so long descent after so many generations?

If to do this while the Synagogue was scarce laid in her grave: what to do it after she is putrified and consumed quite, to rake her up now again after so many hundred years [g]?

If for doing it but indirectly, by nothing but his example, what to him that professes it, makes a doctrine of it? Consider these points well.

This party here stands charged with this fault, that of *Christian men,* the *people of God, his Majesty's subjects,* he seeks to make little better than Jews.

This he doth in two points, and when it takes him in the head, he may do in two, and two, and two more; (we see a third is newly discovered, not heard of till this day;) and so

[c] Gal. ii. 12.
[d] [Ibid.] ver. 11.
[e] [Ibid.] ver. 14.
[f] [Ibid. ver. 18.]
[g] [He refers probably to S. Augustine's words, "Proinde nunc quisquis Christianorum, quamvis sit ex Judæis, similiter ea celebrare voluerit, tanquam sopitos cineres eruens, non erit pius deductor vel bajulus corporis, sed impius sepulturæ violator.'—S. Aug. Epist. lxxxii. (ad Hieron.) § 16. Op., tom. ii. col. 293. B.]

become a perfect Maran[h]: seeing there is no more reason for that one than for that other; for these than for the rest.

1. One is, *Christians are bound to abstain from those meats which the Jews were forbidden in Leviticus.*

2. The other, that *they are bound to observe the Jewish sabbath.* Of either of these briefly: of the Jewish meats first.

First, if we be Christians we cannot but give ear to Christ our Saviour, who in the seventh of Mark[i] *calls all the people together, and when they were come about Him all, He bids them, Hearken unto Me every one of you,* and *mark it well:* What? *That there is nothing, that goeth into the mouth, that defileth the man.* And this is our ground: *Sermo Christi omnes cibos mundans,* saith Gregory Thaumaturgus more than 1300 years since[j].

The Apostle giveth the reason of this speech of our Saviour's. For *I know,* (saith he,) *and I am fully persuaded in Christ, that of itself there is nothing unclean*[k]. And if not, then it cannot make unclean: that which is *clean* cannot defile any.

And indeed should we grant ought were in itself unclean, as Tertullian well saith, *rediret contumelia in Creatorem*[l], the blame must light upon God that made it such. Such a *god, creator immundi,* the Manichees had: we have none such: the true God is not so; His creatures *clean, all.*

For which cause when, after the Flood, God licensed the eating of creatures that had life, He doth it in these terms, *Every thing that liveth shall be meat for you*[m]; *Every thing.* And he adds, to explain it, *Even as the green herb have I given you them: Every thing now,* as before every green herb. Suppose every *wholesome herb* there: so here, every *wholesome meat.* For *herbs* there are, as well as *meats,* noisome and venomous.

Thus stood it then at the first. This, the *law of nations.* This, all the *religion* of meats under Melchisedek's priesthood.

---

[h] [A name for Renegade Moors. See Du Cange's Glossary, sub voc. 'Marani.']

[i] Mark vii. 14.

[j] ['Αλλὰ καὶ ὁ Σωτὴρ ὁ πάντα καθαρίζων τὰ βρώματα, (φησι) Οὐ τὸ εἰσπορευόμενον κοινοῖ τὸν ἄνθρωπον, κ. τ. λ.— S. Greg. Thaum. Epist. Canon. Can. i. apud Bever. Pan. Can. tom. ii. p. 24. B.]

[k] Rom. xiv. 14.

[l] ["Ne dum quædam impura et non munda dicuntur, institutio illorum infamem reddiderit institutorem."—Novatian.] l. de Cibis Judaïcis, [cap. ii. ad calc. Op. Tertull. p. 732. B. "Culpa factorum in artificem redundabit."—Ibid. C. "Ne in auctorem culpa revocetur." cap. iii. p. 733. A.]

[m] Gen. ix. 3.

But after this, under Aaron's, when a *partition-wall* was set up, some were forbidden.

1. True: but I ask first, To whom? Not to the posterity of Japhet, or Cham; nor to the posterity of Sem, but of one son of five. To no other nation of the earth but to the people of the Jews that were *circumcised.*

Begin there then: be *circumcised,* or this belongs not to you. To that people it was given: to others, not.

And it is the common tenet of all divines, fathers, and schoolmen, that the Levitical law standing, all the rest did eat: and none did sin in so eating, no other people did sin in eating those meats but the Jews only. It concerned not others (the book of Leviticus); touched them not; they were not to take notice of it: they kept on still the law of the ninth of Genesis.

2. To the Jews then. But was it to last for ever (this) with them? to have no end? Ask the Jews: and I will have none but the Jews themselves answer this question.

They have an authentical exposition or commentary on the Psalms, (they call it Midrash Tillim[n],) compiled out of and approved by all their Rabbins. In the 146th Psalm, upon that verse[o], *Dominus solvit compeditos,* "The Lord looseth the *bound;*" they ask: How is Israel *bound?* How will God *loose* them, or when? Their answer is: *Bound* they be (the Jews) from divers kinds of meats, of beasts, fowl and fish. And when or how shall they be *loosed?* By the Messias (say they) when he comes. For He shall loose them from this bond, and restore them to the free use of all. So at His coming they hope to be free. And if we believe He is come, we are to hold ourselves free: (even holding that they hold.) And he that thinks Christ is come, and yet holds himself bound to them, in so holding is not only a Jew, but worse than any Jew: worse to Christ than they to their Messias.

3. Thirdly, I say, seeing they were not *prohibita, quia mala,* (for *evil* they were not,) this was no *moral law.* Being *mala, quia prohibita,* it must needs be a *ceremonial,* to endure but a time, as the name gives[p]. That is, to endure no longer

---

[n] מדרש התלים. [i.e. Exercitatio in Psalmos Magna. fol. בן בן verso. Venet. 1546.]

[o] Ver. 8.

[p] Ἀπὸ τῆς μονῆς εἰς καιρὸν, i. e. a duratione ad tempus.

than the prohibition did. And that no longer than the *law of ordinances* whereof it is a part.

Now of that law Christ was the end. *The handwriting of ordinances* [q], that, *sustulit de medio,* saith the Apostle; *He took that away, cancelled it, nailed it to His cross.* Sure if He took anything away, that He took away; or else we be Jews still, not in this point only, but in all other as well as this. But *we are dead to it,* and *it to us,* as Saint Paul there saith [r].

Will ye see this plainly? Will ye hear it from heaven? Saint Peter, as it should seem, *at the coming down of the great vessel like a sheet with all manner of beasts, unclean as well as clean, in it* [s], stood persuaded the *Levitical law* of abstaining had held still: but *the voice from heaven* informed him otherwise; bade him, *Rise, kill, eat* [t]: *not fearing* (saith Austin) *any Jewish observances* [u]. And when he alleged *the difference of clean and unclean,* which *he had ever kept* [v], he was answered, that difference was gone; *God had cleansed all in the sheet.* Now, *what God had cleansed, he nor any from thenceforth to hold common or unclean* [w]: *and this was done thrice* [x]. That word from heaven was *litis decisorium,* made an end of this matter.

Ensuing this voice, we see that, in the fifteenth chapter of the Acts, in the first Council held by the Apostles themselves, S. Peter calls it, to *tempt God* and to *overload men,* to require it now [y]. Saint James calls it, *to disquiet* and *trouble them with more than needs* [z]. They all call it, in their Epistle Synodical, ἀνασκευάζειν, that is, *a ravelling out of that had been well knit before* [a], to enjoin any such thing.

To the Holy Ghost and to them it seemed good, to restrain no kind of creatures, *so it were not offered to Idols, nor strangled* [b]. And if so, then any, (though clean): if not so, then none; no kind at all. (And yet this was but for the time neither, nor but for honour of the funerals [c].)

---

[q] Χειρόγραφον ἐν δόγμασι. Col. ii. 14, 15.
[r] Col. ii. 20.
[s] Acts x. 11, 12.
[t] [Ibid.] verse 13.
[u] ["Fortassis ergo et Petro ita dictum est, *Occide et manduca;* ut non jam teneret observationes Judæorum." —S. Aug. Serm. cxlix. cap. iv. Op., tom. v. col. 1018. C. See also Serm. ci. in Appendix of the same volume, col. 2591. D.]

[v] Acts x. 14.
[w] [Ibid.] ver. 15.
[x] [Ibid.] ver. 16.
[y] Acts xv. 10.
[z] [Ibid.] ver. 19.
[a] [Ibid. ver.] 24.
[b] [Ibid.] ver. 28, 29.
[c] [i. e. The honourable burying of the Law, now dead. See S. Aug. Epist. lxxxii. (ad Hieronym.) § 16. Op., tom. ii. col. 293. A.B.]

1. Upon this, we have Saint Paul full for it. *Whatsoever is sold in the shambles, that eat ye*[d]. And to whom this? To the Corinthians. And at Corinth, all sorts of meat were there sold (it is well known); the Jews were not *clerks of the market* there.

2. Again, to Timothy for Ephesus. *Every creature of God is good, and nothing* ἀπόβλητον, *to be cast away, to be refused, being received with thanksgiving*[c]. *Every creature.*

3. Again, to Titus, for Candy. *To the clean, all are clean*[f]: What would we more? *All, every,* and *whatsoever;* who can devise terms more general?

On the other side, he is direct; he would have none to make *a matter of religion* of meats and drinks.

The kingdom of God is neither meat nor drink[g].
Meat makes us not accepted to God, no meat[h].
If we eat this meat, we are not the less in his favour:
If we eat not that, we are not the more.

Tertullian saith well: *Qui per escas colit Deum, prope est, ut ventrem pro Deo habeat*[i]: If we make a religion of meats, we are not far from making our *belly* our *god*.

But what if any should, for all this, think thus? (as sure some there were, even then, that seemed so to think:) Doth the Apostle give any way? Doth he not upbraid them, *that being with Christ dead to these ordinances, they should fall to dogmatizing thus, Taste not, touch not*[k]: *Taste not* such a meat; *Touch not* such a dead thing, it will make you unclean. For these must follow one another; they be in the same place of the same chapter, so interlaced, there is no severing them. By holding the chapter of Jewish meats[l], we must fall further into these phrensies, and go from *Taste not,* to *Touch* not[m]. And if we touch a *dead hare, mouse,* or *mole,* or an *oyster-shell, then are we unclean, and must wash our clothes, and so remain unclean till the sunset*[n]. If a trap chance to kill a *mouse,* it is unclean; it must be broken all to pieces.

And as we may not eat *swan* or *heron*, &c.[o], or any *shellfish*[p], so we must eat *grasshoppers*, and *beetles*, and *dorrs*[q], instead of them.

[d] 1 Cor. x. 25.
[e] 1 Tim. iv. 4.
[f] Tit. i. 15.
[g] Rom. xiv. 17.
[h] 1 Cor. viii. 8.
[i] ["Ut Dominum habeat ventrem suum." Novatian.] l. de Cibis [Judaicis, cap. v. ad calc. Op. Tert. p. 734.B.]
[k] Col. ii. 20, 21.
[l] Levit. xi.
[m] [Ibid.] ver. 26. 31.
[n] [Ibid.] ver. 33.
[o] [Ibid.] ver. 18, 19.
[p] [Ibid. ver. 9—12.]
[q] ['Locusts,' ibid.] ver. 22.

These must go together; these, and twenty fooleries more. There is no end of *error*.

But for us in these latter times the Apostle saith plainly, *There shall come some such as shall teach to abstain from meats as unlawful, which God hath created to be received with thanksgiving by them that believe and know the truth*[r]*:* and then adds for his reason, *for every creature is good,* and *none to be refused*.

But those that thus shall teach, he brandeth with five evil marks. 1. That they shall be *apostates*[s], or *depart from the faith*. 2. That, *led by spirits of error*[t]. 3. That (the *devil's doctors* they be) preach *the doctrine of devils*. 4. That, *lying hypocrites* they be, *teach lies in hypocrisy*[u]. 5. That, what part soever else they have not, they *have their consciences seared with a hot iron*. Such as were the Marcionites and Manichees of old; and such as now this party here, to make up the number.

And thus the Scripture leaves this matter.

Now, if you desire to know what the Church's tenet hath been concerning this point.

1. In the midst of the *persecution*, there is a book in Tertullian, the title of it is, *De Cibis Judaicis*, which I believe this man never saw: it is directly to this point. And it is not long, for it was but an Epistle. It will serve to satisfy any man that will but read it, that this man speaks he knows not what; that the whole Primitive Church was wrong, if he be in the right.

For the after-times of the Church, I will trouble you but with one example, one authority, and one censure against him. The example is famous in the Ecclesiastical Story[x], of Spiridon, a worthy Bishop (as was any in the first great Council of Nice), a man indued with the spirit of *prophecy,* and with the gift of working miracles. There came to him a stranger, weary and faint; and it was Lent. He at the present provided of no other meat, but of some pork in a powdering tub[y]; that he caused to be boiled, and set on the table; fell to himself first and willed him to do the like.

---

[r] 1 Tim. iv. 3.
[s] Ἀποστήσονται.
[t] 1 Tim. iv. 1.
[u] [Ibid.] ver. 2.

[x] Sozom. [Hist. Eccl.] lib. i. cap. xi. [p. 24.]
[y] [A salting tub.]

And when he strained a little, and said, he was a Christian; *So much the rather* (saith the Bishop) *because you are so, are you not to refuse: for* (saith he, and gave it for his reason) *To the clean, all things are clean*[z]. So, with him, pork was *inter munda*.

2. The authority shall be Saint Augustine's against Faustus the Manichee[a], tainted with this very phrensy, (a full testimony for the Church's practice then:) *Quis jam hoc Christianus observat, ut Leporem non edat?* What Christian man is there now, that observes this, that he will not eat of a hare? And he goes further, (which shows plainly the restraint of the xv. of the Acts was but for a time,) yea, though the hare be *manu a cervice percussus, et nullo cruento vulnere occisus,* killed with a *blow on the neck,* and no *blood* of it let out. But if any should be so simple, *a cæteris irridetur,* (saith he further,) all Christians else would scorn him; and adds for his reason, *Ita omnium animos in hac re tenuit sententia veritatis, 'Nihil quod per os intrat coinquinat hominem,' nullam cibi naturam, quam societas admisit humana, condemnans.* So hath the sentence of the truth (that is, Christ) possessed all men's minds for this matter: (what sentence is that?) *Nothing that goeth in at the mouth defileth the man:* which sentence condemneth no kind of meat, that the society of mankind hath admitted of.

3. The censure is of the Council of Gangræ, (within two or three years as ancient as the first Council of Nice; Hosius was present at both,) holden against Eustathius, of this man's mind, as it seemeth: it is the second canon[b]; and in the great authentic book of the Church, read in the Fourth General Council of Chalcedon, the lxi.[c] *If any man shall*

---

[z] Titus i. 15.

[a] [" Quis jam hoc Christianus observat, ut turdos vel minutiores aviculas non attingat, nisi quarum sanguis effusus est, aut leporem non edat, si manu a cervice percussus, nullo cruento vulnere occisus est? Et qui forte pauci adhuc tangere ista formidant, a cæteris irridentur; ita omnium animos in hac re tenuit illa sententia veritatis, *Non quod intrat in os vestrum, vos coinquinat, sed quod exit;* nullam cibi naturam, quam societas admittit humana, sed quæ iniquitas admittit peccata, condemnans." — S. Aug. contr. Faust.] lib. xxxii. cap. 13. [Op., tom. viii. col. 700. B.C.]

[b] [Εἴ τις ἐσθίοντα κρέα χωρὶς αἵματος καὶ εἰδωλοθύτου καὶ πνικτοῦ, μετ' εὐλαβείας καὶ πίστεως, κατακρίνοι, ὡς ἂν διὰ τὸ λαμβάνειν ἐλπίδα μὴ ἔχοντα, ἀνάθεμα ἔστω.—Conc. Gangr. Can. ii.—Conc., tom. ii. col. 416. D.E.]

[c] [On the subject of this 'great authentic Book of the Church,' the Codex Canonum Ecclesiæ Universæ, see Bp. Beveridge's Annot. in Can. Chalc. i. (Annot. in Pand. Can. ad calc. tom. ii. p. 108.) and Cod. Canon. Eccl. prim. vind. et illustr., lib. ii. cap. v. § vi. p. 64. Oxon. 1848. The Canon is numbered as above in Justelli Bibl. Jur. Can. tom. i. p. 41. Paris. 1660.]

condemn any Christian for eating any flesh (except as the Apostles had before except), *as having no hope to please God for his so eating;* what then? *Anathema sit,* Be he *accursed,* that shall so condemn any.

And so, with that censure, I leave this first opinion.

The other, that *Christian men are bound to the Jew's Sabbath.* I had thought he had held both to that and to the Sunday too: and if that be his opinion, then is he a flat Ebionite (one of the first heresies that ever was condemned), that made a piece of *linsey-woolsey*[d] of *Christian religion,* as appeareth by Eusebius[e].

But if to no other but that of the Saturday, then is he *vere baptizatus Judæus,* a very christened Jew, a Maran, the worst sort of Jews that is.

The Apostle (*inter alia*), reckoning up divers others, concludes with the Sabbath; and immediately upon it adds, *Which all are but shadows of things to come* (Sabbath and all); *but the body is Christ*[f]. The *body* had, the *shadow* to vanish: that *which was to come,* when it is come, to what end any figure of it? it ceaseth too. That to hold the *shadow of the Sabbath* is to continue, is to hold *Christ the body* is not yet come.

It hath ever been the Church's doctrine, that Christ made an end of all Sabbaths, by His Sabbath in the grave. That Sabbath was the last of them. And, that the Lord's Day presently came in place of it: *Dominicus Dies, Christi resurrectione declaratus est Christianis, et ex illo cœpit habere festivitatem suam*[g], saith Austin. The *Lord's Day* was, by the resurrection of Christ, declared to be the *Christian's Day;* and from that very time (of Christ's *resurrection*) it began to be celebrated, as *the Christian Man's Festival.*

For the Sabbath had reference to the old Creation: but in Christ *we are a new creature*[h]; a new creation by Him, and so to have a new *Sabbath:* and *vetera transierunt,* No reference to the old, we.

[d] [Stuff made of linen and wool mixed.]

[e] [Καὶ τὸ μὲν Σάββατον, καὶ τὴν Ἰουδαϊκὴν ἄλλην ἀγωγὴν ὁμοίως ἐκείνοις παρεφύλαττον· ταῖς δ' αὖ κυριακαῖς ἡμέραις ἡμῖν τὰ παραπλήσια εἰς μνήμην τῆς τοῦ Κυρίου ἀναστάσεως ἐπιτελοῦσι.— Euseb. Hist. Eccl.] lib. iii. cap. 27. [pp. 121, 122.]

[f] Col. ii. 16, 17.

[g] [S. Aug.] Epist. [lv. al.] cxix. cap. xiii. [Op., tom. ii. col. 204. A.]

[h] 2 Cor. v. 7.

By whom He made the worlds[i], saith the Apostle of Christ: so, two worlds there were. The first, that ended at Christ's *passion*, saith Athanasius[k]; and therefore then the sun, without any eclipse, went out of itself. The second, which began with Christ's *resurrection:* and that day, *initium novæ creaturæ,* the beginning (and so, the *Feast*) of them that are *in Christ a new creature.*

It is deduced plainly.

The Gospels keep one word, all four: tell us, Christ rose μίᾳ σαββάτων, *Una Sabbatorum;* that is, after the Hebrew phrase, the first day of the week.

1. The Apostles, they keep their meetings on that day: and Saint Luke keeps the very same word exactly, μίᾳ σαββάτων, (to exclude all error.) On that day they were συνηγμένοι[l], that is, held their *Synaxes,* their solemn *Assemblies;* to preach, to pray, to break bread, or celebrate the Lord's Supper[m], δειπνὸν κυριακὸν ἐν ἡμέρᾳ κυριακῇ, the Lord's Supper, on the Lord's Day[n]; for these two only, (1) the *Day,* and (2) the *Supper,* have the epithet of κυριακὸν, *Dominicum,* in the Scriptures; to show *Dominicum* is alike to be taken in both.

This for the *practice* then.

2. If you will have it in *precept:* The Apostle gives it (and in the same word still), that against μίᾳ σαββάτων, the day of their Assembly, *Every one should lay apart what God should move him to offer to the collection for the saints, and then offer it*[o]: which was so ever in use. That, the day of oblations. So have you it, in practice and in precept, both. Even till Socrates's time, who keeps the same word still[p].

This day, this μία σαββάτων, came to have the name of *Dies Dominicus* in the Apostles' times, and is so expressly called then, by Saint John in the Revelation, i. 10.

And that name, from that day to this, it hath holden still; which continuance of it, from the Apostle's age, may be deduced down, from father to father, even to the first Council of Nice; and lower, I trust, we need not follow it. No doubt is made of it since then, by any that hath read anything.

[i] Heb. i. 2.
[k] [See S. Athan. de Sabbatis et Circumcisione, § 1. Op., tom. ii. p. 55. A.B. But it is doubtful whether this treatise was written by S. Athanasius.]
[l] Act. xx. 7.
[m] 1 Cor. xi. 20.
[n] Apoc. i. 10.
[o] 1 Cor. xvi. 2.
[p] [Socr. Hist. Eccl.] lib. v. cap. 22. [p. 294.]

I should hold you too long, to cite them in particular. I avow it on my credit, there is not any ecclesiastical writer in whom it is not to be found.

Ignatius[q] (whom I would not name, but that I find his words in Nazianzen[r]), Justin Martyr[s], Dionysius Bishop of Corinth, in Eusebius[t], lib. iv., Irenæus[u], Clemens Alexandrinus[x], Tertullian[y], Origen[z], Cyprian[a], every one.

And that we may put it past all question, Justin Martyr, who lived the very next age to the Apostles, and Tertullian, who lived the next age to him, both say directly, The solemn Assemblies of the Christians were that day ever, on *Sunday*, τῇ τοῦ Ἡλίου ἡμέρᾳ, saith Justin[b]; *Die Solis*, saith Tertullian, and leaves the Jews to their *Saturn*: (either, in their Apology for the Christians, offered by them to the Emperor. Justin made two; in his *Second*. Tertullian but one, the xvi. chapter of his[c].) That of the true day there can be no manner of doubt.

A thing so notorious, so well known even to the *heathen* themselves, as it was (in the Acts of the Martyrs) ever a usual question of theirs (even of course) in their examining. What? *Dominicum servasti?* Hold you the Sunday? and their answer known; they all aver it, *Christianus sum, intermittere non possum;* I am a Christian, I cannot intermit it: Not the *Lord's Day* in any wise. These are examples enough. I will add but an authority and a censure, and so end.

[q] [Κατὰ κυριακὴν ζωὴν ζῶντες.—S. Ignat. Epist.] ad Magnesianos. [§ 9. Cotel. Patr. Apost. tom. ii. p. 20., and compare the following passage in the interpolated Epistle to the Magnesians. Καὶ μετὰ τὸ σαββατίσαι, ἑορταζέτω πᾶς φιλόχριστος τὴν κυριακὴν, τὴν ἀναστάσιμον, τὴν βασιλίδα, τὴν ὑπάτην τῶν πασῶν ἡμερῶν.—Ibid. p. 57.]

[r] [Ἡ καινὴ παρῆν ἡμέρα τῆς ἑορτῆς, ἣν οὕτως ὀνομάζομεν πρώτην κυριακήν.—S. Greg. Naz. Orat. xix.] Hom. Epitaph. in Patrem. [Op., tom. i. p. 305. C. See also Orat. xliii. in Novam Dominicam, ibid. p. 700. A.]

[s] Apol. ii. [See below, note [b].]

[t] [Τὴν σήμερον οὖν κυριακὴν ἁγίαν ἡμέραν διηγάγομεν.—Dion. Cor. Ep. ad Rom. apud] Euseb. [Hist. Eccl.] lib. iv. cap. 23. [p. 187.]

[u] [Τὸ δὲ ἐν κυριακῇ μὴ κλίνειν γόνυ, σύμβολόν ἐστι τῆς ἀναστάσεως.—S. Iren. fragm. Op., p. 342., quoted in Pseudo-]Justin.[Respons. et Quæst. ad Orthodoxos. Quæst.] 115. [apud S. Justin. Op., p. 490. A.B.]

[x] [Οὗτος ἐντολὴν τὴν κατὰ τὸ εὐαγγέλιον διαπραξάμενος κυριακὴν ἐκείνην τὴν ἡμέραν ποιεῖ.—S. Clem. Alex.] Strom. [lib.] vii. [cap. 12. p. 877.]

[y] [" Non Dominicum Diem, non Pentecosten, etiam si nossent, nobiscum communicassent."—Tert.] de Idol. [cap. xiv. Op., p. 94. B. "Die Dominico jejunium nefas ducimus."—Tert.] de Cor. Mil. [cap. iii. Op., p. 102. A.]

[z] [Ἐὰν δέ τις πρὸς ταῦτα ἀνθυποφέρῃ τὰ περὶ τῶν παρ' ἡμῖν κυριακῶν.—Orig.] con. Celsum, [lib.] viii. [sect. 22. Op., tom. i. p. 758. F.]

[a] [" Dominico legit interim nobis." — S. Cypr.] Epist. xxxiii. [xxxviii. Fell. Op., p. 75.]

[b] [S. Just. Mart. Apol. i. sect. 67. Op., pp. 83. D. 84. A.]

[c] [Tert. Apol. cap. xvi. Op., p. 16. B.]

The authority I will refer you to is of the great Athanasius. Great for his learning, for his virtue, for his labour, and for his sufferings; but above all, great for his *Creed*.

Tertullian had written, as a book, *De Cibis Judaicis*, which we have[d], so another, *De Sabbato Judaico*, which we have lost. But it is supplied by Athanasius's book, *De Sabbato et Circumcisione*[e], (for so he puts them, and so they must go together, *Circumcision* and the *Sabbath*) in which he is so clear and so full for the abolishing of the *Jew's Day*, and the succeeding of the *Lord's Day* in place of it, as no man can wish more. And the treatise is no long one neither.

Now, as in the other of meats, so in this, will I end with the censure. It is of the Council of Laodicea, more ancient than the first of Nice[f], and of so special account, as we find it cited by Saint Basil[g]; nay, as we find four of the Canons made in this Council taken out of it, and transferred, and made four of the Canons of the great Council of Nice[h]. Such was the authority it was had in. It is the xxix. Canon, and of the authentical great book acknowledged in that of Chalcedon the cxxxiii.[i] This it is: That *Christian men may not judaize, or grow Jews; that is, not make the Sabbath, or Saturday, their day of rest; but that they are to work on that day* (this comes home), *giving their honour of celebration to the Lord's Day. And if any in this point be found to judaize, Let them be Anathema Deo et Christo, to God and Christ both*[k].

So, to his two opinions, here are two Anathemas, by two ancient Councils, above all exception. And no other censure shall need.

---

[d] [See it quoted above, p. 85.]
[e] [See S. Athanasii Op., tom. ii. pp. 55—59.]
[f] [The old date of this Council was A.D. 320, but it is inferred by Bp. Beveridge from the mention of the Photinians in the 7th Canon, and from other reasons, that this Council was held about A.D. 365. Vide Annot. in Pand. Can. p. 193. It is generally placed after A.D. 360, or 370. See Mansi Conc. tom. ii. p. 393.]
[g] [S. Basil. Epist. ad Amphil. Can. i. (Bev. Pand. Can., tom. ii. p. 48.) rejected the Baptism of the Montanists, and so agreed with the Council of Laod. Can. viii.—Conc., tom. i. col.

1510. C.]
[h] [Compare Can. Nic. ii. = Laod. iii.
iv. —— xii.
xvii. —— iv.
xiv. —— vii.
[i] [See it quoted under this number in Justelli Bibl. Jur. Can. tom. i. p. 52.]
[k] ["Ὅτι οὐ δεῖ Χριστιανοὺς Ἰουδαΐζειν, καὶ ἐν τῷ σαββάτῳ σχολάζειν, ἀλλὰ ἐργάζεσθαι αὐτοὺς ἐν τῇ αὐτῇ ἡμέρᾳ· τὴν δὲ κυριακὴν προτιμῶντας, εἴγε δύναιντο, σχολάζειν ὡς Χριστιανοί· Εἰ δὲ εὑρεθεῖεν Ἰουδαϊσταί, ἔστωσαν ἀνάθεμα παρὰ Χριστῷ.— Conc. Laod. Can. xxix. Conc., tom. i. col. 1501. C.]

A SPEECH
DELIVERED IN THE STARR-CHAMBER, CONCERNING VOWES, IN THE COVNTESSE OF Shrewsburies Cafe.

BY THE R. HONORABLE AND R. FATHER IN God, Lancelot, late Bifhop of *Winchefter*, deceafed.

A Speech delivered in the Star-Chamber, concerning Vows, in the Countess of Shrewsbury's Case[a].

THIS Right Honourable and Noble Countess standeth convict of an act of *disobedience;* which, by divers circumstances, is grown to a *contempt.* This her contempt receiveth a great aggravation, by a relapse; for, having fallen into the like heretofore, (and even concerning the same party,) and being convented then for it, (though not in the right place, so mildly was she dealt with,) and then showed the censure due to her fault, (even no other than is now set on her,) and yet graciously spared then: upon mature consideration, she came to see her own error, and did both acknowledge it, and promise, for ever after to hold herself bound to answer in like case: and both these, under her hand (as, by an Act of Council, appeareth).

Thus then to recidivate, and to go against her own act and promise, upon favour then received: to dash now this second

---

[a] [This lady was Mary, wife of Gilbert, seventh Earl of Shrewsbury, and the youngest daughter of Sir William Cavendish, by the well-known Elizabeth Hardwick. She was imprisoned in the Tower, June 15, 1611, (see More's Letter to Sir Ralph Winwood,--Winwood, State Papers, vol. iii. p. 281,) for refusing to answer the Lords of the Council respecting the secret marriage of the Lady Arabella Stuart (the daughter of her sister, Elizabeth Cavendish, and Charles Stuart, Earl of Lennox) and William Seymour (created in 1640 first Marquess of Hertford, and in 1660 Duke of Somerset). In Trinity Term, 1612, (10 Jac. I.) she was again examined before a select Council at York House. (See Howell's State Trials, vol. ii. p. 76, Lond. 1816, which contains Coke's account of the case from his 12th Report.) She was charged with having twice refused, at Whitehall, and at Lambeth, to make any answer. She grounded her refusal on the privileges of nobility, and would not sign the paper containing her evidence. It was resolved by the Council, that if a sentence should be given in the Star-Chamber judicially, she should be fined 20,000*l*. and imprisoned during the King's pleasure. It appears that she was still in prison May 6, 1613. See a Letter from Mr. John Chamberlain to Sir Ralph Winwood. (Winwood, vol. iii. p. 454.) Collins states in his Peerage, (vol. iii. p. 27, Lond. 1812,) that after that time she was released without further proceedings. There is a charge given against her in the Star-Chamber, printed in the Cabala, p. 369, which is ascribed to Lord Bacon, and as such printed in his Works, (vol. iii. p. 265, Lond. 1778,) where it is added by the editor:—"As if this was not a sufficient warning, she afterwards reported that the Lady Arabella left a child by her husband; for which and her repeated obstinacy she incurred a greater censure in the same court." It is to this latter censure that this speech of Bishop Andrewes seems to refer.]

time, against this *petra scandali*[b], this rock of offence, it must needs make it more grievous.

But as if all that hath been said were not enough, my Lady doth yet further aggravate her offence, than all this, (which I was right sorry to hear;) that she refuseth to answer or to be examined, because (forsooth) there is a *vow* upon her,—*hoc prætexit nomine culpam*[c].

Thus to do, is to draw over her contempt as a veil, so religious a thing as a *vow* is: to make *Sacramentum pietatis, vinculum iniquitatis*, (as Saint Austin saith,) a sacred act of piety, to become a bond to iniquity.

Of which it may well be asked, that which the Prophet doth, *Is it a small thing to grieve men, that she will grieve God also*[d]? Men with contempt of authority; God, with abuse of his holy *vows?* This last pertains to us, to take off this mask, and to let her see (if it please God to open her eyes); or else, to let others see, and to satisfy them, that this of all others, is the worst.

That she can pretend no such *vow*, for she can make no such: the making of any such *vow* cannot be avowed.

And, if she will make it for all that, that it is utterly void; as, not only *vain*, and so not to be regarded; but further, even *a sin*, to make any such *vow*. A sin, to make it. For, no religion at all, neither of this realm, nor of Rome itself, will warrant it, none but disavow it; and a greater sin to keep it: and so to be repented of, as highly offending God.

1. *Vows* are lawful to be made, if they be made lawfully. A *vow* is that to God, that a promise is to *man*; even, *a deliberate promise to God*, (so we define it.) For God is (in our law) a person capable of a *promise*, and of any devise or conveyance else.

He that promises (if it be but to *man*), binds himself; makes himself debtor of his promise, to him he promises: if it be to God, much more.

And if to *man* he break his truth, so by promise plight, it is *perfidia:* but if to God, it is so too, in a far higher degree.

2. *Vows*, then, are to be *made*, and are to be *kept*, if they be

[b] [1 Pet. ii. 9.]   [c] [Virg. Æn. iv. 172.]   [d] Isaiah vii. 13.

made aright. But, how (say you) shall we know, whether they be right made? If they be made of a right matter. Look then to *materia voti*. For the *vow* is, as the *matter* is, ever. Every *beast* is not meet for *sacrifice*; nor everything *matter* meet for a *vow*.

Jacob, that made the first, made it *to pay tithes*[e]: (not Abraham's tithes, tithes by due; he was bound to them; but) a *votive tithe*. For so are *tithes* by *vow*.

David *vowed a vow to the God of Jacob*[f], that he would *build him a Church*. Paying of *tithes*, building of *Churches*, are a good matter, both : and so these *vows* good.

But there was a wealthy widow, (Micah's mother,) she *vowed* 1,100 *pieces of silver, to make a molten image*[g]. The matter of her vow was *idolatry*.

There were *forty of the Jews that vowed never to eat or drink till they had killed Saint Paul*[h]. The matter of their vow was *murder*.

Absalom, he made a vow, and he *must go to Hebron to pay it*[i]; under colour whereof he went about to dispossess King David of his crown. The matter of this vow was *high treason*.

These they called *vows*. These vows, the matter of them was naught : and so, damned *vows*; and so, no vows *vovenda*, but *devovenda* rather. For such *vows* there are, he is cursed that makes them; there are *vows* that are *abomination to God*.

The reason whereof is : If we promise man aught, it must be of something *that pleaseth him*, that he will accept. To promise one a thing that will displease him, a displeasure or a shrewd turn; that is not to promise, but to *threaten* him. So it is with God. If we promise him aught, (as when we *vow*, we promise,) it must be *de re grata*, of something welcome to him.

And so now we have the full definition of a vow; that it is *a deliberate promise to God, made of something acceptable to Him* : else it is a *threat* and no *vow*.

Nothing is acceptable to Him but that which is good. If we pay Him aught (we call it *paying our vow*), we must

[e] Gen. xxviii. 22. [f] Psalm cxxxii. 2. [g] Judges xvii. 3.
[h] Acts xxiii. 12. [i] 2 Sam. xv. 7.

pay him in his own money; else will God reject it, and say, *Vota vestra non respiciam,* (as in Amos v.[j]) not once look at them. Then can no unlawful thing be matter of a *vow*. If that be lawful that is required, the *vow* against it cannot be lawful; and so, no *vow*.

So that howsoever my Lady saith, *she gives to Cæsar that which is Cæsar's*[k]: I know not that. But she giveth to God that which is *not* God's, if she gave him this for a *vow*.

Let us see, then, what is the matter of my Lady's *vow*. This, that *she will not be examined; she will answer no interrogatories*.

Thus doth my Lady speak to God: *O Lord, I promise thee, that being never so lawfully examined, I will not answer*. Doth my Lady think this acceptable to God? It is not, verily. This is no *materia votiva*: and so, this no *vow*.

For, is this a good and just promise? Then may any make the like; nay all, if they will. Now, if all should make the like, not to answer any, then were justice quite overthrown, and could not proceed. The overthrow of justice can be no matter of vow.

Justice proceeds upon examining. Nay, without examining, it cannot proceed. Inquiry must go before it, else it is not justice. Take away this then; let every offender become such a votary as my Lady; no man examined; all will be at a stand: this Court, all Courts, may be shut up.

To this tendeth my Lady's vow; that, no examination, and so no justice. This is not *res Deo grata*: so this, no vow, no promise; rather threatens God with the subversion of justice.

All laws lay a punishment for delaying, for *retardati processus;* but for *annullatio processus,* the final disappointing the whole proceedings, yet much more.

This (I say) cannot be *res Deo grata;* which I show plainly. God Himself, sitting in judgment, did practise this; did *examine,* did *minister interrogatories*. He needed it not: He knew everything perfectly, not only when, but before it was done. Yet did He *interrogate,* albeit He needed not. And no reason to be rendered of it; but only, in so proceeding Himself in His, to teach us how to proceed in ours. In Adam's offences, his interrogatories were, *Ubi es?* and then,

[j] [Amos v. 22.]   [k] Matt. xxii. 21.

Quis indicavit tibi[1]? The very same are propounded to my Lady: Madam, where is *this supposed child?* Madam, *who told you* such a child there is? that the Lady Arabella had a child? If my Lady will not answer these, (God's own questions and none other, not a syllable added) what is this, but with her *vow* to stop God's mouth sitting in judgment? for she will answer neither.

In the case of the *five cities*, God saith, *Descendam, et videbo utrum ita*[m] : I will *go down* and *see*, whether it be so, as is reported. What needed He? He could have seen well enough, and sit still and never stirred. No reason of this neither, but to guide us, how to deal in matters before us: to *descend* into them, to *see* the bottom of them, of any dangerous report. No way for us to *see*, but by *examining* and *interrogating*. So that my Lady refusing this, what is it, but with her *vow* to put out Justice's eyes? which cannot please God; and no more can her *vow*, whereof this is the matter.

I will go from God's practice to his express commandment in his law, which is plain, Deut. xiii. Upon an offence, saith God, *Interrogabis solicite*, the word is היטב[n], that is, *Thou shalt interrogate, well* and *thoroughly interrogate;* so is the word most properly שאלת. And again, in the xvii. *Inquires diligenter, Thou shalt make diligent inquiry*[o].

Now, by the same commandment that God wills the Judge, *Thou shalt ask*, he wills my Lady, Madam, you shall answer. If the Judge be bound to do the one, by God's express charge, my Lady is bound to do the other. *Tenetur respondere:* and so not to vow the not doing of that which God expressly would have done.

Yea, upon any offence, there is power given to the Judge indefinitely to adjure any party (that knoweth aught concerning the matter) to come forth and bear witness in it; and if any hear that adjuration, and hath seen or known of it, if that party utter it not, *portabit iniquitatem suam*[p] : and so is my Lady like to bear her sin, if she answer not. Not her *vow*, but her sin in making this vow. I know not: the bearing her censure may trouble her more : but in the end, when the sin comes to be borne, it will prove far the heavier

---
[1] Gen. iii. 9, 11.   [m] Gen. xviii. 21.   [n] Deut. xiii. 14.
[o] Deut. xvii. 4.   [p] [Lev. v. 1.]

and the harder so to be borne, far the more insupportable. No bond against this bond (I am sure) : this, the bond of all justice.

So that, what doth my Lady with her vow? *The judgments in earth are God's* q, (as Josaphat said well.) *Justice* and equity uphold all things r, as is well said in Job xxxvi. The law is God's law. She makes a fair *vowing*, if she vow down all these. If, with her vow, she destroy the *judgment*, which is God's. If, with her vow, she shake these two *pillars*, which bear up all. If, with her vow, she run full against God's law. Thus saith the law, *Thou shalt ask.* Thus saith my Lady, *Ask not;* if you do, I will not answer. This is, to condemn the law of God itself. And can this vow, or can the matter of it please God?

I will go from matter of justice, to matter of estate. And this I say, that if a man, when he suspects his neighbour, that he hath put his hand to his goods s; if a man when he suspects his wife, (only out of the spirit of jealousy fallen upon him t;) if, in either of these cases, they shall bring the party to examination: if in these, one is to answer, if at all any to answer, much more, when the safety of the blood royal u, when the quiet of thousands depends on it; then, no *vow*, no excuse to serve.

q 2 Chron. xix. 6.
r Job xxxvi. 17.
s [Exod. xxii. 11.]
t [Numb. v. 19.]
u [The father of Arabella Stuart, Charles, fifth Earl of Lennox, was great grandson, through his mother, (a daughter of Margaret, Queen of Scotland, by her second husband, Archibald Douglas, Earl of Angus,) to King Henry VII.; and was himself a younger brother of Henry Darnley, the father of King James I. This proximity to the throne had rendered Arabella Stuart an object of suspicion both to Queen Elizabeth and her successor. During Elizabeth's reign, her presumptive claims to the crown had been publicly brought forward by Parsons, in his "Conference about the next succession of the Crown of England," published by him in 1593, 1594, under the name of Nicholas Doleman, (part ii. p. 124.) Shortly after James's accession, it was the main object of the plot of Sir Walter Ralegh, and Lord Cobham, to place her on the throne of England, (see State Trials, i. 212, 213.) Her innocence was asserted, on Ralegh's trial, by Cecil, one of the commissioners, and by the Earl of Nottingham, who was in the court, where Arabella herself was also present (ibid. 222); and no trace of evidence has been found, which tends to involve her as an active party in this design.

Her near connexion with the crown, and the prominent manner in which her name had been brought forward, rendered her marriage a question of great importance. Elizabeth had prevented her union with Esmé Stuart, Duke of Lennox, which James wished to effect, and also with a son of the Earl of Northumberland. James, on his accession, treated her at first with suspicion, but afterwards received her into some degree of favour, and, as appears from her own letter to the King, printed by Mr. Lodge, (Portraits, Mem. of Ar. Stuart,) gave her permission to marry, only restricting her choice to his own

I will give you but two examples: 1. One before; 2. The other under the Law.

1. Before, it pleased Joseph (it but pleased him; there was no true cause; but it pleased him) to suspect his brethren for spies; he questions them, makes them answer: they deny it. He puts them to it *sub attestatione juramenti*[v]. This, is further than my Lady was required; yet, they made no *vow* not to answer. And this was by the *Law of Nature*.

[2.] Under the Law of God: King Ahab thought he had cause to know what was become of Elias: Obadiah (that was his *lord's steward,* and one that feared God) he tells Elias himself, *There was no country in the kingdom, to which the king had not sent, to know whether he were not there, and kept close by them*[x]*:* and *he made them answer, and when they were examined,* and denied it, (and there were among them, those *seven thousand that never bowed knee to Baal*[y]*;*) *he put them to it upon their oaths.* And they had not the knowledge to make a *vow* against it (as my Lady hath), and to discharge themselves by that.

God did it Himself, only to teach judges to do it. His practice is plain: His law is plain, both for matter of *law,* and for matter of *state ;* that this *vow* hath not the *matter* of a *vow;* and so is a vow without matter; and so none at all.

Then was it asked, Who shall dispense with my Lady for her vow? Nobody shall need. It needs no *dispensation:* it cannot bind: it is no vow. It hath not the *matter* of a *vow.* He that takes away that *matter,* takes away the *bond:* for he takes away the being; and that which *is not,* cannot *bind;* it subsists not; for nothing subsists without a *matter. Non ens nihil operatur.*

Again, the nature of a *promise,* (and so of a *vow,*) is, *if* he *to whom it is made, will accept it, then it binds;* if he will not, then it is not obligatory, then binds it not. But it hath been showed, God will not, cannot ever accept of this[z].

subjects. The circumstances of her marriage, her cruel treatment, her escape, her subsequent imprisonment in the Tower, and her death, in hopeless idiotcy, need not be dwelt on. Lodge (as above) states that, when the powers of her mind were gone, she made some strange and incoherent accusations against several persons, and among others the Countess of Shrewsbury.]

[v] Gen. xlii. 9.
[x] 1 Kings xviii. 10.
[y] 1 Kings xix. 18.
[z] Non debet voveri Deo, quod displicet Deo. Quod sibi persolvi non vult, voveri non vult. [See S. Ambr. de Off. Ministr. lib. iii. cap. xii. (sect. 79.) Op., tom. ii. col. 127. D.]

It is against His practice, against His law, flat. So it *binds* not, so needs no dispensation.

But if I might advise, let my Lady rather seek how to be assoiled of her *sin* in making this vow, the matter whereof is so plainly repugnant to all these. It needs no *dispensing*, as a vow; it needs *repenting*, as a *sin*.

I will hope, she made it not with that due deliberation and other things requisite to a vow making. But I will add this, that for my Lady to persevere in it, that this can please God, for any to vow never to be *examined*, never to *answer* wittingly; for my Lady to attribute to God this mind, to think Him to be such a one, as such a *vow* can please Him, let her look to it, for it will amount to little less than *blasphemy*. For, it is as much as to *avow, that God loves not justice:* would have it defeated, at our pleasure; would have none done.

I will yet further say this, that as it was *sin* to my Lady to *make this vow*, so will it be a far greater, and more grievous sin, to *keep it*. Let not my Lady add sin to sin, *bind one sin to another*. It is enough for her, that she hath offended in *making* it; that is the one half: if she go forward, and persist in the *keeping* it, it will be double that: better leave at half.

What is then to be done? To *repent* of that is past. To go no further, and to keep it no longer. It is Saint Austin's maxim, *Injusta vincula [dis]rumpit justitia* [a]. Her *bond* is unjust, let *justice* break it in sunder, and spare not.

These are our grounds in *Divinity*, gathered by Isidore; this the Church's rule: *In malo promisso, rescinde fidem* [b]. Albeit, Saint Austin saith well, *Si ad peccatum faciendum adhibetur fides, mirum si fides appellanda est* [c]. It were strange any should call that *faith*, that is abused to commit any sin, as this of my Lady's is. *In turpi voto muta decretum* [b]; that comes to this matter clearly. *Quod incautys*

---

[a] [S. Aug. Serm. lxxxii. (al. xvi. de Verb. Domini.) Op., tom. v. col. 634. C, quoted in Decret. Par. ii. Caus. xi. Quæst. iii. cap. xlviii. ' Cœpisti.' Corp. Jur. Can. tom. i. col. 939.]

[b] [" In malis autem promissis rescindatur fides, in turpi voto muta decretum, quod incaute vovisti, non facias. Impia est promissio, quæ scelere impletur." S. Isid. Hisp. Synon. lib. ii. cap. x. Op., p. 224. E. See also Decret. Par. ii. Caus. xxiii. Quæst. iv. cap. v. 'In malis.'—Corp. Jur. Can. tom. i. col. 1264. This note, it will be observed, refers to several passages in this paragraph, all from S. Isidore.]

[c] [S. Aug. de Bono conjugali, cap. iv. Op., tom. vi. col. 545. D. See also Decret. Par. ii. Caus. xxii. Quæst. iv. cap. xx. 'Si ad peccatum.'—Corp. Jur. Can. tom. i. col. 1268.]

vovisti ne facias[b], (which I will yet hope is my Lady's case.) And the ground of all is, *Quia impia est promissio, quæ scelere impletur*[b]. For *impious* is that *promise* that cannot be fulfilled but with all these. *Tolerabilius est* (saith Saint Ambrose in his Offices) *promissum non facere, quam facere quod turpe est*[d].

The case is plain. Herod vowed, *whatsoever he was asked*, he would give it Herodias's daughter[e]. It was unadvisedly vowed, too indefinite; a *vow* would not be ἀόριστον, *indefinite*. *Whatsoever*. (Jepthe's fault too[f].) Saint John Baptist's head was no *matter* of a *vow*. Well, *Infertur disco prophetæ caput; et hoc æstimatum est esse fidei, quod fuit amentiæ*[g].

David vowed the like, (in a manner,) *to be the death of Nabal*[h]. But upon better advice, (being put in mind by Abigail, it would be no scruple nor upbraiding to his conscience, if he *shed no blood,* and so kept not his heady vow,) he did not keep it. And in not keeping it, did well; is commended, and propounded for imitation, to all *votaries* of that kind. And such, I conceive my Lady's *vow* to be: upon spleen, rather than anything else.

Mine advice then shall be to my Lady, out of the words of the Prophet Amos. God saith there, *He will not regard any such vows*[i]. How shall we then help it? *Let my judgment* (saith He) *run down like the water, and righteousness like a mighty stream.* That is, you stop the course of justice, with this *vow* of yours it cannot *run*. Let *justice* have her course, and let that be the breaking off of your *vow*. If you will needs have it a *vow*, let it be but the *Nazarite's vow*, but for a time: let it expire, it is more than time it so did. Return to your former promise, made advisedly, and lawfully: you were (then) well persuaded; break not your lawful promise then, with this unlawful *vow* of yours now.

Assuring you, Madam, there is no Christian divine, but will assure you, this vow is void: and you may safely vow, never to make any such vow more.

[d] [S. Ambr. de Off. Ministr. lib. iii. cap. xii. (sect. 76.) Op., tom. ii. col. 127. A. See also Decret. Par. ii. Caus. xxii. Quæst. iv. cap. viii. 'Unusquisque.'—Corp. Jur.Can. tom. i. col. 1265.]
[e] Matt. xiv. 7.
[f] Judges xi. 31. [See S. Ambr. de Off. Ministr. lib. iii. cap. xii. (sect. 78.) Op., tom. ii. col. 127. B. C. D.]
[g] [S. Ambr. ibid. (sect. 77.) Op., tom. ii. col. 127. A.B.; and Decret. as quoted above, note [d].]
[h] 1 Sam. xxv. 22. [See S. August. Serm. cccviii. § 2. Op., tom v. col. 1835. B. C.]
[i] [Amos chap.] v. 22.

FINIS.

A DISCOURSE,

WRITTEN BY DOCTOR ANDREWES,

BISHOP OF ELY,

AGAINST SECOND MARRIAGE, AFTER SENTENCE OF DIVORCE WITH A FORMER MATCH,

THE PARTY THEN LIVING.

IN ANNO 1601[a].

THE Question is, whether upon adultery proved, or sentence recorded, a man be set at liberty, that he may proceed to contract with another.

[¹ ['take it', MS. Lansd.]] First, I take[1] the act of adultery doth not dissolve the bond of marriage; for then it would follow, that the party offending would not, upon reconciliation, be received again by the innocent to former society of life, without a new solemnising of marriage, insomuch as the former marriage is quite dissolved, which is never heard of, and contrary to the practice of all Churches.

Secondly, the sentence, as I take it, doth not relieve, for there is no lawful sentence of any court in case of divorce, but it ever containeth an express inhibition to either party to marry with another, with intimation in flat terms, that from the time that either of them shall go about any other marriage, *quod ex tunc prout ex nunc, et ex nunc prout ex tunc*, (it is the style of the court,) that present sentence shall be void to all purposes, and they in the same case as if it had never been given.

---

[a] [This tract is now printed for the first time from a MS. in the British Museum, Birch MSS. 4149. art. 38. p. 320. The volume in which it is found, consists of a large collection of copies of papers on matters of State in the reign of King James I., in the hand of Ralph Starkie, a celebrated transcriber of that period. It comes next to a defence of the second marriage of the Earl of Devon.

There is another copy in a later hand in Bp. Kennet's collections, vol. xxiv. (Lansd. MSS. 958.) There are slight variations between the two MSS., and in each errors of transcription, so that they have been here used to correct each other, the various readings being only noted where they were important, or where the true reading was doubtful. The spelling has of course been modernized.

It is remarkable that both copies speak of Dr. Andrewes as Bishop of Ely; from which we must infer, either that the date ought to have been 1610, or (which is more probable) that these copies, or those from which they were transcribed, were made after his elevation to that see.]

These both failing, the word of God is sought to; where, let me tell you first, that during the primitive Church, ever till now of late, the judgment of the divines and the present practice of the law ecclesiastical were both one; and great reason why; for well known it is, that the authority of the fathers was the ground of the ancient canons, by which the law in this case is ruled. So that but for the conceit of some latter divines, there need not be sought any opposition between law and divinity in this question, nor that pitiful distraction happen, which we daily see, Divines to give their hands for licence to that, for which law will convent men, and censure them too.

But, in my opinion, second marriages (where either party is living) are not warranted by the word of God. The ground of which opinion is, that one may not in any wise have two wives at once; for by the original institution, there can be but two in one flesh. But a man having one wife already, which, notwithstanding she hath profaned marriage with another, is not thereby become the wife of him with whom she now liveth, but remaineth his wife whose first she was, and whose only she can be while she liveth.

The word of God is plain for this in St. Paul, Rom. vii. 2, *The woman is bound to the man so long as she liveth, so that if while she liveth she become another man's, she shall be holden an adulteress;* from which words the vow of marriage seemeth to have been framed, which is solemnly made in the congregation by either party, *forsaking all other to keep only to her so long as both shall live.* And again, *to have and to hold, for better for worse, till death:* these plainly show the band is only broken by death, and that though she become another man's, yet is she not become his wife.

Now, upon this dependeth the next rule of the word of God (1 Cor. vii. 11), that a woman of herself departing, or put away by her husband, is commanded either to be reconciled, or to remain unmarried: which commandment of the Apostle's must be understood of the case of adultery; for were it any other cause but that wherein Christ hath given leave to depart or to put away, the Apostle would not have put it upon either, or upon one, but would simply and absolutely have commanded her to be reconciled, as indeed in all other cases she is bound to seek it, and is not less at liberty.

You may imagine that favourers of those kind of marriages will say somewhat to these places, by way of evasion; for what is so plain, but by man's wit somewhat may be said to it? But that his meaning is the direct meaning of the ancient writers, and that these in this sense understand these places, and that both when they were met together in councils, and in their several writings, I refer you to the Council of Eliberis (which is as ancient as the first General Council of Nice), the 9th Canon[b]; and to the Council of Milevitum, where S. Augustine and Optatus were present, and subscribed the 17th Canon[c]; and to Origen's 7th Homily upon Matthew[d]; and to St. Hierome's Epistle to Amandus[e]; St. Ambrose upon the 1 Cor. vii.[f]; to Innocentius the First, (who lived a little before St. Augustine,) in his Epistle to Ercusius, 9th sect.[g]; to St. Augustine's book, De Adulterinis Conjugiis ad Colentium [*leg.* Pollentium], lib. ii. cap. 4[h], whose meaning and interpretations I prefer, and wish all (I may prevail with) to lean[1] to, rather than opposite ones[2] of latter times.

Likewise, it cannot be denied, but that the fathers do allege and understand these two places, the one in Mark x. 11, the other in Luke xvi. 18, as they stand in plain and full terms, that a man having put away his wife cannot marry again. For as for the place in Matthew xix. 9, where it seemeth to be qualified with (*unless it be for*

[1] ['leave', MS. Lansd. qu. 'cleave'.]
[2] ['than the expositions', MS. Lansd.]

[b] ["Item fœmina fidelis, quæ adulterum maritum reliquerit fidelem, et alterum ducit, prohibeatur, ne ducat; si duxerit, non prius accipiat communionem, nisi, quem reliquerit, prius de sæculo exierit; nisi forte necessitas infirmitatis dare compulerit." Conc.Elib. Can. ix.—Conc., tom. i. col. 971. D.]

[c] [" Placuit, ut secundum Evangelicam et Apostolicam disciplinam, neque dimissus ab uxore, neque dimissa a marito alteri conjungantur."— Conc. Milev. Can. xvii.—Conc., tom. ii. col. 1541. E]

[d] [Ἤδη δὲ παρὰ γεγραμμένα καί τινες τῶν ἡγουμένων τῆς ἐκκλησίας ἐπέτρεψάν τινα, ὥστε ζῶντος τοῦ ἀνδρὸς γαμεῖσθαι γυναῖκα, κ. τ. λ. — Orig. Comm. in Matth. xix. Op., tom. iii. p. 647. Paris. 1740. It is called Tractatus in S. Matth. vii. in Editt. Vett. Latt. Erasmi, tom. ii. p. 67. Basil. 1571.]

[e] [" Quamdiu vivit vir, licet adulter sit, licet sodomita, licet flagitiis omnibus coopertus, et ab uxore propter hæc scelera derelictus, maritus ejus reputatur, cui alterum virum accipere non licet."—S. Hier. Ep. lv. (al. cxlvii.) ad Amandum, § 3. Op., tom. i. col. 296. A.]

[f] [" Non .. permittitur mulieri, ut nubat, si virum suum causa fornicationis dimiserit."—S. Ambr. (seu potius Hilar. Diacon.) in 1 Cor. vii. 10, 11. Op., tom. ii. Append. col. 133.]

[g] [" Qui ergo vel (quæ viro vel, *in marg.*) uxore vivente, quamvis dissociatum videatur esse conjugium, ad aliam copulam festinarunt, neque possunt adulteri non videri."—Innoc. I. Epist. iii. ad Exuperium, § 6.—Conc., tom. ii. col. 1256. C.]

[h] [" Nullius viri posterioris mulier uxor esse incipit, nisi prioris esse desiverit. Esse autem desinet uxor prioris, si moriatur vir ejus, non si fornicetur."—S. Aug. de Conj. Adult. lib. ii. cap. 4. Op., tom. vi. col. 686. B.C.]

adultery), which place is all the show that can be made for these marriages, they follow the rules both of divinity and reason (which is) when there is any diversity in places, first to expound the lesser number by the greater, and not contrary; that is, one evangelist by two, and not two by one; secondly, to expound the former writer (which it is granted, Matthew was) by the latter, as both Mark and Luke were, and not contrary, especially where both may stand, as here, they interpreting it thus: He that putteth away his wife (which but for adultery is not lawful) and marrieth another, committeth adultery himself.

Now, if you ask why that exception might not have been left out in Matthew (seeing it maketh the matter ambiguous), they answer, that in Matthew it was necessary that our Saviour Christ should add it, for that these very words (*he that putteth away his wife, except it be for adultery*) contain the direct answer to the Pharisee's question, Whether a man for any cause might put away his wife? whereunto but for this clause no answer had been made. But in the other two Evangelists, where no such question is moved, nor like occasion offered, there it is left out, both in St. Mark, where the disciples asked Him about it, and in St. Luke, where He simply delivereth[1] the doctrine, no man moving any doubt about it to[2] Him.

Some of the reasons why the ancient writers cannot favour this exposition, which giveth liberty to second marriages, be these:

First, our Saviour Christ meant[3] plainly in that place to restrain the commonness of divorces among the Jews; but divorces are not restrained, this exposition holding, inasmuch as He hath[4] left it still in the pleasure of every lewd man or light woman, who committing the sin with another, may dissolve as many former marriages as they like[5]: for being weary of the first, it is but to be lewd of her body, and presently the bond is broken, and liberty given to make a new choice of another, and being weary of that, of a third, and fourth. Jerome in Matt. xix.[i]

[1] ['delivered', MS. Lansd.]
[2] ['unto', MS. Lansd.]
[3] ['means', MS. Lansd.]
[4] ['it has', MS. Lansd.]
[5] ['list', MS. Lansd.]

[i] [" Ubiquumque est igitur fornicatio, et fornicationis suspicio, libere uxor dimittitur. Et quia poterat accidere, ut aliquis calumniam faceret innocenti, et, ob secundam copulam nuptiarum veteri crimen impingeret, sic priorem dimittere jubetur uxorem, ut secundam, prima vivente, non habeat."—S. Hier. Comm. in S. Matth. xix. 9. (lib. iii.) Op., tom. vii. p. 146.]

Secondly, it is not our Saviour Christ's will to make the committing of sin gainful or beneficial to any offender. But this exposition holding, the guilty person must gain thereby; for so¹ the committing of adultery do dissolve marriage, then maketh it the persons in the same case they were before they were married; and so may either, as well the guilty as the innocent, marry, which is the very benefit the adulterer propounds to himself. Ambrose^k.

Thirdly, this exposition holding, and adultery dissolving marriage, not only that absurdity would follow, (which I in the beginning mentioned,) that no Christian might receive his wife, having been faulty, except a new marriage were celebrated between them, (a thing never heard of;) but that which is more gross, that the innocent party, if he could have knowledge of his wife's body, having been false this way, should in so doing commit adultery himself, inasmuch as he hath had the use of her that now is none of his. None of his (I say), because their marriage was utterly dissolved by the act precedent of his wife. Augustine¹.

Now, to conclude: there be two divers things in that place of St. Matthew: the putting away of his wife, and the taking of another. And in the midst of these standeth the exception, (if it be not for adultery.) To speak truth, it cometh a little too soon, for if it had been stayed till the end of the sentence, thus: He that putteth away his wife, and taketh another, committeth adultery himself, except it be for adultery, it had sounded for them. But now it cometh in thus: *He that putteth away his wife, except for adultery, and marrieth another*, &c.; that is, the exception standing behind the first, and going before the second. Sure it is not clear and plain; for as it may by some be understood to limit the former only, (and so the old writers do generally restrain it, as before it hath been said.) Therefore, here it is doubtful at least, since divines differ about it.

LANCELOT ANDREWES.²

Anno 1601.

¹ ['for if,' MS. Lansd.]

² ['Lancelot Ely', MS. Lansd.]

^k [The reference seems to be to S. Ambr. Expos. S. Luc. (cap. xvi.) lib. viii. § 4. Op., tom. i. col. 1471. B. though the meaning appears to be mistaken.] cap. xii. (§ 13.) (Op., tom. vi. col. 668. B.C.) is probably the passage intended. Compare de Nupt. et Concup. lib. i. cap. x. (§ 11.) Op., tom. x. col. 615. B.]

¹ [S. Aug. de Conj. Adult. lib. i.

ARTICLES

To be enquired of by the Church-Wardens and Sworne-men in the Primary Visitation of the Right reuerend Father in GOD,

LANCELOT, *Lord Bishop of Winton,*
within the Diocesse of Winchester,
Anno 1619.

The Tenor of the Oath of the Churchwardens and Sworn-men.

You shall swear, that upon due consideration of these Articles given you in charge, you shall present every such person of or within your Parish, as you shall know to have committed any offence, or omitted any duty mentioned in any of these Articles, or which are publicly defamed, or vehemently suspected of any such offence or negligence. So help you God by the contents of his holy Gospel.

ARTICLES.

¶ *Touching the Church.*

1. WHETHER is your Church or Chapel, with the Chancel thereof, and every part of either of them, well and sufficiently repaired, the windows well glazed, the floors paved plain and even, without dust, or anything noisome or unseemly?

2. Whether is your Churchyard well fenced with walls, rails, pales, as hath been accustomed? if not, whose default is it?

3. Whether hath there been any fighting, chiding, brawling, or quarrelling, any plays, feasts, temporal courts or leets, lay juries, musters, or other profane usage in your Church or Churchyard; or have any trees been felled in your Churchyard, and by whom?

4. Whether is the mansion house of your Parson, Vicar, or Curate, with all the buildings thereto belonging, your Parish Almshouse and Church house sufficiently repaired, maintained, and to their right uses, that is, to godly uses employed?

5. Whether have you in your Church the Bible in the largest Volume, the Book of Common Prayer lately authorized by his Majesty, the Books of Homilies allowed, the two Psalters, a convenient Pulpit for the Preaching, a decent seat for the Minister to say Service in, conveniently placed, a strong chest with a hole in the lid, and three locks and keys, one for the Minister, the other for the Churchwardens, for the Alms of the poor, and the keeping of the Register Book of the Christenings, Marriages, and Burials?

6. Whether have you in your Church a Font of stone for

Baptism, set in the ancient usual place, a decent Table for the Communion conveniently placed, covered with silk, or other decent stuff in time of Divine Service, and with a fair linen cloth over that at the Administration of the Communion?

7. Whether have you all such Bells, ornaments, and other utensils as have anciently belonged to your Church, a Communion Cup of silver, with cover, a fair standing pot or stoop of silver or pewter for the Wine upon the Communion Table, a comely Surplice with large sleeves, a Register Book of parchment for Christenings, Marriages, and Burials, a book for the names of all strange Preachers, subscribed with their names, and the name of the Bishop or others by whom they had Licence?

8. Whether is your Alms for your poor, (quarterly at the least,) distributed by you, the Churchwardens, and the Minister, in the presence of six of the chief Parishioners, to your poor? And are weekly the names and surnames of all persons Married, Christened, and Buried, and of their Parents, with the day and year, entered in your said parchment book, and every leaf being full, subscribed by you, the Minister and Churchwardens?

9. Whether are all your seats in your Church in good repair, cleanly kept, conveniently placed, and the Parishioners in them, or elsewhere, orderly set, and whether is there any contention or striving for any seat or place among them?

10. Whether in any of your Churches the partition between the Chancel and the body of the Church be taken away; and how long since, and by whom the same hath been so taken away? And if it hath been taken away, to what other use or benefice of the Church hath the same been converted?

¶ *Touching the Ministry, Service, and Sacraments.*

1. Whether is the Common Prayer said or sung by your Minister both morning and evening distinctly and reverently, every Sunday and Holy day, and on their eves, and at convenient and usual times of those days, and in most convenient place of the Church for the edifying of the people?

2. Whether doth your Minister observe the Orders, Rites, and Ceremonies prescribed in the Book of Common Prayer, in reading the Holy Scriptures, Prayers, and Administration of the Sacraments, without diminishing, (in regard of Preaching or any other respect,) or adding anything in the matter or form thereof?

3. Whether doth your Minister on Wednesdays and Fridays, (not being Holy days,) at the accustomed hours of Service resort to the Church, and say the Litany prescribed, and doth your Clerk or Sexton give warning before by tolling of a Bell on those days?

4. Whether doth your Minister, as oft as he administereth the Communion, first receive it himself? Whether doth he use any Bread or Wine newly brought, before the words of Institution be rehearsed, and the Bread and Wine present on the table? Whether doth he deliver the Bread and Wine to every Communicant severally?

5. Whether doth your Minister give warning publicly in the Church at Morning Prayer the Sunday before he administereth the Communion, for the better preparation of the Parishioners?

6. Whether hath your Minister admitted to the Communion any notorious Sinner, openly known or defamed, or any who hath openly and maliciously contended with his neighbour, before repentance and reconciliation made and done by appointment of the Ordinary?

7. Whether hath your Minister admitted to the Communion any Churchwarden or Side-man, who hath wittingly and willingly neglected, contrary to his oath, to present any public offence, or scandal, being moved to present either by some of his neighbours, the Minister, or his Ordinary?

8. Whether hath your Minister administered the Communion to any but such as kneel, or do any refuse to kneel? Hath he administered to any who refuseth to be present at public prayer, or is there any who hath depraved the Book of Common Prayer, Administration of the Sacraments, or the Rites and Ceremonies prescribed, or the Articles of Religion agreed upon, or the Book of Ordering Priests and Bishops, or spoken against his Majesty's Supremacy, or have any been for these causes repelled, and what be their names?

9. Whether hath your Minister more Benefices than one? if he have, how far distant are they, how often is he absent in the year? when he is absent, hath he an allowed Preacher for his Curate?

10. Whether is your Minister an allowed Preacher? If he be, doth he every Sunday in your Church, or some other near adjoining, (where no Preacher is,) preach one Sermon every Sunday?

11. Whether doth your Minister, being no Preacher allowed, presume to expound the Scripture in his own Cure, or elsewhere? Doth he procure every month a Sermon to be preached in his Cure by Preachers lawfully licensed, and on every Sunday when there is no Sermon, doth he or his Curate read some one of the Homilies prescribed?

12. Whether is your Curate allowed by the Ordinary, under his hand and seal, to serve for your Cure, and whether doth he serve two Churches or Chapels in one day?

13. Whether doth your Minister, in saying the public Prayers, and administering the Sacraments, wear a decent Surplice with sleeves, and being a Graduate, doth he wear therewith a hood, by the order of the Universities, agreeable to his Degree?

14. Whether hath your Minister, or any other Preacher in your Church, preached anything to confute and impugn any Doctrine delivered by any other Preacher, and hath he and they used the Prayer for Christ's Catholic Church, &c. as is prescribed by the Canon?

15. Whether hath or doth any preach in your Church, which refuseth to conform himself to the Laws, Rites, and Ordinances established, or which hath not first showed a sufficient Licence?

16. Whether doth your Minister in his Sermons, four times in the year at least, teach and declare the King's Majesty's power within his Realms to be the highest power under God, to whom all within the same owe most loyalty and obedience, and that all foreign power is justly taken away?

17. Whether doth your Minister every Sunday and Holy day, half an hour before Evening Prayer or more, examine and instruct the youth in the Ten Commandments, the Belief,

the Lord's Prayer, and the Catechism, set forth in the Book of Common Prayer?

18. Whether hath your Minister married any which have not been three several Sundays or Holy days asked in your Church in the time of Divine Service (without Licence), and hath he, either with Licence or without, married any, whereof neither dwelt in your Parish, or with any Licence but only from the Lord Archbishop of Canterbury, the Bishop of the Diocese, or his Chancellor?

19. Whether hath your Minister, either with Licence or without, married any at any other time than between the hours of eight and twelve in the forenoon, or in any private house, or before their parents and governors (the parties being under the age of twenty-one years) have testified their consent?

20. Whether doth your Minister declare to the people every Sunday at the time appointed, what holy days and fasting days be the week following? Doth he, being a Preacher, confer with all recusants and persons excommunicate or suspended? Being no Preacher, doth he procure a sufficient Preacher to reclaim them thereby?

21. Whether doth your Minister keep a note of all persons excommunicate, and once every six months doth he denounce them which have not obtained their absolution, on some Sunday in service time, that others may be admonished to refrain their company?

22. Whether doth your Minister, having notice given him, diligently visit the sick (the disease not being infectious)? doth he instruct and comfort them? doth he then move them to make their testaments, and remember the poor, and other works of charity?

23. Whether hath your Minister refused to baptize any child brought to the Church upon any Sunday or Holy day, or to bury any corpse brought into the Church or Churchyard, or to Church any women, having had convenient warning thereof?

24. Whether hath your Minister, being truly informed of the danger of death of any infant unbaptized, and being desired to go to the place where the child is, to baptize it, neglected to go, by means whereof the child died unbaptized?

25. Whether doth your Minister at any time preach or administer the Communion in any private house, except when any are so impotent that they cannot go to Church, or very dangerously sick?

26. Whether hath your Minister held or appointed any public fast, or been present at any? Doth he or any other in your Parish hold any lecture or exercise, without the licence of the Bishop under his hand and seal, or attempt by fasting or otherwise to cast out any devils?

27. Whether hath there been any secret conventicles or meetings in your Parish by any Priest, Ministers, or others, tending to the depraving of the form of prayer, doctrine, or government of the Church?

28. Whether doth your Minister in his journey wear a cloak with sleeves, called a Priest's cloak?

29. Whether doth your Minister resort to any taverns or alehouses, or doth he board or lodge in any such place? Doth he use any base or servile labour, drinking, riot, dice cards, tables, or any other unlawful games? Is he contentious, a hunter, hawker, swearer, dancer, suspected of incontinence, or hath given any evil example of life?

30. Whether is there in your Parish any Minister or Deacon who hath forsaken his calling, using himself in his course of life as a gentleman or other layman?

Touching Schoolmasters.

1. Whether have you in your Parish any Schoolmaster who teacheth either in public school or in private house? Is he of sound religion, or doth he give any evil example of life? Is he allowed by the Ordinary? or doth your Minister or Curate teach? and is he allowed in like manner?

2. Whether doth your Minister or Schoolmaster who teacheth, teach the Catechism by authority set forth?

Touching the Parish Clerk and Sexton.

1. Whether have you a Parish Clerk sufficient for his place, of the age of twenty years at the least? Is he of honest conversation? Can he read, write, and sing? Is he diligent

in his office, and serviceable to his Minister, and not given to over much drink, or any other vice?

2. Whether doth your Clerk meddle with anything above his office, as churching of women, burying of the dead, reading of prayers, or such like?

3. Whether doth your Clerk or Sexton keep your Church clean, the doors safe locked? Is anything by his default lost or spoiled in the Church? Doth he suffer unseasonable ringing, or any profane exercise in your Church?

4. Whether doth your Clerk or Sexton, when one is passing out of this life, neglect to toll a bell, having notice thereof; or the party being dead, doth he suffer more than one short peal, and before his burial one, and after the same another?

5. Whether doth any of your Parish refuse to pay unto the Parish Clerk or Sexton such wages as are unto them due, and have been accustomably paid?

Touching Parishioners.

1. Whether hath any in your Parish spoken against, or any way impugned the King's Majesty's Supremacy in causes ecclesiastical, the Truth and Doctrine of the Church of England, the form of God's worship contained in the Book of Common Prayer and Administration of the Sacraments?

2. Whether hath any in your Parish spoken against or impugned the Articles of Religion agreed upon Anno 1602, the Rites and Ceremonies established in the Church, the government by Archbishops, Bishops, Deans, Archdeacons, and others that bear office in the same?

3. Whether any have in your Parish spoken against or impugned the Form of making and consecrating Bishops, Priests, or Deacons, or have any separated themselves from the society of the Congregation and combined in a new Brotherhood, or depraved the Synod lately held by the King's authority?

4. Whether doth any in your Parish profane, violate, or misspend the Sabbath, or Holy day, or any part of them, using offensive conversation, or worldly labour in those days, or any of them?

5. Whether hath any in your Parish in the time of

Divine Service covered his head, (albeit he hath no infirmity, in which case a cap or night-coif is allowed,) or is there any who hath not reverently knelt when the General Confession, Litany, and other prayers are read, and which have not stood up at the saying of the Belief?

6. Whether hath any in your Parish disturbed the Service or Sermon by walking, talking, or any other way, or departed out of the Church during the Service or Sermon without some urgent cause, or loitered about the Church or Church porch?

7. Whether do all Parishioners receive the Holy Communion thrice every year at the least, whereof the Feast of Easter to be one, and have all being of the age of eighteen years duly received or not?

8. Whether hath any Parent been urged to be present, or admitted to answer as Godfather for his own child, or hath any Godfather or Godmother made any other answer or speech than is prescribed by the Book, or have any been admitted for such a Baptism, who have not first received the Communion?

9. Whether do all Fathers, Mothers, Masters, Mistresses come, and cause their children, servants, and apprentices to come duly to the Church, and according to the Minister's direction to be instructed and catechised, or who be they that have not obeyed the Minister therein?

10. Whether have any persons married together within the degrees of Consanguinity or Affinity prohibited, set forth in a Table, appointed to be placed in every Church?

11. Whether have any persons, once lawfully married, forsaken each other, or do live asunder without the authority of the Ordinary, or do any, being divorced or separated, marry again, the former wife or husband yet living?

12. Whether have any been married in the times wherein marriage is by law restrained, without lawful licence; viz. from the Saturday next before Advent Sunday, until the fourteenth of January; and from the Saturday next before Septuagesima Sunday, until the Monday next after Low Sunday; and from the Sunday next before the Rogation Week, until Trinity Sunday?

13. Whether hath any of your Parish unreverently used

your Minister, or have any laid violent hands upon him, or disgraced his office and calling, by word or deed?

14. Whether have you in your Parish any dweller or sojourner, a maintainer of Popish Doctrine, or suspected to keep schismatical books, or to favour any heresy or error?

15. Whether have you any common resorters to your Church, which are not of your Parish, or do any such receive the Communion amongst you? what be their names, and of what Parishes are they?

16. Whether have any in the time of Service opened their shops, exercised their trade, used any gaming, been in any tavern or alehouse, or otherwise ill employed?

17. Whether are there in your Parish any adulterers, fornicators, incestuous persons, bawds, receivers, close favourers, conveyers away, or which suffer to depart any incontinent person unpunished, any blasphemers, common swearers, drunkards, ribalds, usurers, malicious slanderers, scolds, or sowers of discord, or any defamed of the said crimes?

18. Whether do any in your Parish administer the goods of the dead without authority, or suppress their will and testament? have any executors neglected to perform their wills, especially in paying of legacies given to the Church, to the poor, or to any other charitable or godly uses?

19. Whether do any refuse to pay to the reparations, ornaments, and other things required in your Church, as they are sessed by a lawful Vestry, or any other dwelling out of your Parish which hold land in your Parish?

20. Whether hath any person suspended or excommunicated been suffered to hear Divine Service or the Sermon, to receive the Sacraments, to be married or churched, or have any excommunicate been buried in Christian burial?

21. Whether have any in your Parish been christened, churched, buried, or received the Communion, or been married out of your Church (both parties dwelling in your Parish)?

22. Whether have all women in your Parish delivered of child come at convenient time after to Church to give thanks, and have they been Churched according to the form of the Book of Common Prayer?

23. Whether hath the perambulation of the circuit of your Parish been observed once every year? if not, whose default is it?

24. Whether have any in your Parish given the Church-wardens, or Side-men, or any of them, evil words for doing their duty, according to their oath and conscience, in making presentment for any fault?

Touching Churchwardens and Sworn-men.

1. Whether do any in your Parish take upon them to be Churchwarden or Side-man, which are not lawfully chosen by the Minister and Parishioners according to the Canon, or do any continue that office longer than one year, except they be chosen again, and are all such officers chosen yearly in Easter Week?

2. Whether do your Churchwardens, within one month at the most after their year ended, before the Minister and Parishioners, give up a just account of all such money and other things as they have received and bestowed? have they delivered all remaining in their hands belonging to their Church or Parish, by bill indented, to the next Church-wardens?

3. Whether have the Churchwardens, with the advice of the Minister, from time to time provided a sufficient quantity of fine white bread and wholesome wine for the number of Communicants?

4. Whether do the Churchwardens and Sworn-men, before every Visitation, and at other times when there is just occasion, meet and confer about their presentments and the answering of these Articles, and who hath (after notice given him of the time and place) carelessly absented himself?

5. Whether the forfeiture of twelve pence for absence from Church, appointed by Statute for the use of the poor, be taken and levied by the Churchwardens, and employed according to the said statute, and whether is the same forfeiture taken of all persons which stand wilfully suspended or excommunicated?

6. Whether have any Churchwardens lost, sold, or detained any goods, ornaments, bells, rents, or implements of the Church?

7. Whether do the Churchwardens and Side-men, about the midst of Divine Service, usually walk out of the Church, and see who are abroad in any alehouse, or elsewhere absent or evil employed, and whether have they presented all such to the Ordinary?

8. Whether do you know or have heard a fame of any offence committed or duty omitted by any of your Parish before your time, and heretofore not presented to the Ordinary, or as yet not reformed, and whether have you presented the same?

9. Finally, do you know of any matter or cause which is a breach of the Laws Ecclesiastical here not expressed?

FINIS.

ARTICLES

To Be Enquired

of by the Churchwardens and Sworne-men, *in the Triennial Visitation of the* Right Reuerend Father in God,

Lancelot *Lord Bishop of Winton,* within the Diocesse of Win-chester.

Anno 1625.

The Tenor of the Oath of the Churchwardens and Sworn-men.

You shall swear, that upon due consideration of these Articles given you in charge, you shall present every such person of or within your Parish, as you shall know to have committed any offence, or omitted any duty mentioned in any of these Articles, or which are publicly defamed, or vehemently suspected of any such offence or negligence. So help you God by the contents of His holy Gospel.

ARTICLES.

Touching the Church.

1. WHETHER is the body of the Church and the Chancel thereof in good reparation, decently kept, as well within as without, the roofs so that it rain not in, the windows well glazed, the floors plain and even paved, the pews and seats orderly set, well maintained, clean and sweet kept, without dust or anything noisome or unseemly? and whether is there any striving or contention for sitting in pews, and by whom? Whether is there any new pews erected in places where none were before, or old altered? By whom and by what authority? Is there a partition between the body of the Church and the Chancel, and, if not, when and by whom, and by what authority, was it taken down? Is the Steeple in good repair, and the ancient number of Bells still kept, without diminishing? If not, what is the defect, and by whose default is it?

2. Whether have you in your Church the whole Bible of the largest volume, the Book of Common Prayer, two Psalters, the Book of Constitutions and Canons, all fairly and substantially bound?

3. Whether have you a comely large Surplice, with wide and long sleeves, and what it costs by the yard? a higher Pulpit for preaching, a lower to say Service in, a Font of stone, with a cover, set in the ancient usual place, a decent Table for the Communion, *and what it is worth to be prized?* Whether is the Communion Table abused by sitting on it, throwing hats on it, writing on it, or otherwise, as is not agreeable to the holy use of it? Have you a carpet of silk or other decent stuff, continually lying on it in the time of

Divine Service, with a fair linen cloth at the time of Communion, *and what might either of them be worth?* Have you a fair Communion Cup of silver, with a large cover of silver, to deliver the bread? and a flagon of silver or tin, for the wine to be set on the Communion Table?

4. And whether have you a registrar book of parchment for Christenings, Marriages, and Burials? and whether is the same kept in all points according to the Canons in that behalf provided? Another book wherein strange preachers are to subscribe their names, and the name of the Bishop by whom they were licensed? A chest as well for keeping the books and ornaments of the Church, as the said registrar? Another strong chest with a hole in the lid for the alms, with three locks and keys, one for the Minister, the other two for the Churchwardens? A Table set of the degrees wherein by law men and women are prohibited to marry?

5. Whether have any bells, ornaments, or other utensils, anciently belonging to your Church, been aliened, and by whom?

6. Whether is your Churchyard well fenced with walls, pales and rails, as hath been accustomed, and kept without abuse? And, if not, by whose default?

7. Whether hath any person encroached upon the Churchyard? And if any, who it is? Or have your Ministers, Churchwardens, and Parishioners jointly, or severally, made any lease or leases for term of years, or otherwise, of your Churchyard, or any part thereof? And whether have any trees therein growing been felled, and by whom?

8. Whether hath there been any quarrelling, or striking, brawling, or reviling; any plays, temporal courts, leets, lay-juries, musters, or other profane usages, in your Church or Churchyard?

9. Whether is the mansion house of your Parson, Vicar, or Minister, with all the housing thereunto belonging, well and sufficiently repaired? And whether have you any Almshouse or Church house in your Parish, and they well maintained, and employed to those godly uses whereto they were intended?

10. Whether is your Church full, or vacant of an Incum-

bent? If vacant, who receiveth the fruits thereof, and who serveth the Cure, and by what authority? And whether is it a Parsonage, Vicarage, or Donative, or Appropriation?

11. Whether have you a Terrier, or any ancient true note of all the Glebes, Grounds, and portions of Tithes, to your Parsonage or Vicarage belonging, taken by the view of honest men of your parish? And in whose hands is it? And whether is there a copy thereof laid up in the Bishop's registry? If none such be made, you the Churchwardens and Sidemen, together with your Parson, Vicar, or Minister, are to make diligent inquiry of the premises, as they are known by metes, bounds, and inclosures; and to make, sign, and bring in the said Terrier at the time of this your presentment, or within a time after to be prefixed.

12. Whether hath there not any of the said Glebe, or other grounds thereto belonging, been concealed, aliened, exchanged, or by collusion recovered or gotten from the Incumbent?

13. Whether be any of the profits, tithes, or other commodities ecclesiastical, taken and converted to the use and benefit of Patrons, or such as pretend themselves to be, and by them received and detained? And how long have they been so detained, to your knowledge?

Touching Ministers, Service, and Sacraments.

1. Whether is your Parson, Vicar, or Minister, a Graduate of one of the Universities, or not? And if yea, of what degree? Was he admitted into Holy Orders by any corrupt means of gift or promise? Or came he to his Benefice by any compact for money, or for releasing the Patron's or any other Tithes, directly, or indirectly, as you have credibly heard? Is he a Preacher licensed? And if so, by whom?

2. Whether hath he more Benefices than one? If he have, what is his other Benefice, and how far distant? How often and how long is he absent in the year? When he is absent, hath he an allowed Preacher for his Curate?

3. Whether is his Curate allowed by the Ordinary under his hand and seal? Whetherd oth he serve two Cures in one day? What is his Curate's name, and how long hath

he been Curate? And who was your Curate before, and what is become of him?

4. Whether doth your Minister, being no Preacher allowed, presume to expound the Scripture, in his own Cure, or elsewhere? And being no Preacher, whether doth he procure a Sermon every month in his Cure, by Preachers licensed? or in default thereof, read some of the Homilies prescribed?

5. Whether doth your Minister, every Sunday and Holy day, half an hour before Evening Prayer, examine and instruct the youth of the Parish in the Ten Commandments, the Belief, the Lord's Prayer, and the Catechism, set forth in the Book of Common Prayer?

6. Whether doth he distinctly and reverently every Sunday and Holy day, and on their eves, and other days appointed by the Book of Common Prayer, (as on Wednesdays and Fridays,) say and celebrate Divine Service both morning and evening, at fit and usual times on those days?

7. Whether doth he observe the Orders, Rites, and Ceremonies prescribed in the Book of Common Prayer, in reading Public Prayers and the Litany, in administering the Sacraments of Baptism and the Lord's Supper, in solemnizing Matrimony, in visiting the Sick, burying the Dead, Churching of women, in such manner and form as in the said book enjoined, without omission or addition?

8. Whether doth he, in the time of Divine Service, wear a Surplice both morning and evening, and never omit the same in ministering the Sacraments and other Rites of the Church?

9. Whether doth he, in regard of preaching, diminish Divine Service or Prayer, *that the Creed be not said, and the Commandments read every Sunday,* whereby the Parishioners may lose the knowledge of them both, which it most of all concerns them to know?

10. Whether doth he bid Holy days and Fasting days as by the Book of Common Prayers is prescribed?

11. Whether doth he baptize any in a private house, but in case of necessity?

12. Whether doth he refuse to baptize any Infant in his Parish, having been informed of the weakness of the said

child? And whether the child through his default died without Baptism?

13. Whether doth he use the sign of the Cross in Baptism, or baptize any child in a basin or other vessel, and not in the usual Font?

14. Whether doth he baptize any that were not born in the Parish?

15. Whether doth he admit any father to be Godfather to his own child? or any that have not received the Holy Communion?

16. Whether doth your Minister, before the several times of the administration of the Lord's Supper, admonish and exhort his Parishioners, if they have their consciences troubled and disquieted, to resort unto him, or some other learned Minister, and open his grief, that he may receive such ghostly counsel and comfort, as his conscience may be relieved, and by the Minister he may receive the benefit of absolution, to the quiet of his conscience, and avoiding of scruple? And if any man confess his secret and hidden sins, being sick or whole, to the Minister, for the unburthening of his conscience, and receiving such spiritual consolation; doth, or hath the said Minister at any time revealed and made known to any person whatsoever, any crime or offence so committed to his trust and secresy, contrary to the 113 Canon?

17. Whether doth he give warning, the Sunday before, to his Parishioners, that they may prepare themselves for the Communion the Sunday following?

18. Whether doth he administer so oft, as that every Parishioner may receive the Communion thrice, at least, every year, whereof Easter to be one?

19. Whether hath he debarred any of his Parish from the Holy Communion, who are not publicly infamous for some notorious crime?

20. Whether doth he receive to the Holy Communion any being not of his own Cure, but coming from other Parishes?

21. Whether doth he receive the Holy Communion himself first, kneeling? Or deliver it to any other, but such as kneel? or to any that refuse to be present at public prayers?

22. Whether doth he use the words of Institution every time that the bread and wine is received?

23. Whether doth he deliver the bread and wine to every communicant severally?

24. Whether hath he married any without a Ring? or without Banns published three several Sundays or Holy days in time of Divine Service, in the several Churches or Chapels of their several abodes? or, in times prohibited, without a Licence first obtained from the Bishop or his Chancellor? or before the hour of eight, or after the hour of twelve in the forenoon? or in any private house? or married any under the age of twenty-one years, before the consent of their parents or governors first to him signified?

25. Whether doth your Minister (having notice given him), visit the sick diligently, (the disease not being infectious?) Doth he instruct and comfort them? Doth he move them to make their Testaments, and to remember the poor, and other works of charity?

26. Doth he refuse to bury any, who ought to be interred in Christian burial? or defer the same longer than he should? or bury any in Christian burial, that by the Canons of the Church ought not so to be buried?

27. Doth your Minister carefully look to the relief of the poor, and from time to time call upon his Parishioners to give somewhat according to their ability?

28. Whether doth your Minister, being a Preacher, confer with all Recusants, or persons excommunicated, or suspended: and being no Preacher, procure a sufficient Preacher to reclaim them?

29. Whether doth he keep a note of persons excommunicate, and denounce them once a month on some Sunday in Service time?

30. Whether doth he hold or appoint any Fasts, Prophecies, or Exercises, or hath been present at any?

31. Whether hath there been any Conventicles or Meetings by any Ministers now silenced or suspended, or others, in any private house, to deprave the Book of Common Prayer, or the doctrine and discipline of the Church of England, or to use any other form than is therein appointed?

32. Whether doth your Minister use decency or comeliness

in apparel, and wear a cloak with sleeves (called a Priest's cloak), in his going abroad?

33. Whether doth he board or lodge in any Tavern or Ale-house, or resort thither commonly? or use any base or servile labour, not seemly for his calling, or any dice, cards, tables, or other unlawful games? Is he one that plies not his study, a hunter, hawker, dancer, swearer, usurer, or suspected of incontinency, or any ways offensive or scandalous to his function or ministry?

34. Whether doth he admit any women gotten with child out of matrimony, to be churched without licence?

35. Whether doth he baptize any in private houses (but in case of necessity), or church any woman, or minister the Communion to any persons?

36. Whether doth he go in perambulation in the Rogation week, using the prayers and thanksgiving to God for his blessings, or otherwise entreat His grace and favour, if there be fear of scarcity?

37. Whether is there in your Parish any Minister or Deacon that hath forsaken his calling, or that useth himself in his course of life as a Gentleman or a Layman?

Touching Schoolmasters.

1. Is there in your Parish any Schoolmaster who teacheth in a public School, or any other which teacheth in private houses? Have they the licence of the Bishop?

2. Are they conformable to the sound Religion now established, and receive the Holy Communion? Do they bring their Scholars to Church to hear Divine Service and Sermon? Are they diligent to benefit their Scholars in learning? Do they instruct their Scholars in the grounds of Religion, in the Catechism contained in the Book of Common Prayer, once every week, or teach any other Catechisms besides, or read unto them privately any unlawful books?

3. Do they teach children in any Papist's or Sectary's house that come not to Church? What are their names, and how long have they so taught?

Touching Physicians and Surgeons.

Have you any in your Parish that practise Physic or Surgery, not being a Doctor in either of the Universities, or otherwise licensed? Or that have left their trade, and, taking upon them to profess Physic or Surgery, abuse the people?

Touching the Clerk and Sexton.

1. Have you a fit Parish Clerk, aged twenty years at least, able to read, write, and sing? Is he serviceable to the Minister, not given to drink or any other vice? Doth he meddle with anything above his office, as to Church women, read Prayers, bury the Dead, or such like?
2. Doth he, or the Sexton, keep the Church clean, and the doors locked? Is anything of the Church spoiled or lost by his default, or any profane exercises in your Church?
3. Doth he neglect to toll a Bell, when any person is passing out of this life?
4. Are the Clerk and Sexton's wages duly paid unto them without fraud, as hath been accustomed?

Touching the Parishioners.

1. Are there abiding or resorting to your Parish, any that defend any Heresies, contrary to the faith of Christ and true Religion?
2. Do any of your Parish, or that sojourns therein by the space of a month, being sixteen years of age or upward, neglect to resort to your Church on Sundays and Holy days, at Morning and Evening Prayer?
3. Are there any noted to come late, or to depart before Service be done?
4. Are there any that persuade others to forbear coming to Church, or to receive the Communion in such wise as is appointed by the Book of Common Prayer?
5. Are there any that deprave or speak against the government now established in the Church? or separate themselves from the society of the Congregation, and combine themselves with a new Brotherhood?

6. Are there any that sell or disperse any forbidden books or libels of any Sectaries, touching the religion or government of the Church?

7. Do any of the Parish mis-spend or profane the Lord's day, Sunday, or any Holy day, using any worldly labour, or exercising their trades, or any offensive games, upon any of those days?

8. Are there any that do not reverently behave themselves during the time of Divine Service, devoutly kneeling when the Confession of Sins, the Litany, the Ten Commandments, and other Prayers and Collects are read? and using all due and lowly reverence, when the blessed name of our Lord Jesus Christ is mentioned? and standing up when the Articles of the Belief and the Gospel are read? or that cover their heads in the time of Divine Service; unless it be in case of necessity, wherein a nightcap or coif is allowed? or that give themselves to walk or babble, and be not attentive during the time of Prayers, or the Word read or preached? or that kneel not devoutly at their receiving of the Communion? or that receive it not thrice every year, whereof once at Easter?

9. Whether any of your Parishioners send not their children and servants to be catechised on Sundays and Holy days? or whether such children and servants, being sent, refuse to come? or being come, refuse to learn and be instructed in the same?

10. Whether have there been any persons married together within the degree of consanguinity or affinity prohibited, set forth in a Table, appointed to be placed in every Church?

11. Whether have any been married, in the times wherein marriage is by Law restrained, without lawful licence?

12. Whether have any been married in private houses; or any known or suspected to have been married by any Popish Priest: or in any other order than is appointed by the Church of England?

13. Whether have any persons, once lawfully married, forsaken each other, or do live asunder, without a sentence given by the Ordinary? Or do any, being divorced or separated, marry again, the former wife or husband yet living?

14. Whether have all women in your Parish delivered of child, come, at convenient time after, to give thanks? And have they been churched according to the form of the Book of Common Prayer?

15. Whether do any in your Parish refuse to have their children baptized, or to receive the Communion of your Minister, because he is no Preacher?

16. Whether do any bring strange Ministers into their own houses, to baptize their children privately according to their own fancies? Or receive any child or children born elsewhere, to be baptized in your Parish? If so, who were they that received any such, and whose child or children were so baptized, and what was the name of the child, and who baptized it? And whether do you know of your own knowledge, that the parents of such child or children were married together? And where, when, and by whom?

17. Whether have any in your Parish been christened, churched, buried, or received the Communion, out of your Parish Church, or been married out of your Church, one or both parties not dwelling in your Parish?

18. Whether have you any common resorters to your Church which are not of your Parish? or do any such receive the Communion amongst you? What be their names, and of what Parishes are they?

19. Whether have you in your Parish any Popish Recusants, of insolent behaviour, or that do boldly busy themselves in seducing others, either abroad, or in their own families, by instructing their children in Popish religion; or refusing to entertain any (especially into place of trust), but such as concur with them in opinion? And what be their names that so do?

20. How long have the said Recusants abstained from Divine Service, or the Holy Communion?

21. Whether be any such Recusants married, or their children christened, or any of them buried, by any other than your Minister? Where, when, and by whom? And what certificate have you received thereof? And whether hath any of their children remained unbaptized above one month, or hath not been baptized in your Parish Church? You shall present how the children of such as refuse to come

to Church, are brought up? How many children they have? Under what Schoolmaster or Tutor? Where and in what School? And what those children's names are?

22. Whether hath any person suspended or excommunicated, been suffered to hear Divine Service, or the Sermon, to receive the Sacraments, to be married, or churched? Or have any, dying excommunicate, been buried in Christian burial?

23. Whether hath any of your Parish irreverently used your Minister, or laid violent hands upon him? or disgraced his office and calling, by word or deed?

24. Whether are there in your Parish any adulterers, fornicators, incestuous persons, bawds, receivers, close favourers, conveyers away, or which suffer to depart any incontinent person unpunished: any blasphemers, common swearers, ribalds, drunkards, usurers, malicious slanderers, scolds, or sowers of discord, or any defamed of the said crimes?

25. Whether have the said parties offending in, or suspected of fornication, adultery, incest, or keeping of a bawdy-house, or any other Ecclesiastical crime, been presented since the last Visitation? And have they, being presented, done public penance for the offence? If not, what are their names, and what was the offence? What Parish were they then, or are they now of?

26. Whether have any person or persons suspected or detected of incontinency, and therefore departing, returned again to your Parish? In what place are they now abiding, as you know, or have heard? Or have they done any penance? And what penance?

27. Whether is there any in your Parish that hath used Sorcery or Witchcraft, or been suspected of the same? Or that hath used any charms or unlawful prayers? Or is there any that have resorted to any Sorcerers or Witches for help and counsel? And what are the names both of such as use it, and of such as resort to them?

28. Whether are there in your Parish any Wills not yet proved, or goods of the dead dying intestate left unadministered, neither of both being proved or administered by the authority of the Ordinary? and whether do any ad-

minister the goods of any person deceased without authority, or suppress their Will or Testament? Or hath any Executor neglected to perform their Wills, especially in paying of Legacies given to the Church, to the poor, or to any other charitable or godly uses?

29. Whether do any refuse to pay to the reparations, ornaments, and other things required in your Church, as they are sessed by a lawful Vestry? or any other dwelling out of your Parish, which hold land in your Parish?

30. Whether have any in your Parish given the Churchwardens or Sidemen, or any of them, evil words for doing their duty, according to their oath and conscience, in making presentment for any fault?

Touching the Churchwardens.

1. Whether do any in your Parish take upon them to be Churchwarden or Sideman, which are not lawfully chosen by the Minister and Parishioners, according to the Canon? or do any continue that office longer than one year, except they be chosen again? and are all such officers chosen yearly in Easter-week?

2. Whether do your Churchwardens, within one month at the most after their year ended, before the Minister and Parishioners, give up a just account of all such money and other things as they have received and bestowed? Have they delivered all remaining in their hands belonging to their Church or Parish, by Bill indented, to the next Churchwardens?

3. Whether have the Churchwardens, with the advice of the Minister, from time to time provided a sufficient quantity of fine white bread, and wholesome wine, for the number of Communicants?

4. Whether do the Churchwardens and Sworn-men, before every Visitation, and at other times when there is just occasion, meet and confer about their Presentments, and the answering of these Articles; and who hath (after notice given him of the time and place) carelessly absented himself?

5. Whether is the forfeiture of twelve-pence for absence from Church, appointed by Statute for the use of the poor, taken and levied by the Churchwardens, and employed according to the said Statute: and whether is the same forfeiture taken of all persons which stand wilfully suspended or excommunicated?

6. Whether have any Churchwardens lost, sold, or detained any goods, ornaments, Bells, Belfry, Rents, or implements of the Church?

7. Whether do the Churchwardens and Sidemen, about the midst of Divine Service, usually walk out of the Church, and see who are abroad in any Ale-house, or elsewhere absent, or evil employed: and whether have they presented all such to the Ordinary?

8. Whether do you know or have heard a fame of any offence committed, or duty omitted by any of your Parish, before your time, and heretofore not presented to the Ordinary, or as yet not reformed; and whether have you presented the same?

Touching Ecclesiastical Officers.

1. Whether do you know or have heard of any payment, composition or agreement, to or with the Chancellor, Register, or other inferior Officers Ecclesiastical, for suppressing or concealing of any excommunication, or other Ecclesiastical censure, of or against Recusants, or any other offenders? Or for not certifying of Recusants to the Ordinary? Or for not serving of Process without a sum of money or other consideration received, or promised to any of them in that respect? And by whom?

2. Have they heard any matter of office privately in their chambers without their sworn Register's or their Deputies' presence?

3. Whether hath any mis-liver or mis-doer lawfully presented, and confessing the fault for which he or she was so presented, or being thereof otherwise convicted, had his or their penance, or any part thereof, omitted? If so,

you shall present the name of the party or parties who have so omitted their penance, or any part thereof.

4. Hath any person within your Parish paid or promised any sum of money, or other reward, for commutation of penance for any crime of Ecclesiastical cognisance? If so, then with whom, when, and for what? And how hath the same been employed?

5. Finally, do you know of any matter or cause, which is a breach of the Laws Ecclesiastical here not expressed?

FINIS

NOTES

ON

THE BOOK OF COMMON PRAYER,

Form of Consecrating Church Plate,

&c.

NOTES

ON

THE BOOK OF COMMON PRAYER.

[THE following Notes were written by Bishop Andrewes in his own Book of Common Prayer. The original has not been found, nor is there anything known of it. There are, however, three distinct and apparently independent transcripts still extant; and a fourth was in the hands of Dr. Nicholls. That the transcripts are independent, is inferred from their mutual variations.

The first was made by Bishop Cosin into an interleaved folio Book of Common Prayer, A.D. 1619; which also contains annotations and collections of his own. In the margin opposite to the note of Bishop Andrewes on *Ceremonies*, he wrote, "All the notes which have this mark ?W?, are taken out of my Lord of Winchester's, Bishop Andrewes', Service Book, written with his own hand."

A second was in the possession of a Clergyman, in the year 1710, who had also a MS. vol. of Notes on the Common Prayer by Bishop Cosin, as appears from the following notice by Dr. Nicholls, prefixed to the Additional Notes at the end of his Commentary on the Book of Common Prayer. Lond. 1710. "?W? signifies MS. notes of Bishop Andrewes, partly taken out of the Library of my Lord Bishop of Durham, and partly out of a MS. communicated by the Rev. Mr. C. Neil, Vicar of Northallerton, in Yorkshire."

From this MS. we must suppose that Nicholls printed some notes of Bishop Andrewes', which are omitted in Bishop Cosin's transcript, but are found in the other extant copies; with which, however, Dr. Nicholls was not acquainted. This gives some value to Dr. Nicholls' readings, as they may be derived from this lost MS.; but from the inaccuracy with which he edited Bishop Cosin's Notes, we cannot be certain that his printed Notes exactly represent the MS.

A third transcript, in a beautiful contemporary hand, is preserved in the Archiepiscopal Library at Lambeth. It is contained, with many other valuable papers, in a volume (MSS. No. 943) to which the following curious history is attached: "This MS. was happily recovered by Abp. Herring from Mrs. Ibbott, widow of Dr. Ibbott, formerly Librarian at Lambeth. This MS., it seems, with some money and papers, was in a box which Abp. Tenison directed his executors to burn without opening; but the box bursting in the fire, the money, and this book which they supposed was forgot by the Abp., was taken out and preserved. Abp. Herring made Mrs. Ibbott a present of five guineas for this book.

"This information I received from the Rev. Mr. Henry Hall, Librarian to Abp. Herring, my immediate predecessor in that office.

"AND. COLTEE DUCAREL,
Lambeth Librarian,
Oct. 15, 1757."

It is stated, in the fly-leaf of the volume, that it was sold by Mr. Edmund Wharton (the father of Henry Wharton) to Mr. Keeble, stationer, and bought of him and bound by Archbishop Tenison. The collections seem to have been made by Sancroft, then to have been Henry Wharton's. Most of the papers are Abp. Laud's. They are described in Mr. Todd's Catalogue as "A collection of papers formerly belonging to Abp. Laud; many of them written with his own hand, and most of them endorsed by him; together with some papers of the Abps. Sheldon and Sancroft, and many of Mr. Chillingworth."

The copy commences at the note on Ceremonies with the following heading: "I H S. Some few notes found in a Common Prayer Book, which Bishop Andrewes used, written with his own hand."

In this transcript, the part of the Prayer Book to which the note refers is given in Latin; *e. g.* "Ad Confessionem," "ad verba," &c.

A fourth transcript is in the British Museum, MSS. Harl. 7311. 7, being a part of the Baker Collection. It is on five leaves, placed with other papers at the end of a folio Book of Common Prayer, 1625. The heading is, "Notes found in Bishop Andrewes's Service Booke, written with his own hand." The Prayer Book in which it is, is annotated by several hands; on one of the first leaves is the following note by Humphrey Wanley :—"This book is noted, for the most part, by the hand of Dr. John Cosin, formerly Bishop of Durham, and was bought by Dr. White Kennet, now Bishop of Peterburgh, who found it by chance, in a private house in Peterburgh aforesaid." The handwriting does not appear to be in any part that of Bishop Cosin.

This transcript very much resembles the Lambeth copy; the parts of the Prayer Book on which the notes are made, being given, as there, in Latin; but there are reasons for thinking, as will appear from the various readings, that it is a distinct copy.

These three transcripts have been collated for the present edition. Nicholls' text is printed as being the *textus receptus,* (except where otherwise noted,) and the various readings given in the notes. References to the pages and columns of Nicholls (N.) are added in the margin.]

THE PREFACE, &c.

Though it be appointed, &c.]

N. 6. b. By virtue of this, those Morning Prayers which are used in Colleges, are for the most part Latin.

And all the Priests and Deacons shall be bound to say daily the Morning and Evening Prayer, except they be let by Preaching or some urgent business.]

Concerning Evening Prayer on Saturdays, there is an express rule in the Primitive Church: *Quod in Sabbatis*

BOOK OF COMMON PRAYER. 145

Evangelium cum aliis Scripturis legi conveniat. Conc. Laodic. Can. 160[a]. [leg. 16.] Intelligunt ea quæ fuere Sabbata Judæorum; nam Can. 29[b]. ejusdem Conc. aperte Patres distinguunt inter Sabbata et Diem Dominicum. Id ipsum semper Officium Precum Nona debet exhiberi, Can. 16. [leg. 18.] ejusd. Conc.[c], id est tertia pomeridiana, more computi ecclesiæ Orientalis.

Of Ceremonies.[d]]   N. 7. a.

Ceremonias definiunt { 1. Decorum. 2. Disciplina. 3. Significatio. }[e]

That they would innovate all things.]

(i.) Non est innovatio dicenda, si quid in melius simpliciter, seu alteratione, seu adjectione fiat. S. Ambr. lib. ii. de Officiis[f]. (ii.) Alteratio enim illa est schismatica innovatio, quæ bene posita destruit, non perficit[g].

N. 7. b. and again, 15. b.

Of the Saints' Days[h].]

Requiritur, ut Parochus quilibet indicet, quæ Festa Dominicam quamque sequuntur, et quota feria celebranda sunt, ut inde simul statuti jejuniorum dies devoto populo innotescant.

De promulgatione festorum et Vigiliarum per Parochum.

N. 11. a. and again, 15. b.

Ideo jejunia in prodromis Festorum; ideo Vigiliæ precesque ab Ecclesia usurpata primum, et statuta nobis.

Ideo ipsa Festa Sanctorum et martyrum celebrantur die proximo illucesente, ut sciamus eos modicum quidem in afflictione, Jejuniis, Vigiliis, Precibus degisse; dein in gloriam et lætitiam translatos, ubi

Ratio Vigiliarum et Festorum.

---

[a] [Περὶ τοῦ, ἐν σαββάτῳ εὐαγγέλια μετὰ ἑτέρων γραφῶν ἀναγινώσκεσθαι.—Conc. Laod.Can. xvi.—Conc.tom.i.col. 1500. B. The Latin in the text is from the version of Dionys. Exiguus. —Ibid. col. 1511. B.]

[b] [Ὅτι οὐ δεῖ Χριστιανοὺς Ἰουδαΐζειν, καὶ ἐν τῷ σαββάτῳ σχολάζειν, ἀλλὰ ἐργάζεσθαι αὐτοὺς ἐν τῇ αὐτῇ ἡμέρᾳ· τὴν δὲ κυριακὴν προτιμῶντας, εἴγε δύναιντο, σχολάζειν ὡς Χριστιανοί.—Conc. Laod. Can. xxix.—Ibid. col. 1501. C.]

[c] [Περὶ τοῦ, τὴν αὐτὴν λειτουργίαν τῶν εὐχῶν πάντοτε καὶ ἐν ταῖς ἐννάταις καὶ ἐν ταῖς ἑσπέραις ὀφείλειν γίνεσθαι.— Conc. Laod. Can. xviii.—Ibid. col. 1500. B.]

[d] [The Lambeth and B. M. copies

AND.—PERRON, ETC.

commence here.]

[e] [The numerals and arrangement in columns are derived from the Brit. Mus. and Lamb. copies.]

[f] [This reference to St. Ambrose seems to be incorrect, as the words cannot be found in the place indicated, though it is the one given in all the transcripts.]

[g] [In B.M. this stands as two notes, i. on 'presume to alter,' ii. on 'would innovate.' In the Lambeth MS. it is on the words 'presume to alter,' and 'enim' is omitted.]

[h] [The following note is not in the B. M. or the Lambeth copy; the side notes are in the margin of the Durham MS., but omitted by Nicholls.]

L

totos feriarum dies agunt; atque inde Deo gloriam, nobis exemplum.

Quare ad quædam festa non jejunatur. Illud tamen notandum, quod neque Vigiliæ, neque Jejunia, sed solæ Preces præcedant quædam Festa: neque enim ad Festum Michaelis et Omnium Angelorum jejunatur, aut vigilatur propter rationes prædictas. Quinetiam licet prædictæ rationes in Festis S. Marci, Philippi et Jacobi, eorumque quæ post Domini Natalem usque ad Epiphaniam observantur, obtineant; tamen ex antiquissimis canonibus vetantur ad hujusmodi Festa Jejunia, propter reverentiam majorum solennitatum, Paschatis scilicet et Nativitatis.

Anathema enim dixerunt sancti Patres vel intra Pascha et Pentecostem [i], vel intra Natalem et Epiphaniam jejunantibus. Et fieri nequit, ut Festa S. Marci, Sanctorum Philippi et Jacobi, aliter contingant quam intra dies Paschatis et Pentecostes.

N. 18. a. *The Minister . . . shall use such ornaments . . . as were in use by authority of Parliament in the second year of the reign of King Edward the Sixth.*]

Mention is there made of surplice [j], tippet, hood, *pro cujusque gradu* [k].

MORNING AND EVENING PRAYER.

The Minister shall read with a loud voice some one of these Sentences.]

N. 18. b. Adde huc, quod [l] ad invitandam pœnitentiam egregia sunt misericordiæ et longanimitatis encomia. Psal. lxxviii. 38. Jer. iii. 7. 12 [m]; Heb. iv.

Dearly beloved Brethren.]
'Ικεσία nititur his locis S. Scripturæ [n];

---

[i] ['Pentecosten,' MS. Durh.]
[j] ['cope, surplice,' MS. Durh.]
[k] [This note is not in B. M. or Lambeth MS. Bishop Cosin added to it, 'I find not that. J. C.;' and in a later hand, 'But the Act of Parliament (I see) refers to the Canon, and until such times as other order shall be taken.']

[l] ['Adde huc, quod' not in Lamb. MS.]
[m] ['12.' not in MS. B.M.]
[n] [The texts are thus arranged in columns in the Durh. MS. In the B. M. they are written continuously 1, 2, 3, 4, 5, 6; and in the Lambeth MS. 1, 4, 2, 5, 3, 6, showing that this and the B. M. copy were distinct tran-

[1.] Job. xxxi. 27.   [4.] Levit. v. 5.
[2.] Prov. xxviii. 13.   [5.] Dan. ix. 18.
[3.] Luke xv. 18.   [6.] Acts xix. 18.[o]

A general Confession.]
Suis quisque verbis resipiscentiam profitetur [p]. Basil. ad Neocæsar. Ep. 69 [q]. Idem Reg. Contract. 288 [r].

Most Merciful Father	mercy itself [s].	N. 19. a.
we have erred and strayed	we have [t] wittingly and willingly run from.	
like lost sheep	like untamed heifers, Jer. xxxi. 18. Deut. iii. 15.	
the devices and desires	absurd devices, brutish desires.	
we have offended	we have been offended at.	
we have left undone	not done at all [u].	
we have done	done nothing but [x].	
there is no health	no [y] hope of health.	
miserable offenders	yea most miserable.	
that be penitent	that desire to be penitent, wish they were, would be glad if they were so [z], fear they are [a] not enough; are sorry that they are no more.	
according to thy promises	most precious, most gracious, most sweet.	

The Absolution—Remission of Sins, to be pronounced by the Minister alone.]
And because he speaks it *authoritativè*, in the Name of

---

scripts. The numerals are prefixed, to exhibit this; they are not in Nicholls, or in the MSS.]

[o] ['20.' MS. B.M.]
[p] ['confitetur.' MS. B.M.]
[q] [Τὴν νύκτα διενεγκόντες μεταξὺ προσευχόμενοι, ἡμέρας ἤδη ὑπολαμπούσης, πάντες κοινῇ, ὡς ἐξ ἑνὸς στόματος καὶ μιᾶς καρδίας, τὸν τῆς ἐξομολογήσεως ψαλμὸν ἀναφέρουσι τῷ Κυρίῳ, ἴδια ἑαυτῶν ἕκαστος τὰ ῥήματα τῆς μετανοίας ποιούμενοι.—S. Basil. Ep. ccvii. (al. 63.) ad Clericos Neocæsarienses, § 3. Op., tom. iii. p. 311. C.]
[r] [Ἀναγκαίον τοῖς πεπιστευμένοις τὴν οἰκονομίαν τῶν μυστηρίων τοῦ Θεοῦ, ἐξομολογεῖσθαι τὰ ἁμαρτήματα, οὕτω γὰρ καὶ οἱ πάλαι μετανοοῦντες ἐπὶ τῶν ἁγίων εὑρίσκονται πεποιηκότες.—S. Ba-

sil. Reg. brevius Tractatæ, Interr. et Resp. cclxxxviii. Op.,tom. ii. p. 516.D.]
[s] [In B. M. this is entitled 'Paraphrasis,' and the note marks are numerals. In Abp. Laud's Devotions, (Works, vol. iii. *ad init.*) there is another version of this Paraphrase. It is called 'Confessio cum precatione per L. A. W. (*i. e.* Lanc. Andrewes Winton.')]
[t] ['we have' om. B. M. and Lamb.]
[u] ['we have' added by Nicholls in this and the next clause.]
[x] ['nothing but done.' MS. Lambeth.]
[y] ['nor' MS. Durh.]
[z] ['penitent, who would rejoice they were so,' MS. Lambeth.]
[a] ['bee' MS. B. M.]

Christ and His Church, he must not kneel, but stand up. For authority of absolution[b], see Ezek. xxxiii. 12. Job xxxiii. 23. Numb. vi. 24.[c] 2 Sam. xii. 13. John xx. 23.

The Lord's Prayer [d].]

Προσευχή.   Præceptum Christi[e].

Our Father,   Etsi læsus est, Pater est.
which art in Heaven,   Eminenter, non inclusive.
Hallowed be Thy Name,   In me, per me, super me.
Thy kingdom come,   Ut destruatur regnum peccati, per quod regnavit[f] mors et Diabolus.
in earth   In me, qui sum terra.
in Heaven.   A[g] sanctis angelis.
Give us this day our daily   Pro necessitate.
bread.   Proprium, licite[h] acquisitum, supercœlestem[i] et corporeum.
Forgive us our trespasses,   Talenta dimitte.
Lead us not: nec[k] sinas intrare ductos pronosque.

from evil,   ab authore mali { extra { Diabolo, mundo : intra nobismet ipsis[l].

a malo { culpæ, pœnæ, omni } per[m] { gratiam, misericordiam, pacem.

For thine is the kingdom [n].]

Gloria Patri.] Doxologia a sanctis olim[o] patribus contra virus Arianum præscripta et retenta. [p] Consule Hookerum[q].

---

[b] ['And for authority of absolving' MS. B.M. 'For the authority of absolving' MS. Lamb.]

[c] [Chron. vi. 24. added here in B. M. and Lamb. MSS.]

[d] [There is here in Nicholls a note wrongly marked as Andrewes'; it is Cosin's own note in the interleaved Prayer Book of 1636: and the error is probably one of the press, ? W ? being put for C†. In Abp. Laud's Devotions, (Works, vol. iii. p. 1,) there is a Paraphrase of the Lord's Prayer, so closely resembling that which follows, (though with improved readings,) as to make it almost certain that it was transcribed from Bishop Andrewes' own copy of the Prayer Book.]

[e] ['Domini.' MS. Lambeth.]

[f] [So in MSS. Nicholls printed 'regnant.']

[g] ['In et a' MS. Lamb.]

[h] ['licitis' MS. Lamb.]

[i] ['supercœleste' in all the MSS.]

[k] ['ne' B. M.]

[l] ['nobis ipsis' MS. B. M. 'intra .. ipsis,' not in MS. Lamb.]

[m] [Nicholls repeated 'per' three times, as do the Durham and Lambeth MSS., the B. M. is as here printed, which is Andrewes' usual mode.]

[n] [The rest of the note as printed in Nicholls is not Andrewes', it is wrongly added there, being out of Cosin's notes in the Prayer Book of 1636.]

[o] ['olim' om. MS. B. M.]

[p] ['consule Hookerum.' om. B. M. and Lamb. MSS.]

[q] [The Laws of Eccles. Polity, Book V. ch. xlii. § 8. sqq. ed. Keble.]

Psalms[r].]   N. 20. a.

Ψαλμωδία veterum Christianorum, quacum Liturgiam inchoare solebant. [Quid si *Introite* olim dictum, quod in Introitu Ecclesiæ cani solitum, qualia sunt Psalmistæ Cantica Graduum.] [s]

On the Rubric of Lessons and Hymns.]   N. 21. a.

Qui sequitur ordo intermiscendi Psalmos cum Lectionibus, nititur can. 17. Concilii Laodiceni, his verbis: In conventu fidelium nequaquam Psalmos continuare conveniat, sed per[t] intervallum[u] per Psalmos singulos[v] recenseri debeant Lectiones[x]. Hæc a sanctissimo concilio statuta anno Domini 368[y]. Quod non oportet Plebeios Psalmos cantare in Ecclesia, nec libros præter canonem legi, sed sola sacra volumina N. T. vel V. Idem Concil. can. 10.[z]

The Third Collect for Grace[a].]

THE LITANY.   N. 23. a.

Λιτανείαι a Græco Μηνιαίῳ[b].

The Litany to be[c] said or sung in the midst of the church. Injunct. Elizab.[d]

The Priest goeth from out of his seat into the body of the church, and ([e]at a low desk before the chancel door, called the fald-stool) kneels and says or sings the Litany.

Vide[f] Prophetam Joel, de medio loco inter porticum et altare, ubi sacerdotes et prophetæ ingemere et ingeminare[g]

---

[r] ['Ad Venite exultemus.' B. M. and Lamb. MSS.]
[s] [The words in brackets added in Lambeth MS.]
[t] [om. B. M.]
[u] ['intervallo' MS. B. M.]
[v] ['singulos' om. MS. B. M.]
[x] [Περὶ τοῦ μὴ δεῖν ἐπισυνάπτειν ἐν ταῖς συνάξεσι τοὺς ψαλμούς, ἀλλὰ διὰ μέσου καθ' ἕκαστον ψαλμὸν γίνεσθαι ἀνάγνωσιν.—Conc. Laod. Can. xvii.—Conc. tom. i. col. 1500. B.]
[y] ['A°. 80.' MS. B. M.]
[z] ["Ὅτι οὐ δεῖ ἰδιωτικοὺς ψαλμοὺς λέγεσθαι ἐν τῇ ἐκκλησίᾳ, οὐδὲ ἀκανόνιστα βιβλία, ἀλλὰ μόνον τὰ κανονικὰ τῆς καινῆς καὶ παλαιᾶς διαθήκης.—Conc. Laod. Can. lix. — Conc. tom. i. col. 1508. A.]
[a] [The following note on this Collect is inserted in MS. Durh., but with a line drawn through it, as if of erasure. "This Collect is in some places, by laudable custom, repeated of the people, as the Confession is. And thus in St. Gregory under Paul's, by Dr. White. Mart. 1621." It is not in Nicholls, nor in B. M., nor Lambeth MS.]
[b] [For Μηνιαίῳ, Nicholls has Λιτανεύω. This note is not in B. M. MS.]
[c] ['is to be.' B. M. and Lamb. MSS.]
[d] [Injunctions given by the Queen's Majesty anno Dom. 1559. § 18. Wilkins' Concilia, vol. iv. p. 184.]
[e] [In B. M. and Lamb. MSS. the parenthesis begins before 'called.']
[f] ['Vide etiam' B. M. MS.]
[g] ['et ingeminare' om. B. M. MS.]

jussi, Parce, Domine, Parce populo tuo, &c. temporibus[h] jejuniorum[i].

N. 23. b. 1. *By the mystery of Thy holy Incarnation;* 2. *By Thy holy Nativity,* 3. *and Circumcision;* 4. *By Thy Baptism;* 5. *Fasting,* 6. *and Temptation;* 7. *By Thine Agony,* 8. *and bloody Sweat;* 9. *By Thy Cross,* 10. *and Passion;* 11. *By Thy precious Death,* 12. *and Burial.*] His 12 Deus in carne manifestatus[j].

1. *By Thy glorious Resurrection,* 2. *and Ascension,* 3. *and by the coming of the Holy Ghost.*] His tribus justificatus in spiritu. 1 Tim. iii. 16.

N. 24. a. *That it may please Thee to succour all that are in danger . . . that travel by land, or by water; all women labouring of child; all sick persons, and young children . . . all prisoners and captives.*] Ecclesia[k] pia mater in hoc versiculo[l], septem personas, quas vocant canonici miserabiles, commemorat, dignasque existimat duplici privilegio, viz.: solenni publicarum precum intercessione[m] et carnium esu tempore quadragesimali.

Prayer for the Clergy and People.

N. 24. b. *All Bishops and Curates.*] Ministri nunc appellantur, quos olim ecclesia veriori nomine Curatos dixit, propter animarum curam: non ergo hic subsidiarii solum intelligendi[n], sed ipsi quibus cura incumbit.

At the end of the Litany.

Here the Minister riseth[o], and if there be a sermon an Introit is sung; and after sermon they ascend with three adorations towards the Altar. If both Ministers or Priests[p], the one at one[q] end, the other at the other, representing the two Cherubims at the mercy-seat: if one be but a Deacon, he kneels at the door.

---

[h] ['in temporibus' MS. B. M.]
[i] [Nicholls gives this paragraph in English.]
[j] ['justificatus.' MS. Lamb.
[k] ['Et ecclesia' MS. Lamb.]
[l] ['hoc sequenti versiculo' MS. B. M. 'hoc et sequenti versiculo' MS. Lamb.]
[m] [So in MS. Lamb. 'interesse.' Nicholls, and MS. Durh., om. B. M.]
[n] [So in MSS. 'non ergo subsidiarii solum hic intelligendi' Nicholls.]
[o] [This note is inserted in B. M. and Lambeth MSS. at the beginning of the office for the Holy Communion, and begins thus,—'After an Introite is sung the Priests ascend (Priest ascends.' MS. B. M.) &c.]
[p] ['If both be priests' Lamb. and B. M. MSS.]
[q] ['the one' Lamb. MS., 'then the one' B. M. MS.]

THE HOLY COMMUNION.

N. 35. a.

De apparatu ante Eucharistiam faciendo.] Post finitam primam partem Liturgiæ (quam olim Missam Catechumenorum vocabant [r]) jam [s] nostro more sequitur concio: concionem tertia hæc quæ subsequitur Eucharistiæ peragendæ forma. Recte concio peragitur ante Eucharistiam. Notandum [t] tamen in veteri [u] et primæva Ecclesia concionem primo mane habitam fuisse [x] (quam Tractatum nuncupabant); ad eam [y] cum Christianis audientes, energumeni, Judæi, Ethnici, promiscue admittebantur: et [z] istis egressis, vel exactis, post tractatum, pergebatur ad secundam Liturgiæ partem, Missam Catechumenorum dictam, eam scilicet quacum nos incipimus. Sed illis initium erat, *Venite exultemus:* nobis *Confessio publica generalis,* propter male abolitas [a] publicam ἐξομολόγησιν, et privatam auricularem. Tertio, ipsis catechumenis exactis, ad sacram Synaxim, i. e. εὐχαριστίαν [b], soli ii, qui erant a scelere puri, et baptizati se [c] recipiebant [d], quæ ideo dicta est Missa Sanctorum. Quæ omnia aperte [e] mandantur fieri secundum ordinem prædictum, can. 19. Concil. Laodic. [f]

If any person be an open and notorious evil liver.]

N. 36. a.

Our law in [g] England will not suffer the Minister to judge any man a [h] notorious offender, but him who is convicted by some legal sentence.

And not him that is obstinate.]

It seems, he may rather make open protestation [i] of his obstinacy, than repel him with safety by [k] the common [l] law.

---

[r] ['appellabant' Lambeth MS.]
[s] ['eam' Nicholls.]
[t] [om. Lambeth MS.]
[u] ['in veteri tamen' Lambeth MS.]
[x] ['fuisse constat' Lambeth MS.]
[y] ['ad eam' Nicholls, and 'ad quam' Durh. B. M. and Lamb. MSS.]
[z] ['et' om. MSS. Durh. and B. M.]
[a] ['abolitas male' Lambeth MS.]
[b] ['Euch^m.' Lambeth MS.]
[c] [om. Lambeth MS.]
[d] ['recipiebantur' Lambeth MS.]
[e] [om. Lambeth MS.]
[f] [Περὶ τοῦ, δεῖν ἰδίᾳ πρῶτον μετὰ τὰς ὁμιλίας τῶν ἐπισκόπων, καὶ τῶν κατηχουμένων εὐχὴν ἐπιτελεῖσθαι· καὶ μετὰ τὸ ἐξελθεῖν τοὺς κατηχουμένους, τῶν ἐν μετανοίᾳ τὴν εὐχὴν γίνεσθαι· καὶ τούτων προσελθόντων ὑπὸ χεῖρα, καὶ ὑποχωρησάντων, οὕτως τῶν πιστῶν τὰς εὐχὰς γίνεσθαι, κ. τ. λ. — Conc. Laod. Can. xix.—Conc. tom. i. col. 1500. C.]
[g] ['of' B. M. and Lamb. MSS.]
[h] ['as a' Nicholls.]
[i] ['profession' B. M. MS.]
[k] ['at' Nicholls.]
[l] ['common' om. B. M. MS. 'the common' om. MS. Lamb.]

N. 38. a. *Shall say the Lord's Prayer, with this Collect* [m].]

In sacra synaxi nihil canitur, quod alias fieri solet; sed omnia graviter et severe peraguntur cum affectu potius quam modulatione [n]. Cum non est communio recte sequimur Prophetici Regis morem. Ps. cxviii. 25.

N. 38. b. *Then shall the Priest rehearse distinctly all the Ten Commandments.*]

The Priest, after the Collect, descends to the door of the *Septum*, makes a low adoration towards the Altar; then turns to the people, and standing in[o] the door, readeth the Ten Commandments, as from God, whilst[p] they[q] lie prostrate to the end[r], as to God speaking[s].

Then shall follow the Collect.]

Facta[t] adoratione ut prius, Minister ascendit, et genuflectit.

Immediately after the Collect, the Priest shall read the Epistle.]

Here the other Priest, or if there be none[u], he that executeth[v], descendeth[w] to the door, adoreth[x], and then turning readeth[y] the Epistle and Gospel.

N. 39. a. *And, the Epistle ended, he shall say the Gospel*[z].]

In the reading[a] the holy Gospel, and never else[b], is Adoration made[c] at the name of Jesus; for then[d] only is it in its[e] right exaltation; and then men stand[f] in a posture ready to make reverence.

The Epistle and Gospel being ended, shall be said the Creed.] [*Ad, Laus tibi Domine.* MSS. Lamb. and B. M.]

Ὑμνολογία post Evangelium, Graduale[g].

[m] [This note is not in B. M. or Lamb. MS.]
[n] ['modulate.' Nicholls.]
[o] ['at' MS. B. M.]
[p] ['whiles' MS. Durh. 'while' B. M.]
[q] ['while the people' MS. Lamb.]
[r] ['to the end,' om. MS. Lamb. 'end of them,' MS. B. M.]
[s] ['as answering to God.' MS. B. M. 'as answering and speaking to God.' MS. Lamb.]
[t] ['Tum facta' B. M. and Lamb. MSS.]
[u] ['not another,' MSS. B. M. and Lamb.]
[v] ['executes.' MSS. Durh., Lamb. and B. M.]
[w] ['descends' MS. B.M.]
[x] ['adores' MSS. Durh., Lamb. and B. M.]
[y] ['reads' MSS. B. M. and Lamb.]
[z] [Not noted as Andrewes' in Nicholls.]
[a] ['In reading of.' MS. Lamb.]
[b] ['Gospel only.' B. M. and Lamb. MSS.]
[c] ['made only' MS. Lamb.]
[d] ['for that then' B. M. and Lamb. MSS.]
[e] ['his' MSS. Durh. and Lamb., 'the' B. M.]
[f] ['and for that men stand then' MS. B.M.]
[g] ['graduate.' MS. B. M.]

[*Ad Symbolum*. MSS. Lamb. and B. M.] Adorat[h], ascendit, et legit Symbolum Nicænum, populo adhuc stante.

After the Creed. [*Ante Offertorium.* MS. Lamb.]   N. 40. b.

Lecta Confessione Nicæna; the Priest adores. Then he removes the basin from the back of the Altar to the forepart. Then[i] the Bishop[j] ascends with treble[k] Adoration, and lastly kneels down at the Altar.

Into his hands the Priest from a by-standing table on the south side, reaches[l] first the Wafer Bread, in a canister close covered, and lined with linen[m]. 2dly[n]. The Wine in a barrel on a cradle with four feet[o]. These the Bishop offers[p] in the name of the whole congregation, upon the Altar.

Then he offers[q] into the basin for himself, and after him the whole congregation, and so [r] betake themselves to their[s] proper and convenient place [t] of kneeling.

Bishops[u] and Priests only within the *septum*[x]; Deacons at the door; the Laity[y] without; the Priest meanwhile[z] reading the peculiar sentences for the Offertory. *Solis ministerio sacro deditis ad Altare ingredi et communicare licet.* Conc. Laod. can. 19[a].

Saying one or more of these Sentences following.]

Instead of these, read the peculiar Sentences for the Offer- N. 41. b. tory[b], *ut infra*, and some of these immediately before the Benediction, for the Poor[c].

Peculiar Sentences for the Offertory[d].   N. 42. a.

In process of time it came to pass, that Cain brought of the fruit of the ground an offering unto the Lord. And Abel

---

[h] ['Tum adorat,' MSS. B. M. and Lamb.]
[i] ['Then' om. Nicholls.]
[j] ['Bishop, if present' MSS. B. M. and Lamb.]
[k] ['triple' MS. B. M.]
[l] ['reacheth' MSS.]
[m] ['fine linen.' MSS. B. M. and Lamb.]
[n] ['Then' MSS. B. M. and Lamb.]
[o] [See the plan of Bishop Andrewes' Chapel, appended to his Life, prefixed to this volume.]
[p] ['offereth' MSS.]
[q] ['offereth' MSS.]
[r] ['and then they' MSS. B. M. and Lamb.]
[s] ['their own' MS. B. M.]
[t] ['places' MS. B. M.]

[u] ['The Bishops' B. M.]
[x] [See the plan of Bishop Andrewes' Chapel.]
[y] ['and the Laity' MS. B. M.; 'and Laity' MS. Lamb.]
[z] ['meantime' MS. Lamb.; 'in the meantime' MS. B. M.]
[a] [Μόνοις ἐξὸν εἶναι τοῖς ἱερατικοῖς εἰσιέναι εἰς τὸ θυσιαστήριον, καὶ κοινωνεῖν.—Conc. Laod. Can. xix.—Conc. tom. i. col. 1500. D.]
[b] [After 'Offertory,' the note is in Durh. and Lamb. MSS. 'instead of those that are printed, whereof some may be read ('whereof many are for the poor' MS. Lamb.) at the end before the Benediction.' See below, p. 158.]
[c] [This note omitted MS. B. M.]
[d] [The introduction of these sen-

brought also of the firstlings of his flock, and of the fat thereof. And the Lord had respect unto Abel and his offering. Gen. iv. 3, 4.[e]

Speak unto the children of Israel, that they bring me an offering: of every one[f] *that giveth*[g] *it willingly with his heart they*[h] *shall take my offering.* Exod. xxv. 2.

Three times in the year shall all the males appear before the Lord thy God in the place which He shall choose; and they shall not appear before the Lord empty. Every man shall give according as he is able, and according to the blessing of the Lord thy God which He hath given thee. Deut. xvi. 16, 17.

All things come of Thee, O Lord, and of thine[i] *own we give unto thee*[j]*. I have offered willingly in the uprightness of mine*[k] *heart of*[l] *all these things. Now*[m] *also have I seen thy people, which are found here to offer unto thee willingly*[n] *with joy.* 1 Chron. xxix. 14, 17.

We made statutes for ourselves, to give by the year the[o] *third part of a shekel, for the service of the house of our God.* Neh. x. 32.

Give unto the Lord, ye families of the people, give unto the Lord glory and power[p]*. Give unto the Lord the glory of*[q] *his Name; bring an offering, and enter into his courts.* Psal. xcvi. 7, 8.

As Jesus sat over against the Treasury, he beheld how the people cast money into it: and many rich men cast in much: and he saw also a certain poor widow which cast in[r] *two mites. And he said, Of a truth I say unto you, that this poor widow hath cast in more than they all: for they*[s] *of their superfluity cast into*[t] *the offerings of God; but she of her penury hath cast in all the*[u] *living that she had.* Mark xii. 41.

tences was proposed by Bishop Cosin in 1662; see the MS. alterations submitted by him to the Bishops, in a Book of Common Prayer preserved in his Library at Durham. D. iii. 3.]

[e] [In the MSS. the references are in the margin, and, as in Nicholls, at the beginning of the texts.]
[f] ['man' MS. B. M.]
[g] ['gives' MS. B. M.]
[h] ['ye' MS. B. M.]
[i] ['thy' MS. B. M.]
[j] ['give thee' MSS. B. M. and Lamb.]
[k] ['my' MSS. B. M. and Lamb.]
[l] [om. MS. B. M.]
[m] ['For' Nicholls.]
[n] ['offer willingly' MS. Lamb.]
[o] ['a' Nicholls.]
[p] ['Give... power,' omitted in MS. Lamb.]
[q] ['due unto' MS. Lamb.]
[r] ['in thither' MS. B. M.]
[s] ['they all' MS. B. M.]
[t] ['in into' MS. Lamb.]
[u] ['her' MS. Lamb.]

Now after many years I came and brought[x] *alms to my nation, and offerings*[y]. Acts xxiv. 17.

Then shall the Churchwardens, &c.]

Sapit hæc collectio per capita Genevensem illum per Ecclesias tumultuaria forma discurrendi morem.

Pay to the Curate.] N. 42. a. b.

They should not pay it[z] to the curate alone[a], but to God upon the altar; from whence the curate has[b] his warrant to take it, as deputed by Him, and as the Apostle plainly alludes[c], 1 Cor. ix. 13, 14; Heb. xiii. 10. And this is not[d] to be forgotten, though it be forgone[e], that whosoever gave any lands or endowments to the service of God, he gave it in a[f] formal writing, as nowadays between man and man[g], sealed and witnessed. And the tender of the gift was *super altare*, and[h] by the donor upon his knees.

Let us pray for the whole state.] N. 42. b.

Ὑπερέντευξις[i]. Diaconi voce indici solebat. S. Aug. Ep. 119.[j] Ἱερὰ εὐχὴ Dionysii[k].

Pro Collectâ. N. 44. a.

That he may receive the benefit of absolution.]

It is most expedient that this be read, to induce the people that they bethink themselves of the sovereign benefit of absolution by their penitent confession.

Dr. White, in his "Way to the Church," quotes all this latter part of the Exhortation[l], showing, against the slander of the Jesuits, that we abolish not, but willingly retain the doctrine of confession. § 40. 231.[m]

Then shall the Priest say this exhortation.] Stans recitabit[n].

[x] ['came and' om. MS. B. M.; 'brought up' MS. Lamb.]
[y] ['alms and offerings to my nation.' MS. B. M.]
[z] ['these offerings' MS. B. M.; 'their offerings' MS. Lamb.]
[a] ['only' MSS. B. M. and Lamb.]
[b] ['hath' MSS.]
[c] ['alluded' MS. Durh.; 'alludeth' MSS. B. M. and Lamb.]
[d] ['Nor is this' MS. B. M.]
[e] ['though forgone,' MS. B. M.]
[f] ['a.' om. Nicholls.]
[g] ['as .... man' om. MS. B. M.]
[h] ['and' om. MS. B. M.]
[i] ['Ὑπερέντευξις.' om. MS. B. M.; all as far as 'Collecta.' om. MS. Lamb.]
[j] [.... 'communis oratio voce Diaconi indicitur.' — S. Aug. Epist. lv. (al. cxviii.) ad Inquisit. Januarii, lib. ii. cap. xviii. § 34. Op., tom. ii. col. 212. A.]
[k] [S. Dionys. Areop. de Eccles. Hierarch. cap. iii. § 2. Op., tom. i. p. 188. A. ad. Venet. 1755.]
[l] ['confession. And it is' MS. B. M. omitting the intervening words.]
[m] [The Way to the True Church, by John White, D.D. Works, p. 122. Lond. 1624.]
[n] [Not in Lamb. or B. M. MSS.]

N. 44. b. *Draw near.*
Forte non est opus his verbis, quia jam accesserunt. [Aut omnes, aut per vices ad septum accedentes genuflectebant, et Euchar. sub utraque specie percipiebant º.]

Then shall this general Confession . . . by one of the Ministers.]
The other priest (if there be a second), or he that executeth[p], descendeth[q] to the door, and there, kneeling, saith the Confession, the people repeating after him.

Almighty God.] Ἐξομολόγησις.
[Absolution.] Then shall the Priest stand up.] Ἀπολυτικὸν[r], in quo absolvit stans[s].

Lift up your hearts.]

N. 45. a.   Ἀνάσχωμεν τὰς καρδίας[t]. *Sursum corda*[u]. Aug. de Ver. Relig. cap. 3[v].
Sequentia[w] jubilans.

Then shall the Priest, kneeling down (before "We do not presume.")] Descendit, repetit[x] solus.
Prayer of Consecration.]
Sancta Sanctis. Aug. Epist. 57 [y].
The Priest, standing up, shall say the Prayer of Consecration.]

N. 45. b.   [z] Here the Priest, having made adoration, poureth water upon[a] the napkin ready for that[b] purpose, and cleanseth[c] his hands: mystice respiciens illud Psalmi, *Lavabo in innocentia*

º [Words in brackets added in MS. Lamb.]
p [' executes ' MS. Durh.]
q [' descends' MS. B. M.]
r [Ἀπολυτικὴ, MS. Lamb.]
s [A note occurs here in Nicholls, beginning *Succedit præfatio cujus*, which is wrongly marked as Andrewes', being a note of Bishop Cosin's in another interleaved book of 1636.]
t [Ἀνάσχωμεν τὰς καρδίας. omit. MS. Lamb.]
u [Ut quotidie per universum orbem humanum genus una pene voce respondeat, *Sursum corda se habere ad Dominum.* — S. Aug. de Vera Religione, cap. iii. § 5. Op., tom. i. col. 1211. A.]
v [This reference omitted in MS. Lamb.]
w [' Hæc et sequentia' MS. B. M.]
x [' et repetit' MS. B. M. which puts this note as a continuation of the last, on *Sursum corda*.]
y [In the margin of MS. Durh. at the Prayer of Consecration, but omitted by Nicholls. In MS. B.M. at 'We do not presume.' The reference to S. Aug. connects it with 'Let us give thanks to our Lord God.'
'Nosti autem in quo sacrificio dicatur, Gratias agamus Domino Deo nostro.' — S. Aug. Ep. clxxxvii. (al. lvii.) ad Dardanum, cap. vi. § 21. Op., tom. ii. col. 1027. B.]
z [This note is not found in the Durham book, but it is in Nicholls; it is in the B. M. and Lamb. MSS. Nicholls probably derived it from the MS. communicated by the Rev. C. Neil.]
a [' on ' B. M. and Lamb. MSS.]
b [' the ' MS. Lamb.]
c [' cleaneth ' Nicholls.]

manus meas, et sic introibo ad altare Dei, ut annunciem[d] *vocem εὐχαριστίας.* Ps. xxvi. 6. Moraliter et decore, uti[e] cum magnatibus accubituri sumus[f].

Postea panes e canistro in patinam ponit: dein vinum e doliolo[g], adinstar Sanguinis erumpentis[h], in calicem haurit; tum aquam e Triconali[i] scypho[k] immiscet; postremo omnibus[l] rite, et quam fieri potest decentissime atque aptissime[m] compositis, stans pergit et peragit.

In rariore solennitate hic pergit Episcopus et consecrat.

Thanks, He brake it.]   N. 47. b.

Sic nos ejus ductu et exemplo qui hic præsidet[n].

The Blood . . . unto everlasting life.]   N. 49. a.

To this prayer[o] of the Priest every communicant should say *Amen*; and then, and not before, take the Sacrament of him[p]. Universam Ecclesiam, accepto Christi Sanguine, dicere asserit Augustinus ad Orosium, Quæst. 49[q]. Quare duo hic egregia[r] habemus. 1. Universam[s] Ecclesiam participem esse Calicis[t]. 2.[u] Cum accipiunt[x] dicere[y], Amen.

Et quamquam[z] Schismatici cavillantur debitum genuflexionis ritum[a], orantibus[b] quis alius gestus[c] usurpandus, nisi supplicatorius?

Ad Orat. Dom.] Embolismus, oratio Dominica[d].

We most heartily thank thee[e].]   N. 51. b.

When the Psalm is ended, let the Deacon say, Let us give

---

[d] ['ut sic annunciem' MS. B. M.]
[e] ['ut' MS. Lamb.]
[f] ['sumus' om. MS. B. M.]
[g] ['dolio' MS. B. M.]
[h] ['dirumpens' MS. B. M.; 'erumpens' MS. Lamb.]
[i] ['triclinari' MS. B. M.]
[k] ['cypho' MS. B. M.]
[l] ['omnia' MSS. B. M. and Lamb.]
[m] ['atque aptissime' om. MS. B. M.]
[n] [At that time there was no rubric enjoining this. This note is omitted MS. Lamb.]
[o] ['these prayers' MS. Lamb.]
[p] ['of him' om. MS. Lamb.]
[q] [Dialog. Quæstionum lxv. sub tit. Orosii percontantis et S. August. respondentis, opus spurium seu consarcinatum.—Quæst. 49. Op., tom. vi. (Append.) col. 1094. C. Cf. autem locum unde desumptum est. "Habet enim magnam vocem Christi sanguis in terra, cum eo accepto ab omnibus gentibus respondetur, Amen." — S. Aug. cont. Faust. Manich. lib. xii. cap. 10. Op., tom. viii. col. 382. B.]
[r] ['Secundum morem universæ ecclesiæ. Augustin. ad Oros. quæst. 49. Universa Ecclesia, accepto Christi sanguine, dicit Amen. Ubi duo egregia (notatu digna, MS. Lamb.,) &c.' MSS. B. M. and Lamb.]
[s] ['Universalem' Nicholls.]
[t] ['sanguinis' MS. B. M.]
[u] ['Et 2.' MS. Durh.]
[x] ['accipiant' MS. Durh.; 'acceperint' MS. Lamb.]
[y] ['omnes dicere' MSS. B. M. and Lamb.]
[z] ['quamvis' MS. B.M.]
[a] ['debitum genuflexionis ritum cavillantur,' MS. B.M.]
[b] ['orantibus tamen' MS. B.M.]
[c] ['quis alius gestus orantibus' MS. Lamb.]
[d] [Only found in MS. Lamb.]
[e] [This note omitted MS. Lamb.]

thanks to Him who has made us worthy to receive His holy Mysteries, &c. Clem. Const. Ap. lib. viii. cap. 20.[f]

N. 52. a. *Glory be to God on High.*]
[g] Socrat. vi. 8.[h] Hymnus Angelicus. Ἀντιφωνὰ post Communionem. D. Hilarii Pictav.[i] S. Chrys. ad Antioch. 57[j].

Before the Blessing.]
Here the congregation ariseth, and having made their adoration[k], they go towards their seats to a little[l] private devotion. In their way, at the foot of the choir, stands the *cippus pauperum*, into which every man puts a small piece of silver[m]; whilst[n] the Priest, standing still[o] at the Altar, readeth the exhortatory sentences for alms[p], *ut supra*.

At the Blessing.]
When[q] all are composed in[r] their seats, he proceeds to the Blessing[s].

N. 53. b. *And there shall be no celebration . . . a great number.*]
Communionis tempore dum populus conveniat. Gelas.[t]

---

[f] [Καὶ ὁ διάκονος λεγέτω παυσαμένου τοῦ ψάλλοντος . . . . εὐχαριστήσωμεν τῷ καταξιώσαντι ἡμᾶς μεταλαβεῖν τῶν ἁγίων αὐτοῦ μυστηρίων.—Const. Apost. lib. viii. can. 13, 14. — Conc. tom. i. col. 486. A.]

[g] [This reference is put after in MSS. Lamb. and B. M.]

[h] [Ἰγνάτιος Ἀντιοχείας τῆς Συρίας, τρίτος ἀπὸ τοῦ ἀποστόλου Πέτρου ἐπίσκοπος, ὃς καὶ τοῖς ἀποστόλοις αὐτοῖς συνδιέτριψεν, ὀπτασίαν εἶδεν ἀγγέλων, διὰ τῶν ἀντιφώνων ὕμνων τὴν ἁγίαν Τριάδα ὑμνούντων. κ. τ. λ. — Socrat. H. E. lib. vi. cap. 8. p. 322.]

[i] [Audiat orantis populi consistens quis extra ecclesiam vocem, spectet celebres hymnorum sonitus, et inter divinorum quoque sacramentorum officia responsionem devotæ confessionis accipiat.—S. Hil. in Ps. lxv. § 3. Op., tom. i. col. 196. C.]

[j] [The Homilies of S. Chrysost. ad Pop. Antioch. after the 22d, which used to pass under the name of S. Chrysostom, are made up from passages out of his other works. (See above, p. 40.) The passage here referred to occurs in Hom. lv. (al. lvi.) in S. Matt. § 5. Op., tom. ii. p. 353. ed. Sav.

The references stand thus, 'Hilar. Chrys. Socrat.' in MSS. B. M. and Lamb.

The words, 'A Hymn appointed by Clement, Const. lib. vii. cap. 47.' which are printed by Nicholls as part of Andrewes' note, are not so in MS. Durh., but a remark added by Bishop Cosin. It is not in MS. Lamb. or B. M.]

[k] ['have all made adoration' MS. Lamb.]

[l] ['and use their' MSS. B.M. and Lamb.]

[m] ['his money' MSS. B. M. and Lamb.]

[n] ['whiles' MS. Durh.]

[o] ['still' om. MS. B. M.]

[p] [That is, our present offertory sentences, see above, p. 153.]

[q] ['And when' MS. B.M.]

[r] ['at' MS. Lamb.]

[s] ['the blessing is given.' MSS. B. M. and Lamb.]

[t] [This note is omitted in MS. Lamb.]

A COPPIE OF THE FORME USED BY THE LO: BISHOP OF ELYE IN CONSECRATING THE NEWE CHURCH PLATE OF THE CATHEDRALL CHURCH OF WORC[R].

[THE form used by Bishop Andrewes in consecrating Plate for the Altar, now first printed, as used by him, is preserved amongst the MSS. collections of Henry Wharton, in the library of the Archbishop of Canterbury at Lambeth (MSS. No. 577. pp. 113—115.) The volume, of which it is a part, is described by Wharton as a collection of instruments and records of the greatest value, made in the handwriting or by the care of Archbishop Sancroft. On the fly-leaf is written, "Collectio plurium Instrumentorum et Monumentorum maximi pretii, facta vel manu vel cura R. R. P. Willelmi Sancroft, Archiep[1] Cant." By the side of this is written by another hand, "Mr. Wharton's own hand," and below it by another, "Collectore Henrico Wharton G. Arch. Cant. a sacris domestico." Many of the documents are transcribed by Archbishop Sancroft himself; others by (apparently) employed transcribers; sometimes a scrivener's hand completes what the Archbishop had begun to copy. Others are earlier MSS. on paper of varying sizes bound up together. There is another order of consecrating plate for the altar, and several forms of consecrating churches; e. g. of the church and church-yard of Foulmire in com. Buckingham, by William Barlow, Bishop of Lincoln, 1º. Novemb. Viz. Fest. Omn. SS[m]. 1610; of the Chapel of St. Peter's College, Cambridge, by Francis White, Bishop of Ely, 1632; of St. John's Church, Leeds, by Archbishop Neile of York, 1634; and immediately afterwards of his chapel at Aberguilly, by Archbishop Laud. In the same handwriting as the form of consecrating plate now printed, and, occupying one fasciculus with it, is the service for the consecration of the Church of Dore in Herefordshire, by Theophilus (Field) Bishop of St. David's, acting for Bishop Wren, March 22, 1634. The handwriting appears to be of that date.

This form of consecrating Communion plate seems to have been regarded as a model, and is frequently alluded to: e. g. such consecration was charged against Archbishop Laud at his trial; his answer was, "All that I used was according to the copy of the late Reverend Bishop of Winchester, Bishop Andrews, which I have by me to be seen, and which himself used all his time." (Laud's Troubles, chap. xxii. p. 313. See also Cant. Doom, pp. 469, 470, 499, 503.) The same is stated by Heylin. (Cyprianus Anglicus, p. 94.) And Neal's description of what was done, accords with our form. (Neal's History of the Puritans, vol. ii. p. 567. Lond. 1837.) At Canterbury, the same writer says, the cathedral was furnished "according to Bishop Andrewes' model," and "all the vessels underwent a solemn consecration." (Ibid.) Again, in the life of Kettlewell, prefixed to the edition of his works, p. 56. (Kettlewell's Works, vol. i.), is an account of the consecration of a new set of communion plate for the Church at Coleshill, by Archbishop Sancroft, in the first year of the reign of James II.; the words of the prayers are given, and evidence that it was Andrewes' form which was used. "For the perpetual testification whereof there was an instrument drawn up in the Latin tongue, and signed by the consecrator, with the archiepiscopal seal thereto affixed. The copy of which instrument or act (dates and names omitted) was, in the beginning of this century, made public by Mr. Richard Tisdale, Chaplain to the late Bishop of Norwich (Lloyd); as was also the entire form of the consecration which was then used." The publication referred to is entitled, "Form of Dedication and Consecration of a Church or Chapel;" published in 1703.

The service is substantially the same as this of Bishop Andrewes, which was indeed, as it now appears, in Archbishop Sancroft's possession. Thus it is sanctioned by the use of these two Archbishops.

The circumstances which occasioned the Bishop of Ely to consecrate the communion plate in Worcester Cathedral are not known.

Another copy of this office is found in MSS. Harl. Numb. 3795. Art. 8, the various readings of which are here noted.]

The order of consecrating Plate for the Altar.

The plate to be consecrated is placed upon a Table about the middle of the quire before the beginning of Divine Service.

Immediately after the Nicene Creed, and the pronouncing of this sentence, Let your light so shine before men, &c., *the Presenter of the plate being in his choral habit (if he be a Churchman) cometh forth, and standing by the said Table, after obeisance first to God, and to the Bishop, saith,*

Presenter. Reverend Father in God, in the name of the Dean and Chapter of the Cathedral Church of Worcester: I humbly beseech your Lordship that some vessels prepared for the use of that Church here ready may be presented unto the Lord, and by your sacred office may receive an holy dedication unto godly[a] divine service.

The Bishop. We are ready to do what you desire in a matter so well becoming them in whose name you come, and (as we assure ourselves) so acceptable unto God for the service of his holy Church. First, therefore, let us begin with prayer.

O Eternal God, Lord of all power and glory, prostrate here before thy throne of grace, we beg thy heavenly mercy,

[a] ['God's.' MS. Harl.]

and humbly call upon thee for thy divine acceptance. Lord, bow down thine ear and hear us. Open, Lord[b], thine eyes, and behold thy poor servants, and have respect unto the[c] supplications which, in full assurance of thy blessed Son's merits, we presume to make before thee. Take away the stony heart out of the midst of us, and give us hearts truly sensible of thy Divine Majesty. Let thy Holy Spirit help our infirmities. Lord, increase our faith, order our devotions, make us zealous for thy glory, and give us to revive[d] in the service of thy most blessed name, through Jesus Christ our Lord. *Amen.*

The said Presenter taketh in[e] *his hands,*
 First, the paten[f], *and (after obeisance) cometh up to the Bishop standing before the midst of the Altar, and kneeling down saith,*

I offer this unto thee and thy holy service, O Lord God Almighty.

The Bishop receiveth them and turneth to set them on the Altar, his Chaplains standing on each side of the Altar in their formalities, and in the mean time[g] *saying* alternatim,

a. He rained down manna on them for to eat, and gave them bread from heaven. *Psal.* lxxviii. 25, 26.

b. So man did eat Angels' food, and he sent them meat enough.

In the mean while the Presenter is ready again with the chalices covered, and kneeling down[h], *saith,* (ut prius).
Whiles the Bishop sets them on, the Chaplains pronounce,

a. That he may bring food out of the earth, and wine that maketh glad the heart of man. *Psal.* civ. 15.

b. We will be glad and rejoice in thee: we will remember thy love more than wine. *Cant.* i. 4.

The Presenter as before offereth the flagons, which while the Bp.[i] *sets on, the Chaplains say,*

a. They shall be satisfied with the plenteousness of thy

[b] ['O Lord,' MS. Harl.]
[c] ['their' MS. Harl.]
[d] ['rejoice' MS. Harl.]
[e] ['into' MS. Harl.]
[f] ['patens,' MS. Harl.]
[g] ['while' MS. Harl.]
[h] [om. MS. Harl.]
[i] [The word 'Bp.' is not in either MS.]

house, and thou shalt give them drink of thy pleasures as out of the river. *Psal.* xxxvi. 8.

b. Eat, O friends, drink and be replenished, O beloved. *Cant.* v. 1.

The basin is offered next by the Presenter, which, when the Bishop hath taken, the Chaplains say,

a. An offering of a free heart will I give thee, and praise thy name, O Lord, because it is so comfortable. *Psal.* lviii. 6.

b. Let the freewill offering [k] of my mouth please thee, O Lord, and teach me thy judgments. *Psal.* cxix. 108.

The Presenter bringeth the candlesticks, and the Bishop setteth them on; the Chaplains say [l],

a. Thy word is a lantern unto my feet, and a light unto my path [m]. *Psal.* cxix. 5.

b. For in thee is the fountain of light [n], and in thy light shall we see light. *Psal.* xxxvi. 9.

Lastly he bringeth the censer [1], *which the Bishop likewise sets on, and the Chaplains say,*

[1] The censer was my Lo: own [o].

a. While the king sitteth [p] at his table, my spikenard sendeth out the smell thereof. *Cant.* i. 12.

b. Let my prayer be set forth before Thee as the incense, and let the lifting up of my hands be as the [q] evening sacrifice. *Psal.* cxli. 2.

Then the Bishop layeth his hands upon every piece again, and, standing, saith,

O Lord, heavenly Father, we most meekly beseech Thee favourably to accept these holy offerings now presented unto Thee: Thine, O Lord, be all the [r] glory in all our approaching [s] unto thee, the honour thine alone in all our service [t] of Thee. Grant, most gracious Lord, that what we have now faithfully offered unto Thee in the uprightness of our hearts, may be religiously preserved from all profane and secular uses, and may ever continue in that holy service whereunto they are now dedicated, through Jesus Christ our Lord. *Amen.*

[k] ['offerings' MS. Harl.]
[l] ['saying,' MS. Harl.]
[m] ['paths.' MS. Harl.]
[n] ['life,' MS. Harl.]
[o] [This is a marginal note in the Lambeth MS.]
[p] ['sits' MS. Harl.]
[q] ['an' MS. Harl.]
[r] ['be the' MS. Harl.]
[s] ['approachings' MS. Harl.]
[t] ['services' MS. Harl.]

The Benediction.

We bless Thee, O Lord, for thy blessings upon us, and for that it hath pleased Thee to put into the hearts of thy humble servants to make these holy dedications unto thy Divine Majesty. Look down, Lord, in mercy upon them, and bless them with the riches of thy goodness. Bless them in their persons and in their substance, and in all that belongs unto them, or that they give[u] their hands unto. And grant, we beseech Thee, that by the reverend and holy use of these offerings, Thy praise and glory may now and ever be set forth in thy Church, and that thy daily service may therein be performed in the beauty of holiness, as becometh[x] so holy and glorious a God; through Jesus Christ our Lord. *Amen.*

This done they proceed to read the other sentences[y] for the ordinary offerings, and so go on with the rest of the Communion[z].

[u] ['put' MS. Harl.]
[x] ['becomes' MS. Harl.]
[y] ['services' MS. Harl.]
[z] ['of Communion.' MS. Harl.]

THE MANNER OF INDUCTION

PRESCRIBED BY THE

RIGHT REV. LANCELOT ANDREWES, BISHOP OF CHICHESTER, ELY, AND WINCHESTER.

[This Form of Induction is found in the same volume as the Consecration of Church Plate. It immediately follows the Manner of Consecrating the Church and Churchyard at Foulmire, by Bishop W. Barlow. They are both transcribed by Archbishop Sancroft; and before the Manner of Induction he has written the memorandum, "This I found also in the same book." What that book is, has not been discovered.]

THE neighbour minister, that inducts you, let him read in the Church Porch (the Church being empty and the door locked) the Mandate *ad Inductionem, verbatim.*

That done, let him give you hold of the ring or key, and say,

By virtue hereof, I, C. D. give you, I. N. real, actual, and corporal possession of this Parish, together with all and singular the tithes, rights, and commodities of and belonging to the same.

Then unlock the door, and go into the Church alone, and lock or bolt the door, and execute these particulars, which you shall write on the backside of your mandate, viz.—

Accepi clavem, intravi solus, oravi, tetigi sacra, pulsavi campanas, In nomine Patris, Filii, et S. S^{ti}. Amen.

        Per me,   I. N.

Then let it be endorsed also, that such a day of such a year, C. D. did induct I. N. into the Church of A. in the county of B. and unto him hath given real, actual, and corporal possession of that Parsonage, and of all the rights and appurtenances of the same.

In witness whereof I have hereunto subscribed my name.

        By me,   C. D.

In the presence of us

A

MANUAL OF DIRECTIONS

FOR THE

SICK.

NOTICE.

[THIS Edition of the Manual for the Sick is reprinted from that published by Richard Drake in 1648; being, as he explains in his Preface, the first complete Edition.

The Prayers for the Morning, Evening, and Holy Communion, which were originally subjoined to it, with a fresh title, but continuous paging, were inserted in their proper places in the Edition of the Private Devotions, published a few months afterwards by the same Editor, and ceased from that time to form a part of this Manual.

The Manual for the Sick has, in the subsequent reprints, been subjoined to the Private Devotions, though retaining incorrectly its original title-page.

Richard Drake, the Editor of this Work, and the original translator of the Private Devotions, was admitted a Scholar of Pembroke College, Cambridge, on Dr. Watts's foundation, March 15th, 1626 (see Wilson's Merchant Tailors' School, p. 558); was afterwards Rector of Radwinter (Walker's Sufferings, par. ii. p. 230); created D.D. by Royal Mandate, Aug. 2d, 1660, (Wood's Ath. Ox. iii. 282); appointed Prebendary of North Alton, in the Church of Salisbury, Sept. 9th, 1660, (Walker, *ibid.*) He appears to have resigned this last preferment, March 23d, 1662, on being nominated Chancellor of the same Church. The latter dignity he retained till his death, when he was succeeded (Le Neve, Fasti Eccl. Angl. p. 269) by Seth Ward, Nov. 5th, 1681. It may be added, that he was one of Walton's assistants in editing the well-known London Polyglott.]

A MANUAL OF DIRECTIONS FOR THE SICK.

With many Sweet *Meditations* and *Devotions* of the
R. Reverend Father
in God,
LANCELOT ANDREWS,
late L. Bishop of
Winchefter.

To which are added *Praiers*
for the *Morning, Evening,* and
H. Communion.

Translated out of a *Greeke
MS.* of *His Private
Devotions.*

By *R. D.* B.D.

TO THE CHRISTIAN READER.

THE great errand of our coming into this world, is but to prepare ourselves for a better. Which being the chief scope and aim of this Manual, I cannot but commend his pious intention, who formerly presented it to public view. But, observing a great want of that impression; besides many literal imperfections, omissions and misquotations of Holy Scriptures therein, and generally so great a want of that care and exactness which was due to any piece of him, to whom it claimed relation, and which made the child so unlike the father, I counselled this Second Edition of it, assuring myself that it would be an acceptable service to the Church of God, and not a little engage the world in a reverend estimation of this holy Prelate, who not only taught them the way to Heaven by his incomparable Sermons, but also assisted them in it by his Example and Devotions.

It hath been too great a fault in all ages, to wrap up their drugs in gold, and to vent false wares under glorious titles, imposing on the world, and on famous authors, many broken and imperfect relics.

That this Reverend Father hath suffered somewhat by this false play, is too notorious in the world. And in the former impression of this Manual there were some crude additions, which, though not justifiable by any authentic evidence or remain of his, were yet imposed on him and us, and dared to call him master.

These being hence remanded to their proper place of silence and obscurity, I give you this as his genuine issue. Which I am the rather induced to believe so, not only by the internal arguments, the spirit and genius, the method and piety thereof, but also, by the external testimony and conveyance of it to us, as his, under the fair hand of his amanuensis; from which, collated with another manuscript, and that in print, I give you this corrected.

That it was conceived and used by him in his ordinary Visitation of the Sick, when he was Vicar of St. Giles Cripplegate, though I take it for no good topic to gain your entertainment of it by, yet this persuasion it may happily beget, that all the business of a parish priest is not confined to the pulpit; but that there is other business, if the people could think on it, wherein to employ men of that profession: which, if so well attended as it ought, we should not hear of so many scandalous complaints against a lazy Clergy, nor be so much infested by sacrilegious intruders into our sacred office.

Your pardon, if I tell you what I mean, not in mine own, but his expressions, who knew better what belonged to the court of conscience:—

"I take it to be an error, to think the fruits of repentance, and the worth of them, to be a matter any common man can skill of well enough; needs never ask S. John, or S. Paul what he shall do; knows what he should do as well as S. Paul, or S. John either. And that it is not rather a matter, wherein we need the counsel and direction of such as are professed that way. Truly it is neither the least, nor the last, part of our learning to be able to give an answer and direction in this point. But therefore laid aside and neglected by us, because not sought after by you. Therefore not studied, but by very few, *quia nemo nos interrogat*, because it is grown out of request quite.

"We have learned, I know not where, a new, a shorter course, which flesh and blood better likes of. To pass the whole course of our life, and, in the whole course of our life, not to be able to set down, where, or when, or what we did, when we did that which we call repenting. What fruits there came of it; what those fruits might be worth. But even a little before our death, (and as little as may be,) not till the world hath given us over, then, lo, to come to our *quid faciemus?* to ask, What we shall do? When we are able to do nothing; and then must one come, and (as we call it) speak comfortably to us, that is, minister to us a little Divinity Laudanum, rather stupefactive for the present, than doing any sound good, and so take our leaves to go meet with *Ira ventura.*

"This way, this fashion of repenting, Saint John knew it not; it is far from his *fructus dignos;* St. Paul knew it not; it is far from his *opera digna.* And I can say little to it, but I pray God it deceive us not. It is not good trying conclusions about our souls [a]."

This I take for so fair an item to a tender and pious Christian, as I doubt not of diverting him thereby from deferring the making of his accounts even with Heaven, till the cross, or bed of sickness call upon him. Sure, that is no time or place, to contest with two such enemies, as are infirmities and sins: and an age is too short a time to provide ourselves in for eternity.

With this protest and caveat against this unchristian course and fashion of the world, I commend this to you as your *vade mecum;* and as your faithful friend and counsellor. Which, though it speak in special to the sick, will be found upon serious thoughts, to be serviceable to all estates and conditions whatsoever, whether in sickness or health, prosperity or adversity; making in us such deep impresses of the Divine excellency, and our human frailty, as must needs force us from the cobweb comforts of this, to the desire of enjoying those more solid and immutable in a better world, in the expressions and with the longings of the Royal Prophet, "My soul is athirst for God, yea even for the living God. When shall I come to appear before the presence of God!" *Psal.* xlii. 2.

I need not mind you of the reading of the Psalms after the old translation of the Liturgy. For, besides that there was no other then in being, the constant use of those expressions, to which the Church was so habituated in her daily Offices, had made them so familiar and known to all, that any other reddition of them might have been taken for the greatest injury and invasion that could possibly have been made upon devotion.

---

[a] See Bishop Andrewes's Eighth Sermon of Repentance and Fasting. [Works, vol. i. pp. 450, 451.]

One presumption I shall promise myself your pardon of, my affixed titles and inscriptions, they being wholly designed out of charity, for the better use and service of the many; who, not being able to digest and apply what is given in gross, may, under these special and distinct heads, find matter proper for their meditations and devotions, according to their several exigencies.

The forms of Morning and Evening Prayer, being very lame and broken in the former Edition, I give you here complete and perfect. To which I have added, as the crown and complement of all our services, his Devotions for the Holy Communion; all translated out of the Greek copy of his Amanuensis. You will need no other reason of the addition of this last, when I shall tell you, that (besides that I find it in Latin annexed with the Manual for the Sick) the participation of that sacred mystery is the most proper companion for persons in that condition, as being the Viaticum of the soul, and a Pledge of the Resurrection.

I shall add no more, but the promise of my prayers for a blessed improvement of this intended for your good; and a desire of your for him, who accounts himself happy in nothing more than the prayers of Christian people, as the highest obligation that can possibly be laid upon,

Your most humble Servant
in our Lord Jesus,
R. D.

April 21*st*, 1648.

THE CONTENTS OF THIS MANUAL.

	PAGE
INQUIRIES to be made concerning the Party	177
General Considerations of the Mortality of Man	178
Comfortable Scriptures to be used to the Sick Party	178
Several Duties recommended to the Sick	180
Propositions and Inferences to be made to the Sick	181
Concerning the Wisdom and Providence of God, in the ordering of all Afflictions in general, and this in special	181
Concerning the Fatherly Affection and Love of God	182
Concerning the Patience and Thankfulness required in the Sick	182
Concerning the Contrition and Repentance of the Sick	183
Concerning the Belief of the Sick	185
Concerning the Sick Party's forgiving Offenders against him	186
Concerning the Sick Party's Desire of Forgiveness from them whom he hath offended	186
Prayers and Expressions of the Soul's affiance in God	187
The Commendation of the Sick Party to the blessed Trinity	188
A Profession of the Christianity of the Sick Party demonstrated in many special Graces	189
Heads of Comfort to be administered from the consideration of $\begin{Bmatrix} \text{GOD,} \\ \text{CHRIST} \end{Bmatrix}$	190
A Collection of Prayers out of the Psalter, suitable to the exigences of the Sick	191
A Prayer to be used by the Priest, begging pardon of his own unworthiness, and acceptance of his Devotions for the Sick	200
A Litany for the Sick Person in danger of Death	200
An humble Recognition of Human Frailty, and a deprecation of falling from God	204
An affectionate Recommendation of the Sick Person to God's Mercy, grounded upon his special Relations to God, and the sincerity of his Soul	204
A Prayer for Mercy and Divine Assistance to uphold the Sick Person in his present Affliction	206

	PAGE
A Prayer for the Grace of God, and the Pardon of the Sins of the Sick Party	207
Commendatio Animæ; or, the Recommending of the Soul to God	209
Comfortable Scriptures to be applied to the Friends of the Deceased Party	210
A general Confession of Sins collected out of the Holy Prophets and Apostles	210
A Confession of Sins, according to the Branches of the Decalogue	213
The Triumph of Mercy in many Gradual Expressions and Remembrances, propounded to us in the Holy Scriptures	216
Spiritual Comforts and Confidence issuing from the contemplation of God's Goodness	220
Devout Ejaculations grounded on the consideration of our Human Frailty, and the Divine Providence and Mercy	221

A MANUAL
FOR THE SICK.

SET thine house in order, for thou shalt die. 2 *Kings* xx. 1. *P. Isa.* xxxviii. 1.

Is any sick among you? Let him call the Priests of the Church, and let them pray over him.

And the prayer of faith shall save the sick, and the Lord shall raise him up.

And if he have committed sins, they shall be forgiven him. *S. James* v. 14, 15.

Inquiries to be made concerning the Parties.

     1. Sex.
     2. Age.
     3. Condition of life.

Whether { 1. Learned, instructed?
    2. Sound in { Mind? / Memory? }
    3. The sense of hearing perfect?

Whether { 1. Patient, or unquiet?
    2. Cheerful, or deject?

If being well he found comfort

  In { Hearing, / Reading, / Repeating particulars.

Whether any material point, whereof to be admonished? To take occasion out of his own words.

General Considerations of the Mortality of Man.

What man is he that liveth, and shall not see death? *Psal.* lxxxix. 48.

It is appointed to men once to die. *Heb.* ix. 27.

I am a stranger with Thee, and a sojourner, as all my fathers were. *Psal.* xxxix. 14.

Here we have no continuing city. *Heb.* xiii. 14.

The night cometh, when no man can work. *S. John* ix. 4.

If the tree fall toward the south, or toward the north, in the place where the tree falleth there it shall be. *Eccl.* xi. 3.

Comfortable Scriptures to be used to the Sick party.

The mountains may remove, and the hills may fall down, but my mercy shall not depart from thee, nor the covenant of my peace come to nothing, saith the Lord, that hath compassion on thee. *P. Isa.* liv. 10.

Heaven and earth shall pass, but my word shall not pass. *S. Matt.* xxiv. 35.

All the promises of God are in Him Yea and Amen. *2 Cor.* i. 20.

In Whom we have most great and precious promises, that we should be partakers of the divine nature. 2 *S. Pet.* i. 4.

I have heard Ephraim lamenting thus; Thou hast corrected me, and I was chastised, as an untamed heifer.

Convert Thou me, and I shall be converted. For Thou art the Lord my God.

Surely, after that I had converted, I repented: I smote upon my thigh: I was ashamed, yea even confounded, because I did bear the reproach of my youth.

Since I spake to him, I still remembered him: therefore my bowels are troubled for him: I will surely have compassion on him, saith the Lord. *P. Jerem.* xxxi. 18—20.

I will visit their offences with the rod, and their sin with scourges:

Nevertheless my mercy will I not utterly take from him; nor suffer my truth to fail. *Psal.* lxxxix. 32. [33.]

My son, refuse not the chastening of the Lord, neither be grieved with His correction.

For the Lord correcteth Him whom He loveth, even as the father doth the child, in whom, *for all that,* he delighteth. *Prov.* iii. 11, 12.

Behold, blessed is the man whom God correcteth; therefore refuse not thou the chastening of the Almighty.

For He maketh the wound, and bindeth it up; He smiteth, and His hands make whole again.

He shall deliver thee in six troubles, and in the seventh the evil shall not touch thee. *Job* v. 17—19.

Forget not the consolation that speaketh unto you as unto children;

My son, despise not the chastening of the Lord; neither faint when thou art corrected of Him.

For whom the Lord loveth He chasteneth; and scourgeth every son whom He receiveth.

If you endure chastening, God offereth Himself unto you, as to a son: for what son is he whom the father chasteneth not?

If therefore ye be without correction, whereof all are partakers, then are ye bastards, and not sons.

Moreover, we have had the fathers of our bodies, who corrected us, and yet we gave them reverence; should we not much rather be in subjection to the Father of Spirits, that we might live?

For they, verily, for a few days chastened us after their own pleasure; but He chasteneth us for our profit, that we might be partakers of His holiness.

Now no chastening for the present seemeth joyous, but grievous; yet afterwards it bringeth the quiet fruit of righteousness to them who are thereby exercised.

Wherefore lift up the hands that hang down, and the weak knees. *Heb.* xii. 5—12.

And ye now are in sorrow, but I will see you again, and your hearts shall rejoice, and your joy shall none be able to take from you. *S. John* xvi. 22.

For a little while have I forsaken thee, but with great compassion will I gather thee.

For a moment, in mine anger, I hid my face from thee, but with everlasting mercy will I have compassion on thee, saith the Lord thy Redeemer. *P. Isa.* liv. 7, 8.

Modicum et videbitis Me. S. Jo. xvi. 16.

Blessed is the man whom Thou chastisest, O Lord, and teachest him in Thy law;

That Thou mayest give him rest in the days of evil. *Psal.* xciv. 12, 13.

But when we are judged we are chastened of Thee, that we should not be condemned with the world. 1 *Cor.* xi. 32.

They that sow in tears shall reap in joy. *Psal.* cxxvi. 6.

The Lord hath chastened and corrected me, but He hath not given me over unto death. *Psal.* cxviii. 18.

My brethren, count it exceeding joy when ye fall into divers *afflictions:*

Knowing that the trial of your faith bringeth forth patience.

And let patience have her perfect work, that ye may be complete, entire, lacking nothing. *S. Jam.* i. 2—4.

Blessed are they that mourn, for they shall be comforted. *S. Matt.* v. 4.

When I am weak, then am I strong. 2 *Cor.* xii. 10.

Thou, Lord, upholdest all such as are falling, and liftest up those that be down. *Psal.* cxlv. 14.

Thou healest the broken in heart, and givest medicine to heal their sickness. *Psal.* cxlvii. 3.

My flesh and my heart faileth; but be Thou the strength of my heart, and my portion for ever. *Psal.* lxxiii. 25.

As mine outward man doth wear and decay, so let mine inward man renew daily.

O let this light affliction, which will quickly be over, cause unto me a far more excellent and eternal weight of glory. *2 Cor.* iv. 16, 17.

Several Duties recommended to the Sick.
Prayer.

Pray unto the Lord, if haply this may be forgiven thee. *Acts* viii. 22.

For this cause shall every one that is godly make his *prayer* unto Thee. *Psal.* xxxii. 6.

Alms.

Blessed is the man that considereth the poor and needy. *Psal.* xli. 1.

By mercy and truth are sins cleansed and forgiven. *Prov.* xvi. 6.

Break off thine unrighteousness by mercy to the poor. *P. Dan.* iv. 27.

They showed the garments which she had wrought with her own hands. *Acts* ix. 39.

Πέντε τάδε.

I. Except ye *repent,* ye shall all likewise perish. *S. Luke* xiii. 5.

II. Without *faith* it is impossible to please God. *Heb.* xi. 6.

III. If I have all *faith,* and no *love,* it profiteth me nothing. 1 *Cor.* xiii. 2.

IV. We are saved by *hope*. *Rom.* viii. 24.

V. Hope thou in the Lord, and be *doing good*. *Psal.* xxxvii. 3.

And they shall come forth, that have *done good,* to the resurrection of life. *S. John* v. 29.

Make you friends of the unrighteous mammon, that, when you must hence, they may receive you into everlasting tabernacles. *S. Luke* xvi. 9.

Zaccheus stood forth, and said unto the Lord, Behold, Lord, the half of my goods I give to the poor, and if I have taken any thing from any man by false accusation, I restore him fourfold. *S. Luke* xix. 8.

Propositions and Inferences to be made to the Sick.

Concerning the Wisdom and Providence of God in the Ordering of all Afflictions in general, and this *in special.*

1. You are persuaded that no sickness or cross cometh by chance to any.

2. But you believe, that it is God who sendeth them, without whose Providence they fall not on us.

3. You acknowledge God to be most wise, and to suffer nothing to befal us, but when it is expedient it so should.

4. Therefore, God having sent this His visitation to you at this time, that it is expedient for you thus to be sick.

Say,

I know, O Lord, that Thy judgments are just, and that Thou of very faithfulness hast caused me to be troubled. Psal. cxix. 75.

Concerning the Fatherly Affection and Love of God.

1. You know, and confess, that God to all, but to Christian men especially, carrieth the affection of a *Father* toward his children.

2. You know also, that a father, whether he make much of his child, or whether he chasten him, continueth a father in both; and loveth him in the one no less than in the other.

3. Think the same of God, as touching yourself: that, while He gave you good days, He loved you; and that now He sendeth you some evil, He loveth you also; and would not have sent this evil, but to be a cause unto you of a greater good; that, being called home thereby, you might be at peace with Him.

Say,

Before I was troubled, I went wrong; but now shall I learn thy word. Psal. cxix. 67.

Concerning the Patience and Thankfulness required in the Sick.

1. You are not only to take it patiently, (*I held my peace, and opened not my mouth, because it was Thy doing.* Psal. xxxix. 9. *It is the Lord, let Him do what seemeth good in His eyes.* 1 Sam. iii. 18.)

2. But even to give Him thanks for it, as for a wholesome medicine;

The Lord hath given, and the Lord hath taken away: as it pleaseth the Lord so is it come to pass: blessed be the name of the Lord. Job i. 21.

I will take this cup of salvation, and give thanks to the name of the Lord. Psal. cxvi. 12.

3. Especially for that we, in the time of our health forgetting Him, yet He is so merciful that He giveth us not over with the world: but for all we have oft grieved *his Holy Spirit,* and fallen from grace, He visiteth us again, and offereth it afresh unto us.

4. That, if His will had not been to show mercy by this chastisement, He could and would have suddenly taken you away with a quick destruction; and not have given you this time to bethink yourself, and to seek and sue to Him for grace.

Say,

When I am judged, I am chastened of the Lord, that I might not be condemned with the world. 1 Cor. xi. 32.

God's very punishment is a part of His mercy. Psal. lxxxix. 32.

It is a great mercy of the Lord that we are not suddenly consumed. Lament. iii. 22.

For giving you a time and space. Rev. ii. 21.

O tarry thou the Lord's leisure, be strong, and He shall comfort thine heart, and put thou thy trust in the Lord. Psal. xxvii. 16.

O cast thy burthen upon the Lord, and He shall refresh thee, and shall not suffer the righteous to fail for ever. Psal. lv. 23.

O put your trust in Him alway, ye people: pour out your hearts before Him; for God is our hope. Psal. lxii. 8.

He will not alway be chiding, neither keepeth He His anger for ever. Psal. ciii. 9.

In His wrath He will remember mercy. P. Hab. iii. 2.

Heaviness may endure for a night, but joy will come in the morning. Psal. xxx. 5.

For a little while have I forsaken thee, but with great compassion will I gather thee.

For a moment in Mine anger I hid My face from thee, but with everlasting mercy have I had pity on thee, saith the Lord thy Redeemer. P. Isa. liv. 7, 8.

Concerning the Contrition and Repentance of the Sick.

Do you acknowledge yourself not to have lived so well as you ought? But to have sinned, done amiss, and dealt wickedly?

Do you call to mind the years of your life spent amiss in the bitterness of your soul?

Do you desire to have your mind illuminated by God, touching those sins you never knew; or which you once knew, but have now forgotten; that you may repent of them?

1. Do you desire to feel greater sorrow in your soul for your sins committed than you do? 2. Would you be glad if you did feel it? 3. And, are you grieved that you feel it not? that you are no more grieved?

Be there, or is there any special sin, that doth lie heavy on your conscience, for the which you need, or would require the benefit of private *Absolution?*

Say,

Thou with rebukes dost chasten man for sin, and makest his beauty consume as a moth fretting a garment. Psal. xxxix. 12.

There is no health in my flesh, by reason of Thy wrath: neither is there any rest in my bones, by reason of my sin. Psal. xxxviii. 3.

Lord, be merciful unto me: heal my soul, for I have sinned against Thee. Psal. xli. 4.

Lord, I confess my wickedness; and am sorry for my sin. Psal. xxxviii. 18.

I call to mind the misspent years of my life in the bitterness of my soul. P. Isa. xxxviii. 15.

My misdeeds have prevailed against me: O be Thou merciful unto my sin. Psal. lxv. 3.

For Thy Name's sake, O Lord, be merciful unto my sin, for it is great. Psal. xxv. 10.

O remember not the offences and frailties of my youth; but, according to Thy mercy, think Thou upon me, O Lord, for Thy goodness. Psal. xxv. 6.

Namely, O Lord, and specially in ——— be merciful unto me.

Herein the Lord be merciful unto His servant. 2 Kings v. 18.

O Lord, lay not ——— to my charge. Acts vii. 60.

If Thou, Lord, be extreme to mark what is done amiss, O Lord, who may abide it? Psal. cxxx. 3.

O enter not into judgment with Thy servant: for no flesh is righteous in Thy sight. Psal. cxliii. 2.

My confusion is daily before me, and the shame of my face hath covered me. Psal. xliv. 16.

My heart is disquieted within me, and the fear of death is fallen upon me.

Fearfulness and trembling are come upon me, and a horrible dread hath overwhelmed me. Psal. lv. 4, 5.

The Lord is nigh unto them that are of a contrite heart; and will save such as are of an humble spirit. Psal. xxxiv. 18.

A broken and contrite heart, O Lord, wilt Thou not despise. Psal. li. 17.

Repent you of these your sins?
That is,

1. Have you a purpose to judge yourself for them if you live? 1 *Cor.* xi. 31.

2. And to inflict upon yourself punishment for committing them, according as you shall be directed? 2 *Cor.* vii. 11; *Lev.* v. 18.

3. Are you resolved, if God send you life hereafter, to amend and live more carefully? and to avoid both those means and occasions that may provoke you to sin again? and those signs and marks which testify you delight in it?

4. Do you holily promise thus much in the presence of God, His grace aiding you?

5. Do you desire, if God send you health again, to be specially put in mind thereof?

Turn us, then, O God our Saviour, and let Thine anger cease from us. Psal. lxxxv. 4.

Concerning the Belief of the Sick.

Believe you the Christian Creed, or Confession of our most Holy Faith, once delivered to the Saints?

Believe you that you cannot be saved, except you did believe it?

Are you glad in your soul, and do you give God hearty thanks, that in *this faith* you were *born*, have *lived* in it, and now shall *die* in the same?

Do you yourself desire, and do you wish us to desire at the hands of God, that this Faith may not fail you, until the hour, and in the hour of death?

If your sense fail you, or if the pain of your disease, or weakness otherwise, so work with you, as it shall happen you with your tongue to speak aught otherwise than this your faith or religion would; Do you renounce all such words as none of yours? and is it your will we account of them as not spoken by you?

Is there in your mind any scruple, touching any matter of faith or religion?

Say,
Lord, I believe, help Thou mine unbelief. S. Mark ix. 24.

Concerning the Sick Party's forgiving Offenders against him.

Do you forgive them that any manner of way have offended you, as freely as you would be forgiven at God's hand?

Do you likewise desire of God, that He would forgive them?

That amends which they are bound to make you, in that they have offended you, are you content to remit them also?

Are you willing that so much be showed them from you, that you have forgiven them freely and fully, and desire God to do the like?

Say,

Father, forgive them: they knew not what they did. S. Luke xxiii. 34.

O Lord, lay not these sins to their charge. Acts vii. 60.

Concerning the Sick Party's Desire of Forgiveness from them whom he hath offended.

You yourself living in the world, it cannot be but some you have offended; Do you desire that all such as you have offended would pardon and forgive you?

Do you remember or call to mind any person or persons in special, whom you have so offended?

Will you that so much be signified to them in your name, that you desire them to forgive you?

Inasmuch as the offences against the Seventh Commandment, of getting any children by the act of adultery committed with the wife of another man; and against the Eighth Commandment, touching men's goods; and against the Ninth, touching men's credits or good names, are not by God forgiven, unless restitution be made to the parties wronged; Are you ready and willing to restore and make satisfaction to such as you have wronged, in thrusting in a child begotten by you, likely to deprive the true children of the party, and begotten by him, of a child's part and portion? And, to such as you have wronged in their goods? And, to satisfy those whom you have any way touched in their good name? And that without all fraud or delay?

Can you call to mind any persons in particular, whom you have so offended?

Prayers and Expressions of the Soul's Affiance in God.

And now, Lord, what is my hope? Truly my hope is in Thee. *Psal.* xxxix. 8.

Thou that art the hope of all the ends of the earth, and of them that remain in the broad sea. *Psal.* lxv. 5.

Though He kill me, yet will I trust in Him. *Job* xiii. 15.

Though I walk through the vale of the shadow of death, yet will I fear no evil. *Psal.* xxiii. 4.

Lord, thou knowest whereof we be made; Thou rememberest that we are but dust. *Psal.* ciii. 14.

Call to mind we are but flesh; but a wind that passeth away and cometh not again. *Psal.* lxxviii. 40.

Remember, Lord, of what time I am: what our substance is: Wherefore hast Thou made all men for nought? *Psal.* lxxxix. 46.

Lord, consider my complaint, for I am brought very low. *Psal.* cxlii. 7.

Let my present misery more prevail to move compassion, than my sinful life past to provoke Thine indignation.

Lord, how long wilt Thou be angry with Thy servant that prayeth? *Psal.* lxxx. 4.

Behold, I show the lowliness of a suppliant: show not Thou to me the rigour of a Judge.

Ne, quæso, premat sententia Judicis,
Quem sic submittit petitio supplicis.

O deliver not Thine *own inheritance* over into the *will* of Thine enemy. *Psal.* lxxiv. 20.

I am Thine; O save me. *Psal.* cxix. 94.

I am Thine; carest Thou not that I perish? *S. Mark* iv. 38.

Behold, O Lord, how that I am Thy servant, and the son of Thine handmaid. *Psal.* cxvi. 14.

Thy unprofitable evil servant, *S. Matt.* xviii. 32; yet Thy servant.

Thy lost unkind child, *S. Luke* xv. 24; yet Thy child.

Though I have not showed to Thee the duty and affection

of a son, yet do not Thou cast from Thee the natural kindness and compassion of a father.

The Commendation of the Sick Party to the Blessed Trinity.

Into thine hands I commend myself, as unto a faithful Creator. 1 *S. Pet.* iv. 19.

Receive, O Lord, Thine own image, not made by any strange god, but by Thyself, the only true and living God.

Despise not, O Lord, the work of Thine own hands. *Psal.* cxxxviii. 8.

Lord, I am *created* to Thine own image. *Gen.* i. 27.

Suffer not, O Lord, suffer not Thine own image to be utterly defaced:

But renew it again in righteousness and true holiness. *Eph.* iv. 24.

Into Thy hands I commend myself, for Thou hast *redeemed* me, O Lord, Thou God of Truth. *Psal.* xxxi. 6.

Behold, O Lord, I am the price of *Thy Blood*, of Thy most precious blood. 1 *Cor.* vi. 20.

Suffer not so great a price to perish. Suffer not that to be cast away, that Thou hast so dearly bought.

O Lord, Thou camest down from heaven, to *redeem* that which was lost. *S. Luke* xix. 10.

Suffer not that to be lost which Thou hast *redeemed.*

Behold, O Lord, Thou art in the midst of us: Thy Name is called upon by us. (*P. Jer.* xiv. 9.) We are called by Thy Name (*P. Dan.* ix. 19), *Christians.*

For Thy Name's sake, be merciful unto us. *Psal.* xxv. 10; lxxix. 9.

Spare Thine own Name in us,

And do not, good Lord, so remember our sins, that, by remembering them, Thou forget Thine own Name.

Lord, we call upon Thy Name.

There is no Name under heaven whereby we can be saved, but only *It*. *Acts* iv. 12.

Though we be unfaithful, yet Thou art true, and canst not deny *Thine own Name.* 2 *Tim.* ii. 13.

Into Thy hands I commend myself, as to my true and only *Sanctifier*.

Lord, I have been the temple of Thy *Holy Spirit*. 1 *Cor.* iii. 16.

Though it hath been polluted through my frailty, yet, O Lord, destroy it not; but dedicate it, hallow it anew, and sanctify it to Thee. Yet once again make an *encœnia* of it.

Spare us, good Lord.

Spare { Thine own { Handywork, Image, Name, The price of Thine own blood in us.

The good Lord be merciful to every one that prepareth his heart to seek the Lord God, the God of our fathers, although he be not according to the cleanness of the sanctuary. 2 *Chron.* xxx. 18, 19.

Behold, O Lord, a bruised reed;
    Break it not.
Behold smoking flax;
    And yet, O Lord, quench it not. *P. Isa.* xlii. 3; *S. Matth.* xii. 20.

Profession of the Christianity of the Sick Party demonstrated in many special Graces.

Lord, I have never denied Thy Name; but confessed It ever.

And, in the confession and invocation of It, I desire to spend my last breath, and to depart this life.

Lord, I have desired to fear Thy Name. *Nehem.* i. 11.

My soul hath been desirous to long after Thy Commandments. *Psal.* cxix. 20.

Lord, I do acknowledge my wickedness, and am sorry (*cogitabo, anxius ero*, take thought) for my sin. *Psal.* xxxviii. 18.

Lord, I believe; help Thou mine unbelief. *S. Mark* ix. 24.

Lord, I hope verily to see the goodness of the Lord in the land of the living. *Psal.* xxvii. 15.

Let not this hope confound me, nor make me ashamed. *Psal.* cxix. 116.

Lord, I freely forgive whomsoever I have ought against, those poor *pence* or *mites* they owe me. *S. Matt.* xviii. 28.

Lord, I held my peace; and opened not my mouth at *Thy chastisement;* because it was Thy doing, O Lord. *Psal.* xxxix. 10.

Lord, *I seek Thee;* and Thou never failest them that seek Thee. *Psal.* ix. 10.

I come unto Thee; and of them that come to Thee, Thou castest none out. *S. John* vi. 37.

Nevertheless, though I am sometime afraid, yet put I my trust in Thee. *Psal.* lvi. 3.

O Lord, in Thee have I trusted, let me never be put to confusion. *Psal.* xxxi. 1; and lxxi. 1.

Heads of Comfort to be administered from the Consideration

of { GOD.
     { CHRIST.

God is

A Creator (בורא), and so faithful. 1 *S. Pet.* iv. 19.

A Possessor or Owner. *Gen.* xiv. 19. (קונה)

    I am Thine. *Psal.* cxix. 94.

    Part of Thy possession.

A Redeemer *at large,* (פרק). *Psal.* cxxx. 7.

A Redeemer (גאל) *as of the same flesh and blood.* Job xix. 25.

        Christ is a Mediator;

Between God and us,

    His Priesthood and Sacrifice.

        A Lion;

Between us and Satan,

    His Kingdom and Conquest.

        A Lamb;

Between us and Sin,

    His Innocency.

Between us and our concupiscence,

    His Charity.

Between us and the punishment due to our sins,

    His Passion and blood-shedding satisfaction.

Between us and our conscience, and the Judgment of God,

    His Advocateship.

Between us and our want of righteousness,

    His absolute and complete Obedience.

Between us and our want of desert of the eternal reward,
  His Merit.
Between us and our want of fervour in praying,
  His Intercession.
Between us and our want of sorrow in repenting,
  His Agony and Bloody Sweat.

These { recount, show, offer, set between.

A Collection of Prayers out of the Psalter, suitable to the Exigencies of the Sick.

Psal. vii.

O Lord my God, in Thee have I put my trust: save me from them that *seek after my soul*, and deliver me. *Ver.* 1.

Lest he devour my soul like a lion, and tear it in pieces, while there is none to help. *Ver.* 2.

Psal. xviii.

The sorrows of death compassed me *round about;* the overflowings of ungodliness made me afraid. *Ver.* 3.

The snares of death overtook me; the pain of hell *gat hold upon* me. *Ver.* 4.

Psal. cxvi.

I have found trouble and heaviness, and I will call upon the name of the Lord.

O Lord, I beseech Thee, deliver my soul. *Ver.* 4.

Psal. xviii.

Hear my voice, O Lord, out of Thy holy temple: let my complaint come before Thee; let it enter even into Thy ears. *Ver.* 6.

Send down from on high, and deliver me: take me out of many waters. *Ver.* 16.

Psal. cxvi.

Gracious is the Lord, and righteous; yea, our God is merciful. *Ver.* 5.

The Lord preserveth the simple; I am in misery, *but He will think upon me.* *Ver.* 6.

Turn again then to thy rest, O my soul; for the Lord hath *regarded* thee. *Ver.* 7.

Psal. xxii.

My God, my God, look upon me; why hast Thou forsaken me? and art so far from my health, and from the words of my complaint? *Ver.* 1.

O my God, I cry in the day-time, and Thou hearest not; and in the night-season also *I have no audience.* *Ver.* 2.

Yet Thou continuest holy, O Thou Worship of Israel. *Ver.*3.

Our fathers hoped in Thee; they trusted in Thee, and Thou didst deliver them. *Ver.* 4.

They called upon Thee, and were holpen; they put their trust in Thee, and were not confounded. *Ver.* 5.

But Thou art He that took me out of my mother's womb; Thou wast my hope, when I hanged yet upon my mother's breasts. *Ver.* 9.

I have been left unto Thee ever since I was born: Thou art my God even from my mother's womb. *Ver.* 10.

O go not *far* from me, for trouble is hard at hand; and there is none to help me. *Ver.* 11.

Deliver my soul from the sword; my darling from the power of the dog. *Ver.* 20.

Save me from the lion's mouth: *deliver me* from among the horns of the unicorns. *Ver.* 21.

Psal. xxv.

For Thy Name's sake, O Lord, be merciful unto my sin, for it is great. *Ver.* 10.

O turn Thee unto me, and have mercy upon me; for I am desolate and in misery. *Ver.* 15.

The sorrows of my heart are enlarged: O bring Thou me out of my troubles. *Ver.* 16.

Look upon my adversity and misery, and forgive me all my sin. *Ver.* 17.

O keep my soul, and deliver me: let me not be confounded; for I have put my trust in Thee. *Ver.* 19.

Psal. xxviii.

Unto Thee *do* I cry, O Lord, my strength; think no scorn of me; lest, if Thou make as though Thou heardest not, I become like them that go down into the pit. *Ver.* 1.

Hear the voice of my humble petition, when I cry unto

Thee; when I hold up my hands toward the mercy-seat of Thy holy temple. *Ver.* 2.

Psal. xxvii.

O hide not Thou Thy face from me; nor cast Thy servant away in displeasure. *Ver.* 10.

Thou hast been my succour : leave me not, neither forsake me, O God of my salvation. *Ver.* 11.

Psal. xl.

Withdraw not Thou Thy mercy from me, O Lord; let Thy loving-kindness and Thy truth alway preserve me. *Ver.* 14.

For innumerable troubles are come about me; my sins have taken such hold upon me, that I am not able to look up; yea, they are more in number than the hairs of my head, and my heart hath failed me. *Ver.* 15.

O Lord, let it be Thy pleasure to deliver me; make haste, O Lord, to help me. *Ver.* 16.

As for me, *though* I be poor and in misery, yet the Lord careth for me. *Ver.* 20.

Thou art my Helper and Redeemer : make no long tarrying, O my God. *Ver.* 21.

Psal. xxxi.

O Lord, my hope hath *ever* been in Thee. I have said, Thou art my God. *Ver.* 16.

My time is in Thy hand, O deliver me, *and be merciful unto me*. *Ver.* 17.

Show Thy servant the light of Thy countenance; and save me for Thy mercies' sake. *Ver.* 18.

Psal. xxxviii.

Forsake [me] not, O Lord my God; be not Thou far from me. *Ver.* 21.

Haste Thee to help me, O Lord God of my salvation. *Ver.* 22.

Psal. liv.

Save me, O God, for Thy Name's sake; and *deliver* me in Thy strength. *Ver.* 1.

Hear my prayer, O God; and hearken unto the words of my mouth. *Ver.* 2.

Psal. lv.

Hear my prayer, O God, and hide not Thyself from my petition. *Ver.* 1.

Take heed unto me, and hear me, how I mourn in my prayer, and am vexed. *Ver.* 2.

Psal. lxi.

Hear my crying, O God; give ear unto my prayer. *Ver.* 1.

From the ends of the earth will I call unto Thee, when my heart is in heaviness. *Ver.* 2.

Psal. lix.

O Lord, *let me* make my prayer unto Thee, in an acceptable time. *Ver.* 13.

Hear me, O God, in the multitude of Thy mercies; even in the truth of Thy salvation. *Ver.* 14.

Take me out of the mire, that I sink not: O let me be delivered from them that *seek my soul*, and out of the deep waters. *Ver.* 15.

Let not the water-flood drown me, neither let the deep swallow me up: and let not the pit shut her mouth upon me. *Ver.* 16.

Hear me, O Lord, for Thy loving-kindness is comfortable; turn Thee unto me, according to the multitude of Thy mercies. *Ver.* 17.

Hide not Thy face from Thy servant, for I am in trouble: O haste Thee and hear me. *Ver.* 18.

Draw nigh unto my soul, and save it: O deliver me. *Ver.* 19.

As for me, when I am poor and in heaviness, Thy help, O God, shall lift me up. *Ver.* 30.

Psal. cix.

But deal Thou with me, O Lord God, according to Thy Name, for sweet is Thy mercy. *Ver.* 20.

O deliver me, for I am helpless and poor; and my heart is wounded within me. *Ver.* 21.

I go like the shadow that departeth; and am driven away as the grasshopper. *Ver.* 22.

My knees are weak through fasting; my flesh is dried up for want of fatness. *Ver.* 23.

Help me, O Lord my God: O save me according to Thy mercy. *Ver.* 25.

And *men* shall know how that this is Thy hand; and that Thou, Lord, hast done it. *Ver.* 26.

Psal. lxxiv.

O God, wherefore art Thou absent from us so long? Why is Thy wrath so hot against the sheep of Thy pasture? *Ver.* 1.

O think upon Thy congregation, which Thou hast purchased and redeemed of old. *Ver.* 2.

O deliver not the soul of Thy turtle-dove unto the multitude of Thine enemies; and forget not the *distressed of Thy servants* for ever. *Ver.* 20.

O let not the simple go away ashamed; but let the poor and needy give praise unto Thy Name. *Ver.* 22.

Psal. lxxx.

Turn us again, O Lord God of Hosts; show the light of Thy countenance, and we shall be whole. *Ver.* 3, 7, 19.

Psal. lxxxv.

O forgive the offences of Thy *servants,* and cover all their sins. *Ver.* 2.

Take away all Thy displeasure, and turn Thyself from Thy wrathful indignation. *Ver.* 3.

Turn us then, O God our Saviour, and let Thine anger cease from us. *Ver.* 4.

Wilt Thou be displeased at us for ever? and, wilt Thou stretch out Thy wrath from one generation to another? *Ver.* 5.

Wilt Thou not turn again, and quicken us: that Thy people may rejoice in Thee? *Ver.* 6.

Show us Thy mercy, O Lord: and grant us Thy salvation. *Ver.* 7.

Psal. lxx.

Haste Thee, O Lord, to deliver me; make haste to help me, O Lord. *Ver.* 1.

Psal. xliv.

Up, Lord, why sleepest Thou? awake, and be not absent from us for ever. *Ver.* 23.

Wherefore hidest Thou Thy face, and forgettest our misery and trouble? *Ver.* 24.

For our soul is brought low, even unto the dust: our belly cleaveth unto the ground. *Ver.* 25.

Arise, and help us; and deliver us for Thy mercies' sake. *Ver.* 26.

Psal. lxxxvi.

Bow down Thine ear, O Lord, and hear me: for I am poor and in misery. *Ver.* 1.

Preserve Thou my soul, for Thou *gavest it me:* my God, save Thy servant who putteth his trust in Thee. *Ver.* 2.

Be merciful unto me, O Lord: for I will call daily upon Thee. *Ver.* 3.

Comfort the soul of Thy servant: for unto Thee, O Lord, do I lift up my soul. *Ver.* 4.

For Thou, Lord, art good and gracious, and of great mercy to all them that call upon Thee. *Ver.* 5.

Give ear, Lord, unto my prayer: and ponder the voice of my humble desires. *Ver.* 6.

In the time of my trouble I will call upon Thee, for Thou hearest me. *Ver.* 7.

For, Thou, O Lord God, art full of compassion and mercy: long-suffering, plenteous in goodness and truth. *Ver.* 15.

O turn Thee then unto me, and have mercy upon me: give Thy strength unto Thy servant, and help the son of Thine handmaid. *Ver.* 16.

Show some good token upon me for good, that they *who love Thee* may see it, and be *glad,* because Thou, Lord, hast holpen me and comforted me. *Ver.* 17.

Psal. cxlii.

I cried unto the Lord with my voice: yea, even to the Lord did I make my supplication. *Ver.* 1.

I poured out my complaint before Him, and showed Him of my trouble. *Ver.* 2.

When my spirit was in heaviness, Thou knewest my path. *Ver.* 3.

I looked also upon my right hand, and *lo,* there was none that *could help me. Ver.* 4.

I had no place to fly unto; and none *was able to relieve* my soul. *Ver.* 5.

I cried unto Thee, O Lord, and said, Thou art my hope and my portion in the land of the living. *Ver.* 6.

O consider my complaint, for I am brought very low. *Ver.* 7.

Bring my soul out of prison, that I may give thanks unto

Thee: which thing if Thou wilt grant me, then shall the righteous resort unto my company. *Ver*. 9.

Psal. cxli.

My eyes look unto Thee, O Lord God; in Thee is my trust; O cast not out my soul. *Ver*. 9.

Psal. lxxxviii.

O Lord God of my salvation, I have cried day and night before Thee; O let my prayer enter into Thy presence; incline Thine ear unto my calling. *Ver*. 1.

For my soul is full of trouble, and my life draweth nigh unto hell. *Ver*. 2.

Lord, I have called daily upon Thee, I have stretched out mine hands unto Thee. *Ver*. 9.

Dost Thou show wonders among the dead? or, shall the dead rise up again, and praise Thee? *Ver*. 10.

Shall Thy loving-kindness be shown in the grave? or Thy faithfulness in destruction? *Ver*. 11.

Shall Thy wonderful works be known in the dark? or Thy righteousness in the land where all things are forgotten? *Ver*. 12.

Unto Thee *do* I cry, O Lord; and early shall my prayer come before Thee. *Ver*. 13.

Lord, why abhorrest Thou my soul? Why hidest Thou Thy face from me? *Ver*. 14.

I am in misery, and like unto him that is at the point to die: even from my youth up Thy terrors have I suffered with a troubled mind. *Ver*. 15.

Thy wrathful displeasure goeth over me; and the fear of Thee hath undone me. *Ver*. 16.

Psal. cxli.

Lord, I *will* call upon Thee, haste Thee unto me; and consider my voice when I cry unto Thee. *Ver*. 1.

Let my prayer be set forth in Thy sight as the incense: let the lifting up of my hands be as an evening sacrifice. *Ver*. 2.

Psal. lxxix.

Lord, how long wilt Thou be angry? and, shall Thy jealousy burn like fire for ever? *Ver*. 5.

O remember not *mine* old sins, but have mercy upon *me*, for *I am* come to great misery. *Ver*. 8.

Help *me*, O God of *my* salvation, for the glory of Thy Name: O deliver *me*, and be merciful to *my* sins, for Thy Name's sake. *Ver.* 9.

Psal. cxliii.

Lord, I stretch forth mine hands unto Thee; my soul gaspeth unto Thee, like a thirsty land. *Ver.* 6.

Hear me, O Lord, and that soon, for my spirit waxeth faint: hide not Thy face from me, lest I be like unto them that go down into the *silence*. *Ver.* 7.

Psal. xiii.

How long wilt Thou forget me, O Lord, for ever? How long wilt Thou hide Thy face from me? *Ver.* 1.

How long shall I seek counsel in my soul, and be so vexed in my heart? How long shall mine enemies triumph over me? *Ver.* 2.

Consider and hear me, O Lord my God; lighten mine eyes, that I sleep not in death. *Ver.* 3.

Psal. xxx.

In my prosperity I said, I shall never be removed: Thou, Lord, of Thy goodness hadst made my *state* so strong. *Ver.* 6.

Thou didst turn away Thy face from me, and I was *sore* troubled. *Ver.* 7.

Then cried I unto Thee, O Lord; and gat me unto my Lord right humbly. *Ver.* 8.

What profit is there in my blood, if I go down into the pit? *Ver.* 9.

Shall the dust give thanks unto Thee? or, shall it declare Thy truth? *Ver.* 10.

Hear, O Lord, and have mercy upon me; Lord, be Thou my helper. *Ver.* 11.

Psal. lxxvii.

I will cry unto God with my voice, even unto God will I cry with my voice, and He shall hearken unto me. *Ver.* 1.

In the time of my trouble I sought the Lord; my sore ran and ceased not: in the night season my soul refused comfort. *Ver.* 2.

When I am in heaviness, I will think upon God; when my heart is vexed, I will complain. *Ver.* 3.

Thou holdest mine eyes waking; I am so feeble that I can *scarce* speak. *Ver.* 4.

I have considered the days of old, and the years that are past. *Ver.* 5.

I call to remembrance my song; and in the night I commune with my heart, and search out my spirits. *Ver.* 6.

Will the Lord absent Himself for ever? and will He be no more intreated? *Ver.* 7.

Is His mercy clean gone for ever? Is His promise come utterly to an end for evermore? *Ver.* 8.

Hath God forgotten to be gracious? and will He shut up His loving-kindness in displeasure? *Ver.* 9.

And I said, It is mine own infirmity; but I will remember the years of the right hand of the Most High. *Ver.* 10.

2 *Chron.* xx.

O God, there is no strength in us: neither do we know what to do; but only we lift up our eyes unto Thee. *Ver.* 12.

Psal. xxxv.

Lord, how long wilt Thou look upon this? *Ver.* 17.

This Thou hast seen, O Lord; hold not Thy tongue then; go not far from me, O Lord. *Ver.* 22.

Psal. lxix.

Save me, O God; for the waters are come in, even unto my soul. *Ver.* 1.

Psal. lxviii.

Let God arise, and let His enemies be scattered; let them also that hate Him, flee before Him. *Ver.* 1.

P. Isa. xxxviii.

Lord, it oppresseth me; answer for me. *Ver.* 14.

Psal. xxxviii.

Thou shalt answer for me, O Lord my God. *Ver.* 15.

Psal. cxxx.

Out of the deep have I called unto Thee, O Lord: Lord, hear my voice. *Ver.* 1.

O let Thine ears consider well the voice of my complaint. *Ver.* 2.

Psal. lxxix.

O let the sorrowful sighing of the prisoners come before Thee; according to the greatness of Thy power, preserve Thou those that are appointed to die. *Ver.* 12.

A Prayer to be used by the Priest, begging Pardon of his own Unworthiness, and Acceptance of his Devotions for the Sick.

O Lord, it is a great presumption, that one sinner should dare to commend another to Thy Divine Majesty; especially, the greater, the less; and, who would not fear to undertake it? But Thy commandment it is, by Thy holy Apostle, *When any is sick, that the Priests should be called for;* that they should pray for the sick party, and that their prayers Thou wilt receive; and save and forgive the sins of the party so prayed for.

And now behold, O Lord, we that are no way meet, but unworthy, utterly unworthy, to sue for ought for ourselves, charity and compassion so binding us, are enforced to become suitors to Thee for others.

Even, O Lord, for this Thy servant, ready to depart this world.

To Thee we hope, to Thee we desire, to Thee we intreat and pray in all meek manner, and even from the bottom of our hearts.

O Lord, that which justly Thou mightest deny to our unworthiness, deny not, we beseech Thee, to Thine own gracious goodness.

O Lord, forgive us our sins, our great and grievous sins, oft, and many times committed; long, many years most wretchedly continued; so that we may be meet to pray for others; that so we may make our prayer unto Thee, in an acceptable time.

Graciously look upon our afflictions.
Pitifully behold the sorrows of our hearts.
Mercifully forgive the sins of Thy people.
Favourably with mercy receive our prayers.
Both now and ever vouchsafe to hear us, O Christ.
Graciously hear us, O Christ.
Graciously hear us, O Lord Christ.

A Litany for the Sick Person in Danger of Death.

O God the Father of Heaven,
   Have mercy upon him.
   Keep and defend him.

FOR THE SICK.

O God the Son, Redeemer of the World,
> Have mercy upon him.
> Save and deliver him.

O God the Holy Ghost, proceeding from the Father and the Son,
> Have mercy upon him.
> Strengthen and comfort him.

O Holy, Blessed, and Glorious Trinity,
> Have mercy upon him.

Remember not, Lord, his offences.

Call not to mind the offences of his forefathers; but spare him, good Lord, spare Thy servant, whom Thou hast redeemed with Thy precious blood, and be not angry with him for ever.

From {
 Thy wrath and heavy indignation;
 The guilt and burthen of his sins;
 The dreadful sentence of the last judgment;
}
> Good Lord, deliver him.

From {
 The sting and terror of conscience;
 The danger of impatience, distrust or despair;
 The extremity of sickness, anguish, or agony, that may any way withdraw his mind from Thee;
}
> Good Lord, deliver him.

From the {
 Bitter pangs of eternal death;
 Gates of hell;
 Power of darkness;
 Illusions and assaults of our ghostly enemy;
}
> Good Lord, deliver him.

By Thy manifold and great mercies;

By the manifold and great merits of JESUS Christ Thy Son;

By His {
 Agony and bloody Sweat;
 Strong Crying and Tears;
 Bitter Cross and Passion;
 Mighty Resurrection;
 Glorious Ascension;
 Effectual and most acceptable Intercession and Mediation;
}

By the graces and comforts of the Holy Ghost;
> Good Lord, deliver him.

For
- Thy Name's sake;
- The glory of Thy Name;
- Thy loving mercy;
- Thy truth's sake;
- Thine own self.

In this
- Time of his most extremity;
- His last and greatest need.

In the
- Hour of death, and
- Day of judgment.

Good Lord, deliver him.

Deliver him, O Lord, from all danger and distress; from all pains and punishments, both bodily and ghostly. Amen.

As Thou didst deliver

Noah from the flood;
So save and deliver him.
Lot from the fire of Sodom;
So save and deliver him.
Isaac from present death;
So save and deliver him.
Job from all his temptations;
So save and deliver him.
Moses from the hand of Pharaoh;
So save and deliver him.
Daniel from the lions' den;
So save and deliver him.
Jonas from the belly of the whale;
So save and deliver him.

And, as Thou hast delivered Thy blessed Saints and Servants from all their terrors and torments;

So deliver his soul, and receive it to Thy mercy.

We sinners do beseech Thee to hear us, good Lord.

That it may please Thee to remember him with the favour Thou bearest unto Thy people, and so visit him with Thy salvation.

We beseech Thee to hear us, good Lord.

That it may please Thee to save and deliver his soul from the power of the enemy; lest, as a lion, he devour it, and tear in pieces, if there be none to help.

We beseech Thee to hear us, good Lord.

That it may please Thee to be merciful, and to forgive all

his sins and misdeeds; which, by the malice of the devil, or by his own frailty, he hath at any time of his life committed against Thee.

We beseech Thee to hear us, good Lord.

That it may please Thee not to lay to his charge, what in concupiscence of the eye, pride of life, vanity or superfluity, he hath committed against Thee.

We beseech Thee to hear us, good Lord.

That it may please Thee not to lay to his charge, what in the fierceness of his wrath, or in the eagerness of an angry spirit, he hath committed against Thee.

We beseech Thee to hear us, good Lord.

That it may please Thee not to lay to his charge, what in vain and idle words, in the looseness and slipperiness of the tongue, he hath committed against Thee.

We beseech Thee to hear us, good Lord.

That it may please Thee to make him partaker of all Thy mercies and promises in Christ Jesus.

We beseech Thee to hear us, good Lord.

That it may please Thee to vouchsafe his soul the estate of joy, bliss, and happiness, with all Thy blessed Saints, in Thy heavenly kingdom.

We beseech Thee to hear us, good Lord.

That it may please Thee to grant his body rest and peace, and a part in the blessed resurrection of life and glory.

We beseech Thee to hear us, good Lord.

Son of God, we beseech Thee to hear us.

O Lord God, Lamb of God, that takest away the sins of the world,

Have mercy upon us.

Thou that takest away the sins of the world,

Have mercy upon us.

Thou that takest away the sins of the world,

Grant him Thy peace.

Thou that sittest at the right hand of God the Father,

Have mercy upon us.

Lord, have mercy upon us.

Christ, have mercy upon us.

Lord, have mercy upon us.

Our Father, who art in heaven, &c.

O Lord, deal not with him after his sins.

Neither reward him according to his iniquities.

O God, merciful Father, that despisest not the sighing of a contrite heart, nor the desires of such as be sorrowful, mercifully assist our prayers, which we make before Thee; at such times specially, when our greatest and most grievous extremities are ready to oppress us. And, O Lord, graciously hear us, that those evils, those illusions, terrors, and assaults, which Thine or our enemy worketh against us, may be brought to nought, and by the providence of Thy goodness may be dispersed, that we Thy servants, being swallowed up with no temptations, may evermore give thanks unto Thee in Thy Holy Church, through JESUS Christ our Lord. *Amen.*

An humble Recognition of Human Frailty; and a Deprecation of falling from God.

In the midst of life, we are in death: of whom then may we seek for succour, but of Thee, O Lord, who, for our sins, art most justly displeased with us?

Yet, O Lord most holy, O Lord most mighty, O holy and most merciful Father, deliver us not over to the bitter pains of eternal death.

Thou knowest, Lord, the secrets of our hearts; shut not up against us the ears of Thy mercy; but spare us, O Lord most holy, O Lord most mighty, O immortal and most merciful Father.

Thou most worthy Judge eternal, suffer us not in our last hour for any pains of death to fall from Thee.—*Ch. Engl. Office for Burial.*

An affectionate Recommendation of the Sick Person to God's Mercy, grounded upon his special Relations to God, and the Sincerity of his Soul.

I.

We commend unto Thee, O Lord, the soul of this Thy servant.

He is

The work of Thy hands;

Despise not, O Lord, the work of Thine own hands. [*Psal.* cxxxviii. 8.]

The likeness of Thy image; [*Gen.* i. 27.]
Suffer not, O Lord, Thy image to be utterly defaced.
The price of Thy blood; [1 *Cor.* vi. 20.]
Let not so great a price be cast away.
A Christian;
The name of Thy Son is called upon him;
For Thy Name's sake, be good unto Thy Name.
He is Thine, O save him. *Psal.* cxix. 94.
Give not over that Thine is into the will of the enemy. [*Psal.* xli. 2.]

Though he hath sinned, yet Thy Name hath he not denied; but called upon it, and confessed it unto his life's end; and there is no other name under heaven but Thine whereby he hopeth to be saved. *Acts* iv. 12.

Though he hath sinned, yet he hath not hid his sin (*Job* xxxi. 33), nor excused it (*Psal.* cxli. 4), but hath confessed and been sorry for it, and wisheth even tears of blood, wherewith to lament it.

Though he hath sinned, yet others also have sinned against him, whom he from the heart forgiveth, and desireth forgiveness of them at Thy gracious hands.

O stablish Thy word with Thy servant (*Psal.* cxix. 38); and let him not be disappointed of his hope. *Psal.* cxix. 116.

Though he hath sinned, yet in Thee he trusteth; O suffer him not for ever utterly to be confounded. [*Psal.* xxxi. 1.]

Though he hath sinned, yet he seeketh Thee: and Thou, Lord, never failest them that seek Thee. *Psal.* ix. 10.

Though he hath sinned, yet he cometh to Thee: and of them that come to Thee, Thou castest none out. S. *John* vi. 37.

II.

O Lord,
Let not the guiltiness of a sinner more prevail to condemn, than the gracious goodness of a most merciful Father to acquit and to pardon.

O let not the *unrighteousness* of man make the *goodness* of God of none effect. *Rom.* iii. 3.

O Lord, do not so remember the unkindness of this Thy child, that thereby Thou forget the compassion and kindness of a Father.

Do not so think upon our sins, that Thou thereby forget Thine own nature and property, which is alway to have mercy.—*Ch. Engl. Liturgy.*

Do not so remember our sins, that Thou thereby remember not Thine own name, which is JESUS, a most loving and kind Saviour.

III.
Lord,

If Thy life in our life hath not sufficiently appeared, yet let not Thy death lose the full power and effect thereof in our death also.

Suffer not, O Lord, in both, so great a price to perish.

Lose not, O Lord, that which Thou hast redeemed; since Thou camest to redeem that which was lost. S. *Matth.* xviii. 11; S. *Luke* xix. 10.

That which was so dear to Thee to redeem, suffer not to be lost as a thing of no value.

A Prayer for Mercy and Divine Assistance to uphold the Sick Person in his present Affliction.

Have mercy upon him, O Lord; consider the pains which he suffereth, Thou who only dost deliver from the gates of death. *Psal.* ix. 13.

Show Thy marvellous loving-kindness, Thou that art the Saviour of them that put their trust in Thee. *Psal.* xvii. 7.

O keep him as the apple of Thine eye: hide him under the shadow of Thy wings. *Psal.* xvii. 8.

O let Thy merciful loving-kindness be his comfort, according to Thy word unto Thy servant. *Psal.* cxix. 76.

He is troubled above measure. (*Psal.* cxix. 107.) O be merciful to him according to Thy goodness.

O consider his *adversity, and deliver him:* for he is brought very low. *Psal.* cxlii. 7.

His eyes long sore for Thy word, saying, O when wilt Thou comfort me? *Psal.* cxix. 82.

His eyes are wasted away with looking for Thy health, and for the word of Thy righteousness. *Psal.* cxix. 123.

O think Thou upon him, O Lord, as concerning Thy word, wherein Thou hast caused him to put his trust. *Psal.* cxix. 49.

O look Thou upon him, and be merciful unto him, as Thou usest to do to those that love Thy name. *Psal.* cxix. 132.

Cast him not away in the time of his *weakness;* forsake him not now, when his strength faileth him. *Psal.* lxxi. 8.

In the multitude of the sorrows that are in his heart, let Thy comforts, O Lord, refresh his soul. *Psal.* xciv. 19.

O Lord, when it oppresseth, comfort Thou him. *P. Isa.* xxxviii. 14.

O Lord, let Thy strength be made perfect in his weakness. 2 *Cor.* xii. 9.

Let not temptation *oppress* him, but such as is incident to *Thy children:* but, as Thou art faithful, O Lord, so suffer him not to be tempted above what he is able. But, good Lord, with the tentation *give a happy issue,* that he may be able to overcome it. 1 *Cor.* x. 13.

O Lord, though he be *afflicted* on every side, yet let him not be distressed: *though in want of some of Thy comforts, yet not of all:* though *chastened,* yet not forsaken: though cast down, yet not perish. 2 *Cor.* iv. 8, 9.

A Prayer for the Grace of God, and the Pardon of the Sins of the Sick Party.

Remember him, O Lord, with the favour Thou bearest unto Thy *children:* O visit him with Thy salvation.

That he may see the felicity of Thy chosen, and rejoice with the gladness of Thy *Saints,* and give thanks with Thine inheritance. *Psal.* cvi. 4, 5.

O remember not his *former* sins, but have mercy upon him, *O Lord,* and that soon; for he is come to great *extremity.*

Help him, O *Lord* God of his salvation, for the glory of Thy Name: O deliver him, and be merciful to his sins, for Thy Name's sake. *Psal.* lxxix. 8, 9.

Call to remembrance, O Lord, Thy tender mercies, and Thy loving-kindness, which hath been ever of old.

O remember not the sins and offences of his youth, but according to Thy mercy think Thou upon him, O Lord, for Thy goodness. *Psal.* xxv. 5, 6.

Cleanse him, O Lord, from his secret sins. *Psal.* xix. 12.

From whatsoever he hath offended,

By $\begin{cases} \text{thought, word, or deed,} \\ \text{ignorance or error, frailty or negligence;} \end{cases}$

In excess, or in defect;

By { leaving good undone, or
     doing evil ;
In public or private;
By day or night;
Against { Thee,
         his { neighbour,
              own body ;
By himself, or by others;
Before or since his effectual calling;
Remembered or forgotten;
From them all cleanse him, O Lord, even from them all;
Lay none of them to his charge;
Cast them behind Thee; [*Is.* xxxviii. 17.]
Bury them; drown them; [*Micah* vii. 19.]
Scatter them as the mist, and as the morning cloud; [*Is.* xliv. 22.]
Make them to vanish away, and come to nothing.
And whereinsoever his conscience most accuseth him, therein, O Lord, be Thou most merciful.

O enter not into judgment with Thy servant. If Thou shouldst, no flesh should be righteous in Thy sight. *Ps.* cxliii. 2.

If Thou, Lord, shouldst be extreme to mark what is done amiss, O Lord, who may abide it? *Psal.* cxxx. 3.

But, *good Lord,* one deep calleth another (*Psal.* xlii. 9): the deep of our misery, the deep of Thy mercy.

Wherein sin hath abounded, there let grace over-abound. *Rom.* v. 20.

And in and through all sins and offences, O Lord, let Thy mercy triumph over Thy justice. *S. James* ii. 13.

O Lord, hear; O Lord, forgive; consider, O Lord, and do it. *P. Dan.* ix. 19.

Delay, not, O Lord, for his spirit waxeth faint: turn not Thy face away from him, lest he be like unto them that go down into the pit. *Psal.* cxliii. 7.

Be favourable, O Lord, be favourable;

For Thy { Name's
         Truth's   } sake;
         Mercies'

For Thy { many
         great   } mercies' sake.
         wonderful

Lord, Thine own self, O Lord;
Our { Creator and Redeemer; Lord / King } and our { Father; God.

COMMENDATIO ANIMÆ;

Or, the Recommending the Soul to God.

LORD, now lettest Thou Thy servant depart in peace. *S. Luke* ii. 29.

Into Thy hands, O Lord, we commend his spirit; for Thou hast redeemed it, O Lord, Thou God of truth. *Psal.* xxxi. 6.

Bring his soul out of prison, that it may praise Thee. *Psal.* cxlii. 9.

O deliver him from this body of death. *Rom.* vii. 24.

Say unto his soul, I am thy salvation. *Psal.* xxxv. 3.

Say unto him, This day shalt thou be with Me in Paradise. *S. Luke* xxiii. 43.

Let him now feel the salvation of JESUS.

Let him now feel the anointing of Christ; even the oil of gladness wherewith Thou art anointed. [*Psal.* xlv. 8.]

Guide Thou him through the vale of the shadow of death. *Psal.* xxiii. 4.

Let him see the goodness of the Lord in the land of the living. *Psal.* xxvii. 15.

O Lord, command his spirit to be received up to Thee in peace.

O Lord, will him to come to Thee. *S. Matt.* xiv. 28.

Lord JESU, receive his spirit. *Acts* vii. 59. And open to him the gates of everlasting glory.

Let Thy good Spirit conduct him into the land of righteousness, (*Psal.* cxliii. 10,) into Thy holy hill, (*Psal.* xv. 1,) and heavenly kingdom.

Send Thine angel to meet him, and to bring him into Abraham's bosom. *S. Luke* xvi. 22.

Place him in the habitation of light and peace, of joy and gladness.

Receive him in the arms of Thy mercy; and give him an inheritance with Thy Saints in light. *Coloss.* i. 12.

There to reign with Thy elect Angels, Thy blessed Saints departed, thy holy Prophets, and glorious Apostles, in all joy, glory, felicity, and happiness for ever and ever. *Amen.*

Comfortable Scriptures to be applied to the Friends of the deceased Party.

Precious in the sight of the Lord is the death of his saints. *Psal.* cxvi. 13.

I heard a voice from heaven, saying, Write, Blessed are the dead, who die in the Lord: for they rest from their labours, and their works follow them. *Rev.* xiv. 13.

A General Confession of Sins, collected out of the Holy Prophets and Apostles.

P. Moses.

We have sinned, O Lord.

Thou hast set our faults before Thee, and our secret sins in the light of Thy countenance. *Psal.* xc. 8.

Return, O Lord; how long? and be merciful toward Thy servants. *Psal.* xc. 13.

H. Job.

I have sinned: what shall I do unto Thee, O Thou preserver of men? Why hast Thou set me as a mark against Thee, that I am become a burthen to myself? *Job* vii. 20.

That I have offended Thee, woe is me. *Job* x. 15.

Have mercy upon me, O Lord, and restore unto me my righteousness again. Say, concerning me, O Lord, Deliver him, for I have received a reconciliation. *Job* xxxiii. 24, 26.

Yet, if Thou kill me, I will put my trust in Thee. *Job* xiii. 15.

P. David.

My misdeeds have prevailed against me.

O be Thou merciful unto my sin. *Psal.* lxv. 3.

I have gone astray like a sheep that is lost.

O seek Thy servant, for I do not forget Thy Commandments. *Psal.* cxix. 176.

We have sinned with our fathers: we have done amiss, and dealt wickedly. *Psal.* cvi. 6.

For Thy Name's sake, O Lord, be merciful unto our sin; for it is great. *Psal.* xxv. 10.

My foot hath slipped.

Let Thy mercy, O Lord, lift me up. *Psal.* xciv. 18.

P. Isai.

Behold, Thou art angry; for we have sinned: we have been as an unclean thing; and all our righteousness as a defiled cloth.

We all fade away as a leaf; and our iniquities, like a wind, have taken us away.

But now, O Lord, Thou art our Father: we are the clay and Thou art the potter: we all are the work of Thy hands.

Be not angry, O Lord, above measure; neither remember our iniquity for ever. Lord, we beseech Thee, remember we are all Thy people. *Ch.* lxiv. *ver.* 5, 6, 8, 9.

P. Jeremy.

Lord, our iniquities are against us: our rebellions are many; we have sinned against Thee.

Yet deal with us according to thy Name: for Thou, Lord, art in the midst of us, and Thy Name is called upon us.

O Lord, forsake us not.

O Lord, the hope of Israel, the Saviour of it in the time of trouble, forsake us not. *Chap.* xiv. *ver.* 7, 8, 9.

P. Daniel.

We have sinned, O Lord, we have transgressed, and done wickedly: yea, we have rebelled, and have departed from Thy precepts, and from Thy judgment.

O Lord, righteousness belongeth unto Thee, but unto us confusion and shame of face, because of all the offences we have committed against Thee.

Yet compassion and forgiveness is with Thee, O Lord, our God: though we have rebelled against Thee: O Lord, according to all Thy goodness I beseech Thee, let Thine anger and Thy wrath be turned away from me, and cause Thy face to shine upon Thy servant. O my God, incline

Thine ear and hear, open Thine eyes, and behold my afflictions.

For, we do not present our supplications before Thee for our own righteousness, but for Thy manifold and great mercies.

O Lord hear, O Lord forgive.

Consider and do it, O Lord.

Defer not for Thine own sake, O my God. *Chap.* ix. *ver.* 5, 7, 9, 16, 17, 18, 19.

P. Jonas.

O Lord, in following vanities, I have forsaken mine own mercy: for which I am cast out of the sight of Thine eyes.

Yet I remember Thee, O Lord; yet will I look yet again toward Thy holy temple.

O Lord, hear, and have mercy. *Chap.* ii. *ver.* 4, 8.

Prodigal Child.

Father, I have sinned against heaven and against Thee.

I am no more worthy to be called thy son.

But forgive me; and make me as one of the meanest of Thy hired servants. *S. Luke* xv. 18, 19.

God be merciful to me a sinner. *S. Luke* xviii. 13.

JESU, Master, have mercy upon us. *S. Luke* xvii. 13.

Have mercy on me, O Lord, Thou son of David. *S. Matt.* xv. 22.

O Lord, help me. *Ver.* 25.

O Lord, even the little whelps eat of the crumbs of Thy table. *Ver.* 27.

S. Paul.

O Lord, I am carnal, and sold under sin :

And in me (that is, in my flesh) dwelleth no good. *Rom.* vii. 14, 18.

The good thing I do not, which I would: the evil that I would not, that do I. *Ver.* 15.

Though I consent to the Law, according to the inner man, *Ver.* 22.

Yet I feel another law in my *nature* rebelling against the law of my mind, and leading me captive to the law of sin. *Ver.* 23.

O wretched man that I am, who shall deliver me from this body of death? *Ver.* 24.

But, this is a true saying, and by all means worthy to be received,

That JESUS Christ came into the world to save sinners, whereof I am chief. 1 *Tim.* i. 15.

S. Peter.

We have spent the time past of our life, after the lusts of the heathen; walking in wantonness, lust, surfeiting, uncleanness, and other excesses. 1 *S. Pet.* iv. 3.

But, Thou hast redeemed us, O Lord, by the precious blood of Christ, the undefiled Lamb. 1 *S. Pet.* i. 18, 19.

Have mercy upon us in that Name, besides which Thou hast given none under heaven, whereby we must be saved. *Acts* iv. 12.

S. John.

If we say we have no sin, we deceive ourselves, and the truth is not in us. 1 *S. John* i. 8.

If our hearts condemn us not, God is greater than our heart, and knoweth all things. 1 *S. John* iii. 20.

But, we confess our sins, and confessing them, we have an Advocate with the Father, JESUS CHRIST, the righteous, and He is the propitiation for our sins. 1 *S. John* ii. 1, 2.

S. James.

In many things we sin all. *Chap.* iii. *ver.* 2.

But, Lord, let Thy mercy triumph over Thy justice. *Chap.* ii. *ver.* 13.

A Confession of Sins according to the branches of the Decalogue.

I.

I have, touching Thee, O Lord, been full of roving imaginations, and evil thoughts.

I have not studied to seek and know Thee, as I ought.

Knowing Thee, I have not glorified Thee, nor given thanks to Thee accordingly.

I have doubted of Thy promises, and not trusted to Thy help.

I have made flesh mine arm, and hoped for prosperity from man, rather than from Thee.

I have not performed the duty of Invocation with that reverence I ought.

I have not been thankful: specially not for Thy chastisements.

II.

I have not worshipped Thee in spirit and truth.

I have drawn near to Thee with my lips, but my heart hath been far from Thee.

I have been more careful of the outward ceremonial part of Thy worship, than of the inward and spiritual.

III.

I have not with due regard taken Thy Name into my mouth.

I have with rash oaths and eager execrations oft abused it.

I have not given occasion to others to sanctify Thy Name; but have caused it to be evil spoken of, through mine evil dealing.

I have not duly regarded and reverenced those things, whereon Thy Name is imprinted.

IV.

I have not to Thy Sabbath or Sanctuary brought that care which I should.

I have not spared to absent myself from Thy holy assemblies, without sufficient cause.

I have not spent the days assigned to holy exercises, upon them chiefly; but have in them too much intended mine own private business.

I have been content in them with the use of the means alone, without any practice at all.

V.

I have not so reverently spoken, nor so dutifully carried myself toward some whom Thou hast placed over me, as was meet I should.

I have not so carefully prayed for them, as was requisite.

I have not opposed them, who unreverently in terms used them.

Chiefly those who have had me in government touching my soul.

VI.

I have not wished or provided for the good of my neighbours as I should, but rather maligned, been angry, and quarrelled with them; and sought revenge upon every light injury.

I have not had that compassion on the poor that I should; nor ministered to their necessities.

I have not defended them against the wrongs of others, as I might.

I have not rejoiced in the good success of my neighbour; but envied his welfare.

VII.

I have not possessed my vessel in holiness and honour, nor preserved it from pollution, as the temple of God should be.

I have suffered my fancy to wander licentiously.

Mine ears and tongue I have not kept as I should.

I have not eschewed the occasions of lust, nor made the covenant with mine eyes that I should.

I have not brought under my body, nor kept it in subjection with such abstinence as I should.

I have more studiously, and with more cost, intended my flesh than my spirit.

VIII.

I have not reckoned godliness gain; nor been content with my estate, but wished an higher.

I have not been so exact, in paying and dealing with those I have dealt withal, as in justice I was bound.

I have by undue means interverted, to my use, that which was not mine.

I have not of that, whereof I had more than enough, been willing to part with, to the relief of the needy.

IX.

I have not been so studious of speaking the truth, as I should.

I have been desirous to seem, and to be reputed more than I was.

I have not had that care of the good name of my brother, I was bound.

I have not so hated flattery, as I should.

I have not so stood for, and defended the truth, as was meet I should.

X.

I have been full of wandering desires, wicked affections, unlawful concupiscences, evil suspicions and surmises, and inordinate lust, touching my neighbour, and that which is his.

The Triumph of Mercy, in many gradual Expressions and Remembrances, propounded to us in the Holy Scriptures.

God,
In His mercy,
is,

Ἐπιεικής. 2 *Cor.* x. 1. *Gen.* xviii. 32.
Takes all in the better part.
If it will admit any good sense, so he construes it.
Πραΰς. 2 *Cor.* x. 1.
Meek. Not irritable: not easily stirred up or provoked.
Παρορᾷ. *Wisd.* xi. 24.
Sees and *sees* not: makes as if he did not see.
Ὑπεριδών. *Acts* xvii. 30.
Overlooks. Looks beyond our sins; looks not at them.
Ὑπερβαίνων. *P. Micah* vii. 18.
Passeth by (or over) them.
Dissimulat peccata propter pœnitentiam.
Ἀνοχή. *Rom.* ii. 4.
When He cannot but see, yet *He forbears*, is *patient.*
Μακροθυμία. *Rom.* ii. 4. *Neh.* ix. 21, 30.
Forbears long, suffers long, many times, many years.
Πῶς; *P. Hos.* vi. 4. and xi. 8.
When he can suffer no longer, yet stands (as over Ephraim) asking, *How shall I?* stays yet.
Exspectat ut misereatur. P. Isa. xxx. 18.
When he can forbear no longer, but punish He must, He

doth it *not from the heart*, (Lament. iii. 33,) but *against his will.*

When He punisheth: He doth it,

Not suffering His *whole* displeasure to arise, (*Psal.* lxxviii. 39,) containing Himself and His anger.

Not according to our deserts, (*Psal.* ciii.10,) nothing so much.

Not long: it endures but a *moment* in comparison, *Psal.* xxx. 5, and ciii. 9, and *P. Isa.* liv. 7, 8.

He thinks every stripe *two*, (*P. Isa.* xl. 2;) is quickly weary.

In His wrath He *remembers mercy.* *P. Hab.* iii. 2.

Repents Him of the evil. *P. Joel* ii. 13.

Is *moved* with the *sight* of *our misery.* *Psal.* cvi. 43, 44.

Is $\left\{ \begin{array}{c} soon \\ easily \end{array} \right\}$ appeased.

P. Isa. xxx. 18, and lv. 7. *S. Matth.* xi. 30.

Hath *mercy.* חסד

  Multitudes of it.

    רחמים [*Psal.* li. 1.]

The *bowels* of $\left\{ \begin{array}{l} \text{Compassion. } S. \textit{ Luke } \text{xv. 20.} \\ \text{A } \textit{parent.} \text{ } \textit{Psal.} \text{ ciii. 13.} \\ \text{A } \textit{mother.} \text{ } \textit{Isa.} \text{ xlix. 15.} \end{array} \right.$

Hath *compassion.*

Many bowels. Πολυεύσπλαγχνος, *S. James* v. 11, *secundum Edit. Complut.*

Forgives, pardons. *S. Matt.* xviii. 27.

Is *reconciled.* 2 *Cor.* v. 19.

Takes into *favour again.* *S. Luke* xv. 22, 23.

Receives to *grace.* *Rom.* iii. 24.

All have sinned, and *are defective in giving glory to* God. *Rom.* iii. 23.

In His *Angels* He found *folly;* and the *stars* are *not clean* in His sight. *Job* iv. 18, and xv. 15, and xxv. 5.

But, God hath not made all men for nought. *Psal.* lxxxix. 46.

Yet, if God should be extreme to mark what were done amiss, who were able to abide it? *Psal.* cxxx. 3.

If He should enter into judgment with His servants, no flesh should be found righteous in His sight. *Psal.* cxliii. 2.

None were able to answer one *for* a thousand. No not *Job* himself. *Job* ix. 3.

Therefore God hath shut up all under sin, that He might have mercy upon all. *Rom.* xi. 32.

He would have all to be saved. 1 *Tim.* ii. 4.

He would have none to perish; but *to turn to Him by* repentance. 2 *S. Pet.* iii. 9.

He would not the death of a sinner; but, that He might turn to Him, and live. *P. Ezech.* xxxiii. 11.

All that, 1, know their sin. *Psal.* li. 3.

Know it, and, 2, *acknowledge it.* *Psal.* xxxii. 5. *S. Luke* xv. 18.

Acknowledge it, and, 3, *be sorry for it.* *Psal.* xxxviii. 18.

Be sorry for it, and, 4, *be ready to leave it.* *Prov.* xxviii. 13.

Not only to leave it, but, 5, *to judge* themselves for it. 1 *Cor.* xi. 31. *P. Ezech.* xxxvi. 31. 1 *Cor.* ix. 27.

And to, 6, *punish* themselves for it. 2 *Cor.* vii. 11.

By the, 1, *fruits of mortification.* *P. Joel* ii. 12, 13. *P. Jonah* iii. 5, accompanied with,

2. Prayer. *Psal.* xxxii. 7. *Acts* viii. 22.

3. Alms. *P. Isa.* lviii. 7. *Prov.* xvi. 6. *P. Dan.* iv. 27.

At the, 4, *estimation* of the *Priest.* *Levit.* vi. 6.

5. Who may *forgive* us in the *person of Christ.* *S. John* viii. 11, and xx. 23. 2 *Cor.* ii. 10.

Which His mercy is not only for common and ordinary sinners, but for the chief.

Such as { Manasses.
         Paul.

Such as { David.
         Peter.

Such as { Rahab.
         Mary Magdalen.

Such as { Jonas.
         The thief on the cross.

Such as { The Corinthians. 1 *Cor.* v. 1.
         The Corinthians. 1 *Cor.* vi. 11.

Et hæc eratis.

Such as the Jews, His { Betrayers.
                       Murderers. *Acts* iii. 13, 14, 15.

David was a man according to God's own heart.

Christ is the Son of David.

And David *forgave* Shimei. 2 *Sam.* xix. 23.
And *wept* for his rebellious son Absolom. 2 *Sam.* xviii. 33.

The Preface or Style of the Law.

The Lord, the Lord,
Gentle and merciful,
Patient, and of much mercy,
Who keepeth mercy for thousands, and forgiveth. *Exod.* xxxiv. 6, 7.

The discourse of Elihu.
Job xxxiii. 23, 24.

If there be a messenger with Him, an interpreter, one among a thousand, to show unto man his uprightness.

Then He is gracious unto him, and saith, Deliver him from going down to the pit; I have found a ransom.

Taste and see how *gracious* the Lord is. *Psal.* xxxiv. 8. 1 *S. Pet.* ii. 3.

His mercy is *sweet*. *Psal.* cix. 20.

His mercies are *many*.

There is a *multitude* of them. *Psal.* lxix. 17; and v. 7; and li. 1.

There is a *plenteous* redemption. *Psal.* cxxx. 7.

His mercies are *great*. *Psal.* lxxxvi. 5; and cxix. 156.

Have a *magnitude*.

Great in ⎧ *height*. *Psal.* ciii. 11; cviii. 4; xxxvi. 5.
⎨ *depth*. *Psal.* xlii. 9.
⎩ *length*. *Psal.* xxvi. 3; and *Psal.* cxxxvi.

There is *no end* of His salvation. *Psal.* lxxi. 13.

Mercy shall be set up for *ever*. *Psal.* lxxxix. 2.

His mercy is *over all* His works. *Psal.* cxlv. 9.

As is His majesty, *so* is His mercy. *Ecclus.* ii. 18.

His property is to have mercy. *P. Isa.* xxviii. 21.

He is the *Father* of mercies. 2 *Cor.* i. 3.

He is *Mercy itself*. *Psal.* lix. 17.

He was so merciful, that He *forgave* their misdeeds, and destroyed them not.

Yea, many a time *turned He His wrath away;* and would not suffer His *whole* displeasure to arise.

For He considered they were but *dust.* *Psal.* lxxviii. 38, 39, 40.

The Lord *waiteth,* that He may have mercy on you. *P. Isa.* xxx. 18.

In the Father of the lost child, His image. *S. Luke* xv. 22.

Without shedding of blood there is no remission *of sins.* *Heb.* ix. 22.

God hath shut up all under sin, that He might have *mercy* upon all. *Rom.* xi. 32.

Where sin aboundeth, there *grace* doth over-abound. [*Rom.* v. 20.]

Mercy triumpheth over justice. *S. James* ii. 13.

In this God set forth His *love* to us ward, that, when we were His enemies, Christ died for us. *Rom.* v. 8.

This is a true saying, and of all men worthy to be received, that JESUS Christ came into the world to save sinners. 1 *Tim.* i. 15.

Christ died once for our sins, the just for the unjust, that He might *offer* us unto God. 1 *S. Pet.* iii. 18.

We have an advocate with the Father, JESUS Christ the righteous;

And He is the propitiation for our sins; and not for ours only, but for the sins of the whole world. 1 *S. John* ii. 1, 2.

I came not to call the righteous, but sinners to repentance. *S. Matt.* ix. 13.

Come unto Me, you that travail, and be heavy laden, and I will *refresh* you. *S. Matt.* xi. 28.

Of them that come to Me, I will cast none out. *S. John* vi. 37.

Thou never failest them that seek Thee. *Psal.* ix. 10.

Spiritual Comforts and Confidence issuing from the contemplation of God's Goodness.

Why art thou so heavy, O my soul? and why art thou so disquieted within me?

O put thy trust in God; for I shall yet give Him thanks: for He is the light of my countenance, and my God. *Psal.* xlii. 6, 7, 14, 15; and xliii. 5, 6.

Return then to thy rest, O my soul; for the Lord hath *been gracious to* thee. *Psal.* cxvi. 7.

If the Lord had not helped me, it had not failed, but my soul had been put to silence.

In the *midst* of the *troubles* that *were* in my heart, Thy comforts have refreshed my soul. *Psal.* xciv. 17, 19.

Nevertheless, though I be sometimes afraid, yet put I my trust in *the Lord*. *Psal.* lvi. 3.

Nevertheless, my soul, wait thou still upon *God;* for *of Him cometh my salvation.*

He *verily* is my *Hope*, and my *strength :* He is my defence, so that I shall not *greatly* fall. *Psal.* lxii. 5, 6.

Let us *go with boldness* to the throne of Grace, that we may *find* mercy in the time of need. *Heb.* iv. 16.

Devout Ejaculations, grounded on the consideration of our Human Frailty, and the Divine Providence and Mercy.

I.

Lord of life and death, of sickness and health, and all things thereto belonging;

By Whose appointment we are born; and again, by Whose appointment we die:

Our time is in Thy hand (*Psal.* xxxi. 17), and unto Thee belong the issues of death. *Psal.* lxviii. 20.

Thou that hatest nothing that Thou hast made, [*Wisd.* xi. 24,] nor dost utterly forsake the work of Thine own hands: [*Psal.* cxxxviii. 8.]

Thou that art a defence for the oppressed; a refuge in *the needful* time of trouble.

Thou never failest them that seek Thee. *Psal.* ix. 9, 10.

And to Whom none ever prayeth without hope to be heard: *Thou that hast promised,*

The poor shall not alway be forgotten; *that* the patient abiding of the meek shall not perish for ever, *Psal.* ix. 18.

For the comfortless trouble's sake of the needy: and *for* the deep sighing of the poor. *Psal.* xii. 5.

Arise, O Lord:

And *men* shall know that *it* is Thy hand, and that *it* is Thy hand, and that Thou, *Lord, that* hast done it. *Psal.* cix. 25.

II.

O Lord, Whose mercy reacheth to the heavens, and Whose faithfulness to the clouds; *Psal.* xxxvi. 5; and lvii. 11.

Of Whose mercies there is neither number nor end;

The greatness of Whose goodness is not shut up under any time;

Who callest into Thy vineyard even at the eleventh hour; *S. Matt.* xx. 6, 7.

Who rulest not with rigour, but with meekness dost govern the things Thou hast made;

Thou that killest and revivest; that bringest to the gates of death, and bringest back again; [1 *Sam.* ii. 6.]

Thou that hatest nothing that Thou hast made;

That hast shut up all under sin, that Thou mightest have mercy upon all. *Rom.* xi. 32.

LORD,

The *Saviour* and the saving health of all Thy *faithful*;

The *Fountain* of grace and goodness;

The *Father* of mercies, and *God* of consolation; 2 *Cor.* i. 3.

Thou that upholdest all such as are falling, and liftest up those that be down; *Psal.* cxlv. 14.

Thou that healest the broken in heart; and givest medicine to heal their sickness; *Psal.* cxlvii. 3.

The comfort of them that be in heaviness,

The strength of them that be in weakness,

The health of them that be in sickness,

 Hear, O Lord, and have mercy;

 Look down from heaven:

 Behold and visit;

Visit with Thy salvation. [*Psal.* cvi. 4.]

A MANUAL

OF

PRIVATE DEVOTIONS

AND

MEDITATIONS.

NOTICE.

[THE following is a Reprint of the Translation of Bishop Andrewes' Private Devotions, originally published by Richard Drake, in 1648.

It has been already stated that he had a few months previously edited the Manual for the Sick, and that he had appended to it the Prayers for the Morning, Evening, and Holy Communion, to which he appears then for the first time to have gained access, but which he immediately afterwards removed from thence, and inserted (as they here occur) in their proper places.

This Edition was reprinted together with the Manual for the Sick, in 1674 and 1692. The former Edition appeared during the lifetime of the original Editor, but, from the many and grievous misprints, evidently not under his superintendence.

An imperfect Edition had been previously put forth by the same Publisher, varying, however, so much from the Edition followed in the present reprint, as to render collation quite impossible.

It was published under the title of,

" *The Private Devotions of the Right Reverend Father in God Lancelot Andrewes, late Bishop of Winchester.* Lord, I have called daily upon Thee; I have stretched out my hands unto Thee. *Psal.* lxxxviii. 9. *London, Printed for Humphrey Moseley, and are to be sold at his shop at the Princes Arms, in St. Pauls Churchyard. An. Dom.* 1647."

It was introduced by the following Preface, from

The Stationer to the Christian Reader.

The life of this Reverend Father was a life of Prayer. Five hours in a day he spent in his Devotions, and for divers months before his dissolution he gave himself wholly up to converse with God. It is most remarkable, and may instruct posterity, that when sickness had deprived him of his voice, yet his eyes and hands prayed; and when both they failed, his heart still prayed, till it pleased God to accept it as his last sacrifice. This testimony and character of his holy Piety, we received from learned Bishop Buckeridge, who being well acquainted with his life, commended his precious memory to posterity in a funeral Sermon, one of the last offices which, as men and Christians, we are wont to pay to Honour and Virtue. In the evening of his life he was seldom seen without these devotions in his hand; he penned them in Greek, and in that language presented them to his God; the reason it is not for me to determine; whether it were for that the clearest evidences of our salvation are delivered to us in that tongue, or whether amongst those fifteen he was master of, he chose this language as the most copious to express the fulness of his soul. It appears not as yet who translated this manual of devotions; some of his learned Friends (to whom the world owes much for the benefit of this publication) informed me, that they found them written with his own hand, from whence they had the happiness to transcribe them. It is not improbable that we are indebted to the same hand for the translation to whom we owe the original; since I could never yet learn that any have laid claim thereunto; it being no new thing in this ambitious age, for men to endeavour to translate fames, as well as books, it may seem strange in these *extempore* times, for me to send these set forms to the press, since I am not ignorant how of late it hath been hotly disputed, whether it be better to pray to God with consideration or without, against this wild fancy I conceived I could not oppose any argument above the example of this learned Doctor of our Church.

Who, though he was so universal in all holy dimensions, you may be pleased to observe the reverential addresses of his soul in these his approaches to the highest Majesty; he well knew the distance between heaven and earth, betwixt God and himself, which I hope will be a motive to every pious Christian, as Solomon saith, not to be rash with his mouth, Eccles. v. 2.

I must clearly confess, when these copies came first to my hand, I resolved to imprint them in my own heart; but, considering with myself that no man might better excuse the divulging of so usual a book, than one of my profession, and withal that there were divers manuscripts dispersed abroad, and the Church might be deprived of this genuine edition, and I of mine own right, I thought this publication absolutely necessary, being confident that no man could justly except against this Reverend Author, who both abroad and at home was acknowledged, for his piety and learning, to have been one of the oracles of the Church ; much less against these his devotions, which are for the most part selected out of the Holy Scripture.

And whereas he freely wrote his controversies and sermons for the benefit of others, these pieces, I suppose, cannot be too well thought of, which he kept peculiar to himself, having appropriated and consecrated them to his private use for the employment of his own soul.

This treasure, so piously laid up in his lifetime, I thought good not to keep wrapt up in a napkin from the public, enjoy it thankfully, to the glory of that God who kindled these holy fires in his soul, and let the memory of the devout Author, in spite of ignorance and malice, be perpetuated and blessed by after ages ; as for me, I shall never desire any higher recompence, than to be in some measure serviceable to the Church, and to be esteemed

Your faithful Servant,

HUM. MOSELEY.]

A MANUAL

OF

THE PRIVATE

DEVOTIONS

AND

MEDITATIONS

OF

The Right Reverend

Father in God
LANCELOT ANDREWS,
late *Lord BISHOP* of
Winchester.

Tranflated out of a fair *Greek MS.*
Of His Amanuenfis.

By *R. D.* B.D.

TO HIS HIGHNESS

THE PRINCE OF WALES.

Sir,

It was the special command of your Royal Father, our most Gracious Sovereign, to the Bishops of London and Ely, now with God, to take care, that, of the innumerable papers of this reverend Prelate, none should be committed to the press, but such as they found perfected by his accurate hand.

In prosecution whereof, we are much bound to their care and faithfulness for the communication of his incomparable Sermons and Discourses, which now enrich the world with piety and learning; and put it to the wonder, to see the quintessence of the Fathers and school distilled through his limbeck, in so fit language and expressions, to the great advantage of the Church of God.

Why this most excellent piece of his Devotions was not by them presented with the rest, the language, wherein it was conceived, and used by him, will give abundant satisfaction to Your Highness; his Greek had been but a barbarian unto them, whose benefit was chiefly intended in all the publications of his works. Nor is Your Highness now to be assured, that they, who were employed in that service, were wise and honourable persons; that they well knew their work, and did it.

And truly, Sir, the commands of His Majesty shall ever be so sacred to me, and the judgment of those Reverend Prelates so much esteemed by me, that I should not have presumed on this essay, had not the honour of this renowned Bishop been eclipsed, by obtruding on the world some broken parcels, miserably defaced by a careless press, under the glorious name of Bishop Andrews.

If this be thought no sufficient ground for this high presumption, I shall proceed, in my presumption on Your Highness, to be a mediator to your most glorious father, for his gracious pardon to a sinner, who, not being without great hopes of advancing piety by his sin, is confident of obtaining your princely interposition, that it is *felix error*. And that the benefit hereof so much redounding to the glory of God, by promoting Christian people in devotion, it would have been a greater sin against the public, to detain so precious a jewel from improvement: it being the peculiar happiness of sacred commodities, to be made better by their using.

And, to whom should devotion address herself for patronage in this age of irreligion and profaneness, in this great invasion upon God, the King, the Church, and whatsoever is called holy, if not to Your Highness? It will be no sin in us, to look for the righting and maintenance of them all, from your princely arm, assisted with the power of Heaven.

Ride on, great Prince, upon the horses of salvation, and the Lord of Hosts fight your battles. May the sword of the LORD and Prince CHARLES be mighty in operation, for the redemption of His Sacred Majesty, and the restitution of this Church and Kingdom to their ancient liberty and glory. May honour, prosperity, and peace so accompany and crown your pious, Christian, and princely undertakings, that our eyes may once more see the KING upon his throne, gloriously triumphing in the affections of his subjects, happily united in the indissoluble bonds of love and loyalty.

This is the sum of all our desires, and the daily prayer of him, whose highest ambition is, not to be utterly incapable of doing service to the Church of God, and of approving himself,

  Sir,
   Your Highness's
    Most humble
     and most loyally devoted
      Orator and Servant,
       RICHARD DRAKE.

TO THE CHRISTIAN READER.

AMONG the many blessings, for which I am eternally indebted to Heaven, I ever highly esteemed the possession of this precious treasure, this sacred relic of the most Reverend Bishop Andrews. Which, being used by him, in his most secret conference with his God, not only acquaints us with the devotion of his soul, but also gives us an example, how earth may traffic and communicate with heaven.

Had you seen the original manuscript, happy in the glorious deformity thereof, being slubbered with his pious hands, and watered with his penitential tears, you would have been forced to confess, that book belonged to no other than pure and primitive devotion.

Of that, having had the happiness to obtain a copy under the fair hand of his amanuensis, I should not so long have detained from you the communication thereof, but that some reasonable and just arguments effectually prevailed with me.

But at last, finding a great invasion made upon his honour, I resolved to pay my due respects to his precious memory, and to exercise so much charity, which I had learned from his Devotions, towards others, as not to engross to my own private use and benefit, what I was confident would be most serviceable and welcome to the Church of God.

From the general inspection of those his set and sacred forms, as you are convinced of his piety, so you may learn his judgment concerning *ex tempore* conceptions, and undigested prayers.

I am confident he had as great abilities of expressing himself to purpose without premeditation, as any rabbi that pretends to the highest pitch of inspiration. But his devotion had not taught him to cast off his humility; nor was he so little acquainted with his God and himself, as not to know his distance, and to keep it. It had been a sin to him to appear before his God empty, or with that which cost him nothing.

There is too much of a Pharisee in him that dares trust to his memory, his fancy, or invention, before the Majesty of heaven; when even his most premeditated and weighed thoughts, though clothed in the best attire of language, would be esteemed by himself too too unworthy to be offered to his Prince. And yet, such is the irreligion of this age, the most high God must take up and be content with that homely entertainment, which my Lord or Lady, forsooth, would not receive from their most faithful servant without great scorn and indignation.

But it is the highest pitch of sacrilege to make the Scripture patronise impiety. They abuse the text, and the Apostle, that urge his, *I will pray with the spirit*, to justify enthusiasm in praying, unless they will, what never any brain-sick novelist attempted, interpret to us, *I will sing with the spirit*, with their extemporary music.

His reading had not taught this learned Father to make such wild conclusions; nor would his piety permit him to license them to others, or himself. Hence is it, that in his addresses to his God, his heart was kindled, first, with holy fire. Nor would he then present his thoughts upon the altar, till he had weighed them in the balance of the sanctuary, and by committing them to faithful writing, left no room for fruitless matter, or idle words.

The truth hereof will evidently appear in the ensuing prayers; where you may see the actings of the spirit, to the height of the Apostle's sense. The matter, form, and phrase of his Devotions, all borrowed from the Sacred Scriptures, the holy Fathers, and primitive Liturgies, cherished with those flames of actual intention, burning charity, and profound humility, will give the most invincible assurance, that he, that prayed thus, made good S. Paul's, *I will pray with the spirit*.

Nor did his method vary from him neither; *prayers, supplications, intercessions,* and *giving of thanks*, make up the body of his Devotions. That was his unquestionable directory in these his sacred forms: where you shall ever find his faith, his hope, and charity, that sacred triad of supernatural and theological virtues, in the highest pitch of elevation.

And now, I think, there need no arguments to persuade your acceptation, and improvement of them. It is enough that you *know the man and his communication.* Thus did he discourse with God, and so may you: building confidently on this infallible oracle, that the *effectual fervent prayer of a righteous man availeth much;* that, *like a prince it hath power with God,* and conquers heaven.

The citations of the Sacred Scriptures, the Holy Fathers, and Primitive Liturgies; the very few additions thus [ ] included in the body of the text; together with some titles and annotations, by way of exposition or illustration, intended for your greater benefit, are all my ἐθελοθρησκεῖαι, my voluntary oblations; or, if you please to call them so, presumptions; which if I may obtain your pardon for, you see the terms on which I dare commend these Devotions to the truly pious soul. What is amiss you may assure yourself is not in Greek, is not the Bishop's; the English may have faults, but that is mine; and, I shall not doubt your charity in covering them will extend itself to him, who had not now been guilty of them, but out of charity to you. To which if you shall add the recommendation of him in your prayers, who shall never be unmindful of you in his, you shall eternally oblige in the most sacred bonds,

Your most humble
Servant in our
Lord Jesus,
RICH. DRAKE.

On the Nativity of
S. Jo. Baptist, 1648.

S. *Hieron.*

Oras?
Loqueris cum Sponso.
Legis?
Ille tecum loquitur.

Epist. [xxii.] *ad Eustoch. Virg.* [§ 25.
Op., tom. i. col. 107. A.]

Gul. Parisiensis.

Lectio Orationem
    impinguat.
Lectionem Oratio
    illuminat.

De Rhetor. Divina, cap. 30. [Op.,
tom. i. p. 370. col. 1. H.]

S. Gregor. Nazianz.

Τάξις ἀρίστη παντὸς ἀρχομένου καὶ λόγου καὶ πράγματος, ἐκ Θεοῦ τε ἄρχεσθαι καὶ εἰς Θεὸν ἀναπαύεσθαι. Orat. Apologet. Prima. [Op., tom. i. p. 1. A.]

St. Bernard.

Noli vilipendere Orationem tuam, quoniam Ille, ad quem oras, non vilipendit eam: sed, antequam egrediatur de ore tuo, Ipse scribi eam jubet in Libro suo. Et unum e duobus indubitanter sperare debemus, quoniam aut dabit nobis *quod petimus*, aut *quod nobis* noverit esse *utilius*. Meditat. Devotiss. [al. *Piissimæ* incert. auct.] *cap.* 6. [§ 18. apud S. Bern. Op., tom. ii. col. 340. E.]

THE CONTENTS OF THIS MANUAL.

	PAGE
THE Times of Prayer	241
The Places of Prayer	241
The Gestures of the Body, denoting the Affections of the Soul	242
Prayers Preparatory to all our Devotions	243
At our Entrance into the Church	243
Morning Prayer	244
Prayers for { Sunday	250
Monday	266
Tuesday	275
Wednesday	281
Thursday	291
Friday	298
Saturday	306
A Form of Prayer for all the World, and particularly for our special Relations	313
A Recommendation of ourselves and ours to God's blessing	314
Prayers preparatory to all our Thanksgivings	315
A Form of Thanksgiving for Temporal and Spiritual Blessings	315
A Litany to be used upon special Occasions of Public or Private Humiliation	319
Hosanna in the Highest; or, a Supplication for Spiritual Blessings	323
Hosanna upon Earth; or, a Supplication for Temporal Blessings	325
Evening Prayer	327
A Prayer for all Estates	332
Prayers for the Holy Communion	333
Special Duties recommended to Christian People	337

MEDITATIONS AND DEVOTIONS.

As for me, God forbid that I should sin against the Lord in ceasing to *pray* before Him for you, and to *shew* you the good and the right way. 1 *P. Sam.* xii. 23.

But we will give ourselves continually to *prayer,* and to the *ministry* of the *word. Acts* vi. 4.

[*The Times of Prayer.*]

Pray { *Always. S. Luke* xviii. 1.
        Without ceasing. 1 *Thess.* v. 17.
        At all seasons. Ephes. vi. 18.

Three times a day he used to kneel on his knees, and to *pray,* and to *give thanks* before his God, as he used to do afore-time. *P. Dan.* vi. 10.

Evening, and *morning,* and *noon* will I pray, and cry aloud, and He will hear my voice. *Psal.* lv. 18.

Seven times a day do I praise thee. *Psal.* cxix. 164.

1. In the *morning,* a great while before day. *S. Mark* i. 35.
2. In the *dawnings* of the morning. *Psal.* lxiii. 7. *secund.* LXX.
3. At the *third hour* of the day. *S. Mark* xv. 25. *Acts* ii. 15.
4. About the *sixth hour. Acts* x. 9.
5. At the hour of prayer, being the *ninth hour. Acts* iii. 1.
6. At *evening. Gen.* xxiv. 63.
7. By *night. Psal.* cxxxiv. 2.

At *midnight. Psal.* cxix. 62. *Acts* xvi. 25.

[*The Places of Prayer.*]

In *all places,* wheresoever I record *My Name,* I will come unto thee, and I will bless thee. *Exod.* xx. 24.

Congregation.
In the *assembly* of the righteous, and in the *congregation*. Psal. cxi. 1.

Closet.
Enter into thy *closet*, and when thou hast shut the door, pray in *secret*. S. Matt. vi. 6.

Housetop.
He went up on the *housetop* to pray. Acts x. (9.)

Temple.
They went up into the Temple. Acts iii. 1.

Sea-shore.
We kneeled down on the *shore*. Acts xxi. 5.

Garden.
Christ in the *garden*. S. John xviii. 1. collated with S. Matt. xxvi. 36.

Bed.
Upon their *beds*. Psal. cxlix. 5.

Wilderness.
Christ withdrew himself into the *wilderness*, and prayed. S. Luke v. 16.

Pray *every where*, lifting up holy hands, without wrath and doubting. 1 Tim. ii. 8.

[*The* Gestures *of the* Body, *denoting the* Affections *of the* Soul.]

1. *Bowing* of the *knees*.

Falling on the { *Knees.*
                  Face.

Humility and *dejection* of *soul*.

    My *soul* is brought low even unto the *dust;* my *belly* cleaveth unto the ground. Psal. xliv. 25.

2. *Bowing* of the *head*.
    Shamefastness.
    Heaviness.

3. *Smiting* on the *breast*.
    * *Indignation.*

4. *Trembling*.
    * *Fear.*

5. *Sighing, Wringing* of the *hands*.
     Sorrow.

6. *Lifting up* of the $\begin{cases} Eyes. \\ Hands. \end{cases}$
     * *Vehement desire.*

7. *Chastising* and keeping the body under.
     * *Revenge.*

     * 2 *Corinth.* vii. 11.

[*Prayers Preparatory to all our Devotions.*]

O Thou that hearest prayer, unto Thee shall all flesh come; *Even my flesh shall come.*

My misdeeds prevail against me; O be Thou merciful unto my sins. *Psal.* lxv. 2, 3.

Thou shalt open my lips, O Lord: and my mouth shall shew Thy praise. *Psal.* li. 15.

[*At our Entrance into the Church.*]

As for me, I will come into Thy house, even upon the multitude of Thy mercy; and in Thy fear will I worship towards Thy holy Temple. *Psal.* v. 7.

O Lord, hear the voice of my humble petitions, when I cry unto Thee; when I hold up my hands toward the *mercy-seat* of Thy holy Temple. *Psal.* xxviii. 2.

We wait for Thy loving-kindness, O God, in the midst of Thy Temple. *Psal.* xlviii. 8.

Be mindful of the brethren who are present, and join together in prayer with us now:

Remember their devotion and their zeal.

Be mindful of them also who upon good cause are absent:

And have mercy upon them and us, according to the multitude of Thy mercies, O Lord.

We bless Thee

for our $\begin{cases} \text{Godly Princes,} \\ \text{Orthodox Prelates,} \end{cases}$

and for the founders of *this* Thy holy habitation.

Glory be to Thee, O Lord, glory be to Thee; glory be to Thee, because Thou hast glorified them; for and with whom we also glorify Thee.

Let Thine eyes be open, and Thine ears graciously attent, to hear the prayer which Thy servant prayeth in this place, wherein Thy Name is called upon. 2 *Chron.* vi. 20, 33, 40.

Woe is me, I have sinned against Thee, O Lord,
I have sinned against Thee:
O how evilly have I done;
And yet Thou hast not requited me, according to my sins. *H. Job* xxxiii. 27. *secund.* LXX.

But I am ashamed,
And turn from my wicked ways,
And return to my own heart,
And with all my heart I return to Thee,
And seek Thy face;
And pray unto Thee:
    saying,
I have sinned, I have done perversely, I have committed wickedness;
Lord, I know the plague of my own heart, and, behold, I return unto Thee with all my heart, and with all my might.
And now, O Lord, in Thy dwelling place, the glorious throne of Thy kingdom in heaven, hear the prayer and supplication of Thy servant.*
And be merciful unto Thy servant, and heal his soul. *Psal.* xli. 4.

* [*K. Solomon's Prayer at the Dedication of the Temple,*
    1 Kings viii. and 2 Chron. vi.]

I dare not so much as lift up mine eyes unto heaven,
But standing afar off,
I smite upon my breast,
And say with the publican,
God be merciful to me a sinner. *S. Luke* xviii. 13.
To me, a greater sinner than the publican, be merciful as to the publican.

The earnest desire of man shall be to Thy praise, and the continuance of that desire shall hold a festival to Thee. *Psal.* lxxvi. 10. *secund.* LXX.

[*Morning Prayer.*]

Glory be to Thee, O Lord; glory be to Thee: glory be to Thee, who hast given me sleep, for the refreshing of my weakness, and for the ease of my labours of this flesh subject to weariness.

* That this day, and every day may come on perfect, holy, peaceable, healthful, and without sin,

 Grant, Lord, we beseech Thee.

* That an angel of peace, a faithful guide, a guardian of our souls and bodies, may pitch a tent about us, and ever suggest what is needful for my salvation,

 Grant, Lord, we beseech Thee.

* The pardon and remission of all sins, and of all transgressions,

 Grant, Lord, we beseech Thee.

* What things are good and profitable to our souls, together with peace in this world,

 Grant, Lord, we beseech Thee.

* That we accomplish the rest of our life in repentance and godly fear, in health and peace,

 Grant, Lord, we beseech Thee.

* What things are true, what are honest, what are just, what are pure, what are lovely, what are of good report, wherein there is virtue, wherein there is praise, that we may reckon of these things to do them, *Philip.* iv. 8.

 Grant, Lord, we beseech Thee.

* A Christian end of our life, without sin, without shame, and, if Thou think good, without pain, and a good apology at the dreadful and terrible tribunal of our Lord Jesus Christ,

 Grant, Lord, we beseech Thee.

   * *S. Chrysost. Liturgy.*

O Being above all being, O uncreated Nature, Thou Framer of the whole world,

 I set Thee, Lord, before me. *Psal.* xvi. 9.
 I lift up my soul unto Thee. *Psal.* xxv. 1.
 I fall down on my knees and worship Thee. *Psal.* xcv. 6.
 I humble myself under Thy mighty hand. 1 *S. Pet.* v. 6.
 I stretch forth my hands unto Thee,
 My soul [is] for Thee, as ground without water. *Psal.*cxliii.6.
 I smite upon my breast, and say with the publican,
 God be merciful unto me a sinner, *S. Luke* xviii. 13.
 To me altogether a sinner;

To me the chief of sinners, 1 *Tim.* i. 15.

To me, a greater sinner than the publican, be merciful as to the publican.

O Father of mercies,

I beseech Thee, by Thy fatherly bowels of compassion,
 Despise me not;

An unclean worm. *Psal.* xxii. 6.

A dead dog. 2 *P. Sam.* ix. 8.

A stinking carcass.
 Despise me not,

The work of thy hands. *Psal.* cxxxviii. 8.

Thine own image. *Gen.* i. 27.
 Despise me not,

Though I bear the brands of mine iniquity.

Lord, if Thou wilt, Thou canst make me clean:

Lord, speak the word only, and I shall be cleansed. *S. Matt.* viii. 2, 8.

And Thou, O Saviour Christ,
 O Christ my Saviour,

Saviour of sinners, of whom I am chief, 1 *Tim.* i. 15.
 Despise me not,

Despise me not,
  O Lord,

The price of Thine own blood;

Upon whom Thy Name is called;
  O Lord,

Despise me not.

But look upon me with those Thine eyes, with which Thou lookedst

upon { Mary Magdalene at the feast,
Peter in the high-priest's hall,
The thief on the cross:
  That, with

The thief, I may humbly call upon Thee, saying, Lord, remember me in Thy kingdom; *S. Luke* xxiii. 42.

Peter, I may weep bitterly. *S. Matt.* xxvi. 75. And, oh that mine eyes were a fountain of tears, that I might weep day and night! *P. Jer.* ix. 1.

Mary Magdalene, I may hear Thee saying, Thy sins are

forgiven thee. And that with her I may love much, because my many and manifold sins are forgiven me. *S.Luke* vii. 47, 48.

And Thou, all-holy, and gracious, and quickening Spirit,
    Despise me not:
Despise me not,
Thine own { Inspiration, Holy thing;
But turn Thee again, O Lord, at the last, and be entreated to look upon Thy servant. *Psal.* xc. 13.

Blessed art Thou, O Lord our God, the God of our fathers,
Who turnest the shadow of death into the morning. *P. Amos* v. 8.
And renewest the face of the earth. *Psal.* civ. 30.
Who hast dispelled the darkness, by the presence of the light;
Who separatest the night, and bringest in the day;
Who hast lightened mine eyes, that I sleep not in death. *Psal.* xiii. 3.
Who hast delivered me from the terrors of the night; and from the pestilence that walketh in darkness. *Psal.* xci. 5, 6.
Who hast driven sleep from mine eyes, and slumber from mine eyelids. *Psal.* cxxxii. 4.
Who makest joyful outgoings of the morning and evening. *Psal.* lxv. 8.
For I laid me down and slept; and rose up again. *Psal.* iii. 5.
And Thou, Lord, madest me dwell in safety. *Psal.* iv. 9.
For I waked and beheld; and my sleep was sweet unto me. *P. Jerem.* xxxi. 26.

O Lord, blot out as a night-mist mine iniquities. *P. Isa.* xliv. 22.
Scatter my sins as a morning cloud.
Grant that I may become a child of the light, and of the day. 1 *Thess.* v. 5.
That I may walk soberly, chastely, and honestly, as in the day. *Rom.* xiii. 13.
Vouchsafe to keep me this day without sin. *Te Deum.*
Uphold me when I am falling, and lift me up when I am down. *Psal.* cxlv. 14.

That I may never harden my heart, as in the provocation, *Psal.* xcv. 8, with the temptation or deceitfulness of any sin. *Heb.* iii. 8, 13.

Moreover, deliver me this day

From
{ The snare of the hunter,
The noisome pestilence,
The arrow that flieth by day,
Mischance,
The noon-day destruction. *Psal.* xci. 3, 5, 6.

Preserve this day from any evil of mine; and me from the evils of the day.

Let not my days consume in vanity, nor my years in trouble. *Psal.* lxxviii. 33.

Let one day certify another. *Psal.* xix. 2.

Let this day add some knowledge or practice to yesterday.

Psal. cxliii.

O let me hear Thy loving-kindness betimes in the morning, for in Thee is my trust: shew Thou me the way that I should walk in, for I lift up my soul unto Thee. *Ver.* 8.

Deliver me, O Lord, from mine enemies: for I fly unto Thee to hide me. *Ver.* 9.

Teach me to do the thing that pleaseth Thee, for Thou art my God:

Let Thy loving Spirit lead me forth in the way of righteousness. *Ver.* 10.

Quicken me, O Lord, for Thy Name's sake: and for Thy righteousness' sake bring my soul out of trouble. *Ver.* 11.

Remove from my mind, *thoughts* that are *without understanding*. *Wisd.* i. 5.

Inspire *good thoughts* into me, even such as shall be *well-pleasing* unto Thee.

Turn away mine *eyes*, lest they behold *vanity*. *Psal.* cxix. 37.

Let mine *eyes* look after that which is *right*, and mine *eyelids* after *just* things. *Prov.* iv. 25.

Hedge in mine *ears* with thorns, that they listen not to *foolish discourses*.

In the morning give me an *ear* to hear with; and open mine *ears* to the *doctrine* of *Thy oracles*. *P. Isa.* l. 4, 5.

Set a watch, O Lord, before my *mouth*: and a door, with a guard, about my *lips*. *Psal.* cxli. 3.

Let my *speech* be seasoned with salt, *Col.* iv. 6, that it may minister *grace* unto the hearers. *Ephes.* iv. 29.

Let me do nothing that shall make my *heart* ache, or be a scandal to me. 1 *P. Sam.* xxv. 31.

But let my *doings* be such, for which Thou mayest *remember me for good*: And spare me according to the greatness of Thy mercy. *H. Nehem.* xiii. 22, 31.

Into Thy hands I commend

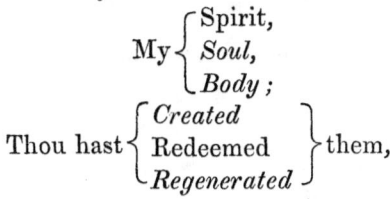

O Lord, Thou God of truth. *Psal.* xxxi. 6.

And, with myself, I *commend unto Thee* all mine, and all that belong unto me.

Thou, O Lord, hast graciously given them unto Thy servant. *Gen.* xxxiii. 5.

Preserve us, O Lord, from all evil: O Lord, I beseech Thee, keep our souls. *Psal.* cxxi. 7.

Keep us from falling, and present us faultless before the presence of Thy glory, *S. Jude* ver. 24, at that day, 2 *Tim.* i. 18.

O Lord, preserve my going out, and my coming in, from this time forth for evermore. *Psal.* cxxi. 8.

Prosper, I beseech Thee, Thy servant this day: and grant him mercy in the sight of all he shall meet with. *P. Nehem.* i. 11.

Haste Thee, O God, to deliver me: make haste to help me, O Lord. *Psal.* lxx. 1.

O turn Thee unto me, and have mercy upon me; give Thy strength unto Thy servant, and help the son of Thine handmaid. Shew some good token upon me for good; *that I be not put to shame in the sight of them that hate me;* because Thou, Lord, hast holpen me, and comforted me. *Psal.* lxxxvi. 16, 17.

☉ a

By the tender mercies of our God, the Day-spring from on high hath visited us.   *S. Luke* i. 78.

Glory be to Thee,
    O Lord,
Glory be to Thee,
Who createdst the *Light,* to enlighten the world.   *Genes.* i. 2.
  The *Visible* Light:
  The beams
    of the sun;
  The flame
    of fire;
  The day and night;
  The evening and morning.
  The *Intelligible* Light;
    That which is
    ⎰ Known of God.   *Rom.* i. 19.
    ⎱ Written in the Law.   *S. Luke* x. 26.
  The oracles
    of the Prophets;
  The melody
    of the Psalms;
  The instruction
    of the Proverbs;
  The knowledge
    of Histories.
  The *Eternal* Light,
    without any evening.
God is the Lord, who hath shewed us *light:* keep an holy-day, full crowding up even to the horns of the altar. *Psal.* cxviii. 27.

   [a] [☉ The planetary character or hieroglyphic of 𝕾𝖀𝕹𝕯𝕬𝖄𝕰, called in Holy Scripture, The First Day, *Genes.* i. 5; The First Day of the Sabbath, 1 *Cor.* xvi. 2; and, The Lord's-Day, *Revel.* ii. 10.]

By Thy *Resurrection* raise us unto newness of life, affording unto us the means of repentance.

O God of peace, who didst bring again from the dead the Lord Jesus Christ, the great Shepherd of the sheep, through the blood of the everlasting Testament;

Make us perfect in every good work, to do His will, working in us that which is well-pleasing in His sight, through Jesus Christ; to whom be glory for ever and ever. Amen. *Heb.* xiii. 20, 21.

O Thou, who, upon *this* day, didst send down Thy most Holy Spirit upon Thy disciples, withdraw not the same again from us, but renew it daily in us, *Psal.* li. 10, 11, who call upon Thee.

Merciful and gracious Lord, long-suffering, and of great pity, I have sinned, Lord, I have sinned against Thee.

O wretched man that I am! *Rom.* vii. 24.

I have sinned against Thee, O Lord, I have greatly and grievously sinned; and that by giving heed to vanity and lies. *P. Jonas* ii. 8.

I conceal nothing. *H. Jos.* vii. 19.
I pretend no pretences. *Psal.* cxli. 4.
I give glory unto Thee, O Lord, this day. *H. Jos.* vii. 19.
I confess my sins against myself;
In very deed I have sinned against the Lord; and thus and thus have I done. *H. Jos.* vii. 20.
O what have I done? *P. Jer.* viii. 6, and Thou hast not punished me, as my sins have deserved. *H. Job* xxxiii. 27.

And now what shall I say? or, how shall I open my mouth?
What shall I answer, for I, even I have done it.
I am
 Without $\begin{cases} \text{any pretence,} \\ \text{all excuse.} \end{cases}$ *Rom.* ii. 1.
I am condemned of myself. *Tit.* iii. 11.
My destruction is from myself. *P. Hos.* xiii. 9.
To Thee, O Lord, belongeth righteousness: but to me confusion of face. *P. Dan.* ix. 7.

And Thou art just in all that is come upon me; for Thou hast done right, but I have done wickedly. *H. Neh.* ix. 33.

And now what is my hope? Art not Thou, O Lord?
Surely, my hope is from Thee. *Psal.* xxxix. 7.
Surely, I have hope of salvation,
Surely, Thy loving-kindness vanquisheth the multitude of my sins.

O remember upon what I subsist. *Psal.* lxxxix. 46.

> That I am
> The work
> > of Thy hands,
> The image
> > of Thy countenance,
> The price
> > of Thy blood,
> Called by Thy Name, A sheep
> > of Thy flock,
> A son
> > of Thy covenant.

O despise not the work of Thine own hands. *Psal.* cxxxviii. 8.
Despise not Thy image and likeness.
Hast Thou made me for nought? *Psal.* lxxxix. 46.
Even for nought, if Thou destroy me.
And, What profit is there in my destruction? *Psal.* xxx. 9.

Thy enemies will rejoice at it. *Psal.* xxxv. 19.
Let them not rejoice, O Lord;
Do not gratify Thine enemies with my destruction.

Look upon the face of Thy Christ; *Psal.* lxxxiv. 9.
And by the blood of Thy testament, *P. Zech.* ix. 11.
By His propitiation for the sins of the whole world, 1 *S. John* ii. 2.
Lord, be merciful to me a sinner. *S. Luke* xviii. 13.
Be merciful, O Lord, to me,
the { first, chief, greatest } of sinners.

For Thy Name's sake, O Lord, be merciful to my sin,

For it is $\begin{cases} \text{great, } Psal. \text{ xxv. 11.} \\ \text{very great;} \end{cases}$

Even for that Thy Name, beside which there is no other name under heaven given among men, whereby we may be saved. *Acts* iv. 12.

The *Holy Spirit* Himself helping our infirmities, and making intercession for us, with groanings which cannot be uttered. *Rom.* viii. 26.

For the
Paternal bowels
  of God the Father;
Bleeding wounds
  of God the Son;
Unutterable groans
  of God the Holy Ghost.

O Lord, hear; O Lord, forgive;
O Lord, hearken and do;
Defer not, for Thine own sake, O Lord, O Lord, my God. P. *Dan.* ix. 19.

But, as for me, I do not forget my offences; for they are ever before me. *Psal.* li. 3.

I recount them in the bitterness of my soul. H. *Job* vii. 11.
I am perplexed, I take thought for them. *Psal.* xxxviii. 18.
And turning myself, I mourn. P. *Isa.* xxx. 15. *secundum* LXX.

I am moved with indignations,
$\left.\begin{array}{l} \text{I take vengeance on} \\ \text{I am displeased with} \\ \text{I abhor and chasten} \end{array}\right\}$ myself,

That I do it no $\begin{cases} \text{better.} \\ \text{fuller.} \end{cases}$

I repent, Lord; Lord, I repent:
Help Thou my want of repentance:
And yet more and more
$\left.\begin{array}{l} \text{Pierce} \\ \text{Break} \\ \text{Grind} \end{array}\right\}$ my heart,

Pass by, forgive, and pardon all my transgressions, which make my heart ache, and are a scandal to me. 1 *P. Sam.* xxv. 31.

Cleanse Thou me from my secret faults;

Keep Thy servant also from presumptuous sins. *Psal.* xix. 12, 13.

Make Thy mercies to be admired over me, who am an high and notorious sinner;

And say unto me in due time, Be of good cheer, Thy sins are forgiven thee. *S. Matt.* ix. 2.

My grace is sufficient for thee. 2 *Cor.* xii. 9.

Say unto my soul, I am thy salvation. *Psal.* xxxv. 3.

Why art thou so heavy, O my soul? and why art thou so disquieted within me? *Psal.* xlii. 6, 14, and xliii. 5.

Turn again then unto thy rest, O my soul: for the Lord will be gracious unto thee. *Psal.* cxvi. 7.

* O Lord, rebuke me not in Thine indignation, neither chasten me in Thy heavy displeasure. *Psal.* vi. 1.

* I said, I will confess my sins unto the Lord, and so Thou forgavest the wickedness of my heart. *Psal.* xxxii. 6.

* Lord, Thou knowest all my desire, and my groaning is not hid from Thee. *Psal.* xxxviii. 9.

* Have mercy upon me, O Lord, after Thy great goodness, according to the multitude of Thy mercies, do away mine offences. *Psal.* li. 1.

* Lord, Thou shalt arise, and have mercy upon *me*, for it is time that Thou have mercy upon *me*, yea, the time is come. *Psal.* cii. 13.

* If Thou, Lord, wilt be extreme to mark what is done amiss, O Lord, who may abide it? *Psal.* cxxx. 3.

* Enter not into judgment with Thy servant; for in Thy sight shall no man living be justified. *Psal.* cxliii. 2.

* *Collected out of the Seven Penitentials.*

I lift up my hands, O Lord, unto Thy commandments, which I have loved. *Psal.* cxix. 48.

Open mine eyes, and I shall see. *Ver.* 18.

Incline my heart, *ver.* 36, and I shall affect.

Order my steps, *ver.* 133, and I shall walk in the path of Thy commandments.

O Lord God,

Be Thou my God.
Let me have no other God but Thee;
No other beside Thee;
Nothing else with Thee.

Grant that

I may worship and serve Thee,

With { 1. Truth of spirit;
2. Decency of body;
3. Benediction of mouth;

In 4. Public and private.

Grant also,

That I may render,

5. Honour to my governors,

By obedience and submission to them who have the rule over me, *Heb.* xiii. 17.

Natural affection to those who belong to me,

By taking care of, and providing for them. 1 *Tim.* v. 8.

That I may,

6. Overcome evil with good. *Rom.* xii. 21.
7. Keep my vessel in holiness and honour. 1 *Thess.* iv. 4.
8. Have my conversation without covetousness, and be content with such things as I have. *Heb.* xiii. 5.
9. Profess the truth with charity. *Ephes.* iv. 15.

10. Desire, not { Covet.
Lust in concupiscence. 1 *Thess.* iv. 5.
Walk after my lusts. 1 *S. Pet.* iv. 3.
S. Jude ver. 16.

The Fence of the Law.

[*Give me grace, O Lord,*]

To { Bruise the serpent's head. *Gen.* iii. 15.
Remember the last ends. *Deut.* xxxii. 29.
Cut off the occasions of sin. 2 *Cor.* xi. 12.
Be sober. 1 *S. Pet.* v. 8.

Not to sit idle. *S. Matt.* xx. 6.

To
- Shun wicked company. *Psal.* xxvi. 4, 5. *Tit.* iii. 10.
- Consort with good men. *Rom.* xii. 9.
- Make a covenant with mine eyes. *H. Job* xxxi. 1.
- Bring my body into subjection. 1 *Cor.* ix. 27.
- Set apart times for prayer. 1 *Cor.* vii. 5.
- Withdraw myself for [*the exercise of*] repentance. 2 *S. Pet.* iii. 9.

Hedge up my way with thorns, that I find not the path to follow after vanity. *P. Hos.* ii. 6.

Hold me in with bit and bridle, when I keep not close to Thee. *Psal.* xxxii. 9.

O Lord, compel me to come in unto Thee. *S. Luke* xiv. 23.

Lord, I believe

In Thee, the { Father, Word, Spirit, } One God.

1. That by Thy love and power all things were created.
2. That, by Thy goodness and love to mankind, were gathered together in one all things in Thy Word.

Who,

For us men, and for our Salvation,
was made flesh;
Conceived and Born;
Did Suffer,
was Crucified;
Did Die,
was Buried;
Did Descend;
and Rose again;
Did Ascend,
and Sitteth;
Shall
Return, Reward.

3. That by the illumination and operation of the Holy Spirit, a peculiar people is called, out of the whole world, to be a corporation,

According to
- The belief of the truth. 2 *Thess.* ii. 13.
- Holiness of conversation. 1 *S. Pet.* iii. 2.

By whom we are made partakers
> Of the
Communion } of { Saints,
Remission   { Sins,
  in this present world;
By whom we look
  For { Resurrection of the flesh,
      { Eternal life,
  in the world to come.

This most holy faith, once delivered to the Saints, (*S. Jude*, ver. 3,)
Lord, I believe;
Help Thou mine unbelief, *S. Mark* ix. 24.
Supply the defects of my weak faith. *S. Luke* xvii. 5.
> Grant me also,
To { Love the *Father* for His tender love.
   { Adore the *Almighty*, for His power.
To commit the keeping of my soul to Him, in well-doing, as unto a faithful *Creator*. 1 *S. Pet.* iv. 19.
> Grant me to enjoy
From { Jesus, } Salvation,
     { Christ, } Anointing,
     { the only-begotten Son,
       Adoption.
> To serve the Lord,
For His Conception,
  in faith.
For His Nativity,
  in humility.
For His Sufferings,
  in patience and antipathy to sin.
For His Cross,
  in crucifying all occasions of sin.
For His Death,
  in mortifying the flesh.
For His Burial,
  in burying my bad purposes by good works.
For His Descent,
  in meditation upon hell.

For His Resurrection,
> in newness of life.

For His Ascension,
> in setting my affections on things above.

For His Session,
> in seeking those better things at His right hand.

For His Return,
> in awe of His second coming.

For His Judgment,
> in judging myself, before I come to be judged.

From the Spirit,
> To receive
> The breath of saving grace.
>> To be partaker
> In the Church,
>> of vocation;
> In the Holy Church,
>> of sanctification;
> In the Catholic Church,
>> of distribution and communication,
> Of the
>> Holy mysteries,
>> Prayers,
>> Fastings, groans,
>> Watchings, tears,
> and suffering of afflictions.
> To a firm persuasion of the remission of my sins.
> To a confident hope
> Of { Resurrection / Translation } to life eternal.

O Thou, that art the hope of all the ends of the earth, and of them that remain in the broad sea, *Psal.* lxv. 5.

O Thou, on whom our fathers hoped, and Thou didst deliver them; on whom they trusted, and were not confounded. *Psal.* xxii. 4, 5.

O Thou, who art my hope
> Even from my Youth, *Psal.* lxxi. 4.
>> Mother's breasts,
> On whom I have been left from the womb, *Psal.* xxii. 9, 10.

Be Thou still, and still, my hope and my portion in the land of the living. *Psal.* cxlii. 6.
    My hope is in
      Thy
    Nature, Names,
    Types, Word,
      Deed.
O let me not be ashamed of this my hope. *Psal.* cxix. 116.

O Thou, who art the hope of all the ends of the earth, *Psal.* lxv. 5.
    Remember all Thy creatures for good.
    Visit the world with Thy mercies.
    O Thou preserver of men, *H. Job* vii. 20.
    O Lord, the lover of men,
    Remember all mankind; and
    Thou, who hast shut up all in unbelief, *Rom.* xi. 32.
    Have mercy upon all, O Lord.
    O Thou, who didst die, rise, and revive,
    That Thou mightest be Lord both of the dead and living, *Rom.* xiv. 9.
    Whether we live or die,
    Thou art our Lord. *Ver.* 8.
    Whether living or dying,
      Have mercy upon us, O Lord.
O Thou, the helper of the helpless, the refuge in due time of trouble, *Psal.* ix. 9.
    Remember all who are in any necessity, and stand in need
      of Thy help.
    O Thou, the God of grace and truth, *S. John* i. 14.
    Confirm all who stand in grace and truth. 1 *Thess.* iii.
      2, 13. and 2 *S. Pet.* i. 12.
    Restore all who are sick of heresy and sin. *Gal.* vi. 1.
      and 1 *Tim.* vi. 4.
O Thou, who art the buckler and horn of salvation, through Thy Christ, *Psal.* xxviii. 9.
    Think upon Thy congregation, whom Thou hast purchased
      and redeemed of old. *Psal.* lxxiv. 2.
    Let there be one heart and one soul of all believers.
      Acts iv. 32.

O Thou, who walkest in the midst of the golden candlesticks, *Revel.* ii. 1.
> Remove not our candlestick out of the place thereof. *Revel.* ii. 5.
> Set in order the things that are wanting. *Tit.* i. 5.
> Establish what remains, which Thou mightest reject. *Revel.* iii. 2.

O Thou, who art the Lord of the harvest,
> Send forth labourers *sufficiently enabled by Thee* into Thy harvest. *S. Matt.* ix. 38.

O Thou, who art the portion of them who continually attend in Thy temple, 1 *Corinth.* ix. 13.
> Grant, that
> - Thy Clergy may rightly divide the Word of Truth, 2 *Tim.* ii. 15.
> - They may walk uprightly, according to the same. *Gal.* ii. 14.
>
> Grant, that all they who love Christ may obey and submit themselves to them. *Heb.* xiii. 17.

O Thou, the King of all nations to the ends of the earth,
> Establish all Governments in all the world, as being *Thine own* ordinance, *Rom.* xiii. 2, though an ordinance among men. 1 *S. Pet.* ii. 13.
> Scatter Thou the people that delight in war. *Psal.* lxviii. 30.
> Make wars to cease in all the world. *Psal.* xlvi. 9.

O Lord, who art the hope of the islands, and on whom the isles wait, *P. Isa.* li. 5. and lx. 9.
> Deliver this island and country wherein we dwell, from all distress, danger, and necessity. *S. Chrysost.*

O Thou, who art the Lord of lords, and Prince of princes,
> Be mindful of all princes, to whom Thou hast given right to rule upon earth.
> But, above all, be mindful of our most gracious King, preserved by Thee:
> Work mightily with him, and prosper him in all things:
> Speak good unto his soul, for Thy Church's, and for Thy people's sake.
> Grant unto him a settled peace, which may not be taken away;

That in his prosperity we may lead a quiet and peaceable life, in all godliness and honesty. 1 *Tim.* ii. 2. *S. Chrysost.*

O Thou, by whom all powers are ordained and ordered,

Grant to

All that be in eminency at Court, that they may be eminent in virtue, and in the fear of Thee,

The Council, Thy holy wisdom,

All that are in power and authority over us, that they may have no power to do anything against the truth, but for the truth, 2 *Corinth.* xiii. 8.

The Judges, Thy judgments, that they may judge all persons in all causes, without prejudice and partiality. 1 *Tim.* v. 21.

O God of Sabaoth, Thou Lord of Hosts,

Prosper and strengthen all Christian armies against the enemies of our most holy faith.

Grant to

All the people of this kingdom, to be subject to their prince, not only for *wrath*, but also for *conscience* sake, *Rom.* xiii. 5.

Husbandmen and dealers in cattle, fruitful seasons,

The navy and fishermen, calm seas and happy passage,

Tradesmen, grace, not to overreach one another,

Artificers and workmen, even to the poorest beggars, to do their work, and deal uprightly in their vocations.

O God, the God not of *us* alone, but also of *our seed*,

Bless all the youth among us, that they may grow up in wisdom and stature, and favour with God and men. *S. Luke* ii. 52.

O Thou, who commandest us to provide for our own, 1 *Timoth.* v. 8, and hatest them who are without natural affection,

Remember, O Lord, all my kindred according to the flesh; *Rom.* ix. 3.

Grant that I may speak peace to them, and seek their good.

O Thou, who willest us to recompense them who do good to us,

> Remember, O Lord, for good all whom I have received any benefit from;
> Preserve them, and keep them alive, that they may be blessed upon earth; and deliver Thou not them into the will of their enemies. *Psal.* xli. 2.

O Thou, who hast taught us, that he who provideth not for his own house is worse than an infidel, 2 *Tim.* v. 8.

> Remember, according to Thy good pleasure, all in my family;
> Peace be to my house,
> The Son of peace be with all therein. *S. Luke* x. 5, 6.

O Thou, who hast commanded, that our righteousness exceed the righteousness of sinners, *S. Matt.* v. 20.

Grant, O Lord,

That I may { Love them that love me. *S. Matt.* v. 45.
Never forsake mine, or my parents' friends,
and the children of those friends.

O Thou, who hast commanded us to overcome evil with good, *Rom.* xii. 21, and to pray for them who despitefully use us, *S. Matt.* v. 44.

> Be merciful to mine enemies, O Lord, even as to myself; and bring them, with me, unto Thy heavenly kingdom.

O Thou, who graciously respectest the prayers of Thy servants, which they make for others;

> Remember, O Lord, for good, and shew mercy unto all, who remember me in their prayers; and shew mercy unto all, whom I am desired to remember in mine.

O Thou, who in every good work acceptest of a ready mind; 2 *Corinth.* viii. 12.

> Remember them, O Lord, who, upon reasonable causes, find no leisure to pray; even as Thou dost them who call upon Thee.

Thou wilt arise and have mercy upon all who are in extreme necessity; for it is time that Thou have mercy upon them; yea, the time is come. *Psal.* cii. 13.

> Be merciful to them, O Lord, as to myself in my extremity.

Be mindful,
O Lord,
                    Of
The { Infants, { Children,
     Lads,   Youth,
     Men,   Aged;
            All
In extreme age and weakness;
    The
Hungry,   Thirsty,
Naked,   Sick,
Prisoners,   Strangers,
Harbourless,   Unburied;
                Such as are
Possessed by the Devil, and tempted to make themselves away;
Vexed with unclean spirits; *Acts* v. 16.
In despair;
    Sick in { Soul,
             Body;
Faint-hearted;
In prison and bonds;
Condemned to die;
            All
Orphans, widows;
Strangers;
Travellers by { Land,
                Water;
Women { With child,
        Giving suck;
In hard servitude,
    In the { Mines,
             Galleys;
In solitude.

Thou, Lord, shalt save both man and beast. How excellent is Thy mercy, O God! and, doubtless, the children of men shall put their trust under the shadow of Thy wings. *Psal.* xxxvi. 7.

The Lord bless us, and keep us; the Lord make His face to shine upon us, and be gracious unto us;

The Lord lift up His countenance upon us, and give us peace. *Numb.* vi. 24—26.

Lord, I commend unto Thee
My {
  Soul and body,
  Mind and thoughts,
  Prayers and wishes,
  Senses and members,
  Life and death,
}
My brethren and sisters, and their children,
My friends
  and benefactors,
My family
  and neighbours,
All commended to my prayers,
This my native country, and all Christian people.

Let us lift up our hearts unto the Lord, as it is very meet, right, and our bounden duty that we should *in* all, and *for all things, at* all *times, in* all *places, by* all *means,* ever, every where, every way,
Make mention of Thee,
Confess to Thee,
Bless Thee,
Worship Thee,
Praise Thee,
Sing laud to Thee,
Give thanks to Thee,
The {
  Creator,
  Nourisher,
  Preserver,
  Governor,
  Physician,
  Benefactor,
  Perfecter,
  Lord and Father,
  King and God,
} of all;
The {
  Fountain of Life and Immortality,
  Treasury of eternal good things:
}
  Whom

The {Heavens, and the heavens of heavens,
Angels, and all the Celestial Powers sing praise unto ;
Uncessantly crying one to another,
(And we, base and unworthy we,
    with them, under their feet,)
       Holy, Holy, Holy,
Lord God of Hosts,
Heaven and earth is full of the Majesty of Thy glory.
   P. Isa. vi. 3.
Blessed be the glory of the Lord from His place. *P. Ezech.* iii. 12.

For His {Divinity,
Incomprehensibleness,
Sublimity,
Dominion,
Almightiness,
Eternity,
Prevision and Providence.

   My God, my
Strength and Stay,
Refuge and Deliverer,
Helper and Defender,
Horn of Salvation,
   And, my Lifter up.   *Psal.* xviii. 1.

☾ ᵃ

My voice shalt Thou hear betimes, O Lord; early in the morning will I direct my prayer unto Thee, and Thou wilt look upon me. *Psal.* v. 3.

Blessed art Thou, O Lord, who createdst the firmament of the heaven, *Gen.* i. 6.

The heaven and the heaven of heavens,
The Celestial Powers,
Angels, Archangels,
Cherubim, Seraphim;
   The waters above the heavens,
      Vapours,
      Exhalations,
         From whence
Clouds from the ends of the earth, *P. Jer.* x. 13.
Storms, dew, hail,
Snow as wool,
Hoar-frost as ashes, } *Psal.* cxlvii.
Ice as morsels:
Lightnings, thunder,
Winds out of His treasuries, *P. Jer.* x. 13.
Tempests;
The waters beneath the heavens,
   For { Drink,
          Washing.

P. Moses.

O Lord, I confess my iniquities, and the iniquities of my fathers, with the trespass which I trespassed against Thee, and that I have walked contrary unto Thee. *Levit.* xxvi. 40.

Set not, O Lord, set not my misdeeds before Thee, (my whole age is in the sight of Thy countenance. *Psal.* xc. 8.)

ᵃ [☾ The planetary character or hieroglyphic of 𝔐𝔘𝔑𝔇𝔄𝔍𝔈, called in Holy Scripture, the *Second Day*, Genes. i. 8.]

But pardon the iniquity of Thy servant, according to the greatness of Thy mercy; and as Thou hast forgiven me from my childhood even until now. *Numb.* xiv. 19.

Holy Job.

I have sinned, what shall I do unto Thee, O Thou Preserver of men?

Why hast Thou set me as a mark against Thee, so that I am a burthen to myself?

O put my wickedness out of remembrance, and wash away all my sin. *Chap.* vii. 20, 21.

Deliver me from going down into destruction, for Thou hast found in whom to be appeased. *Chap.* xxxiii. 24.

[*The Canaanitish Woman.*]

Have mercy upon me, O Son of David.

Lord, help me.

Yea, Lord, even the dogs eat of the crumbs which fall from their masters' table. *S. Matt.* xv. 22, 25, 27.

[*The Servant owing Ten Thousand Talents.*]

Lord, have patience with me: yea rather, (I confess I have nothing to pay,) forgive me all my debt, I beseech Thee. *S. Matt.* xviii. 26, 29, 32.

K. David.

1. How long wilt Thou forget me, O Lord, for ever? How long wilt Thou hide Thy face from me?

2. How long shall I seek counsel in my soul, and be so vexed in my heart? (day and night?) How long shall mine enemies triumph over me?

3. Consider and hear me, O Lord my God, lighten mine eyes that I sleep not in death.

4. Lest mine enemy say, I have prevailed against him; for if I be cast down, they that trouble me will rejoice at it.

5. But my trust is in Thy mercy. *Psal.* xiii.

[Lord,] remove far from me,

1. All { Impiety and profaneness,
        Superstition and hypocrisy.

2. Idolatry and self-will-worship.
   3. Rash oaths and cursing.
   4. Withdrawing from, and irreverence in Thy public service. *Heb.* x. 25, 38.
   5. Pride and carelessness.
   6. Strife and wrath.
   7. Wantonness and uncleanness.
   8. Idleness and deceit.
   9. Lying and slandering.
   10. All wicked and unbeseeming imaginations.

   All
Lascivious thoughts,
Filthy desires.

   Give me
   1. Piety and true godliness.
   2. Grace to adore and worship Thee.
   3. Not to speak,
  but with blessing;
 Not to swear,
  but with religion.
   4. Decent confession in the congregation.
   5. True natural affection, and a tractable disposition.
   6. Patience and meekness.
   7. Chastity and temperance.
   8. Contentation and goodness.
   9. Truth and integrity.
   10. Good thoughts, and perseverance to the end.

I BELIEVE in God,
 I. The Father
  Almighty,
  Maker of { Heaven,
      Earth.
 II. JESUS Christ, His only-begotten Son,
  Our Lord.
     Who [b]
  Was { 1. Conceived by the Holy Ghost,
     2. Born of the ever-Virgin Mary,
  3. Suffered under Pontius Pilate,

[The articles of Christ's Humiliation.]

Was {
 4. Crucified,
 5. Dead,
 6. Buried.
}
Who ^c
1. Descended into hell,
2. Rose from the dead,
3. Ascended into heaven,
4. Sitteth on the right hand,
5. Shall come thence again,
6. To judge the { Quick, Dead. }

III. The Holy Ghost.

The { 1. Holy   2. Catholic } Church.
     3. Communion of Saints.

The Forgiveness of sins.
The Resurrection of the body.
The Life everlasting.

And now, What is my hope?
Art not Thou, O Lord?
Surely my hope is from Thee. *Psal.* xxxix. 8.
In Thee, O Lord, have I put my trust, *Psal.* xxxviii. 15.
Let me never be confounded. *Psal.* xxv. 1

Let us beg of the Lord,
  For all creatures,
    the gift of
Healthful ⎫
Fruitful   ⎬ times.
Peaceful ⎭
  For all mankind,
    Not Christians,
{ Atheists, Ungodly,
      Heathens,
  Turks, Jews, }
    Conversion;
    Christians,

---

^c [(The articles of Christ's) Exaltation.]

{ Labouring under { Infirmities,
                   Sins,
          Restoration ;
  Endowed with { Grace,
                 Truth,

    Confirmation ;
Help and comfort to all men and women labouring under
    Dejection of mind,
    Infirmity of body,
    Poverty, trouble;
Thankfulness and moderation to all that enjoy,
    Cheerfulness of mind,
    Health of body,
    Plenty of estate,
    Freedom from trouble ;
    For the Church
Catholic,
    Confirmation, and
    Enlargement ;
Eastern,
    Deliverance, and
    Unity ;
Western,
    Perfection, and
    Peace ;
British,
  { Supply of what is wanting,
    Establishment of what remains.

    [*Let us beseech the Lord,*]
  For the { Bishops,
         Presbyters,
And all the people that love Christ ;
    For all estates
Throughout the world,
  { Christian and other,
    Neighbouring,
    This, among us ;
    For all in authority.

Our King, preserved by God,
The { Queen,
{ Prince,
Courtiers, Counsellors,
   Judges, Magistrates,
People, Under-Officers,
   Husbandmen,
Dealers in cattle,
   Fishermen,
Merchants, Tradesmen,
     Artificers,
  Even to the { Labourers,
            { Poor;
For the succession and good education of all the
  Royal seed,
   Noble branches;
  Students
          { Universities,
          | Inns of Court,
  In the { Schools,
          | Shops in the
                   { City,
                   { Country;
For all who are recommended to my prayers,
By kindred or alliance,
    My { Brethren,
        { Sisters,
The blessing of God be upon them and upon their children;
By the obligation of any benefit received from them,
  Do Thou requite them all, O Lord, according to that good I have received from them;
   Even all who have ministered to my necessity in carnal things;
By Tuition and Charge;
  " All instructed, and at any time,
  " Ordained by me.
    " My { College,
       { Parish.
" The Collegiate Church

of {
"Southwell,
"S. Paul,
"Westminster.

"The Dioceses of
{
"Chichester,
"Ely,
"Winchester.

The {
"Clergy,
"Laity,
"Officials,
"Governors of them,

"The Deanery of the King's Chapel,
"The Colleges committed to
"My Visitation,[d]
My Family;
By moral friendship,
   All that love me, though some of them unknown to me;
By Christian charity,
   All that hate me without a cause; and some for truth and righteousness' sake;
By neighbourhood,
   All that live quietly and harmlessly by me;
By promise,
   All whom I have undertaken to remember in my prayers;
By mutual office,
   All that remember me in their prayers; and desire the like of me;
For those, who, for want of their own leisure, and upon reasonable causes, are hindered from coming to prayers;
For those, who have nobody to pray for them in particular;
For those, who at present labour under,
{
Extreme necessity,
Great affliction;

For those, who undertake any great design, whereby glory may come to the name of God, or some great good to the Church;
For those, who have done any notable good work for the Church, or poor;

---

[d] [Instead of the Bishop's particular relation marked thus " put in your own]

For those, who at any time have been scandalized by me,
in $\begin{cases} \text{Word,} \\ \text{Deed.} \end{cases}$

Psal. lxvii.

God be merciful unto me, and bless me,
Shew me the light of His countenance, and be merciful unto me. *Ver.* 1.

God, even our God, give me His blessing. *Ver.* 6.
God bless me. *Ver.* 7.

Receive, O Lord, this my supplication,
Direct my life in Thy commandments,
Sanctify my soul,
Purify my body,
Rectify my thoughts,
Cleanse my desires,
   Renew
My $\begin{cases} \text{Soul} \\ \text{Mind} \\ \text{Heart} \end{cases}$ and $\begin{cases} \text{Body,} \\ \text{Spirit,} \\ \text{Reins,} \end{cases}$
My whole man.
For, if Thou wilt, Thou canst.

   The 1. Lord, the Lord,
     2. God,
     3. Compassionate,
     4. Merciful,
     5. Long-suffering,
      Abundant
   in $\begin{cases} \text{6. Goodness,} \\ \text{7. Truth,} \end{cases}$
     8. Keeping mercy for thousands,
Forgiving $\begin{cases} \text{9. Iniquity,} \\ \text{10. Transgression,} \\ \text{11. Sin,} \end{cases}$
     12. Not clearing the guilty,
     13. Visiting the iniquity of the fathers upon the children. *Exod.* xxxiv. 6, 7.

I will always give thanks unto the Lord : His praise shall ever be in my mouth. *Psal.* xxxiv. 1.

> Glory be to God in the Highest,
>> On earth peace,
>>> Good-will towards men. *S. Luke* ii. 14.

^eAngels,   *Tuition ;*

Archangels, 1 *Thessal.* iv. 16.
                                        Illumination ;

Virtues, 1 *S. Pet.* iii. 22.
                                        Miracles ;

Thrones,
                                        Judgment ;

Dominions,
                                        Beneficence ;

Principalities,
                                        Government ;

Powers, *Coloss.* i. 16.
                                        Against Devils ;

Cherubim,
                                        Knowledge ;

Seraphim,
                                        Charity.

^e [The Hierarchy of Heavenly Essences, commonly called the Nine Orders of Angels, with their distinct operations.]

♂ ᵃ

O GOD, Thou art my God; early will I seek Thee. *Psal.* lxiii. 1.

Blessed art Thou, O Lord, who didst gather the waters into the sea, and make the dry land appear,

Who didst cause the earth to bring forth

Herbs ⎱
Trees ⎰ yielding fruit, *Gen.* i. 9, 11.

Depths and seas, as in a bottle, *Psal.* xxxiii. 7.

Lakes, rivers, fountains;

The ⎰ Continent,
Earth, ⎱ Islands;

Mountains, hills, valleys.

Arable, meadows, woods;

Green things, ⎰ Corn, Grass, Herbs, Flowers,

For ⎰ Food, Pleasure, Medicine;

Trees, for ⎰ Fruit ⎰ Wine, Oil, Spices; Timber;

Things under the earth,

⎰ Stones,
⎱ Metals and minerals,
Coals.

Blood and fire, and vapour of smoke, *Acts* ii. 19.

K. David.

Who can tell how oft he offendeth? O cleanse Thou me from my secret faults.

ᵃ [♂ The planetary character or hieroglyphic of 𝕿𝖀𝕰𝕾𝕯𝕬𝖄𝕰, called in Holy Scripture, the *Third Day*, Genes. i. 13.]

Keep Thy servant from presumptuous sins; lest they get the dominion over me. *Psal.* xix. 12, 13.

For Thy Name's sake, be merciful unto my sin, for it is great. *Psal.* xxv. 10.

My sins have taken such hold upon me, that I am not able to look up:

Yea, they are more in number than the hairs of my head; and my heart hath failed me.

O Lord, let it be Thy pleasure to deliver me; make haste, O Lord, to help me. *Psal.* xl. 15, 16.

Show Thy marvellous loving-kindness upon me, Thou that art the Saviour of them that put their trust in Thee. *Psal.* xvii. 7.

I said, Lord, be merciful unto me; and heal my soul, for I have sinned against Thee. *Psal.* xli. 4.

K. Solomon.

I have sinned; but I am ashamed, and turn from my wicked ways; and return unto my heart; and with all my heart I return unto Thee;

And seek Thy face, and pray unto Thee; saying,

I have sinned, I have done perversely, I have committed wickedness.

Lord, I know the plague of mine own heart.

And, behold, I return unto Thee, with all my heart, and with all my strength.

And now, O Lord, from Thy habitation, and from the throne of Thy glorious kingdom in heaven, hear Thou the prayer and the supplication of Thy servant.

[b] And be merciful unto Thy servant; and heal his soul. 1 *Kings* viii. and 2 *Chron.* vi.

The Publican.

God be merciful to me a sinner. *S. Luke* xviii. 13.

Be merciful to me the chief of sinners. 1 *Tim.* i. 15.

The Prodigal.

Father, I have sinned against Heaven, and against Thee;
I am no more worthy to be called Thy son;

[b] *Psal.* xli. 4.

Make me one of Thy hired servants;
Make me one, *though even the last, and the least of them all.* S. Luke xv. 18, 19.

Psal. xxx.

What profit is there in my blood, when I go down to the pit? *Ver.* 9.

Shall the dust give thanks unto Thee? or shall it declare Thy truth? *Ver.* 10.

Hear, O Lord, and have mercy upon me; Lord, be Thou my helper. *Ver.* 11.

Turn my heaviness into joy. *Ver.* 12.

[O Lord, forgive me,]

My $\begin{cases} \text{Thoughts, slips,} \\ \text{Guilt, falls,} \\ \text{Sins, transgressions,} \\ \text{Iniquities, abominations.} \end{cases}$

[Work in me]
Carefulness,
Clearing of myself,
Indignation,
Fear,
Vehement desire,
Zeal,
Revenge, 2 *Corinth.* vii. 11.

FAITH.

I. The Deity.
$\begin{cases} \text{Love,} \\ \text{Power,} \\ \text{Providence.} \end{cases}$

II. Salvation, Anointing, Adoption,
Dominion,
Conception, Birth,
Sufferings,
Cross, Death, Burial,
Descent, Resurrection,
Ascension,

Session, Return,
   Judgment.
III. Inspiration and Sanctification.
 Calling out of ⎫
 Sanctifying in ⎬ the world.
 Communion of { Saints,
       Holy Mysteries.
 { Forgiveness of sins,
  Resurrection,
  Life eternal.

Be Thou my Hope, O Thou that art the Hope of all the ends of the earth,
And of them that remain in the broad sea. *Psal.* lxv. 5.

[Bless, O Lord,
   All]
 { Thy creatures,
  Mankind,
  Compassed with infirmities;
     { Catholic,
The Church { Eastern,
      Western,
      British;
   { Bishops,
The { Presbyters,
    Clergy,
    People that love Christ;
All estates of the world,
 { Christian,
  Neighbour,
  Our;
   Godly { Princes,
       Kings;
    Our
Counsellors,
Judges,
Magistrates,
 Commanders at { Land,
        Sea;

Commonalty.
   Succession,
     Learning;
All, in the ⎰ Court,
         ⎨ City,
         ⎱ Country;
All who any way minister
To our ⎰ Souls ⎰ Food,
      ⎱ Bodies ⎨ Raiment,
             ⎱ Health;
   Things for this life.
[All whom we are bound to pray for
     ⎧ Nature,
     ⎪ Good turns,
     ⎪ Charge ⎰ Formerly,
     ⎪   ⎱ At present,
By] ⎨ Friendship,
     ⎪ Charity,
     ⎪ Neighbourhood,
     ⎪ Promise,
     ⎩ Mutual respects;
    All who
Find no pleasure to pray,
Are in ⎰ Great want,
      ⎱ Extreme necessity.

Psal. cxxi.

The Lord be my keeper; the Lord be my defence upon my right hand. *Ver.* 5.

The Lord preserve me from all evil; yea, the Lord keep my soul. *Ver.* 7.

The Lord preserve my going out, and my coming in, from this time forth for evermore. *Ver.* 8.

O Lord, Thou knowest how, Thou art able and willing to do good to my soul:

I, wretched man that am! *Rom.* vii. 24, neither know how, nor am able, nor, as I ought, willing to do it.

Do Thou, O Lord, I beseech Thee, in Thy unspeakable

loving-kindness, so order and dispose of me, as Thou knowest to be best pleasing to Thee, and most expedient for me.

Goodness, grace, love;
Kindness, humanity; *Tit.* iii. 4.
Gentleness, meekness; 1 *Cor.* x. 1.
Forbearance, long-suffering; *Rom.* ii. 4.
    Manifold mercies,
                    1 *S. Pet.* i. 3.
    Great mercies,
             Psal. li. 1.
Compassions, *Rom.* xii. 1.
Multitude of compassions, *Psal.* li. 1.
Bowels of compassions, *Col.* iii. 12.
Tenderness of ⎫
Abundant tender ⎬ Compassions, *S. Jam.* v. 11.
    ⎧Passing by, *P. Mich.* vii. 18.
In ⎨ Overlooking, *Acts* xvii. 30.
    ⎩Conniving, *P. Isa.* lvii. 11.
Many ⎧Times,
       ⎩Years, *H. Nehem.* ix. 28, 30.
Unwillingly [*angry,*] *Lament.* iii. 33.
Not [*suffering His*] whole [*displeasure to arise,*] *Psal.* lxxviii. 39.
Not according [*to my desert,*] *Psal.* ciii. 10.
Not always, *Psal.* ciii. 9.
In wrath [*remembering*] mercy, *P. Hab.* iii. 2.
Repenting of the evil, *P. Joel* ii. 13.
[*Thinking every stripe*] two, *P. Isa.* xl. 2.
              ⎧Pardon,
[*Receiving*] to ⎨ Reconciliation,
              ⎩Propitiation.[c]

---

[c] [See the Triumph of Mercy in the Bishop's Manual for the Sick, *supra*, p. 216.]

☿ a

IN the morning watches I thought upon Thee, O Lord;
Because Thou hast been my helper. *Psal.* lxiii. 7, 8.

Blessed art Thou, O Lord, who createdst the two lights,

The {Sun, Moon;

The {Greater, Lesser;

And the stars; *Genes.* i. 16.

For {Light, Signs, Seasons;} *Ver.* 14.

For {Spring, Summer, Harvest, Winter;

For {Days, Weeks, Months, Years;

And to rule over

The {Day, Night.} *Ver.* 18.

P. Isaiah.

Behold, Thou art wroth, for we have sinned:

We are all as an unclean thing, and all our righteousnesses as filthy rags:

We all fade as a leaf; and our iniquities, like the wind, have taken us away.

But, now, O Lord, Thou art our Father:

We are the clay, we all are the work of Thy hands.

Be not wroth with us very sore:

Do not suddenly remember our sins:

But behold, look upon us, O Lord, we are all Thy people. *Chap.* lxiv. 5, 6, 8, 9.

---

a [☿ The planetary character or hieroglyphic of WEDNESDAY, called in Holy Scripture, the *Fourth Day*, Genes. i. 19.]

P. Jeremiah.

Though our iniquities testify against us, O Lord, show mercy to us, for Thy Name's sake;

For our backslidings are many; we have sinned against Thee.

Yet Thou, O Lord, art in the midst of us, and Thy Name is called upon among us;

O forget us not.

O Lord, our confidence, who savest us in the time of trouble,

Why art Thou as a foreigner in the land?

Or as a native, that comes but to his inn?

As one that is fallen into a sleep?

As a man that is not able to save? *Chap.* xiv. 7—9.

O Lord, forgive our iniquities; and remember our sins no more. *Chap.* xxxi. 34.

S. Paul.

Lord, I am carnal, sold under sin:

In me (that is, in my flesh) dwelleth no good thing.

For, the good that I would, I do not; but the evil that I would not, that I do.

I consent unto the law, that it is good;

And I delight in the law, after the inner man:

But I see another law in my *members*, warring against the law of my *mind;* and bringing me into captivity to the law of sin.

O wretched man that I am! who shall deliver me from the body of this death?

I thank God through JESUS Christ. *Rom.* vii. 14, 16, 18, 19, 22—25.

Because, where sin abounded, grace did much more abound. *Chap.* v. 20.

O Lord, Thy graciousness leadeth me unto repentance. *Rom.* ii. 4.

O give me repentance, that I may recover myself out of the snare of the devil, who am taken captive by him at his will. 2 *Tim.* ii. 25, 26.

S. Peter.

The time past of my life is sufficient to have wrought the will of my lusts;

When I walked in lasciviousness, revellings, banquetings, and all excess of riot, 1 *Epist.* iv. *chap.* 3 *ver.*

O Lamb of God, without blemish, and without spot,

Who redeemedst me with Thy precious Blood, 1 *Epist.* i. *chap.* 18, 19 *ver.*

For that same Blood, have mercy and save me;

For that Blood, and for that Name of Thine, beside which there is no other under heaven, given among men, whereby we must be saved. *Acts* iv. 12.

K. David.

God, Thou knowest my simpleness; and my faults are not hid from Thee. *Psal.* lxix. 5.

Lord, all my desire is before Thee, and my groaning is not hid from Thee. *Psal.* xxxviii. 9.

Let not them who trust in Thee, O Lord God of Hosts, be ashamed for my cause:

Let not them who seek Thee be confounded through me, O Lord God of Israel.

Take me out of the mire, that I sink not;

O let me be delivered from them that hate me, and out of the deep waters.

Let not the water-flood drown me; neither let the deep swallow me up; neither let the pit shut her mouth upon me. *Psal.* lxix. 6, 15, 16.

1. Pride,
    an 1. Amorite;
2. Envy,
    an 2. Hittite;
3. Anger,
    a 3. Perizzite;
4. Gluttony,
    a 4. Girgashite;
5. Wantonness,
    an 5. Hivite;

6. Worldly carkings,   a 6. Canaanite;

7. Lukewarm carelessness,   a ᵇ 7. Jebusite.

1. Humility,
2. Mercy,
3. Patience,
4. Temperance,
5. Chastity,
6. Contentation,
7. Alacrity and Diligence.

I BELIEVE

In the { Father, Affection and good-will; Almighty, Saving power; Creator, Providence; }

To { Preserve, Govern, Perfect } The world;

In { JESUS, Salvation; Christ, Anointing; The only Son, Adoption; }

To our Lord, service [*is due.*]

In His { Conception, Birth, } The purging of our unclean conception and birth;
Sufferings, That, what we should, we might not;
Cross, The curse of the law;
Death, The sting of death;
Burial, Eternal corruption in the grave is taken away;

ᵇ [The VII. cursed nations. *Deut.* vii. 1.]

In His
- Descent,
  - That, whither we should [go], we might not;
- Resurrection,
  - As the first-fruits of them that sleep;
- Ascension,
  - To prepare a place for us;
- Session,
  - To appear, and make intercession [for us];
- Coming again,
  - To take, to Himself those that are His;
- Judging,
  - To render to every one according to His works;

In the Holy Ghost,
   Power from on high, outwardly and invisibly,
              But,
Powerfully and manifestly, converting unto holiness;
            The Church,
The mystical body of them, who are called out of the whole world, to a corporation,
   According to { Faith, Holiness;
The Communion of Saints, the members of that body,
A mutual participation in the holy mysteries;
            To a
Full persuasion of the Remission of sins,
   Hope of { Resurrection, Translation,
    To life eternal.

My trust is in Thy mercy, for ever and ever. *Psal.* lii. 9.
How excellent is Thy mercy, O God! *Psal.* xxxvi. 7.
If I have any hope, it is in Thy mercy.
Let me not be ashamed of this my hope. *Psal.* cxix. 116.

We beseech Thee, O Lord, remember all for good;
Have mercy upon all, O Lord;
Be reconciled to us all.
Settle the multitudes of Thy people in peace;

Dissipate all scandals;
Cease all wars;
Stop all rising heresies.

O God, our Saviour, and the hope of all the ends of the earth, *Psal.* lxv. 5.
Grant unto us Thy peace and love.

Remember to crown the year with Thy goodness. *Psal.* lxv. 12.
For the eyes of all wait upon Thee; and Thou givest them their meat in due season;
Thou openest Thy hand, and fillest all things living with Thy gracious bounty. *Psal.* cxlv. 15, 16.

Remember Thy holy Church, from one end of the world unto the other;
And give peace unto her whom Thou hast purchased with Thy precious Blood;
And establish her unto the consummation of the world.

Remember all who bring forth fruit, and do good works in Thy holy Churches;
Them also who are mindful of the poor and needy;
Reward them with Thy rich and heavenly gifts;
Give them
For { Earthly, heavenly,
Corruptible, incorruptible,
Temporal, eternal blessings.

Remember them who lead their lives
in { Virginity,
Chastity, and
Mortification.
Them also who in honourable marriage, in piety, and the fear of Thee.

Remember every Christian soul, who being in
any { Affliction,
Trouble,
Agony,
stands in need of Thy mercy and help.

Remember our brethren, who are

in {
  Captivity,
  Prisons,
  Bonds,
  Bitter servitude.
}

Giving {
  Conversion to all who go astray;
  Health to the sick;
  Deliverance to the captives.
}

Remember all pious and faithful kings, to whom Thou hast given a right to reign upon earth.
And chiefly, O Lord,
Remember our most gracious King, preserved by Thee;
Establish his throne;
Subdue to him all his enemies;
Speak good to his soul, for Thy Church's, and all Thy people's sake.
Give him long peace, which may not be taken away,
That under his happy government we may lead peaceable and quiet lives, in all godliness and honesty. 1 *Tim.* ii. 2.

Remember, O Lord, all principalities and powers; and all that be in place at Court;
Those who are of the Council;
Or in the seats of judgment;
And all that fight Thy battles for us, by land or sea.

Furthermore, be graciously pleased, O Lord, to remember

The {
  Holy Fathers of the Church;
  Venerable Presbytery, and all the Clergy,
}
Who rightly divide the Word of Truth, 2 *Tim.* ii. 15, and walk uprightly according to the same. *Gal.* ii. 14.

Remember, O Lord, our brethren, who are present, and join together in prayer with us, in this holy hour,
Remember their devotion and their zeal.

Remember them also who upon good cause are absent;
And have mercy upon them and us, according to the multitude of Thy mercy.
Fill our garners with all good;
Preserve our married people in peace and concord;
Cherish up all infants;

Instruct the youth;
Strengthen the aged;
Comfort the faint-hearted;
Gather the dispersed;
Bring back again them that are gone astray;
Unite them to the
Holy,
Catholic, } Church;
Apostolic
Deliver all that are possessed with unclean spirits;
Sail with all that go by sea;
Travel with all that go by land;
Take care of the widows;
Defend the orphans;
Set the captives at liberty;
Heal the sick.

Remember, O God, all
Who are { Questioned at the bar of justice;
         { Condemned to the mines and galleys;
Who are in { Banishment;
            { Any other { Affliction,
            {   { Necessity,
            {   { Distress;
            { Need of Thy great mercy;
Who { Love } us;
    { Hate }

All recommended by us Thy unworthy servants, to be remembered in our prayers.

Remember, O Lord our God, all Thy people; and pour upon them all the riches of Thy mercy; giving to all their desires tending to salvation.

Remember, O God, all, whom we, through ignorance, forgetfulness, or multitude of names, have not remembered;
Thou knowest the condition and name of every one;
Thou knowest every one, from his mother's womb.

For Thou, O Lord, art the
Helper } of the { Helpless;
Hope   }   { Hopeless;
The Saviour of them who are tossed with tempests;

The Haven of them who sail;
The Physician of them who are sick;
Be Thou all to all, Thou who knowest every one,

His { Desires,
Habitation,
Wants.

O Lord, deliver this city, and all the country wherein we dwell,

From { Pestilence, famine,
Earthquakes,
Inundations,
Fire, sword,
Foreign invasion, and
Civil insurrections.

Appease the schisms of the Churches;
Abate the insolencies of the Heathen;
And receive us all into Thy kingdom, owning us for children of the light;
And grant unto us Thy peace and love, O Lord our God.

Remember, O Lord our God, all spirits and all flesh, whom we have remembered, and whom we have not remembered.

O Lord, make the end of our life Christian, acceptable to Thee; and, if Thou think good, without pain, in peace; gathering us together under the feet of Thy elect, when Thou wilt, and as Thou wilt, only without shame and sin.[c]

The glorious majesty of the Lord our God be upon us;
Prosper Thou the work of our hands upon us:
O prosper Thou our handy-work. *Psal.* xc. 17.

Lord, be Thou
    Within me,
        to strengthen me;
    Without me,
        to keep me;
    Above me,
        to protect me;

---

[c] [Collected out of the Liturgies St. James, Basil, and Chrysost.]

Beneath me,
> to uphold me.

Before me,
> to direct me;

Behind me,
> to reduce me;

Round about me,
> to defend me.

Blessed be Thou, O Lord God of Israel, our Father, for ever and ever.

To Thee, O Lord, belongeth

Majesty,   Power,
Glory,   Victory,
Strength,   Confession;

For Thou art Lord over all, in heaven, and on earth. 1 *Chron.* xxix. 10, 11.

Every king and nation trembleth at Thy presence. *P. Isa.* lxiv. 2.

Thine, O Lord, is the kingdom and exaltation

over all { Things; Dominion; }

Riches are from Thee, and honour from Thy presence;

Thou reignest over all, O Lord;

Thou hast dominion over all dominion;

And in Thy hand is power and might;

And in Thy hand it is to make great, and to give strength to all:

And now, O Lord, we confess to Thee, and praise Thy glorious Name. 1 *Chron.* xxix. 12, 13.

♃ ᵃ

LET us be satisfied with Thy mercy, O Lord, in the morning. *Psal.* xc. 14.

Blessed art Thou, O Lord, who broughtest forth, out of the waters, every

Living creature that moveth, and the whales, and winged fowls;

And blessedst them, so that they were fruitful, and did multiply. *Gen.* i. 20—22.

The Graduals.

Set up Thyself, O God, above the heaven;
And Thy glory above all the earth. *Psal.* cviii. 5.

By Thy *Ascension* draw us unto Thee, O Lord. *S. John* xii. 32.

That we may set our affections on things above, and not on things of the earth. *Coloss.* iii. 2.

By the wonderful mystery of Thy holy Body, and Thy precious Blood, instituted in the *evening of this day*, O Lord, have mercy.

P. Ezekiel.

As I live, saith the Lord God, I will not the death of a sinner, but that the wicked turn from his ways, and live.

Turn ye, turn ye from your evil ways; for why will ye die, O house of Israel? *Chap.* xxxiii. 11.

P. Jeremiah.

Turn Thou us unto Thee, O Lord; and so shall we be turned. *Lam.* v. 21.

P. Ezekiel.

Turn us from all our transgressions; and let not iniquity be our ruin. *Chap.* xviii. 30.

ᵃ [♃ The planetary character or hieroglyphic of 𝕿𝖍𝖚𝖗𝖘𝖉𝖆𝖞𝖊, called in Holy Scripture, the *Fifth Day*, Genes. i. 23.]

P. Daniel.

I have sinned, I have done unjustly, I have been ungodly, in departing from Thy precepts and Thy judgments.

O Lord, righteousness belongeth to Thee: but to me confusion of face, as at this day: because of our unfaithfulness, for which Thou hast cast us off.

O Lord, to us confusion of face, and to our princes; because we have sinned against Thee.

O Lord, Thy righteousness is in all things:

According to all Thy righteousness, let Thine anger and Thy fury be turned away:

And cause Thy face to shine upon Thy servant.

O my God, incline Thine ear, and hear;

Open Thine eyes, and behold my desolation.

O Lord, hear, O Lord, forgive, O Lord, hearken; hearken, O Lord, and do; do, and defer not; for Thine own sake, O Lord, O Lord my God.

For Thy servant is called by Thy name. *Chap.* ix. 5, 7, 8, 16—19.

S. James.

In many things we offend all. *Chap.* iii. 2.

Lord, let Thy mercy triumph over Thy justice, *in my sins.* *Chap.* ii. 13.

S. John.

If I say that I have no sin, I deceive myself, and the truth is not in me.

But I confess my sins, *many and grievous;* and Thou, O Lord, art faithful and just to forgive my sins *to me confessing them.* 1 *Epist. chap.* i. 8, 9.

But even for this I have an Advocate, with Thee, *to Thee,*

Thine only-begotten Son the Righteous.

Let Him be the propitiation for my sins, who is for the sins of the whole world. 1 *Epist. chap.* ii. 1, 2.

K. David.

Will the Lord absent Himself for ever? and will He be no more entreated?

Is His mercy clean gone for ever? and is His promise come utterly to an end for evermore?

Hath God forgotten to be gracious? and will He shut up His loving-kindness in displeasure?

And I said, now I began: this is the change of the right hand of the Most High. *Psal.* lxxvii. 7—10.

[*O Lord, give me grace to lay aside*]
Every weight, and the sin that doth so easily beset me, *Heb.* xii. 1.

All filthiness, and superfluity of naughtiness, *S. James* i. 21.

The lust of the { Flesh, Eye,

And the pride of life ; 1 *S. John* ii. 16.

Every motion both of flesh and spirit, which is contrary to the will of Thy holiness.

[*Give me grace also*]
[b] 1. To be poor in spirit ;
That I may have my part in the kingdom of heaven.
2. To mourn ;
That I may be comforted.
3. To be meek ;
That I may inherit the earth.
4. To hunger and thirst after righteousness ;
That I may be filled.
5. To be merciful ;
That I may obtain mercy.
6. To be pure in heart ;
That I may see God.
7. To be a peacemaker ;
That I may be called a child of God.
8. To be ready to suffer persecution for righteousness' sake ;
That my reward may be in the kingdom of heaven. *S. Matt.* v.

Coming unto God
   I believe
      That { He is ;
             He is a rewarder of them who diligently seek Him. *Heb.* xi. 6.

[b] [The eight Beatitudes.]

I know that
My Redeemer liveth. *H. Job* xix. 25.
He is Christ, the Son of the living God. *S. Matt.* xvi. 16.
He is indeed the Saviour of the world. *S. John* iv. 42.
He came into the world to save sinners; of whom I am chief. 1 *Tim.* i. 15.
We believe, that through the grace of our Lord JESUS Christ, we shall be saved, even as our fathers. *Acts* xv. 11.

I know that *this* my flesh, which hath shared in all, shall rise again upon the earth. *H. Job* xix. 25.
I believe verily to see the goodness of the Lord, in the land of the living. *Psal.* xxvii. 15.

Our heart shall rejoice in Him, because we have hoped in His holy Name. *Psal.* xxxiii. 20.

In the Name,

of the {
  Father,
  Saviour, Mediator,
  Intercessor, Redeemer:
  Double Paraclete,
}

Under the figures,

of a { Lamb, Dove.

Let Thy merciful kindness, O Lord, be upon us; like as we do put our trust in Thee. *Psal.* xxxiii. 21.

^c In the peace of God, let us pray
For the peace which is from *above,* and for the salvation of our souls;
For the peace of the *whole world;*
For the establishment of the Churches of God; and the union of them all;
For *this* holy place; and all that enter into it, with faith and reverence;
For our holy fathers the Bishops; the venerable Presbytery, and Deaconry in Christ;
For the whole Clergy and Laity;
For *this* holy mansion; all *this* city and country; and all faithful people who dwell therein;

^c [Collected out of S. James and Chrysost. Liturgy.]

For good temperature of the air;
Fruitful seasons; peaceable times;
For all who travel by land or by water;
For all who are sick, ill at ease, and in captivity; and for their safety:
> Help and save us;
Have mercy on us; and keep us by Thy grace, O God.
Neither are we unmindful to bless Thee, for the most holy, pure, highly blessed, the Mother of God, Mary the eternal Virgin, with all the Saints:
Recommending ourselves and our whole life to Thee, O Lord, our Christ and God:
For to Thee belongeth glory, honour, and worship.

The grace of our Lord JESUS Christ, and the love of God, and the communion of the Holy Ghost, be with me, and with us all. Amen. 2 *Cor.* xiii. 14.

I commend both myself, and mine, and all that I have, to Him who is able to keep from falling, and to present me faultless before the presence of His glory;
To the only wise God, and our Saviour;
To whom be glory and majesty, dominion and power, now and for ever. Amen. *S. Jude* 24, 25.

O Lord, my God,
    For my
  Being, life,
  Endowment with reason,
  Nourishment,
  Preservation,
  Guidance,
  Education,
  Civil government and religion;
    For Thy
  Gifts of { Grace, Nature, The world;
  For my { Redemption, Regeneration, Catechising;

For Thy { Calling,
Recalling,
Manifold recalling me again and again;

For Thy
Forbearance,
Long-suffering,
Long-suffering towards me,
Many { Times,
Years,
Even until now;

For all whom I have received
any { Good
Benefit } from;

For them, if any, whom I have done any good unto;
For the use of Thy present good things;
For Thy promise, and my hope of enjoying future good things;

For my
Good and careful parents,
Gentle masters,
Ever-memorable benefactors,
Brethren of the Clergy, who are of one mind,
Understanding auditors,
True friends,
Faithful servants;

For all who have any way benefited me,
By their { Writings,
Sermons,
Discourses,
Prayers,
Examples,
Reproofs,
Injuries;

For all these, and for all other,
Known or unknown,
Manifest or secret,
Remembered or forgotten by me,
From whom I have willingly or unwillingly received good,
I praise Thee,
I bless Thee,
I give Thee thanks;

And I will praise and bless, and give Thee thanks, all the days of my life.

What am I? and what is my father's house? *2 P. Sam.* vii. 18.

That Thou shouldest look upon such a dead dog as I am. *2 Sam.* ix. 8.

What reward shall I give unto the Lord, for all the benefits that He hath done unto me? *Psal.* cxvi. 11.

What thanks can I render unto God, for all wherein He hath
$$\left.\begin{array}{l}\text{Spared}\\\text{Forborne}\end{array}\right\}\text{me until now?}$$

Holy, Holy, Holy,

Thou art worthy, O Lord our God, to receive glory, and honour, and power;

For Thou hast created all things; and for Thy pleasure they are, and were created. *Rev.* iv. 8, 11.

♀ [a]

IN the morning shall my prayer come unto Thee. *Psal.* lxxxviii. 13.

Blessed art Thou, O Lord, who didst bring forth of the earth
$\left\{\begin{array}{l}\text{Beasts,}\\\text{Cattle,}\\\text{Creeping things,}\end{array}\right.$ *Gen.* i. 24, 25.

For $\left\{\begin{array}{l}\text{Nourishment,}\\\text{Clothing,}\\\text{Help;}\end{array}\right.$

And didst make man after Thy image, to have dominion over the earth, and didst bless him. *Gen.* i. 26, 28.

[b] The consultation [*of the blessed Trinity about him*]. *Gen.* i. 26.

The work of his hands. *Psal.* cxxxviii. 8.

The breath of life. *Gen.* ii. 7.

The image of God. *Gen.* i. 26.

The setting him over Thy works. *Gen.* i. 28, and *Psal.* viii. 6.

The charge to the Angels concerning him. *Psal.* xci. 11.

Paradise. *Gen.* ii. 8.

[b] Heart,		Reins,
Eyes,		Ears,
	Tongue,	
Hands,		Feet.
	[b] Life,	
Sense,		Reason,
Spirit,		Freewill,
Memory,		Conscience.

[a] [♀ The planetary character or hieroglyphic of 𝔉𝔯𝔦𝔡𝔞𝔦𝔢, called in Holy Scripture, the *Sixth Day*, Genes. i. 31: and the Παρασκευή and Προσάββατον, *the Day of Preparation,* and *the Day before the Sabbath,* in the Holy Evangelists.]

[b] [Special heads of meditation.]

                ᶜ That which is
Known of God, *Rom.* i. 19.
Written in the law ; *S. Luke* x. 26.
        The oracles
                        of the Prophets ;
                The melody
                        of the Psalms ;
        The instruction
                        of the Proverbs ;
        The knowledge
                        of histories ;
        The service
                        of sacrifices.

Blessed art Thou, O Lord, for Thy great and precious promise, on *this* day, concerning *that life-giving seed, Gen.* iii. 15.

And for the fulfilling thereof in the fulness of time, *Gal.* iv. 4, upon *this* day.

Blessed art Thou, O Lord, for Thy holy passions on *this* day.

Oh, by Thy saving passions on *this* day, save us, O Lord.

P. Hosea.

I have stood out against Thee, O Lord ; *Chap.* xiii. 16.
But I return unto Thee.
I am weakened by mine iniquities ;
But, I take with me words, and turn to Thee, saying,
Forgive my sin, and receive my prayer ;
So will I render to Thee the fruit of my lips. *Chap.* xiv. 1, 2.

P. Joel.

Spare, O Lord, spare ;
And give not Thine heritage to reproach *among Thine enemies. Chap.* ii. 17.

P. Amos.

O Lord, O Lord, be gracious ; cease, I beseech Thee.
By whom shall Jacob arise ? For he is small.
Repent, O Lord, concerning this. Let it not be. *Chap.* vii. 2, 3.

                ᶜ [Special heads of meditation.]

P. Jonah.

Observing vanity and lies, I have forsaken mine own mercy :

And I am cast out of Thy sight.

But, when my soul fainted within me, I remembered the Lord.

I will look yet again toward Thy holy temple.

Thou hast brought my life from corruption. *Chap.* ii. 4, 6—8.

P. Micah.

Who is a God like unto Thee, who passest by the iniquities of the remnant of Thine heritage?

Thou wilt not always retain Thine anger, for a testimony [*against us*], because Thou delightest in mercy.

Turn again, and have mercy upon us, O Lord; drown our iniquities, and cast all our sins into the depths of the sea,

According to Thy truth and mercy. *Chap.* vii. 18—20.

P. Habakkuk.

O Lord, I have heard Thy *speech*, and was afraid ;
I have considered Thy *works*, and was astonished ;
In wrath remember mercy. *Chap.* iii. 2.

P. Zechariah.

Behold me, O Lord, clothed with filthy garments.

Behold Satan standing at my right hand. *Chap.* iii. 1, 3.

And by the blood of Thy Covenant, O Lord, *Chap.* ix. 11.

In that fountain opened for the purging of all uncleanness, *Chap.* xiii. 1.

Take away mine iniquities, and cleanse my sins,

Save me, as a brand plucked out of the fire. *Chap.* iii. 2.

Father, forgive me ; for I know not, in truth I know not, what I have done, in sinning against Thee. *S. Luke* xxiii. 34.

Lord, remember me, when Thou comest into Thy kingdom. *S. Luke* xxiii. 42.

Lord, repay not mine enemies their sins. *Acts* vii. 60.

Repay me my sins, O Lord,

By $\begin{cases} \text{Thy } sweat, \text{ and great drops of blood;} \\ \text{The } agony \text{ of Thy soul.} \end{cases}$ *S. Luke* xxii. 44.

By Thy
{
Head, crowned with thorns, *S. Matt.* xxvii. 29, set on with staves,
Weeping eyes, Heb. v. 7.
Ears, filled with revilings, *S. Matt.* xxvii. 39.
Mouth, given vinegar and gall to drink, *Ver.* [34,] 48.
Face, shamefully defiled by spitting, *Ver.* 30.
Neck, loaded with the burthen of the cross, *S. John* xix. 17.
Back, furrowed with stripes and wounds, *Psal.* cxxix. 3, and 1 *S. Pet.* ii. 24.
Hands and *feet* digged, *Psal.* xxii. 17.
Strong *cry, Eli, Eli, S. Matt.* xxvii. 46, and *Heb.* v. 7.
Heart, pierced with the spear, *S. John* xix. 34.
Water and *blood* running out, *Ver.* 34.
Body broken,
Blood shed.
}

Psal. lxxxv.

Lord, forgive the offences of Thy servant; and cover all his sins. *Ver.* 2.

Take away all Thy displeasure; and turn Thyself from Thy wrathful indignation. *Ver.* 3.

Turn me, O God of our salvation; and let Thine anger cease from us. *Ver.* 4.

Wilt Thou be angry with us for ever; and wilt Thou stretch out Thy wrath from one generation to another? *Ver.* 5.

O God, Thou wilt turn again, and quicken us; and Thy people shall rejoice in Thee. *Ver.* 6.

Shew us Thy mercy, O Lord; and grant us Thy salvation. *Ver.* 7.

The works of the flesh :
  Adultery,
  Fornication,
  Uncleanness,
  Lasciviousness,
  Idolatry,
  Witchcraft,
  Hatred,

Variance,
Emulation,
Wrath, Strife,
Sedition,
Heresies,
Envyings,
Murders,
Drunkenness,
Revellings, and such like.   *Galat.* v. 19-21.

The fruits of the Spirit:
  Love, joy, peace,
      Long-suffering,
  Gentleness, goodness,
      Faith,
  Meekness,
  Temperance.   *Galat.* v. 22, 23.

The spirit
  Of { Wisdom,
      Understanding,
      Counsel,
      Might,
  Of { Knowledge,
      Godliness,
      The fear of the Lord.   *P. Isa.* xi. 2.

The gifts of the Spirit:
  The word of
    Wisdom;
  The word of
    Knowledge;
      Faith;
  The gifts of healing;
  The working of
    Miracles;
    Prophecy;
  Discerning of spirits;
  Divers kinds, and interpretations of tongues.   1 *Cor.* xii. 8—10.

LORD, I believe,
That Thou didst *create* me;
  Despise not the work of Thine own hands.
That, according to Thy image and likeness;
  Suffer not Thy likeness to be blotted out.
That Thou didst *redeem* me with Thy blood;
  Suffer not the price of Thy redemption to be lost.
That Thou didst set me out for a *Christian*, after Thine own *name*;
  Despise not me, who am called by Thy name.
That Thou didst *sanctify* me in the regeneration;
  Destroy not me, whom Thou hast sanctified.
That Thou didst ingraff me in the good olive-tree, *Rom.* xi. 24, as a member of the mystical body;
  Cut not off a member of Thy mystical body.

O think upon Thy servant, as concerning Thy word, wherein Thou hast caused me to put my trust. *Psal.* cxix. 49.
My soul fainteth with longing for Thy salvation; and I have a good hope because of Thy word. *Ver.* 81.

Let us pray,
For the prosperity and strengthening of all Christian armies against the enemies of our most holy faith,
  For our holy fathers, and all our brethren in Christ,
  For all that hate us, and love us,
  For all that have mercy upon us, and minister unto us,
  For all whom we are desired to remember in our prayers,
  For the redemption of the captives,
  For our fathers and brethren who are absent,
  For all seafaring persons,
  For all who are cast upon the bed of sickness,
  For plenty of the fruits of the earth,
  For the souls of all orthodox Christians.
Let us commemorate
  Our { Godly kings,
        Orthodox prelates,
The founders of *this* holy habitation,
Our parents, and all our forefathers and brethren who are gone before us.

Let Thy mighty hand, O Lord, be my defence;
Thy mercy in Christ, my salvation;
Thy all-true word, my instruction;
The grace of Thy quickening Spirit, my consolation, unto the end, and in the end.

> Let the
> Soul of Christ
> > sanctify me;
> Body of Christ
> > strengthen me;
> Blood of Christ
> > redeem me;
> Water of Christ
> > cleanse me;
> Stripes of Christ
> > heal me;
> Sweat of Christ
> > refresh me;
> Wounds of Christ
> > hide me.

The peace of God, which passeth all understanding, keep my heart and mind in the knowledge and love of God. *Phil.* iv. 7.

[d] O Lord, who didst not despise, nor forsake man, transgressing Thy commandment, and falling;

But, as a tender-bowelled father, didst visit him sundry ways;

Giving him *that* Thy great and precious promise, concerning the *blessed* quickening *Seed;*

Opening unto him a door of faith and repentance unto life;

And in the fulness of time sending the same Thy Christ, to take the seed of Abraham;

And, by the *oblation* of His *life*, to fulfil the *obedience* of the law;

And, by the *sacrifice* of His *death*, to take away the *curse* thereof;

By His *death* to *redeem* the world;

[d] James' Liturgy.

And, by His *resurrection* to *quicken* the same :

Who didst all things to this end, to bring back mankind to Thee, that he might be partaker of the Divine nature, and of eternal glory;

Who didst attest the *truth* of Thy Gospel,

By many and manifold *miracles* ;

By the ever memorable *conversation* of Thy *saints;*

By their supernatural *patience,* under torments ;

By the most wonderful *conversion* of the whole world unto the obedience of faith,

Without { Strength, Rhetoric, or Force;

Blessed, praised, celebrated, magnified, highly exalted, glorified, and hallowed be Thy Name; the mention and memory, and all the monuments thereof, both now and for ever.

Thou art worthy to take the book, and to open the seals thereof;

For Thou wast slain, and hast redeemed us to our God by Thy blood, out of every kindred, and tongue, and people, and nation.

Worthy is the Lamb that was slain, to receive power, and riches, and wisdom, and strength, and honour, and glory, and blessing.

To Him that sitteth upon the throne, and to the Lamb, blessing, and honour, and glory, and power, for ever and ever. *Revel.* v. 9, 12, 13.

Salvation to our God, who sitteth upon the throne, and to the Lamb. Amen.

Blessing, and glory, and wisdom, and thanksgiving, and honour, and power, and might, be unto our God, for ever and ever. Amen. *Revel.* vii. 10. 12.

♄ [a]

O LORD, have mercy upon us, for we have trusted in Thee:
Be Thou our arm *every* morning; and our salvation in the time of trouble. *P. Isa.* xxxiii. 2.

Blessed art Thou, O Lord, who didst rest the seventh day from all Thy works;
And didst bless, and sanctify it. *Gen.* ii. 2, 3.

Of { [b] [*The Institution and Rites of*] the Sabbath.
The rest in the returns thereof.

Of the { Death and Burial of Christ.
Ceasing of sin [*thereby*].

Of those who are [*gone*] before us, [*and are*] at rest [*from their labours.*]

P. Ezra.

O my God, I am ashamed, and blush to lift up my face to Thee;
For mine iniquities are increased over my head;
And my trespasses are waxed great unto the heavens.
Since the days *of my youth* I am in a great trespass, even to this day;
And I cannot stand before Thee, because of this. *Chap.* ix. 6, 7, 15.

K. Manasses.

I have sinned above the number of the sands of the sea;
My transgressions are multiplied; and I am not worthy to look up, and to see the height of heaven, because of the multitude of mine iniquities:
Neither have I any release; for I have provoked Thy wrath, and done evil before Thee; not doing Thy will, nor keeping Thy commandments.

---

[a] ♄ [The planetary character or hieroglyphic of 𝕾𝖆𝖙𝖚𝖗𝖉𝖆𝖞𝖊, called in Holy Scripture, the *Seventh Day*, Gen. ii. 2, and the *Holy Sabbath*, Exod. xvi. 23.]

[b] [Heads of meditations and devotions.]

And now I bow the knee of my heart, beseeching Thee of grace.

I have sinned, O Lord, I have sinned, and I acknowledge mine iniquities.

But, I humbly beseech Thee, forgive me, O Lord, forgive me; and destroy me not with mine iniquities;
Be not angry with me for ever, by reserving evil for me;
Neither condemn me into the lower parts of the earth:
For Thou art the God, even the God of them that repent;
And Thou shalt shew in me all Thy goodness, if Thou wilt save me, that am unworthy, according to Thy great mercy:
And I will praise Thee for ever.

Lord, if Thou wilt, Thou canst make me clean:
Lord, speak the word only, and I shall be healed. *S. Matt.* viii. 2, 8.

Lord, save me. *S. Matt.* viii. 25.
Carest Thou not that we perish? *S. Mark* iv. 38.

Say unto me, Be of good cheer; thy sins are forgiven thee. *S. Matt.* ix. 2.

JESUS, Master, have mercy on me. *S. Luke* xvii. 13.
JESUS, Thou Son of David, have mercy on me. *S. Mark* x. 47, 48.

JESUS, Thou Son of David;
Thou Son of David.

Lord, say unto me, Ephphatha. *S. Mark* vii. 34.
Lord, I have no man [*to do it*]. *S. John* v. 7.

Lord, say unto me, Thou art loosed from thine infirmity. *S. Luke* xiii. 12.

Say unto my soul, I am thy salvation. *Psal.* xxxv. 3.
Say unto me, My grace is sufficient for thee. 2 *Cor.* xii. 9.

Psal. lxxix.

Lord, how long wilt Thou be angry, for ever?
Shall Thy jealousy burn like fire?
O remember not our old sins; let Thy mercies, O Lord, speedily prevent us, for we are come to great misery.

Help us, O God our Saviour, for the glory of Thy Name;
O Lord, deliver us, and be merciful to our sins, for Thy Name's sake. *Ver.* 5, 8, 9.

All my debts,
Faults, Defects,
Slips, Falls,
Offences, Stumblings,
Transgressions,
Sins, Wickednesses,
Ignorances, Iniquities,
Ungodliness, Unrighteousness,
Abominations;
The Guilt
Graciously forgive,
Pardon, Remit,
Pass by, Spare,
Be merciful,
Repay not, Impute not,
Remember not.

The filthiness
Pass by, Pass over,
Look beside, Look beyond,
Cover, Wash away,
Blot out, Cleanse.

The damage,
Release, Heal,
Save from,
Take $\begin{cases} \text{away,} \\ \text{upon Thee,} \end{cases}$
Cancel, Frustrate,
Disappoint,
Bring to nought.

Let them not be found,
Let them not be.

[*Give me grace*] to add

To $\begin{cases} \text{Faith, virtue;} \\ \text{Virtue, knowledge;} \\ \text{Knowledge, temperance;} \\ \text{Temperance, patience;} \\ \text{Patience, godliness;} \\ \text{Godliness, brotherly kindness;} \\ \text{Brotherly kindness, charity;} \end{cases}$

And, not forgetting that I am purged from my old sins, to give diligence to make my calling and election sure, 2 *S. Pet.* i. 5, 6, 7, 9, 10, by good works. 1 *Tim.* ii. 10.

I believe in Thee the *Father*.
> Behold then, if Thou be a Father, and we children,
> As a father pitieth his own children, *Psal.* ciii. 13, let Thy bowels yearn upon us, O Lord.

I believe in Thee the *Lord*.
> Behold then, if Thou be a Lord, and we servants,
> Our eyes wait upon Thee, our Lord, until Thou have mercy upon us. *Psal.* cxxiii. 2.

I believe, that, were we neither sons, nor servants, but dogs only,
> It should be lawful for us to eat of the crumbs that fall from Thy table. *S. Mark* vii. 28.

I believe, that *Christ* is the Lamb of God.
> O Lamb of God, that takest away the sins of the world, *S. John* i. 29.
> Take mine away also.

I believe that JESUS *Christ* came into the world, to save sinners. 1 *Tim.* i. 15.
> Thou who camest to save sinners,
> Save even me, the first and chief of sinners.

I believe that *Christ* came to save that which was lost. *S. Matt.* xviii. 11.
> Thou, who camest to save that which was lost,
> Suffer not, O Lord, that to be lost, which Thou hast saved.

I believe, that the *Spirit* is the Lord and Giver of life. [*Nicene Creed.*]
> Thou, who gavest me a living soul, *Gen.* ii. 7.
> Grant that I may not receive this my soul in vain.

I believe, that the *Spirit* communicates grace in the holy mysteries.
> Grant that I may not receive the grace of them, nor the hope of His holy mysteries in vain. 2 *Cor.* vi. 1.

I believe, that the *Spirit* maketh intercession for us, with groans that cannot be uttered. *Rom.* viii. 26.

Grant, O Lord, that I may be partaker of that His intercession, and of those His groans.

Our fathers hoped in Thee, they trusted in Thee, and Thou didst deliver them:
They called upon Thee, and were holpen; They put their trust in Thee, and were not confounded. *Psal.* xxii. 4, 5.
As Thou didst our fathers in the former generations, even so, O Lord, deliver us, who trust in Thee.

O heavenly KING,
Establish all our Christian kings;
Confirm the faith;
Assuage the rage of the heathen;
Set the world at peace;
Graciously preserve *this* holy habitation;
And, according to Thy goodness and love to man, receive and protect us in our orthodox faith, and in repentance.

Let the *power* of the *Father* guide me;
Let the *wisdom* of the *Son* enlighten me;
Let the *operation* of the *Spirit* quicken me.

Preserve my soul,
Strengthen my body,
Elevate my senses,
Order my conversation,
Compose my manners,
Bless my works,
Perfect my prayers,
Inspire
    Holy thoughts,
Pardon
    what is past,
Rectify what is present,
Prevent
    what is to come.

To Him, that is able to do exceeding abundantly above all that we ask or think, according to the power that worketh in us,

To Him be glory in the Church, by Christ JESUS, throughout all ages, world without end. Amen. *Ephes.* iii. 20, 21.

Blessed, praised, celebrated, magnified, exalted, glorified, hallowed be Thy Name,
     O Lord,
The mention, the remembrance, and every memorial of it,

For the
{
1. Patriarchs'
  Honourable senate;
2. Prophets'
  Ever-venerable quire;
3. Apostles'
  All-glorious company;
4. Evangelists;
5. Martyrs'
  Most noble army;
6. Confessors;
7. Doctors'
  Assembly;
}

For, 8, them that give themselves to the exercise of devotion;
For the beauty of, 9, Virgins;
For the delicious order of, 10, Infants;

For their
{
1. Faith, 2. Hope,
3. Labours, 4. Truth,
5. Blood, 6. Zeal,
7. Diligence, 8. Tears,
9. Chastity, 10. Glory.
}

    Glory be to Thee,
     O Lord,
    Glory be to Thee,
    Glory be to Thee,
Because Thou hast glorified them, for and with whom we also glorify Thee.

Great and manifold are Thy works, Lord God Almighty;
Just and true are Thy ways, O Thou King of Saints:
Who shall not fear Thee, O Lord, and glorify Thy Name?
For Thou only art holy;
For all nations shall come, and worship before Thee,

For Thy judgments are made manifest. *Rev.* xv. 3, 4.

Praise our God, all ye His servants, and ye that fear Him, both small and great.

Allelujah ;

For our Lord God omnipotent reigneth ;

Let us be glad and rejoice, and give honour to Him. *Rev.* xix. 5, 6, 7.

Behold, the tabernacle of God is with men, and He will dwell with them ;

And they shall be His people, and God Himself shall be with them ;

And He shall wipe away all tears from their eyes ;

And there shall be no more death, nor crying; neither shall there be any more pain ;

For the former things are passed away. *Rev.* xxi. 3, 4.

[*A Form of Prayer for all the World, and particularly for our special Relations.*]

Do good, O Lord, and visit with Thy mercies

All { Creatures,
      Mankind ;

The { World,
      Habitable part thereof ;

The
States of the world ;
Catholic Church ;
      Christianity ;

All particular { Churches,
                States ;

Our { Church,
      State,
      Country ;

The several Orders in either of them ;
      The sacred ;
The several persons in those Orders ;

The { King,
      Prince ;

The {
  a City,
    [*wherein I was born.*]
  b Parish,
    [*wherein I was baptized.*]
  c Two Schools,
  d University,
  e College,
    [*wherein I was brought up*[a].]

" The parish of St. Giles [*Cripplegate*], committed to my charge,

" Pembroke Hall ;

[*a* London.] *b* [All-Hallows, Barking.] *c* [Merchant-Tailors, and St. Paul's] *d* [Cambridge.] *e* [Pembroke Hall.]

"The
Three churches
"Of {Southwell, S. Paul, Westminster;
"The three dioceses
"Of {Chichester, Ely, Winchester [b];
My {Family, Kindred;
All that have {Shewed mercy, Administered
To me;
My {Neighbours, Friends;
All commended to my prayers.

[A Recommendation of ourselves and ours to God's blessing.]

O Lord, I commend unto Thee
My
Soul and body,
Mind and thoughts,
My
Wishes and prayers,
Senses and members,
Words and deeds,
Life and death;

My brethren, and sisters, and their children;
My {Benefactors, Well-willers, Family, Neighbours, Country;
All Christian people.

---

[b] [Instead of the Bishop's particular relations marked thus ("), put in your own.]

O Lord, I commend unto Thee

My $\begin{cases} \text{Motions and opportunities;} \\ \text{Resolutions and undertakings;} \\ \text{Going out and coming in;} \\ \text{Sitting down and rising up.} \end{cases}$

[*Prayers preparatory to all our Thanksgivings.*]

Thou, O Lord, art worthy to be praised; and unto Thee shall the vow be performed. *Psal.* lxv. 1.

Worthy art Thou, O Lord, our holy God, to receive glory, and honour, and power. *Rev.* iv. 11.

O Thou that hearest prayer, unto Thee shall all flesh come:
Even my flesh shall come:

My misdeeds prevail against me; O be Thou merciful unto my sins. *Psal.* lxv. 2, 3.

That I may come to confess to Thee, with all Thy works; and with all Thy saints to bless Thee.

Thou shalt open my lips, O Lord; and my mouth shall shew Thy praise. *Psal.* li. 15.

[*A Form of Thanksgiving for Temporal and Spiritual Blessings.*]

My soul praiseth the Lord, for that He hath done good

To all $\begin{cases} \text{Creatures,} \\ \text{Mankind;} \end{cases}$

To the $\begin{cases} \text{World,} \\ \text{Habitable part thereof;} \end{cases}$

To the
States of the world;
Catholic Church;
   Christianity;

To all particular $\begin{cases} \text{Churches,} \\ \text{States;} \end{cases}$

To our $\begin{cases} \text{Church,} \\ \text{State,} \\ \text{Country;} \end{cases}$

To the several Orders in either of them;
   The sacred;

To the several persons in those Orders;

To the { King, Prince;

To the { City, [*wherein I was born.*] Parish, [*wherein I was baptized.*] Two schools, University, College, [*wherein I was brought up.*]

To my { Family, Kindred;

To all that have
Shewed mercy,
Administered to me;

To my { Neighbours, Friends;

To all commended to my prayers.

For that He hath shewed mercy to me

In my { Soul, Body, Goods;

For the gifts of { Nature, Grace, The world;

For all things wherein

I have { Received benefit, Been successful,

{ Formerly, At present;

For the good, if any, which I ever did;

For my

Health,	Good name,
Sufficiency,	Safety,
Liberty,	Quiet.

Thou hast not cut off, as a weaver, my life; but, from day even to night, Thou preservest me. *P. Isa.* xxxviii. 12.

Thou hast graciously given me life and breath, until this hour.

From my childhood, from my youth upward, even until now, *to old age.* *Psal.* lxxi. 15, 16.

Thou hast held my soul in life, and Thou wilt not suffer my foot to slip. *Psal.* lxvi. 8.

Delivering me

From
- Dangers,
- Diseases,
- Poverty,
- Servitude,
- Public shame,
- Evil accidents.

Not giving me up to perish in my sins.
Always waiting for my conversion.

Leaving in me

A
- Turning to my heart,
- Remembrance of the last ends [c].

Some
- Shame,
- Horror,
- Trembling,

} for my sins past.

O give me oftener and greater, greater and oftener, more and more, O Lord.

Giving me good hopes of the remission of them, by repentance, and by the works thereof, through the power of the most holy keys, and sacraments in Thy Church.

So that, day by day, for these Thy benefits, which I remember;

And so also for many more forgotten, by reason of their multitude, and my forgetfulness;

For them bestowed on me,

- Willing,
- Knowing,
- Asking,

Not
- Asking,
- Knowing,
- Willing,

I confess and give thanks to Thee, I bless and praise Thee, as is meet, every day.

[c] [Death, Judgment, Heaven, Hell.]

And I pray with all my soul, and with all my mind I pray.

Glory be to Thee,
O Lord,
Glory be to Thee,
Glory be to Thee,

And glory be to Thy most holy Name,

For all Thy Divine perfections in them,

For Thy unspeakable and unexpressible goodness and mercy toward sinners, and the unworthy,

And even toward me, altogether the most unworthy of all sinners.

Yea, O Lord,

For this and for the rest,

Glory and praise, and blessing, and thanksgiving, with the voices, and the harmony of the voices, of angels and men; of all Thy saints in heaven, and of all Thy creatures, whether in heaven or earth,

And, under their feet, of me, an unworthy and miserable sinner, Thy poor creature, both now in this day and hour, and daily unto my last breath, and unto the end of the world, and for ever and ever. Amen.

[*A Litany to be used upon special occasions of Public or Private Humiliation.*]

O FATHER, who didst create,
  Destroy not him, whom Thou didst create :
O Son, who didst redeem,
  Destroy not him, whom Thou didst redeem :
O Spirit, who didst regenerate,
  Destroy not him, whom Thou didst regenerate.
Remember not, Lord, our offences, nor the offences of our forefathers, neither take Thou vengeance on our sins ;
        on $\begin{cases} \text{Their,} \\ \text{Mine.} \end{cases}$
Spare us, good Lord.
    Spare $\begin{cases} \text{Them,} \\ \text{Me.} \end{cases}$
Spare Thy people ; and, in Thy people, me Thy servant, whom Thou hast redeemed with Thy precious blood ; and be not angry with us for ever.
        Be merciful,
        Be merciful,
Spare us, O Lord,
And be not angry with us for ever.
        Be merciful,
        Be merciful,
Have mercy on us, O Lord,
And be not angry with us very sore,
      Not very sore, O Lord,
Deal not with me according to my sins,
Neither reward me after mine iniquities,
But deal with me according to Thy great mercy,
And reward me after the multitude of Thy compassions ;
Even according to that great mercy,

And after that multitude of compassions,
As Thou didst deal with our fathers in the generations of old.
By whatsoever is dear unto Thee,
From all evil and adversity,
In all times of necessity,
From the evil and adversity at this present time,
Stand up, O Lord, rescue and save me,
Deliver me, O Lord,
And destroy me not.
    In the
Bed ⎫   ⎧ Sickness,
Hour ⎬ of ⎨ Death,
Day ⎭   ⎩ Judgment,
In *that* terrible and dreadful *day,*
Deliver me, O Lord, and save me
       ⎧ Beholding the stern countenance of the Judge,
From ⎨ Standing on the left hand,
       ⎩ Hearing that fearful sentence,
Depart from Me. *S. Matt.* xxv. 41.
      ⎧ Bound in the chains of darkness, 2 *S. Pet.* ii. 4.
From ⎪ Cast out into outer darkness, *S. Matt.* xxv. 30.
being ⎨ Tormented in the bottomless pit of fire and brim-
      ⎪   stone, where the smoke of torments ascendeth
      ⎩   up for ever and ever. *Rev.* xiv. 10, 11.
      Be merciful,
      Be merciful,
        Spare us.
Deliver us, O Lord, and save us; and destroy us not for ever; not for ever, O Lord.

And, that this may not be,
Remove far from me, O Lord,
* 1. Hardness of heart,
* 2. Want of remorse after sinning, *Ephes.* iv. 19.
* 3. Obduration of heart, *S. Mark* iii. 5, and vi. 52.
* 4. Setting light by Thy threatenings,
* 5. A seared conscience, 1 *Tim.* iv. 2.
* 6. A reprobate mind; *Rom.* i. 28.
The sin against the Holy Ghost; *S. Matt.* xii. 32.
The sin unto death; 1 *S. John* v. 16.

DEVOTIONS. 321

The four crying sins [a].

* The six forerunners of the sin against the Holy Ghost.

From the grievous and terrible evils

From
- Pestilence, famine, war;
- Earthquakes, inundations, great fires;
- Plague of immoderate rains;
- Drought;
- Corrupting winds, blasting;
- Thunder, lightning, tempest;
- Epidemical, acute, and evil diseases;
- And from sudden death;

[*Good Lord, deliver us.*]

From pernicious evil in the Church,

From
- Private interpretations, 2 *S. Peter* i. 20.
- Innovations in holy things,
- Strange doctrines, 1 *Tim.* i. 3.
- Doting about questions, and making endless strifes; 1 *Tim.* vi. 4.

From
Heresies,
Schisms,   } Public and private;
Scandals,

[*Good Lord, deliver us.*]

From the
- Deifying of kings, *Acts* xii. 22.
- Flattering of the people, *S. Mark* xv. 15; *Acts* xii. 3, and xxiv. 27.
- Profaneness of Saul, 1 *P. Sam.* xiv. 5.
- Scorns of Michal, 2 *P. Sam.* vi. 16.
- Fleshhook of Hophni, 1 *P. Sam.* ii. 13.

[*Good Lord, deliver us.*]

From the
- Massacre of Athalia, 2 *Kings* xi.
- Priesthood of Micha, *Judg.* xvii. 10.
- Combination of Simon [Magus], *Acts* viii. 18, and Judas [Iscar.], *St. Matt.* xxvi. 16.
- Doctrine of the unlearned and unstable, 2 *S. Pet.* iii. 16.

---

[a] [1. Voluntary murder, *Gen* iv. 20, 21. 2. Unnatural lusts, *Gen.* xviii. 20, 21. 3. Oppression of the poor, the fatherless and widows, *Exod.* xxii. 22, 23, and *Deut.* xv. 9. 4. Detention of the wages of the labourers, *Deut.* xxiv. 15, and *S. Jam.* v. 4.]

From the { Pride of novices, 1 *Tim.* iii. 6.
People that strive with the priest, *P. Hos.* iv. 4.

[*Good Lord, deliver us.*]

From pernicious evils in the state,

From { Anarchy, multitude of kings,
Tyranny, Asshur, Jeroboam, Rehoboam, Gallio, Haman;

From the {
Dangerous counsel of Achitophel, 2 *P. Sam.* xvi. 21.
Foolish counsel of Zoan, *P. Isa.* xix. 11, 13.
Statutes of Omri, *P. Mic.* vi. 16.
Judgments of Jezreel, 2 *Kings* x. 7.
Floods of Belial, *Psal.* xviii. 4.
Plague of Peor, *Numb.* xxv.
Valley of Achor, *H. Josh.* vii. 26.
Pollution of { Blood, Seed;

[*Good Lord, deliver us.*]

From { Foreign invasion, civil war,
Displacing of good and upright magistrates,
Exalting of bad and corrupt men into office,

[*Good Lord, deliver us.*]

From an uncomfortable life,

In { Sadness of spirit,
Infirmity of body,
Ill report, want,
Danger, servitude, tumults,

[*Good Lord, deliver us.*]

From death

In { Sin, shame,
Torture,
Distraction,
Filthiness,
Violence,

For treason;

From Sudden } Death;
Eternal

[*Good Lord, deliver us.*]

HOSANNA IN THE HIGHEST,

[*Or, a Supplication for Spiritual Blessings.*]

REMEMBER me, O Lord, according to the favour that Thou bearest unto Thy people;
Visit me with Thy salvation,
That I may
See the felicity of Thy chosen,
Rejoice in the gladness of Thy people,
Give thanks with Thine inheritance. *Psal.* cvi. 4, 5.
For there is a glory to be revealed, 1 *S. Peter* v. 1.
And, when the Judge cometh, *Acts* x. 42.
Some shall
See His face with joy; *H. Job* xxxiii. 26.
Be placed on His right hand; *S. Matt.* xxv. 33.
Hear that most sweet voice,
Come, ye blessed; Ver. 34.
Be caught up in the clouds, to meet the Lord; 1 *Thess.* iv. 17.
Enter into His joy; *S. Matt.* xxv. 21.
Enjoy the vision of Him;
Be ever with Him. 1 *Thess.* iv. 17.
These only, only these are blessed among the sons of men.
O give to me, the meanest of them all, the meanest place there, under their feet, under the feet of Thy elect, of the meanest of them.
And, to this end,
Let me find grace in Thy sight, that I may serve Thee acceptably, with reverence and godly fear. *Heb.* xii. 28.
But let me find this grace also, that I may not receive that grace in vain, 2 *Cor.* vi. 1.
Nor fall short of it, *Heb.* xii. 15.
Much less so neglect it, 1 *Tim.* iv. 14.
As to fall quite from it; *Gal.* v. 4.
But to stir it up, 2 *Tim.* i. 6.
So as to grow in it; 2 *S. Pet.* iii. 18.

Howsoever, to continue still in it, *Acts* xiii. 43, to the end of my life.

And, O make up the defects of Thy graces in me;

Of
- Faith; increase my little faith. *S. Luke* xvii. 5.
- Hope; confirm my trembling hope.
- Love; kindle the smoking flax thereof. *S. Matt.* xii. 20.

Shed abroad in my heart the love of Thee, *Rom.* v. 5.

That I may love Thee,

My { Friend, in / Enemy, for } Thee.

O Thou, who givest grace to the humble. *S. James* iv. 6.

Give me grace to be humble.

O Thou, who never failest them that fear Thee,

Let my heart rejoice in the fear of Thee. *Psal.* lxxxvi. 11. *secundum LXX.*

Let this my fear be my confidence; *H. Job* iv. 6.

Let me fear one thing only; not to fear anything more than Thee.

As I would that men should do unto me, so let me likewise do to them. *S. Matt.* vii. 12.

Nor let me think of myself more highly than I ought; but let me think soberly. *Rom.* xii. 3.

Give light to them who sit in darkness, and in the shadow of death,

Guide our feet in the way of peace, *S. Luke* i. 79.

That we may

Be like minded one towards another, *Rom.* xv. 5.

Rightly divide, 2 *Timoth.* ii. 15.

Uprightly walk, *Gal.* ii. 14.

Edify one another, 1 *Thess.* v. 11.

With one mind and one mouth glorify God; *Rom.* xv. 6.

But, if anything prove otherwise,

Let us walk by the same rule, whereto we have attained, *Phil.* iii. 16.

Let us hold fast

Order, *Coloss.* ii. 5; 1 *Corinth.* xiv. 40.

Decency, 1 *Corinth.* xiv. 40.

Steadfastness. *Col.* ii. 5.

HOSANNA UPON EARTH,

[*Or, a Supplication for Temporal Blessings.*]

REMEMBER, O Lord, to crown the year with Thy goodness. *Psal.* lxv. 11.
For the eyes of all wait upon Thee, O Lord;
Thou givest them their meat in due season;
Thou openest Thy hand, and fillest all things living with Thy gracious bounty. *Psal.* cxlv. 15, 16.
Vouchsafe us therefore, O Lord,
The blessings of heaven, and of the dew from above;
The blessings of the springs of the deep from beneath;
The returns of the sun;
The conjunctions of the moon;
The benefits of the rising mountains, and of the lasting hills;
The fulness of the earth, and of all that breeds therein; *Deut.* xxxiii. 13—16. *secundum LXX.*

{ Fruitful seasons,
Temperate airs,
Plenty of corn,
Abundance of fruits,
Health of body, and
Peaceable times;

Good and { Fair government,
Wise counsels,
Just laws,
Righteous judgments,
Loyal obedience,
Due execution of justice,
Sufficient store for life,
Prosperous issue,
Happy births,

Good and { Fair plenty
Due breeding } of children.
Right institution

That our sons may grow up as the young plants; and that our daughters may be as the polished corners of the temple.

That our garners may be full and plenteous with all manner of store; that our sheep may bring forth thousands.

That our oxen may be strong to labour; that there may be no decay; no leading into captivity; and no complaining in our streets. *Psal.* cxliv. 12—14.

One thing have I desired of the Lord, which I will require; that I may dwell in the house of the Lord all the days of my life, to behold the fair beauty of the Lord, and to visit His temple. *Psal.* xxvii. 4.

Two things will I require of Thee, O Lord; deny me them not before I die.

Remove far from me vanity and lies;

Give me neither poverty, nor riches.

Feed me with food convenient for me.

Lest I be full and deny Thee, and say, Who is the Lord?

Or lest I be poor and steal, and take the name of God in vain. *Prov.* xxx. 7—9.

Let me learn how to abound, and let me learn also how to want:

And in whatsoever state I am, therewith to be content. *Phil.* iv. 11, 12.

And, beside what I have, never either to desire, or expect, any earthly, transitory, corruptible thing.

Give me

A holy life

In {
Godliness,
Gravity,
Purity,
All goodness,
Cheerfulness of mind,
Health of body,
Good name,
Content, safety,
Liberty, quiet;
}

A happy death,

Eternal life.

[EVENING PRAYER.]

Having passed over this day, Lord, I give thanks unto Thee.
The evening draweth nigh, make it comfortable.
An evening there is, as of the day, so of this life.
The evening of this life is old age:
Old age hath seized upon me; make that comfortable.
Cast me not away in the time of age:
Forsake me not when my strength faileth me; *Psal.* lxxi. 9.
Be Thou with me until old age, and even to hoar hairs do Thou carry me. *P. Isa.* xlvi. 4.
Do Thou do it, do Thou forgive,
Do Thou receive and save me, O Lord.
Tarry Thou with me, O Lord, for it is toward evening with me: and the day is far spent, *S. Luke* xxiv. 29, of this my toilsome life.
Let Thy strength be made perfect in my weakness. 2 *Cor.* xii. 9.

The day is vanished and gone; so doth my life vanish; my life no life.
The night is coming on, and so doth death; death without death.
The end, as of the day, so of our life, is at hand.
We therefore, remembering this, beseech Thee, O Lord, that the end of our life being Christian, and acceptable to Thee, without sin, without shame, and, if it please Thee, without pain, Thou wouldst guide us in peace, O Lord our Lord; gathering us together under the feet of Thine elect, when Thou wilt, and as Thou wilt, only without shame and sin.

Grant that we may remember the days of darkness, that they are many, *Eccles.* xi. 8, that we be not cast out into outer darkness, *S. Matt.* xxii. 13, and xxv. 30, and that we may remember to prevent the night, by doing some good.
Judgment is at hand,
Grant us, O Lord, that we may make a good and acceptable account at the dreadful and terrible tribunal of Jesus Christ.

In the night I lift up my hands toward Thy sanctuary, and bless the Lord. *Psal.* cxxxiv. 2.

The Lord hath granted His loving-kindness in the day-time, and in the night-season will I sing of Him, and make my prayer unto the God of my life. *Psal.* xlii. 10.

As long as I live will I magnify Thee on this manner, and lift up my hands in Thy name. *Psal.* lxiii. 5.

Let my prayer be set forth in Thy sight as the incense; and let the lifting up of my hands be an evening sacrifice. *Psal.* cxli. 2.

Blessed art Thou, O Lord our God, the God of our Fathers,

Who didst create the interchanges of the day and night;

Who givest us occasions of songs in the night; *H. Job* xxxv. 10.

Who hast delivered us from the evil of this day;

Who hast not cut off, like a weaver, my life, nor in this day before night didst make an end of me. *P. Isa.* xxxviii. 12.

Lord, as we add days to our *days,* so we add sin to our sins. *Ecclus.* v. 5.

A just man falleth seven times a day, *Prov.* xxiv. 16; but I, a wretched sinner, seventy times seven times, *S. Matt.* xviii. 22, wonderfully and horribly, O Lord. *P. Jerem.* v. 30.

But I turn from my wicked ways, and bewailing them, *P. Isa.* xxx. 15, I return to my heart, *P. Isa.* xlvi. 8, and turn to Thee with all my heart, *Deut.* xxx. 2, O Thou who art the God of them that repent, O Saviour of sinners.

And evening after evening I return, with the utmost strength of my soul; and, out of the deep, my soul crieth unto Thee. *Psal.* cxxx. 1.

Lord, I have sinned against Thee, I have sinned grievously against Thee:

Forgive, forgive; alas, alas! woe worth my miserable condition!

I repent, woe is me, I repent; spare me, O Lord;

I repent, woe is me, I repent; help my want of repentance.

Have pity, spare me, O Lord;

Have pity, be merciful unto me.

I said, Lord, be merciful unto me, heal my soul, for I have sinned against Thee. *Psal.* xli. 4.

Have mercy upon me, O Lord, after Thy great goodness; according to the multitude of Thy mercies do away mine offences. *Psal.* li. 1.

Forgive my guilt,
Heal my sores,
Take out the stains,
Deliver me from shame,
Rescue me from the tyranny of sin,
And make me not an example.

Deliver me, O Lord, from my necessity, *Psal.* xxv. 16.
Cleanse me from my secret faults,
Keep Thy servant also from presumptuous sins. *Psal.* xix. 12, 13.

Impute not to me the wanderings of my *mind, Wisd.* iv. 12, nor my idle *words, S. Matt.* xii. 36.

Stop the black and filthy inundation of unclean and wicked *thoughts.*

O Lord, my destruction is from myself. *P. Hos.* xiii. 9.
Whatsoever I have done amiss, graciously pardon;
Deal not with us after our sins,
Neither reward us after our iniquities. *Ch. Eng. Litany.*

Mercifully look upon our infirmities, and for the glory of Thy most holy Name, turn from us all those evils and afflictions, which to our sins, and to us for them, are most justly and worthily due.

And, O Lord, give rest to me that am weary; renew my strength to me that am tired with labour,
Lighten mine eyes that I sleep not in death, *Psal.* xiii. 3.

Deliver me from the terrors of the night, and from the pestilence that walketh in darkness, *Psal.* xcviii. 5, 6.

Grant me wholesome sleep, and to pass this night without fear.

Thou Keeper of Israel, who dost neither slumber nor sleep, *Psal.* cxxi. 4.

Preserve me *this night* from all evil; O Lord, keep my soul, *Ver.* 7.

Visiting me with the salvation of Thy children:

Open my understanding in the visions of the night. *H. Job* xxxiii. 15, 16.

But, if not this, for I am not worthy,

I am not worthy,

Yet, O Lord, Thou lover of men, let my sleep be a rest, as from labours, so from sin;

Even so, O Lord.

And sleeping, let me not dream of anything

That may { Offend Thee, Defile myself.

Let not my loins be filled with illusions, *Psal.* xxxviii. 7, but rather let my reins chasten me. *Psal.* xvi. 8.

Preserve me, without grievous fear, from the dismal sleep of sin; and lay asleep in me all earthly and wicked imaginations;

Give me sweet sleep, free from all carnal and diabolical fancies.

Lord, restrain the malice of my never-sleeping invisible enemies; and the inclinations of my sinful flesh, O Thou who madest me.

Let the wings of Thy mercy shadow me, *Psal.* xvii. 8, and xci. 4.

Raise me up in due time in the hour of prayer; and grant that I may be early up, *Psal.* lxiii. 1, at my praises and worship of Thee.

Bless, O Lord, Thy creatures; Mankind.

All in affliction or prosperity; error or truth; sin or grace.

 The universal
  Church:

The Eastern, Western,
 This among us.

Prelates, clergy, laity.

The governments of the earth;

Christian; about us;
 Our.
   The

King, Queen, Prince.

All in authority and eminency.

Counsellors, judges,

Magistrates, officers,
  People.
Husbandmen, merchants, artificers,
Even to the { Labourers,
             { Poor,
All whom { Kindred,
         { Good turns,
         { Ministering in carnal things,
Charge { Formerly,
       { Now,
Moral friendship,
Charity,
Neighbourhood,
My promise,
Their desire,
Want of their own leisure,
Compassion on them being in extremity,
Worthy acts,
Good works,
Scandal given to,
Want of any else to pray for them commends to my prayers.

Lord, into Thy hands I commend *myself*,
My { Spirit,
   { *Soul*,
   { *Body*,
Thou hast { *Created*   } them,
          { *Redeemed* }
O Lord, Thou God of truth. *Psal.* xxxi. 6.

And, together with myself, all mine, and all that belong unto me:

Thou, O Lord, hast graciously given them unto Thy servant. *Gen.* xxxiii. 5.

Preserve my lying down, and my rising up, *Psal.* cxxxix. 1, from this time forth for evermore. *Psal.* cxxi. 8.

Grant that I may remember Thee upon my bed, *Psal.* lxiii. 7, and search out my spirit, *Psal.* lxxvii. 6; that I may rise again, and still be with Thee. *Psal.* cxxxix. 18.

I will lay me down in peace, and take my rest, for it is Thou, Lord, only that makest me dwell in safety. *Psal.* iv. 9.

[A Prayer for all Estates.]

[Bless, O Lord,]
The world,
The habitable part thereof,

The
- Church,
- Kingdom,
- Throne,
- Altar,
- Council-table,
- Judgment-seat,
- Universities,
- Shops;

All
Infants, children,
Striplings, youth,
Men grown in years,
Old men, infirm men;

The
Possessed, faint-hearted,
Sick, prisoners,
Orphans, widows,
Strangers;

All
Travellers by { Land, Water; }
Women { With child, Giving suck; }
In { Hard servitude, Solitude; }
Heavy-laden.

PRAYERS FOR THE HOLY COMMUNION,

[*Before the Receiving of the Blessed Sacrament.*]

O LORD, I am not fit, nor worthy that *Thou* shouldest come under the filthy roof of the house of my soul, *S. Matt.* viii. 8, because it is wholly desolate and ruinous; neither hast *Thou*, with me, a fit place where to lay *Thy* head; *S. Matt.* viii. 20.

But, as *Thou* didst vouchsafe to be laid in a *stable* and *manger* of unreasonable beasts, *S. Luke* ii. 7.

As *Thou* didst not disdain to be entertained even in the house of Simon the leper, *S. Matt.* xxvi. 6.

As *Thou* didst not reject the *harlot*, a sinner like unto me, coming unto *Thee*, and touching *Thee*,

As *Thou* didst not abhor *her* foul and profane mouth, *S. Luke* vii. 36, 38.

Nor yet the *thief* on the cross, confessing *Thee*; *S. Luke* xxiii. 43.

Even so vouchsafe to admit me also, an over-worn, miserable, and out of measure sinful creature, to the receiving and communicating of the most pure, most auspicious, quickening and saving *mysteries* of *Thy* most holy Body and *precious Blood* [a].

Attend, O *Lord* our *God*, from *Thy* holy habitation, and from the glorious throne of *Thy* kingdom, and come and sanctify us.

O *Thou* who sittest on high with the Father, and art here invisibly present with us, come and sanctify these gifts here presented, and those also by and for whom, and the end whereto they are brought hither [b].

---

[a] S. Chrysost. Liturgy.   [b] S. Chrysost. and S. Basil's Liturgy.

And grant us to partake of them

In { Faith, that need not be ashamed,
    Love, without dissimulation; *Rom.* xii. 9.

For the { Keeping of the commandments,
         Stirring up of all spiritual fruits,
         Healing of soul and body;

For a { Symbol of our communion, *Acts* ii. 42.
        Memorial of Thy dispensation; *S. Luke* xxii. 19.

For the { Shewing forth of Thy death, 1 *Cor.* xi. 26.
          Communion of Thy Body and Blood, 1 *Cor.* x. 16.
          Participation of Thy Spirit, 1 *Cor.* xii. 13.
          Remission of our sins; *S. Matt.* xxvi. 28.

For an amulet against all evil; 1 *Cor.* v. 7.
For the quieting of our conscience; *S. Matt.* xi. 28.

For the { Blotting out of our debts, *Col.* ii. 14; *Acts* iii. 19.
          Purging of our spots, *Heb.* ix. 14.
          Healing of the infirmities of our souls, 1 *S. Pet.* ii. 24.
          Renewing of our covenant, *Psal.* l. 5.
          Viands of our spiritual life, *S. John* vi. 27.
          Increase of strengthening grace, *Heb.* xiii. 9; soul-ravishing comfort, *Psal.* civ. 14.
          Enforcing of our repentance, 2 *Cor.* vii. 9.
          Enlightening of our understanding, *S. Luke* xxiv. 31.
          Exercise of our humility; *S. John* xiii. 11.

For { A seal of our faith, 2 *Cor.* i. 22.
      The fulness of wisdom, *S. John* vi. 35.
      A sufficient account of our oblations; 1 *Cor.* xvi. 1.

For the armour of patience; 1 *S. Pet.* iv. 1.
For the stirring up of our thankfulness; *Psal.* cxvi. 11.

For { Confidence in prayer, *Psal.* cxvi. 12.
      Mutual inhabitation, *S. John* vi. 56.
      A pledge of our resurrection, *S. John* vi. 54.
      An acceptable apology at the bar of judgment, 1 *Cor.* xi. 31.
      A testament of our inheritance, *S. Luke* xxii. 20.
      A type of perfection; *S. John* xvii. 23.

That we with all *Thy Saints*, who, from the beginning,

have pleased *Thee*, may be partakers of *Thy* most pure and eternal good things, which *Thou* hast prepared, O *Lord*, for them that love *Thee*, in whom *Thou* art glorified for ever.

O *Lamb* of *God*, who takest away the sin of the world, *S. John* i. 29, take away mine also, who am a notorious sinner.

We, therefore, O *Lord*, in the presence of *Thy holy mysteries*,
  Being mindful of
  The saving passions of *Thy Christ*,

His ⎰ Life-giving cross,
      Precious death,
      Three days burial,
      Resurrection from the dead,
      Ascension into heaven,
      Session at the right hand of *Thee* the Father,
      Glorious and dreadful return,

Humbly beseech *Thee*, that we receiving a part of *Thy holy mysteries* with a pure testimony of our conscience, may be united to the *holy body* and *blood* of *Thy Christ*.

" Let me so receive these mysteries, that I may be worthy to be engrafted into *Thy body*,
" Which is the *Church;*
" That I may become one of *Thy members*,
" And Thou my *Head;*
" That I may remain with *Thee*,
" And *Thou* with me;
" That now, not I in *myself*,
  " But *Thou* in *me*,
  " And I in *Thee*,
" May for ever continue in an indissoluble bond of love.
" Wash out the stains of my old and fresh sins;
" Never let any sinful spot abide, where so pure sacraments have entered.
" Through this *sacred mystery*, which I here call to mind,
" Bury me, already dead to this world, with *Thee* in *Thy* grave [c].

---

[c] [These prayers (thus " marked) are not in the Greek, but in the Latin MS.]

And receiving *this sacrament* not unworthily, let us procure *Christ's* dwelling in our hearts, *Ephes.* iii. 17, and be made a temple of Thy Holy Spirit. 1 *Cor.* vi. 19.

Even so, O *Lord.*

And make not any one of us guilty of these *Thy dreadful and heavenly mysteries;* nor weak in soul or body, by our unworthy partaking of the same. 1 *Cor.* xi. 27, 29, 30.

But grant, that, to our utmost and last gasp, we may worthily receive the hope of these *Thy mysteries,*

To our { Sanctification, Illumination, Strengthening;

To the ease of the burthen of our many sins;
As a preservative against all the assaults of the devil;
As a deletory and impediment of our evil customs;

For the { Mortification of our lusts, Keeping of *Thy* commandments, Increase of *Thy* divine grace, and Possession of *Thy* kingdom.

[*After the Receiving of the Blessed Sacrament.*]

"It is good for me to hold me fast by God, and to put my trust in the God of my salvation [d].

We have now, O *Christ* our *God,* finished and perfected, according to our ability, the *mystery of Thy dispensation.*

For we have { had the *memorial* of *Thy death;* seen the *type* of *Thy resurrection;* been filled with *Thy endless life;* enjoyed *Thy never-failing dainties;*

Whereof vouchsafe to make us all partakers in the world to come.

The good *Lord* pardon every one that prepareth his heart to seek the *Lord God* of his fathers, though he be not cleansed according to the purification of the *sanctuary.* 2 *Chron.* xxx. 18, 19.

[d] [In the Latin, not in the Greek MS.]

[*Special Duties recommended to Christian people.*]

I. What shall I do to inherit eternal life?
   1. Keep the commandments. *S. Mark* x. 17, 19.

II. What shall we do?
   2. Repent, and
   3. Be baptized every one of you. *Acts* ii. 37, 38.

III. What must I do to be saved?
   4. Believe on the Lord Jesus Christ. *Acts* xvi. 30, 31.

IV. What must we do?
   1. He that hath
      Two { Coats, Meats, }
   Let him give to him that hath none;
     To the people.
   2. Require no more than that which is appointed you:
     To the publicans.
   3. Do violence to no man, neither accuse any falsely:
   4. Be content with your wages:
     To the soldiers.
   S. Luke iii. 11, 13, 14.

1. Knowledge of the righteousness [*of God*].
   For { Fear, Humility, Repentance, Fasting, Prayers, Patience, }
   As a sacrifice.

2. Faith in the mercies [*of God*].

For { Hope,
Comfort,
Thanksgiving,
Alms,
Hymns,
Obedience,
As an Oblation.

FINIS.

I.

INDEX OF TEXTS TO SERMONS.

II.

GENERAL INDEX TO SERMONS,

&c.

☞ The Texts of SERMONS are distinguished by an asterisk.

INDEX OF TEXTS TO SERMONS.

GENESIS.

Genesis	Vol. Page
i. 1.	i. 85; iii. 242
2.	i. 273; iii. 169, 184, 197, 206, 242, 251, 257, 274, 354, 387
3.	iii. 169, 242, 257, 370; iv. 205; v. 316, 317, 370, 509
4.	iii. 370
5.	ii. 393
6.	iv. 205
7.	iv. 205
8.	ii. 393
9.	iv. 205
11.	v. 365
14.	i. 245; v. 509
20.	iii. 207
26.	iv. 205, 330; v. 207, 365, 410, 457, 462, 504
27.	v. 463
31.	v. 314
ii. 4.	v. 387
5.	v. 509
7.	iii. 207, 265; iv. 330; v. 462
9.	i. 129; iv. 110
17.	i. 181, 435
iii. 1.	v. 200, 443, 482, 495
2, 3.	v. 86
4.	i. 180; iii. 122
5.	i. 22, 206, 226; ii. 165, 215; iii. 71; v. 228
6.	i. 33, 173, 380, 417, 443; ii. 165; iii. 228; v. 520, 540
8.	i. 6; v. 318
9.	i. 6; iv. 123
10.	iii. 335; iv. 123
11.	v. 81
14.	i. 6; iv. 8, 9, 13, 15, 17
15.	i. 53, 72, 93, 104; iii. 10; iv. 15, 17, 345; v. 479, 505
19.	i. 123, 185; ii. 216; v. 407, 411, 544
22.	i. 22
24.	i. 210, 272
iv. 4.	v. 284
5.	v. 285, 434
7.	v. 87
8.	iv. 10; v. 434

Genesis	Vol. Page
iv. 9.	ii. 20; v. 427
10.	iii. 321; v. 81
12.	iv. 197
13.	iv. 328; v. 97
20—22.	ii. 7; v. 347
23.	v. 14
24.	v. 436
26.	ii. 7, 34; v. 326, 347
v. 22.	i. 361
24.	ii. 217
vi. 2.	v. 540
5.	v. 306
6.	iii. 213; v. 221
8.	v. 309
12.	v. 227
viii. 7.	iii. 256
11.	iii. 197, 252; iv. 253
ix. 2.	v. 492
6.	iv. 187, 196
25.	iii. 258; iv. 20
27.	i. 239; iii. 237
x. 8.	ii. 11
9.	i. 242; iv. 15, 58
xi. 3.	i. 242
4.	iii. 196
7.	i. 273; iii. 139
xii. 8.	v. 327
10.	v. 414, 498
17.	iv. 71
xiii. 16.	i. 130
xiv. 1—16.	iii. 230
14.	i. 324
14—16.	iv. 48
16.	iv. 388
18.	i. 168, 220
19.	ii. 257; iv. 324
23.	v. 548
xv. 1.	i. 416; v. 450
5, 6.	i. 130
6.	i. 13; v. 114
7.	i. 9
9, 10.	iii. 91
11.	v. 338
12.	ii. 232
17.	i. 124
xvii. 6.	v. 170
19.	i. 128

INDEX OF TEXTS.

Genesis	Vol. Page	Genesis	Vol. Page
xviii. 2.	i. 211	xxviii. 20, 21.	v. 359
3.	i. 133	xxx. 37.	ii. 6
5.	i. 133	xxxi. 24.	iv. 60
10.	i. 128	53.	v. 72, 74, 556
19.	v. 114	xxxii. 1.	v. 523
23.	iv. 210, 251, 253	6.	v. 15
24.	iv. 253	10.	i. 8; ii. 10; iv. 325;
25.	i. 124; ii. 150; iv. 192, 210		v. 306, 461
		11.	iv. 210
27.	i. 4, 8, 37, 123; v. 322, 364, 365	26.	i. 13; iii. 81; v. 331, 557
		28.	ii. 6
xix. 16.	i. 10	36.	v. 512
17.	ii. 62; v. 488, 541	xxxiii. 1.	ii. 41
20.	i. 160	5.	iii. 365; v. 313
22.	iv. 388	9.	ii. 91; iii. 365; v. 313, 416
24.	iii. 307	13.	ii. 23
26.	ii. 66	xxxiv. 2.	iv. 191
xx. 7.	v. 231, 356	11.	iv. 191
xxi. 17.	v. 529	13.	i. 407
18.	ii. 62	23.	ii. 46; iii. 276
24.	v. 72	24.	iv. 192
xxii. 1.	v. 443	25.	iv. 133, 191
2.	v. 510	30.	iv. 189
7.	ii. 201; iv. 213; v. 510	31.	iv. 192
8.	iv. 213; v. 510	xxxv. 16, 17.	iv. 343
9.	i. 301	18.	iv. 353
13.	iii. 299	19.	i. 157
14.	iv. 213; v. 510, 529	22.	iv. 57
16.	v. 72	xxxvi. 1.	iii. 64
18.	i. 13, 72, 104, 239; v. 505	xxxvii. 5.	v. 550
xxiii. 6.	iv. 48	9.	iv. 229
xxiv. 2.	i. 129; v. 79	xxxviii. 16.	iv. 57
3.	i. 129; v. 72, 79	28.	i. 162
5, 8.	v. 80	xxxix. 9.	v. 80
43.	i. 137	20.	ii. 392
50.	v. 299	xl. 15.	ii. 328
55.	i. 137	20.	i. 73
57.	i. 137	21.	i. 84
xxv. 6.	v. 377	xli. 4.	v. 32
23.	ii. 407	21.	v. 32
30.	i. 381, 401; iii. 75	35, 36.	v. 422
32.	i. 386	38.	iv. 214
33.	v. 81	44.	v. 150, 543
34.	v. 420	45.	i. 33; iv. 214
xxvi. 1.	v. 414, 498	51.	v. 455
4.	i. 129, 130	xlii. 2.	v. 414
11.	iv. 69	21.	v. 87
28.	iv. 48	32.	iv. 186
31.	v. 72	xliii. 1.	v. 498
xxvii. 12.	v. 535	11.	i. 445
22.	ii. 45	12.	v. 500
28.	v. 415	xliv. 10.	v. 210
29.	v. 207	xlv. 21.	v. 313
34.	v. 100	24.	i. 17; ii. 374
36.	ii. 6	27.	i. 68; ii. 245; iii. 295
37.	v. 318	xlvii. 25.	iv. 380; v. 135
38.	i. 351, 371; v. 100, 542	29.	v. 79
39.	v. 415	xlviii. 7.	i. 157
xxviii. 11.	ii. 275		
12.	i. 3, 23, 222; iv. 229; v. 408	EXODUS.	
13, seq.	iv. 229	i. 16.	iv. 210
17.	ii. 232	ii. 3.	i. 159, 202

INDEX OF TEXTS. 343

Exodus	Vol. Page	Exodus	Vol. Page
ii. 5, 6.	iv. 248	xvii. 9.	i. 327 ; v. 53
8.	i. 137	11.	v. 403
10.	iii. 351	12.	ii. 275
11.	ii. 9	13.	i. 326
13.	ii. 9 ; iv. 391	14.	i. 228
14.	iv. 278 ; v. 164	15.	ii. 22
21.	i. 239	xviii. 5.	i. 241
iii. 2.	ii. 177 ; iii. 124	14.	ii. 113
6.	v. 498	18, etc.	ii. 113
14.	iii. 374 ; iv. 278	23.	i. 26
iv. 3.	ii. 20	xix. 1.	iii. 147
6.	ii. 31	4.	iv. 327
14.	ii. 34.	12.	i. 31 ; iv. 55, 69
20.	iv. 13	13.	v. 142
24.	v. 228	xx. 1, seq.	v. 130, 433
v. 2.	i. 310 ; v. 249, 335	2.	iii. 52
3.	v. 228	3.	iii. 228 ; v. 365
12.	i. 169, 273 ; ii. 22	4.	v. 171
vii. 11.	v. 534	5.	iii. 214 ; iv. 328, 374 ; v. 171, 197
12.	v. 447, 556		
viii. 8.	ii. 68	6.	iv. 328
19.	iv. 208 ; v. 447	17.	v. 410
ix. 8.	v. 225	20.	iv. 380
27.	i. 310 ; iii. 84 ; v. 335	24.	v. 357, 384
28.	v. 335	xxi. 13.	v. 225
x. 16.	ii. 326	xxii. 11.	v. 80
xi. 10.	v. 447	28.	v. 245
xii. 2.	iv. 206	xxiii. 13.	v. 73
3, seq.	iv. 204	15.	i. 332
4, 5, seq.	i. 105	16.	iii. 115
6, 7.	iii. 210	17.	iv. 381
8.	i. 433	20.	v. 382—384, 523, 529
11.	ii. 249	xxiv. 8.	iii. 91
12.	i. 453	18.	i. 378
13.	ii. 153 ; v. 226	xxv. 2, seq.	i. 239
19.	ii. 302, 303	20.	iii. 251
22.	iii. 347	22.	iii. 10
23.	i. 428 ; iv. 204	32.	iii. 372
26.	ii. 292	40.	ii. 179 ; iv. 144
27.	ii. 299	xxvi. 34.	v. 98
29.	ii. 292	xxviii. 12, seq.	i. 25
36.	i. 239	29.	i. 25
xiii. 15.	ii. 296, 297	36.	iii. 206 ; iv. 374 ; v. 385
18.	ii. 23	37.	iii. 206
xiv. 10, seq.	iv. 380	xxxi. 3.	iii. 207
15.	v. 340	xxxii. 1.	i. 37
19, seq.	ii. 25	6.	i. 132 ; iv. 218 ; v. 497
20.	ii. 17	9.	ii. 25
21.	v. 510	10.	v. 339
22.	ii. 17	19.	ii. 349 ; v. 505, 551
xv. 9.	i. 334	22.	ii. 25, 26
10.	ii. 192	28.	v. 551
11.	i. 337 ; iv. 222, 340	29.	i. 323
xvi. 2.	v. 414, 497	xxxiii. 3.	ii. 25
3.	ii. 63	15.	v. 218
20.	ii. 349 ; v. 494, 528	17.	iii. 20
24.	ii. 349	18.	v. 464
27.	v. 528	22.	ii. 262
33.	ii. 349	23.	ii. 262 ; v. 382
xvii. 2.	v. 497	xxxiv. 1.	ii. 256
6.	ii. 33	4.	ii. 349
7.	v. 445, 497, 498, 513	6.	iv. 324
8.	i. 324, 326, 332	33.	iii. 312

INDEX OF TEXTS.

Exodus	Vol. Page
xxxv. 23, 27.	v. 38
xxxvii. 7, 8.	iii. 242
9.	iii. 242 ; iv. 324

LEVITICUS.

i. 4	ii. 297
ii. 1.	ii. 350
iii. 2.	ii. 297
3.	v. 66
iv. 5, 6.	v. 93
20.	v. 231
v. 1.	iv. 141 ; v. 76, 80
4.	v. 76
6.	ii. 350 ; v. 356
15.	iii. 329
18.	iv. 449, 450
vi. 3, 5.	v. 76
9.	ii. 350
12.	iii. 126
vii. 15.	v. 66
16, 17.	ii. 296
viii. 12.	i. 76
14.	ii. 297
xii. 50.	ii. 350
xiii. 45.	iii. 32 ; v. 225
46, 52, 54.	v. 225
xiv. 41, 45.	v. 225
xvi. 8.	i. 26 ; iv. 393
9.	i. 26
10.	i. 105
29.	i. 378, 388, 432
xvii. 11.	iii. 354
xviii. 5.	ii. 216
xix. 12.	v. 74
17.	v. 432
xxii. 15.	ii. 350
28.	iv. 211
32.	v. 78
xxiii. 5.	iv. 400
10.	ii. 212, 329
11, 14.	ii. 213
15.	iii. 115
16.	iv. 400
xxv. 9.	iii. 299
25.	ii. 259
xxvi. 12.	v. 463
26.	v. 417, 508
40.	v. 429, 430
42.	v. 430

NUMBERS.

v. 18.	v. 79
19.	v. 79, 80
vi. 3, 4.	i. 373
23.	iii. 81
24—26.	v. 463
27.	iii. 187 ; v. 68
viii. 7.	iii. 347
ix. 18, 20, 23.	v. 142

Numbers	Vol. Page
x. 1, 2.	* v. 141
3, 4.	v. 208
10.	iv. 217 ; v. 151
35.	iii. 222
xi. 6.	iii. 160
12.	i. 25 ; ii. 21
14.	i. 25
16.	iii. 198, 207
17.	iii. 207
18.	ii. 63
25.	iii. 131, 184
29.	iii. 314
33.	v. 507
34.	ii. 67
xii. 3.	ii. 24 ; iv. 8. 248 ; v. 551
14.	v. 100
15.	i. 449
xiii. 19.	ii. 4
23.	i. 237
33.	v. 13
xiv. 4.	ii. 63
xv. 34.	iii. 327
xvi. 1 seq.	v. 497
2.	iv. 10, 18
3.	iv. 12, 54, 286, 306 ; v. 233
10.	v. 63
12 seq.	ii. 21
14.	v. 168
15.	iv. 8 ; v. 551
21.	iv. 69
22.	v. 426
24—26	iv. 93, 309
28.	v. 247
29.	ii. 70 ; iv. 13, 19
29, 30.	v. 247
32.	iv. 34
33.	iv. 294
41.	ii. 25 ; iv. 41
46.	v. 228
47, 48.	v. 230
xvii. 8.	ii. 20, 349
xviii. 32.	v. 78
xix. 1, 2, seq.	i. 105
xx. 2, 3.	v. 414
10.	v. 533
11.	v. 532
13.	v. 152
xxi. 4, 6.	v. 497
8, 9.	ii. 128
14.	i. 334
xxii. 3.	i. 336
5.	i. 328
6.	iv. 7
17.	v. 545, 550
19 seq.	iv. 9.
23.	iii. 335 ; iv. 309 ; v. 542
25, 27.	v. 542.
xxiii. 7.	i. 242
8.	iv. 351
10.	ii. 82 ; v. 531
21.	ii. 11 ; v. 182
25.	v. 7
xxiv. 9.	iv. 194

INDEX OF TEXTS.

Numbers	Vol. Page
xxiv. 14 seq.	iii. 207
17.	i. 237, 238, 240, 244, 254
xxv. 1.	v. 495
5.	v. 233
6.	v. 227, 230
7, 8.	v. 232
9.	v. 223
14.	v. 227
xxvii. 16.	v. 426
17.	ii. 11, 33
21.	i. 105
xxviii. 3, 9, 10.	v. 354
xxix. 1.	v. 141
xxx. 2.	v. 73, 75
3.	v. 73
xxxi. 6.	v. 151
16.	iv. 82
xxxii. 23.	v. 87
xxxv. 25.	ii. 153
28.	iii. 209

DEUTERONOMY.

	Vol. Page
i. 2.	ii. 23
iv. 1.	v. 189
6.	ii. 316
19.	iii. 388; v. 316
29.	v. 329
32.	ii. 411; iv. 215; v. 154
v. 6, seq.	v. 433
27, 28.	v. 193
vi. 13.	v. 73, 78
16.	v. 513
vii. 15.	v. 332
viii. 2.	v. 533
3.	v. 418, 506, 527, 533
4.	v. 510
ix. 4.	iii. 342
6.	i. 13
9.	v. 491
x. 12.	v. 324, 330
17.	iii. 330
18.	v. 418
xii. 8.	v. 79, 172, 228, 240
xiii. 3.	v. 494
6.	ii. 267
xv. 4.	v. 44
11.	v. 46
xvi. 10.	iii. 115; v. 67
11.	iv. 217
19.	v. 540
xvii. 6.	iii. 353
14, seq.	v. 170
16.	ii. 32, 193
20.	iv. 291; v. 17
xviii. 18.	i. 24, 77, 104, 106, 165
xix. 14.	v. 135
15.	iii. 248
xx. 1—4.	i. 321
xxii. 6.	iv. 211
8.	v. 518
xxiii. 9.	✶ i. 321

Deuteronomy	Vol. Page
xxv. 1.	v. 116
2.	i. 449
xxvi. 8.	iv. 86
13.	v. 133
xxvii. 1, seq.	v. 433
13.	iv. 8
15—26.	v. 434
16.	iv. 20
24.	iv. 60, 194
25.	iv. 194
26.	v. 115, 427, 434
xxviii. 12.	ii. 5.
23.	v. 407
xxix. 19.	i. 363; v. 16, 99
20.	v. 99
29.	iv. 373; v. 347, 398
xxxi. 6.	v. 529
14.	ii. 252
19.	ii. 3; v. 204
xxxii. 2.	iii. 305, 326
4.	v. 471
5.	ii. 26
6.	ii. 25; v. 366
7.	ii. 65
8.	v. 552
11.	i. 26
15.	v. 421
17.	v. 229
22.	ii. 86, 94
29.	i. 425; ii. 93
32.	ii. 62; iii. 71
35.	iv. 187
49.	v. 540
51	v. 386
xxxiii. 2.	iv. 252
5.	iv. 291; v. 150
7.	ii. 5, 6; v. 212
8.	v. 384
10.	i. 296; v. 355
11.	ii. 35
17.	iv. 368
19.	v. 4
26.	iii. 225
27.	ii. 12
xxxiv. 9.	iv. 253

JOSHUA.

	Vol. Page
i. 17.	v. 154
ii. 1.	i. 241
vi. 4.	iii. 299
vii. 5.	i. 325, 327
6.	i. 379
11, 12.	i. 335
19.	v. 75, 459
21.	v. 540
26.	i. 332
x. 13.	v. 407, 408
xvi. 36.	v. 468
xix. 15.	i. 157
xxii. 11.	v. 185
12.	i. 324

Joshua	Vol. Page	Judges	Vol. Page
xxiii. 7.	v. 73	xix. 1 seq.	v. 170, 241
xxiv. 1, 28.	v. 154	22—30.	i. 335
		25 seq.	ii. 11
JUDGES.		30.	v. 181
		xx. 1.	i. 324
iii. 1.	v. 537	10, 17.	i. 327
9, 15.	v. 244	26.	i. 379
21.	iv. 160, 251	40.	iii. 317
iv. 9.	i. 326	xxi. 25.	v. 170
19.	i. 366		
19—21.	v. 558		
v. 2.	i. 337; v. 220	RUTH.	
7.	iv. 20		
9.	i. 337; v. 220	i. 4.	i. 241
15.	i. 23, 273; v. 210	20.	i. 39
16.	i. 331; v. 209, 219	ii. 4.	i. 148
20.	i. 336; v. 212	20.	ii. 225
21.	i. 336; iii. 66	iii. 12.	ii. 259
23.	i. 327; iv. 8, 13; v. 137, 208, 212, 220		
24.	v. 220	1 SAMUEL.	
30.	iv. 337		
31.	iv. 13, 17, 200; v. 256	i. 7.	i. 385
vi. 11.	i. 75	11.	iii. 85
36 seq.	ii. 386; v. 530	15.	i. 385
37.	i. 71	ii. 6.	iii. 89
vii. 20.	i. 332; iv. 13	12.	i. 288
viii. 2.	iii. 77	15 seq.	v. 14
19.	v. 74	16.	iii. 167; v. 134
22.	v. 170	24.	i. 305
ix. 1 seq.	v. 552	30.	v. 389, 465
2.	i. 411; v. 170	iii. 5.	v. 504
3 seq.	v. 75	9.	iv. 378
4.	iv. 308; v. 207	17.	v. 80
5.	iv. 28	18.	i. 6
13.	iii. 71	iv. 18.	iii. 296
15.	ii. 317; iii. 254; iv. 254; v. 9, 542	19.	iv. 343
		21.	iv. 353
23.	i. 336; v. 219	v. 2—4.	v. 556
48.	v. 503	vi. 9.	v. 225
53.	ii. 13	19.	i. 33
x. 14.	v. 556	vii. 3.	v. 556
xi. 1.	i. 75	12.	ii. 5
xiii. 5.	i. 75	viii. 5.	ii. 115
15.	i. 211	18.	iv. 286
16.	v. 545	19.	ii. 9, 26; v. 537
22.	i. 272	20.	ii. 26
xv. 4.	i. 271; iv. 248	ix. 2.	iv. 323
14.	i. 191	21.	v. 11
xvi. 3.	ii. 233	24.	v. 543
16.	v. 537	x. 1.	i. 76
18.	iv. 351	6.	iii. 271
19.	ii. 409	9.	iii. 271; iv. 58
25.	ii. 172, 329; v. 534	10.	iii. 118, 271; iv. 58
29.	ii. 6, 172; v. 534	11.	iii. 271; v. 521
30.	ii. 172, 354; v. 534	26.	ii. 8; v. 133
xvii. 1 seq.	ii. 11	27.	i. 199; v. 133, 542
2.	v. 80, 170	xi. 5.	iv. 37; v. 210, 543
4.	v. 240	xii. 3, 4.	iv. 39
5.	v. 170	21.	iii. 399
6.	ii. 33; ✱ v. 169	23.	ii. 115; v. 339, 355
xviii. 1.	v. 170	xiii. 1.	iv. 37
15—27.	v. 240	9.	iv. 38

INDEX OF TEXTS. 347

1 Samuel	Vol. Page	1 Samuel	Vol. Page
xiii. 13.	i. 351	xxv. 17.	v. 16
14.	i. 229; ii. 19; iv. 10, 81, 173; v. 117, 250, 282, 368	23.	i. 329
		31.	i. 361; iii. 204
19.	v. 506	32 seq.	v. 79
22.	ii. 12	36.	ii. 41; v. 15
xiv. 4.	v. 535	41.	ii. 327
13.	v. 535	xxvi. 8.	iv. 92, 155
18.	ii. 11	8, 9.	✳ iv. 24
19.	ii. 11; v. 323, 345	9.	iv. 44, 57, 172, 242, 308; v. 132
24.	i. 386		
28.	v. 79	10.	iv. 31
44.	v. 74	11.	iv. 172
xv. 4.	v. 542	16.	iv. 172
9.	ii. 13, 327; v. 229	19.	i. 274
11.	iii. 213	21.	iv. 115
17.	ii. 32, 283; iv. 15, 38	xxviii. 2.	iv. 134
23.	iii. 255	6.	v. 330
29.	i. 321; iii. 213	7.	v. 500
30.	i. 411	14.	i. 407
xvi. 1.	v. 399	15 seq.	v. 522
4.	iv. 84	19.	v. 500
6.	ii. 283; iii. 330; iv. 80	xxix. 4.	ii. 283
7.	iii. 330, 333	xxx. 1—20.	iii. 230
12.	iv. 28, 80	xxxi. 4.	ii. 172
13.	iii. 118; iv. 83	7.	ii. 4
14.	iii. 259; iv. 38, 58, 81		
23.	iv. 27		
xvii. 28.	ii. 283	2 SAMUEL.	
36.	iii. 86		
37.	v. 513	i. 10.	iv. 63, 113
49.	i. 167; iv. 27	12.	i. 385
50.	v. 513	13.	iv. 63
54.	iii. 229	14.	iv. 34, 172
xviii. 6.	iv. 27	16.	iv. 172
7.	iv. 27, 323	18.	ii. 12
10.	iii. 191	20.	i. 39
11.	ii. 13; iv. 27	21.	iv. 32, 63
17.	ii. 12	ii. 4.	iv. 94.
19.	ii. 12	8.	ii. 283
25.	iv. 27	14, 26.	i. 330; ii. 4
xix. 1, 5.	iv. 27	iii. 7.	v. 16
10.	ii. 13; iv. 27	12.	ii. 4
15.	iv. 27	27.	v. 251
xx. 3.	iv. 113, 213	33.	ii. 173
27.	v. 13	35	i. 368, 379
33.	ii. 13; iv. 37	36.	i. 379
xxi. 4.	ii. 12	39.	ii. 24; iv. 253
xxii. 7.	ii. 102; v. 543	iv. 4.	iii. 372; v. 319
8.	ii. 15	5.	iv. 133; v. 252
9.	iii. 65; v. 251	5—12.	iv. 132
17.	ii. 13, 35	12.	iv. 18, 19, 33, 71; v. 248
18.	iv. 38	v. 2.	ii. 284; iv. 15
22.	ii. 126	3,	iv. 94
23.	iv. 38	6, 7.	iii. 222
xxiii. 6.	iv. 39	vi. 1—19.	iii. 222
12.	v. 251	7.	iii. 34, 390
xxiv. 2.	iv. 158	16.	ii. 12; v. 250
5—8.	✳ iv. 153	19.	iii. 222
6.	iv. 167, 172	20.	i. 39; v. 17, 250, 554
11.	iv. 158, 165	22.	i. 141; ii. 325; iv. 375; v. 250, 554
18, 20.	iv. 28		
xxv. 9.	iv. 173	vii. 14.	i. 291
10 seq.	ii. 109	18.	iv. 290

INDEX OF TEXTS.

2 Samuel	Vol. Page
vii. 19.	i. 59; iv. 290; v. 254
20.	v. 255
27.	v. 338
viii. 15.	ii. 14; v. 105
17.	iv. 209
ix. 7.	v. 437
x. 4.	v. 243
xi. 2.	v. 495, 514
4.	v. 537
11.	i. 336
21.	ii. 13, 65.
xii. 5—7.	ii. 129
7.	ii. 151; iv. 118
13.	i. 189; ii. 297; v. 93
16.	i. 385, 443
30.	iv. 113
31.	v. 243
xiii. 24.	v. 543
28.	iv. 21
39.	iii. 298
xiv. 10.	v. 543
20.	i. 4; v. 544
23.	iii. 298
24.	v. 374
32.	v. 378
33.	iii. 298
xv. 1 seq.	iv. 21
2—6.	iv. 12
3.	ii. 14; iv. 306
4.	v. 542
5.	ii. 326
7.	i. 407; ii. 47
8.	iv. 21, 89
10.	iv. 21; v. 248
11.	iv. 307
12.	v. 248
15.	v. 555
25.	v. 340, 343
26.	v. 340
31.	ii. 286
xvi. 7.	ii. 58; iv. 306, 308
9.	iv. 34
11.	v. 550
13.	iv. 8
17.	iv. 12
21.	iv. 308
22.	iv. 12
xvii. 14.	iv. 350; v. 247.
23.	iv. 34
25.	ii. 286
xviii. 2.	i. 241
3.	ii. 15; iv. 106, 209, 258
5.	v. 368, 430
8.	iv. 272
9.	i. 336; iv. 18, 34
10.	iv. 7
14.	iv. 33, 34
32.	iv. 3; ✱ v. 256
33.	v. 251
xix. 14.	v. 219
21.	iv. 49, 57
23.	v. 437
27.	v. 184

2 Samuel	Vol. Page
xx. 1.	i. 325; ii. 286; iv. 11, 14, 120, 306, 308; v. 131, 247
9, 10.	v. 251
12.	ii. 127
14.	iv. 308
21.	ii 15; iv. 18, 19, 33, 92; v. 247
24.	iv. 209
xxi. 7, 8, 11.	iv. 118
16.	iv. 89
17.	iii. 371; iv. 15; v. 317
xxii. 2.	ii. 7
5.	i. 329, 335
xxiii. 3.	ii. 7; v. 206
8.	ii. 14; iv. 209
15.	v. 528
18.	iv. 172
19.	ii. 224
xxiv. 1 seq.	i. 387
10.	iv. 107, 166
17.	v. 230
25.	i. 172

1 KINGS.

i. 5.	iv. 18, 280
7.	iv. 80, 281, 308; v. 248
50.	v. 247
ii. 5 seq.	ii. 15; iv. 192
9.	v. 247
23.	i. 325
25.	iv. 18
27.	iv. 281
28—34.	iv. 33
32.	iv. 97
34.	iv. 18, 19
43.	v. 81
46.	iv. 71; v. 247
iii. 9—12.	ii. 103
26.	iv. 272
iv. 30.	i 245
v. 7.	i. 240
8.	iii. 386
10.	i. 240
11.	iii. 386
13.	i. 240
vii. 21.	ii. 7
viii. 18.	ii. 351; v. 307
27.	i. 204; v. 373, 407
31.	v. 79, 80
32.	v. 116
37.	v. 230, 452
38.	i. 333; iv. 166, 270; v. 227, 230, 352, 452
39.	v. 230, 452
49.	v. 431
59.	iii. 4
x. 1.	i. 241; v. 543
9.	v. 105, 184
xi. 14.	v. 181

INDEX OF TEXTS. 349

1 Kings	Vol. Page	2 Kings	Vol. Page
xii. 3.	iv. 308	viii. 22.	iv. 251
4.	iv. 306	ix. 37.	v. 466
6.	iv. 120	x. 8.	v. 550
7.	v. 555	18.	i. 407
8.	v. 207	20.	v. 155
10, 11.	ii. 23	xi. 1.	iv. 28, 287; v. 550
xiii. 4.	ii. 31; iv. 131	12.	ii. 13
5.	v. 502	16.	iv. 160
xiv. 15.	ii. 22; v. 241	20.	iv. 251
xv. 1.	iv. 20	xii. 21.	iv. 133; v. 248
26.	v. 184	xiii. 14.	i. 326, 328; ii. 9; v. 37
30.	v. 245	xiv. 9.	v. 15, 542
xvi. 9.	v. 248, 252	10.	ii. 5
15.	iv. 289	25.	ii. 391
18.	iv. 34	26.	iv. 176
xvii. 4.	v. 46	xv. 8.	iv. 289
9.	i. 241; v. 46	13.	iv. 289
14, 15.	v. 508	19, 20.	v. 138
23.	ii. 292	xvii. 41.	v. 556
xviii. 10.	v. 80	xviii. 4.	ii. 336
xix. 5.	v. 529, 555	xix. 3.	iv. 344
8.	v. 491	31.	i. 92
11.	iii. 118, 267; v. 318	xx. 3.	i. 229
12.	i. 105; iii. 267; v. 318	8—11.	ii. 386
16.	i. 76	xxiii. 31.	iv. 289
18.	ii. 333; v. 554	xxv. 8 seq.	iv. 210
xx. 11.	i. 332; ii. 5		
32, 33.	iii. 42	**1 CHRON.**	
xxi. 2.	v. 540		
4.	i. 385		
7.	v. 14	iv. 4.	i. 157
9.	i. 408; ii. 47	xi. 2.	ii. 284
13.	iv. 14	10 seq.	ii. 14
20.	v. 447	15.	i 324
27.	i. 371, 387, 388, 443	17.	i. 168
xxii. 8.	v. 7	20—47.	iv. 209
11.	v. 18	xii. 17.	v. 74
13.	v. 7	18.	ii. 5; iv. 14, 173
16.	v. 76, 80	xiii. 1 seq.	iv. 116
22.	v. 446, 447	2.	ii. 13
27.	v. 16	3.	ii. 11, 13
31.	v. 242	10.	iv. 56
		xv. 1 seq.	iv. 116
		4.	v. 155
2 KINGS.		10.	iv. 284
		xvi. 1.	iv. 72
i. 2, 3.	v. 331	3.	iii. 222, 239
ii. 9.	iii. 135	5.	iv. 72
11.	ii. 329; iii. 52	22.	✶ iv. 43; v. 132
16.	iii. 224	23.	iv. 72
iii. 14.	v. 496	36.	v. 468
iv. 7.	v. 429, 442	37, 42.	iv. 72
27.	iii. 327; v. 340	xvii. 1.	ii. 55
40.	iii. 71; v. 509	23.	v. 470
v. 13.	ii. 343	xx. 6.	i. 324
15.	i. 241	xxi. 1.	v. 233
27.	iv. 20	7.	v. 226
vi. 9.	v. 246, 501	8.	v. 233
17.	v. 532	14.	v. 228
27.	v. 453, 463	16.	i. 14; v. 226
32.	v. 532	18.	i. 240
33.	v. 482, 499	30.	v. 226
vii. 9.	i. 65	xxiii. 2, 3, 6.	v. 155

1 Chron.

	Vol. Page
xxiv. 1 seq.	iv. 116
xxv. 1 seq.	iv. 116
xxvi. 1 seq.	ii. 13; iv. 117
15, 16.	v. 208
xxviii. 1 seq.	iv. 116
xxix. 11.	v. 136, 458, 469
12.	v. 136
14.	v. 44, 417
23.	iv. 14, 53

2 CHRON.

vi. 8.	ii. 352
13.	v. 329
41.	iii. 237
42.	iv. 49
ix. 8.	iv. 284
20.	v. 493
x. 14.	v. 184
xiii. 5.	ii. 76
7.	v. 207
17.	v. 184
xv. 2.	i. 151
3.	ii. 33
14.	v. 155
15.	v. 78
xvi. 12.	i. 317; v. 226, 507, 511
xvii. 2.	ii. 9
xix. 5.	ii. 9
6.	ii. 32
7.	iii. 330
8.	v. 76
11.	ii. 32; v. 509
xx. 3.	i. 335, 387; v. 155, 491
12.	v. 327
14.	i. 326
15.	i. 332
26.	i. 332
37.	iv. 350
xxii. 10.	v. 181
xxiii. 9, 10.	v. 530
xxiv. 5.	v. 155
25.	v. 252
xxv. 3.	v. 248
6.	v. 138
8.	i. 327
xxvi. 16.	iii. 390
16—21.	iv. 38
xxix. 15.	v. 155
xxx. 19.	iii. 152
xxxiv. 29, 30.	v. 155
xxxvi. 13.	v. 75
16.	v. 464
19.	ii. 349
22.	iv. 234

EZRA.

i. 1.	iv. 234, 236
iii. 4.	v. 266
iv. 5.	v. 10

Ezra

	Vol. Page
v. 13.	iv. 402
vi. 12.	iv. 402
vii. 9.	ii. 30
viii. 21.	i. 388
x. 2.	v. 80, 333
5.	v. 80

NEHEMIAH.

i. 11.	i. 229; v. 41
iv. 1.	ii. 325
v. 12.	v. 80
vi. 6.	ii. 58
10, 12.	v. 525
18.	v. 80
vii. 39 seq.	v. 155
64, 65.	v. 155
viii. 9.	iv. 217
10.	iv. 217, 405
ix. 1, 2.	i. 389
3.	v. 354
xiii. 11.	v. 155
16.	v. 493

ESTHER.

ii. 21.	iv. 11, 12, 62, 92, * 127, 198; v. 240, 248
22.	iv. 92, 127, 308; v. 246
23.	iv. 19, 33, 71, 92, 127; v. 248
iii. 1.	ii. 325; iv. 391; v. 543
5 seq.	iv. 210, 392
6.	iv. 130, 309
7.	iv. 367, 389
8.	iv. 392
9.	ii. 46
12, 13.	iv. 386
iv. 3.	iv. 369, 404
11.	iv. 134; v. 362
14.	iv. 141; v. 41
16.	i. 378, 387, 389
v. 14.	iv. 396
vi. 1.	ii. 21; iv. 396
6.	v. 10
8—11.	iii. 271
vii. 3.	iv. 396, 397
4.	iv. 396
6.	iv. 392
7.	iv. 350
9.	iv. 396
10.	iv. 386, 396; v. 543
viii. 9, 10.	iv. 396
ix. 17—22.	iv. 150
20.	v. 155
21.	iv. 386
22.	iv. 151
25.	iv. 397
26.	iv. 204
31.	* iv. 385

INDEX OF TEXTS. 351

JOB.

Job	Vol. Page
i. 1.	i. 241; iii. 334
6.	v. 232
8.	ii. 257; iii. 341; v. 117
9.	ii. 257; v. 31, 482
10.	iii. 225; v. 521
11.	iv. 59, 431
12.	v. 240, 445, 484, 552
18, 19.	iv. 210
21.	i. 162; iii. 366; v. 28, 314, 400
22.	v. 529
ii. 3.	ii. 257; v. 557
4.	ii. 104, 257, 327; iii. 208, 225; v. 50, 240
5.	iv. 59; v. 513
7.	v. 552
10.	v. 529
iii. 3, 5, 6.	iv. 206
iv. 6.	iv. 301
8.	iv. 131
16.	iii. 199, 268
18.	ii. 259; iii. 374; iv. 325; v 109, 426
19.	i. 5; v. 372
v. 6.	v. 226, 484
7.	v. 104, 110, 226
vi. 15.	ii. 68
15—17.	iii. 159
15—20.	ii. 373
26.	ii. 255
vii. 1.	v. 480
3.	i. 48
7.	ii. 64
20.	ii. 258; v. 238
viii. 8.	ii. 65, 411, 418
9.	ii. 64
14.	ii. 374; v. 24
ix. 3.	i. 280; v. 429
11.	iii. 15, 115; v. 217
15.	iii. 341; v. 117
20.	v. 429
28.	iii. 341
30.	iii. 247, 347
x. 9.	ii. 64
15.	iii. 341; v. 117
xi. 12.	ii. 28; v. 401
xii. 2.	iii. 327; v. 197
7.	i. 349
18.	iv. 289
xiii. 15.	ii. 400; iv. 364
26.	v. 426
xiv. 2.	iii. 374
4.	i. 4; iii. 244
xv. 15.	ii. 259; iv. 325; v. 109
16.	i. 331; v. 428
xvi. 2.	iii. 160
19.	i. 416
20.	i. 369; ii. 263
xvii. 14.	i. 4; ii. 101; iii. 54
xviii. 14.	ii. 194
xix. 21.	ii. 139

Job	Vol. Page
xix. 23—27.	
25.	i. 123; ii. 198
27.	ii. 208
xx. 10.	v. 25
11.	v. 87
12, 13.	v. 86
14.	v. 511
29.	iv. 398
xxi. 15.	v. 326, 547
xxii. 3.	i. 354
13, 14.	v. 373
xxiii. 12.	v. 419
xxiv. 13.	v. 319
xxv. 4.	ii. 259
5.	ii. 259; v. 109
xxvi. 7.	ii. 278
xxvii. 3.	v. 345
8.	v. 26
10.	v. 354
xxviii. 5, 6.	v. 507
28.	iii. 335
xxix. 11.	v. 34
xxxi. 1.	ii. 263; v. 447, 541
7.	v. 541
9.	v. 541
22.	ii. 320
24.	v. 19, 527
25, 28.	v. 507
37.	v. 518
xxxii. 8.	iii. 133
21, 22.	v. 106
xxxiii. 7.	ii. 30
15.	i. 104
23.	v. 93
24.	i. 184; ii. 258; v. 93, 429
26.	i. 436; ii. 264; v. 431
27.	iii. 399; v. 309
28.	v. 309
33.	v. 557
xxxiv. 19.	iii. 330
31.	ii. 258
xxxv. 11.	i. 2
xxxvi. 7.	iv. 53, 58, 284
xxxvii 5, 6.	v. 375
9.	iii. 266
xxxviii. 6.	ii. 278
7.	i. 211, 292
9.	i. 204
28.	iii. 52; v. 365
31.	v. 375
xxxix. 27.	i. 85
xl. 27.	i. 336
xli. 24.	ii. 127
34.	v. 392
xlii. 6.	i. 372
8.	v. 356
10.	v. 557

	Vol. Page
	✱ ii. 252

PSALMS.

i. 1.	iv. 189
3.	i. 432; iv. 220
4.	iv. 179

Psalms	Vol. Page	Psalms	Vol. Page
ii. 3.	ii. 21	xix. 8.	v. 319
6.	v. 392	10.	ii. 103 ; v. 419
7.	i. 53, 109, 164 ; ii. 375 ; iii. 57, 257	13.	iv. 305 ; v. 444, 521
8.	i. 286 ; iv. 283	14.	ii. 256
11.	iii. 24, 78 ; iv. 219	xx. 2.	iv. 117
12.	i. 62	5.	iv. 120
iii. 1.	iv. 9, 10	6.	ii. 32 ; iv. 68
8.	v. 238	7.	i. 332 ; iv. 107 ; v. 508
iv. 6.	iii. 368 ; v. 312	8.	ii. 6 ; iv. 107, 109, 368 ; v. 106
v. 3.	v. 474	9.	iv. 115 ; v. 238, 349
12.	ii. 7	xxi. 1.	iv. 6, 23, 332
vi. 2.	v. 359	1—4.	✶ iv. 101
6.	i. 448	2.	v. 353
vii. 4.	iv. 27 ; v. 469	3.	ii. 19, 241 ; iv. 53, 284
5.	v. 469	5.	iv. 108
8, 9.	v. 5	6.	iv. 105
13.	iv. 368	7.	iv. 118, 136
14.	iv. 346	8.	iv. 106, 118
16.	iv. 91 ; v. 253	9, 10.	iv. 118
viii. 1, 2.	iii. 270	11.	iv. 91, 115, 118, 398
3.	i. 14	12.	iv. 118 ; v 247
4.	i. 91, 112, 204 ; iv. 330	13.	iv. 214
6.	iv. 330	xxii. 1.	ii. 139
ix. 10.	iii. 14, 340	6.	i. 92 ; ii. 165, 275
13.	ii. 328 ; iv. 266	14.	ii. 5, 170
15.	iv. 268, 368	15.	ii. 5
17.	i. 362 ; ii. 264	16.	ii. 121, 170, 277
x. 4.	v. 18	20.	ii. 293
16.	iv. 375	21.	iv. 367
xii. 4.	ii. 340 ; iv. 11 ; v. 461	27.	i. 241
xiv. 4.	v. 323	xxiii. 2.	i. 168 ; ii. 24
5.	i. 403	4.	ii. 400
xv. 1.	ii. 321 ; v. 219	6.	i. 99 ; iv. 267
1 seq.	ii. 3	xxiv. 1.	v 28, 382, 552
2.	v. 425	5.	v. 109, 326
4.	v. 75	6.	i. 259, 309 ; ii. 317 ; v. 326
xvi. 2.	ii. 334, 368 ; v. 107, 284, 307, 382	xxv. 17.	v. 444
		22.	v. 469
3.	v. 408	xxvi. 5.	v. 221
6.	i. 182 ; iv. 398	6.	iii. 359
8.	ii. 137 ; v. 376	11.	i. 107
9.	i. 98, 129 ; ii. 266, 357 ; iii. 10 ; iv. 218	12. Vulg.	i. 344
		xxvii. 1.	v. 104
10.	ii. 260, 397 ; iii. 61, 65, 313	4.	v. 377, 415
11.	i. 320, 360 ; ii. 184, 260 ; iii. 213 ; iv. 383 ; v. 382	8.	v. 330
		9.	v. 403
xvii. 7.	v. 256	10.	v. 374
14.	v. 454	11.	iii. 97
xviii. 2.	iv. 290 ; v. 18, 248	13.	ii. 25 ; iii. 120, 226
10.	iii. 118, 251 ; v. 528	14.	v. 474
14.	iv. 248	xxviii. 5.	ii. 127
28.	v. 319	8.	v. 238
39.	iv. 284	xxix. 1, 2.	v. 460
44.	iv. 218	9.	v. 357
45.	v. 242, 252	xxx. 3.	iv. 289
46—48.	i. 337	5.	iv. 268 ; v. 455
50.	i. 337 ; v. 238, 256	6.	iii. 173, 336
xix. 1.	v. 372	9.	i. 180 ; iii. 399
2.	iv. 95, 118	11.	iii. 17
3.	iii. 139	12.	ii. 337
4.	i. 234 ; ii. 19 ; iv. 139	xxxi. 4.	i. 362
5.	i. 142	15.	i. 268 ; iv. 394

INDEX OF TEXTS.

Psalm	Vol. Page
xxxii. 3.	v. 353
4.	v. 225
5.	v. 353, 429, 431
6.	i. 443; v. 353, 429, 431
9.	i. 15; ii. 9, 28; v. 401
xxxiii. 9.	i. 301; iii. 146; v. 509
10.	ii. 6
11.	v. 397
12.	v. 245
17.	v. 238
xxxiv. 7.	v. 523
8.	i. 134; ii. 205, 268, 301; iii. 161
9.	v. 510
12.	i 429
14.	i. 191, 223; ii. 249
xxxv. 3.	v. 238, 487
10.	iv. 238, 275; v. 255, 349
13.	i. 388; v. 341, 359, 474
27.	iv. 220, 405
xxxvi. 6.	iii. 32; v. 237, 398
7.	iv. 108; v. 237
9.	ii. 198
xxxvii. 3.	v. 31
5.	v. 27
15.	iv. 23, 97, 253
xxxviii. 4.	iv. 321, 329
5.	v. 227
9.	v. 337
15.	v. 125
18.	v. 429, 442
xxxix. 1.	i. 336
2.	v. 399
3.	iii. 137, 199; v. 339, 354, 359, 504
5.	i. 48
6.	iii. 374
7.	v. 310
12.	v. 377
xl. 2.	ii. 275
6.	i. 151, 183, 247, 274, 281; iii. 21; v. 260
7.	i. 7, 62, 247, 265, 276; ii. 162, 176; v. 135
9, 10.	iv. 118
12.	v. 96, 338
17.	v. 416
xli. 1.	v. 4, 274
3.	v. 475
4.	v. 224
9.	iv. 31, 92
13.	v. 470
xlii. 1.	v. 472
2.	v. 378
3.	v. 221
4.	iv. 181
6.	v. 540
10.	v. 221
xliii. 8.	iv. 175
xliv. 1.	iv. 329
4.	i. 129; v. 256
5.	iv. 9
6.	i. 332; iv. 107, 280

Psalm	Vol. Page
xliv. 22.	ii. 11
23.	v. 214
32.	v. 64
xlv. 1.	ii. 14; iii. 139; iv. 110; v. 349
2.	iii. 121
3.	ii. 9
6.	i. 114; ii. 38
7.	ii. 56, 236; iv. 46, 85, 123; v. 488
8.	iii. 286, 288; v. 543
9.	v. 543
xlvi. 4.	i. 193; iii. 268
xlvii. 2.	i. 367, 466
5.	iii. 227
7.	ii. 19; iv. 283, 375; v. 335, 349, 360, 473
8.	iv. 55
9.	i. 241
xlviii. 2.	iv. 226
7.	iii. 118; v. 238
8.	iii. 21, 250
xlix. 7.	ii. 258
8.	ii. 258; iii. 65; iv. 253
12.	i. 15, 206
14.	ii. 85
15.	ii. 328
16.	v. 21
18.	v. 7
20.	i. 349; v. 520
l. 1.	v. 215
5.	v. 67
10.	i. 447
15.	v. 324, 460
18.	iv. 141
21.	v. 533
23.	i. 211; v. 282
li. 1.	iv. 113; v. 318, 368
3.	iii. 94
5.	i. 4; iii. 244
6.	i. 409; iii. 393; v. 210
8.	i. 68
10.	iii. 126, 191, 194; v. 310
11.	iii. 184
12.	iii. 111, 194; v. 410
15.	v. 338
17.	i. 371, 381, 409, 445; v. 281
lii. 1.	iii. 399
3, 4.	i. 341
liii. 1, 3.	i. 310
6.	iv. 120
liv. 3.	iv. 37
lv. 6.	ii. 319; iii. 255; v. 334, 376
9.	ii. 387
12.	iv. 10, 88
13.	v. 200
14.	v. 200, 251
15.	iv. 311
17.	v. 354, 356
22.	v. 368
lvi. 8.	i. 369
lvii. 1.	iv. 37, 50, 158, 181

AND.—PERRON, ETC. B B

INDEX OF TEXTS.

Psalm	Vol. Page	Psalm	Vol. Page
lvii. 4.	iv. 177, 181	lxviii. 22.	iii. 74
5.	iii. 225; v. 469	26.	iv. 108, 212, 218
8.	ii. 337; iii. 122; iv. 181	27.	iv. 212
11.	iv. 181; v. 411	28.	iv. 107, 212; v. 255
lviii. 4.	iii. 389	30.	ii. 25
5.	i. 68; ii. 15; v. 504	lxix. 1.	v. 338
8, 9.	iv. 213	4.	ii. 395; v. 429, 545
10.	ii. 71	9.	v. 359
11.	iv. 213	10.	i. 367, 411
lix. 1.	iv. 9	21.	i. 147
5.	v. 444	22.	i. 401; v. 517
9.	ii. 6; v. 465	26.	ii. 124
11.	iv. 196	32.	i. 312
16.	iii. 42	lxxi. 8.	iv. 339
17.	v. 110	16.	v. 108, 117, 283
lx. 2.	ii. 13	18.	ii. 73
6	i. 237	20.	ii. 401; iii. 61; iv. 266, 366, 368
9	i. 237; iii. 62, 65		
11.	i. 79; iii. 67; v. 104, 110, 238	23.	iv. 218
		lxxii. 6.	ii. 24; iii. 267; iv. 254
lxi. 6.	iv. 116	7.	iii. 243
lxii. 3.	iv. 18; v. 247	10.	i. 237, 243
4.	ii. 273	11.	i. 241; v. 446
8.	v. 472	14.	ii. 15
9.	i. 5; ii. 59	16.	i. 171
10.	v. 12	18.	iv. 208
11.	v. 504	19.	v. 470
lxiii. 1.	v. 472	lxxiii. 13, 14.	v. 547
3.	iii. 267	15.	v. 156
9, 10.	iv. 140	20.	iv. 232
11.	iv. 97; v. 72, 75	24.	ii. 24
lxiv. 3, 4.	ii. 123	25.	v. 32
8.	iv. 213; v. 246	lxxiv. 1.	ii. 273
9.	ii. 285; iv. 98	4.	iv. 366
lxv. 1.	iv. 337	12.	ii. 18, 30; v. 480
2.	i. 41; ii. 98; v. 335, 353, 426	18.	i. 180
		lxxv. 1.	ii. 7
3.	v. 469	2.	ii. 15
7.	ii. 21; iv. 97	3.	ii. ✶ 3, 284
10.	v. 407	4.	ii. 13
11.	iv. 206	6.	ii. 14; iii. 388; iv. 279
lxvi. 1.	iii. 299	8.	iii. 71
4.	iv. 215	9, 10.	ii. 7
8, 16.	v. 388	lxxvi. 1.	ii. 34; iii. 237, 310; iv. 127
18.	v. 68, 315, 320, 441		
18—20.	v. 322	2.	iii. 238; v. 219
lxvii. 1.	v. 415	12.	ii. 20
2.	iii. 310; v. 387, 469	lxxvii. 7.	i. 180; ii. 16; v. 333
6.	v. 407	8.	i. 180; ii. 16
lxviii. 1.	iii. 236; iv. 198; v. 338, 487	9.	ii. 16; v. 333
		10.	iii. 138; v. 333
2.	iv. 198; v. 487	13.	ii. 23
4.	v. 376	14.	ii. 20
6.	iii. 114, 238; v. 219	15.	ii. 19, 27
9.	iii. 226	18.	ii. 20
12.	iii. 235	19.	ii. 20, 21
13.	iii. 233, 252, 253	20.	i. 170; ii. 16, 20, 273
16.	iii. 237	lxxviii. 8.	i. 306; iv. 144
17.	iii. 223	9.	ii. 6
18.	iii. 108, 126, 129, 134, 136, ✶ 221, 315, 320, 362, 385; iv. 237; v. 315	13, 14.	i. 315
		19.	i. 309
		20.	v. 510, 513
20.	ii. 194; iv. 350	23.	v. 417

INDEX OF TEXTS.

Psalm	Vol. Page	Psalm	Vol. Page
lxxviii. 24.	i. 315; v. 510	lxxxix. 8.	iii. 84
25.	i. 174; v. 419, 510	15.	i. 61; iv. 83, 100
27.	i. 315	19.	iv. 80
30.	v. 29, 421	20.	iv. 53, 55, 284
31.	v. 421	20—23.	* iv. 76
33.	i. 48, 308, 309	21.	iv. 85, 130; v. 250
34.	* i. 305	22.	iv. 130, 290; v. 250, 253
36.	i. 309, 318	23.	iv. 91, 106, 130; v. 250
39.	v. 333	27.	iv. 124
52.	ii. 18, 273	29.	ii. 20
54.	ii. 24	32, 33.	iv. 227
57.	ii. 63; iii. 125	34.	v. 75
71.	iv. 78, 113	38.	iv. 75
72.	ii. 32	43.	ii. 6
lxxix. 8.	iv. 267; v. 438	44.	iv. 75, 289
9.	v. 461	45.	iv. 75
13.	ii. 273	47.	i. 12, 180, 274
lxxx. 1.	ii. 19, 273; iii. 85	51.	iv. 97
2.	v. 372	52.	v. 470
4.	v. 431	xc. 1 seq.	v. 348
13.	ii. 9	4.	v. 48
lxxxi. 7.	ii. 407	9.	i. 300; iii. 272, 391
10.	iv. 110; v. 324, 325, 338, 420	10.	ii. 294
		11.	i. 427; ii. 155; v. 427, 429
lxxxii. 1.	ii. 22; * v. 203		
1—8.	ii. 14	xci. 3.	v. 529
2.	v. 220	5.	ii. 294; v. 529
5.	v. 210, 211	6.	ii. 294; iv. 40
6.	i. 109, 292; iv. 14, 32, 52, 55, 132, 284, 285, 304; v. 17, 76, 180, 206, 244	9, 10.	v. 532
		11.	iv. 68, 181
		13.	iv. 61, 337
		16.	v. 51
lxxxiii. 5—8.	v. 211	xcii. 9.	iv. 10, 17, 179
13.	i. 336	11.	iv. 150
17.	iv. 17	xciii. 1.	i. 193; iv. 280
lxxxiv. 2.	iv. 105; v. 378	xciv. 11.	v. 305
3.	i. 351	12, 13.	v. 455
5.	iii. 49, 226	15.	i. 362
6.	ii. 293	19.	iii. 158; iv. 305, 455; v. 319
9.	iii. 259		
10.	iv. 117	xcv. 1 seq.	ii. 3
11.	v. 315, 352, 390, 396, 413, 415	2, 3.	v. 555
		6.	ii. 334; iv. 374; v. 462, 555
lxxxv. 1, 2.	v. 98		
8.	iii. 199; v. 101	7.	i. 301, 330; ii. 11, 273; iii. 22, 78, 86; iv. 43, 44; v. 462
9.	i. 182; v. 411		
10, 11.	* i. 175		
10.	i. 97; v. 111, 524	8.	i. 115, 301, 330; iv. 44
13.	i. 188, 191	10.	i. 345; ii. 19; v. 197
lxxxvi. 2.	v. 249	11.	ii. 319; v. 152, 197, 535
9.	v. 460	xcvi. 9.	iv. 374
11.	v. 464	11.	i. 216
13.	ii. 401; iv. 266; v. 520	xcvii. 1.	ii. 19; iv. 280
17.	ii. 386, 400; iv. 213	5.	iv. 374
lxxxvii. 2.	iv. 226	11.	iii. 373; v. 319
4.	i. 155, 173, 240, 298; iii. 56	xcviii. 1.	iv. 100
		xcix. 1.	ii. 19, 20; iv. 280; v. 391
5.	i. 240; ii. 349	3.	iv. 378; v. 383
7.	v. 98	4.	ii. 14
lxxxviii. 5.	iii. 88	8.	v. 224
8.	iii. 293; v. 86	c. 3.	ii. 27; iii. 86, 210; iv. 280
lxxxix. 1.	iv. 99, 275		
2.	iv. 275	ci. 1—8.	ii. 3, 14; v. 523

INDEX OF TEXTS.

Psalm	Vol. Page	Psalm	Vol. Page
ci. 5.	v. 13	cx. 2.	v. 406
cii. 4.	i. 385; v. 429	3.	i. 71, 163, 235, 292;
27.	ii. 18; v. 256, 374		v. 135, 406
ciii. 1.	iv. 275; v. 255	4.	i. 24, 77, 104; v. 72, 75
4.	iv. 113	cxi. 1.	iv. 373; v. 357
7.	ii. 30	2.	v. 360
8, 10.	v. 523	4.	iv. 204, 382
14.	iii. 152; v. 333, 486	5.	v. 415
16.	i. 5	9.	ii. 334; iv. 378; v. 78, 383
20.	i. 4; v. 407, 409		
22.	v. 357	10.	iii. 335, 337; v. 197
civ. 3.	ii. 278	cxii. 9.	v. 271
11.	iv. 326	cxiii. 2, 3.	v. 386
15.	iii. 162; v. 417	7.	iii. 331
21.	v. 325, 413	cxiv. 3.	iv. 234
24.	iv. 325	5.	iii. 244
25.	v. 493	8.	i. 370
27.	i. 268; v. 421, 507	cxv. 1.	i. 225; iv. 268, 281; v. 37, 123, 375, 387, 400, 461, 465
28.	i. 268; v. 417, 507		
29.	v. 510		
30.	iii. 112, 184, 189, 191	3.	v. 397
cv. 3.	i. 316	7.	iii. 193
4.	i. 313, 314	10.	ii. 283
15.	iii. 32; iv. 31, 49, 132, 166, 211; v. 245	11.	iii. 67
		12.	ii. 283
18.	iii. 293	16.	v. 28
26.	ii. 30	cxvi. 7.	i. 222; ii. 319
29.	iii. 351	10.	i. 253; iii. 193
45.	v. 427	12.	i. 29, 62, 83; ii. 134, 382; iii. 237, 320
cvi. 4, 5.	v. 469		
10.	v. 475	13.	i. 84, 169; ii. 134, 382; iii. 79, 300, 321; iv. 124, 376
15.	v. 418		
23.	i. 335; v. 231		
28.	v. 227	15.	iii. 9; iv. 173
29.	v. 418	16.	iii. 293; iv. 228; v. 249, 457
29, 30.	* v. 223		
30.	i. 335	cxvii. 1.	iv. 337; v. 386
44.	iv. 321	cxviii. 1--4.	iv. 208, 221
48.	v. 468	2.	iv. 274
cvii. 1.	ii. 240	6.	iv. 209
6.	iv. 268	8—10.	iv. 207
9.	i. 278	11.	iv. 209
10.	v. 317	12.	iv. 207, 209, 213; v. 435
20.	iii. 342		
35.	iv. 234	13.	iv. 207, 209; v. 486, 521
41.	ii. 273	15.	iv. 105, 121, 180, 208, 217, 406
cviii. 1.	ii. 39; iii. 122; v. 338		
2.	iii. 122; v. 107	16.	iv. 180, 208, 259
4.	iv. 324	17.	iv. 204, 207
5.	iii. 174	19.	iv. 217, 218
9.	iii. 66, 73	22.	i. 241; ii. * 270, 426; iv. 15, 212, 220
cix. 4.	v. 327, 353		
5.	iv. 88	23.	iv. 98, 228; v. 253
7.	i. 401; v. 328, 346	23, 24.	* iv. 203
11.	v. 511	24.	ii. 270, 406, 426; iv. 181
11—15.	iv. 33		
17.	iv. 336	25.	ii. 282; iv. 219; v. 255
18.	iii. 286	26.	ii. 282
24.	i. 368, 448	27.	iv. 217, 221
27.	iv. 214; v. 246	cxix. 4.	v. 400
29.	iv. 214	5.	v. 410
cx. 1.	ii. 338, 370; iii. 307, 313; iv. 9, 337; v. 393	20.	v. 410
		32.	v. 85

INDEX OF TEXTS.

Psalm	Vol. Page	Psalm	Vol. Page
cxix. 36.	v. 553	cxxxii. 3.	i. 434; ii. 13; v. 250
37.	v. 469	4.	i. 434; ii. 113; v. 250
40.	iii. 152	5.	v. 250
49.	v. 470	6.	i. 160, 172; ii. 349
54.	iv. 72, 75	8.	ii. 7
60.	v. 411	11.	i. 72, 104
62.	v. 356	12.	i. 104
67.	iii. 173; v. 369	14.	v. 221
70.	iii. 294; v. 99	17.	v. 246
71.	iii. 173	18.	ii. 20; iv. 123
72.	ii. 103	cxxxiii. 1.	ii. 243; iii. 51, 238; v. 219
83.	i. 448		
93.	iii. 126	2.	ii. 56, 247; iii. 136; v. 219
94.	iv. 327		
98—100.	v. 505	3.	ii. 56, 247; iii. 120
105.	iii. 372; v. 319	cxxxiv. 1.	iv. 221
106.	v. 75	cxxxv. 6.	v. 397, 406
131.	iii. 178, 198; v. 341	7.	iii. 119
132.	ii. 137; v. 125	15.	v. 18
136.	i. 369	19.	ii. 283
148.	v. 356	cxxxvi. 1.	iv. 260, 275, 340; v. 523
164.	v. 356	4.	iv. 221
165.	ii. 245; v. 5	5, 7.	iv. 326
175.	iv. 115	10.	iv. 337
cxx. 5.	i. 246; iii. 238; v. 220, 377, 410	11.	iv. 234
		12.	iv. 221
cxxi. 1.	iv. 227; v. 376	15.	iv. 221, 234
2.	v. 376	19.	iv. 234
cxxii. 3.	ii. 247; v. 219	20.	iv. 234, 337
4, 5.	ii. 32	23, 24.	iv. 221
6.	ii. 247	25.	v. 416, 481
cxxiii. 1.	v. 325, 349	cxxxvii. 1.	iii. 291; iv. 226
cxxiv. 1.	iv. 228, 329	2.	i. 391; iii. 291
2.	iv. 228	4.	iv. 227
3.	iv. 334	5.	ii. 32
4.	iv. 321	7.	i. 161, 238; ii. 349, 351; iii. 65; iv. 210, 253; v. 211, 520
6.	iv. 367		
7.	iv. 228, 397		
8.	v. 386	cxxxviii. 2.	ii. 282; iv. 376, 378
cxxv. 1.	iv. 221	8.	iii. 228; iv. 327; v. 365, 457, 462
3.	iv. 394, 405; v. 557		
cxxvi. 1.	iv. 215, 226, 353	cxxxix. 7.	iii. 134, 251
1—4.	* iv. 223	8.	v. 373
2.	iv. 215, 231	cxl. 1 seq.	iv. 48
3.	iv. 216, 231	cxli. 2.	i. 390; v. 230, 324, 325, 344, 355
4.	iii. 229; iv. 231		
6.	i. 421	3.	v. 338, 469
cxxvii. 1.	ii. 6	4.	v. 338
2.	v. 417	7.	iii. 293; iv. 238, 336
5.	v. 505	cxlii. 7.	v. 86, 99
cxxviii. 2.	v. 417, 420	cxliii. 2.	v. 117, 282
cxxix. 1, 2.	iv. 227	7.	v. 359
3.	ii. 277	8.	iii. 41
5.	ii. 170; iv. 16—18	10.	iii. 97; v. 469
6.	iv. 17	12.	v. 457
7.	i. 268	cxliv. 1 seq.	ii. 14
cxxx. 1.	i. 364; v. 340	3.	i. 53
3.	iv. 255	4.	i. 5, 53
4.	v. 373, 535	5.	i. 61; iv. 14; v. 246
7.	ii. 197; iii. 306, 371; v. 318	6.	iv. 34; v. 246
		7.	iv. 93, 131; v. 241, 246
cxxxi. 1.	iii. 32	8.	v. 251
2.	iv. 113; v. 542	10.	i. 321; v. 235

INDEX OF TEXTS.

Psalm	Vol. Page
cxliv. 11.	v. 75, 241, 242, 251, 254
12—14.	v. 244
15.	v. 30, 244
cxlv. 1 seq.	v. 421
8.	v. 436
9.	iv. 99, 109, 262, 270, *318, 363; v. 523
10.	iv. 327, 331, 337; v. 392
11.	v. 392
12.	iv. 337
13.	iv. 283; v. 466
14.	iv. 332
15.	i. 268; v. 316, 422, 469
16.	i. 268
17.	i. 181
18.	v. 474
cxlvi. 3.	ii. 375
4.	i. 362; ii. 267, 375
10.	ii. 18
cxlvii. 9.	iii. 325; iv. 326; v. 323, 334, 415
10.	v. 238
15.	iii. 118
20.	i. 2; ii. 34, 57; iii. 310, 331; iv. 47, 268, 332, 338
cxlviii. 1—13.	i. 221
5.	i. 110; iv. 274, 284
6.	i. 110; iv. 274
8.	v. 407
11.	iv. 274
cl. 4, 5.	i. 221
6.	ii. 339; iv. 337

PROVERBS.

i. 7.	iii. 335; iv. 299
8.	i. 392
ii. 14.	v. 99
iii. 5.	v. 401
7.	iii. 335
9.	i. 263
10.	i. 269
14.	ii. 315
16.	v. 21
28.	v. 39, 135
29.	iii. 212
34.	i. 161; iii. 196; v. 309
iv. 17.	v. 420, 500, 511
23.	iii. 291
v. 8.	v. 447
15.	v. 33
16.	v. 33, 422
22.	i. 57; ii. 360; iii. 293; v. 86
vi. 2.	iv. 140
4.	v. 429
6.	i. 349
23.	iii. 372
26.	i. 91; ii. 114
27.	v. 447
vii. 22.	iii. 294; v. 531
27.	iii. 328

Proverbs	Vol. Page
viii. 2.	iv. 277
14.	iv. 280
15.	* iv. 277; v. 210, 243, 297, 552
22.	i. 235
31.	ii. 275
ix. 10.	ii. 103
x. 22.	v. 511
xi. 17.	i. 443
21.	iv. 186, 195, 198, 308; v. 80
28.	v. 18
29.	i. 423
xii. 2.	v. 309, 311, 327, 403, 424
10.	iv. 268, 335
18.	iv. 60
20.	ii. 247
xiii. 10.	ii. 404; v. 15
12.	i. 69, 129; iv. 110; v. 334
17.	i. 68
xiv. 13.	i. 72
15.	i. 253; ii. 45
16.	v. 225
22.	i. 342; iii. 329
27.	iii. 357
30.	iv. 123
xv. 16, 17.	ii. 243
xvi. 1.	v. 304
2.	iv. 250
6.	i. 443; v. 439
9.	v. 304
10.	iv. 214, 369
14.	ii. 372
24.	i. 68; iv. 123
33.	iv. 350
xvii. 1.	ii. 243
12.	i. 185
15.	v. 116
19.	v. 15
25.	i. 392
xviii. 1.	ii. 67
8.	iii. 271
10.	ii. 7; v. 27, 106, 344, 383, 424
11.	v. 19
14.	ii. 144; iii. 204; v. 333
16.	iii. 395
19.	iv. 186
xix. 2.	ii. 313
12.	ii. 14
17.	v. 278
xx. 8.	iii. 152; v. 115
9.	v. 115
15.	ii. 103
17.	v. 420, 500, 511
27.	iii. 372; v. 319, 366
28.	ii. 15
xxi. 1.	iv. 228, 234, 285, 396
13.	v. 328
30.	v. 397
31.	i. 332; iv. 350
xxii. 1.	v. 382
2.	ii. 82

INDEX OF TEXTS. 359

Proverbs	Vol. Page	Ecclesiastes	Vol. Page
xxii. 22.	v. 323	vii. 17.	iv. 310
xxiii. 4, 5.	v. 19	29.	v. 54
13.	v. 402	viii. 2.	v. 76, 78
xxiv. 11.	iv. 140	9.	iv. 327
12.	iv. 140, 141	12.	iii. 335
16.	v. 428	ix. 4.	ii. 207, 225
21.	v. 130	8.	ii. 231; iii. 9
21—23.	* iv. 297	11.	v. 28, 303, 417
26.	ii. 42	15, 16.	v. 303
29.	v. 437	x. 18.	ii. 21
xxv. 11.	i. 420; ii. 212	19.	v. 10, 212
27.	v. 397	20.	iv. 132, 213; v. 245, 246
xxvi. 11.	i. 348	xi. 1.	v. 278
13.	ii. 212	7.	iii. 292, 370; v. 317
23.	ii. 47	8.	ii. 64
25.	ii. 47; v. 251	xii. 1.	iii. 178; v. 531
xxvii. 1.	iv. 219; v. 422	7.	v. 378, 408
4.	iv. 28	11.	iii. 141
24.	v. 20	12.	ii. 105
xxviii. 13.	v. 441	13.	iii. 333
14.	iii. 335		
21.	v. 546		
xxix. 18.	iii. 312	SONG OF SOLOMON.	
24.	v. 80		
xxx. 1.	i. 144, 150, 332; ii. 6	i. 3.	i. 77; ii. 312; iii. 286; iv. 58; v. 386, 424, 430
2.	v. 107		
4.	ii. 282; v. 107	4.	i. 257; v. 379
5.	v. 504	15.	iii. 252
7.	v. 337	ii. 2.	i. 137
8.	v. 12, 415, 421, 453, 469	4.	i. 208; ii. 224
9.	v. 12, 415, 453	9.	v. 213
11—14.	ii. 388	14.	iii. 254
13.	v. 13	iii. 1.	i. 312, 315; iii. 173
15.	iii. 400; v. 35	1—4.	iv. 82
17.	iv. 20	4.	iii. 36
19.	v. 497	11.	v. 543
25.	v. 422	iv. 1.	iii. 252
28.	v. 542	3.	iii. 76
31.	ii. 5; iv. 11, 19, 31	4.	v. 503
xxxi. 3.	iv. 88, 293	v. 2, 5.	iii. 254
6.	iii. 162	10.	i. 158; iii. 75
		12.	iii. 251, 252, 254
		vi. 4.	ii. 101
ECCLESIASTES.		9.	iii. 254
		13.	i. 278; ii. 163
i. 1.	iv. 277	viii. 1.	i. 37
2.	ii. 24	6.	ii. 104, 225
4.	ii. 294		
6.	iii. 120		
9.	ii. 65	ISAIAH.	
iii. 1.	i. 268, 351, 383; v. 170		
3.	iv. 252	i. 3.	i. 199, 349
4.	i. 385	4.	i. 326
11.	iii. 133	12.	i. 382
iv. 12.	ii. 108; iv. 265; v. 108	17.	iii. 338
14, 49.	i. 255	18.	iii. 75
v. 1.	iii. 34	20.	v. 350
4, 5.	v. 79	24.	i. 326; iii. 85
8.	i. 224; v. 206	ii. 3.	i. 300; iii. 111
13.	v. 187	4.	i. 330
vi. 2, 3.	v. 29	iii. 7.	i. 168
vii. 1.	v. 382	10.	iii. 34
6.	i. 72; iii. 268; iv. 105	iv. 5.	i. 346

INDEX OF TEXTS.

Isaiah	Vol. Page	Isaiah	Vol. Page
v. 2.	i. 448	xxvi. 16.	v. 353
4.	iii. 71	18.	iii. 192, 337; v. 353
10.	i. 421	19.	ii. 192, 231, 264, 376, 399; iii. 16
18.	v. 538		
vi. 1.	i. 105; v. 117	xxvii. 9.	iii. 347; v. 119, 425, 442
2.	ii. 160; iii. 251; iv. 325; v. 117, 232, 350, 409	xxviii. 6.	ii. 7
		9.	iii. 137
3.	i. 212, 227, 326; iii. 206, 354; iv. 373; v. 350, 385, 387, 389, 460, 463	16.	ii. 265, 274; iii. 115; v. 341, 557
		21.	v. 89
5.	i. 326; v. 117	xxix. 8.	iv. 230
6.	iii. 124	9.	iii. 132
7.	iii. 141	10.	iii. 191
8.	iii. 306	11.	v. 506
9.	iii. 204	13.	iv. 379; v. 232, 329, 464, 473
vii. 4.	i. 332		
8.	ii. 283	15.	v. 221
9.	i. 20, 138, 272, 328; ii. 7, 63	16.	ii. 286
11.	i. 21, 145, 210, 234; v. 530	22.	i. 123
12.	i. 149	xxx. 11.	i. 308; iii. 216
13.	iii. 212	18.	i. 346, 451; iv. 110
14.	i. 23, 72, 76, ✶ 135, 149, 153; v. 109, 110	21.	i. 166, 318, 339, 361, 451; ii. 23, 407; iii. 199; v. 442
15.	i. 144, 147		
20.	i. 331; v. 223	33.	ii. 87
viii. 6.	iii. 268	xxxii. 2.	iv. 325
8.	i. 151	5.	v. 105
10.	i. 150	14, 15.	iii. 312
13.	v. 388	17.	v. 110, 555
18.	i. 298; ii. 218	xxxiii. 1.	iv. 268
20.	i. 378; iii. 353; iv. 401	6.	iii. 335
21.	ii. 400; iv. 115	14.	i. 426; ii. 94
ix. 3.	i. 28, 61, 70; v. 387	xxxvi. 6.	ii. 374; v. 26
6.	i. ✶ 18, 82, 104, 236; ii. 22, 196; iii. 108; v. 185	7.	iv. 375
		12.	ii. 5
7.	i. 12, 19, 23, 59	13.	iii. 324
10.	ii. 358	14.	i. 335
12.	v. 229, 234	xxxvii. 2—4.	iv. 343
x. 5.	i. 330	3.	i. 141, 308; iv. 266, ✶ 341, 361; v. 304
xi. 1.	i. 163, 186, 235		
2.	iii. 134, 176, 335, 357; v. 388, 390	4.	iv. 344, 358; v. 231, 339, 356
10.	i. 240; ii. 183	6, 7.	i. 326
xii. 3.	iii. 351; v. 504	9.	iv. 343
xiv. 14.	i. 206; v. 520	22.	iv. 343
xvi. 1.	i. 65	23.	v. 228
xix. 14.	iii. 191	25.	iv. 342
23.	i. 221	29.	iv. 343
xxi. 12.	i. 312, 313, 315	31.	i. 424
xxii. 12.	i. 381, 387	36.	iv. 350; v. 226, 228
15.	ii. 325	xxxviii. 2, 3.	v. 230
16.	iii. 389	14.	iii. 252; iv. 118; v. 125, 334, 446, 487
22.	ii. 14		
23.	ii. 10	15.	i. 369
xxiii. 3.	v. 4	xxxix. 2.	v. 540
4.	v. 493	8.	v. 136
8.	v. 4	xl. 3.	i. 451
xxiv. 16.	i. 370	6.	i. 5, 37; ii. 378; iii. 308; v. 17
xxv. 8.	ii. 256		
xxvi. 1.	ii. 5	7, 8.	v. 17
12.	iii. 98, 393; v. 114, 304, 403	12.	i. 276
		16.	iii. 246
13.	iii. 394; v. 392	22.	v. 329

… INDEX OF TEXTS. 361

Isaiah	Vol. Page	Isaiah	Vol. Page
xli. 11.	i. 332	liv. 10.	v. 471
23.	i. 18	lv. 3.	iv. 94, 99, 180
xlii. 2.	iii. 267	6.	i. 314
3.	i. 126; v. 309, 340, 538	7.	iii. 68
6.	i. 240	10, 11.	v. 198
8.	iii. 187; v. 123, 391, 465, 545	lvi. 7.	i. 133; iv. 218, 376; v. 357
xliii. 6.	i. 240	10.	v. 516
11.	i. 79; ii. 332, 336; v. 237	12.	i. 313
18.	i. 70; ii. 127	lvii. 15.	i. 161, 165; iii. 174, 253
23.	v. 555	16.	iii. 196
24.	v. 534, 555	lviii. 1.	v. 7, 156
25.	v. 90, 461	3.	i. 383, 411
xliv. 22.	iii. 266, 269	5.	v. 360
28.	ii. 9	7.	i. 443; v. 67, 439
xlv. 1.	iv. 49, 51, 57	8.	i. 254, 416
2.	iii. 73	lix. 1.	v. 25, 533
8.	i. 185; v. 109	2.	iii. 87, 425
15.	i. 37	5.	iii. 399; iv. 131
19.	i. 311	7.	iv. 186, 188
23.	ii. 334; v. 72, 123	11.	iii. 252, 256
24.	ii. 338; v. 113, 123, 284	21.	iii. 198
		lxi. 1.	i. 78; iii. 184; v. 85
25.	v. 123	8.	iii. 184
xlvi. 8.	i. 361; iii. 295	lxii. 2.	iii. 248
9.	ii. 65	3.	iii. 248; iv. 53, 114, 285
10.	v. 399	4.	iv. 343; v. 400
xlvii. 1.	ii. 352; iv. 343	6.	ii. 64; v. 356
xlviii. 11.	v. 430	11.	iii. 61, 62
16.	iii. 188, 204	lxiii. 1—3.	*iii. 06
17.	·iii. 399; v. 347	3.	i. 26, 169; ii. 171; iv. 22; v. 488
18.	ii. 248		
xlix. 4.	v. 198	4.	iii. 78
6.	i. 71, 240; ii. 391	14.	ii. 23
7.	v. 471	16.	i. 120; v. 366, 374
8.	iv. 102	17.	v. 368
15.	i. 2; v. 375, 472	lxiv. 1.	i. 61
16.	ii. 132, 178	4.	v. 375
23.	ii. 27; iv. 16; v. 180, 248	6.	iii. 243; v. 109, 284, 309
		8.	iii. 228
l. 4.	iii. 141	lxv. 1.	i. 259, 317; iii. 14, 118
8.	i. 150	5.	iii. 32
li. 1.	ii. 275	11.	iv. 268, 280
9.	iii. 73; iv. 19, 86; v. 372	16.	v. 471
		24.	iv. 111; v. 362
21.	i. 412; iii. 132, 314	lxvi. 1.	i. 161; v. 213, 373
22.	iii. 72; v. 518	2.	i. 161; iii. 253; v. 341
lii. 7.	i. 69; ii. 249	7.	iv. 348
liii. 1.	iv. 86	8.	i. 431
3.	i. 92, 160, 204	12, 16.	i. 193
4—6.	ii. 126, 150	24.	iv. 93; v. 86
5.	i. 92; ii. 180		
6.	ii. 29, 297, 395; iii. 87, 246	JEREMIAH.	
6 seq.	i. 25		
7.	i. 206; ii. 151, 296, 396; iii. 61	i. 8.	iv. 303
		18.	ii. 9
8.	i. 163	ii. 10.	i. 348; iv. 127, 215
10.	i. 171, 184; ii. 121; v. 83	12.	i. 349
		17.	iii. 374
12.	i. 169; iii. 71	19.	i. 371; v. 86
liv. 5.	v. 556	22.	i. 113; iii. 247, 347

AND.—PERRON, ETC.   C C

INDEX OF TEXTS.

Jeremiah	Vol. Page	Jeremiah	Vol. Page
ii. 24.	i. 310	xxvii. 6.	v. 249
27.	v. 550	xxviii. 2, 3.	v. 470
28.	i. 272	6.	v. 470, 472
iv. 1.	i. 363	xxix. 7.	v. 183, 358
2.	*v. 71	xxx. 21.	i. 165
22.	v. 401	24.	i. 75; v. 88
31.	iv. 343	xxxi. 12.	iii. 16
v. 4, 5.	ii. 276	15.	i. 238; iv. 210
7.	v. 73	19.	i. 371, 372
9.	i. 441	20.	v. 429
25.	i. 272; v. 425	22.	i. 20; iv. 215
31.	i. 425; ii. 94; iii. 316	31.	i. 169
vi. 10.	v. 17	33.	iii. 192; v. 462
11.	v. 221	34.	v. 442
14.	v. 110	xxxiii. 11.	v. 465
16.	ii. 65, 411	xxxv. 6.	i. 391
24.	iv. 333	xxxvi. 9.	i. 379
29.	i. 360; iii. 269	xli. 1.	v. 181
viii. 4.	i. 340, 360; ii. 62	2.	v. 252
4—7.	i. 338	xlv. 5.	i. 315
5.	i. 340	xlvi. 11.	v. 227
6.	i. 345	18.	iii. 85
7.	i. 348, 357, 394, 432	xlix. 31.	v. 41
8.	i. 340, 349	l. 23.	i. 330
22.	v. 227, 333, 507	29.	i. 326
ix. 1.	i. 370		
23.	v. 313		
x. 2.	iii. 376; v. 375	LAMENTATIONS.	
14.	v. 401		
16.	i. 326	i. 12.	ii. 128, *138
23.	v. 304	13.	ii. 145
xi. 19.	ii. 165	ii. 2.	ii. 360
xii. 9.	iii. 252	9, 10.	iv. 210
xiii. 16.	i. 313	21.	iv. 266
17.	i. 369	iii. 22.	iv. *261, 289, 319, 363
18.	v. 466	27.	v. 289
xiv. 7.	v. 125	41.	v. 325, 349, 376
xv. 1.	v. 231	44.	v. 425
19.	i. 307, 377, 405; iii. 269, 345; v. 509	iv. 9.	iv. 227
		14.	iii. 75
xvii. 1.	ii. 256	20.	ii. 10, 148; iv. 49, 57
5.	v. 527	v. 12.	iv. 210
9.	iii. 193	21.	v. 310
xviii. 6.	v. 307		
8.	v. 81		
12.	v. 88	EZEKIEL.	
18.	iv. 60; v. 231, 537		
20.	v. 231	i. 15, 16.	iv. 239
xxii. 15.	ii. 41	20.	v. 208
18.	ii. 148	ii. 9, 10.	v. 426
29.	i. 185; v. 411	iii. 19.	i. 376
30.	iv. 290	iv. 16.	v. 417
xxiii. 5.	i. 76, 104, 163; v. 105, 109, 111	viii. 12.	v. 554
		ix. 2.	iii. 210
6.	i. 77; v. *104, 284	4.	i. 205; ii. 76, 163
7.	ii. 369; v. 104	7.	iii. 210
8.	ii. 369	x. 14.	i. 85
16.	v. 118, 124	xi. 3.	ii. 20; iii. 391, 396; v. 15
21.	iii. 288	xiii. 3.	i. 171; iii. 133
24.	iii. 134; v. 213, 373	19.	v. 546
27.	v. 124	xiv. 3.	i. 334; v. 447, 532
28.	i. 399, 422; iii. 274, 313	8.	iv. 141
xxiv. 2.	i. 448	xvi. 4 seq.	i. 38

INDEX OF TEXTS. 363

Ezekiel	Vol. Page
xvi. 6.	iii. 244
49.	ii. 92; v. 421
xvii. 15.	v. 75
16, 18, 19.	v. 105
xviii. 20.	i. 181
21.	i. 350
24.	ii. 73
30.	v. 88
31.	v. 310
32.	i. 345
xx. 46.	iii. 135
xxi. 9, 10.	ii. 15
xxiii. 36.	iv. 343
xxviii. 12.	v. 4
14.	v. 41
xxxiii. 11.	i. 270; v. 345
14.	v. 100
30.	i. 407
31.	i. 407; v. 188, 360
32.	i. 407; iv. 378; v. 198, 360
xxxiv. 5, 6.	ii. 22
20, 21.	ii. 9
23.	i. 65
xxxvi. 20.	v. 387
22.	iii. 342
25.	iii. 135
26.	iii. 192
31.	v. 100
xxxvii. 7.	i. 326
7—9.	iii. 112
22.	v. 185
26.	iii. 90
xxxix. 7.	iv. 378
xlvii. 3—5.	i. 60

DANIEL.

i. 4.	i. 245
6.	i. 244
15.	v. 509
18.	i. 379
ii. 31.	iv. 229
32 seq.	ii. 63; iv. 229
33.	v. 239
34.	ii. 274
38.	ii. 283
iii. 1.	iv. 227; v. 132
6.	iv. 227
8 seq.	v. 199
15.	v. 249
17, 18.	iv. 364
25.	v. 529
27.	iv. 212
28.	v. 529
29.	iv. 402
iv. 5.	iv. 229
12.	iv. 325
17.	iv. 53, 280
24.	i. 360
25.	iv. 53

Daniel	Vol. Page
iv. 27.	i. 352, 443, 445; v. 100, 274, 333, 439
30.	v. 461
32.	iv. 53
v. 1 seq.	v. 132
2.	i. 335
5.	ii. 266
7.	iii. 76
19.	v. 543
21.	v. 547, 552
25.	iv. 289; v. 215
26.	ii. 266; iv. 68
27.	i. 306, 447; iv. 175
29.	ii. 89
vi. 7.	v. 343
10.	v. 329, 354
15.	iv. 143
16.	ii. 392
18.	ii. 21; v. 543
22.	v. 529
23.	ii. 328
vii. 9.	v. 117
10.	v. 232, 481, 557
24.	iv. 369
ix. 7.	v. 117
8.	v. 461
18.	v. 117, 457
19.	v. 462
23.	v. 117
24.	i. 20; v. 117, 343
25.	i. 20, 76, 93, 104, 167, 238; iii. 68, 77
26.	i. 104; ii. 121, 150
27.	iv. 211
x. 3.	i. 368, 379, 394
7 seq.	i. 105
xii. 2.	ii. 357
7.	v. 72, 79
11.	v. 516

HOSEA.

i. 6.	iv. 343
9.	ii. 17
11.	ii. 283
ii. 8.	v. 416
15.	i. 427; ii. 209, 266, 319, 391; iii. 5, 308; v. 302
21.	v. 417
22.	v. 417
iv. 4.	v. 15, 176
6.	iii. 389
v. 5.	i. 207; v. 15
6.	i. 313, 319
10.	iv. 380
15.	i. 311
vi. 2.	ii. 360
4.	ii. 68; iii. 194; iv. 382
5.	v. 16
vii. 1.	ii. 306

364 INDEX OF TEXTS.

Hosea	Vol. Page	Amos	Vol. Page
vii. 5.	iv. 218; v. 421, 543	viii. 14.	v. 73
7.	v. 176	ix. 11.	i. 273
14.	v. 335, 383		
viii. 4.	iv. 287		
10.	iv. 286	JONAH.	
11.	i. 415; v. 447		
ix. 14.	iv. 359	i. 2.	i. 240
x. 1.	i. 172, 422	3.	iii. 324
2.	iii. 133	4, 5.	ii. 393
3.	ii. 20; v. 178, 182	12.	ii. 244, 393, 396
9.	v. 180	17.	ii. 192
xi. 1.	i. 292; ii. 139	ii. 2, 6.	ii. 396
4.	ii. 9, 14, 101	8.	i. 148; ii. 68
5.	v. 183	10.	ii. 192, 233, 328, 329, 357,
xiii. 2.	ii. 12		397
9.	iv. 142; v. 308, 312	iii. 3.	ii. 234
11.	iv. 286; v. 183	4.	i. 393, 429, 431; iii. 324
14.	ii. 256; iii. 229	5.	i. 379, 387, 432, 442;
xiv. 2.	i. 381; iii. 199; v. 338		ii. 399; iii. 334
		6.	i. 443
		7.	iv. 402
		8.	i. 443
JOEL.		9.	iii. 340
		iv. 6.	i. 452; iii. 391; v. 48, 542
i. 14.	i. 379, 404	7.	ii. 379; iv. 107
17.	iii. 259	8.	v. 48
ii. 1.	i. 39	9.	iii. 396
3.	i. 225	10.	iii. 325; iv. 107; v. 243,
11.	i. 358, 368; iii. 317		542
12.	i. 375, 385, 387, 432	11.	iii. 325; iv. 251; v. 243
12, 13.	* i. 356		
13.	i. 373		
15.	i. 308, 323, 367, 378, 404,	MICAH.	
	433		
17.	i. 443		
28.	iii. 135, 184; v. 351	ii. 1.	v. 19
30.	iv. 210	10.	ii. 320
31.	iii. 321	13.	iii. 51, 226
32.	v. 324	iii. 10.	iv. 316
iii. 9.	i. 323	iv. 3.	i. 330
		v. 2.	i. 104, 121, *153, 237, 238,
			292; iii. 92
AMOS.		vi. 5.	ii. 9
		7.	i. 183; v. 435
i. 1.	i. 224	8.	iii. 237
3.	i. 330	16.	i. 297; iv. 379; v. 464
11.	i. 335		
ii. 13.	v. 534, 555		
iii. 2.	iii. 331	NAHUM.	
6.	v. 450		
iv. 6—12.	v. 229	i. 1, 3, 4.	i. 442
v. 18.	v. 395	ii. 3.	iii. 77
25, 26, 27.	v. 69	iii. 8.	ii. 6
vi. 1.	ii. 87		
1—6.	i. 308		
4.	ii. 93	HABAKKUK.	
13.	v. 18		
vii. 2.	v. 452	i. 14.	ii. 11; iv. 15; v. 14
25.	i. 161	16.	iv. 280; v. 507, 527
viii. 1, 2.	ii. 68	ii. 2.	ii. 180
5.	i. 378	3.	ii. 265; iii. 115
6.	v. 546	11.	iv. 238, 263
11.	v. 419	13.	i. 326; iii. 85

INDEX OF TEXTS.

Habakkuk	Vol. Page
iii. 2.	i. 204; iv. 326
8.	v. 227
13.	iv. 49

ZEPHANIAH.

i. 5.	v. 73, 556
12.	v. 483
iii. 3.	v. 14

HAGGAI.

i. 1.	ii. 330
2.	v. 409
6.	v. 417
14.	ii. 349
ii. 4.	i. 326
7.	i. 76
7—9.	i. 238
8.	i. 240; v. 28
13.	iv. 32
16.	i. 421

ZECHARIAH.

i. 6.	i. 326
9.	i. 105
ii. 8.	v. 368
10.	i. 206
13.	i. 37; ii. 160; iv. 161, 281
iii. 1.	ii. 183
2.	iv. 264
8.	i. 186
9.	ii. 274, 277
iv. 7.	ii. 76, 282, 360
9.	ii. 162
10.	i. 124, 160; ii. 284; iii. 368; iv. 208; v. 314
v. 1—4.	v. 76
vi. 12.	i. 76, 163, 235
vii. 3.	i. 378
5.	i. 378, 379, 412
6.	i. 412
8.	i. 378
17.	i. 378
viii. 19.	i. 394
23.	ii. 5, 331
ix. 11.	ii. 134; iii. 348
12.	i. 77
x. 4.	ii. 279
xi. 4.	ii. 12
7.	ii. 29, 280; iii. 387
10.	ii. 280
13.	i. 318, 448; iii. 142
14.	ii. 280
xii. 10.	ii. ✻119, 120; iii. 198, 314, 385; v. 311, 351, 403
11.	ii. 131

Zechariah	Vol. Page
xiii. 1.	i. 113; ii. 134, 372; iii. 247, 348, 359
4.	i. 408
7.	iii. 88; iv. 15; v. 90, 93

MALACHI.

i. 4.	iii. 64
6.	iv. 381; v. 369, 373, 464, 556
7.	iv. 375
8.	i. 318, 448; iv. 375; v. 329
13.	iv. 375, 382
14.	i. 326, 367; iii. 85; iv. 375; v. 459
ii. 3.	iv. 218
5.	v. 93
7.	i. 168; iii. 68, 76; v. 355
10.	v. 556
iii. 6.	iii. 373
10.	ii. 53
14.	v. 483
iv. 2.	i. 201; iii. 326, 336
6.	v. 533

TOBIT.

ii. 4.	i. 395

JUDITH.

vii. 30.	iii. 114; iv. 381

WISDOM.

i. 5.	iii. 252
12.	i. 169, 273; ii. 22; iii. 77; v. 53
xi. 20.	i. 47
xiii. 10.	ii. 375
xv. 12.	v. 76

ECCLESIASTICUS.

iii. 27.	i. 366
x. 9.	i. 185
xiii. 1.	i. 364
xix. 1.	ii. 409
xxiv. 35, 38, 43, 44, 61, 63.	ii. 423
xxv. 13.	iii. 291; iv. 166
xxxiv. 2.	ii. 374
xxxvii. 3.	iv. 135
xlvii. 2.	iv. 373; v. 248
6, 7.	iv. 102

BARUCH.

i. 11.	v. 76

INDEX OF TEXTS.

1 MACCABEES.

1 Maccabees	Vol.	Page
xiv. 44.	v.	156, 165

2 MACCABEES.

i. 10.	iv.	50

S. MATTHEW.

i. 1.		i. 80
5.		i. 241
6.		i. 244
18.		i. 136
20.		iii. 171
21.	i. 75; ii. 330; iii. 68, 347; iv. 254; v. 98, 119, 239	
22.		i. 137, 142
23.	i. 135, 138, 153	
26.		i. 153
ii. 1.	i. 154, 162, 276; ii. 349	
1, 2.		*i. 233, 249
1 seq.		v. 552
2.		i. 94, 166
3—8.		i. 243
4, 5.		i. 154
6.	i. 155—158, 164	
8.		ii. 46
9.		i. 155, 170
10.		i. 40; v. 370
11.		i. 40; ii. 335
14.		iii. 63
15.		ii. 139; v. 496
16.	ii. 46, 210; v. 550	
18.		i. 161
23.		ii. 234
iii. 2.	i. 418, 419, 424	
3.		iii. 117
4.		v. 492
6.		iii. 243
7.		i. 419; ii. 294
7, 8.		*i. 417
8.		i. 422, *435
9.	i. 423, 428; v. 502	
10.		i. 426; v. 347
11.	i. 447; iii. 302, 351; iv. 85; v. 306	
12.	i. 377, 426; v. 443, 484, 494	
13.		ii. 373
14.		iii. 244
15.	i. 90; ii. 396; iii. 73, 245; v. 458, 517	
16.		iii. 196
17.	i. 142, 218, 222, 299; ii. 150; iii. 51; v. 487, 488	
iv. 1.	i. 416, 388; v. 446, *479	
2.		i. 388; *v. 490
3.		i. 401; v. 482
4.		*v. 501
5.		v. 488

S. Matthew	Vol.	Page
iv. 5, 6.		*v. 512
6.		iv. 68
7.		*v. 525
8.		v. 488
8, 9.		*v. 536
9.	iii. 394; iv. 281; v. 483, 539, 543	
10.		v. 539
10, 11.		*v. 549
11.		v. 481, 557
15.	i. 19; ii. 234; iii. 293	
16.		v. 393
18, 21.		i. 159
v. 3.		iii. 291; v. 271
3 seq.		v. 388
4—6.		i. 374
6.		v. 419
7.		v. 440
8.		v. 391
9.	i. 225; ii. 246, 247; iv. 245	
12.		v. 454
13.		i. 358; ii. 105
14.	ii. 105; iii. 371; v. 317	
15.	i. 404, 438; iii. 370, 398	
16.		i. 411; v. 387
17.		v. 72
18.		v. 471, 553
19.		v. 324
20.		v. 76
22.		v. 482
23.		v. 433
24.		i. 223; v. 433
25.		v. 87
26.		v. 429
28.		iii. 213; v. 385
29.		v. 436
33.		v. 72, 75
34.		v. 72, 73, 373
35, 36.		v. 73
44.		v. 370
45.	iii. 326; v. 422, 436	
46.	ii. 107; iii. 145	
48.		v. 315, 410
vi. 1.		iii. 339
2.	i. 382, 404, 423; ii. 94	
5.	i. 377, 382, 404, 411; iii. 339; v. 496	
6.	v. 344, 357, 473	
7.	v. 68, 346, 449, 496	
9.	iv. 378; v. 214, 323, 360	
10.		v. 314
11.		v. 29, 314
12.		v. 115
13.	iv. 267; v. 29, 391, *449 *458, *467	
14.		v. 68, 440
15.		v. 68, 440, 475
16.	i. 323, 367, *375, *398; ii. 90, 305; iii. 339; v. 439	
19.		v. 22, 375, 379
20.		v. 22, 50
21.		iii. 49; v. 379
23.		v. 335

INDEX OF TEXTS. 367

S. Matthew	Vol. Page	S. Matthew	Vol. Page
vi. 24.	v. 556	xi. 12.	ii. 135
25.	iv. 167	14, 15.	v. 6
26.	i. 349, 432; v. 375, 406, 409, 422	18.	i. 432, 446
27.	v. 417	19.	ii. 45; iv. 316
29.	v. 553	25.	i. 161
32.	v. 422	26.	i. 159
33.	i. 281, 318; ii. 316; v. 360, 390, 396, 413, 511	28.	i. 26, 76; ii. 62; v. 99
34.	v. 449	29.	i. 205; ii. 319, 342; iii. 196, 253; iv. 256; v. 10, 487
vii. 6.	iii. 217; v. 321, 328	30.	iii. 151
7.	i. 30; iv. 110, 111; v. 302, 309, *321, 332, 342, 343	xii. 6.	ii. 350
		10.	ii. 386
8.	i. 30; v. 322, 330	20.	iii. 125, 152, 182, 253
9.	iii. 366; v. 500, 502	22.	ii. 386
10.	iii. 366	24.	i. 330, 402; v. 189
12.	v. 434	25.	i. 270
14.	ii. 314	31.	iii. 184
16.	v. 273	32.	iii. 184, 212
19.	v. 347	37.	v. 116
21.	ii. 340, 396, 400	38.	i. 204; ii. 386
22.	iii. 319	39.	ii. 405
24.	v. 193, 197	39, 40.	* ii. 383
26.	v. 197	40.	ii. 192
27.	v. 49	41.	i. 242; ii. 394, 401, 402
viii. 2.	v. 363, 372, 518	42.	i. 73, 242, 261; ii. 247, 398; iv. 277, 314; v. 33, 190
3.	i. 95		
8.	i. 447; v. 306		
9.	i. 430; ii. 21	43.	ii. 319; iii. 358; v. 443
10.	ii. 265	44.	v. 443
11.	i. 243, 258	45.	ii. 75
12.	i. 358; iii. 371	48.	i. 99
25.	iv. 238	49.	i. 29, 99
26.	ii. 396	50.	i. 29; v. 194
29.	i. 28, 80, 318; v. 111, 409, 503	xiii. 3.	i. 421
		12.	iii. 154
30.	v. 552	17.	ii. 134
31.	iv. 335; v. 484	20.	ii. 68
32.	v. 239, 445, 552	22.	v. 21
34.	iii. 216, 350; v. 218	25.	v. 495
ix. 8.	iii. 269; iv. 286	29.	iv. 211
14.	i. 381; iv. 160	30.	i. 283
14 seq.	i. 385	31.	i. 358
15.	i. 367, 381, 391; iii. 158, 164	32.	i. 159
		38.	iii. 111
16.	v. 57	39.	ii. 365; v. 47
17.	i. 381	41.	v. 392, 394, 558
20.	iii. 37	42.	v. 558
21.	i. 7; iii. 25	43.	iii. 372
33.	iv. 215	44.	ii. 315
36.	ii. 29, 33; iv. 336	48.	v. 394
37.	v. 35	xiv. 6, 7.	i. 30
x. 6.	iii. 135	17.	v. 508
7.	i. 418; v. 95	21.	v. 481, 508
8.	iii. 384	23.	v. 323
16.	iii. 252	29 seq.	v. 403
20.	iii. 156, 189, 284	30.	ii. 340; iv. 118
28.	i. 312; iii. 336; v. 553	31.	i. 10
29.	iii. 325; iv. 326; v. 224	xv. 9.	v. 55
30.	v. 523	14.	i. 166; v. 516
31.	iii. 325; v. 224	18, 19.	iv. 346
42.	ii. 97; v. 309	22—27.	v. 331
xi. 7.	ii. 74; v. 480, 481	xvi. 1 seq.	ii. 388

368 INDEX OF TEXTS.

S. Matthew	Vol. Page	S. Matthew	Vol. Page
xvi. 4.	ii. 389	xx. 28.	i. 58
6.	ii. 304	40.	v. 364
12.	ii. 304; v. 55	xxi. 5.	iv. 256
13, 16.	iii. 324	9.	i. 414; iv. 219, 220; v. 238
17.	iii. 133, 254, 324; v. 337, 401	13.	v. 296, 357
18.	i. 21; ii. 7, 275; iii. 327	16.	iv. 219
19.	ii. 339; iii. 250; v. 83, 86, 89, 95	19.	i. 421, 422
		21.	ii. 317; v. 346
22.	i. 368, 449; ii. 73, 104, 108; v. 101, 229, 496	23.	iv. 278
		25.	iii. 119
23.	ii. 113, 313; v. 550	33, 34.	v. 427
24.	v. 400	35.	i. 105
26.	i. 184; ii. 111; iii. 400; v. 545, 547	37.	i. 115; v. 217
		38.	i. 105; iv. 28
27.	iii. 94	42.	ii. 284
28.	i. 62	xxii. 12.	ii. 306
xvii. 1.	i. 96	13.	v. 319
2.	i. 38, 96; ii. 262; iii. 75, 260	19.	iii. 366; v. 130
		20.	iv. 98
4.	ii. 262; iii. 47, 173	21.	iii. 368; iv. 300, 373; v. *127, 132
5.	i. 21, 59, 106, 218, 299; iii. 299; v. 189, 350, 484	23 seq.	v. 347
		30.	ii. 230, 231
21.	i. 389	32.	i. 129
27.	v. 138	36, 37.	i. 418
xviii. 3.	i. 206	38.	iv. 305
6.	i. 160; ii. 74	xxiii. 5.	ii. 352; iv. 372
13, 14.	i. 26	7.	ii. 305
15.	ii. 26	8.	v. 370
15 seq.	v. 157	12.	v. 520
16.	i. 94	14.	i. 407; ii. 352; v. 69, 515
17.	v. 63	15.	v. 518
18.	v. 83, 86, 102	17.	ii. 352; v. 197
20.	i. 151; v. 107, 214	23.	ii. 410; v. 189, 515
21.	v. 438	25.	iv. 381
22.	v. 96, 438	26.	v. 84
24.	i. 280; v. 96, 367, 426, 429, 435	27.	ii. 305
		33.	i. 426
26.	v. 554	34.	iii. 82
27.	v. 367, 437, 440	37.	i. 345; ii. 242; iv. 254, 327; v. 398, 402
28.	iv. 336; v. 434, 435		
29.	v. 428	xxiv. 2.	iv. 264
32.	v. 431, 438	8.	iii. 317
34.	v. 438, 440	15.	iv. 211, 212
xix. 4.	v. 143	23.	i. 259; ii. 29; iii. 345
6.	iii. 349; iv. 300; v. 131, 135, 193	24.	ii. 29
		28.	i. 85
8.	ii. 411; iv. 128	31.	i. 283
11.	iv. 116	36.	i. 4
12.	i. 339, 368; v. 352	37.	iv. 334
19.	ii. 112	38.	iv. 397
24.	ii. 88	51.	i. 402; ii. 48, 60; iv. 121
28.	ii. 375	xxv. 2.	v. 197
30.	i. 102, 229, 277; ii. 160; iii. 382; v. 171	4.	i. 319
		9.	iii. 147; iv. 270
xx. 6.	v. 483	11.	i. 351
15.	v. 283	12.	i. 319, 351; iii. 178, 210
20.	v. 336, 346, 542	14.	iii. 315
21.	v. 542	15.	iii. 307, 366, 386, 389
22.	iv. 250; v. 324, 328, 336, 376, 443, 473	15 seq.	v. 427
		18.	iii. 338; v. 278
23.	v. 336	19.	v. 319
26.	v. 150		

INDEX OF TEXTS. 369

S. Matthew	Vol. Page
xxv. 21.	i. 63, 80, 416; ii. 308; iii. 210; v. 326
23.	i. 415, 416; v. 221
26.	v. 220
27.	v. 46, 319
30.	iii. 259, 338
32.	i. 283
33.	ii. 250
34.	ii. 382; iii. 210, 227; v. 391, 396
35.	i. 172
36.	i. 173
37.	v. 278
40.	i. 162; iv. 106
41.	ii. 192; v. 201
42, 43.	i. 173
44.	v. 278
45.	i. 162
xxvi. 7.	iii. 10
8.	i. 407; ii. 43
9.	v. 131
13.	iii. 44; v. 194
15.	iii. 395; v. 546, 547
17.	ii. 299
26.	i. 31, 83, 113; iii. 34, 278, 279, 355
27.	i. 113; iii. 71
28.	i. 83, 116, 247; ii. 134, 153, 355; iii. 279, 321; v. 94
30, 31.	v. 495
33.	ii. 63; iii. 173, 336
36.	iii. 70, 247, 348
38.	ii. 123, 144
39.	ii. 298; iii. 71; v. 340, 359
40.	v. 488
41.	v. 333, 344, 402, 443, 504
48.	iv. 146, 148
51.	iv. 146
53.	i. 149, 211; ii. 129
56.	ii. 240; iii. 74
61.	ii. 346
69.	iii. 138, 153
72.	ii. 240
73.	iii. 358, 365
75.	i. 446; v. 488
xxvii. 19.	ii. 147
21.	i. 414
24.	ii. 126
25.	ii. 146
26.	ii. 170
29.	ii. 277; iii. 68
32.	ii. 326
40.	v. 488
42.	ii. 331; v. 502
45.	ii. 231
46.	ii. 124, 139, 146, 179; iii. 55, 74; v. 359
47.	ii. 277
48.	i. 147
49.	ii. 124
50.	iii. 269; v. 502

S. Matthew	Vol. Page
xxvii. 51.	ii. 277, 356, 394; v. 502
52.	ii. 356, 394
54.	ii. 129
57.	ii. 89
60.	i. 243; ii. 278
64.	v. 189
66.	ii. 398
xxviii. 1.	iii. 6
2.	ii. 213, 233, 328; iii. 78; v. 502
6.	ii. 208
9.	ii. 238; iii. 18, 28, 31, 35
12.	i. 222
13.	ii. 233
17.	ii. 190
18.	i. 28; ii. 279; v. 392
19.	i. 288; iii. 44, 185, 242; v. 5, 91, 463
20.	i. 147; v. 486

S. MARK.

i. 1.	i. 80
4.	i. 434
15.	i. 418, 434; v. 58
22.	i. 430
24.	i. 213
35.	v. 323, 344, 355
ii. 9.	v. 227
10.	v. 90
12.	iv. 215
18.	ii. 44
20.	i. 379
25.	ii. 65
iii. 17.	iv. 245
iv. 5, 6, 8.	iii. 321
19.	v. 495
24.	v. 188, 192
28.	i. 268
38.	ii. 156; v. 452, 463
39.	i. 95
v. 26.	v. 227, 511
31.	iii. 37
vi. 17.	v. 543
20.	i. 407; v. 515
21.	i. 73
23.	i. 84; v. 80, 326, 546
25.	v. 543
26.	v. 81
27.	v. 81, 543
28.	i. 407
vii. 3.	v. 526
4.	v. 57
18.	i. 405
19.	ii. 51
27.	v. 557
viii. 11.	ii. 388; v. 518
12.	v. 535
15.	ii. 305; v. 414
33.	v. 503
ix. 3.	iii. 9, 75
6.	iii. 30

AND.—PERRON, ETC. D D

S. Mark	Vol. Page
ix. 22.	v. 363, 372
23.	i. 139
24.	iii. 152, 153
26.	ii. 338; iv. 210; v. 409
43.	iii. 321
44.	i. 426; iii. 204
46.	i. 426
49.	iii. 125, 126
50.	ii. 239, 247
x. 2.	v. 347
37.	iv. 249
38.	ii. 108, 169
40.	iv. 249
xi. 24.	v. 474
25.	v. 341, 438
xii. 10.	ii. 284
24.	v. 505
42.	ii. 53; v. 273
44.	i. 229, 451; ii. 103
xiii. 4.	i. 155
21.	iv. 47
37.	v. 91
xiv. 3.	iii. 25
3 seq.	ii. 225
4.	ii. 226; iii. 311
4—6.	*ii. 37
5.	ii. 226
6.	ii. 53
8.	i. 229, 451; ii. 103; iii. 152
9.	ii. 59
13.	iii. 359
21.	iv. 13
24.	iii. 359
33.	ii. 123, 144
34.	ii. 123
36.	i. 27
50.	ii. 240
58.	ii. 346
63.	v. 515
70.	iii. 358
71.	ii. 235
xv. 16, 18, 19.	ii. 329
22.	iii. 247
29, 36.	ii. 146
39.	ii. 148
xvi. 1.	iii. 26
1—7.	ii. 221
3.	ii. 295; iv. 228
6.	ii. 321; ii. 208, 266
9.	ii. 223, 238; iii. 4
11.	ii. 190
12.	iii. 15
15.	iii. 122, 123
17.	i. 205

S. LUKE.

i. 10.	v. 230, 324
12.	ii. 232
17.	iii. 134
18.	v. 535
20.	v. 533

S. Luke	Vol. Page
i. 28.	i. 97
29.	i. 73; ii. 232
31.	i. 69, 72, 135
31 seq.	i. 27
34.	i. 138
35.	i. 138; iii. 146, 184
36.	i. 138
37.	i. 139
42.	i. 163
43.	i. 11
44.	i. 125
45.	i. 206
46.	i. 29; iv. 119, 259; v. 383
47.	iv. 105, 108, 119; v. 383
48.	i. 206; ii. 325
51.	iv. 75, 91
53.	i. 278
68.	i. 29; ii. 365
69.	iv. 368
71.	iv. 363
72.	iv. 362, 363
74, 75.	iii. 231, *iv. 361
76.	i. 428
78.	i. 12, 105, 112, 124, 142, 186, 188, 235; ii. 238, 371; iv. 279, 322, 332, 362
79.	i. 35, 77, 167, 189, 191; ii. 249
ii. 1.	i. 71, 242; iii. 324; v. 128, 130
5.	v. 138
7.	i. 24, 70, 158, 161, 197, 209, 242; ii. 249, 327
9.	i. 3
10.	i. 27, 122; ii. 230
10, 11.	i. *64, 212
11.	i. 27, 122, 160; ii. 148
12.	i. 170, 197, 199, 234; ii. 342; iv. 331
12—14.	*i. 196
13.	i. 3, 10, 117, 142
14.	i. 3, 29, 82, 117, 122, 189, 209, *215, 218, 277; ii. 243, 244, 321, 338; iii. 98, 100; v. 389, 404, 551
15.	i. 170, 210
19.	i. 255
20.	i. 213, 253
21.	i. 55
22.	iii. 148
25.	i. 27
26.	iv. 49
29.	i. 128, 129, 191, 222; ii. 258; v. 395
30.	i. 79, 127
32.	i. 240; ii. 391
34.	i. 207, 226
35.	ii. 123
37.	i. 380, 381; v. 323
46.	ii. 249
51.	ii. 326
iii. 4.	v. 287
6.	i. 90

INDEX OF TEXTS. 371

S. Luke	Vol. Page
iii. 8.	i. 172; v. 100
10.	i. 365, 441, 450
12.	i. 441, 450
14.	i. 335, 441, 450
16.	i. 279; iii. 245; v. 347
21.	i. 433
21, 22.	✱iii. 241
22.	iii. 184, 251, 260, 264, 286, 309
iv. 1.	i. 410, 433
8.	v. 503
13.	v. 536
18.	iii. 184, 305; iv. 254; v. 85, 97
18, 19.	✱iii. 280
19.	v. 495
20.	v. 555
21.	i. 153, 321; iii. 222, 281; iv. 203, 314
23.	iii. 291
25.	i. 241; iii. 249, 294; v. 97, 424
26.	v. 97
27.	i. 241; iii. 294; v. 97
29.	iv. 89
34.	ii. 243
v. 8.	iii. 270; v. 91, 428
9.	v. 56
16.	i. 410
26.	iv. 215
37.	v. 56
vi. 1.	iv. 242
12.	v. 344
24.	v. 48
26.	i. 413
35.	ii. 115
36.	iv. 339
38.	iv. 105, 121; v. 48
41, 42.	ii. 26
46.	ii. 340
48.	ii. 267
vii. 3.	iii. 398
4.	iii. 341
5.	i. 279
6.	iii. 341
14.	i. 95; ii. 193
30.	iii. 247
32.	iv. 261
35.	ii. 281; iv. 294
37.	ii. 223; iii. 5
38.	i. 369
39.	ii. 58
41.	v. 96, 426, 428
46.	ii. 54, 225; iii. 25
47.	ii. 38; iii. 6, 28; v. 437
48.	v. 101, 442
viii. 10.	i. 33
18.	v. 188, 192
31.	v. 503
32.	v. 451
46.	ii. 204
54.	ii. 193
ix. 1.	v. 63

S. Luke	Vol. Page
ix. 2.	v. 95
9.	v. 534
32.	v. 328
33.	v. 328, 474
36.	v. 488
49.	v. 63
51.	v. 517
53.	iv. 242, 243
54.	iii. 256; iv. 263; v. 318, 346
54—56.	✱ iv. 241
55.	iii. 256
56.	iv. 245
58.	iv. 246; v. 499
62.	ii. 74
x. 1.	v. 63
5, 6.	ii. 247
9.	i. 418; v. 397
18.	v. 520
20.	v. 21
21.	i. 12; v. 359
24.	i. 61
26.	v. 143
27.	v. 348
31.	i. 183, 273
32.	i. 183, 273; ii. 127
34.	iii. 295; iv. 84
37.	i. 263; ii. 56; iv. 144, 157
40.	ii. 58; v. 341
42.	i. 132; ii. 34; iii. 366; v. 190, 192, 194, 314, 345, 377, 415
xi. 1.	v. 324, 332, ✱342, 343, 346
2.	v. 68, 343, ✱351, ✱362, ✱372, ✱381, ✱390, ✱396, ✱405
3.	✱v. 413
4.	v. ✱424, 426, ✱432, ✱441
5.	v. 331
11.	v. 328, 375
12.	v. 328, 366
13.	iii. 198, 376; v. 309, 314, 364, 375, 377, 452
14.	v. 348
20.	ii. 387
22.	iii. 229
23.	i. 272
24.	iii. 191
25.	v. 520
26.	iii. 218; v. 537
27.	v. 196
28.	v. 193
29.	ii. 388
31.	iii. 34
32.	v. 101
41.	v. 439
42.	i. 229
43 seq.	iv. 9
47.	i. 229
52.	v. 97, 100, 190, 191
xii. 1.	i. 377, 400; ii. 305
5.	i. 426
12.	iii. 188

372 INDEX OF TEXTS.

S. Luke	Vol. Page
xii. 18.	v. 38, 278
19.	ii. 91; iii. 365; v. 34, 278, 313, 422, 506, 508
20.	iv. 397; v. 23
24.	i. 349
32.	i. 228; iii. 92, 93
38.	v. 356
42.	v. 421
46.	i. 320
47.	i. 191; iii. 152; iv. 326; v. 24
48.	i. 15; v. 38
49.	iv. 259
50.	ii. 113, 176, 350; iii. 247
xiii. 3.	i. 429
4.	v. 426
5.	i. 429
7.	i. 439; ii. 40; iii. 389
25.	v. 200
26.	iii. 319; v. 200
28.	ii. 85
32.	i. 261; ii. 176; iii. 225, 367; v. 315
xiv. 15.	v. 419
18.	v. 409
23.	i. 324; ii. 306; v. 401
31.	v. 212
xv. 2.	i. 98
5.	i. 6, 280; iii. 89
6.	iv. 98
7.	i. 213
9.	iv. 98
10.	iii. 299, 379; v. 557
13.	v. 319, 378
18.	iii 51; iv. 14; v. 367, 368
19.	v. 306
20.	iii. 258, 298; iv. 272; v. 322, 430
21.	i. 447; ii. 31
22.	ii. 224; iii. 298
24.	ii. 242
28.	i. 3
31.	i. 82; ii. 102; iii. 53
32.	iv. 98; v. 330
xvi. 1.	v. 457
2.	i. 279
9.	i. 279; ii. 80; iv. 117; v. 272
14.	v. 16, 17
15.	ii. 87
16.	v. 348
19.	v. 33
20, 21.	v. 277
22.	ii. 82; v. 21
23.	i. 130
24.	ii. 85; v. 38, 277
25.	✱ii. 78; iii. 375; v. 277, 558
26.	i. 37; ii. 85; iii. 65
27, 28.	ii. 80
29.	v. 191
30.	ii. 345
xvii. 5.	v. 310
10.	i. 279; ii. 242; v. 457

S. Luke	Vol. Page
xvii. 13.	v. 475
14, 15 seq.	ii. 107
16.	ii. 134; iv. 245
18, 19.	v. 460
21.	v. 393
22.	i. 121
26, 28.	iv. 334
29.	iv. 397
32.	✱ii. 61
35.	ii. 72
37.	i. 86, 155, 174, 282; ii. 302, 318; v. 376
xviii. 1.	v. 354
2.	v. 330
3—5.	v. 274, 330
5.	v. 331
5—7.	v. 330
10.	i. 443; v. 63
11.	iii. 342; v. 13, 428, 538
12.	i. 401, 412; v. 492
13.	i. 371, 443; iv. 166; v. 341, 358, 428
14.	i. 190; iii. 342; v. 322
21.	i. 384
xix. 3.	i. 127
4.	iv. 323
8.	i. 443, 448; v. 34
9.	i. 127; iv. 99; v. 34
13.	iii. 366, 386
14.	i. 325; ii. 21, 276; iv. 11; v. 392
20.	iii. 396
22.	iv. 140, 143; v. 168, 438
23.	iii. 399; v. 427
27.	i. 325
38.	iv. 221
40.	iv. 238
41.	i. 351, 354, 425; v. 339
42.	i. 351, 354, 425; ii. 244; v. 15
44.	v. 15
xx. 4.	iii. 250
17.	ii. 284
20.	v. 127
35.	i. 15, 451; iii. 341; v. 308
36.	ii. 217; v. 407, 460
39.	v. 193
xxi. 2.	iii. 366
4.	ii. 103; v. 67
15.	iii. 141
19.	v. 456
25.	i. 201
28.	ii. 136; iii. 209; v. 395
33.	i. 21, 255
34.	i. 329, 382; v. 421
35.	v. 395
xxii. 3.	ii. 52; iv. 133, 189
7.	ii. 299, 303
15.	ii. 176, 295, 350
19.	i. 83; ii. 300, 343; iii. 161; v. 91, 95, 260
20.	iii. 72
24.	i. 7

INDEX OF TEXTS.

S. Luke	Vol. Page
xxii. 27.	ii. 249
31.	v. 443, 446, 494
32.	iii. 327; v. 355
37.	iii. 306
40.	v. 353, 446
41.	v. 329, 344
42.	v. 379, 399, 400, 408
43.	v. 557
44.	i. 26; ii. 123, 144, 277, 298, 356
46.	v. 344
49, 51.	iv. 254
53.	i. 122; ii. 149; iii. 67, 227; v. 483, 517
61.	i. 9; ii. 137
62.	i. 9
64.	iii. 68
xxiii. 2.	v. 129
4.	ii. 296
8.	i. 133
11.	i. 260
14, 15.	ii. 126, 148, 296
30.	iii. 47
31.	v. 480
33.	ii. 249; v. 456
34.	ii. 112, 113; iii. 56, 156; v. 359
41.	ii. 395
42.	v. 391
43.	v. 322
44.	i. 40
46.	iii. 56
48.	i. 122; ii. 158, 181
xxiv. 1.	ii. 241, 376
4.	iii. 15
5.	iii. 319, 321
6.	ii. 208, 318
11.	i. 200; ii. 190
13.	ii. 190, 321
15.	ii. 238
16.	iii. 15, 21, 66
17.	iii. 18
21.	ii. 207, 375, 392
26.	ii. 389
28.	v. 218
29.	iii. 47, 168; v. 218
30.	ii. 322
31.	ii. 205
32.	ii. 137, 156, 374; iii. 22
34.	ii. 238
35.	ii. 322; iii. 22
36.	iii. 18
37—40.	iii. 31
38.	v. 308, 494
39.	iii. 27
41.	ii. 190
47.	ii. 402; iii. 235; v. 98
49.	iii. 135, 144, 195, 271, 274; v. 403
50.	iii. 81

S. JOHN.

S. John	Vol. Page
i. 1.	i. 85, 181; ii. 162; iii. 10, 68
3.	i. 90, 91, 110; iv. 283
9.	i. 110; iii. 317, 319, 370; v. 352
10.	iv. 255
11.	ii. 145; iv. 255
12.	i. 23, 98, 109, 150, 297; ii. 218
13.	v. 366, 400
14.	i. 16, 22, 39, 49, 53, 56, 79, 80, *85, 86, 106, 132, 146, 187, 237, 276; ii. 183; iii. 10, 148, 159, 169, 198, 285, 308; v. 194, 344
16.	i. 49, 63, 96, 106; iii. 151, 307; v. 309, 403
17.	i. 96; iii. 151; v. 315, 348
18.	i. 94; v. 365, 382
26.	ii. 249; v. 217
29.	i. 65, 112, 183, 433; ii. 197, 295, 296; iii. 253; iv. 254, 329; v. 119
32.	iii. 171, 354; iv. 253
33.	iii. 125, 251, 257
41.	i. 198; iv. 82
46.	i. 158
51.	i. 3
ii. 1.	ii. 234
10.	v. 502, 558
11.	v. 502
13.	ii. 290
15.	v. 551
17.	ii. 346
18.	ii. 344
19.	ii. 263, *344
20.	ii. 346
21.	ii. 345, 346
iii. 3.	ii. 371; v. 366, 393
5.	iii. 170, 176, 185, 248, 250; v. 366, 393, 470
6.	v. 379
8.	iii. 115, 120, 176, 204, 251, 357, 369; v. 100, 285, 335, 352, 484
14.	ii. 120, 133, 142, 302; v. 480
16.	i. 12, 28, 40, 92; ii. 175, 180, 369; iii. 245; v. 398
19.	v. 317
21.	iii. 370
27.	iii. 369; v. 315, 348
31.	v. 348, 349, 379, 402
32.	v. 187
34.	i. 49, 97; iii. 154, 251; iv. 85, 344
35.	i. 28
iv. 2.	v. 95
6.	v. 498
7, 8.	iv. 245
9.	iv. 244
10.	iii. 232, 361; v. 327

374 INDEX OF TEXTS.

S. John	Vol. Page
iv. 14.	iii. 308, 355
15.	iii. 351
22.	iv. 250, 257
23.	v. 380
24.	i. 91; iii. 204; v. 231, 360, 468, 473
25.	i. 75; iii. 328
34.	v. 410
35.	iii. 111
42.	i. 76
v. 3.	i. 353
4.	i. 311; iii. 295, 356
14.	iii. 353; v. 227
17.	i. 110; iii. 381, 391
19.	v. 305
22.	iii. 152
24.	ii. 193
29.	v. 197
39.	v. 505
44.	v. 388
45.	iii. 158
vi. 12.	i. 273; ii. 40; v. 422
14.	i. 133
15.	v. 344
24.	ii. 268
26.	i. 313; ii. 102; v. 409
27.	i. 76, 170; iii. 219, 355
31.	i. 173
32.	i. 169, 173
33.	i. 169; ii. 205; v. 384
34.	iii. 351
35.	i. 160, 248; iii. 239; v. 419, 504
37.	i. 76; v. 323
38.	v. 407
39.	v. 398
41.	i. 173, 248
44.	v. 379
48.	i. 169, 173; ii. 33
49.	i. 281
50.	ii. 322, 427; v. 419
51.	i. 30, 173, 238, 281; ii. 33; iii. 58; v. 481
53.	v. 470
54.	ii. 268, 403
56.	i. 100; ii. 205, 265, 289; iii. 34
57.	ii. 220
58.	ii. 427
60.	i. 168, 358; v. 201, 409
62.	iii. 37
63.	ii. 205, 220; iii. 37, 143, 170, 192, 200, 273, 355, 357
70.	i. 15; v. 494
vii. 3.	iii. 398
4.	v. 503
6.	i. 265
8.	i. 48
12.	i. 413
32.	v. 191
37.	i. 134; iii. 179
37—39.	iii. 249
39.	iii. 197, 262, 305

S. John	Vol. Page
vii. 42.	i. 154, 160
46.	iii. 76; v. 191, 193
48.	ii. 276
52.	i. 158
viii. 1—9.	ii. 388
11.	v. 101, 442
12.	v. 317, 335
21.	i. 313
23.	v. 520
24.	v. 87, 98
33.	i. 120
34.	v. 364
35.	iii. 258
36.	v. 454
39.	i. 14, 120, 428
40.	i. 14, 120
44.	iv. 210, 254; v. 364
46.	ii. 126
48.	iv. 245
53.	i. 120
56.	i. 15, 20, *118; ii. 91
58.	iii. 374
59.	iv. 89
ix. 6.	v. 509
7.	iii. 288
22.	ii. 240
24.	v. 459
31.	v. 322
x. 3.	iii. 388
7.	iii. 388; v. 327
10.	ii. 329
11.	i. 65
16.	ii. 281; iii. 135
17.	v. 263
18.	ii. 129, 331; iii. 89; v. 263
28.	i. 26
30.	iii. 188
31.	iv. 89
32.	ii. 58
34.	v. 206
35.	i. 92, 294; iv. 284, 293, 300; v. 206, 525
36.	iv. 278
38.	ii. 342; iii. 397
xi. 2.	ii. 37, 54
4.	v. 333
12.	ii. 213
21.	iii. 172
23.	ii. 198
25.	ii. 203, 253; iii. 27
26.	v. 310
31.	ii. 225
32.	iii. 47
36.	i. 148; ii. 132, 181; iii. 7
41.	v. 345, 359
42.	v. 345, 350
43.	ii. 193
44.	ii. 329
48.	ii. 46, 282; iii. 133
49.	ii. 276; iii. 327
50.	ii. 45, 276; iii. 167
55.	ii. 290
xii. 3.	iii. 10, 40

INDEX OF TEXTS. 375

S. John	Vol. Page
xii. 4.	ii. 43
5.	i. 407
6.	ii. 46, 47
8.	v. 43
15.	iv. 221
19.	ii. 46
20.	i. 242
23.	i. 48, 242
24.	i. 169, 281; iii. 71
27.	i. 222; ii. 123, 144
30.	iii. 257
32.	ii. 159, 176, 182, 312
41.	i. 212; v. 350
xiii. 1.	ii. 163; iii. 376
5.	ii. 327
7.	iii. 328
10.	iii. 358
15.	i. 432; ii. 160, 342; v. 503
17.	v. 194, 397
18.	iv. 11
23.	ii. 347
25.	iii. 219
27.	ii. 352; v. 494
29.	ii. 40; v. 33, 67
35.	i. 42
xiv. 2.	i. 11; iii. 158, 226
3.	i. 11, 152; iii. 51, 227
5.	i. 165; v. 324
6.	i. 96, 166, 177, 185, 219, 245; iii. 276, 356; v. 190, 327, 471
8.	i. 109; ii. 261; iii. 53; v. 327
9.	i. 109
11.	ii. 342
15, 16.	✶ iii. 145
16.	iii. 115, 188, 221
17.	iii. 155, 182, 221
26.	iii. 155, 156, 171, 176, 178, 184, 188, 189, 191, 207, 369
27.	i. 222; ii. 244
28.	iii. 50
30.	ii. 148; v. 392, 480, 538, 545
xv. 1.	i. 169; ii. 281; iv. 254
3.	i. 116
4.	ii. 62
5.	i. 280; ii. 203; iii. 70, 279, 392; v. 304, 305, 306
13.	ii. 104, 109, 130, 180; iii. 149
15.	iii. 43
24.	ii. 112
25.	iv. 88
26.	iii. 156, 171, 176, 178, 184, 188, 189, 264, 284, 358; v. 471
xvi. 2.	iii. 165
6.	iii. 164
7.	iii. ✶162, 184, 188; v. 316
8.	iii. 177, 188, 207
11.	i. 376
12.	iii. 328; v. 352

S. John	Vol. Page
xvi. 13.	iii. 175, 188, 189, 207
14.	iii. 179, 189
16.	v. 455, 536
21.	i. 73; iv. 346
22.	i. 72; iv. 122, 205, 240
23.	v. 328, 350, 470, 473
24.	i. 69; v. 331
28.	i. 110
33.	ii. 244, 245; v. 454, 486
xvii. 3.	i. 193; v. 481
5.	v. 359, 464
15.	v. 457
17.	iii. 143, 156; v. 389
20.	iii. 249; v. 359
21.	ii. 244; iv. 285
24.	i. 152; iii. 90
xviii. 1.	v. 344
1 seq.	ii. 244
3.	v. 494
5.	i. 149
6.	ii. 129, 338
8.	i. 58; ii. 197, 396; iii. 88; v. 429
22.	ii. 150
28.	ii. 299
30.	v. 499
36.	i. 24
38.	i. 312; ii. 315
40.	i. 414; ii. 146, 276
xix. 3.	i. 260
5.	ii. 143, 147, 148, 183, 260
10.	ii. 21, 119; iii. 272, 365; v. 313, 543
11.	ii. 21; iii. 365; iv. 52; v. 313, 416
13.	iii. 247
13 seq.	iii. 70, 348
15.	ii. 146
22.	ii. 148
29.	ii. 171; ii. 277
30.	i. 26, 107; ii. 113, 163; iii. 49, 169, 225
34.	i. 113; ii. 122, 134, 178, 398; iii. 70, 247, 348, 349
35.	i. 94; ii. 78
36.	ii. 295
37.	ii. 136, 237
39.	i. 40, 243; ii. 226; iii. 19
xx. 1.	iii. 74
4.	ii. 315
8.	iii. 7, 8
11—17.	✶ iii. 3
12.	ii. 230; iii. 23
14.	iii. 23, 66
15.	ii. 192; iii. 23, 45
16.	iii. 23
17.	ii. 218; iii.✶ 23, ✶39, 232
18.	iii. 42
19.	ii. 223, ✶238, 240, 281
21.	iii. 100, 281; v. 82, 92, 96
22.	iii. 135, 184, 188, 193, 254, ✶260, 309; v. 83, 92, 96
23.	iii. 254, 262; ✶ v. 82

INDEX OF TEXTS.

S. John	Vol. Page
xx. 25.	ii. 190
26.	iv. 245
27.	iii. 27, 35
28.	ii. 133, 183; iii. 30
30.	v. 496
xxi. 7.	iv. 247
15.	ii. 223
16.	iii. 86, 327
20.	ii. 74, 223
21.	v. 409

ACTS.

i. 1.	ii. 163
1 seq.	ii. 311
3.	iii. 36
5.	iii. 305
6.	iii. 114; v. 542
7.	i. 50; iii. 114, 328
8.	v. 91
9.	i. 94; ii. 334; iii. 223, 224
11.	i. 205, 256; ii. 142; iii. 225, 227
15.	ii. 235
18.	iv. 19, 34
25.	ii. 287; iv. 98, 294
ii. 1.	iii. 115, 252; v. 219, 345
1—4.	iii. *108, 241
2.	iii. 125, 195, 268
3.	iii. 125, 176, 184, 193, 197, 242, 253, 256, 260, 264, 309, 333, 361; v. 317
4.	ii. 339; iii. 123, *130, 277, 358
5.	iii. 111, 207, 310, 324
6.	v. 191
8.	iii. 207
11.	ii. 339; iii. 108, 313
13.	v. 191
15.	iii. 147, 178; v. 354
16—21.	*301
17.	v. 351
18.	iii. 310
20.	iii. 322
24.	ii. 167, 398; iii. 66; iv. 233, 367
26.	ii. 398
31.	ii. 260; iii. 313
33.	iii. 116, 181, 306, 308
34.	iii. 313
37.	i. 423; ii. 131, 137, 156; iii. 125, 198; v. 101
38.	iii. 236; v. 94
41.	iii. 242, 254, 358
42.	v. 54, *63
44.	ii. 41
46.	iii. 114, 128, 254; v. 67
iii. 1.	v. 354, 357
2.	iii. 290
6.	ii. 103
15.	i. 80; ii. 165; v. 97
19.	ii. 197; v. 97
21.	i. 270; ii. 220; iii. 298, 300

Acts	Vol. Page
iv. 10.	ii. 270
11.	ii. 270, 274, 284
12.	i. 77; ii. 332; v. 106, 383
13.	iii. 270
24.	iii. 114, 123
25.	i. 197
27.	i. 77, 286
31.	iii. 127
32.	ii. 247
36.	iii. 175
37.	ii. 52
v. 3.	ii. 52
4.	iii. 184
5.	iv. 249
28.	v. 5
29.	iii. 256
37.	v. 128
39.	ii. 210; iv. 19, 293
41.	iii. 157
vi. 4.	v. 355
5.	v. 58
10.	iii. 134
15.	i. 4.
vii. 22.	i. 245
37.	i. 24
43.	i. 242; v. 69
51.	iii. 196
52.	ii. 353; iii. 236, 283
54.	i. 371
55.	i. 97
viii. 6.	iii. 114
9.	i. 171; v. 9
13.	iii. 355
17.	i. 193
18.	iii. 395; v. 546
19.	v. 11
20.	iii. 362; iv. 8; v. 51, 548
22.	i. 442; v. 100, 431
23.	iii. 113, 197, 293, 355; v. 56, 86
27.	i. 244, 261; ii. 89; iii. 290, 324, 332
28, 30.	v. 473
31.	i. 171; v. 473
33.	i. 201
34.	i. 19, 135; ii. 119; iii. 61
ix. 1.	ii. 115; iii. 358
3—6.	v. 303
4.	i. 9; ii. 50; iii. 226
5.	iv. 19, 293; v. 397
6.	i. 440; ii. 340; v. 190
15.	v. 117, 384, 454
36.	iii. 290
37—41.	v. 279
40.	v. 329
x. 1.	iii. 324, 332
2.	iii. 334, 339
3.	i. 395; iii. 339
4.	i. 279; v. 279, 298; v. 341
5.	iii. 324; v. 90
6.	iii. 290, 295, 325, 337; v. 90
9.	i. 395; v. 354, 357, 492
11.	i. 274

INDEX OF TEXTS. 377

Acts	Vol. Page	Acts	Vol. Page
x. 15.	iv. 378; v. 78	xviii. 17.	ii. 12
25.	v. 554	24.	i. 245
26.	iii. 328; iv. 281	26.	iii. 182
30.	iii. 339; v. 492	xix. 1—3.	*iii. 180
32.	iii. 270, 295; v. 90	2.	iii. 170
34.	iii. 290	4.	iii. 243, 244
34, 35.	*iii. 323	6.	iii. 115, 127
36.	iii. 369	9.	iii. 195
38.	i. 77; ii. 54; iii. 338; iv. 33	15.	v. 522, 526
		23.	v. 147
43.	iii. 324	24.	ii. 102
44.	iii. 115, 118, 127, 198, 323	25.	ii. 46; iii. 195
xi. 2.	iii. 327	27.	iii. 275
12.	iii. 188	28.	i. 413
14.	v. 191	32.	i. 413; ii. 25
18.	iii. 324	39.	v. 148
26.	v. 366, 386	40.	v. 152
xii. 3.	iii. 275; iv. 131	xx. 9.	v. 530
5.	v. 358	16.	iii. 358
7, 8.	iv. 236	19.	v. 329
9.	iv. 236	20.	v. 347
22.	i. 226; v. 388, 542, 544	21.	iii. 121; v. 58
xiii. 2.	i. 379; iii. 188; v. 266, 323	22.	iii. 207; v. 484
3.	i. 379; v. 491	28.	iii. 188, 234; v. 463
7.	i. 244	29.	ii. 9; v. 55
10.	iv. 8	30.	iv. 11, 160; v. 55, 58
11.	iv. 249	32.	ii. 204
22.	iv. 81	35.	v. 460
33.	ii. 230, 330, 376; iii. 5, 57	xxi. 9, 10.	iii. 312
35.	ii. 260	14.	v. 399
36.	iii. 388	16.	ii. 62
39.	v. 115	26.	v. 357
41.	iv. 216, 268	28.	v. 63
43.	iii. 220	xxii. 16.	iii. 248; v. 94
xiv. 11.	v. 207, 388	23.	ii. 25
14.	i. 225, 226	xxiii. 3.	v. 80
15.	v. 388	8.	iv. 372
17.	iii. 353; v. 375, 407, 418	14.	i. 408; v. 80
27.	i. 236, 239, 252; v. 302	xxiv. 16.	i. 381
xv. 9.	iii. 310, 352	17.	i. 172
10.	i. 25; iii. 151	25.	i. 314, 350, 356, 431; ii. 11; iii. 198, 334
11.	v. 468		
16.	i. 273	26.	v. 11
20.	v. 59	27.	ii. 320
21.	iii. 116	xxv. 11.	v. 137
28.	i. 357; iii. 184, 188; v. 60	23.	v. 543, 553
		xxvi. 8.	i. 138
30, 32.	v. 63	9.	iii. 329
xvi. 6, 7.	iii. 207	20.	i. 440, 447; v. 100
14.	ii. 89; iii. 290	24.	i. 245; ii. 191
25.	v. 356	25.	i. 311
30.	i. 440; iii. 290	26.	i. 40, 94, 234; iii. 110
xvii. 11.	i. 244	27.	iii. 290
15.	v. 63	28.	i. 350, 364; iii. 198; iv. 372; v. 193, 409
20.	i. 420		
21.	i. 346	29.	i. 364
27.	iii. 15	xxvii. 21.	i. 385
28.	v. 62, 305, 378	23, 24.	v. 533
32.	ii. 191	29.	v. 533
34.	i. 244, 245; ii. 89; iii. 290; iii. 332	30, 31.	iv. 68; v. 533
		32.	v. 533
xviii. 11.	ii. 98	xxviii. 4, 6.	i. 414
14, 15.	v. 105		

AND.—PERRON, ETC.   E E

378 INDEX OF TEXTS.

ROMANS.

Romans	Vol. Page
i. 8.	ii. 63
14.	iii. 123 ; v. 427, 434
16.	i. 202 ; iii. 398
19.	iii. 334
20.	i. 36
23.	v. 385
24.	v. 401, 545
31.	v. 374
ii. 4.	i. 424 ; v. 374, 521, 533
5.	ii. 152 ; v. 51
9.	v. 86, 87
13.	v. 194
14.	v. 307
15.	i. 290, 361 ; iii. 334 ; v. 115
17.	v. 199
22.	i. 363 ; ii. 47, 351
24.	ii. 341 ; iii. 212 ; v. 387
iii. 2.	i. 149, 189 ; ii. 360 ; iii. 313
4.	i. 179, 294 ; v. 471
8.	iv. 211
15.	iv. 186
19.	v. 115
21.	v. 114
22.	i. 27
23.	i. 436
25.	ii. 169 ; iii. 351, 357 ; v. 441
26.	v. 112
27.	i. 287 ; v. 124, 313
28.	v. 555
31.	iii. 352 ; v. 438, 498
iv. 1.	v. 114
3.	i. 13, 130 ; v. 114
5.	v. 112, 114
6, 8, 9, 10.	v. 114
11.	i. 128 ; iii. 219 ; iv. 193 ; v. 114
12.	i. 14, 250, 251, 256 ; iii. 95
16.	v. 114
17.	i. 18
18.	ii. 266
21—24.	v. 471
25.	ii. 199, 298, 362
v. 2.	iii. 220, 258
3.	v. 456, 485, 493, 557
4.	v. 493, 557
5.	ii. 209, 267, 375 ; iii. 108, 121, 189, 192, 197, 207, 363 ; v. 310, 337, 352, 459
8.	ii. 151
10.	ii. 115 ; iii. 149, 257
12.	ii. 214 ; v. 227
14.	ii. 193, 216 ; v. 392
15.	ii. 153, 216, 328
16.	ii. 218 ; v. 116, 313
17.	v. 109, 318
20.	i. 343
21.	v. 392, 393, 396
vi. 1.	v. 535
3.	iii. 247 ; v. 431

Romans	Vol. Page
vi. 4.	ii. 206 ; v. 463
5.	ii. 192
6.	ii. 200
9—11.	*ii. 187
9.	ii. 398
11.	ii. 188, 194 ; iii. 49
12.	ii. 200 ; v. 392, 444
13.	ii. 263 ; iv. 187
14.	i. 333
18—20.	iv. 372
19.	i. 333, 368 ; ii. 335 ; iii. 169, 214 ; v. 52, 336, 340, 354, 444
21.	ii. 40 ; iii. 399
22.	i. 434 ; v. 305
23.	i. 181 ; ii. 327 ; iii. 269 ; v. 260
vii. 10.	v. 521
12.	v. 401
14.	i. 57 ; ii. 256 ; iii. 208 ; v. 401
16.	v. 400, 408
17.	v. 307
18.	i. 92 ; ii. 63 ; v. 303, 307
19.	v. 304
20.	v. 444
22.	i. 128 ; v. 400, 408
23.	i. 93, 176 ; ii. 258 ; iii. 208, 228 ; v. 400
24.	iii. 293 ; v. 99, 410, 451
viii. 1.	v. 366
3.	iii. 284, 308, 390 ; v. 315
7.	i. 92 ; v. 304
9.	iii. 170, 192, 193, 284
11.	ii. 219 ; iii. 191
12.	v. 427
14.	v. 484
15.	i. 27, 300 ; iii. 51, 55, 111, 195, 258, 335, 337 ; v. 61, 468
16.	iii. 158, 188
17.	i. 60 ; iii. 258 ; v. 309, 368
18.	i. 279, 447 ; v. 309, 456
20.	ii. 257 ; v. 394
21.	iii. 230 ; v. 394
22.	i. 125 ; iii. 209
23.	ii. 70, 219 ; iii. 209, 252
24.	ii. 380 ; iii. 352
26.	iii. 158, 170, 191, 207, 253, 362 ; v. *332, 333, 342, 346, 370
28.	ii. 71 ; v. 484
29.	i. 54 ; ii. 218 ; iii. 57, 245 ; v. 113, 410
32.	i. 7, 28 ; ii. 133, 184 ; v. 362
33.	v. 115, 116
34.	v. 116
37.	i. 150 ; iii. 75
39.	i. 150
ix. 1.	v. 76
4.	i. 189

INDEX OF TEXTS. 379

Romans	Vol. Page
ix. 5.	ii. 366; iii. 187; iv. 324; v. 470
7.	i. 13
18.	v. 533
19.	v. 397, 398
23.	iv. 325
29.	i. 11; iv. 255, 264, 388
x. 1.	i. 230
2.	i. 231; iv. 250
3.	iii. 342
4.	i. 106
6.	i. 171; iii. 270; v. 90
6—8.	v. 436
8.	i. 93, 171, 276; v. 90
10.	i. 251; v. 553
12.	iii. 310
13.	iii. 312, 320; v. 190
14.	iii. 117, 320, 339; v. 107, 190, 531
15.	ii. 243, 249; iii. 288, 312
17.	v. 196
18.	iii. 116, 139, 183, 266; v. 408
25.	i. 277
xi. 16.	ii. 213, 216, 236
17, 18.	v. 307
20.	iii. 336
20—22.	ii. 72
22.	ii. 63
25.	ii. 391; iii. 136, 237
29.	iii. 376
32.	iii. 332; iv. 330; v. 370
33.	iii. 33; iv. 398
34.	v. 397
36.	iv. 285
xii. 1.	i. 262, 381; iii. 212; v. 231, 262, 264, 265, 288, 344, 354, 360
3.	iii. 289; v. 15
5.	v. 265, 457
6.	i. 449; v. 64, 265
7, 8.	v. 64
10.	v. 370
11.	iii. 124
12.	i. 69, 126; v. 358
13.	v. 41
14.	iv. 8
18.	i. 230; v. 143, 221
21.	v. 210
xiii. 1.	iv. 282, 285; v. 132, 178, 206, 243, 313
2.	iv. 14, 19, 132, 284
4.	i. 178; iii. 334, 388; iv. 15, 187, 279, 284; v. 136, 179, 180, 243
5.	v. 135, 139
6.	v. 136, 137, 180, 243
7.	iv. 304; v. 130, 132, 134, 136, 139
8.	v. 429
9.	iii. 148
13.	ii. 88
14.	i. 368

Romans	Vol. Page
xiv. 9.	i. 80; ii. 279
11.	ii. 334, 338
17.	v. 394
xv. 3.	v. 359, 428
4.	ii. 266; v. 223
6.	ii. 251; iii. 114, 123
8.	iii. 388
13.	iii. 85; v. 463
17.	ii. 33
26.	i. 230
28.	i. 172, 443
30.	iii. 363
xvi. 18.	v. 554
20.	i. 167; v. 393

1 CORINTHIANS.

i. 3.	ii. 368
13.	v. 526
13 seq.	iii. 187
16.	iii. 290
17.	v. 355
21.	iii. 79
24.	v. 454
25.	i. 202; iv. 293; v. 97
26.	i. 244
30.	i. 188; iii. 276, 329; v. 112, 124, 284
31.	v. 124
ii. 2.	i. 36; ii. 122, 159
8.	i. 80; ii. 165
9.	i. 416; iv. 235, 312; v. 314, 375, 395
10.	i. 34; v. 337
11.	v. 337, 350
12.	iii. 133, 175, 195, 275, 358
14.	iii. 192; v. 304, 305, 401
iii. 3.	i. 16
6.	iii. 15
9.	ii. 273; v. 90, 93
11.	v. 49
16.	iii. 159, 237; v. 366
17.	v. 366
19, 20.	v. 305
22.	i. 28
iv. 1.	i. 43, 282
3.	i. 414; ii. 59
4.	v. 115, 117
7.	iii. 365, 368; v. 29, 274, 313
9.	v. 443, 557
11.	v. 498
20.	v. 483
v. 1 seq.	v. 81
2.	i. 370; v. 482
5.	iii. 170; v. 233, 401
7.	i. 404, 433; ii. 193, 212, 251, 290, 406, 416, 426; iii. 111, 162
7, 8.	✶ii. 290
8.	ii. 251, 406, 416, 426; iv. 121

INDEX OF TEXTS.

1 Corinth.	Vol. Page
v. 12.	v. 63, 98
13.	v. 98
vi. 3.	ii. 33
5.	ii. 111; iv. 64, 127, 364
7.	v. 187
11.	v. 106, 125, 383
12.	iii. 167
13.	i. 444
16.	i. 99
18.	v. 551
19.	ii. 347; iii. 159, 197; v. 366, 462
20.	i. 263; v. 228, 231, 366, 383, 457, 462, 554
vii. 3.	ii. 331; v. 134
5.	i. 350, 369, 380, 390, 453
6.	iv. 365
7.	iii. 385
10.	v. 59
14.	i. 141
23.	v. 547
25.	v. 59
28.	iv. 365
31.	ii. 294
32.	v. 307
35.	v. 60
viii. 1.	v. 495, 517
2.	v. 302
5.	ii. 368
7.	v. 333
ix. 7.	i. 327
8.	v. 57, 521
9.	ii. 105; iii. 308; iv. 144; v. 237, 368
10.	ii. 206, 207; v. 237
16.	v. 135
25.	i. 387
27.	i. 380, 381, 442, 445, 446; v. 233
x. 2.	iii. 248
3.	iii. 143, 179, 199, 239; v. 469
4.	i. 169; ii. 33, 256, 269, 274, 279; iii. 128, 179, 239; v. 280, 469
5.	iv. 218
7.	iv. 363
11.	i. 305; ii. 139, 303
12.	ii. 62; iii. 199
13.	ii. 138; iii. 199; v. 446, 472, 484, 557
16.	i. 16, 113; ii. 300, 382; iii. 72, 78, 239, 321; iv. 376; v. 66, 67
17.	i. 282; ii. 289; iii 128
21.	iii. 71
21 seq.	ii. 301
22.	i. 331, 339; iii. 212; v. 534
23.	iii. 167; v. 59
31.	v. 386
33.	iii. 400
xi. 3.	iii. 10
4, 5.	ii. 407

1 Corinth.	Vol. Page
xi. 13.	v. 60, 232
14.	i. 384; v. 62
16.	i. 392; ii. 251, *404; v. 60, 61
17.	ii. 408; v. 62, 209
19.	v. 62
20.	v. 59, 360
21.	v. 59
22.	i. 305
23.	i. 397
24.	i. 31, 116; ii. 300, 302, 355
25.	i. 113; ii. 300; iii. 351
26.	ii. 120, 300
30.	v. 228
31.	v. 100, 217, 233
32.	v. 225, 456
xii. 2.	v. 484
3.	ii. 340; iii. 154; v. 341, 402
4.	iii. 134, 233, 255, 285, 314, 362
4–7.	*iii. 377
4—11.	iii. 306
5.	iii. 108, 169, 314
6.	iii. 314, 392
7.	iii. 129, 134, 385
10.	iv. 251
11.	iii. 169, 307, 357, 358, 385
12.	ii. 50
13.	i. 62; ii. 205; iii. 102, 128, 144, 161, 239, 260; v. 66
17.	i. 420; iv. 377; v. 192
23.	v. 137
27.	v. 407
28.	iii. 315; v. 62, 64
29.	iii. 314
xiii. 1.	i. 4, 40; ii. 335; iii. 122, 132; v. 350
2.	i. 34; v. 305
3.	ii. 106; v. 305
5.	iii. 30
9.	i. 104; iii. 327
10.	i. 106; iii. 367
12.	i. 127, 134; ii. 78
13.	ii. 114
xiv. 1.	iii. 385
8.	v. 148
14.	v. 68
15.	v. 68, 329, 335, 340, 349, 360, 472, 473
16.	v. 63, 468, 472, 475
25.	ii. 341; v. 221, 387
29.	iii. 314
31.	iii. 314, 367
32.	iii. 315
33.	v. 135
34.	iii. 313
36.	ii. 408
38.	iii. 389
40.	iii. 386; v. 60, 148, 232, 458
xv. 1 seq.	ii. 203, 312
6.	ii. 190, 235

INDEX OF TEXTS. 381

1 Corinth.	Vol. Page
xv. 9.	v. 306, 308
10.	ii. 98; iii. 98; iv. 284; v. 114, 308, 404
14.	ii. 256
17—19.	ii. 209
20.	ii. *206, 312, 357; iii. 148
22.	iii. 245
23.	ii. 219, 236, 312
25.	v. 463
26.	ii. 245; v. 393, 457
27.	i. 275; ii. 332
28.	i. 63, 283; v. 393
31.	ii. 105, 207; v. 72, 73, 74
32.	ii. 207; iii. 183; iv. 210
33.	v. 62
36.	ii. 192, 213
41.	i. 220, 371; v. 318
42.	ii. 358
42 seq.	ii. 267
43.	ii. 231, 288, 358
45.	ii. 215; iii. 21, 100; v. 306, 483, 496
47.	i. 80; ii. 216; iv. 169; v. 379
48.	v. 379
49.	v. 379, 408
50.	i. 98, 410
51.	i. 33
52.	v. 146
53.	ii. 253, 263, 378; iii. 29
54.	i. 37; ii. 256; iii. 66, 228
55.	ii. 194, 256; iii. 66, 229; v. 486
56.	iii. 229; v. 84
58.	ii. 199, 207; v. 47, 326
xvi. 2.	v. 266
12.	ii. 99
22.	iii. 148; v. 61

2 CORINTHIANS.

i. 3.	iii. 84, 371; v. 318, 368, 455
4.	v. 455
9.	iv. 114
12.	iii. 133, 158
15.	v. 308
20.	i. 10, 20, 185; ii. 370; v. 471, 476, 552
22.	iii. 207
23.	v. 72, 74
ii. 1.	v. 309
2.	iv. 120
3.	iv. 120; v. 332
5.	v. 332
6.	i. 460; v. 309
7.	i. 449; v. 100, 517
10.	v. 91
11.	v. 480
14.	ii. 38

2 Corinth.	Vol. Page
ii. 15.	i. 68; v. 198
16.	ii. 236; iii. 40, 290; v. 305, 308
iii. 5.	ii. 203; iii. 95, 154; v. 301, 311, 314, 321, 342, 402
6.	iii. 170, 191, 192, 207, 273, 357; v. 305, 526
13.	iii. 312
15.	i. 137
17.	iii. 188
iv. 4.	iii. 394; v. 242, 317, 392
6.	i. 212; ii. 325; iii. 372; v. 509
7.	v. 239, 457
10.	i. 42; ii. 269
11.	i. 42
13.	iii. 193, 357; v. 468
14.	iii. 74
15.	v. 40
16.	i. 128; ii. 268; v. 408
17.	i. 31; v. 275, 334, 455, 456, 465
18.	iii. 366
v. 1.	v. 48
4.	ii. 262
5.	iii. 108, 170, 219
10.	v. 115, 215
11.	i. 358, 415, 427; iii. 316, 334
13.	i. 311
14.	ii. 213; v. 484
16.	iii. 37, 173
17.	i. 277; iii. 242, 258
18.	v. 93
19.	i. 276; ii. 332; v. 93, 95
20.	v. 84, 323, 330
21.	i. 56, 146; ii. 297, 395; iii. 87, 148, 244, 246; v. 112, 113, 359
vi. 1.	ii. 204; iii. 220, 398; v. 90, 93, 309, 326, 398
2.	i. 63, 318, 320, 322, 434; ii. 153; iii. 298, 343; iv. 102
5.	i. 379
8.	ii. 59
14.	i. 307
15.	i. 288, 332; iv. 14, 292; v. 61
18.	v. 463
vii. 1.	i. 112
4.	v. 456
8, 9.	i. 374
10.	i. 372, 446
11.	i. 372, 373, 380, 386, 388, 441, 452; v. 100, 101, 233
viii. 3.	i. 448
4.	iii. 276
12.	i. 229; iii. 152, 340; v. 438
23.	ii. 50
ix. 5.	ii. 382; v. 135
6.	v. 38, 47, 275

INDEX OF TEXTS.

2 Corinth.	Vol. Page
ix. 7.	v. 39, 135, 273, 410
8.	v. 39, 135
10.	v. 416
12.	v. 266
15.	i. 29
x. 4.	i. 323 ; ii. 8 ; iii. 118 ; v. 503
5.	v. 16, 302
6.	iv. 249
8.	iii. 399 ; v. 89
10.	ii. 99
14.	iii. 234, 390
17.	iii. 210
xi. 4.	iii. 345, 356 ; iv. 256
6.	ii. 99
8.	ii. 99 ; iii. 391
9.	ii. 99
10.	iv. 102
11.	v. 74
12.	ii. 59, 100, 114
14.	i. 407 ; v. 452, 522
26.	v. 22
27.	i. 379
29.	ii. 105
30.	v. 22
xii. 2.	i. 36 ; iii. 32 ; v. 407
4.	v. 375
7.	i. 362 ; iii. 174 ; v. 17, 337, 438, 454, 484, 537, 557
7—9.	v. 474
9.	i. 202, 452 ; iii. 136 ; v. 337, 340, 346, 431, 557
11.	ii. 99
14.	i. 313 ; ii. 98, 102, 107 ; v. 368, 375
15.	✱ii. 98
xiii. 1.	iii. 185
4.	ii. 215
10.	ii. 14 ; iii. 399 ; iv. 187, 402
11.	ii. 243

GALATIANS.

i. 4.	v. 522
6.	iii. 345 ; v. 522
9.	v. 61
15.	iii. 277
16.	iii. 277 ; v. 401, 409, 411
20.	v. 74
ii. 2.	iii. 331
4.	v. 58
6.	iii. 331
9.	iii. 277, 309 ; iv. 247
15.	i. 242 ; ii. 391
20.	i. 144 ; ii. 265
21.	iii. 352
iii. 1.	ii. 120 ; v. 445
3.	ii. 74 ; v. 539
8.	iii. 352
9.	i. 13, 128
10.	v. 427

Galatians	Vol. Page
iii. 13.	ii. 167, 174, 297 ; v. 113
15.	v. 199
16.	iii. 187
17.	iii. 332
19.	iii. 151
20.	i. 146
23.	i. 57 ; v. 86, 115
24.	i. 49
26.	v. 370, 378
27.	iii. 246, 257
28.	ii. 279
iv. 2.	i. 50 ; ii. 365
4.	i. 13, 26, 28, 69, 106, 186, 292 ; iii. 180 ; v. 115, 170, 479
4, 5.	✱i. 45
5.	i. 56 ; iii. 258
6.	i. 60 ; iii. 108, 156, 189, 284 ; v. 337, 370
7.	iii. 258
9.	i. 213 ; iii. 20, 192, 249, 355
10.	i. 119
14.	v. 464
19.	i. 206 ; v. 194
24.	i. 300
25.	i. 239
26.	i. 169 ; ii. 380
28.	i. 300 ; v. 377
29.	ii. 407
v. 3.	i. 12, 55 ; iii. 151 ; v. 429
3 seq.	ii. 306
4.	iii. 220
6.	i. 14, 121 ; iii. 193, 337 ; v. 364
7.	ii. 76, 182
9.	ii. 306
11.	ii. 167
12.	ii. 306 ; iv. 16 ; v. 61, 63
13.	v. 60
15.	v. 432
17.	ii. 246 ; iii. 152 ; v. 334, 400, 444
19.	i. 42
22.	ii. 101 ; iii. 129, 134, 233, 238, 252
24.	i. 380 ; v. 431
vi. 1.	iii. 354 ; v. 482
3.	v. 302
6.	v. 41
7.	v. 198
8.	i. 4 ; ii. 51
9.	v. 330
10.	i. 280 ; v. 276
12.	iii. 398
15.	ii. 372 ; iii. 169 ; iv. 331
16.	v. 59
17.	ii. 166

EPHESIANS.

i. 3.	ii. 367, 368 ; v. 377
4.	i. 164 ; v. 383

INDEX OF TEXTS.   383

Ephesians	Vol. Page
i. 5.	i. 110
6.	i. 96, 302; iii. 341, 342; v. 383
7.	iii. 343
10.	i. 71, *265; ii. 162
14.	iii. 91, 209, 298
18.	i. 128; v. 38
21.	v. 457
22.	ii. 211; iii. 124, 245; v. 345, 407, 457
23.	i. 63, 277; iii. 245
ii. 1.	ii. 402
2.	v. 392
3.	i. 141, 210; ii. 151, 372
4.	i. 12; ii. 175, 180
6.	i. 115
7.	ii. 197
8.	iii. 368; v. 310
10.	iii. 94; iv. 331
12.	i. 50, 57, 145; iii. 257
14.	i. 23, 71, 188, 216, 222, 272; ii. 245, 275, 279; iii. 88, 253, 310; v. 104, 468
15.	iii. 88; v. 157
16.	iii. 88
19.	iii. 257
20.	v. 49
21.	v. 468
iii. 5.	i. 290
6.	i. 41, 242
7.	i. 41; iii. 289
8 seq.	iii. 277
9.	i. 33, 41
14.	v. 329, 376, 555
15.	v. 374
17.	ii. 203; v. 49
18.	i. 34; ii. 180
20.	ii. 197; v. 326
iv. 3.	iii. 114, 238
7.	iii. 386
8.	i. 94; iii. 136, 142, 221, 231, 233
9.	ii. 275, 328; iii. 55, 224, 225
10.	iii. 224, 237
11.	. iii. 142, 204; v. 64
12.	iii. 97
13.	i. 47, 195, 206
14.	v. 55, 486, 539
15.	i. 266; ii. 236
16.	i. 266; iii. 96
18.	v. 318
19.	iii. 350; v. 99, 446
20.	ii. 251; iii. 345
22.	v. 408
23.	iii. 192, 271, 273, 274
24.	v. 408
25.	v. 75
26.	iv. 136, 195
28.	v. 422
29.	iii. 215, 358
30.	i. 62; ii. 268; iii. 108, 169, 191, *201, 215; v. 221

Ephesians	Vol. Page
iv. 31.	iii. 193, 215
32.	v. 433
v. 2.	i. 28, 144, 184; ii. 164, 200, 265; iv. 259; v. 260
3.	iii. 30, 193
6.	v. 227, 531
8.	v. 320
13.	v. 317
14.	ii. 219
16.	ii. 12
17.	v. 397
28.	i. 9
29.	i. 9, 97
32.	ii. 394, 402
vi. 11.	v. 494
12.	i. 79; ii. 33; iii. 373
13.	iii. 160
15.	i. 36
16.	ii. 7; iv. 248; v. 480, 502, 504
17.	v. 525
18.	i. 328; v. 68, 357, 358
19.	v. 358

PHILIPPIANS.

i. 3, 4.	v. 358
6.	iii. 95, 304
7.	ii. 77
15.	i. 230, 231
16.	ii. 45
18.	v. 13, 191
23.	ii. 350; v. 378, 395
ii. 1.	iii. 147
3.	iii. 399
5.	ii. 182, 281, 313, 325, 342; iv. 240
6.	i. 206, 286; ii. 175, 325
7.	i. 52, 93, 206; ii. 172, 327; iii. 284; v. 479
8.	i. 29, 206; ii. 167, 197, 277, 322, 325, 327; iii. 149; iv. 331; v. 517
9.	i. 147; ii. 197, 241, 280, 323, 328; iii. 29; v. 123, 386
10.	ii. 280, 324, 333; v. 123, 406
11.	ii. 280, 324
12.	iii. 336
13.	i. 229; iii. 95; v. 303, 304, 402
14.	v. 409
15.	v. 317, 387
17.	i. 250
20.	i. 301
21.	ii. 314; v. 427
22.	i. 301
iii. 8.	v. 109, 390
9.	v. 113
10.	ii. 204; iii. 22

Philippians	Vol. Page	Colossians	Vol. Page
iii. 11.	v. 518	iii. 23.	v. 135, 410
12.	i. 16; iii. 329	iv. 14.	iii. 175
13.	ii. 72; iii. 95		
15.	i. 36; iii. 329		
16.	v. 483		
18.	v. 62	\multicolumn{2}{c}{1 THESSALONIANS.}	
20.	ii. 316; iii. 119; v. 379, 407	i. 3.	i. 172; iii. 193
21.	i. 4, 92, 98, 299; ii. 114, 206; iii. 260	ii. 5.	v. 74
		13.	v. 504
iv. 2.	v. 516	iii. 5.	v. 444, 498
4.	iv. 109	11.	iii. 392
6.	v. 351	iv. 3.	v. 370, 400, 411, 448
7.	ii. 243; v. 110	4.	iv. 374
9.	ii. 247; iii. 85	6.	v. 500
10.	i. 172	13.	iii. 17
12.	v. 409, 518, 541	17.	i. 195; ii. 264
13.	ii. 203; v. 308	18.	ii. 198
15.	v. 313, 319	v. 2.	i. 134; v. 395
18.	i. 172, 445; iii. 99	3.	iv. 390
22.	i. 244; iii. 290	5.	v. 320
		8.	ii. 373
		11.	ii. 273
\multicolumn{2}{c}{COLOSSIANS.}	12.	v. 15
		17.	v. 354
i. 3.	v. 358	18.	v. 68
10.	i. 440	19.	ii. 219; iii. 124, 220
12.	i. 29; ii. 224; iii. 372; iv. 394; v. 308, 319, 389	23.	ii. 85
		24.	v. 471
13.	v. 319		
15.	v. 345		
16.	i. 90; ii. 162	\multicolumn{2}{c}{2 THESSALONIANS.}	
17.	i. 90, 135		
18.	i. 266; ii. 272, 279, 394; iii. 57; v. 507	i. 5.	i. 452; iii. 341
		7.	v. 52
19.	i. 277	8.	v. 52, 395
20.	i. 69, 180, 189; ii. 167, 169, 251, 350; iii. 88	11.	i. 230, 452
		12.	v. 389, 465
21.	i. 276	ii. 3.	iii. 269
22.	i. 276	4.	iv. 147
23.	v. 49	7.	i. 34, 41
ii. 3.	i. 22, 106, 203; ii. 103, 349; v. 346, 349	8.	iii. 119, 269
		9.	i. 18
8.	v. 55	11.	iii. 191
9.	i. 49, 51, 276; ii. 347; iii. 10, 307	16.	v. 309, 319
		iii. 2.	ii. 9
10.	ii. 279	3.	v. 472
11.	iii. 249	6.	v. 63
14.	i. 12, 54, 55, 146; iii. 66, 229; v. 115, 426, 429	10.	v. 420, 530
		11.	iii. 391
15.	ii. 397; iii. 66	12.	v. 420
17.	i. 96	16.	iii. 85
18.	ii. 314; iii. 275		
19.	iii. 96		
21.	ii. 314; v. 60	\multicolumn{2}{c}{1 TIMOTHY.}	
23.	ii. 314		
iii. 1.	i. 269; ii. 199; iii. 48, 119	i. 1.	ii. 207, 375
1, 2.	*ii. 309	7.	v. 15
2.	i. 269; v. 378	8.	iii. 366
5.	v. 18, 553	9.	i. 54
12.	iii. 166	13.	v. 286
13.	v. 433	14.	ii. 197; iii. 371
14.	iii. 367		

INDEX OF TEXTS.

1 Timothy	Vol. Page
i. 15.	i. 13, 27, 309; ii. 254; iii. 370; v. 91, 428
17.	i. 224
19.	v. 484
ii. 1.	iv. 72; v. 95, 107, 244, 334, 357
1 seq.	ii. 8
2.	iv. 374, 402; v. 68, 137, 244, 334, 394
5.	ii. 250
6.	ii. 179
8.	v. 357
iii. 9.	ii. 10
16.	i. 1, 3, 231, 276; ii. 199, 210; iii. 109, 329; iv. 308; v. 194, 517
iv. 1.	iii. 191, 357; v. 55
2.	v. 99
3.	v. 493
4.	v. 420
5.	iii. 143; v. 420
6.	v. 419
7.	i. 42; ii. 10; v. 194, 195
8.	i. 20, 34
9.	ii. 254
10.	i. 76; ii. 265; iv. 331; v. 248
11.	v. 59
13.	ii. 105
14.	ii. 220
15.	v. 532
16.	iii. 77
v. 4.	v. 136
8.	v. 422
15.	v. 550
17.	v. 65
19.	v. 63
22.	v. 97
23.	i. 368; ii. 105; v. 333
24.	v. 298
vi. 2.	v. 59
5.	v. 76
6.	i. 34; v. 544
8.	v. 418, 421, 544
9.	iii. 243; v. 7, 52
10.	ii. 123
12.	i. 14
13.	v. 8, 52
15.	ii. 19; v. 8
16.	i. 37, 121; v. 8, 318, 466
17—19.	*v. 3
19.	v. 50
20.	iii. 345; v. 35, 55, 105

2 TIMOTHY.

i. 6.	iii. 124, 220, 385
7.	iii. 195
10.	ii. 193
12.	i. 134
18.	i. 134

2 Timothy	Vol. Page
ii. 4.	v. 480
8.	ii. 268
13.	v. 471
18.	ii. 312
19.	iii. 320
25.	i. 357; v. 370, 505
26.	v. 86, 370, 453, 495
iii. 2—4.	v. 493
3.	v. 482
4.	v. 14
5.	i. 38, 407; ii. 47; iii. 275, 333
6.	v. 484
7.	v. 198
8.	ii. 35; v. 61
12.	v. 454
13.	ii. 387
16.	v. 3
17.	v. 38
iv. 2.	iii. 182
3.	i. 316; v. 61, 229
6.	ii. 350
7.	ii. 76, 183
10.	iii. 164
11.	i. 245
13.	ii. 102
16.	ii. 63
vi. 20.	v. 198

TITUS.

i. 9.	iii. 141; v. 308
12.	v. 420
14.	v. 55
16.	ii. 340; iii. 193
ii. 11.	i. 40, 243, 251; v. 309, 403
12.	v. 309, 448
13.	i. 251; ii. 210, 265, 366
14.	iii. 94, 462
iii. 3.	v. 432
4.	i. 40; iii. 237
5.	i. 113, 141; ii. 219, 372; iii. 101, 170, 185, 191, 242, 250, 258, 348
7.	ii. 365
8.	iii. 399; v. 39
13.	i. 245; iii. 175

HEBREWS.

i. 1.	iii. 276, 304
1—3.	*i. 102
2.	i. 28, 80
3.	i. 36, 59, 60, 114, 164; v. 507
4.	iv. 50; v. 106, 207
5.	i. 90, 286, 293; ii. 376; iv. 50; v. 365
6.	i. 14, 98, 211, 250; iii. 10
7.	v. 317, 535
7 seq.	ii. 311

386 INDEX OF TEXTS.

Hebrews	Vol. Page	Hebrews	Vol. Page
i. 9.	i. 142	vii. 7.	ii. 366
13.	i. 115	9.	v. 138
14.	i. 4; iii. 370, 388; v. 316, 409	10.	iii. 81; v. 138
		13, 14.	ii. 284
ii. 1.	ii. 64	17.	iii. 158
2.	i. 91	18.	i. 289
4.	iii. 235	19.	i. 168, 291; iii. 366; v. 315
7.	i. 91, 92, 204		
9.	ii. 171	22.	v. 115
10.	i. 59, 298	23, 24.	i. 78
11.	i. 15, 54, 203; iii. 43	25.	i. 78; v. 263
14.	i. 9, 10, 16; ii. 194; iii. 66, 229, 246; v. 393	28.	i. 78
		viii. 5.	ii. 281
15.	ii. 232	6.	i. 169
16.	i. *1, 27, 53, 82, 90, 130; v. 88	9.	i. 11; iii. 257
		13.	i. 289
17.	i. 9; iii. 225	ix. 5.	i. 4; ii. 348
iii. 1.	i. 62; iii. 288	11.	ii. 361; iii. 158, 300
4.	ii. 278	12.	ii. 322; v. 263
5.	i. 105; v. 348	14.	i. 113; ii. 205; iii. 102, 354, 359
7.	v. 190		
11.	ii. 319; v. 535	15.	iii. 169
13.	i. 64, 301, 345; iv. 123; v. 422	22.	i. 112, 183; iii. 88, 247; v. 83
15.	i. 301; v. 415	24—26.	v. 263
18, 19.	ii. 319	27.	ii. 216, 360; v. 213
iv. 2.	v. 505, 525	28.	ii. 197, 300
5.	iii. 210	x. 1.	i. 96, 239
8.	i. 169; ii. 330	4.	i. 183; ii. 300; iii. 347
9.	iii. 10; v. 535	5.	i. 132, 151, 293; v. 260
11.	iii. 210	9.	i. 247
12.	iii. 271; v. 504	10.	i. 83, 116, 247; ii. 220; iii. 143, 343
15.	i. 146, 165; iii. 152; v. 486	12.	iii. 52
16.	iii. 152; iv. 328; v. 347, 363, 365	14.	v. 263
		19.	i. 41
v. 1.	i. 165; v. 230	20.	i. 38, 41—43, 95, 274; iii. 226
2.	iii. 152; iv. 281; v. 333		
4.	iii. 273, 288, 386	22.	ii. 299
7.	i. 26, 371; ii. 171; iii. 156; v. 329, 339	23.	v. 471
		25.	i. 282; iii. 114; v. 62, 516
9.	i. 79, 165; ii. 331; iii. 182	26.	v. 431
vi. 1.	i. 357, 418, 437; ii. 209; iii. 95; v. 58, 410	27.	v. 87
		29.	ii. 134; iii. 91, 218, 302; v. 386
2.	iii. 191		
4.	ii. 322; v. 419	32.	ii. 65
6.	i. 360; ii. 125	37.	i. 274
8.	i. 421	39.	iii. 114, 273
9.	ii. 343	xi. 1.	i. 128, 251, 253; ii. 209
10.	ii. 223, 263; iii. 14, 40	4.	i. 324; v. 285
11.	v. 301	6.	iii. 339
15.	ii. 265	7.	i. 324
16.	v. 73	9.	v. 48
17.	i. 28, 179	10.	i. 130
18.	ii. 381; v. 367, 459	11.	v. 471
19.	i. 34 ii. 267, 373, 381; v. 459, 484	13.	i. 127, 130
		15, 16.	v. 378
20.	i. 114; ii. 236; iii. 148, 226, 381	17.	ii. 201
		19.	ii. 201, 287, 400; iv. 206
vii. 2.	i. 179; iii. 238; iv. 287; v. 110, 185	23.	iv. 345
		24.	v. 541
3.	iv. 285	25.	i. 336; v. 32, 541
4.	i. 78	27.	i. 128; ii. 177; v. 217

INDEX OF TEXTS.

Hebrews	Vol. Page
xi. 32.	i. 324; ii. 7
35.	ii. 218
38.	v. 498
xii. 1.	i. 94; ii. 219, 235
2.	ii. 19, 120, 142, *158, 160
3.	ii. 130, 167, 177, 182; iv. 331
4.	ii. 104
9.	v. 374
11.	v. 367
12.	v. 329
14.	ii. 246; iii. 190; iv. 373
15.	iii. 220; v. 219
16.	i. 402; v. 420, 547
17.	i. 351; iii. 82; v. 100
18.	v. 544
20.	iv. 55
22.	ii. 380
23.	v. 408, 468
24.	iii. 156, 161, 321
28.	iii. 98; iv. 381; v. 309
29.	iv. 263
xiii. 2.	v. 276
3.	ii. 139, 142
5.	v. 529
7.	i. 170
8.	i. 236; ii. 253; iv. 108, 220
9.	i. 169; ii. 205; iii. 162; v. 55, 507
10.	ii. 301
14.	ii. 294; v. 378
15.	v. 281
16.	i. 381; iii. 99, *259, 268
17.	i. 170; ii. 19; iii. 167; iv. 11
18.	iii. 167
20.	i. 65; iii. 91, 348; v. 484
20, 21.	* iii. 80
21.	iii. 393
22.	iii. 97; v. 41
24.	i. 170

S. JAMES.

i. 3.	v. 443
4.	v. 445
5.	v. 31, 547, 553
6.	v. 474
11.	v. 23
12.	v. 444, 557
13.	iii. 373
14.	v. 445, 483
16, 17.	* iii. 361; *v. 311
17.	i. 29; iii. 309, 381, 384; iv. 280, 285; v. 27, 308, 316, 317, 321, 332, 342, 365, 416
18.	i. 96, 298; iii. 369; v. 262, 316, 509
19.	v. 188, 189
21.	i. 16; iii. 79, 199; v. 186, 188, 189, 191, 199, 444

S. James	Vol. Page
i. 22.	*v. 186
23.	ii. 64; v. 199, 277
24.	ii. 64; v. 277
25.	v. 194
26.	iii. 216
27.	i. 42; v. 36
ii. 6.	v. 14
8.	iii. 111
10.	v. 115
12.	i. 191
13.	iii. 152; iv. 270, 328; v. 111, 438, 440
15.	v. 268
16.	iv. 275; v. 268
17.	iii. 194; v. 36
18.	i. 42, 99, 250, 256, 439; iii. 150, 193, 194; v. 196, 400, 554
22.	i. 14; ii. 182; iii. 94
iii. 2.	i. 339; iii. 153, 270; v. 91, 428
6.	i. 361; ii. 294, 319; iii. 122, 197
8.	ii. 39
9.	iv. 7
11.	v. 312
15.	ii. 316; iv. 291
16.	iii. 100
17.	iv. 299
18.	iv. 287
iv. 3.	ii. 248; v. 328, 346, 473
5.	iii. 191, 197, 358, 368, 376; iv. 301; v. 525
6.	i. 234, 333, 339; ii. 262; iii. 91, 203, 232; iv. 290
7.	v. 551
8.	i. 359; v. 397
9.	i. 359
10.	ii. 342
12.	v. 210
14.	v. 23
17.	i. 191; v. 194
v. 7.	i. 172
9.	v. 87
10.	ii. 65, 160
13.	v. 353
14.	v. 95
17, 18.	iii. 249

1 S. PETER.

i. 3.	ii. 198, 200, 253, 266, 267, 322; v. 375
3, 4.	* ii. 364
4.	ii. 329, 366; v. 368, 375, 466
5.	i. 290; ii. 380
7.	i. 250; v. 443, 494
9.	ii. 162
12.	i. 3, 187
13.	iii. 40; v. 309, 310
17.	iii. 336; v. 369

INDEX OF TEXTS.

1 S. Peter	Vol. Page
i. 18.	i. 58; ii. 27, 258
19.	i. 52, 112; ii. 27, 134; iii. 228, 244; v. 457, 463
23.	i. 298; v. 194
24.	ii. 878
25.	iii. 198
ii. 2.	iii. 244; v. 354
4.	ii. 278
5.	ii. 273, 277; v. 262, 344, 360
7.	ii. 284
9.	iii. 372; v. 178, 262, 319, 462
11.	i. 389; ii. 246; iii. 228; v. 377, 448
13.	iv. 292, 302; v. 132, 135, 178, 206
15.	iv. 284; v. 37, 181, 400, 411
16.	i. 407; ii. 47
17.	v. 131
18.	v. 132
19.	i. 201; v. 456
20.	i. 201, 319; v. 455
21.	i. 30; ii. 179, 200
22.	iii. 67, 244, 253
23.	iv. 8
25.	ii. 34
iii. 1.	v. 387
4.	iii. 196
7.	v. 345, 433
9.	ii. 366
15.	ii. 209; v. 386
18.	ii. 395
20.	iii. 248
21.	iii. 248, 250
iv. 1.	i. 328; ii. 181, 200; v. 431, 481
2, 3.	v. 441
4.	iv. 307
6.	ii. 201
10.	iii. 155, 276, 371, 398; v. 94, 318, 357, 411
11.	iii. 141
12.	ii. 407; iv. 10
15.	iii. 392
18.	i. 353
19.	v. 471
v. 3.	v. 57
4.	i. 65; ii. 19; v. 466
5.	iii. 174; v. 310, 461
6.	ii. 342
7.	v. 368
8.	v. 452, 480, 491, 498, 504
9.	v. 491
10.	ii. 182

2 S. PETER.

i. 1.	i. 16, 34, 59; ii. 101; iii. 367; v. 58, 109, 146, 190, 366, 369, 444, 557

2 S. Peter	Vol. Page
i. 5, 6.	i. 206; v. 531
12.	v. 339
14.	i. 425
17—19.	i. 255
19.	i. 19, 20, 30, 235, 236, 238, 250, 251; iii. 303, 372; v. 191, 202, 318
20.	i. 154; v. 133, 275, 276
21.	i. 105
ii. 4.	i. 7; v. 426
5.	v. 116
7.	ii. 104; v. 514
8.	ii. 104
9.	v. 454, 464
10.	v. 137
11.	i. 4
14.	iv. 8
15.	i. 242, 349; ii. 88
16.	i. 349
18.	v. 206
19.	v. 555
20.	v. 442
22.	i. 348; v. 243, 442
iii. 1.	v. 190
5, 6.	v. 250
8.	i. 268; v. 48
9.	i. 268, 270, 350, 369, 390, 452
10.	i. 134
11.	i. 42; v. 207
16.	v. 57, 64, 526
18.	v. 220

1 S. JOHN.

i. 1.	iii. 31; iv. 265
2.	i. 86
3.	i. 94, 95
5.	iii. 370, 373; v. 317
7.	i. 113, 116; iii. 247, 352
8.	i. 189, 339; iii. 153, 270; v. 91, 428
9.	v. 125, 429, 472
ii. 1.	i. 44, 174, 248; ii. 343; iii. 22, 157, 176, 225, 266, 353; v. 115
2.	i. 77; ii. 392; v. 430
7.	iii. 362; v. 468
9.	iii. 371; v. 318
12.	v. 106
13, 14.	v. 239, 251
15.	v. 293
16.	i. 441; v. 496
17.	ii. 294
20.	ii. 38; iii. 176
27.	iii. 125, 191, 197
iii. 1.	i. 40, 51, 92, 148; ii. 180; iii. 86, 149, 150; v. 106, 369, 471
2.	i. 101; v. 106
3.	ii. 269; iii. 352
4.	v. 104, 110

INDEX OF TEXTS.   389

1 S. John	Vol. Page
iii. 7.	v. 114, 531
8.	ii. 354; iv. 329; v. 479, 531
14.	i. 42
17.	iii. 366; v. 21, 314, 315
18, 19.	v. 437
iv. 1.	iv. 251
2.	iii. 154
3, 6.	iii. 356
8.	i. 40
9.	i. 294; v. 309
10.	ii. 176
13.	ii. 42
18.	i. 69, 291; ii. 228
20.	iii. 150
v. 3.	iii. 151
4.	ii. 191; iii. 118; v. 498
6.	iii. 248, *344; iv. 254, 301; v. 471
7.	iii. 188, 248, 353
8.	iii. 248, 354
14.	v. 328, 473
15.	v. 473
18.	iv. 74; v. 239

2 S. JOHN.

1.	i. 244; ii. 89; iii. 290
10.	v. 62

3 S. JOHN.

10.	v. 482

S. JUDE.

6.	i. 6; ii. 360; v. 17, 88, 426
8.	iv. 303; v. 137
9.	ii. 35; v. 480, 522
10.	v. 15, 401
11.	i. 344; iv. 11, 54, 306; v. 63, 152
12.	i. 307; v. 59
13.	iii. 371
14.	i. 124, 426; iii. 116; v. 61
15.	i. 124
19.	iii. 170, 192, 216, 273, 354, 384
20.	ii. 273
23.	iv. 388
25.	i. 225

REVELATION.

i. 3.	v. 193
4.	iii. 134
5.	iii. 57, 352; iv. 375
7.	ii. 136, 237, 264
8.	ii. 75, 162
10.	ii. 426; v. 384
11.	ii. 162

Revelation	Vol. Page
i. 15.	v. 221
17.	ii. 162
18.	ii. 194, 339; iii. 46, 296
ii. 7.	i. 129
9.	v. 210
10.	ii. 194
14.	v. 55, 58
17.	iii. 232; iv. 312
21.	i. 315, 393; v. 434
22, 23.	i. 315
24.	i. 34, 401; iii. 349
iii. 1.	iii. 134; v. 105
2.	i. 451; v. 100
4.	i. 451; iii. 9
7.	ii. 339
8.	v. 454
12.	ii. 361
14.	ii. 162; v. 471
17.	iii. 291, 293; iv. 333
18.	v. 175
20.	v. 302, 330
21.	i. 115; ii. 164, 184
iv. 1.	iii. 250
6, 7.	i. 85
8.	ii. 338, 354, 385, 387
10.	ii. 336, 338; iv. 374; v. 329, 555
11.	v. 382, 389, 409
v. 1—7.	iii. 76
5.	iii. 74, 229; iv. 121; v. 480
6.	iii. 74
8.	ii. 336; v. 230
9.	ii. 338
12.	ii. 296
14.	ii. 336
vi. 4—8.	ii. 294
6, 10.	v. 452
16.	ii. 136; v. 395
17.	i. 437
vii. 1—3.	iii. 210
9.	iii. 9
11.	ii. 336
12.	v. 460, 465, 475
14.	iii. 75, 249, 352
16.	v. 457
17.	ii. 249; v. 457
ix. 2.	v. 241
3.	i. 376; iv. 209; v. 241
11.	v. 239
x. 5.	v. 79
6.	i. 63, 163, 283, 317; v. 72
7.	i. 43
xi. 3.	iii. 64
xii. 2.	iv. 343
3.	ii. 401; iii. 73
4.	v. 539
9.	v. 480
10.	iii. 158; v. 115, 482
12.	v. 255
xiii. 1.	iv. 281
8.	i. 164; ii. 296
11.	iv. 281

Revelation	Vol. Page	Revelation	Vol. Page
xiii. 17, 18.	v. 554	xix. 12.	iv. 55, 283
xiv. 4.	i. 170; iii. 9; v. 298	16.	iv. 284; v. 459, 466
6.	i. 71; iii. 92, 298	xx. 2.	ii. 339; v. 484, 557
11.	iii. 64; iv. 383	3.	ii. 339
13.	iii. 9	5.	ii. 402; iii. 49; v. 298
18—20.	iii. 78	6.	ii. 199, 237, 312, 362; iii. 10, 83, 84; v. 452
xv. 3.	ii. 338; iii. 337, 352		
4.	iii. 337	13.	ii. 399
xvi. 1.	iv. 329	14.	ii. 194
1—17.	ii. 293	xxi. 4.	v. 457
2.	v. 226	6.	ii. 162
10.	ii. 338	8.	ii. 194
xvii. 4.	v. 544	14.	v. 49
5.	i. 34; iv. 308	27.	i. 112; iii. 250; v. 425
9.	iv. 481	xxii. 1.	iii. 307
12.	iv. 369	7.	v. 394
14.	i. 78	9.	i. 14
xix. 3.	iii. 321	12.	i. 31, 283
4.	v. 476	13.	ii. 162
7.	ii. 308	16.	i. 235, 251, 252; ii. 211
9.	ii. 308; iii. 63	17.	i. 247
10.	i. 19, 153; ii. 119, 271; iii. 63, 222, 312; v. 545, 554	20.	iii. 168, 359; v. 394

II.

GENERAL INDEX TO SERMONS

AND

MINOR WORKS.

INDEX TO BISHOP ANDREWES' SERMONS,

&c.

A.

Aaron, his apparel, typical meaning of, i. 25; one of God's hands, ii. 17, 29, 30; why his rod budded, ii. 20; his rod inflicts Church censures, ii. 28; and thus makes men fruitful, ii. 34. The hand of Ecclesiastical government, ii. 32, equal with Moses, ii. 33; supplies spiritual wants, ii. 33; with Moses makes a complete government, ii. 34; needs Moses' aid, ii. 35; steadies his hand, ii. 35; has the same enemies, ii. 35, 36; his house the Ecclesiastical estate, ii. 283; his rod, the type of Christ's Priesthood, ii. 349; its blossoming again, the type of his Resurrection, ii. 349; his ointment a type of the Holy Ghost, iii. 238.

Abaddon, a name of Satan, v. 239.

Abel, why his sacrifice better than Cain's, v. 285.

Abimelech, why kings of Canaan so called, ii. 24.

Abishai, his advice to David, iv. 24; rejected, iv. 25, 29, 30; condemned out of his own mouth, iv. 34.

Abner, angry at reproof, v. 16.

Abraham, Christ took on Him the seed of, i. 1; works of, must be done by the seed of, i. 14; rejoiced to see Christ's day, i. 118, 119, 123; saw it by faith, i. 128; religion of, one with ours, i. 119; believed in the judgment, i. 124; his joy like that of the unborn Baptist, i. 125; according to the Fathers, saw Christ's birth at Mamre, i. 128; rejoiced not to hear that his seed should be as the dust of the earth, but as the stars of heaven, i. 130; rejoiced that his seed should be his Saviour, i. 130; our light greater, i. 131; now in God's presence, ii. 78; his bosom a place of comfort, ii. 78; his sons often forgetful, and need warning, ii. 79; a rich man, ii. 88; kind to the poor, ii. 92; his faith, ii. 201; in taking the five kings, a type of Christ, iii. 230; though rich here, blessed hereafter, v. 34; the different portion he bestowed on Isaac, and on his other children, v. 377.

Absalom, the several degrees of acceptance illustrated in his case, iii. 298; rebelled from ambition, iv. 12; a meaning in his being killed with three darts, iv. 17; God's judgment signally manifested in his case, iv. 18.

Absolution, conferred at Easter, ii. 426, 427; power of, when given to the Apostles, v. 95, 96; discretion needed in applying it, v. 97; given to the members of the Church, if they are repentant, v. 98, and forsake their sins, v. 100, 101; conveys remission at once, v. 102.

Abstenti, distinguished from *excommunicati,* v. 63.

Acceptable, year of the Lord, why so called, iii. 298, 299; day, the day of Pentecost, iii. 343.

Acceptance, several degrees of, iii. 298; illustrated by the case of Absalom, iii. 298; what temper is accepted with God, iii. 332, 339, 340; implies that God might reject, if he pleased, iii. 340, 341; relates not to human merit, but to the Divine purposes, iii. 341; leaves all in God's hands, iii. 342; is only through Christ, iii. 342; leads on to the Sacraments, iii. 342, 343.

Account, we must take account with ourselves, ii. 189.

Achan, enticed by the eye, v. 540.

Actions, good, evil spoken of, ii. 39, 57.

Adages, by unhappy, Satan breathes infection and poison, ii. 3.

Adam, in him we came by our attainder, ii. 209, 216; our fall in, compared with our Resurrection in Christ, ii. 214; his rising, was his fall, ii. 215; what he lost in falling, ii. 217, *seq.*; by drinking the cup of devils became a degenerate vine, iii. 71; brought forth wild grapes, iii. 71; in losing his joy, lost Paradise, iv. 123; teaches us the danger of doing what is good in one's own eyes, iv. 162; his temptations and our Lord's compared, v. 497; whether he sinned by gluttony or by distrust, v. 497.

Administrations, signify outward call-

394 INDEX TO SERMONS, ETC.

ing, as gifts, inward qualification, iii. 380; come from Christ, iii. 381, 386, 388; divided, not scattered at random, iii. 388.

Adoption, the words of the Father to the Son at His baptism our words of adoption. iii. 258, 259.

Adoration, to be used in entering God's house, iv. 374; practice of the Primitive Church, iv. 374; of angels in heaven, and saints on earth, iv. 374, 375.

Adrian the Sixth, owned man's want of righteousness, v. 121.

Adverbs, God loves better than verbs, ii. 105; v. 405.

Adversity, the effect of perversity, v. 334; and of sin, v. 353.

Aërius, opposed the keeping of Easter, ii. 416.

Æschylus, parallel between Ps. lxxviii. and Persæ, i. 310.

Affections, to be set above, ii. 309, 310, 313—315; especially at Easter, ii. 321; and in the Holy Communion, ii. 321, 322.

Afflictions, force men to seek God, i. 310, 311; compared to darkness, v. 319; a means of trying us, v. 443.

Agag, Saul too merciful to, ii. 13.

Agapæ, not observed at the present day, v. 59.

Agar, warned to return, ii. 62.

Agatho, Pope, admitted that the Sixth General Council was summoned by the Emperor, v. 160.

Agde, Council of. See *Council of Agde.*

Agere and *facere* contrasted, v. 195.

Agrippa, half-hearted, iii. 198.

Ahab, angry at Micaiah's reproof, v. 7, 16; delivered up to temptation, v. 447; enticed by the eye, v. 540.

Ahashuerosh, meaning of, ii. 284.

Ahasuerus, his danger and deliverance both recorded, iv. 129; the same as Artaxerxes, iv. 130; why his deliverance specially recorded, iv. 143, 144.

Ahijah, God's messenger to Jeroboam, ii. 12.

Ahimelech, Saul too severe in punishing him, ii. 13.

Ahithophel, his miserable end, iv. 313, 314.

Aix-la-Chapelle, Council of. See *Council of Aix-la-Chapelle.*

'Ἀκουσταί, distinguished from ἀκροαταί, v. 191.

'Ἀκροαταί, distinguished from ἀκουσταί, v. 191.

Alaric, summoned the Council of Agde, v. 162.

Alcuin, how he explains the words ' palmares posuisti dies meos,' i. 48.

Alkum, the meaning of, ii. 5.

Allegiance, true, springs from the fear of God, iv. 302.

Allen, Cardinal, why sent into the Low Countries, and thence into England, iv. 256.

Alms, one of the fruits of repentance, i. 442, 443; are swallowed up by luxury, ii. 92; a part of righteousness, iii. 338, 339; a help to prayer, v. 341; a means of obtaining forgiveness, v. 439.

—— a part of our daily sacrifice, v. 267, 268, 278; acceptable to God, v. 272, 279, 280; accompany us to His tribunal, v. 272; draw consolation out of greatest misery, v. 273; rules for distributing them, v. 273, 274; to be done in secret, v. 275; never to be forgotten, v. 275, 276. (*From Bishop Buckeridge's Funeral Sermon.*)

Almshouses, great increase of in England, v. 37.

Alpha, and Omega, Christ, why called, ii. 75, 162.

Altar, S. Paul speaks of the Christian, ii. 301.

—— not merely spiritual, but external, v. 259; common to all Christians, v. 259. (*From Bishop Buckeridge's Funeral Sermon.*)

Ambition, the cause of Absalom's rebellion, iv. 12; might have led David to kill Saul, iv. 28; is gratified at any cost, v. 550.

Ambrose, S., held that unbelief foils the Incarnation, i. 27; on the lowliness and glory of the cradle of Christ, i. 209; his interpretation of the words, 'I will pour out of my Spirit,' iii. 305; owned the imperfection of his own righteousness, v. 118; presided at the Council of Aquileia, v. 161.

Amen, of early Christians sounded like thunder, ii. 338.

—— (at the end of the Lord's Prayer), necessary to be understood aright, v. 467; by it we acknowledge the truth of the prayer, and our desire that God would hear it, v. 467; so used elsewhere in Scripture, v. 470; enjoined to be said at the end of all prayers, v. 468; retained untranslated in all languages, v. 468; rests on God's faithfulness, v. 471, 472; to use it aright we must pray by the Spirit, v. 472; according to God's will, v. 473; intelligently, v. 473; for a good purpose, v. 473; with confidence in God, v. 474; to be applied to every clause of the Lord's Prayer, v. 474, 475; as an expression of thanks, v. 475.

Anabaptists, in error on the Incarnation,

INDEX TO SERMONS, ETC. 395

i. 53, 186; revived the heresy of Valentinus, i. 140; misinterpret the passage, Acts ii. 17, 18, iii. 313; deny all secular jurisdiction, iv. 11; oppose the very estate of kings, iv. 11; their new parity, and confusion, iv. 54; would destroy kingly power, iv. 300.

'Ανάγειν and εἰσφέρειν, compared in respect of temptation, v. 485.

Ananias, a Church-robber, ii. 52.

Anarchy, desired by Satan, v. 241.

Ancyra, Council of. See *Council of Ancyra*.

Andrewes, Lancelot, his funeral sermon preached by John Buckeridge, Bishop of Ely, v. 257, *seq.*; his birth-place, v. 288; his early ability, v. 289; his schoolmasters, v. 289; his gratitude to them, v. 289; admitted of Pembroke Hall, v. 290; where he founded two fellowships, v. 290; attended the Earl of Huntingdon into the north, v. 290; patronised by Walsingham, v. 290; his further preferments, v. 290, 291; his oriental learning, v. 291; his industry, v. 291, 292; an encourager of learned men, v. 292; refused the Bishoprics of Ely and Salisbury, v. 292; appointed Bishop of Chichester A.D. 1601, Lord Almoner A.D. 1605, Bishop of Ely A.D. 1609, Winchester A.D. 1618, Dean of the Chapel A.D. 1619, v. 292; restored his Prebendal houses, and Episcopal Palaces, v. 293; entertained King James at Farnham, v. 293; entrusted the care of his estates to his steward, v. 294; his charity to his kindred, v. 294; to the parishes in which he lived, and to poor scholars, v. 295; his bequests, by will, v. 294, 295; his painful preaching, v. 295; his hatred of usury, simony, and sacrilege, v. 296; his life a life of prayer, v. 296, 297; his death a loss to the Church, v. 297. (*From Bishop Buckeridge's Funeral Sermon.*)

———— *Nicholas*, the Bishop's brother, died shortly before him, v. 297. (*From Bishop Buckeridge's Funeral Sermon.*)

———— *Thomas*, the Bishop's brother, died shortly before him, v. 296. (*From Bishop Buckeridge's Funeral Sermon.*)

Angels, Holy, Christ took not the nature of, i. 1, 5; the preeminence of Christians above, i. 2; incapable of envy, i. 3; compared with men, i. 4; what they are, i. 4; Heaven the abode of, i. 4; below us only by the Incarnation, i. 5; adore our nature in the personal union with the Deity, i. 14; the Fathers note that they assume a lower position towards man in the Holy Trinity, i. 14; our flesh in the Incarnate Son, adored by, i. 98; stand before the Throne as ministering spirits, i. 115; pass from an army into a choir at the Nativity, i. 210; in arms ever since the Fall, i. 210; order amongst, i. 211; sang at the world's birth, and a new song at Christ's birth, i. 211; rejoice in our good, i. 213; we are more like when we come fresh from Holy Eucharist, i. 214, 231; lovers of peace, i. 225; called Sons of God, i. 292; fit messengers of Christ's Birth and Resurrection, ii. 230; being found in the grave, a ground of assurance to us, ii. 230; as also the mode of their appearing, ii. 230, 231; their white clothing a token of joy, ii. 231; their gracious message, ii. 232—235.

Angels, could not redeem others, as needing a Redeemer themselves, ii. 259; use reverence in heaven, ii. 336, 338; strange occupants of a tomb, iii. 9; their coming to Christ's tomb an omen of good, iii. 9; their white clothing a type of the Resurrection, iii. 9; their sitting a type of rest, iii. 10; why they sat at the head and foot of Christ's tomb, iii. 10; had no rivalry for the best place, iii. 10; they do service to Christ as God, and as man, iii. 10; they guard our dead bodies, iii. 10; and will present them alive, iii. 10; ministering spirits, iii. 370; not made ministers of reconciliation, v. 90; employed to inflict plagues, v. 226; how they obey God's will in heaven, v. 407—409; employed in confessing God's glory, v. 469; have no need of prayer, v. 460; their charge over us, v. 522, 523.

———— *fallen*, Christ suffered not for, i. 6; their own tempters, and less to be pitied than man, i. 11; their fall hopeless, ii. 192; had no remission of their sin, v. 88, 426.

Anger, leads us to inflict punishment, iii. 214; in what sense ascribed to God, iii. 213, 214; God's, caused by sin, v. 227; how to be appeased, v. 230—233.

Animals, instinct of, a lesson to sinful man, i. 350, 351.

Anointed, kings God's anointed, iv. 25, 32, 43, 44, 49, 52, 53; so called by Fathers and Councils, iv. 49; so were the Patriarchs, iv. 47, 49; other persons anointed, though not so termed, the Lord's, iv. 50; God's, not to be assaulted by men, iv. 169; great force of this word to prevent rebellion, iv. 172.

Anointing of the Holy Spirit makes men's hearts ready to be kindled, iii. 125; our anointing drops of Christ's, iii. 281; the peculiar work of the Holy Ghost, iii. 285; why the work of the Holy Ghost compared to, iii. 286; some few drops of it fall on us, iii. 287.

—————— ceremony of, only declares a man to be king, does not make him so, iv. 51; may be used or not, iv. 51, 52; serves to show that kings are God's after a peculiar manner, iv. 54; this anointing gives not a spiritual grace, iv. 56, 57, but a just title, iv. 58.

Antevorta and *Postvorta*, iv. 233.

'Ἀπέχειν and ἔχειν distinguished, ii. 90.

Apocrypha cited frequently by the Fathers, v. 61.

'Ἀπολαβεῖν and λαβεῖν distinguished, ii. 90.

Apollos found the Corinthians difficult to please, ii. 98; soon left them, ii. 98; knew at first only John's Baptism, iii. 182.

Apollyon, a name of Satan, v. 239.

'Ἀποφθέγγεσθαι, this word explained, as used of the disciples at Pentecost, iii. 140,141; implies uttering weighty words, iii. 140, 141, 277.

Apostasy, does not unmake a king, iv. 57.

Apostles, first doubted of Christ's resurrection, then preached it, ii. 190, 191; sat with closed doors, for fear of Jews, ii. 242; almost dead with fear, ii. 245; revived by hope, ii. 245; handed down customs to the Church, iii. 410, 414; how long their age extends, ii. 414; Easter observed by them, ii. 424; received at Pentecost courage, iii. 138, language, iii. 138, 139, discretion, iii. 139, learning, iii. 140; their 'sound' went out to the end of the world, iii. 139; preferred their own safety to love of Christ, iii. 153; troubled at not keeping Christ's commands, iii. 153; specially needed a comforter, iii. 156; gained a double Comforter in the coming of the Holy Ghost, iii. 157; mistaken in not wishing for Christ's departure, iii. 165; seemed to be satisfied with only His carnal presence, iii. 172; needed, therefore, His withdrawal, iii. 172, 173; full of carnal fancies, iii. 173; none in the Church now, iii. 233; their office a proof of Christ's Godhead, iii. 270; appointed to it soon after they had sinned, iii. 270;
needed the breath of the Spirit, in order to speak, iii. 266; the grace of Apostleship, what it is, iii. 277; commissioned by Christ after His resurrection, v. 82; power given to them for the remission and retaining of sins, v. 83, not only personally, but to their successors also in the ministry, v. 91, 92, when they received the power of administering the Sacrament, v. 95, and the power of the keys, v. 95, 96; by confessing their sins teach us humility, v. 428.

Apprehension of our nature by Christ, what this means, i. 6—9; of men from error and sin to grace and truth, i. 9; of Abraham, i. 9; of S. Paul, i. 9; of S. Peter, i. 9, 10; from daily dangers the fruit of the Incarnation, i. 10.

Aquarii, their heresy, iii. 350.

Aquileia, Council of. See *Council of Aquileia.*

Aquinas, S. Thomas, on the various reasons for the Eucharist being called a sacrifice, v. 261. (*From Bishop Buckeridge's Funeral Sermon.*)

Aristotle, on the desire of knowledge, i. 33.

Arius, his error confuted by Micah v. 2, i. 163.

Ark, neglected in the time of Saul, ii. 12; its contents types of Christ, ii. 349; the, a type of Christ's body, iii. 16; endured not an unhallowed touch, iii. 34; the, being full, a type of the fulness of God's gifts, iii. 233.

Arles, Council of. See *Council of Arles.*

Arm, and hand, signify different degrees of God's power, iv. 86, 87; signifies offensive power, iv. 97.

Armada, the Spanish, the loss of referred to, iii. 230, 231.

Arnulphus, summoned the Council of Tribur, v. 162.

Arrow, that flies by day, means distant dangers, v. 529.

Arteries, supposed to be air-channels, iii. 101, 265.

Ascension, witnesses of Christ's, i. 94; on the day of, our Lord took possession of heaven in our names, i. 114; Christ's, a greater triumph by reason of His former humiliation, iii. 224; compared to a jubilee and to a triumph, iii. 227.

—————— ours of more value than our Resurrection, iii. 46, 47; follows close on Resurrection, iii. 48; this illustrated from nature, iii. 48; our duty to ascend in mind after Christ, iii. 49.

INDEX TO SERMONS, ETC.   397

Ascension Day, to the disciples a day of sorrow, to Christ a day of triumph, iii. 164; if no Ascension, no Pentecost, iii. 166.
Ash Wednesday, the ancient custom upon, full of meaning, i. 362, 427.
Asking, and *seeking*, and *knocking*, used to show the necessity of earnest prayer, v. 323, 324; how these words depend on each other, v. 325; to be distinguished from each other, v. 325, *seq.*
Assemblies, in whose hands is the calling of them, v. 141, 142; given to Moses, v. 142; necessary both for war and for the Church, v. 145, 146; to be called by the chief magistrate, v. 149, 151, 208; should come together when called, v. 152; should not come together unless duly called, v. 152, 153; instances of religious assemblies being called by kings in the Old Testament, v. 154—156.
Assume, distinguished from 'receive,' iii. 273.
Athanasius, S., his regard for Easter, ii. 420; condemns the Arians for their violences on that day, ii. 420.
Attainder, its nature, ii. 216; Adam's fall an act of, ii. 209, 216.
Attributes of God, ii. 215.
Audæus censured as a heretic, ii. 415.
Augustine, S., on the Fall, i. 11; Abraham's faith, i. 13; responsibilities, i. 15; offering Christ for our price, i. 31; the Incarnation, i. 38; the opinion of philosophers on The Word, i. 88; Christ's 'day' the Nativity, i. 123; hope in death, i. 124; swearing by the thigh, i. 129; believing beyond reason, i. 138; the wise men and scribes, i. 167; on Psalm lxxxv. 11, i. 185, 186; righteousness and peace not separable, i. 191, 192; his rule, 'Distingue tempora et concordabis Scripturas,' i. 200; held Christ's cradle a sign in us, i. 205; various notions of the chief good, i. 219, 272; a good will the gift of God, i. 228; joy in tears of penitence, i. 316; passionate addresses by God, i. 341; repentance, i. 347; the corruption of his times, i. 359; fasting, i. 379, 388; no word of Scripture to spare, i. 420; fruitless hearing, i. 422; his prayer before preaching, i. 424; on hell, i. 426; false repentance, i. 440; calls the inscription the key of every Psalm, ii. 3; on the words, 'Inasmuch as ye have done it,' &c. (Matt. xxv. 40), ii. 27; says that Mary Magdalen was the only person who came to Christ for pardon of sin only, ii. 37; by what words he was converted, ii. 88; explains Job's words, 'In my flesh I shall see God,' 'I shall see God incarnate,' ii. 259; condemns the breaking of Church customs, ii. 412, 429; condemns the Quartodecimans, ii. 419; mentions Easter-tide, ii. 420; speaks of Easter as an Apostolic observance, ii. 424; explains the words, 'Touch me not,' as intended to wean Mary Magdalen from sensual touching, iii. 36; how he explains, 'grieving the Holy Spirit of God,' iii. 214; how he explains the phrase, 'the rich of this world,' v. 20; defines good to be that which is against our will, v. 35; termed life a long disease, v. 50; his opinion of the necessity of the power of the keys, v. 94; owned the imperfection of his own righteousness, v. 118, 121; considered it his righteousness to be forgiven his sin, v. 120; used Psalm lxix. 1, at the beginning of his prayers, v. 338; explains the words, 'groanings that cannot be uttered,' of the prayers of the saints, v. 339; compares prayer to a key that can open and shut heaven, v. 424; explains 'deliver us from evil,' of the evil that is in ourselves, v. 451; regarded the length of Lent only as a positive law, v. 492; on his sick-bed had the penitential Psalms written up, that thence he might refute Satan, v. 505; condemns security of salvation, v. 531.
Augustine, S., on the true nature of sacrifice in the Christian Church, v. 263—265. (*From Bp. Buckeridge's Funeral Sermon.*)
'Αξία and καταξίωσις distinguished, iii. 341.

B.

Babel, curse of it reversed at Pentecost, iii. 123, 139.
Babylon, a type of spiritual enemies, iii. 63; captivity of, more heavy than that of Egypt, iv. 227; deliverance from by gentle means, contrasted with deliverance from Egypt, iv. 234.
Balaam, leagued with Balak against God's people, ii. 9; loved the wages of unrighteousness, ii. 88; yet wished for the death of the righteous, ii. 88; had the spirit of prophecy by the Holy Spirit, iii. 207.
Balak, an evil ruler sent for chastisement, ii. 30; his counsel neither to

bless nor to curse, too commonly followed, v. 7.
Bands and *Beauty*, two staves, signify unity and order, ii. 29.
Bankers, the poor should be our, v. 46.
Baptism, water flowing from Christ's side, a type of, ii. 134; the fulness of forgiveness received therein, ii. 134; the laver of our regeneration, ii. 219; we are made thereby firstfruits to Christ, ii. 219; the fountain opened for sin and uncleanness, ii. 372; most commonly administered at Easter, ii. 426; Holy Ghost received in, iii. 128, 170, 183; Who is there specially mentioned, iii. 184, 185; since it is His 'laver,' iii. 185; we are baptized 'with' Him, not only 'into' Him, iii. 185; our faith in Him there set forth, iii. 185, 186; as God, iii. 186, 187; the words of, show the unity of God, iii. 187; a seal applied only once, iii. 219; WhitSunday the feast of, iii. 242; usually deferred to that time, iii. 242; commission for, in the name of the Trinity, iii. 242; infants require it, iii. 244; Christ's, the strongest reason for ours, iii. 247, 248; Baptism, threefold, of blood, water, and the Spirit, iii. 248; we are freed from the first, the two last concur to a true Baptism, iii. 248, 249; the body of, the baptism of the body; the soul of, the baptism of the soul, iii. 248; in baptism, the hand casts on the water, the Holy Ghost works invisibly, iii. 249; not bare washing, but the giving a fresh colour, iii. 250; of heaven, not of men, iii. 250; by it we put on Christ, and are the sons of God, iii. 257; not merely of His household, but beloved children, iii. 258; from having been servants, iii. 258; Christ's blood applied therein, iii. 260; cannot be repeated, iii. 260; grace poured on us therein, sinks into our soul, iii. 309; water of, not without blood, iii. 352; typified by the 'pitcher of water,' iii. 359; a means for the remission of sins, v. 94.
Baptist, S. John. See *John, S., the Baptist.*
Bar-jona, filius columbæ, iii. 254.
Bartholomew, explained 'Son of rain,' iv. 245.
——— *S., Massacre of*, compared with Gunpowder Treason, iv. 393.
Basil, S., his ἀσκητικά the same as S. Paul's γυμναστικά, i. 42; on humility, i. 206; his testimony to the antiquity of the Doxology, iii. 185, 186; once thought that a man by change of place could avoid temptations, v. 489.
Basilides, his heresy, v. 56.
Beddered, bed-rid, iii. 216.
Bede, the Venerable, the reason given by, for the Jews rejecting Christ, ii. 281.
Beelzebub, why Satan called by this name, v. 538.
Bees, why enemies compared to, v. 435.
Beggars to be made to work, v. 43.
Belial, children of, iv. 14; has no agreement with Christ, iv. 14, 15.
Belief necessary to secure the blessings of baptism, iii. 311.
Bellarmine, Robert, Cardinal, regarded kings as the anointed of the people, not of God, iv. 52; considered that primitive Christians did not rebel, *quia deerant vires*, iv. 249, 354; speaks of S. Peter's twofold office, to feed and to kill, iv. 254; his treasonable speech about deposing kings, iv. 278.
———, admitted that Councils were summoned by the emperors, v. 160.
———, acknowledged the imputation of Christ's merits, v. 119; his conclusions on the subject of Justification, v. 122; owned that it is safest to rely solely on God's mercy, v. 123; asserted that we could claim heaven, *titulo hæreditatis*, and *jure mercedis*, v. 124.
Beneficence, a feeling of the mind, distribution, an act of the hand, v. 269; comes from God, v. 270. (*From Bp. Buckeridge's Funeral Sermon.*)
Bernard, S., on appropriating the Incarnation, i. 29, 140; on 'using' Christ, i. 82; on 'Mercy and Peace' collectaneæ, i. 178; Mercy, Truth, Righteousness, Peace contending, i. 180; Mercy, Truth, &c. if parted, cease to be virtues, i. 194; the cradle of Christ, a sign to be spoken against, i. 207; on fasting, i. 389; the eyes of man, i. 410; owned the imperfection of his own righteousness, v. 118, 121; considered it his righteousness to have his sins forgiven, v. 120; used Psalm lxviii. 1, at the beginning of his prayers, v. 338; his apostrophe to Satan, in a Sermon, when tempted to vainglory, v. 495.
Bethlehem, 'little,' but fruitful, i. 158; why Christ should come out of, i. 160; meaning of, i. 168, 238, 248; the shepherds and wise men found Christ here, so must we, i. 171.
Bezaleel, the Holy Spirit wrought in him, iii. 207.
Bigthan, one of Ahasuerus' chamber-

INDEX TO SERMONS, ETC. 399

lains, iv. 134; his great sin in seeking the king's life, iv. 135; the reason of his doing so, iv. 135, 136; the strange way in which his treason was detected, iv. 138, 139.
Birthday of Christ, not as the Son of God, but as the Son of man, i. 121; joy upon, in heaven and in earth, i. 122.
Births, two, by nature, and by grace, ii. 372.
Bishops succeeded to the Apostles, v. 64.
Bit and *Bridle*, the curb of justice, ii. 9.
Blasphemy, a special cause of God's wrath, v. 227.
Blast and *Breath* distinguished, iii. 266; they mark the two effects of the Holy Spirit, repelling from sin, and remitting it, iii. 266.
Blastus censured as a heretic, ii. 415.
Blessing, part of the Priest's office, iii. 81; enjoined to be used by Jewish Priests, iii. 81; Christ gave a blessing before He left the world, iii. 81; Apostles used it at the end of their epistles, iii. 81; used at the end of the Church's service, iii. 81; now but little thought of, iii. 82.
——— God's, makes natural means nourish us, v. 506—508, 510; will not attend on unlawful means of gain, v. 510, 511.
Blessings, the three great, which have come from God, ii. 365; a blessing pronounced at Christ's birth, and at His resurrection, ii. 365; due from us to God, ii. 366, 367, 381; are of several degrees and kinds, ii. 367; ours optative, God's effective, ii. 367; how we can wish well to God's name, &c. ii. 368; our blessings to be showed by voice, by sacraments, and by good deeds, ii 381, 382; of parent given to Jacob and Esau, v. 414, 415; all from God, v. 416.
Blood, without shedding of, no remission, i. 112; of Christ, the medicine for sin, i. 113; and water the ingredients of that medicine, i. 113; innocent, cries for vengeance, Christ's, for mercy, iii. 321; fit to take away guilt, iii. 347; shed in heathen sacrifices, iii. 347; and by the Jews in theirs, iii. 347; cannot of itself take guilt away, iii. 347; Christ gave it its true power, iii. 347; goes with the water of Baptism, iii. 352, 359; without the Spirit profiteth nothing, iii. 355.
——— the sin of, troubles at the time of death, iv. 184; shedding of, how punished, iv. 197.
Blood and *Water* from Christ's side, the twin Sacraments of the Church, iii. 348; both needed, iii. 350, 351; both go together, iii. 352, 353, 359; the Spirit goes with them, iii. 359.
Boar, a type of outward enemies, ii. 9.
Boaz, one of the pillars at the Temple gate, ii. 7.
——— blessed for having remembrance of the dead, ii. 225.
Bodily signs convey spiritual gifts, iii. 143.
Body, being created by God, should worship God, i. 262; the health of, more attended to than the health of the soul, i. 387; should suffer for the sin it commits, i. 388—440; how it is like a temple, ii. 347; because our souls dwell therein, ii. 347; and God's Spirit, ii. 347; especially when we are in church, ii. 347; will be raised again, the same in substance, not in quality, ii. 358, 361; should be kept as temples of God, not of sin, ii. 361, 362; and temples of Christ's body in the Holy Eucharist, ii. 362; its erect posture teaches us to raise our thoughts from below, iii. 375; members thereof rallied together by danger, v. 209.
Body, Christ's. See *Christ.*
Bondage, Egyptian, Passover close of, ii. 17.
Bosom, the coffer of the heart, ii. 267; our hopes should be laid up there, ii. 267.
Bozrah, Christ coming from, how explained, iii. 61; a very strong city, no escape from it, and so a type of hell, iii. 65.
Braccara, Council of. See *Council of Braccara.*
Bradwardine, Bishop, held the Christian religion to be the best every way, i. 220.
Bramble, parable of, v. 9, 15.
Bread, Christ the true, i. 169; in the Holy Communion a symbol of unity, iii. 239; of life to be toiled for, v. 326; our daily, asked for, after we have prayed to do God's will, v. 415; must be blessed, as well as given by God, v. 418, 423; all our wants included under this term, v. 418; by 'our' bread is meant that which is fit for our sustenance, v. 419, 421; truly 'ours,' as given by God, v. 420, and gained honestly, v. 420; spiritual food meant thereby, v. 419, 421; superabundant, not to be asked for, v. 421; we have a claim for it as God's creatures, v. 422; to be asked for daily, v. 422, 423; nourishes not without God's blessing, v. 506, 508, 510.

Breaking of bread, Christ made known by, iii. 22; signifies the Communion, v. 66; a partaking of Christ's true body, v. 67.

Breath, the instrument both of life and of voice, iii. 121, 193, 304; the Holy Ghost given as, iii. 262; a fit symbol of the Holy Ghost, iii. 265, as being a means of life, iii. 265, 266, and the organ of the voice, iii. 265; marks the gentle working of the Holy Ghost, iii. 266, 267; though seemingly weak, works great things, iii. 268.

Brethren, the disciples so called by Christ, ii. 43; this showed He bare them no grudge, iii. 43, and had no pride, iii. 43; teaches identity of nature, and increased affection, iii. 43.

Britons, the ancient, their weakness in not assembling for common counsel, v. 145.

Broken heart, the Hebrews understand by this a heart broken off from sin, iii. 295.

Buckeridge, John, Bishop of Ely, preached Bishop Andrewes' funeral sermon, v. 257, seq.; his long intimacy with Andrewes, and his high esteem for him, v. 287, 288. (*Funeral Sermon.*)

Builders, we are, in several senses, ii. 273; Scripture instances, ii. 273; the chief Builder is God, ii. 378.

Building, we all are parts of a spiritual, ii. 273; how we are to be built together, ii. 273; states to be as buildings, firm and steady, ii. 274; of strong materials, well compacted, ii. 274.

Burial, places of, why called Cemeteries, ii. 213.

Busybodies condemned, iii. 391.

C.

Cæsar, and *God*, duties to both together not incompatible, v. 130, 131; the duties due to each distinguished, iv. 133, 135.

Cæsarea, a fit place for the descent of the Holy Ghost on the Gentiles, iii. 324; the Nineveh of the New Testament, iii. 324.

Caiaphas, though a bad man, spoke well, ii. 43.

Cain, his progeny skilful as artificers, ii. 7; attended to civil polity, not to God's worship, ii. 34; his doings proceeded from envy, iii. 358.

Caitiff, and *captive*, nearly the same word, iii. 291.

Calamities, temporal, are Satan's claws, v. 452; there is good in them as well as evil, v. 453, 456; we pray only to be delivered from the evil that is in them, v. 453; always to be expected here, v. 454; to be rejoiced at, v. 456.

Calling, outward, necessary for the ministry, iii. 286—288; requisite for doing a work, iii. 382, 383, 386; else there would be disorder, iii. 383, 386, 387; to make light of it a trespass against Christ, iii. 383; a rightful, necessary in secular, much more in spiritual matters, iii. 387; each one should have his own, iii. 389; to be chosen according to a man's gifts, iii. 389, 390; each has its own limits, like the functions of the body, iii. 392.

Calvin, how he explains the phrase, 'the rich of this world,' v. 20.

Candlestick, the seven lights of Moses', compared to the seven lights which God bestows, iii. 372.

Canons, penitential, i. 450; made by the Church in her Councils, v. 146.

Captivity, men by nature in captivity, iii. 208, 227, 292, 293; redemption needed from it, iii. 208; the misery of this captivity, iii. 228; 'led captivity captive,' how explained, iii. 227; illustrated by the capture of a Turkish galley with Christian slaves on board, iii. 230; we were taken Christ's prisoners, iii. 230, that we might serve Him in freedom, iii. 231; compared to a desert, iv. 226; a sore scourge, iv. 227.

Captivity, the Babylonian, not Israel's worst, i. 176; greater than the Egyptian, iv. 227; turning of it, God's work, iv. 228; how it was like a dream, iv. 228, 229; 'turned as the rivers in the south,' how explained, iv. 234; this turning compared with deliverance from Gunpowder Treason, iv. 235, seq.

Carloman summoned a Council in Germany, v. 162.

Carnality, an obstacle to receiving the Holy Ghost, iii. 197.

Carpocrates, his errors, v. 58.

Cart-rope, a temptation compounded of various sins, v. 538.

Casaubon, Isaac, patronised by Bishop Andrewes, v. 292. (*From Bishop Buckeridge's Funeral Sermon.*)

Catesby, one of the Gunpowder conspirators, iv. 289.

Cathari, their errors, v. 59.

Causes, both original and secondary, in everything, iv. 269.

Cemeteries, burial-places why so called, ii. 213.

Censures, various kinds of in the Church, v. 63.

Centurion, did not count himself worthy of Christ's favours, iii. 341.

Ceremonies, easily quarrelled with, ii. 408; this is Satan's first step, ii. 409; vain imaginations respecting them, v. 60; left to the arrangement of the Church, v. 60; to be observed by all its members, v. 60.

Cerinthus, heresy of, i. 90.

Chalcedon, Council of. See *Council of Chalcedon.*

Châlons, Council of. See *Council of Châlons.*

Chance, what seems chance is destiny, iv. 139.

Change, natural to man, only apparent in God, iii. 374.

Changers, in Church and Commonwealth, instances of, iv. 304.

Charge, given to the rich, v. 5; as given by God, to be solemnly attended to, v. 6; concerns the welfare of the rich, both in this world and the next, v. 6; an unwelcome office to give one, v. 7; causes loss of favour, v. 7; Timothy solemnly enjoined to give it, v. 8.

Χάρισμα more than δώρημα, iii 384.

Charities, much increased in England, v. 37.

Charity prays for others, v. 369.

Charlemagne summoned several Councils, v. 162.

Charles the Bald summoned the Council of Meaux, v. 162.

——— *the Fat*, summoned the Council of Cologne, v. 162.

Chastel, Jean, attempted the life of Henry IV., iv. 289.

Cherebert summoned the Council of Tours, v. 162.

Cherethite should ever be a Pelethite, iv. 188.

Cherubim have a flaming sword to repress God's enemies, ii. 17; wings to defend His people, ii. 17, 32.

Childbirth, difficulties compared to, iv. 341—343; Gunpowder Plot compared to a fruitless one, iv. 340, *seq.*

Childebert summoned the 2d Council of Orleans, v. 162.

Children, their birth sometimes a cause of joy, sometimes of sorrow, iv. 345; should return to their fathers, even if they have offended them, v. 368.

Chrism, a holy anointing, iv. 55.

Christ took man's nature, not that of angels, i. 1; spared not Himself to spare man, i. 7; became the seed of Abraham, i. 9; being circumcised, became a debtor to keep the whole law, i. 12, 55; entered bond for us and took our death on Him, i. 13, 55.

——— a Child and Son, i. 21, 22; why

AND.—PERRON, ETC.

both, i. 22; the person of, i. 23, 107; office of Prophet, Priest, and King, i. 23, 24, 76, 104, 108; principality of, not of this world, i. 24; suffered willingly and alone for His government, i. 26; given to all people, Jews and Gentiles, as shown by His name Jesus Christ, i. 27; His humanity our right, His Deity a gift, i. 28; offered in the Lord's Supper, i. 30, 82; our everlasting reward, i. 31.

Christ, how manifested, i. 38, 39; the Substance of all solemnities, i. 45; 'emptied' Himself for us, i. 52; came not empty, i. 86; fulfilled the law, both directive and penal, i. 56.

——— the only Prophet, Priest, and King, i. 77; the Anointed, i. 77; anointed as man, i. 78; the Lord of lords, i. 78; His manhood implied in the name of, i. 80.

——— consubstantial with the Father, as the Son, coeternal as the Word, i. 88; brought us into grace, i. 96.

——— the natures, person, offices, and agency of, described, i. 107, 108; coeternal as the 'Brightness,' i. 108; coequal as the 'Character,' i. 109; consubstantial as the 'Son,' i. 109; the express form of the Father, i. 109; the Light succeeding sparks, the firm impression succeeding shadows, i. 110; the fittest to restore man, since He made him, i. 111; Blood of, the medicine for sin, i. 113; our duty to, as a Prophet, Priest, and King, i. 115; in Person at Mamre with Abraham, i. 128; abhorred not the womb of the Blessed Virgin, i. 140.

——— sought us when we had fled from Him, i. 148; eternal generation of, i. 162—164; our Shepherd and Leader, i. 167; the true Zerubbabel who frees us from the captivity of sin, i. 176; to us born, when to us known, i. 197; worth finding although meanly cradled, i. 203; the Reconciler, Pacifier, and Glorifier, i. 216; had heathen ancestors, i. 241; the Saviour of the great as well as the small, i. 244; the learned as well as unlearned, i. 255; not to be found 'any where,' must be sought, i. 259.

——— His two natures, i. 295, 296; twice called 'Son' by the Father, i. 299.

——— fasted, not for Himself, but for us, i. 388, 389.

——— a rock of Peter and David, Church and Kingdom, ii. 7.

———'Αρχηγὸς, ii. 19; ἀρχιποιμὴν, ii. 19, 35; often preached in pretence, ii 45.

H H

Christ, in correcting His disciples' errors, removed ours, ii. 48; not only tolerated, but approved of S. Mary Magdalene's conduct, ii. 48; what is given to the Church is given to Him, ii. 49; the Church His Body, ii. 50; He is persecuted in His members, ii. 50; He loves His mystical Body better than His natural, ii. 52; nothing given to Him is waste, ii. 50, 51; will reward what is done to Him, ii. 52; gives a dignity to it, ii. 53; to be preferred even to the poor, ii. 53; praises Mary Magdalene, reproves Simon for not anointing Him, ii. 54; He has a right not only to what is needful, but superfluous, ii. 54; analogical instances under the law, ii. 55; He has claims on us, ii. 55; specially on this nation, ii. 56.
—— why called Alpha and Omega, ii. 75, 162, 163.
—— in the history of Lazarus, shows us the sufferings of the next world, ii. 79; gives it as a warning to the rich, ii. 80; compares future torments to fire and thirst, ii. 84.
—— met with unkindness, ii. 107; His love for His enemies, ii. 109, 130, 151, 182; a rule for us, ii. 111, 112; shown on the cross, ii. 113, 180; seen in the wound of His heart, ii. 132.
—— compared to the 'morning hart,' ii. 120, 134, 167; chased all His life through, ii. 120; pierced at last, ii. 120; His death shown forth in the Holy Sacrament, ii. 120, 121; described as 'He whom they pierced,' ii. 121; the mode of His death, ii. 121; He was pierced through and through, ii. 122; in body and soul, ii. 123; by sorrow, as shown in His agony and great cry, ii. 123; by reproach, ii. 124; and ingratitude, ii. 124; not merely by Pilate, the soldiers, &c., ii. 125; but by our sins, ii. 126; and with love, ii. 132; this piercing should cause compassion for Him, remorse for ourselves, ii. 127; a great contempt not to look on Him, ii. 127; and danger to ourselves, ii. 128; we must look at Him attentively, ii. 128, 129; repeatedly, ii. 130; the effect of it, sorrow, ii. 130; mortification, ii. 131; love for Him, ii. 132; belief, ii. 133; hope, ii. 133; accepting His gifts, ii. 134; due return, ii. 134; we must force ourselves to look at Him, ii. 135; we shall have to look at Him hereafter, ii. 136; a terrible sight, if we have not looked at Him before, ii. 136; He looked on S. Peter, ii. 137; the effect of it, ii. 137; is the book of love laid open, ii. 132; out of His side a fountain opened for sin and uncleanness, ii. 134; to Him the Book of Lamentations applied, ii. 128, 139, 140.

Christ applies David's words to Himself, ii. 139; day of His passion the day of God's wrath, ii. 139; no sorrow like His, ii. 139, 140, 154; in what respects, ii. 143, 144; in suffering and in loss, ii. 144, 145; stripped of all comforts as a tree of its leaves, ii. 145, 146; deserted by His Father, ii. 147; not merely an innocent man, ii. 148; His suffering a deep abyss, ii. 149; the cause of it, ii. 149; God's wrath, ii. 149; our sins, ii. 150; He stood between us and God's wrath, ii. 150; His compassion for us, ii. 152; no love like His, ii. 152; Priest and Sacrifice both, ii. 153; complains that His sorrow is not regarded, ii. 154; the creatures regarded it, ii. 155; danger of not regarding it, ii. 155; our best regard due to it, ii. 156.
—— His passion a great sight, ii. 158; to be specially considered on its own day, ii. 157, 159; knowledge of it, perfection of knowledge, ii. 159; in it we see our demerits, ii. 166; to be looked upon, ii. 177; a cure for sin, ii. 179; to be imitated, ii. 179; should cause hatred for sin, ii. 181; the arch-guide, ii. 160; our example, ii. 160; how the author of our faith, ii. 163, 182; how the finisher, ii. 163, 164, 182; disregarded both life and reputation, ii. 165; an agreement between His ransom and our debt, ii. 165; compared to a Lamb, ii. 165; and to a worm, ii. 166; crowned in mockery, ii. 166; His blood the blood of God, ii. 169; how often it was poured forth, ii. 169, 171; its great value, ii. 169; stretched on the cross as on a rack, ii. 170; His death tedious, ii. 171; had a spiritual cross to bear, ii. 171; never complained, ii. 171; died a servile and dishonourable death, ii. 172; made sport of, ii. 173; and despised, ii. 173; He made light of all this, ii. 175; left the joy of heaven, ii. 175; looked forward to greater joy, ii. 175; His joy increased by man's salvation, ii. 176; this why He longed for His death, ii. 176; has graven us in the palms of His hands, ii. 178; His wounds, rubrics, ii. 180; His death compared with Jonas's and the fall of the angels, ii. 192; is seed cast into the ground, ii. 192; manifests His priesthood, ii. 195; a mould in which our life should be cast, ii.

196; He died once to sin, ii. 196, 197; could, had He so willed, have saved us without dying, ii. 196.

Christ, His resurrection, the evidence of it, ii. 190; first doubted, ii. 190; frequency of His appearance, ii. 190; an earnest of ours, ii. 191; our nature raised therein, ii. 192; will be completed at ours, ii. 192; compared to rising from bed, ii. 192; and to the springing of seed, ii. 192; fitly took place in the spring, ii. 192, 231; He will not die again, ii. 192, 193; freed from the dominion of death, ii. 193; constantly spoken of in connexion with His death, ii. 195; sets forth His divine nature, ii. 195; and His kingdom, ii. 195; a mould in which our lives should be cast, ii. 196, 199; took His own life again, ii. 197; raised by God's hand, ii. 197; lives now as the Son of Man, ii. 198; ground of comfort, ii. 198; a rule of life, ii. 199, *seq.*; He is both the Resurrection and the Life, ii. 203, 204; the power it should have over us, ii. 204.

—— the First-fruits, ii. 208, 209, 211, 212; we thus consecrated in Him, ii. 213, 214, 236; His resurrection compared with the sheaf of first-fruits, ii. 213; restored in Him, ii. 209; our resurrection depends on His, ii. 209; risen, a Christian's hope, ii. 209, 365, 366, 374—376; proofs of His resurrection, ii. 210; rose as the Head of a body, ii. 211; our resurrection in Him compared with our fall in Adam, ii. 214, *seq.*; the First-born among many brethren, ii. 218; by His flesh and blood we obtain life, ii. 220.

—— why His resurrection first made known to women, ii. 223; its blessings extend to sinners, ii. 223, 238; willing to be anointed by us, ii. 225, 226; our love to Him to be shown by making sacrifices, ii. 226; those who seek Him will be sure to gain tidings of Him, ii. 229; unlikely that His disciples carried Him away, ii. 233; our forerunner in rising, ii. 234; appeared frequently after His resurrection, ii. 235; five times on the first day, ii. 238; even to those who had denied Him, ii. 235, 238; His passion had not destroyed His compassion, ii. 235.

—— His salutation to the eleven, ii. 238; not a mere salutation, ii. 239, or wish, but an injunction, ii. 239; gave His blessing to those who did not deserve it, ii. 240; on a fitting day, ii. 240; without delay, ii. 241, 248; and thrice, ii. 248; pitied the fears of His disciples, ii. 242; gave Himself up as a peace-offering, ii. 244; Mediator between God and man, ii. 250; frequently spoken of as 'in the midst,' ii. 249, 250, 281.

Christ, His resurrection prophesied of by Job, ii. 253; and His incarnation, ii. 259; completed His work of redemption when he rose again, ii. 259, 260; His resurrection implied His death, ii. 260; having redeemed Himself, is able to redeem us, ii. 260; to show the identity of His body, retained the marks of His passion, ii. 263; our great hope, ii. 266, 268; He dwells in us by His flesh, ii. 268; from which we derive life, ii. 268.

—— the Corner-stone, ii. 270, 274, 275, 281; refused by the builders, ii. 270, 276; at His passion, ii. 271; both by rulers and people, ii. 276; more refused, and more honoured, than any beside, ii. 272; a Stone cut out without hands, ii. 274; a Stone full of eyes, ii. 274, 277; the Stone from which our spiritual drink flows, ii. 275; a type of His humility, ii. 275; of His endurance, ii. 275; and of His firmness, ii. 275; a living Stone, and so felt His wrongs, ii. 277; the very stones felt for Him, ii. 277; exalted by His Father, the chief Builder, ii. 278, 279; what meant by His being 'Head of the Corner,' ii. 279; we must make Him our head, ii. 282; joined together the Lamb of the Passover and the Bread of the Eucharist, ii. 288.

—— the Paschal Lamb, ii. 291, 295; a propitiatory sacrifice, ii. 296; therefore to be eaten, ii. 296; a 'Passover' in His birth, circumcision, resurrection, and ascension, ii. 297; but specially in His death, ii. 297; He then 'passed over' to the state of sinners, ii. 297; but was not 'passed over' Himself, ii. 298; offered *for* us first, *to* us afterwards, ii. 299; His flesh to be eaten, as of a peace-offering, ii. 298, 299; His sacrifice once performed, ii. 300; prefigured in the Passover, ii. 300; commemorated in the Eucharist, ii. 300; and feasted on, ii. 301; as then offered, ii. 302.

—— rose at Easter, ii. 310, 311; should draw us upward, ii. 312; is seated at God's right hand, ii 318; never so near as in the Holy Communion, ii. 322; gracious in offering us the means of grace, ii. 322.

—— His exaltation began at His resurrection, ii. 324; how to be exalted by us, ii. 324; though God, humbled

Himself, ii. 325; for what purpose, ii. 326; even to a disgraceful death, ii. 327; the steps of His humility, ii. 327; exalted, not merely from the grave, but to heaven, ii. 329; His resurrection a kind of nativity, ii. 330; named Jesus on His exaltation, ii. 330; why called Jesus, ii. 331; had this name fully after His resurrection, ii. 331; His chief name, ii. 332; His humanity had the grace of union with the Godhead, ii. 331, 332; His soul and Godhead present with His body and blood, ii. 335; our Lord, as well as our Saviour, ii. 338; over what He is Lord, ii. 339; we are willing to have Him as our Saviour, though not as our Lord, ii. 340; His glory reaches to the Father, ii. 341, 342.

Christ framed His speeches according to the place in which He was, ii. 344; was in the temple when He spoke of raising up the temple of His body, ii. 344; did not thereby command His own death, ii. 351; only foretold it, ii. 353; and permitted it, ii. 353; how the temple of His body dissolved, or destroyed, ii. 345, 350, 351; His words misunderstood by the Pharisees, ii. 346; being zealous for God's house, would not wish it to be destroyed, ii. 346; how His body resembles a temple, ii. 345—350; it was destroyed by a violent death, ii. 351, 355; but which yet was voluntary, ii. 351; for a greater good, ii. 353; the destruction of sin, ii. 354; the parts of His body compared to the different parts of a temple, ii. 355; His body felt its dissolution, ii. 355; evidenced by the bloody sweat, ii. 356; accompanied by a dissolution of nature, ii. 356; He raised this fallen temple, ii. 356, 357; as if death were only a sleep, ii. 357; thus disappointed His enemies, ii. 357; with perfect ease, as shaking off slumber, ii. 357; by His own power, and yet by the Father's, ii. 357, 358; the very same temple in substance, though not in quality, ii. 358; an earnest of His raising His mystical body, ii. 360.

—— He is the means through which our blessings come, ii. 369; began in Jordan the sacrament of our new birth, ii. 373; begotten of the Father eternally, and at His resurrection, ii. 376; His resurrection the ground of our regeneration, ii. 375, 376; leads from hope to enjoyment, ii. 376.

—— why He would give only the sign of Jonah, ii. 384—389; by raising Himself from the dead proved Himself to have come from God, ii. 389; a greater than Jonah, though like him, ii. 394—398; not a sinner, though treated as such, ii. 395; by giving up Himself, stayed the tempest of God's wrath, ii. 396; rose to a higher state, ii. 398; destroyed death, ii. 398; made it a harbour of hope, ii. 398; enjoined the preaching of repentance, ii. 401, 402.

Christ appeared first to Mary Magdalene, iii. 4; blessed the grave, iii. 9; made it a place for angels, iii. 9; His body the true ark, iii. 10; His head the Godhead, His feet the manhood, iii. 10; not taken away from the tomb, but self-raised, iii. 12, 18, 19; how He can be lost by us, iii. 14; found by all who seek for Him, iii. 14; often near us when we know not, iii. 15; why He appeared as a gardener to Mary Magdalene, iii. 15—17; the meaning of His question, 'Why weepest thou?' iii. 17; how He disclosed Himself to her, iii. 20, 23; lost as a dead body, found as a quickening spirit, iii. 21; His word has great power, iii. 21; made known by word and by breaking of bread, iii. 22.

—— made Himself strange to Mary Magdalene, iii. 23, 24; in order to beget reverence, iii. 24, 28, 29; His message to her called Magdalene's Gospel, iii. 24, 51; she desired to touch Him, iii. 25; was not touched by her though the Tree of Life, iii. 27; was afterwards touched by S. Thomas, iii. 27, 28; as the fit cure for his unbelief, iii. 31; raised from the dead not the same as before, iii. 29; therefore, not to be approached as before, iii. 29; but with reverence, iii. 30—32; by us now, iii. 33; not to be approached with a proud foot or stiff knee, iii. 34; specially touched in the Holy Communion, iii. 34; can be touched here truly, because spiritually, since He has ascended, iii. 37; to be reached by faith, iii. 38.

—— honoured Mary Magdalene in making her the bearer of glad tidings, iii. 40, 41; even before she touched Him, iii. 41; wished that no time should be lost, iii. 41; His message sent to His 'brethren,' iii. 42, 43; what implied in His calling them so, iii. 43; called them only 'friends' before, iii. 43: rose in the same nature in which He died, iii. 43; our nature died and rose in His person, iii. 43; this is the ground of our hope,

iii. 43; rose with increased affection, iii. 43; by His ascension showed He had the keys of heaven, by His resurrection that He had the keys of hell, iii. 44; His ascension the main end of His resurrection, iii. 44; valued it more than His resurrection, iii. 46, 47; by speaking to Mary Magdalene of His ascension, He showed that He was not to remain long on earth, iii. 47; and cured His disciples of carnal notions, iii. 47, 48; showed that our ascension would follow close on our resurrection, iii. 48; His resurrection a type of our daily life, iii. 49; natural for Him to ascend to heaven, His former abode, iii. 49; and to His Father, iii. 50; He made heaven our Father's house, iii. 51; all His relationships now made ours, iii. 53; His Father made ours, iii. 53—55, 57, 58; our God made His through the incarnation, iii. 54, 58.

Christ has a Father as being God, had a God as being man, iii. 55, 56; makes us His brethren by adoption, iii. 55; born again at Easter by His resurrection, iii. 57; the firstborn among many brethren, iii. 57; as He took our flesh, so He gives us His flesh, iii. 58.

—— came from Edom (Isa. lxiii. 1) when He rose from the dead, from Bozrah when He vanquished hell, iii. 61; described as a mighty conqueror, iii. 62, 63, 66; made a banner of the cancelled law, iii. 66; compared to David and Deborah, iii. 66; this seemed unlikely after His former defeat, iii. 66, 67; His word truth, His work salvation, iii. 67; His speaking in righteousness and being mighty to save sets forth His nature, His offices, and His benefits, iii. 68; His suffering, a greater miracle than creation, iii. 68; by speaking He saves us from error, by saving He gives the power of grace against sin, iii. 68; speaks little, does much, iii. 68; mighty in saving, not in destroying, iii. 68, 69; saves those only who hear His teaching, iii. 69; why clothed in red garments, iii. 69, 75, 77; was trodden in the winepress of suffering, iii. 70; three several times, iii. 70; trod His enemies in the winepress of His wrath, iii. 70; blood and water that flowed from Him 'the twin sacraments' of the Church, iii. 70, 102; compared to the wine in the cup, iii. 71, and to corn cut down and formed into bread, iii. 71; drank of the cup of vengeance as found among sinners, iii. 72; from His blood pressed out came our cup of the New Testament, iii. 72; He drank ours, that we might drink of His, iii. 72; His cup an antidote to Satan's, iii. 72; first trampled on Himself, then trampled on His enemies, iii. 73, 77, 78; even in the grave, iii. 73; spoken of as a Lamb slain, and as a Lion red with His enemies' blood, iii. 74; trod the winepress of suffering alone, because forsaken by His disciples, iii. 74, and even by His Father, iii. 74; and also the winepress of wrath, iii. 74; this an earnest of our triumph, iii. 74, 75; dyed in His own blood and in that of His enemies, iii. 75; wore our colour (red) that we should wear His, iii. 75; clothed in scarlet as a Doctor, a Priest, and a Conqueror, iii. 76, 77.

Christ, His resurrection should lead us to rise again to good works, iii. 82, 83; His death, to die to sin, iii. 83; first brought down to the grave, then raised, iii. 83; why termed a Shepherd, iii. 85; the great Shepherd, iii. 86; as superintending all the flock, iii. 86; as its owner, iii. 86; as having great love for it, iii. 86; so as to shed His blood, iii. 87; and to spare ours, iii. 88; brought down to the grave for His sheep, iii. 88; 'free among the dead,' *i.e.* set free from the dead, iii. 88; brought back when the ransom was paid, iii. 89; bore His sheep on His shoulders as a type of our resurrection, iii. 90; would not be parted from His sheep, iii. 90; His blood obtained not merely peace, but spiritual gifts, iii. 91; at His birth universal peace, iii. 100; raised Lazarus from the grave, and Magdalene from sin, iii. 101; His blood and Spirit go together, iii. 101; His blood when poured forth ran into two streams, *i.e.* the two sacraments, iii. 101, 102.

—— sent the Holy Ghost as the greatest gift after His ascension, iii. 108, 129.

—— being both the Word and flesh shows us the use of bodily signs, iii. 143; loved us, that we might love Him in return, iii. 148, 149; the greatness of His love, iii. 149; sealed the covenant with the first drops of His blood, iii. 148; gave us seizin of all His gifts at Pentecost, iii. 148; had the law in His hand, so as to mitigate it at His will, iii. 151, 152; contrasted with the severity of Moses, iii. 152; accepts a ready will, iii. 152; knows our weakness, and the nature of our conflict, iii. 152; tempers His judgment with mercy, iii. 152, 153; His intercession the cause of God's blessings, iii. 154; intreats as man, gives as God, iii. 155; likely to be heard because a Son, and because earnest in His prayer, iii. 156; His blood cries for a blessing, iii. 156; a Comforter, as well as the Holy Ghost, iii. 157, 158; our Advocate against Satan, iii. 158; our Intercessor, iii. 158; took possession of heaven in our name, iii. 158; tabernacled (ἐσκή-νωσε), did not dwell among us, iii. 159; specially comforts us in the Holy Sacrament, iii. 161; His flesh and blood the vehicles of His Spirit, iii. 161, 162; took our body, that we might have His Spirit, iii. 162.

Christ, a question whether it were expedient for Him to depart, iii. 164, 167; His ascension a cause of sorrow to the disciples, iii. 164; because they most needed Him at that time, iii. 165; shows both the loss and the gain of His departure, iii. 165; gave good reason for it, iii. 166, 167; the Testator of the New Testament, iii. 169; took our flesh, gave us His Spirit, iii. 170; no incompatibility between Him and the Holy Ghost, iii. 171; retired to make way for the Holy Ghost, iii. 171; by sending Him, showed Himself equal to the Father, iii. 171; His corporal presence less valuable than His spiritual, iii. 172; withdrew from the Apostles, that they might not be foolishly fond of Him, iii. 172; His spiritual presence is sometimes rightly withdrawn, iii. 173; as from the faint-hearted, or the self-conceited, iii. 173; takes away His flesh, to send His Spirit, iii. 174; the Spirit comes by His flesh and blood, iii. 179.

—— His flesh never without the Holy Spirit who conceived it, iii. 199.

—— Redemption His work, iii. 208; how purchased, iii. 209; on what day, iii. 209; fully bestowed at His second coming, iii. 209; without the Holy Ghost, like a deed without a seal, iii. 211.

—— Ps. lxviii. 18, applied to Him by S. Paul, iii. 221; typified by Moses and David, iii. 222; and Abraham, iii. 230; triumphed over His enemies, delivered His people from captivity, iii. 223; His ascension a great triumph, in comparison with His previous humiliation, iii. 224; went up as high, as before He was low, iii. 224, 225; now pleads and intercedes for us, iii. 225; supplies our wants, iii. 226; is our forerunner into heaven, iii. 226; is in heaven in our persons, iii. 227; died as a lamb, rose as a lion, iii. 229; the evidences of His triumph, iii. 229; His gifts compared to largess given at triumphs, iii. 231; He both received and gave these gifts, iii. 231, 232; received of God, to give to man, iii. 234; not merely liberates, but rewards, iii. 232; carried up His flesh, gave us His Spirit, iii. 232, 233; even to His enemies, iii. 235; left us the gifts of His Body and Blood, iii. 239; His Body full of the characters of love, iii. 239; every drop of His Blood a great drop of love, iii. 239; His Body the Spirit of strength, His Blood the Spirit of comfort, iii. 239; ascended, that God might dwell with us, iii. 239; went 'up on high,' that the Spirit might descend, iii. 239.

Christ, Holy Ghost descended on Him at baptism, iii. 241; His Baptism a high mystery, iii. 242; the whole Trinity present thereat, iii. 242; it was the regeneration of the world, iii. 242; naturally needed not baptism, iii. 244; submitted to it as an act of humility, iii. 244; and of justice, iii. 245; and as the head of a new society, iii. 245, 246; gave virtue to Jordan by this act, iii. 245, 246; and to the sacrament itself, iii. 246; 'put us on' in His Baptism, iii. 246; His Baptism cleanses by virtue of His baptism in blood, iii. 247; thrice baptized in blood, iii. 247; the stream of water and blood from His side the true Jordan, iii. 247; His Baptism the strongest reason for ours, iii. 247, 248; prays for the Holy Ghost to be joined to the waters of baptism, iii. 249; the force of His prayer, iii. 249; compared to Elias's, iii. 249; rewarded for His humility by a voice from heaven, iii. 256, 257; this voice for our sake, not His, iii. 257; explained as referring to all Christians, iii. 257; His Baptism not so much His as ours, iii. 257; through His being the beloved Son, we are made so also, iii. 257, 258; God well pleased with us in Him, iii. 259; without Him we could not have been God's sons, iii. 259.

—— received the Holy Ghost once, gave Him twice, iii. 261; by breathing on the Apostles showed His manhood, by His words His Godhead, iii. 264; His breath cured the poisonous breath of the serpent, iii. 266; as necessary for man as his own breath,

INDEX TO SERMONS, ETC. 407

iii. 267; His breath had power, iii. 268; especially after His resurrection, iii. 269; will never fail, iii. 269; gave power thereby to sinful men, iii. 270; gave spiritual breath, as the Father gave natural, iii. 271; reached thereby into the very inward man, iii. 271; thus gave proof of His Godhead, iii. 271; His breath not transubstantiated into the Holy Ghost, yet gave it, iii. 272; this act of His implies necessity of outward call, iii. 272.

Christ, His sermon at Nazareth, iii. 280; said to have been on a year of Jubilee, iii. 281; suited to Whit-Sunday, iii. 281; His inauguration to His office, iii. 282; preaches the Gospel, as Prophet, iii. 283; enlarges prisoners as King, proclaims a Jubilee as Priest, iii. 284; the words of His sermon manifest the Trinity, iii. 284; received the Spirit as man, iii. 284; sending the Spirit shows Him to be Lord, iii. 284; why we ascribe His anointing to the Holy Ghost, and not to the Father, iii. 285; His taking the manhood a work of grace, iii. 285; anointed by the Holy Ghost at His conception, iii. 285, 286; Messias as anointed, Shiloh as sent, iii. 288; therefore called the Apostle of our profession, iii. 288; a Physician of broken hearts, iii. 291, 293; both cures and stops sin, iii. 295; kept His jubilee when He ascended, iii. 300.

—— His flesh exalted on high drew down blessings on ours, iii. 308.

—— without the Spirit avails nothing, iii. 344; the complement of the law, iii. 345; false Christs, iii. 345, not to be mistaken for the true, iii. 346; came by water and blood, iii. 345, 346, 348; saves from sin by taking it away, iii. 347; gave water and blood their power to remove sin, iii. 347; began in the blood of His circumcision and in the water of His Baptism, ended in the water of His tears and in the blood of His passion, iii. 348; is still coming in water and blood, iii. 348, 359; came in His own person, first in blood, then in water, iii. 349; comes to us in water first, iii. 349, 359; heretics sever His natures, iii. 349; must come both in water and blood, to make His work complete, iii. 350; we must come to Him for both of them, iii. 350, 351; cannot be separated, iii. 352; His Blood is drink to nourish, and medicine to purge, iii. 359; appoints our sphere of work in the Church, iii. 381; the essential wisdom of the Father, iii. 382.

Christ refused the request of His disciples to destroy the city of Samaria, iv. 242, 244, 250; wished to break down the separation between them and the Jews, iv. 245; His Spirit is of the dove, not of the eagle, iv. 253; became Son of Man, to save the sons of men, iv. 253; compared to gentle animals, iv. 254; reproved S. Peter for wishing to use the sword, iv. 254.

—— spake in the Proverbs of Solomon, iv. 277; the Wisdom of the Father, iv. 282; the source of kingly power, iv. 282; not by permission, but by commission, iv. 283; the King of all the earth, iv. 282, 283; He reigns by kings, iv. 285; unmakes as well as makes them, iv. 286.

—— compared to a pelican, iv. 331.
—— a pattern of humility, v. 10.
—— when He gave His Apostles the power of remitting sins, v. 82, 83; the Saviour of both body and soul, v. 84; honoured His own human nature by making men the channels of His absolution, v. 90; ratifies in heaven what His Apostles do on earth, v. 103.

—— not merely our Justifier, but our Righteousness, v. 112; shows thus the greatness of the gift, v. 112; is Jehovah our Righteousness, v. 113, 123; both the pattern and efficient cause of our righteousness, v. 113; we need His righteousness to be counted ours, because we look for an eternal reward, which cannot be due to our doings, v. 120.

—— willingly paid tribute, v. 138, 139.
—— the Author of grace, v. 315; the special gift of God, v. 327.
—— His tears intercede for us, when we cannot pray ourselves, v. 339; teaches submission to God's will, v. 340; a pattern in praying, v. 343; prayed in every place, and under every circumstance, v. 344; needed to pray only as a creature, v. 345; was content to follow S. John the Baptist's pattern in preaching and praying, v. 347; an example of every kind of prayer, v. 359.

—— a manifestation of God's love to us, v. 365; our great pattern of obedience, v. 379; has God's kingdom committed to His government, v. 392.

—— grieved for sin committed against God, as though committed against Himself, v. 428; not only satisfies for our sins, but gives us a right to heaven, v. 430; His satisfaction, how applied, v. 430; frees us from curse, v. 434.

Christ, contrasted with Satan, v. 454; how He delivers us, v. 454; when forsaken of God was comforted by patience, v. 455, 456; His dying an assurance of His love, v. 459; His name made up of Hebrew and Greek to show that they were made one in Him, v. 468.

—— began His mission by opposing Satan's power of temptation, v. 479; led by the Holy Ghost to the conflict, v. 481, 483; just after His baptism, v. 487; though before unassailed, v. 487; greatness of His love which led Him thus into hunger, temptation, and the company of Satan, v. 481; His temptation came not by chance, v. 484; it is to be reverenced and to be imitated, v. 485, 486; sanctifies and abates our temptations, v. 486; shows His compassion for us, v. 486; our fellow-helper in temptation, v. 486, 487; began His course with fasting, contrary to the world's fashion, v. 490; length of His fast corresponded with that of Moses and Elias, v. 491; various numbers of days set apart by the Church to commemorate it, v. 492; His three temptations a summary of all He underwent, v. 496, 497; though the Son of God, He suffered want, v. 498; His temptation warns us of Satan's coming, v. 501; chose not to use His power at Satan's request, v. 502; why He answered Satan, instead of driving him away, v. 503; why led by Satan to the pinnacle of the temple, v. 515; Satan had power over His body, v. 516, 517; the reason of all His sufferings, v. 517; answers Satan by Scripture, v. 526, 553; to explain what he had misquoted, v. 526; why carried by Satan to the high mountain, v. 539; in accepting the world from Satan would have lost everything, v. 544, 545; why most offended at Satan's last temptation, v. 550; much offended when God's glory is at stake, v. 551.

—— offered up Himself on the cross as on an altar, v. 259, 260; the only true sacrifice, v. 260; not offered again and again in the Eucharist, v. 261, 262, 266; claims His own, when He requires us to give our alms, v. 274, 275; manifested in the poor, v. 274, 278; our righteousness, v. 284. (*From Bishop Buckeridge's Funeral Sermon.*)

Christi distinguished from *uncti*, iv. 45, 50, 54.

Christians, their duty to bear wrong, ii. 8; their nearness of access to God, v. 365; their dignity as sons of God, and temples of the Holy Ghost, v. 366, 368, 369, 379; still God's children, though sinners, v. 430.

—— the early, their patience contrasted with doctrines of modern Romanists, iii. 254, 255; their numbers and strength, iv. 355.

Christiern IV., King of Denmark, visited England in 1606, v. 235 note; Sermon preached before him, v. 235, *seq.*

Christmas-Day, an annual representation of the fulness of time, i. 45; joy of, i. 62, 70; dignity of, set forth, i. 103; our original uncleanness began to be purged on, i. 114; mistake of those who observe it not, i. 119; spoken of by SS. Irenæus, Augustine, and Cyril, i. 123; made a *dies ludi*, a calf's day, i. 132; called by the Fathers 'Theophania' more often than ' Genethlia,' i. 198; a glorious day in every way, i. 221; fitness of the angelic hymn upon, i. 232; called 'Epiphany' in the East, i. 233; the poorest and emptiest season in nature the fullest and richest in grace, i. 277.

Chrysostom, S. John, his words on Heb. ii. 16, i. 6; on the frailty of man, i. 339; compares men to beasts, i. 349; on the many senses of Scripture, i. 353; on the way we walk, i. 360; on fasting, i. 389; on the History of Dives and Lazarus, ii. 82, 86, 90—92, 94; distinguishes between λαβεῖν and ἀπολαβεῖν, ii. 90; his regard for Easter, ii. 420; explains the words 'touch me not,' as intended to teach reverence, iii. 28, 35; explains 'deliver us from evil,' of the evil one, v. 451; regarded the length of Lent only as a positive law, v. 492.

Church, The, appoints a time for repentance, i. 374; authority of, in discipline, i. 391, 392; has her faults, i. 393; what is given to, is given to Christ, ii. 49, 368, v. 41; Christ's body, ii. 50, 236, 353; Christ persecuted in, ii. 50, 352, iv. 19; all who spoil it are like Judas, ii. 52; it needs anointing, ii. 236; Christ the Head of, ii. 279; many joined together therein, ii. 279; joined to God in one Person, ii. 368; by being therein, we obtain our spiritual blessings, ii. 368; holds out heavenly promises, ii. 380.

—— has her own customs, ii. 410; even in the Apostles' times, ii. 410;

an argument against contentions, ii. 410; both negatively and affirmatively, ii. 411; has power to appoint customs, ii. 412; each particular Church in subordination to the Church Universal, ii. 412.

Church, inaugurated at Pentecost, iii. 116; the Holy Spirit manifested therein, iii. 120; as having converted many nations, now speaks with many tongues, iii. 139.

—— compared to a dove, iii. 254.

—— set up for the good of the world, iv. 16; enemies of, enemies of God, iv. 16; has gained by the support of kings, iv. 16.

—— has authority to institute fast and festival, iv. 400; and to ordain ceremonies, v. 60; can cut off from her fellowship, v. 63; her various kinds of censure, v. 63; her true form of government, v. 63, *seq.*

—— has wars to fight, and laws to make, v. 146.

—— God's kingdom by purchase, v. 462; holy in spite of corrupt members, v. 516.

—— Christ's mystical body, v. 263; offers up herself daily, v. 263—265. (*From Bishop Buckeridge's Funeral Sermon.*)

—— (the building), house of prayer, and not of preaching, v. 357.

—— *the English*, retained fasting, v. 492; for what reason, v. 492, 493.

—— *the Primitive*, why it instituted Lent, v. 492.

—— *the Reformed*, abolished fasting, v. 492.

Churches, Foreign, in England, took good care of their poor, v. 43.

Circumcision of Christ, His coming under the law, i. 55.

Civil duty to do no wrong, ii. 8.

Clement, James, the murderer of Henry III. of France, iv. 36, 289; almost canonized, iv. 36.

Clergy, meanly paid, iii. 142; the several orders of, v. 63.

Cloud, light to Israelites, darkness to Egyptians, ii. 17.

Clovis the First, summoned the first Council of Orleans, v. 162.

—— *the Second*, summoned the Council of Châlons, v. 162.

Cluverius, Philip, patronised by Andrewes, v. 292. (*From Bishop Buckeridge's Funeral Sermon.*)

Cobweb laws, and cobweb divinity, v. 7.

Coins of Emperors, device on, to signify that their power was of God, iv. 114.

Cologne, Council of. See *Council of Cologne.*

Combat between Christ and Satan, a wonderful sight, v. 480.

Comfort, one result of looking at Christ pierced, ii. 137; literally means ' strengthening,' ii. 145; Christ's rising a ground of, ii. 198; spiritual, a light to the soul, iii. 372; in affliction a kind of deliverance, v. 455.

Comforter, the Holy Ghost, why so called, iii. 146, 155—157; Christ one Comforter, the Holy Ghost another, iii. 157.

Comforters, what kind of, sought for by the world, iii. 175.

Comforts, earthly, of little avail, iii. 159; often discomforts, iii. 159; compared to winter brooks, full at the wrong season, iii. 159; soon leave us, iii. 160; soon cloy, iii. 160.

Commandments, better to keep them, than to have Christ with us, iii. 151; Christ's, easy to keep through grace, iii. 151; we should be sorry for not having kept them, iii. 153; all are considered as kept when sins are pardoned, iii. 153.

—————— *the Ten*, given in the singular number, iv. 64; the Fifth, why placed on the confines of the two tables, ii. 10, 11, 284.

—————— distinguished from counsels, v. 59.

Communicate, means to bestow to some good common use, v. 40.

Communion, Holy, imparts the Incarnation, i. 16, 100, 151; offering of Christ in, i. 30, 82; shows the union of Christ's nature with man's, i. 43; public service incomplete without, i. 62; purges us from actual sins, i. 113; makes the Church a Bethlehem, i. 173; symbolized by Christ's cradle, i. 213; fitness of the angelic hymn, as used in it, i. 214—231; and of the star on the vessel containing the sacrament, i. 247; consists of a heavenly and an earthly part, i. 281; refutes Eutychianism, i. 281; reunites scattered man, i. 282; Christ especially touched therein, iii. 34; it most nearly represents Him, iii. 34; to be handled reverently, iii. 34; therein we partake of the substance of the second Adam, iii. 58; are engrafted into Christ, iii. 58; we drink the blood of the true Vine, iii. 77; gain remission of sins, iii. 77; have full communion with Christ, iii. 77; Christ's blood therein the vehicle of the Spirit, iii. 102; best received at

AND. — PERRON, ETC.

I l

Easter, iii. 102; we drink therein of the Spirit, iii. 128; a type of agreement, iii. 128; as shown by kneading of grains into bread, and squeezing the grapes into one cup, iii. 128; called spiritual food, not as being received spiritually, but as conveying spiritual gifts, iii. 144; ordained for our spiritual comfort, iii. 161; Christ given us therein, iii. 161; why instituted in the elements of bread and wine, iii. 162, 239; spiritual meat and drink, iii. 199, 279; a placing Christ, as it were, in our hands, iii. 199; supplies what we have lost of the gift of Baptism, iii. 219; the seal of our redemption, as applying our redemption to us, iii. 219; Christ's blood applied therein, as a supplement of Baptism, iii. 260; means of restoring to baptismal state, iii. 260.

Communion of Saints, its benefit found in intercessory prayer, v. 370.

Company, evil, a kind of leaven, ii. 305; soon infects, ii. 306.

Compassion, is passion at rebound, ii. 123; we should feel it for Christ, ii. 127; most due to the innocent, ii. 129.

——————— a kind of sacrifice, v. 281. (*From Bp. Buckeridge's Funeral Serm.*)

Compunction, one result of looking at Christ pierced, ii. 137.

Conception, the, of our Lord, above nature, i. 138; love of Christ to us shown in, i. 140; that of Christ healed ours, i. 141.

——————— applied to the mind, as well as to the body, iv. 346.

Confession obtains mercy, i. 189; comes best from a humble heart, ii. 338; a part of prayer, v. 358; either of sin, or of thanks, v. 358; both tend to God's glory, v. 459; the latter the best, v. 460.

——————— *seal of*, conceals treason among Romanists, iv. 141.

Confidence, has reference to God's faithfulness, v. 471; must be blended with patient waiting on Him, v. 474; and submission to His will, v. 474.

Constans summoned the Council of Sardica, v. 161.

Constantine, enjoined uniform observance of Easter, ii. 421; spoke of it as an apostolic observance, ii. 424, 425; summoned the Council of Nice, v. 158; also Provincial Councils, v. 161; and the Council of Tyre, v. 161.

——————— *Copronymus* summoned the seventh General Council, v. 160.

Constantinople, Council of. See *Council of Constantinople*.

Contentions, about Church customs even in the Apostles' times, ii. 405, 407; their nature, ii. 407; proceed from ceremonies to sacraments, ii. 409; not to be overlooked, ii. 408, 409.

Contentiousness, the way to be somebody, ii. 408.

Contrition comes from the heart, i. 371.

——————— a kind of sacrifice, v. 281. (*From Bp. Buckeridge's Funeral Sermon.*)

Conversion, the Church's teaching respecting it misrepresented, i. 359, 363; should be without hypocrisy, i. 364.

Cord of vanity, Satan's first temptation, v. 538.

Cords of a man, religion and reason, ii. 9; fair and gentle persuasions, ii. 14.

Corinth, its situation, ii. 100, 108; a sensual place, ii. 110.

Corinthians, unkind to S. Paul, ii. 98; took exceptions to him, ii. 99; hard to please, ii. 99; full of self-love and unkindness, ii. 100; did not requite his love, ii. 107.

Corner, how many Christ joined together therein, ii. 279; symbol of unity, ii. 281.

Coronation of kings of Judah, ceremony in, ii. 13.

Councils, General, useful for overthrowing heresies, and for making Canons, v. 146; called by Christian emperors, v. 157; their decrees made law by Justinian, v. 163; the later were only of the Western Church, v. 157.

——————— *Provincial*, summoned by emperors, v. 160, 161; ordered to be held every year, v. 163.

Council of Agde (A.D. 516), summoned by Alaric, v. 162.

——————— *of Aix-la-Chapelle* (A.D. 816), summoned by Louis I., v. 162.

——————— *of Ancyra* (A.D. 314), held by Eustathius, v. 159.

——————— *of Aquileia* (A.D. 381), summoned by Theodosius, v. 161; presided over by S. Ambrose, v. 161.

——————— *of Arles* (A.D. 813), summoned by Charlemagne, v. 162.

——————— *of Auvergne* (A.D. 535), summoned by Theodobert, v. 162.

——————— *of Braccara* (two), summoned by Spanish kings, v. 162.

——————— *of Chalcedon* (A.D. 451), defined doctrine of Incarnation, i. 91; enjoined observance of Easter, ii. 421; summoned by Valentinian and Marcian, v. 160; first summoned to Nice, then removed to Chalcedon by their command, v. 160; ordered provincial councils to be held yearly, v. 163.

——————— *of Châlons* (circa A.D. 650), summoned by Clovis the Second, v. 162.

Council of Châlons (A.D. 813), summoned by Charlemagne, v. 162.
—— *of Cologne* (A.D. 887), summoned by Charles the Fat, v. 162.
—— *of Constantinople* (the second general, A.D. 381), summoned by the emperor, v. 159; enjoined uniform observance of Easter, ii. 421.
—————————— (the fifth general, A.D. 553), summoned by Justinian, v. 160.
—————————— (the sixth general, A.D. 680), summoned by the emperor, v. 160.
—— *of Elvira* (A.D. 305), held by Hosius, v. 159.
—— *of Ephesus* (the third general, A.D. 431), enjoined uniform observance of Easter, ii. 421; summoned by the emperor, v. 160.
—— *of Gangra* (about A.D. 324), enjoined the keeping of Lent, i. 392.
—— *of Germany* (A.D. 742), summoned by Carloman, v. 162.
—— *of Frankfort* (A.D. 794), summoned by Charlemagne, v. 162.
—— *of Lampsacus* (A.D. 368), summoned by Valentinian, v. 161.
—— *of Lateran* (A.D. 1180), summoned by the pope, v. 163.
—— *of Mâcon, first* (A.D. 581), summoned by Guntram, v. 162.
————————— *second* (A.D. 585), summoned by Guntram, v. 162.
—— *of Mayence* (A.D. 813), summoned by Charlemagne, v. 162.
—————————— (A.D. 847), summoned by Lothaire, v. 162.
—— *of Meaux* (A.D. 845), summoned by Charles the Bald, v. 162.
—— *of Nice* (the first general, A.D. 325), defined the doctrine of the Incarnation, i. 394; enjoined observance of Easter, ii. 420; summoned by the Emperor Constantine, v. 158; three hundred and eighteen Bishops assembled at it, v. 158; the names of some of the chief of them, v. 159; came when called by Constantine, v. 159; its decrees confirmed by him, v. 163.
—————————— (the seventh general, A.D. 727), summoned by Constantine and Irene, v. 160.
—— *of Orleans, first* (A.D. 511), summoned by Clovis the First, v. 162.
————————— *second* (A. D. 533), summoned by Childebert, v. 162.
—— *of Rheims* (A.D. 813), summoned by Charlemagne, v. 162.
—— *of Rome* (A.D. 502), summoned by Theodoric, v. 162.
—— *of Sardica* (A.D. 347), summoned by Constans, v. 161.

Council of Seleucia (A.D. 359), attended by Liberius, v. 161.
—— *of Seville* (A.D. 619), how Isaiah ix. 6 expounded by, i. 21.
—— *of Sirmium* (A.D. 351), attended by Liberius, v. 161.
—— *of Thessalonica* (A.D. 457), summoned by Gratian, v. 161.
—— *of Toledo* (ten), summoned by Spanish kings, v. 162.
—— *of Tours* (A.D. 567), summoned by Cherebert, v. 162.
—————————— *third* (A.D. 813), summoned by Charlemagne, v. 162.
—— *of Tribur* (A.D. 895), summoned by Arnulphus, v. 162.
—— *of Vern* (A.D. 755), summoned by Pepin, v. 162.
—— *of Worms* (A.D. 868), summoned by Louis the Second, v. 162.
Counsel, neglected, brings misery, iv. 297; good, given by fathers to children, iv. 297; the wisest will do well to follow it, iv. 298; arises from the union of wisdom and affection, iv. 298; the result of, is in God's hands, iv. 350.
Counsels distinguished from commandments, v. 59.
Covenant, sufficient for conveying peace, iii. 90; always ratified by blood, iii. 91; may be broken, iii. 91; God's, its purpose to deliver man, iv. 304.
—————————— nature of that made with David, iv. 86; against whom, iv. 88; kept with mercy and truth, iv. 99.
Covetous, shrink at the thought of giving, v. 44.
Covetousness, the motive of many, ii. 46; is as bad as idolatry, ii. 47; fitly called idolatry, v. 553; never waxes old, v. 541.
Cratch, the, of Christ, i. 203; made crosswise, and so the sign of the Cross, i. 201; the sign of His humility, i. 204; a sign to be spoken against, i. 207; likened to the outward symbols of the Holy Eucharist, i. 213.
Creation, the Trinity present at, iii. 242; resemblance between it and Christ's Baptism, iii. 242.
Crescentius censured as a heretic, ii. 415.
Crime, often caused by opportunity, iv. 158, 159.
Cross, story of Dives and Lazarus compared to the arms of a cross, ii. 80, *seq.*; the, a kind of shame, ii. 166, 172; how spoken of by the heathen, ii. 166; the kind of death it indicates, ii. 166—168; Christ stretched on it as on a rack, ii. 170; a tedious kind of death, ii. 170; a spiritual as well as material cross, ii. 171; a servile

punishment, ii. 172 ; an accursed kind of death, ii. 174 ; often turned into a crown, v. 456 ; frees from anguish, v. 456; to be borne in this life, v. 456.
Cross, the altar of Christ, v. 259, 260. (*From Bp. Buckeridge's Funeral Sermon.*)
Crown, placed by God on the head of kings, iv. 114 ; not to be taken off by the people, iv. 114, 115.
Cruciatus, derived from *crux*, ii. 170.
Cup of salvation, memorial of acceptance, iii. 300; to partake of it an effectual mode of invocation, iii. 321 ; and of thanksgiving, iii. 321 ; the blood of that cup will drown the cry of sin, iii. 321.
Cup of vengeance, sinners had to drink of it, iii. 71 ; the fruit of their own inventions, iii. 71 ; Christ drank of it as found among sinners, iii. 71, 72.
Cup-shotten, drunken, v. 15.
Curse, will fall according to the cause, iv. 9.
Cushi, his prayer against David's enemies, iv. 3, 6 ; may be regarded as either a prayer or a prophecy, iv. 6 ; may be applied to other times, iv. 7 ; regarded first as a prayer, iv. 7, *seq.;* as a prophecy, iv. 17, *seq.*
Customs, Church, how proved good, ii. 405, 406, 411, 412 ; to be urged against the contentious, ii. 409, 413 ; not to be set against Scripture, ii. 410 ; not committed to writing, ii. 410 ; ever urged by the Prophets and the Fathers, ii. 411 ; in what matters to be urged, ii. 413.
Cyprian, S., on the virtue appropriate to Christ's birth, i. 30 ; on the Church, i. 391 ; explains 'Deliver us from evil' of every calamity and trial, v. 451, 452.
Cyril, S., of Alexandria, called the nativity Christ's Day, i. 123.
Cyrus, God's shepherd, ii. 9, iii. 85 ; God's anointed, iv. 51 ; His instrument in restoring His people, iv. 228 ; his so doing very marvellous, iv. 231.

D.

Dagger-cheap, v. 546.
Daily Bread, why asked for, v. 422, 423.
Danger rallies together all the members of the body, v. 209.
Daniel, his image a type of declension, ii. 63 ; himself a type of Christ, ii. 328 ; especially in reading the handwriting, iii. 76 ; risked his life rather than neglect prayer, v. 343.
Darkness, akin to evil, iii. 373 ; various kinds of, iii. 371, v. 318, 319 ; contrasted with the many 'lights' that come from God, iii. 371 ; a type of ignorance, v. 317.
Date and Dabitur, two twins, v. 48.
Dathan withstood Aaron, ii. 35.
Datum and Donum distinguished, iii. 366 ; a transitory gift, iii. 366.
David, mercy and truth meet together in his repentance, i. 189.
—— brought songs to perfection, ii. 3, v. 204 ; teaches men to tune themselves and their households, ii. 3, v. 204.
—— resolved to re-establish the pillars of the land, ii. 4, 11 ; how he does it, ii. 8 ; his duty is to uphold them, ii. 10 ; his first act to restore the ark, ii. 13 ; his reverence for it, ii. 12, 13 ; set the Levites in order, ii. 13 ; provided for their maintenance, ii. 13 ; a man after God's own heart, ii. 13 ; executed judgment and justice, ii. 14 ; enjoined the duties of all estates in the land, ii. 14 ; too merciful, ii. 14, 15, 24, 58 ; repaired Saul's ruins, ii. 15, 284 ; changed the nature and name of his country, ii. 15 ; complained against by Shimei, ii. 58 ; his taking the shew-bread, sanctioned by Christ, ii. 65 ; preferred God's word to gold, ii. 103 ; resented Nabal's unkindness, ii. 109 ; originally spoken of in Ps. cxviii., ii. 271 ; how it is applicable to him, ii. 282—284 ; said to be called 'stone' as a term of disgrace, ii. 282 ; fed God's flock, ii. 284, iii. 85.
—— in conquering Edom and Bozrah, a type of Christ, iii. 66, 73 ; also in going up to Mount Zion, iii. 222, 227; and in taking Amalek, iii. 230.
—— used imprecations in his Psalms, iv. 8.
—— surrounded with enemies, iv. 10, v. 251 ; comforted inwardly by them, v. 435.
—— would not sanction Saul's death, iv. 25, 29, 30 ; though he had reason for wishing it, iv. 27, 28 ; and it might have seemed the course of God's providence, iv. 29 ; and though Saul had sought his life, iv. 37 ; persuaded to lay hands on Saul, iv. 157, 158 ; motives for his doing so, iv. 159, 160 ; had set an evil eye against him, iv. 162 ; seemed at first as if disposed to kill him, iv. 163 ; only cut his mantle, iv. 164 ; sorry that he had done so, iv. 164, 166 ; perhaps over scrupulous, iv. 165 ; might have done more, iv. 165 ; would have been more deeply grieved if he had done it, iv. 166 ; contrasted with modern king-

killers, iv. 166, 167; kept his servants from rising against Saul, iv. 168; his passionate abjuration of the act, iv. 168, 169; the reasons of his conduct, iv. 169, 170; a pattern for us, iv. 174.

David, a type of all good kings, iv. 77; twice found by God, iv. 78, 79; appointed by God, not by the people, iv. 80; appointed by God, because worthy, iv. 81; not only found, but anointed, iv. 83; and so not to be touched, iv. 55; the nature of the covenant made with him, iv. 86; many times crowned with God's goodness, iv. 113; sought not the crown for himself, iv. 114; the blessings God heaped on him, iv. 116, 117; an instance of humble adoration, iv. 375; specially protected by God, v. 249, 250; His faithful servant, v. 249, 250.

—— thought more of returning to God's temple than to his own house, v. 343; prayed to God seven times a day, as a prophet of God, v. 356; his affection for his rebellious son Absalom, v. 368, 430; an example of submission to God's will, v. 399.

—— when delivered from persecution fell into presumption, v. 514; led on to various sins, v. 537.

Day, the last, the thought of, will keep us serious, iii. 304, 316; why spoken of in connexion with Pentecost (Acts ii.), iii. 315, 317; signs of its coming, iii. 317.

—— *the Lord's*, has reference to Easter, ii. 426.

Days, some are specially of God's making, iv. 205, 206; God's deed makes God's day, iv. 207.

—— *fixed*, of fast or festival, of use, iv. 399; appointed by Church authority, iv. 399, 400; not by private persons, iv. 401.

—— *the last*, the days of Christ, iii. 304, 315; called the days of the Lord, to show that they are not to be used as we please, iii. 316.

Deacons, are not laymen, but have a step in the ministry, v. 66.

Dead, offices of love to be shown to, ii. 225.

Death, sudden, to be prayed against, ii. 70; fearfulness of, ii. 70; in the act of sin, most dangerous, ii. 70; an unusual, full of terror, ii. 70; most fearful of all things, ii. 167; of what kind the death of the cross, ii. 168; a fall without rising, ii. 191; compared to a great lord, ii. 193; the perils of, different provinces of his kingdom, ii. 193; the king of terrors, ii. 194; the second death, its nature, ii. 194; moral death, what it is, ii. 202; why termed sleep, ii. 213, 214; one of the two great matters in the world, ii. 215; came from Adam, ii. 215; caused by eating the forbidden fruit, ii. 220; not destruction, only a passage, ii. 294, 295; a dissolution of body and soul, ii. 350; and of all present ties, ii. 351; only a kind of sleep, ii. 357, 358; appointed for all men, ii. 360, 361; overcome by Christ, ii. 398; by Him made a harbour of rest, ii. 398; a passage to a haven of happiness, ii. 399; led captive at Christ's ascension, iii. 229; fear of, most fearful, iv. 309, 310; strips us of all our goods, v. 46; both bodily and spiritual, v. 83; divine power alone can cure either, v. 84; has set up a kingdom, v. 392; an enemy to God's kingdom, v. 392; to be prayed against, v. 394.

Deber, the Hebrew word for plague, indicates that it does not come by chance, v. 225.

Debts, by this word in the Lord's Prayer are meant sins, v. 426; how we incur them, v. 427; cannot discharge them of ourselves, v. 428; their greatness set forth, v. 429, 435; can be claimed by God, v. 429; every man a debtor, v. 434; incurred daily, v. 438.

Decrees, God's, many too bold and busy with them, iii. 328.

Dedication, feast of, why appointed, iv. 400.

Defamers are Satan's agents, v. 482.

Δεκτὸς and δεκτέος contrasted, iii. 340.

Deliverance, great, comes from God, iv. 207; of two kinds, the not falling into danger, and the escaping out of it, iv. 332, 367; a ground of joy, iv. 362; arises from God's goodness, iv. 362; deliverance of man, the purpose of God's covenant, iv. 364; the result of it should be our faithful service, iv. 365, 370; from evil, beyond our own power, v. 453; the several ways in which God effects it, v. 454, 455; special reasons why he should deliver, v. 457.

Deluge, the rainbow its close, ii. 17.

Demas, fell back, ii. 75; his works from spirit of the world, iii. 358.

Demetrius feared for the loss of his gain, ii. 46; self-interested, iii. 275.

Depose, people must not depose a king, iv. 114.

Deprecation is for the removing of evil, v. 358.

Desperation, our way lies between it and presumption, v. 535.

Detractors soon become seditious, iv. 303, 304; scripture instances of, iv. 304.
Deventer, the town of, betrayed to the Spaniards, v. 10.
Devil, the spirit that inspires traitors, iv. 87, 135, 189. See also *Satan*.
Devils confessed Christ unwillingly, ii. 338, 339; rejoice in man's misfortunes, iii. 65.
Devotion, the most proper work of holiness, iv. 376; public and private to be distinguished, v. 357; should be joined with reverence, v. 363, 373.
——— a kind of sacrifice, v. 281. (*From Bp. Buckeridge's Funeral Sermon.*)
Dew falling on wool, a good king compared to, ii. 24.
Diabolus means 'defamer,' or spreader of evil reports, v. 482.
Διακονία, the word applied to the highest order of the ministry, iii. 388; to teach humility, iii. 388; to kings, iii. 388; and to Christ, iii. 388.
Διάκονοι, kings so called, v. 180.
Διατάξεις distinguished from ἐπιτάξεις, v. 59.
Didymus, his interpretation of the words, 'I will pour out of my Spirit,' iii. 305.
Disciples, gained the Holy Ghost at Pentecost by their unity, iii. 112, 113, 129; uniformity, iii. 114; and patient waiting, iii. 114, 129.
Discontent weakens faith, v. 547.
Discord, a bar to the entry of the Holy Ghost, iii. 113.
Discretion in the use of a gift, as great a blessing as the gift itself, iii. 140; to be used in applying comfort and absolution, v. 97.
Disease, to, i.e. to put to pain, v. 7.
Disobedience, curses uttered against, v. 427.
Distrust quenches faith, v. 528.
Disunion drives away the Holy Spirit, iii. 238.
Dives, a son of Abraham, ii. 79, 83, 87; had received his good things, ii. 79, 87; their nature, ii. 83; his story, not a parable, ii. 80; compared to a cross, ii. 80, 81, *seq.*; his torments began at once, ii. 84; eternal, ii. 84; contrasted with Lazarus's happiness, ii. 85; without any comfort, ii. 85; punished, not because rich, or over-reaching, or covetous, or lavish, ii. 89; but because he chose his portion in this life, ii. 90; this life, why called his, ii. 91; forgot what he had received, ii. 91; and that he was God's steward, ii. 92; forgot Lazarus, ii. 92; spent all on himself, ii. 92; neglected his own soul, ii. 93; forgot the other world, ii. 93, 94; scorned God's word, ii. 94; a warning to others, ii. 95.
Divinity, the 'back-bone' of the prince's law, ii. 8; many laity wrongly pretend to a knowledge of, v. 15.
Division of place will cause division of mind in God's service, iii. 114.
Dock, 'In nettle, out dock' (a proverb), ii. 202.
Doctors the same as pastors, according to the Fathers, v. 65.
Doctrine, false, a kind of leaven, ii. 304.
Doers of the word have it, as it were, incarnate within them, v. 195; become Christ's kinsmen, v. 195, 196.
Δοκιμασία, signifies a good kind of temptation, v. 443.
Dolichum, what it is, ii. 73, 182.
Donatists, their error concerning the personal holiness of Christ's ministers, iii. 277, 278.
Donum distinguished from *datum*, iii. 366; a permanent gift, iii. 366.
Δωρήματα, why Christian virtues so called, v. 312; distinguished from δόσεις, v. 313; eternal gifts, v. 314, 416.
Δόσις, distinguished from δώρημα, v. 313; transitory gifts, v. 313, 314, 416.
Do this (in the Eucharist), how to be understood, ii. 300.
Doubt, Apostles' doubt of Christ's resurrection, our certainty, ii. 190.
Dove, sets forth the properties of the Holy Ghost, iii. 251, 252, iv. 253; as a bird of purity, of peace, of bright colour, of harmlessness, iii. 197, 252; a type of patience, iii. 252; its silver feathers (Ps. lxviii. 13), how explained, iii. 253; a symbol of the Church, iii. 254; a type of God's gifts, iii. 233; some of them fall on ourselves, iii. 287.
Doxology, ever used in the Church at the end of Psalms, iii. 185, 186; in Lord's Prayer taken from Old Testament, v. 458.
Dream, returning from captivity why compared to, iv. 229; strange things beheld in, iv. 229; true and false dreams compared, iv. 230.
Duty, Christian, to bear wrong, ii. 8; civil, to do no wrong, ii. 8.

E.

Eagles, which fly high and gaze on the sun, a type of Christians, v. 376.
Ear, the sense of faith, iii. 116; of the word, iii. 144.
Earnestness, needful in prayer, v. 329.
Earth, witness to Christ's death, ii. 155,

INDEX TO SERMONS, ETC. 415

173; heart of, compared with the jaws of a whale, ii. 397; how this expression understood by several of the Fathers, ii. 397; implies that the earth has life, ii. 399; and so will give forth her dead, ii. 399; no abiding home, v. 377.

East, the, the fountain of sin and falsehood, i. 242; more favoured than the West in respect of the prophecy of the Star, i. 255.

Easter, Sermons preached at, ii. 185, *seq.;* iii. 1—105; the Christian's Passover, ii. 291; two Passovers in one, ii. 298; looked to by the common people as a time of pleasure, ii. 309; the Christian's duty at, ii. 310; a Dedication Feast for the raising of Christ's Body as a temple, ii. 360; fit season for Holy Communion, ii. 362, 427; for Baptism, ii. 426; and for Absolution, ii. 427; the feast of the resurrection, iii. 17; a time of joy, iii. 18; a kind of second Christmas, iii. 57; Christ's birth from the grave at this time better than His birth at Christmas, iii. 57; the Holy Communion always celebrated at, iii. 58; a special time for good works, iii. 83; and for Holy Communion, iii. 102; compensates for the sorrow of Good Friday, iii. 164.

―― Scripture authority for, ii. 406; apostolic, ii. 424; Church custom, ii. 406; contentions about it, ii. 291, 415; the paschal cycles and epistles appointed the proper season for keeping it, ii. 416, 417; proof of its being kept shown by homilies and other writings of the Fathers, ii. 418, 419; by their practice, ii. 419; by the decrees of Councils, ii. 420, 421; even in time of persecution, ii. 422—424.

Easter tide, noticed by SS. Augustin and Gregory Nyssen, ii. 420.

Ebal, we must creep into, leap into Gerizim (Hebrew proverb), iv. 9.

Ebion held the necessity of Jewish observances, v. 56.

Ἔχειν and ἀπέχειν distinguished, ii. 90.

Eclipses arise from natural causes, and yet may be signs of God's wrath, iii. 317.

Edom, Christ coming from, how explained, iii. 61; a type of our spiritual enemies, iii. 63; the worst enemy of the Israelites, iii. 64; though as near of kin they ought to have been friends, iii. 64; rejoiced in the misfortunes of the Israelites, iii. 65; out of Edom came Doeg, David's greatest enemy, and Herod, the enemy of Christ, iii. 65.

Egypt, deliverance from, a type of our spiritual deliverance, ii. 133, 258; Israel's calling out of, a type of Christ, ii. 140; a type of the world, ii. 293; and of spiritual enemies, iii. 63, 64.

El, this name of God given to men, v. 109; God's name of power, v. 110, 211.

Election, God's, not to be inquired into, v. 398.

Elements in the Holy Communion, work the same effect on the outward, as the Spirit in the inner man, iii. 162.

Elias, his fire not to be called down, iii. 256; not to be quoted as a warrant for persecution, iv. 251; his temper unbefitting the Gospel, iv. 252.

Elizabeth, Queen, her praises, ii. 56, 76; counted perseverance a queenlike virtue, ii. 76; exposed to alluring proffers and tempting dangers, ii. 71.

Elvira, Council of. See *Council of Elvira.*

Emmaus, meaning of, ii. 208.

Emperors, styled θεοφύλακτοι, iv. 108; and θεοστεφεῖς, iv. 114; device on their coins, iv. 114; assembled General Councils, v. 157, *seq.*

Encænia, why appointed, iv. 400.

Encratitæ, their origin, v. 58, 492; their error respecting the necessity of true faith, i. 193; v. 58.

Enemy, distinguished from son of wickedness, iv. 88.

Enemies, spiritual, described under the titles of the temporal enemies of the Jews, iii. 63, 64; especially of Edom, iii. 64, 65.

―― of Christ gained gifts at His ascension, iii. 235, 236; scattered at His resurrection, brought near to Him at Pentecost, iii. 236.

―― by wronging us often do us a service, v. 435; why compared by David to bees, v. 435.

Ἐνέργημα, a work wrought in us and by us, iii. 392; wrought willingly, truly, and actively, iii. 393.

England, the pride and luxury of, v. 15; God's favours towards, v. 29, 30; charities much increased in, v. 37.

Enmity makes us ready for revenge, iv. 26.

Enoch, taught the judgment, i. 124; invoked the name of God, ii. 7, 34.

Enthusiasts have no outward calling to the ministry, iii. 272; their want of submission, iii. 289.

Envy, no feeling of, in the angels, i. 3.

Ephesian disciples, their answer considered, iii. 180, *seq.;* should have received more than John's Baptism, iii. 181, 182; S. Paul bears with their deficiency, iii. 182.

Ephesus, Council of. See *Council of Ephesus.*
Ephod, David's reverence for, ii. 12.
'Επιούσιος, how explained, v. 419, 421; explained by the corresponding words in Syriac and Hebrew, v. 421.
Epiphany, Christmas-day called so in the East, i. 233; glory of, compensates for the humility of Christmas, iii. 164.
Epistle, the, for the day, tells us our duty, ii. 309.
'Επιτάξεις, distinguished from διατάξεις, v. 59.
Erpenius, Thomas, patronised by Andrewes, v. 292. (*From Bp. Buckeridge's Funeral Sermon.*)
Esau, his selling his birthright a lesson on fasting, i. 311; wasteful, ii. 41; Esau's bands, what meant by, ii. 45; had a different blessing from his brother, v. 415; did not acknowledge that all good came from God, v. 416.
Essex, Earl of, his expedition, i. 321.
Etymology, an unsound argument, v. 105.
Eucharist, Holy, our thank-offering for the Incarnation, i. 84; proof of the hypostatical union, i. 281; called Synaxis, i. 282; therein we may partake of Christ's body and blood, ii. 134; stands in the place of the Passover, ii. 299; a memorial sacrifice, ii. 300; cannot be dispensed with, ii. 302; to be received in token of thankfulness, ii. 381, 382; means of raising soul from sin, body from death, ii. 402, 403; always received at Easter, ii. 427; both a memorial and an application of Christ's sacrifice, v. 66; both a sacrifice and a sacrament, v. 67; Christ's body truly present therein, v. 67; almsgiving to be used therein, v. 67; to be frequently partaken of, v. 67; qualifications for receiving it, v. 68; means of obtaining remission of sins, v. 94.
—— a sacrifice as commemorative of Christ's, v. 260—262; not a proper sacrifice, v. 261; a sacrifice of praise, v. 262. (*From Bishop Buckeridge's Funeral Sermon.*)
Εὐδοκία used of God's will, when obeyed readily, v. 405.
Eunuch, the, sought instruction from S. Philip, ii. 119.
Eusebius, on the opinion of philosophers as to the Word, i. 88.
Eustathius, presided at the Council of Ancyra, v. 159.
Eutyches, heresy of, i. 90; the sacraments confute it, i. 281, 282.
Evangelists, none in the Church now, iii. 233.

Eve, enticed by the eye, v. 540; wanted to gain a higher estate, v. 542.
Evil, mortified by Christ's death, iii. 101; akin to darkness, iii. 373; comes not from God, iii. 374; is good to an evil eye, iv. 162; turned away by prevention before, or deliverance afterwards, iv. 233; turned into good by God, v. 303; consists of afflictions and disappointments, v. 334; of sins past, of sins to come, and of punishment, v. 424; not the same as temptation, v. 449, 450; some things evil in themselves, and in their effects, v. 449; of two kinds, sin and its punishment, v. 450; the evil of which we speak in the Lord's Prayer explained by the Greek Fathers to mean Satan, v. 451; it means also our own selves, v. 451; it includes earthly calamities, v. 452; long inflicted will make us Satan's bondmen, v. 453; deliverance from, only from God, v. 453.
Examples, evil, stand as pillars, ii. 71; compared with precepts, iv. 401; store of in the Bible, iv. 401.
Exchange, a heavenly, to do good with our wealth here, v. 45.
Excommunicati, distinguished from *abstenti,* v. 63.
Ἕξεις, not χαρίσματα. iii. 384; why virtues so called by the heathen, v. 312.
Eye, the sense of love, iii. 116; of the sacrament, iii. 144; to do what is good in one's own eyes has a different meaning with different people, iv. 162; evil is good to an evil eye, iv. 162; we must take heed they do not deceive us, iv. 162; the first origin of evil, v. 172; easily deceived, v. 172; doing right in one's own eyes, the evil of, v. 172, 174; one's own deceived by self-love, v. 173; the hand follows its guidance, v. 174, 175; soon enticed to sin, v. 540; Scripture instances of this, v. 540, 541; will not betray, unless the heart is corrupt within, v. 541.
—— spoken of God, notes His knowledge, v. 213.

F.

Facere and *agere* contrasted, v. 195.
Faggot, a type of unity and strength, iv. 196.
Faith, the basis in us of things supernatural, i. 139; must be joined to humility, i. 206; of the wise men, i. 250, 252; distinguished from credulity by having a ground, i. 253; and fear blend well together, ii. 338; comes

by hearing, not by sight, iii. 21; it holds good where sight fails, iii. 21; perfected by works, iii. 94; seldom spoken of by S. John, iii. 345; nowadays has become a virtue of chief request, iii. 345; its value derived from its object, iii. 345; not to be talked of unless we have good works, v. 36; a foundation, v. 49; vain imaginations respecting it, v. 58; manifested by works, v. 196; all articles of, are of a practical character, v. 196; the handle by which to lay hold of the shield of Scripture, v 504; stands between distrust and presumption, v. 528; 'only justifies,' this expression used by several of the Fathers, v. 556.

Faithfulness, both power and will required in it, v. 471; both exist in God, v. 471.

Fall, the, shown by man's fear of angels, i. 67; caused by evil desires of the flesh, i. 89; a division and separation, i. 270, 272; more than remedied, i. 275.

Falling back, the danger and folly of, ii. 74.

Fanatics, their want of mission and submission, iii. 289.

Fasting, degenerated in Bishop Andrewes' time, i. 359; accompanies repentance, i. 365—367, 393; duty and benefits of, i. 367, 378; necessity of, i. 367; kinds of, i. 368, 394, 395; the Church's requirement and mitigation of, i. 368, 394; excuse alleged for neglect of, i. 368; the English Church charged with neglect of, i. 376; encouraged by Christ, i. 378; prescribed by the Law, the Prophets, and the Gospel, i. 378, 379; instances of, under the Law, Prophets, and Gospel, i. 379; constant practice of, in the Church, i. 380; highly esteemed in primitive times, i. 380; virtues exercised in, i. 380, 381; effects of neglecting, i. 381, 382; arguments for, from nature, i. 385, 386; resorted to when danger threatened, i. 387; a remedy to prevent sin, i. 388; Tertullian upon, i. 388, 390; S. Bernard, i. 389; S. Chrysostom, i. 389; set time for, i. 393, 394; fasts here bring feasts in heaven, i. 397; fear of being thought hypocrites deters some men from, i. 401; want of, brings us into the place of hypocrites, i. 402; the charge of Popery deters others, i. 403; the loss of its reward, i. 413; one of the fruits of repentance, i. 443; a part of righteousness, iii. 338, 339; a help to prayer, v. 341; usual in the Church at the beginning of any great work, v. 491; as before the writing of S. John's Gospel, and Simon Peter's disputation with Simon Magus, v. 491; the length of our Lord's corresponded with that of Moses and Elias, v. 491; abolished by the Reformed Churches, v. 492; retained in the English Church, v. 492.

Father, God the, we ascribe to Him what the Son hath by nature, iii. 285.

Father, this word shows God's love for us, v. 363, 367, 368, 391, 459; 'Our Father,' contains a sum both of Law and Gospel, v. 364; a proof He will give us everything that is good, v. 364; not at variance with God's greatness, v. 364; we have Christ's authority for so calling Him, v. 364, 365; shows God not only as our Creator, but as having natural affection for us, v. 365; in what senses God is our Father, v. 365, 366; the nature of His fatherly love, v. 366; and its fruits, v. 367, 368; God distinguished from earthly fathers, v. 374, 375.

Father of lights, God why so called, iii. 369, 370, 372; why Father and not author, iii. 372, v. 316, *seq.*

Fathers, their compassion and their bounty towards their children, v. 367, 368.

Fathers, the, of the Church, on the Temple being built of fruit-bearing trees, i. 172; on Psalm lxxxv., i. 175; use 'Theophania' more often than 'Genethlia' with reference to Christ's birth, i. 198; find the mystery of the Trinity in the angels' song, i. 216; on the Christian law, i. 289; on the grace of tears, i. 370; on fasting, i. 380, 381; their name for hypocrisy, i. 404; the lights of the Church, iii. 287.

Fear in the presence of angels a sign of our fallen nature, i. 67; drives the greater part of men, ii. 9; the bridle of nature, iii. 335, iv. 301; the ground of hope, iv. 301; of God and of the king consistent with each other, iv. 302, 304; a forcible reason for action, iv. 309; to be manifested in worship, iv. 380, v. 554; a motive to prayer, v. 353.

—— of God, how it is the whole duty of man, iii. 333; God to be feared for the evil we may expect from Him, iii. 333; for His power and His justice, iii. 334; a bridle to our nature, iii. 335; the beginning of wisdom, iii. 335, 336; has place under the New Testament, iii. 335, 336, iv. 381; tempers our faith, awakens our carefulness, iii. 336; enjoined by our

Lord himself, iii. 336, 337; acceptable with God, iii. 337; if true, shows itself in righteousness, iii. 338; a sure protection to kings, iv. 303.

Feasts of dedication seasons of joy, ii. 360.

Feed my sheep, this text does not sanction the murder of kings, iv. 161.

Felix, an instance of procrastination, iii. 198.

Fellowship of the Apostles, its benefits, v. 62.

Fifty, the number both of Jubilee and Pentecost, iii. 282.

Finding, joy of, follows care in seeking, iv. 82.

Fire, implies zeal, iii. 124; type of the Holy Ghost, iii. 124, 125.

First-fruits, Christ our, ii. 208, 211, 212; the mode in which they were offered, ii. 212, 213; Easter-day the day of, ii. 212, 213, 219; the pledge of other fruits to come, ii. 212.

Flax, smoking, a remainder of the Spirit, iii. 125.

Flesh, God manifested in, i. 36; manifestation of Christ's in Holy Communion, i. 43; expresses the basest part of man, i. 89; Hebrew word for, the same as for good tidings, i. 89; the Word 'made flesh' refutes the heresies of Manichæus, Cerinthus, Valentinus, Nestorius, Eutyches, i. 90; its vileness and unworthiness taken by Christ, i. 92; our, in Christ, adored by the angels, i. 98; the Sacrament of the Lord's Supper the antitype of His, i. 100; the same that cleansed, now sits on the throne to purge and to exalt, i. 116.

—— will have its part in the resurrection, ii. 262; as having had part in the sufferings of this world, ii. 263; the same will rise, ii. 263; to be exalted by the Spirit, ii. 313; why the Holy Ghost said to be poured on the flesh, not on the spirit, iii. 308, 309; to show that it was through Christ's flesh that grace came to us, iii. 308.

—— we bestow too much care on it, v. 427.

Flowers, a type of our fading state, ii. 378.

Foot, used of God, indicates His presence, v. 213.

Foresight required on our part to further God's providence, iv. 68.

Forgiveness, prayer for, enjoined on all, iii. 153; a help to prayer, v. 341; granted to man only, v. 426; must be asked for others as well as for ourselves, v. 428; given daily on repentance, v. 430; depends on our forgiving our neighbours, v. 430—434, 436, 437; should make us watchful, v. 442, 443; the difference between God's and ours, v. 434; the price we would willingly pay for it, v. 435; our forgiveness of others a token that we are forgiven, v. 436, 437; without forgetfulness only a half-forgiveness, v. 438; the highest kind of mercy, v. 439.

Fornication a special cause of God's wrath, v. 227.

Foster-fathers, kings so called, v. 180.

Foundation, in what sense good works are, v. 48, 49; the next world a firm one, v. 49, 50.

Frankfort, Council of. See *Council of Frankfort.*

Frank-almoigne, riches given by God in this tenure, v. 29.

Friend, a great grief to lose one, iii. 164.

Frugality, should be joined with liberality, ii. 42.

G.

Gabbatha without, Golgotha within, ii. 305.

Galilee, fittest place for Christ to appear in after His resurrection, ii. 234; the meaning of the word, ii. 234; a type of heaven, ii. 236; and of spiritual change, ii. 237.

Gangra, Council of. See *Council of Gangra.*

Garden, a fit place for the resurrection, ii. 231.

Gardener, why Christ appeared in this form to Mary Magdalene, iii. 15.

Garnet, Henry, counted a martyr by the Romanists, iv. 146, 303, 315; the miracle of his straw alluded to, iv. 315; encouraged the Gunpowder Plot, iv. 392.

Gaulonites, maintainers of the liberties of the Jews, v. 128.

Gelasius considered the Holy Eucharist a sign of the hypostatical union, i. 281.

Generation, our natural, of little profit without our regeneration, ii. 371.

Gentiles, types and prophecies of their call, i. 239—242.

Gerizim, we must leap into, creep into Ebal, (Hebrew proverb,) iv. 9.

Germany, Council of. See *Council of Germany.*

Ghost, Holy, uses no waste words, iii. 84; sealed all Christ's promises, iii. 108; the earnest of all that Christ has done for us, iii. 108; His descent a mystery of godliness, iii. 109; fulfilled the promises of the New Testament, iii. 109; the complement of the Gospel, iii. 109; was manifested at Pentecost to the outward senses, iii. 110, 115, 116, 131, 147; why manifested at that time, iii. 110; the disciples prepared to receive Him by their unity, in mind and in place, iii. 112; the essential bond of unity in the Trinity, iii. 113, 147, 238; and of God with man in Christ, iii. 113, 147; will enter only where there is unity, iii. 112, 113, 238; sometimes appears visibly, sometimes known only by His outward effects, iii. 115; why He descended sensibly at Pentecost, iii. 116; sounded forth in all ages of the world, iii. 116; compared to the wind, iii. 117—120; the heart of the Church, iii. 124; abode, not merely lighted, on Christ, iii. 126; He is a constant Spirit, iii. 126; His visible coming not to be looked for again, iii. 127; to be obtained by prayer, preaching, and the sacraments, iii. 127, 128; more surely if we use all three, iii. 128; the blessings of His coming, iii. 128.

Ghost, Holy, the true canonizer of all saints, iii. 130; Whit-Sunday His special day, iii. 130; no speaking of Him without His aid, iii. 131; begins inwardly, works outwardly, iii. 132; differs from men's fancies and humours, iii. 132, 133; characters by which He is to be discerned, iii. 133; fills us not by His Person, but by His gifts, iii. 134; two kinds of gifts, ordinary and supernatural, iii. 134, 135; many in number, iii. 134; divers measures of the Spirit, iii. 135; at Pentecost increased His old gifts and gave new ones, iii. 135; gave the disciples then as much as they could require, iii. 136; gave them courage, language, discretion, learning, iii. 137—140; gives learned speech, not impetuous action, iii. 141; to be obtained by spiritual means and by bodily signs, iii. 143.

———— promised by Christ, iii. 145; under what circumstances, iii. 146; a high honour to Him, iii. 145; the Alpha and Omega of all our festivals, iii. 145; descended on the blessed Virgin, iii. 146; why spoken of as 'the Comforter,' iii. 146, 155—157; given in measure to all but Christ, iii. 154; promised more abundantly to those who use their present gifts, iii. 154; is manifold in His graces, iii. 155; many titles given Him, iii. 155—157; may be had in some of His graces, if not in all, iii. 155; proceeds from both the Father and the Son, iii. 155, 156; equal to them both, iii. 156; comes in His various graces according to our needs, iii. 157; appears in fire to give warmth, in tongues as instruments of consolation, iii. 157; administered great comfort to the Apostles, iii. 157; frames our petitions and witnesses with our spirit, iii. 158; an ever abiding Comforter, iii. 159, 160; superior to earthly comforters, iii. 159, 160.

Ghost, Holy, the great loss of His not coming, iii. 169; present at the creation and at the regeneration of the world, iii. 169; came to complete the work of man's salvation, iii. 169; gives investiture to Christian privileges, iii. 170; and power to Christian ordinances, iii. 170; His coming ends our solemnities, iii. 170; no incompatibility between Him and Christ, iii. 171; was manifested as God after Christ's departure, iii. 171; if Christ had not gone away first, His sending would have been ascribed to the Father alone, iii. 171; more fit than Christ to aid the Apostles in their work, iii. 172; manifested at first visibly, now invisibly, iii. 174; is a Comforter as being true and holy, iii. 175; His various uses, iii. 176; as also His types, iii. 176; and His names, iii. 176; He is our reprover as well as our counsellor, iii. 177; and so in the end our Comforter, iii. 177; should be ever called in to our aid, iii. 177; the time of His coming at Pentecost reads useful lessons, iii. 178; takes of Christ's and gives to us in the holy Sacrament, iii. 179.

———— not conferred by John's Baptism, iii. 181, 182; the special importance of receiving Him, iii. 182, 190; Baptism the way to do so, iii. 183; His Divinity denied by modern heretics, iii. 183; spoken of at the creation, under the law, in the Psalms and in the Prophets, iii. 184; at Christ's Conception and Baptism, iii. 184; frequently in the Acts of the Apostles, iii. 184; specially at our Baptism, iii. 184, 185; His name used in doxology and benediction, iii. 185, 186, 206; is God, since we are baptized into His name, believe in Him, give Him glory, gain from Him blessing, iii. 186, 187; personal acts ascribed to Him, iii. 188; yet He is not a person of or from Himself, iii. 188; as indicated by the very word 'Spirit,' iii. 188; shown to proceed both from the Father and the Son, iii. 188; yet not by generation, but emission, iii. 189; without Him we have not the life of grace, iii. 190; if not received, the Evil Spirit will enter in, iii. 191; in receiving Him we receive all that we need, iii. 191; the work of regeneration, confirmation, renewal, His only, iii. 191; gives life to Christian ordinances, iii. 192; how we know that we have received Him, iii. 192, 193; changes corrupt into clean conversation, iii. 193; makes active in good works, iii. 193; work natural to Him, iii. 194; teaches us to abstain from sin from a regard to God, iii. 195, 196; how we must prepare ourselves to receive Him, iii. 196; obstacles to His reception, iii. 196, 197; means to receive Him, iii. 198—200.

Ghost, Holy, not to be grieved, iii. 201, 206; for the sake of His Person and of His benefits, iii. 202, 203; spoken of as emphatically 'the' Spirit, iii. 202; uncreated, and of the substance of God, iii. 204; like the wind, His substance unseen, power manifest, iii. 204, 205; His effects great, not only at Pentecost, but throughout the heathen world, iii. 205; the source of all graces, specially of holiness, iii. 205, 206; so proclaimed by the seraphim, iii. 206; has manifold names to show His manifold gifts, iii. 206, 207; wrought in Bezaleel and the seventy elders, iii. 207; *Spiritus reflans, afflans*, and *difflans*, iii. 207; 'sealing' is His work, iii. 208, 211; wishes to plant His seal upon the tongue, iii. 215; we should be willing for Him to seal us, iii. 216; prepare ourselves for it, iii. 217; after sealing, His seal not to be broken, iii. 217; or another stamped upon it, iii. 217; if we grieve Him, Satan will enter in, iii. 218; seals by means of Sacraments, iii. 219.

———— the Lord God who was to dwell among men (Ps. lxviii. 18), iii. 221; the true ark of God's presence, iii. 237; we should prepare Him a resting place, iii. 237; the nature of His resting place, iii. 237; should treat Him well when there, iii. 237, 238; compared to Aaron's ointment and the dew of Hermon, iii. 238; will not dwell with disunion, iii. 238.

———— His descent on Christ and on the Apostles compared, iii. 241, 242; works invisibly in Baptism, iii. 249; making it of spiritual value, iii. 249; fit to be the author of regeneration as of creation, iii. 250; giver of natural and of spiritual life, iii. 250; by lighting on Christ shows that He was to abide with men, iii. 251; and that His Baptism was to be with power, iii. 251; came in the form of a bird to show the quickness of His working, iii. 251; why in the form of a dove, iii. 251—253; works in Christians the qualities indicated by the dove, iii. 253; the means of intercourse between Christ in Jordan and the Father in heaven, iii. 257; applies Christ's blood one way in Baptism, and another way in the Communion, iii. 260.

Ghost, Holy, given first by the breath of Christ, afterwards in tongues and a mighty wind, iii. 262; most fitly comes as a breath (*spiritus a spiro*), iii. 262, 265; the very breath (*flamen*) proceeding from the Father and the Son, iii. 262; when breathed, did not merely light upon, but passed into the Apostles, iii. 262; His procession from Christ shown by the words 'Receive ye the Holy Ghost,' iii. 264; sent from the Father as a dove, from the Son as breath, from both as cloven tongues, iii. 264; most properly proceeds from Christ in the remission of sins, iii. 265; gives the life of grace, iii. 266; and the speech of grace, iii. 266; as necessary for man as his own breath, iii. 267; gentle in His operations, iii. 267; soon converted the world to be Christian, iii. 271, 272; to be received, not assumed, iii. 272; distinguished from the spirit of the world, iii. 275; to be sought in the Church, not in the Court, iii. 276; how to distinguish the Holy Ghost, iii. 276; His manifold operations, iii. 276; can be received savingly by all who partake of Christ's Body and Blood, iii. 278, 279; this better than the grace of ordination, iii. 279; proceeds from both the Father and the Son, iii. 284; given by the Son as God, received as man, iii. 284; anointed Christ at His conception, iii. 285; sent Him at His Baptism, iii. 286; sends us, as well as anoints, iii. 289; how received in Holy Orders, iii. 289.

———— the author of life and of prophecy, iii. 304; pouring out of, implies a distinction of persons, iii. 304; and His Godhead, iii. 305; this phrase very suitable for the occasion (Acts ii.), iii. 305; to be understood of the gifts of the Spirit, iii. 305; this phrase further explained, iii. 306;

poured out by Christ, at the will of the Father, iii. 307 ; the whole Trinity thus set forth, iii. 307; poured out from the human nature of Christ upon us, iii. 307, 308; on all flesh, iii. 308, 310; His grace given on us in Baptism, in us in the Eucharist, iii. 309; is from without, not from within us, iii. 309; from above, to initiate us, and teach us submission, iii. 309; poured as a balm to heal our flesh, iii. 311; saves the flesh by spiritualizing it, iii. 311; His gifts various, iii. 314.

Ghost, Holy, His second solemn coming at the call of Cornelius, iii. 323; and on the Gentiles, iii. 324.

—— the complement of the Gospel, iii. 345 ; witnesses for Christ, iii. 353, 354; to His conception and anointing, iii. 354 ; the chief witness both in heaven and in earth, iii. 355 ; gives effect to the other two witnesses, iii. 355, 356; the 'middle term' between God and man, iii. 355; gives a true testimony, iii. 356 ; His truth to be discerned by holy desires, iii. 356 ; and by newness of life, iii. 357; purity of speech, iii. 358; vigour of action, iii. 358; gives seizin of our inheritance, iii. 360.

—— the gift of gifts, iii. 361, 362, 367; many gifts in one, iii. 362; the gift and the giver both, iii. 362.

—— came to establish order in the Church, iii. 378 ; gives the power of working, iii. 381; the essential love of the Father and of the Son, iii. 382 ; the oneness of, contrary to Polytheism, iii. 385 ; without Him our own industry unavailing, iii. 385 ; the sacred breath of Father and Son, iii. 390.

—— the most perfect gift bestowed on man, v. 316 ; compared to light, v. 317 ; gives power to prayer, v. 332, 338, *seq. ;* makes our prayers fervent, v. 336, 337; assures us of adoption and help, v. 333, 334 ; intercedes for us by giving us power to intercede, v. 337 ; makes us attentive in prayer, v. 338 ; works with us, does not take the work out of our hands, v. 341 ; works both on our will and understanding, v. 351; sheds in our hearts the love of good, v. 352.

—— the essential love of God, v. 459 ; works in us God's goodness, v. 459.

—— led Christ to temptation, v. 481, 483 ; no idle spectator of our trials, v. 485 ; turns temptations to our profit, v. 485.

Gideon was not refused a sign, ii. 386.

Gifts of the Holy Spirit, to be filled with them is to be filled with the Holy Spirit, iii. 134 ; not so abundant now as in earlier times, iii. 136 ; why given abundantly at Pentecost, iii. 136.

—— the nature of those given by Christ at His ascension, iii. 233 ; of holiday gifts a working-day account to be given, iii. 234 ; given to each man according to his need, iii. 235 ; the word teaches us that we have nothing of our own, iii. 364, 365, 375, 384 ; some are good, others perfect, iii. 367, 375 ; all from God, iii. 367, 368, 375 ; not from ourselves, iii. 368, 369, 375 ; come not by chance, but by the will of the Sender, iii. 369, 375.

—— signify inward qualifying for an office, iii. 380; their number, iii. 380 ; come from the Spirit, iii. 381 ; to neglect using them an offence to the Spirit, iii. 383, 394 ; come before a calling, iii. 383 ; though bestowed, yet to be sought for, iii. 385 ; divers, from one Spirit, iii. 385 ; different to different persons, iii. 386 ; like worldly gifts, iii. 386 ; in kind and degree, iii. 386 ; divided orderly, not scattered at random, iii. 388 ; gifts and callings are relative, iii. 393, 394, 396 ; possession of, cannot make a true calling, iii. 396 ; not to be buried, iii. 396 ; to be manifested, iii. 397, 398 ; for edification, and not for vain-glory, iii. 398, 399.

—— God's, are grounds of pride to sinful man, v. 10 ; why Christian virtues so called, v. 312 ; all come from God, v. 312, 313; will have to be accounted for, v. 319 ; not to be boasted of, v. 319 ; what gifts we should seek from God, v. 377.

Giving, cheerful, is a fair seed-time, v. 40 ; there is in it an interchange of the giver's grace and the receiver's prayer, iv. 40.

Glory of transfiguration, i. 95 ; of Moses' and of S. Stephen's countenance compared with our Lord's, i. 95 ; of our Lord's miracles, i. 95 ; of the Word of Life witnessed by many, i. 95 ; His, full of grace, i. 96 ; and humility, united by the incarnation, i. 212 ; belongs not to man, i. 224 ; not coveted by God, i. 224 ; lost by seeking, i. 226 ; future, the light of, iii. 372 ; due to God, not to man, v. 387.

Gluttony, a sin of the times, i. 444 ; v. 493.

Gnostics, made knowledge everything, i. 193 ; their origin and errors, v. 58

God, great condescension of, in sending His Son, i. 50 ; no absolute necessity that He should send Him, i. 51 ; made man to satisfy God, i. 81 ; the leaving Him a great evil, the being with Him a great good, i. 145; we left Him, He sought us, i. 148; more glorified by men and angels together, than by either alone, i. 220, 221 ; God and the holy angels have peace, i. 223 ; desires not glory, i. 224 ; receives true glory only from the humble man, i. 229 ; sought by us in times of affliction, i. 307, 308 ; instances of such seeking, i. 310 ; our seeking too commonly like that of Pilate, i. 312 ; to be sought for Himself, i. 313; not always to be found, i. 314, 319 ; His passionate entreaties to men, i. 340, 341, 354.

—— His right hand a hand of power, ii. 16 ; a God of vengeance to His enemies, ii. 16 ; of comfort to His people, ii. 17 ; Moses and Aaron God's hands, ii. 17, 29, 30 ; and afterwards, other rulers, ii. 18 ; He guides these hands, ii. 19 ; the Head of every government, ii. 18 ; the King of all the earth, ii. 19 ; King of kings, ii. 19 ; a ground of comfort and of fear, ii. 19, 20 ; gives nations kings according to their desert, ii. 20 ; the Standard-bearer and Counsellor of His people, ii. 22 ; leads them into all truth, ii. 22 ; the nature of His leading, ii. 22, 23 ; the end of it, ii. 24, 25 ; His word the load-star, ii. 23 ; He the Herdsman, ii. 23 ; the true Shepherd, ii. 23 ; His hands of two kinds, ii. 30.

—— sight of, our chief good, ii. 261 ; seen by Moses, ii. 261, 262 ; the chief Builder, ii. 278.

—— His wrath the cause of Christ's death, ii. 149 ; Christ stepped between it and us, ii. 150 ; His wrath compared to a tempest, ii. 394 ; could not be appeased but by Christ's death, ii. 395; poured forth on sin, ii. 395.

—— His mercy the moving cause of all our spiritual blessings, ii. 366, 369, 370 ; to be blessed by us for all our blessings, ii. 366, 367; the Father who begat us in two senses, ii. 366 ; He blesses us in one way, we Him in another, ii. 367 ; values our wishes for good, ii. 367 ; how we can wish well to His Name, Word, and Person, ii. 368 ; spoken of in the New Testament as the Father of our Lord Jesus Christ, ii. 368 ; this His best title, ii. 369; sets forth the channel of all our blessings, ii. 370.

God, His secret decrees not to be searched into, iii. 32.

—— the Father of all Christians by Christ's Ascension, iii. 51, 53--55 ; ready to receive us to grace and to glory, iii. 51 ; called 'Lord' in the Law, 'Father' in the Gospel, iii. 52 ; Father, in the highest sense, iii. 52 ; Father shows His love, God His power, iii. 53.

—— His titles vary according to His acts, iii. 84 ; why termed the God of Peace, iii. 84; there may be some doubt of His peace, none of His power, iii. 85; if we have His peace, we shall be sure of His power in our behalf, iii. 85 ; took this title since Christ's resurrection, iii. 85 ; as God of Hosts brought Christ to the dead, as God of Peace raised Him up, iii. 89; His will that we do good works, iii. 94 ; can alone fit us to do them, iii. 96 ; His will to be done as well as learned, iii. 97 ; works by outward means and by inward grace, iii. 98; patiently waits for our conversion, iii. 115; will come to us if we wait for Him, iii. 115.

—— gives a day's wages for an hour's work, iii. 153 ; rewards out of His bounty, iii. 153, 154 ; gives in answer to Christ's prayer, iii. 154.

—— the Holy Ghost shown to be, iii. 186, 187 ; God alone believed in and worshipped, iii. 187 ; unity of, shown by words of Baptism, iii. 187.

—— human passions ascribed to Him, iii. 213 ; in accommodation to our infirmity, iii. 214 ; we should endeavour to have in ourselves the same affections against sin, iii. 214.

—— did not dwell among men till Christ's Ascension, iii. 236 ; only visited them, iii. 236; dwells now with us in the Holy Communion, iii. 239.

—— provides religious men of every age with needful means of salvation, iii. 325, 326 ; how to be understood that He is no respecter of persons, iii. 330, 331 ; in what sense to be feared, iii. 333 ; by counting men worthy, makes them worthy, iii. 341.

—— the Author of all good, iii. 363 ; of less as well as of greater grace, iii. 367, 368 ; as well as the Maker of the less and greater animals, iii. 368 ; to be discerned in small things, if we would see Him in greater, iii. 368 ; why spoken of as the Father of Lights, iii. 369, 370, 372 ; is unchanging, iii. 374 ; if He seems to change, the change is in ourselves, iii. 374 ; His wisdom never wanting, and never lavish, iii. 383.

God, His Providence does not work by miracle, iv. 68.

—— His being said to 'seek for' kings shows the value He sets on them, iv. 81; His hand signifies His ordinary, His arm His special providence, iv. 86, 87; both stretched over kings, iv. 90, 91; smites rebels, iv. 92; plagues them both in this and the next world, iv. 93.

—— supplies our wants by anticipation, iv. 110; with the blessing of goodness, iv. 111; appointing and deposing of kings both come from Him, iv. 114, 115; gives them their lives as well as their crowns, iv. 115; heaped great blessings on David, iv. 116, 117; His providence in bringing treachery to light, iv. 138, 139.

—— in leaving us to ourselves, does not give leave to do evil, iv. 162; smites our hearts, that they may smite us, iv. 165, 166.

—— must be seen in small things as well as great, iv. 208; His ordinary works seem small, because usual, iv. 208; His miracles no more marvellous than His ordinary works, iv. 208; salvation, prosperity, and blessing, are from Him, iv. 220; His mercies numerous, iv. 271; most tender, iv. 272; unfailing, iv. 273; how to be acknowledged, iv. 274—276.

—— the source of kingly power, iv. 279—281; His name joined with that of kings, iv. 300; to be feared, iv. 301; His fear the surest protection of kings, iv. 303.

—— reasons for His being exalted, iv. 319; His mercies and His works compared, iv. 320; the nature of His mercies, iv. 322; their extent, iv. 323; speaks to men in human language, iv. 322; has care for His lesser, as well as His greater works, iv. 325; His mercy, the maker and preserver of all things, iv. 326, 327; is greater than His judgment, iv. 328; and than our sins, iv. 328; more able to save than Satan to destroy, iv. 329; greater to man than to the rest of His works, iv. 330; specially to Christians, iv. 331; abhors cruelty, iv. 336; shows His mercy in punishing it, iv. 337; His goodness to this land, iv. 332, 339; controls the issues of all attempts, iv. 350.

—— the true nature of His service, iv. 372, seq.; is displeased with irreverence in worship, iv. 375; His name too often used irreverently, iv. 378.

God, thought of His presence a cure for hypocrisy, iv. 381.

—— makes heirs, v. 24; alone to be trusted in, v. 27; both gives and takes away riches, v. 28; gives all our enjoyments, v. 29; not only necessities, but luxuries, v. 30; can change plenty into want, v. 30; upbraids not when He gives, v. 31; why He gives riches, v. 34; looks for more good deeds from the rich, v. 39.

—— makes His ministers workers together with Him, v. 93; delights in being called the Lord our Righteousness, v. 104, 105; bears not His name for nought, v. 125; His name to be invoked, v. 107; communicates some of His names to men, v. 109.

—— duties to Him and Cæsar not incompatible, v. 130, 131; the duties due to each distinguished, v. 133, 135.

—— a title applied to kings, v. 180; for what reasons, v. 206; no unmeaning term, v. 206; gradations in this honour, v. 207.

—— is on the side of right, v. 212; in danger when that is in danger, v. 212; is said to 'stand' on account of His stability, v. 212, and of His presence, v. 213; His attention, v. 214, and perseverance, v. 214; has no bodily members, v. 213; His glory specially manifested in the congregation, v. 214; the Judge of judges themselves, v. 215; what to be understood by His judging 'in the midst,' v. 216; we must believe in His presence, v. 217, 218, 222; should keep Him by us by unity, truth, and sincerity, v. 219, 220; why He is said to be weary, to grieve, and repent, v. 220, 221.

—— His anger the cause of plagues, v. 226; caused by sin, v. 227; to be worshipped with reverence and decency, v. 231, 232.

—— a general deliverer, v. 237; especially of kings, v. 237, 238, 249; for the good of their people, v. 244; throws round them the safeguard of His word, v. 245; and His special providence, v. 246; overthrows traitors, v. 247.

—— turns men's evil purposes to good, v. 303; the source of true strength, v. 303; begins and carries it on, v. 304; regards and values His own work in us, v. 309; nothing but good comes from Him, v. 311, 312; this should kindle our love, v. 312; every perfect thing from Him, v. 314; His goodness seen in this world, as well as in the next, v. 314; bestows blessings according to His wisdom, v. 316. *God*, why called 'Father of Lights,' v. 316; gives light without heat, v. 318; the lights He kindles within us, v. 319; will call us to account for His gifts, v. 319; exhorts us to pray to Him, v. 322; gives what we ask for, v. 322; even though we are unworthy, v. 322; gives largely, v. 322.

—— invites us all to speak to Him, v. 362; a great blessing looked for by our calling on Him as 'Father,' v. 362, 391; perfect in goodness and power, v. 363; by being called 'Father,' teaches us the love due to Him, v. 363; 'our Father,' our love to our neighbour, v. 364, 369, 370; our approaching near to Him a proof of our Christian dignity, v. 365; in what senses He is our Father, v. 365, 366; unchangeable in love, v. 366, 374; even in chastisement, v. 367; when spoken of as ' in heaven,' we learn His power, v. 372, 373; His power and presence not confined to one place, v. 373; His majesty and mercy both to be considered, v. 374; teaches us thereby to look for heavenly things, v. 375—377, 391; we should long to behold Him, v. 378.

—— His name to be sanctified, v. 381; cannot be prayed to aright, unless His name be honoured, v. 382; needs nothing at our hands, but claims this as His due honour, v. 382, 383; sets the hallowing of His name before His kingdom, v. 382; His name impressed on His Word, Sacraments, &c., v. 384; how His name is to be hallowed, v. 385—387; all glory to be ascribed to Him, v. 387; to be made our fear, v. 388; to be ever blessed, v. 388, 389; His kingdom comes, as His name is sanctified, v. 389, 393; the first blessing we should ask for, v. 390; gives not His glory to another, v. 391; on the coming of His kingdom He will punish the ungodly, v. 395.

—— His will either revealed or secret, v. 397, 398; His secret will concerns not us, v. 397; is unsearchable, v. 398; His revealed will is what is to be regarded, v. 397, 398; we may dissent from His secret will without doing wrong, v. 399; His revealed will to be submitted to, even when it crosses ours, v. 399, 400, 404; is our sanctification, v. 400; He gives us both the will and power to do right, v. 403; His goodness in teaching us to pray for forgiveness, v. 425;

accepts our stubble for His pearls, v. 435.

God the Giver of all blessings, v. 416; in what ways He gives us bread, v. 417.

—— shows mercy to His enemies, v. 436; in what way He is said to tempt us, v. 443, 493, 533; tries us for our good, v. 443, 444, 493; how He suffers us to be led into temptation, v. 446; is both a Giver and a Saviour, (δωτήρ and σωτήρ,) v. 450; keeps us out of temptation, or delivers us under it, v. 451; our great Deliverer from Satan's bondage, v. 453; willing as a Father, powerful as a King, to supply our wants, v. 458, 459, 463, 472; the glory we ascribe to Him a reason why He should relieve our wants, v. 461; it is His nature to be gracious, v. 461; will help us, not for our deserts, but for His name's sake, v. 461, 462; and for His covenant, v. 462; reasons in His nature why He should help us, v. 462; to be loved as a Father, feared as a King, v. 464; His ministers to be reverenced, v. 464; has power of grace to strengthen, of might to punish, v. 464, 465; reserves His glory to Himself, v. 465; differs from earthly kings and fathers, v. 465.

—— produces great results by small means, v. 508; works sometimes without means, v. 509; works sometimes by unlikely means, v. 509; gives both natural and supernatural life, v. 509, 510; always provides for the wants of His people, v. 510; His blessing does not accompany unlawful ways of gain, v. 511; His mercy blended with judgment, v. 523; not to be abused, v. 534; first humbles, then exalts, v. 520; how He can be tempted, v. 528, *seq.;* to be entirely depended on in time of need, v. 529; will not help us if we neglect means, v. 530, 532; knows what we are doing, even when He does not reprove us, v. 533; must not be treated too familiarly, v. 533; not to be trifled with, v. 534; nor to be presumed on, v. 534, 535; rewards better than Satan, v. 547; alone to be worshipped and served, v. 553, *seq.*

—— well pleased with almsgiving, v. 281, contrition, and devotion, v. 281, 282; His rewards exceed our highest deserts, v. 283; cannot be benefited by our good, nor injured by our evil deeds, v. 284; accepts a man's person first, and then his doings, v. 284. (*From Bishop Buckeridge's Funeral Sermon.*)

Godhead, dwelt in Christ by personal union, ii. 348.

Godliness, the Word in the flesh, the mystery of, v. 195.

―――― consists not in mere hearing of sermons, v. 187; to think so, a delusion, v. 187; to do the Word is the mystery of, v. 195.

Gomorrah, grapes of, ii. 62.

Good, of every kind comes from God, iii. 363; even from His very nature, iii. 373; S. Augustine's definition of, v. 35; we shall have to answer for our doing it, v. 36; the power of beginning, completing, thinking, speaking of, and understanding it, is of God, v. 304, 305; is from us, but not of us, v. 307, 308; to be ascribed to grace, v. 308; comes from God, v. 311, 312; comes not by chance, v. 316.

Good, the chief, ancient views upon, and the Truth, i. 219.

Goodness, is true greatness, iii. 92.

―――― an accident with man, of the essence of God, v. 269, 270; all goodness in the creation comes from God, v. 270; is diffusive towards man, and unites us to God, v. 271. (*From Bishop Buckeridge's Funeral Sermon.*)

Good news, its reviving power, iii. 295.

Goods of this world to be valued, because we can do good with them, v. 314, 315; the heathen questioned their goodness, v. 314.

―――― our, belong, strictly speaking, to the poor, v. 271; given to the poor, are well laid out, v. 278, 279; become thus heavenly riches, v. 279. (*From Bishop Buckeridge's Funeral Sermon.*)

Good works, to do them is not mere abstinence from evil, v. 34; good works, not good words, to be regarded, v. 37; to be done readily, v. 39; to the church, v. 41; to the poor, v. 43; in what sense a foundation, v. 48, 49.

Gospel, the, for the day, tells us what was done for us, ii. 309; addressed to all classes, including the poor, iii. 290; the nature of its proclamation, iii. 296, 297; comes with a ransom in one hand, and the keys of death in the other, iii. 296; one of God's lights, iii. 372.

Government, rod of, miraculous, ii. 20; why compared to bands, ii. 30, 31; in a well ordered, the Holy Ghost bestows gifts, Christ assigns places, God effects the work, iii. 379.

Governors, their constant anxiety, ii. 20, 21; given special strength to bear it, ii. 21; their power given from above, ii. 21, 22; why called God's hands, ii. 31; they must be guided by God, ii. 31, and active, ii. 31.

Gowries, conspiracy of, iv. 4, 5; compared to Absalom, iv. 20, 21, and to Abishai, iv. 40, 41; sons of wickedness, iv. 96; frustrated by God, iv. 96; compared to Bigthan and Teresh, iv. 148; contrasted with David, and David's men, iv. 177, 178; compared to Simeon and Levi, iv. 198, 199.

Grace, without truth, nothing, i. 96; we were out of, and without it, before the Incarnation, i. 96; opposed to the law, i. 96; and Truth, met together in the Incarnation, i. 97; wherein our Lord's fulness of, differed from that of His blessed mother and S. Stephen, i. 97; the sacrament of the Lord's Supper the conduit-pipe of, i. 100; active and passive, iii. 151; v. 403; active, helps us to keep the Commandments, iii. 151; v. 403; passive, abates the rigour of our account, iii. 151; v. 403; court of, is higher than the court of justice, iii. 152; sorrow for sin is there accepted, iii. 153; the gift of, the gift of gifts, iii. 207; different varieties of, reproving, guiding, quickening, teaching, &c., iii. 207; the very breath of the Holy Spirit, iii. 219; applied to both the understanding and the affections, iii. 219; not to be received in vain, or neglected, iii. 220; *gratis data* and *gratum faciens* distinguished, iii. 263, 276, 318; iv. 56, 57; of Apostleship, what is its nature, iii. 277; the grace of their spiritual function, not inward holiness, iii. 277; added to perfect both nature and the law, iii. 366; acts both on the understanding and the will, iii. 367; to grow therein, the perfection of this life, iii. 367; the breath of the Spirit, iii. 367; gives inward light, iii. 372; not tied to means, v. 92, 507; perfects nature, v. 306, 315; takes away sin, and bestows inherent virtue, v. 315; is manifold, v. 318; being asked for, must be used, v. 329; needed to do God's will, v. 425; hindered by sin, v. 425; a sovereign balm, v. 507.

Grapes, in reading we gather, by study we press them, iii. 77.

Gratian summoned a Council at Thessalonica, v. 161.

Grave, made by Christ a womb for our second birth, ii. 399; blessed by Christ, iii. 9; made a place for angels,

iii. 9, and of rest in hope, iii. 10; called an assembly, v. 213.

Graving, how inscriptions graven among the Hebrews, ii. 255.

Gregory, S., the Great, on the return we should make for grace, i. 15; terms love a son's motive, i. 301; on the words, 'They have their reward,' i. 415; feared he had 'received his good things' on becoming pope, ii. 88; explains the words, 'Touch me not,' as teaching that there was no leisure for S. Mary Magdalene so to do, iii. 35; would have no hand in any man's blood, iii. 254 ; iv. 355; compared with Gregory VII., iii. 255; passages cited from him on the question of justification, v. 121.

—— *VII.* compared with S. Gregory the Great, iii. 255.

—— *S., Nazianzen,* on the honour due to Bethlehem, i. 162; his statement, that God and the angels know no discord, i. 225; calls rulers the images of God, compares them in their several orders to pictures of different sizes, ii. 31; once thought that a man by change of place could avoid temptations, v. 489.

—— *S., Nyssen,* mentions Eastertide, ii. 420.

—— *of Valentia,* owns that we cannot claim reward, except by Divine promise, v. 122.

Grief, in what sense ascribed to God, iii. 213, 214; v. 220.

—— the deepest least easily uttered, iii. 340.

Grieve, neither great nor good persons should be grieved, iii. 203, 212 ; the Holy Ghost not to be grieved, iii. 201, 202, 206; this but a trifling request, iii. 203, 212, 213; we grieve Him specially by unholy language, ii. 215; in what sense grieving Him to be understood, iii. 213, 214; it is to cause Him to withdraw, as if in grief, iii. 214 ; we should be grieved with ourselves for sin, iii. 214, 215 ; should ever have a will not to grieve the Spirit, iii. 218.

Grotius, Hugo, patronized by Andrewes, v. 292. (*From Bishop Buckeridge's Funeral Sermon.*)

Groundsill of our nature our conception, healed by Christ's, i. 141.

Guides, the office of Christ's ministers to be, i. 170; we must not look for other, but only pray that these may lead us right, i. 170.

Gunpowder Treason, hypocritical fast before it, i. 408; wickedness of its plotters, iv. 210; from Satan, iv. 209, 210, 212; compared with instances of cruelty in Scripture, iv. 210; would have destroyed innocent and guilty together, contrary to Christ's rule, iv. 211; called 'the abomination of desolation,' iv. 211; kept secret under an oath, iv. 211, 265 ; known to, and justified by, the Jesuits, iv. 211 ; deliverance from it only from God, iv. 212—214, 268, *seq.;* and of His mercy, iv. 270; especially considering the then state of morals, iv. 270, 271; its marvellous discovery, iv. 215, 216; deliverance from, compared with Jews' restoration from captivity, iv. 235, *seq.,* 267; the plot compared with John's and James's wish to call fire from heaven, iv. 257, 258; the danger it caused, iv. 263, *seq.;* a mixing together of religion and sedition, iv. 308; suddenly detected, iv. 312 ; greatness of deliverance from, iv. 333, *seq.;* its great cruelty, iv. 334, 335 ; its failure compared to a fruitless childbirth, iv. 340, *seq.;* how disclosed, iv. 351; compared to shipwreck in the very harbour, iv. 352; why it was allowed to go so far, iv. 356, *seq.;* compared with Haman's plot, iv. 389; with Massacre of S. Bartholomew, iv. 393; how frustrated, iv. 395, *seq.*

Guntram summoned two Councils at Mâcon, v. 162.

H.

Hallelujah of early Christians, sounded as the sea, ii. 338.

Hallow, things perfectly hallowed under the law by water, blood, and oil, iii. 354 ; with God, means to make holy, with man, to account holy, v. 384 ; why applied to God's name, v. 385.

Haman endeavoured to bribe Ahasuerus, ii. 46; his cruelty and pride, iv. 392; his design frustrated, iv. 396; his ambition, v. 10.

Hand, and arm, signify different degrees of God's power, iv. 86, 87; signifies defensive power, iv. 97; follows the guidance of the eye, v. 174, 175.

—— spoken of God, indicates His power, v. 213.

Hands, holding up of, the posture of prayer, ii. 249.

—— often laid on for mischief, as well as for good, iv. 130, 131; not to be laid on kings, iv. 131.

Hands, laying on of, applied by many to the act of absolution, v. 97.
Hands of God, Moses and Aaron, ii. 17, 28, 29; His good and bad hands, ii. 30; God rules by their ministry, they by His authority, ii. 31 ; government, why compared to, ii. 30, 31; hands have strength and skill, ii. 32; a type of the equality of ecclesiastical and civil power, ii. 33; neither superfluous, ii. 33; need each other's aid, ii. 35.
Head of the Corner, Christ so called, as joining many in one, ii. 279.
Hearing of the Spirit outward, receiving inward, iii. 200; cannot stand in the place of doing, v. 187—189, 194; not to be confounded with it, v. 199; without doing, a self-deception, v. 196 —198, 200; the key to knowledge, v. 190.
Heart, of wax, what meant by, ii. 5; the place of life and warmth, iii. 124; God's peculiar part of man, iv. 381.
Hearts, how they can be broken, iii. 291; by captivity to sin, iii. 292—294; how to be cured, iii. 295, *seq.;* sorrow of, is overpowering, iii. 291; Christ the Physician of, iii. 291, 293; if hardened, are beyond His cure, iii. 294; broken by a sense of sin, iii. 294; must be broken off from sin, iii. 295; when they smite us, are first smitten by God, iv. 165, 166; their blow the greatest blow of all, iv. 166.
Heathen writers frequently quoted by the Fathers, v. 62.
Heaven, we sit there in Christ, i. 115; open at Christ's prayer, at His Baptism, iii. 249, to show that Baptism is from heaven, not of men, iii. 250, and gives right to enter heaven, iii. 250; the place where God manifests His power, v. 372; His stately dwelling, v. 373 ; our affections to be lifted up to it, v. 376, 391; heavenly things to be sought, v. 376—379; we are its citizens, v. 379; must live by its laws, v. 380.
Heavens, the three, the blessings that come from them severally, v. 375 ; how God's will done in each of them, v. 406, 407; especially in the highest, v. 407, 408.
Heir, Christ both born and made, i. 111 ; Christ made, for us, i. 111, 114.
Heirs, God makes, men make heritages, v. 24.
Hell, the fear of, moves us to repentance, not the loss of heaven, i. 425 ; the fire of, i. 426; full of good purposes, iv. 358.
Henry III. of France murdered by James Clement, iv. 36, 65, 145 ; this approved of by Sixtus V., iv. 146.
Henry IV. of France murdered, May 1610, iv. 47, 65, 74, 145 ; his life previously attempted, iv. 166.
Heresies put an end to by Councils, v. 146. See *Arius, Cerinthus, Eutyches, Manichees, Nestorius, Pelagius, Valentinus.*
Heresy, does not unmake a king, iv. 57.
Heritages, men make, God makes heirs, v. 24.
Hermon, dew of, a type of the Holy Ghost, iii. 238.
Hero, his Pneumatica, iii. 274, 275.
Herod, did not give the true reason for wishing to find Christ, ii. 46; leaven of, ii. 305; courted popular favour, iii. 275.
Herodians, maintainers of royal power, v. 128.
Hezekiah, why he was not refused a sign, ii. 386.
Hilary, S., of Poictiers, on Christ not abhorring the Virgin's womb, i. 140.
Holiness, not our own, but by divine inspiration, iii. 190 ; to be gained by receiving the Holy Ghost, iii. 190 ; God's chief attribute, iii. 206 ; personal, not required to make us means of holiness in others, iii. 278 ; this position illustrated, iii. 278; includes our duty to God, iv. 372; how distinguished from righteousness, iv. 372, 373; to be exhibited in God's public service, iv. 374, *seq.;* no discharge from righteousness, iv. 379.
Holy days, why appointed, iv. 400 ; to be kept holy, as well as passed in relaxation, iv. 402.
Honour, its value above everything beside, ii. 172.
Hope, seasons labour, ii. 206 ; a Christian's, fails not in death, ii. 208 ; Christ risen, a Christian's, ii. 209.
—— the confidence of Job's, ii. 264, 265 ; the Hebrew word used to express it, ii. 266; he laid it up within him, ii. 267; such hope a ground of confidence, ii. 267.
—— expels fear, ii. 266; dwells not in the brain, but in the heart, ii. 268 ; in Christ, should lead to purification, ii. 269 ; a Christian's, a present blessing, ii. 365; a living, and not dead, ii. 375 ; compared to the blossom of a tree, ii. 365; worldly, a waking man's dream, ii. 373 ; has a reviving power, ii. 373, 374; at the time of death, ii. 374 ; from whence it gains its strength, ii. 374 ; we should take care to have it well placed, ii. 374, 375.

Horn of salvation, meaning of, iv. 368.
Hosius, Bishop of Cordova, held the Council of Elvira, and presided at the Council of Nice, v. 159; attended at Ariminum, v. 161.
Hour-glass, the length of a sermon, iii. 232.
Hours, fixed, to be appointed for prayer, v. 354.
Hucking, huxtering, v. 546.
Hugh of S. Victor, on mercy, i. 181; on confession, i. 190.
Humility of the Son of God in becoming a child of man, i. 29, 37, 38, 112; the title to grace, i. 161, 162; taught by the nativity, i. 205, 206; and glory, united by the Incarnation, i. 212; the Bethlehem of virtues, i. 238; the way to exaltation, ii. 342; to be learned from Christ, ii. 342.
Humours, not to be mistaken for the Spirit, iii. 132, 133; the different kinds of, iii. 133.
Hunter, snare of the, means secret dangers, v. 529.
Huntingdon, Henry, Earl of, Andrewes attended him into the North, v. 290. (*From Bp. Buckeridge's Funeral Sermon.*)
Hydroparastatæ, their heresy, iii. 350.
Hypocrisy, the fear of the charge of, deters men from fasting, i. 401; the Fathers' name for, i. 404; examples of, i. 407; a kind of leaven, ii. 305; artificial religion, iii. 194; cured by the thought of God's presence, iv. 381.
Hypocrite, meaning of, i. 406; Judas one, i. 407; a puppet of religion, iii. 274.

I.

Idol, wealth the idol of the worldly, v. 18.
Idolatry pollutes, sacrilege destroys, a temple, ii. 351.
Ignatius's, S., spurious epistle quoted, i. 392, 394.
Ignorance, sin of, i. 343; self-conceited, intoxicates the brain, iii. 314; involuntary, is pardoned, iii. 329; men's, of what is good for them, v. 336.
Imaginations, vain, set up by Satan, v. 55; worshipped, instead of the old images, v. 55, 179; inspired by Satan, wrought out by men, v. 55; both without and within the Church, v. 55—58; respecting repentance and faith, v. 58; things indifferent, v. 59; ceremonies, v. 60; the Apostles' fellowship, v. 62—66; the Eucharist, v. 67, 68; prayers, v. 68.

Immanuel, infers Jesus, i. 143; 'with us,' though not 'like us,' in sin, i. 146; 'with us,' full meaning of, i. 147.
Impatience, likely to lose God's gifts, iii. 114.
Importunity needful in prayer, v. 330, 331.
Imprecations, whether allowable, iv. 7, 8; sometimes quite proper, iv. 8; Scripture instances of, iv. 8; must be involuntary, iv. 9; and against God's enemies, iv. 9, 10, 13.
Incarnation, not an assumption of the person, but the nature of man, i. 8, 9, 89; the root of all conversion, which is a taking of individual man, i. 9; delivers us from death, i. 10; necessity of, i. 10; appropriated by the Holy Communion, i. 16; the double nature manifested all along in the acts of Christ, i. 22; no controversy about it in Andrewes's days, i. 35; S. Paul's charge to Timothy on the, i. 36; desire of, by man, i. 37; God's grace and love appear in, i. 40; a lesson of holiness, i. 42, 99; witnessed by the Holy Communion, i. 43; being 'made,' a great humiliation, i. 52; error of Anabaptists on, i. 53; why the term 'made flesh' is used, i. 90; typified by speech, i. 90; defined by S. Leo and Fourth General Council, i. 91; makes Christ bless our flesh, the Father regard it favourably, sinners to approach, gives hope of the resurrection and of heaven, i. 97, 98; we are to copy it in action, i. 99; of Christ, gives to children of one believing parent a right to Baptism, i. 141; cause of seeing God in the flesh, i. 262; prophesied by Job, ii. 259; the, and the gift of the Holy Ghost compared, iii. 108, 109.
Incense, why prayer compared to, v. 324, 355; its various uses, v. 324.
Inchmeal, ii. 165.
Independents seek to introduce parity into the Church, iv. 12; and so into the commonwealth, iv. 12.
Indifferent things not unlawful, v. 60.
Infants require baptism, iii. 244.
Inferiors envy those above them, v. 542.
Infirmities, spiritual, aided by the Spirit, v. 332, 333; shown in being unable to do good, or to bear evil, things, v. 334.
Infirmity, sins of, i. 343.
Ingratitude wounds deeply, ii. 124.
Inheritance, a Christian's, a future blessing, ii. 365; compared to the fruit or crop, not to the blossom, ii. 365; its

INDEX TO SERMONS, ETC. 429

nature, ii. 366 ; kept in store for us, ii. 366 ; an object of hope, ii. 373 ; comes to us by mercy, ii. 376 ; from a Father to children, ii. 376 ; but only to some who are most highly favoured, ii. 377 ; a 'living' inheritance, because the present possessor still lives, ii. 377 ; given to one, without depriving others, ii. 377 ; its imperishable nature, ii. 378, *seq.;* compared to spring-tide, ii. 379.

Innocency, a stedfast purpose of keeping ourselves clean, iii. 359.

Innocent, the, most deserve compassion, ii. 129.

————— *I., Pope,* requested Arcadius to summon a council, v. 161.

Intercession, practised by our Lord, and by the saints of the Old and New Testaments, v. 355; the duty of God's ministers, v. 355 ; proceeds from charity, v. 358 ; to be used for all classes of persons, v. 358.

Interrogation, use of, the strongest form of prohibition, iv. 35.

Inventions, why sins are so called, v. 228 ; are evil things in religion, v. 229 ; and in common life, v. 229 ; should have judgment executed on them, v. 232.

Irenæus, S., called the Nativity Christ's 'Day,' i. 123 ; on Psalm lxxxv. 11, i. 185; spoke of the Eucharist as consisting of a heavenly and an earthly part, i. 281; his testimony to the Apostolic observance of Easter, ii. 425 ; on the source of kingly power, iv. 53.

Irene summoned the Seventh General Council, v. 160.

Isaac, his offering a type of Christ's, ii. 140 ; his deliverance from death a kind of resurrection, ii. 201, 287 ; the twofold blessing he gave his two sons, v. 414, 415.

Isaiah, the first prophet cited in the Gospel, i. 135 ; speaks much of Christ's nature, person, and offices, iii. 282.

'Ισχὺς and δύναμις distinguished, iv. 86, 87.

Israel, the strength of, the counsel of God, ii. 6 ; a type of wrestling with God in prayer, v. 358.

Israelites, fed miraculously because they followed God's guidance, v. 510.

Ithiel, the meaning of, ii. 6.

J.

Jachin, one of the pillars at the Temple gate, ii. 7.

Jacob, the strength of, the counsel of man, ii. 6, 10 ; overreached Esau and Laban, won by strength from the Amorite, ii. 6 ; had his staff for his flock, his sword for the Amorite, ii. 10 ; the vow of, ii. 45; his censure on Simeon and Levi, iv. 184 ; for the discharging of his conscience, iv. 184 ; offended at their craft against Shechem, iv. 188, 189 ; his words explained, as praying that his own life might be free from treachery, iv. 191 ; turned his death-bed blessing into a curse, iv. 194, 195 ; had a different blessing from Esau, v. 415 ; through his humility gained mercy, v. 461.

Jael, praised for her forwardness, v. 220.

Jah, this name of God given to men, v. 109.

Jambres withstood Moses, ii. 35.

James and John requested fire to fall from heaven, iv. 242, 247 ; their request refused, iv. 243 ; v. 346 ; had ground for indignation, iv. 246 ; expected Christ's thanks, iv. 249 ; had their ignorance reproved, iv. 250 — 254 ; v. 336, 346.

James, King of England, delivered from Gunpowder Plot, ii. 201, 287 ; the day of his accession, ii. 271, 285 ; iii. 282 ; plots laid against his succeeding to the crown, ii. 285 ; the head of three kingdoms, ii. 285; attempted assassination of, by the Gowries, iv. 4, 5, 22 ; his case compared with Saul's, iv. 39, 41 ; his escape marvellous, iv. 73, 74 ; compared with David, iv. 77, 94, 118,119; when crowned in England, and in Scotland, iv. 78, 94, 95 ; protected by God, iv. 86, 87; his deliverances, iv. 94, 95 ; compared to Ahasuerus, iv. 127, 147 ; and to Saul, iv. 154, 175, 179; his skill in detecting the Gunpowder Plot, iv. 259, 269, 395 ; did good service in uniting the two kingdoms, v. 183; and by being of the race royal, v. 184 ; sound in religion, v. 184 ; of good understanding, v. 184; peaceful, v. 185, and a founder of a succession, v. 185; his several deliverances, v. 236, 252—256.

Jannes withstood Moses, ii. 35.

Jealousy, in what sense ascribed to God, iii. 213, 214 ; ever mixed with our love, iii. 214.

Jebus, its meaning, ii. 15.

Jehovah, this name of God never given to any creatures, v. 109; the true root of righteousness, v. 110 ; must become our righteousness, if we are to be saved, v. 111 ; this name belongs to Christ, v. 113.

Jehu, impetuous, ii. 247.

Jeroboam, his contempt for religion, ii. 12; God's message to him, ii. 12; kept up a schism out of policy, ii. 247.

Jerome, S., on Ps. lxxxv. 11, i. 185; on Eph. i. 10, i. 279; on Lent, i. 392, 395; ever haunted by the text, 'Arise from the dead,' ii. 88; his reason why Christ was called the Corner-stone, ii. 208; his tradition, that the whole Church fasted before S. John began to write his Gospel, v. 491.

Jerusalem, its meaning, ii. 15; chosen as the place whence the message of mercy should begin, iii. 235, to show Christ's compassion for His enemies, iii. 235; the holy city, in spite of corruptions, v. 516.

—— early Bishops of, were of the circumcision, ii. 415.

Jesuits, new and old, iii. 256; seek to unhallow the calling of kings, iv. 84; privy to the Gunpowder Treason, iv. 211, 256; justified it as lawful, iv. 211, 256; maintained it under colour of religion, iv. 212, 256, 265; allusions to, iv. 242, 247, 256, 355, 391; counsellors of change in kingdoms, iv. 314, and in the rules of right, iv. 315; traitors to kings, v. 241, 242.

Jesus, why Christ so called, i. 27, ii. 331; the meaning of the word, ii. 137; many called by this name, ii. 330; the highest of Christ's names, ii. 332; by which we most appeal to Him, ii. 332.

—— we should bow thereat, ii. 333; many opposed to this practice, ii. 335; they who dishonour it, will find no comfort by it, ii. 337.

—— *Christ*, moral obligations arising from His various offices and acts, i. 29.

Jews, a foolish people, ii. 25; brutish, ii. 25; spiteful, ii. 25; headstrong in choosing a king, ii. 26; thought they could lead themselves, ii. 26; unworthy of any favours, ii. 27; made God's people, ii. 27; had Moses and Aaron set over them, ii. 27; wished to go back to Egypt, ii. 63; reason given by Bede for their rejecting Christ, ii. 281; why refused a sign, ii. 386—388; guilty not only of spiritual, but of bodily adultery, ii. 388.

—— their ground of quarrel with the Samaritans, iv. 244; compared to ours with the Romanists, iv. 257.

—— their delivery from captivity most marvellous, as their sufferings under it most severe, iv. 224; their danger from Haman, iv. 390, *seq.*

Jews, their lawlessness from wanting a king, v. 170—175, 181; began to be Babel, not Israel, v. 177, 178; more jealous for their own wrong, than for God's dishonour, v. 181.

Job, his wife an instance of relapse, ii. 75; his ground of comfort, ii. 198; though a Gentile, believed in Christ's resurrection, ii. 253; spoke as clearly of it beforehand as any one afterwards, ii. 253; wished to put his belief for ever on record, ii. 254, 255; and to have it graven on stone, ii. 256; to make the gospel equal to the law, ii. 256; as speaking of our Rock, ii. 256, as a standing token of Christ's triumph, ii. 256; his words the 'Epitaph of Death,' ii. 256; the first who spake of a Redeemer, ii. 257; deprecates God as a Judge, ii. 257; confessed his natural bondage, ii. 258, and his hope of pardon, ii. 258; his hope of seeing God Incarnate, ii. 259; called by S. Jerome the Church's champion, ii. 260; the great truths contained in his words, ii. 261; looked to Christ in his own flesh, ii. 262, 263; and for his own good, ii. 264; shows the certainty of his hope by repeating the same words, ii. 264; felt certain of the resurrection, ii. 265; and of his own, ii. 265; though then under trial, ii. 265, 266; pleaded not his own deserts before God, iii. 341; first tempted, then tormented by Satan, v. 450, 451.

John, S., the Baptist, his baptism did not confer the Holy Ghost, iii. 181; the only baptism known to the Ephesian disciples, and to Apollos, iii. 182; rewarded for his humility, iii. 257; taught his disciples a form of prayer, v. 348.

—— *S., the Evangelist*, like the eagle, i. 85; a tradition that he would not begin to write his Gospel till the whole Church had fasted, v. 491.

—— *the Faster*, Patriarch of Constantinople, i. 412.

Jonah, supposed by the Rabbins to be the son of the widow of Sarepta, ii. 392; a type of Christ, ii. 192, 328, 359, 384, *seq.*; in death, burial, and resurrection, ii. 385; as a Prophet to sinners, ii. 390, and to the Gentiles, ii. 391; as the earliest Prophet, ii. 391; as cast out for an expiation, ii. 391, and as restored to life, ii. 392; in the length of his burial, ii. 392; died only in figure, ii. 398; did not rise by his own power, ii. 398, nor to a higher state, ii. 398; a type of great deliverance,

INDEX TO SERMONS, ETC. 431

ii. 400; fitted to be a preacher of repentance, ii. 401; compared with S. Peter, iii. 324, 332; unwilling to deliver his message, v. 8.

Joppa, the call of the Gentiles, both in the Old and New Testament, came from thence, iii. 324, 332.

Jordan, Christ began therein the sacrament of our new birth, ii. 373; might well have started back at Christ's baptism, iii. 244; cleansed by that act, iii. 245, 246; the true Jordan, the blood and water from Christ's side, iii. 247.

Joseph, his selling, a type of Christ's, ii. 140, 328; a shepherd, iii. 85; the evil design of his brethren turned into good by God, v. 303; took not vengeance on his brethren, v. 437.

Joshua, a type of Christ, i. 169.

Josias, his death compared with Christ's, ii. 131, 148.

Joy, both inward and outward, iv. 104, 105, 121, 217, 218; inward shows reality, outward earnestness, iv. 217, 218; the true grounds of, iv. 106—109; a prolonger and cheerer of life, iv. 123; great for a prince's deliverance, iv. 151; to be manifested not in revelry, but in singing God's praises, iv. 218, 219; ever mixed with fear, iv. 219.

Jubilee, Christ's ascension compared to, iii. 227, 231; Christ's sermon at Nazareth preached on a year of, iii. 281; the Jews' last Jubilee, iii. 281, 297; Gospel Jubilee then announced, iii. 281, 297; agrees in number with Pentecost, iii. 282; a season of joy, iii. 282; of restoration and freedom, iii. 297; the height of joy, iii. 297; Jubilee of the Gospel surpasses that of the Law, iii. 298; ushered in with sound of rams' horns, iii. 299; outward exhibition of joy, iv. 105.

Judah signifies confession, v. 358.

—— *Kings of*, ceremony in their consecration, ii. 13, 14.

Judas Iscariot, a hypocrite, i. 407; complained of S. Mary Magdalene's profuseness, ii. 38, 226; seeming goodness of his reason, ii. 42, 43; though he spoke against waste, he wasted Christ's goods, ii. 43; an ill thing for him to reform Mary Magdalene, ii. 43; gave the wrong reason for his finding fault with her, ii. 46; his real motive covetousness, ii. 46; he fell away from worse to worse, ii. 44, 48; was first guilty of sacrilege, then of hypocrisy, ii. 47; a Christ-robber, ii. 52; Satan had filled his heart, ii. 52; made a wrong distinction between duty done to Christ and to the poor, ii. 53; the best way to redress his complaint, ii. 53; faithful for a short time, ii. 68; had the blood of the sacrament without the spirit, iii. 355; his wicked fraternity with Simon Magus, iii. 395; of a covetous spirit, v. 45.

Judge, the unjust, an encouragement to importunity in prayer, v. 330, 331.

Judgment, Abraham believed in, i. 124; taught by Enoch, i. 124.

—— how God's is to be avoided, v. 217, 218; to be inflicted on sin, by public authority, v. 232, and by each man on himself, v. 233.

Julian acknowledged as a king, after his apostasy, iv. 57.

Justice must be satisfied, before Mercy and Truth, Righteousness and Peace, can meet, i. 182; not satisfied by prayer, i. 183; only satisfied in the Christian religion, i. 183; God's cannot be foregone, i. 184; its place in repentance, i. 442; one of the pillars of a land, ii. 9, 10; of two kinds, against outward and inward enemies, ii. 9; fences religion from without, ii. 10; makes, with religion, an arch of government, ii. 10; is goodness to the deserving, iv. 321; an enemy to sin, v. 111; requires to be reconciled with mercy, v. 111.

Justification, the question obscured by the schoolmen, v. 124.

Justinian summoned the Council of Constantinople, v. 160; made into laws the decrees of the first four General Councils, v. 163.

K.

Καταρτίζειν, its senses explained, iii. 95, 96.

Καταξίωσις and ἀξία distinguished, iii. 341.

Keys, power of, how first given, iii. 262; continual need of, iii. 262; the two, of authority and knowledge, v. 96.

Kings defend their people against inward and outward dangers, ii. 9; they wield a sword and a sceptre, ii. 10; are the Lord's anointed, ii. 10; compared to a nail, ii. 10; when there are none, justice and religion both suffer, ii. 11; the 'shout of a king,' joyful, ii. 11; of Judah, ceremony in coronation of, ii. 13; given to nations according to their desert, ii. 20; good kings compared to dew, ii. 24.

Kings, subjects should not rise against, iv. 11, 19; stand in God's place, iv. 13, 14, 19; are called gods, iv. 14; welfare of kingdoms depends on them, iv. 15; terms of dignity given them, iv. 15; their enemies ever overthrown, iv. 18, 19, 33.

—— God's anointed, iv. 25, 32, 43, 44, 48, 49, 52, 53; so termed by Fathers and Councils, iv. 49; not the Pope's anointed, iv. 51; not to be slain, iv. 31, 34, 43, 44; nor to have a hand raised against them, iv. 31, 34; contrary doctrine of Romanists, iv. 36; their callings and persons sacred, iv. 32; share the name of God and of Christ, iv. 32, 33; a near alliance between God and them, iv. 33; both governors and fathers, iv. 48.

—— not the anointed of the people, iv. 52; have their power from God, iv. 53; God's hand has touched them, no other may, iv. 54; taken into connexion with Christ's name, being *Christi*, or anointed, iv. 55, 56; counted by the primitive Church as sacred, iv. 55; cannot cease to be God's anointed, iv. 56; good and bad kings equally God's anointed, iv. 57; not unmade by heresy, iv. 57.

—— not to be touched either by violence, or virulent tongue, iv. 60; in their persons, their estates, or families, iv. 61; not even in will, iv. 62, 63; Popes wished to depose them if heretics, iv. 67; to be prayed for, iv. 69, 72; thanks to be returned for their deliverance, iv. 72, 73; their welfare connected with that of the Church, iv. 72; their preservation a special benefit, iv. 72; no human invention, God's finding, iv. 79, 80, 81; anointed with holy oil, iv. 84; their function holy, iv. 84.

—— their salvation a ground of joy, iv. 106; when preserved by God, to be specially esteemed, iv. 108; their crowns and lives closely connected, iv. 112, 113; titles applied to them, iv. 108, 114; crowned by God, not to be deposed by the people, iv. 114, 115.

—— hands not to be laid on them, iv. 131; why called gods, iv. 132; treason against them may be committed in thought, iv. 132.

—— their murder mentioned, but not sanctioned in Scripture, iv. 160, 161; should be good divines, iv. 161.

—— the origin of their power not accidental, iv. 279; not from themselves, iv. 280; but from God, iv. 281; particularly from Christ, iv. 282; not by permission, but by commission, iv. 283, 284; by His grace, iv. 284; called by His name, iv. 284, 285; He reigns by them, iv. 285; whatever their religion, or their tyranny, iv. 286; but especially by good kings, iv. 287; unmade, as well as made, by Him, iv. 286; distinguished from usurpers, iv. 287; reign by God, both in their first entrance, and in their continuance in their kingdoms, iv. 288, 289; and in their posterity, iv. 290; follow His wisdom as their rule, iv. 291; should be strictly obeyed, iv. 292; anti-christian to plot against them, iv. 293; to oppose them is to oppose God, iv. 293; closely joined to God by Solomon, iv. 299; this connexion not to be severed, iv. 300, 301; are to be feared, iv. 301.

Kings, should use their power to support the truth, iv. 402; can appoint holidays, iv. 402.

—— to be obeyed, though heathen, idolaters, and wicked, v. 132; are God's ordinance, be they personally what they will, v. 133; the honour due to them, v. 137; the protection afforded by them, v. 137.

—— summoned Councils, as well as the emperors, v. 162.

—— the lawlessness of the Jews, for want of, v. 170—175, 181; the benefit of good kings, v. 176; the best mode of ruling a state, v. 176, 177; a means of keeping God's people in due subjection, v. 177; control both the eye and the hand, v. 178; and in matters of religion, v. 179; are called 'gods,' v. 180; foster fathers, v. 180; διάκονοι and λειτουργοί, v. 180; a regular succession of, better than elective rulers, v. 182; to be prayed for, v. 183; any king better than anarchy, v. 183.

—— represent God, v. 207; God's special care, v. 235, 237, 238, 249; as His vicegerents, v. 243; need this protection, v. 239; God wronged in their persons, v. 243; their protection a benefit to their people, v. 244; supporters of religion, v. 245; not all protected by God, v. 252.

—— their name reverenced by those who have not seen their persons, v. 382; not to be deified, v. 388.

—— they and their people bound together by mutual obligations, v. 464.

Kingdom of God, the first blessing we should ask for, v. 390; how it can be said to 'come,' v. 391; is everlasting, v. 391; is a kingdom of glory and power, v. 391; its government committed to Christ, v. 392; its hindrances and enemies, v. 392; prevails not in this world, v. 393; is also a kingdom of grace, v. 393; the tokens of its approach within us, v. 394; we pray that it may 'come' to us, because we cannot by nature come to it, v. 394; the saints long for its coming, v. 394; the door to enter it is the doing of God's will, v. 396, 397; to be willingly submitted to, v. 406; sin a hindrance to, v. 425; different from earthly kingdoms, v. 463, 466; both of might and of glory, v. 463; eternal, v. 466.

Kingdoms set forth under the name of women, iv. 342.

———— offered by Satan to Christ, v. 540, *seq.*; how far his to offer, v. 552; of less value than one soul, v. 545, 553.

Knee, to be bent in worship, ii. 333, 334; especially at Jesus's name, ii. 334—336.

Kneel, some refuse to kneel at the Holy Eucharist, ii. 335.

Knock, we must knock at the gate of God's Mercy, as He knocks at the door of our hearts, v. 302; implies importunity, v. 330.

Knowledge, Christian, to be accounted for, ii. 188; of two kinds, of facts and of causes, ii. 189.

———— required previous to speaking, iii. 137.

————, the key of, needed, to show to whom remission is to be given, v. 97, 100; and for self-guidance, v. 101.

———— *of self* used in a different way by heathens and by Christians, v. 302.

Korah, canonized by the Jews, ii. 26; withstood Aaron, ii. 35; destroyed for gainsaying, iv. 11; Moses cursed him, iv. 13.

L.

Λαβεῖν and ἀπολαβεῖν distinguished, ii. 90.

Label-Christians, such as have not the seal of the Spirit, iii. 216.

Labour, seasoned by hope, ii. 206.

Lactantius on Ps. lxxxv. 11, i. 185.

Ladder of practice and of contemplation, v. 531.

Λαλεῖν distinguished from ἀποφθέγγεσθαι, iii. 139, 141.

Lamech, full of revenge, v. 436.

Lampsacus, Council of. See *Council of Lampsacus.*

Land, A, the cause of its weakness, ii. 4; its pillars, ii. 4, *seq.*

Λαοῖς ἄφεσις, a form of dismissing the people, iii. 81.

Lateran, Council of. See *Council of Lateran.*

Latinus (? *Tatianus*), the founder of the Encratitæ, v. 58.

Λατρεύειν, its meaning, iv. 383.

Law, directive and penal, both satisfied by Christ, i. 56; opposeth grace, i. 96; the Gospel has one, i. 287, 288; disuse of the term, and so of the doctrine, i. 288, 289; God has a statute and a common law, i. 290; ours a law of love, i. 300.

———— fastened to Christ's cross at His ascension, iii. 229; impossible to be performed by nature, iii. 366; perfected by grace, iii. 366; gives light, iii. 372; offered only temporal promises, ii. 380.

———— of supplication, the law of belief, v. 363; and of conduct, v. 406, 430.

Lawlessness, the result of wanting a king, v. 170, 174, 175, 181.

Laws, all, except God's, breed only fear of sin, not hatred of it, ii. 8; they cannot fetter the thoughts, ii. 8; supported by religion, ii. 8; the remedy for evils in the state, v. 210; to give them, the work of God, v. 210.

Lay elders, government by, lately introduced, v. 64; unknown to the fathers, v. 65.

Laymen, pretend wrongly to a knowledge of divinity, and to control the clergy, v. 15; though qualified by knowledge, cannot exercise the priest's office, v. 92.

Lazarus, his story not a parable, ii. 80; compared to a cross, ii. 80; he received evil in this life, ii. 80; can be found by us daily, ii. 96; his resurrection compared to Christ's, ii. 193; his resurrection a less miracle than Mary Magdalene's rising from sin, ii. 203; in a rich man's bosom, a goodly sight both in earth and in heaven, v. 43, 47.

Leading, the nature of God's, ii. 22; the end of all, ii. 24.

Learning does not exclude from Christ, i. 245.

Leaven, its meaning, ii. 292, 303; to be purged out, ere we can keep our Passover, ii. 301, 303, 306; its several kinds, ii. 304; a little does much harm, ii. 306.

Leek-blade, love's purse-strings made of a, (Greek proverb,) ii. 102.

M M

Λειτουργία, the meaning of, iv. 376; who were excluded from it in the Primitive Church, iv. 377.
—— applied to the collection of alms, v. 267. (*From Bp. Buckeridge's Funeral Sermon.*)
Λειτουργοί, kings so called, v. 180.
Lending to others a blessing of God's people, ii. 5. See *Borrow.*
Lent, primitive respect for, i. 374, 391 —395, 432; three Lents kept by Montanists, i. 392; Council of Gangra anathematized those who kept it not, i. 392; why kept before Easter, i. 393; why forty days long, i. 393, 394; the rule for its termination fixed by the Council of Nice, i. 394; has ever been religiously observed, i. 432; at a very fit season of the year, i. 453; its origin, v. 492; only a positive law, not of divine obligation, v. 492.
Leo, S., his reason why fallen angels are not to be pitied, i. 12; his definition of incarnation, i. 91; considered the joy of the nativity retrospective, i. 122; held that Christ's nature was placed for us in the font, i. 150; that Christ when an infant was so little and so great, i. 198; on the desertion of Christ in His last agony, ii. 147.
—— his anxiety about the proper day for keeping Easter, ii. 417; speaks of it as the season for Baptism, Absolution, and Holy Communion, ii. 427.
—— requested Theodosius to summon a Council, v. 161.
Levi and *Simeon* cursed and disinherited by their father, iv. 184, 185; how this curse fulfilled, iv. 195, 197; brethren in violence, iv. 187; their guilt in murdering innocent and guilty alike, iv. 192; the vengeance they took was beyond the offence, iv. 193; their anger implacable, iv. 194; their curse afterwards reversed, iv. 197, 198.
Liberius present at Councils of Sirmium and Seleucia, v. 161; requested Constantius to summon a Council, v. 161.
Liberty, Christian, much abused in denying fundamentals of the faith, iii. 183.
Life, the way of, not easy to find, i. 166.
—— subject to changes, ii. 82; its goods may be received as an earnest or as a reward, ii. 90; short, ii. 96; eternity depends on it, ii. 96; and reputation go together, ii. 165; opposed to death, ii. 215; came from Christ, ii. 215; several kinds of, ii. 217; to regain natural, without spiritual, no blessing, ii. 218; spiritual life given by the Spirit, ii. 219; we gain it by Christ's flesh and blood, ii. 220; correspondence between natural and spiritual, iii. 190, 191; both the work of the same Spirit, iii. 191; spiritual how discerned, iii. 357; by faith and fear, iii. 357; by our speech, iii. 357; what compared to in Scripture, v. 48; natural life, only a long disease, v. 50; much valued, v. 51.
Light, a type of the coeternity of the Son, i. 108; the first of God's gifts to the world, iii. 370; connexion between it and goodness, iii. 370; good on its own account, iii. 370; so perfect, as to be applied to describe God, iii. 370; should remind us of Him, iii. 376; God compared to, v. 316, 317; a type of God's ministers and of holy men, v. 317.
Lights, spoken of in the plural, in the words 'Father of lights,' to show that God's gifts are manifold, iii. 371; and as opposed to various kinds of darkness, iii. 371; the various lights God gives, nature, the law, prophecy, Gospel, grace, comfort, glory, iii. 372.
—— of heaven regarded by the heathen as the causes of good, v. 316; kindled within us by God, v. 319.
Little things not to be despised, instanced in Bethlehem, i. 160.
Lively, a word of greater meaning than 'living,' ii. 373.
Locusts, (Rev. ix. 2,) who meant by, v. 241, 251.
London, the charities there administered, v. 37.
Lord, the, Christ, i. 79; the Divine nature implied in, 80.
Loss of blessing proves its value, v. 170.
Lot, his days like those of the Son of man, ii. 61; vexed with the sins of the wicked, ii. 104; fell into presumption, v. 514; forbidden to look on Sodom on account of his weakness, v. 541.
—— his wife, an instance of faint virtue, ii. 62; our warning, ii. 62; the only Old Testament story Christ tells us to remember, ii. 65; her sin in looking back, ii. 66, 67; out of love for Sodom, ii. 67; her disobedience, ii. 66; her wavering, ii. 67; she fell after having stood long, ii. 68; and in the midst of mercies, ii. 69; the favours before shown her, ii. 69; her punishment death, ii. 70; (1) sudden, (2) in the act of sin, (3) unusual, (4) without burial, ii. 70;

INDEX TO SERMONS, ETC. 435

her pillar said to have existed in the time of Josephus, ii. 71; why a pillar of salt, ii. 71; the lessons to be learnt from her history, ii. 71, 77.
Lot, the, is in God's hands, iv. 394.
Lothaire summoned the Council of Mayence, v. 162.
Louis I. summoned the Council of Aix-la-Chapelle, v. 162.
—— *II.* summoned the Council of Worms, v. 162.
Love, leads the better disposed, ii. 9; is not influenced by hope, ii. 73, 116, 164; has the virtue of the loadstone, ii. 99, 182; S. Paul's for the Corinthians, ii. 98 (see *S. Paul*); ours soon grows cold, ii. 100; for souls the highest, ii. 101, 114; empty-handed, no longer known, ii. 102; it is liberal, ii. 102; showed specially in bestowing oneself, ii. 104; changes the nature of unpleasant things, ii. 106; disregards difficulties, ii. 108, 164, 228; the greatest of virtues, ii. 114; no love bestowed for Christ's sake ever lost, ii. 116; leads to faith, ii. 180; its several designations, ii. 224.
—— evidenced in S. Mary Magdalene, iii. 6—8, 13, 19, 23, 26; hers a contrast to ours, iii. 8; fears and suspects without reason, iii. 18; gives strength, iii. 19; attracts love, iii. 20, 149; forgets not propriety, iii. 30; should not lead us to forget reverence, iii. 30.
—— worldly, is mercenary, iii. 149; should be manifested by some outward sign, iii. 150; makes labour light, iii. 150; is ashamed of the word 'difficulty,' iii. 150; shown by keeping the commandments, iii. 150; an evidence that we have received the Spirit, iii. 192; the first of the fruits of the Spirit, iii. 238; the sign and means of the Holy Spirit's indwelling, iii. 238; towards God, the end of both covenants, iii. 362, 363; the gift of the Holy Ghost, iii. 363; cannot be ours without prayer, v. 310.
—— *God's,* fully manifested in sending His Son, i. 52, 92; is unchangeable, v. 366—368; the fruits of it are compassion and bounty, v. 367, 368.
—— towards God and man, the same temper, though with different objects, v. 268. (*From Bp. Buckeridge's Funeral Sermon.*)
Luke S., the Psalmist of the New Testament, i. 215.
Luther, his saying that every man has a Pope in his own belly, iii. 328.

M.

Mâcon, Council of. See *Council of Mâcon.*
Magdalene, S. Mary, her abundant tears, i. 369.
—— the only person who came to Christ for pardon of sin only, ii. 37; S. John speaks of her as the person who anointed Christ's feet, ii. 37; her profuseness, ii. 38; complained of by Judas, ii. 38, and on other occasions, ii. 58; approved by Christ, ii. 39, 48; her conduct, even if not imitated, to be tolerated, ii. 49; was good to Christ, ii. 53; to follow her example, the best way to redress Judas's complaint, ii. 53; her example to be followed, ii. 59; well spoken of throughout all the world, ii. 59; a well-doer, though a waster, ii. 59; did what she could, ii. 103; her being raised from sin a greater miracle than Lazarus's resurrection, ii. 203, 402; why mentioned as first at the sepulchre, ii. 223, 224; a notorious sinner, ii. 223; made a messenger of good tidings, ii. 235.
—— Christ first appeared to, iii. 4; carried the good tidings to the Apostles, iii. 4, 5; needed Christ most, and therefore sought Him first, iii. 5; went by the common name of sinner, iii. 5; seemed to have want of faith but not of love, iii. 6; proofs of her great love, iii. 7, 8, 13, 19, 23, 26; her going to the tomb, iii. 7; her waiting there, iii. 7; her weeping, iii. 7; her earnest seeking, iii. 8; a contrast to ours, iii. 8; its reward, iii. 9, 23; her sorrow needless, iii. 11; sorrowed more at the loss of Christ's body than at His death, iii. 12; her error in thinking that Christ was gone, iii. 12; not ashamed to own Christ as her Lord, iii. 13; affected neither by the strange sight, nor by the comforting words of the angels, iii. 13; comforted by Christ's own presence, iii. 14; her sorrow a type of the world before Christ, iii. 17; her thoughts full of Christ, iii. 19; how Christ made known to her, iii. 20; she enjoyed a kind of resurrection, iii. 21.
—— repulsed by Christ, iii. 23; then comforted, iii. 24; wished to touch Christ out of pure love, iii. 25; as she had touched Him before iii. 25; forbidden to touch Him, not on His account, but her own, iii. 27; to beget reverence, iii. 24, 28, 29, 35; she erred in judgment, though she exceeded in affection, iii. 29

should not have called Christ 'Rabboni,' or have addressed Him so familiarly, iii. 29, 30; was carried away by her over-joy, iii. 31; touched Him afterwards, when she had learned reverence, iii. 31, 35; to have touched Him would have made her less reverent, iii. 31; was taught at first to seek for a truer spiritual touch of Him, iii. 37, 40.

Magdalene, S. Mary, honoured in conveying Christ's message, iii. 40, 44; and thus brought the first tidings of His resurrection, iii. 40; made 'an apostle to the Apostles,' iii. 44; specially a bearer of good tidings, iii. 44; this a kind of reproach to the Apostles, iii. 44; and a greater honour than touching Christ, iii. 45; the words of this message compared to the 'rongs' of Jacob's ladder, and the wheels of Elijah's chariot, iii. 52.

——————————— her touch irreverent, iv. 61.

Magi, their offerings, how explained figuratively, iii. 338.

Magistrates, their duty to call assemblies both of Church and State, v. 141, 149—151, 208; the term 'gods' applied to, v. 205; yet not all equal, v. 206, 207; S. Gregory Nazianzen's comparison respecting, v. 207; their assembly, God's assembly, v. 209; must stand before God as their Judge, v. 213, 215; in what way distinguished from God, whose name they bear, v. 213; will give account for the way in which they have done His work, v. 216. See *Kings.*

Mahomet destitute of the witness of prophecy, i. 19; could not satisfy God's justice, i. 183.

Malice, an obstacle to receiving the Holy Ghost, iii. 197.

Mamre, Christ in Person at, with Abraham, i. 128.

Man, his nature in the seed of Abraham taken by Christ, i. 1; but not his person, i. 8, 89; compared to angels, i. 4; raised above them by the incarnation, i. 5; fallen, sought for, and sent after, i. 6; spared, i. 7; what was denied to angels was granted to, i. 8; why more to be pitied than the fallen angels, i. 11; and God in one Person, i. 23; Christ, son of, by His birth, i. 23; satisfaction made for him, i. 81; would be as a god, i. 226; works of, rewarded, by the good-will of God, i. 228; a compendium of heaven and earth, i. 275; taught a lesson by the instinct of animals, i. 350, 351; the cistern to receive all God's gifts, iii. 234; lost in sin without Christ's death, iii. 269; the highest of God's works, iv. 330; more mercy shown to him than to the rest, iv. 330; his very form should teach him to look upward, v. 378; the only creature to whom forgiveness is granted, v. 426.

Manichees, held that Christ had no true body, i. 90, 140; considered the creature unclean, i. 405; their heresy, v. 56.

Manna, pot of, type of Christ, ii. 349.

Marcian summoned the Council of Chalcedon, v. 160.

Mariana, John, his infamous doctrines concerning the murder of kings, iv. 66; his book condemned, iv. 66, 67; his saying respecting the use of poison alluded to, iv. 355.

Martha and *Mary* compared, v. 194.

Martyrs, not delivered, but yet not forsaken, ii. 146.

——————, sacrifice never offered to, v. 263; prayers not due to, v. 264. (*From Bishop Buckeridge's Funeral Sermon.*)

Mary and *Martha* compared, v. 194.

Massah, signifies presumption, v. 513.

Mayence, Council of. See *Council of Mayence.*

Means, neither to be neglected nor made too much of, v. 527; to neglect them is to tempt God, v. 528, 530, 532.

Meaux, Council of. See *Council of Meaux.*

Meddlers with sedition censured, iv. 306, 307; how they can meddle with it, iv. 308; their punishment, iv. 309, 310; utter ruin, iv. 310; sudden, iv. 311; and eternal, iv. 311.

Meditation, the uses of, iii. 199.

Meiny, a retinue, v. 17.

Melchizedek, wherein Christ's offering is better than his, i. 168; a type of the Church offering bread and wine, i. 194.

Members of the body rallied together by danger, v. 209.

Mercies, bowels of, force of this expression, iv. 272; the nature of God's, iv. 271—273; how to be acknowledged, iv. 274—276.

Mercy to others draws down God's mercies on ourselves, iv. 275; has misery for its object to work on, iv. 321; this specially marked in the word *misericordia,* iv. 321; opposed to merit, iv. 321; is goodness to the undeserving, iv. 321.

————— God's, the cause of our regeneration, ii. 370; is manifold, ii. 370, 371; iii. 371; its nature, iv. 322; its extent, iv. 323; its works greater than God's other works, iv. 323, 324; is over all things, not merely as superior to, but as protecting them, iv. 324, 325; includes His greater and His lesser works, iv. 326; is the Maker and Preserver of all things, iv. 326, 327; is greater than His judgment, iv. 328; than our sins, iv. 328; and than Satan's power, iv. 329; greater to man than to the rest of His works, iv. 330; specially to Christians, iv. 331; and to particular people, iv. 331, 332; manifested in punishment of wicked, iv. 337; should be exalted by us, iv. 337; should be our pattern, iv. 339; always blended with judgment, v. 523; not to be abused, v. 534, 535.

Mercy and *truth* severed by Adam's fall, i. 180.

Mereri, used by the Fathers in the sense of obtaining, v. 286. (*From Bishop Buckeridge's Funeral Sermon.*)

Meribah, signifies murmur, v. 513.

Merit opposed to mercy, iv. 321; none in our best doings, v. 282, 285. (*From Bishop Buckeridge's Funeral Sermon.*)

Merita, signify in S. Augustine, not dignity of work, but means of obtaining, v. 286. (*From Bishop Buckeridge's Funeral Sermon.*)

Merits not to be relied on, iii. 154.

Meroz cursed for its backwardness, v. 220.

Mesech, the meaning of the word, v. 220.

Micah, his idolatry the result of there being no king in Israel, v. 179, 180.

———, the second prophet cited in the Gospel, i. 153.

Micaiah hated by Ahab, v. 7, 16.

Michal despised David for reverencing the ark and ephod, ii. 12; scorned the priest's dress, v. 17.

Minds to be set above, ii. 309, 310, 313 —315; especially at Easter, ii. 321; and in the Holy Communion, ii. 321, 322.

Ministers, Christ's, their work to set in joint what sin has disjointed, iii. 97; the means they use, iii. 97; the means of rescuing men from Satan, and bringing them prisoners to Christ, iii. 234; are Christian-makers, first by baptism, then by the power of the keys, iii. 262; though themselves not personally holy, may be the channels of grace, iii. 277, 278; compared to seals, which may give a good impression, even though of base metal, iii. 278; to conduits, which make a garden fruitful, though unfruitful themselves, iii. 278; need both unction and mission, iii. 288.

Miracles, lying, cast a doubt on true, i. 18, 19; of Christ, showed His glory, i. 95; no more marvellous than God's ordinary works, iv. 208.

Miseratio, the act, *misericordia,* the habit of mercy, iv. 321.

Misericordia, the habit, *miseratio,* the act of mercy, iv. 321.

Missa est fidelibus used at the end of the service, iii. 82.

Mithridate, an ointment compounded of a bruised viper, a cure for its sting, ii. 15, 214.

Montanists, had three Lents, i. 392; first set apart fourteen days in memory of our Lord's fasting, v. 492.

Mordecai, how he came to detect the treason against Ahasuerus, iv. 138— 140; the pattern of a faithful subject, iv. 140; our example, iv. 140— 142; saved Ahasuerus, though of a different religion, iv. 142.

Morton, Nicholas, an agent of the Pope to promote rebellion in England, iv. 256.

Moses brought Israel to the border to show that the law made nothing perfect, i. 169; a type of Christ, i. 169; by special direction of God made music the conveyer of men's duties, ii. 3; a man of meekness, ii. 24; one of God's hands, ii. 17, 29, 30; why his rod turned into a serpent, ii. 20; equal to Aaron, ii. 33; is a type of the secular arm, ii. 28, 32, 33; gives bodily relief, ii. 33; to lead us against worldly enemies, ii. 33; to decide causes of law, ii. 33; needs Aaron to be joined with him, ii. 33, 34; needs his aid, ii. 35; is jealous of his honour, ii. 35; has the same enemies, ii. 35, 36; beheld God, ii. 261, 262; in the length of his fasting, a type of Christ, ii. 359; a shepherd, iii. 85; would break the bruised reed and quench the smoking flax, iii. 152; a type of Christ in going up from the Red Sea, and receiving the law from Mount Sinai, iii. 222; used imprecations, iv. 8; first put men's duty into music, v. 204; sorely offended at idolatry, v. 551.

Moth, in Matt. vi. 19, 20, understood figuratively by Musculus, v. 22.

Mulcaster, Richard, Andrewes his pupil, and his gratitude to him, v. 289. (*From Bishop Buckeridge's Funeral Sermon.*)

Multitude to be ruled by unity, v. 177.

Murder condemned in every part of Scripture, iv. 186; has a curse on it, iv. 194.
Musculus, Wolfgang, understood the word 'moth,' (in Matt. vi. 19, 20,) figuratively, v. 22.
Music the conveyor of men's duties into their minds, ii. 3.
Mysteries, operative, i. 41; are to be dispensed, i. 43; holy, conduits to convey into us the benefits that come from our Saviour, i. 83.
Mystery of the incarnation, i. 32; imparts a mystery, i. 43; of godliness, i. 34; in the Sacrament of the Holy Communion, i. 43; wherein it differs from a ceremony, i. 41.

N.

Nabal, wasteful, ii. 41; his churlishness, v, 16.
Nail, kings compared to, ii. 10.
Nacah and *Nackah,* their meaning, ii. 28.
Name, used in the singular number in the words of baptism, shows the unity of God, iii. 188.
——— *God's,* too often used irreverently, iv. 378; to be sanctified, v. 381; the hallowing of it set before His kingdom, v. 382; is a strong tower, v. 383; we cannot add holiness to it, v. 383; in glorifying it, we glorify Him, v. 383; to be honoured, by regarding those that bear it, v. 384; things that bear it considered holy, v. 384; why said to be sanctified, rather than glorified, v. 385; how hallowed negatively, v. 385; how positively, v. 387; the punishment for not hallowing it, v. 385; all serious actions to be begun by the use of it, v. 386; to be hallowed at all places, and times, and by all, v. 386; as it is sanctified, His kingdom comes, v. 389, 393.
Names, imposed by God, are no empty sounds, v. 106.
Nardus πιστική, its value, ii. 38; according to Pliny, ii. 41.
Nativity, called by the Fathers 'Theophania,' i. 198; five kinds of peace accompany it, i. 221, 222; reached from Zion to Rahab and Babylon, i. 298, 299.
Nature, Christ took our, i. 1, 8, 89; never to be severed, i. 9, 39, 52, 59; of Christ, i. 21; that sinned, must bear the punishment, i. 22; Adam alienated our, i. 57; we are made partakers of Divine, i. 59; Incarnation exalts our, i. 81, 116; the Divine, exhibited in the creation and in the preservation of all things, i. 110; our, first purged, then exalted, i. 112; the contumelies of our, not refused by Christ, i. 140; glorified by the Incarnation, i. 221; human, like a broken bow, ii. 63; and like flesh which soon corrupts, ii. 63; raised in Christ, ii. 191; disjointed by the fall, iii. 96; good, but imperfect, iii. 366; perfected by grace, iii. 366; the light of, iii. 372; asks for temporal blessings, v. 413, 416.
Natures of Christ, i. 107; in Micah, v. 2; the two set forth, i. 162, 163; His two natures, i. 295, 296.
Neckamoth and *Nekamoth,* their meaning, ii. 17.
Nestorius, his error concerning Christ's person, i. 90; iii. 349.
Nice, Council of. See *Council of Nice.*
Nicolaitans, their licentious doctrines, v. 58.
Ninevites, an example to us of repentance, ii. 399, 400.
Noah, when delivered from the ark, fell into presumption, v. 514.
Novatians, observed Easter, ii. 416.
Novelties, too much hankered after, v. 528.
November, Fifth of, a memorable day, iv. 203; to be held in remembrance, iv. 204; greatness of the danger, iv. 208, 209; a day of rejoicing, iv. 216, 217. See *Gunpowder Plot.*

O.

Oaths, used by the saints in the Old Testament, v. 72; by the Apostles, v. 72; voluntary oaths forbidden by our Lord, v. 73; when lawful, v. 73; in what manner to be taken, v. 74; instances of profane oaths, v. 77; not to be taken needlessly, v. 78; nor without reverence, v. 78, 79; but for a just purpose, v. 79, 80; not for things impossible, or unlawful, v. 80.
Œcumenius, on Hebrews ii. 16, i. 6.
Offices, of Christ, God spoke of, to the fathers in times past, i. 104; of Christ, their nature, i. 108, 296, 297.
Οἰκονομία is a dispensation, not a dissipation, ii. 40.
Oil, a type of sovereignty, iv. 54; taken from the sanctuary to anoint kings, iv. 55; a type of continuance, iv. 84; and of gentleness, iv. 84.
Olive-branch, sign of salvation, not of destruction, iv. 253.
Olympic games referred to by S. Paul, ii. 159.
Omega and *Alpha,* Christ why called, ii. 75, 162, 163.

INDEX TO SERMONS, ETC. 439

Omission, sins of, most condemning, v. 272. (*From Bishop Buckeridge's Funeral Sermon.*)
Operations, the work wrought by 'gifts,' and 'administrations,' iii. 381.
Opportunity often causes crime, iv. 158, 159.
Order highly pleasing to God, iii. 387.
Orders, Holy, whether to be considered as, strictly speaking, a Sacrament, iii. 263; outward, as well as inward, calling necessary in them, iii. 272; convey not personal holiness, but grace for the right exercise of an office, iii. 277, 278; the Holy Ghost how received in, iii. 289; three degrees of, in the Church, iii. 387, 388; the highest but a διακονία, iii. 388.
Orleans, Council of. See *Council of Orleans.*
Overreaching is the bread of deceit, v. 500.
Ox, a type of spiritual labourers, ii. 105.

P.

Papists, men called so for fasting, i. 403. See also *Bellarmine, Jesuits, Mariana, Romanists.*
Parable, history of Lazarus and Dives not a, ii. 80.
Παράκλητος, senses of the word, as applied to the Holy Spirit, iii. 175, 176; implies comfort, iii. 175; invitation, iii. 176, 177; counsel, iii. 176; reproof, iii. 177; a guest, dwelling in us by His grace, iii. 179.
Paraclitus contrasted with *paracletus*, iii. 178.
Pardon, the first degree of acceptance, iii. 298.
Parent, children of one believing, have a right by Christ's Incarnation to the Laver of Regeneration, i. 141.
Paschal cycles, their history and use, ii. 416, 417.
Paschal epistles, Bishops of Alexandria directed to prepare them, ii. 417, 418; of high repute, ii. 418; some of them translated by S. Jerome, ii. 418.
Passion, the day of Christ's, the day of God's wrath, ii. 139.
Passover, close of Egyptian bondage, ii. 17; a 'passing over' to a better land, ii. 193; a feast for Christians, ii. 290; Christ offered up is ours, ii. 291, 295; what is comprehended in the word, ii. 292; ours greater than the Jews', ii. 293, 294; both sacrificed and eaten with us and with them, ii. 299; Eucharist now stands in its place, ii. 299; Jews obliged to partake of, under penalty of death, ii. 302; the rules for its observance, ii. 303; why the Feast and the Lamb have the same name, ii. 307; a season of great change in nature, ii. 307; a type of the great marriage feast, ii. 308; the door-posts marked therein with blood, a type of the Holy Ghost's sealing, iii. 210; feast of, why observed, iv. 204.
Pastors and teachers ordained by the Church after Christ's Ascension, iii. 142.
Pastors the same as Doctors, according to the Fathers, v. 65.
Patience, the way to obtain God's gifts, iii. 114, 129; to be exercised in waiting for an answer to prayer, v. 341; a way in which God helps us to bear affliction, v. 455.
Patriarchs, types of Christ, ii. 139; anointed of God, iv. 47; princes in their generations, iv. 47; exercised fatherhood and government, iv. 48.
Paul, S., his love for Corinthians, ii. 98; how shown, ii. 98; in spite of their coldness, ii. 99; no self-seeker, ii. 99; not overcome by unkindness, ii. 100; loved the Corinthians' souls, ii. 100, 101, 110; had no wealth to bestow, ii. 102, but treasures of wisdom, ii. 103; did not gain their love, ii. 107; the more he laboured, the less cared for, ii. 108; after Christ's example, ii. 112; much loved by Christ when a blasphemer, ii. 115, and for all his labours, ii. 116; insists on the identity of the body at the Resurrection, ii. 263; by speaking of the Christian 'Altar,' compared the Jewish and Christian sacrifices, ii. 301; bore with the deficiency of the Ephesian disciples, iii. 182, 'in meekness instructing' them, iii. 182; his imprecation against Elymas, iv. 8; quoted heathen authors, v. 62; diverted from his evil designs by God, v. 303; acknowledged his own weakness, v. 305, 306; asked improperly for the removal of his thorn in the flesh, v. 337, 346; his shipwreck teaches us the use of means, v. 533.
—— *of Samosata*, his error concerning Christ's nature, iii. 349.
Peace, five kinds effected by means of the Nativity, i. 221, 222; angels lovers of, i. 225; a heaven on earth, i. 225; lost by seeking glory, i. 226; hovers over earth, would alight but cannot, i. 230; the highest of wishes, ii. 243, 244; comprehends every good,

ii. 243; wished for on earth and in heaven, ii. 243; often given by Christ, ii. 244; bought by his cross, ii. 244; a fit wish from Him, ii. 244; for His disciples, ii. 245; He our Peace, ii. 245; suited to Easter, ii. 245, 251; is a kind of resurrection, ii. 245; opposed to suffering, ii. 245, and to fear, ii. 246; the nature of that given by Christ, ii. 246, 247; a means of safety, ii. 247; compared to an everflowing river, ii. 248; stands midway between opposites, ii. 250; God of, why so called, iii. 85; broken between God and men by sin, iii. 87; obtained by Christ's blood, iii. 88; restores from death, iii. 100; sets things straight, iii. 100; fits us for good, iii. 100; universal, at Christ's birth, iii. 100; a fruit of righteousness, v. 109; watchfulness against danger, the best security of, v. 211.

Peace-offering, partly eaten by the offerer, ii. 251, 296, 298; the Christian, Christ's body, ii. 251.

Πειρασμὸς signifies an evil kind of temptation, v. 443.

Pelagius, his heresy, v. 56.

Pelican, a type of Christ, iv. 331.

Pelting, i.e. peddling, v. 544.

Pen of iron, why Job wished to use, ii. 256.

Penances, prayers, fasting, and alms, exterior acts of repentance, i. 381, 441, 442.

Pentecost, why the Holy Ghost then manifested, iii. 110; because the law first given at that feast, iii. 111, 147, 148; it was the feast of harvest, iii. 111, and agreed in number with the year of jubilee, iii. 111, 112, 282; various names of this feast, iii. 115; Christ's coronation day, iii. 136; our duties at this feast, iii. 142—144; the Holy Ghost's first sealing day, iii. 202; both Baptisms, of fire and of water, took place at this feast, iii. 242; prisoners to Satan then set free, iii. 283; a true day of jubilee, iii. 283; an acceptable day, iii. 343.

People, rages as the sea, ii. 20; Jewish people unsteady, ii. 25; brutish, ii. 25; malicious, ii. 25; headstrong, ii. 26.

———— God's, like sheep, ii. 28, 29, 32.

———— their suffrage required to the appointment of a king, according to Bellarmine, iv. 52; should rejoice in a good king, iv. 83; cannot depose a king, iv. 108; should share in his joys and sorrows, iv. 120.

People, madness of, v. 17.

Pepin summoned the Council of Vern, v. 162.

Perfection, angelic, we are most near to, when we come from Holy Eucharist, i. 214; absolute, not to be had in this life, iii. 95; relative there may be, iii. 95; is of grace, not of nature, v. 306, 315; we should proceed in it, v. 315.

Perjury forbidden, v. 74, 75; its several kinds, v. 76; its punishment, v. 77.

Perking, lifting up the head, v. 15.

Perseverance, called by S. Gregory, the preserver of virtues, ii. 72; by S. Augustine, the queen of virtues, ii. 72, 76; by S. Bernard, the only crowned virtue, ii. 72, 77; without it, the just will fall, ii. 73; how to attain it, ii. 74; wicked more persevering in sin, than God's people in good, ii. 75, 111; Satan chiefly set against it, ii. 77.

Person of man, Christ took not, but the nature, i. 8, 9; of Christ, i. 23, 107; of Christ, God spoke of to the fathers in many places, i. 104.

Persons, that God is no respecter of, how to be understood, iii. 330, 331.

Peter, S., first boastful, afterwards fell, ii. 63; first of men at the sepulchre, ii. 224; permitted to see Christ after His resurrection, ii. 235; called Barjona when the keys were given him, iii. 254; timid before Pentecost, courageous afterwards, iii. 138; preached the first Whitsun sermon, iii. 302; prophesied in expounding Scripture rightly, iii. 313; compared to Jonah, iii. 324; gained religious knowledge by degrees, iii. 327; contrasted with the successors in his chair, iii. 328; ignorant at first of God's designs towards the Gentiles, iii. 329; his imprecation against Simon Magus, iv. 8; his fault in dissuading Christ from His passion, v. 228; before his disputation with Simon Magus the whole Church is said to have fasted, v. 491.

Petronius endeavoured to bring Caligula's image into the temple of God, v. 129.

Pew-fellow, i.e. boon companion, ii. 91, v. 33.

Pharisees, mere actors, i. 407; the 'non sicuts' of the world, i. 412; superstitious, ii. 304; hypocrites, ii. 305; good Church destroyers, ii. 352; added to God's word by traditions, v. 57; instances of hearing and not doing, v. 197.

Pharaoh, his frequent relapses, ii. 68;

given up to a hardened mind, v. 447.
Philip, S., instructed the eunuch, ii. 119.
Philo Judæus explains why the Fifth Commandment is placed on the confines of the two tables, ii. 10, 284.
Philosophers distort the sense of Scripture, v. 57.
Phinehas stayed the plague by praying and executing judgment (Ps. cvi. 30), how these phrases reconciled, v. 230 —233; prayed as a priest, v. 230, 231; executed judgment as a magistrate, v. 232, 233.
Φύσησις distinguished from φύσις, iii. 274, and φυσίωσις, iii. 384.
Φύσις distinguished from φύσησις, iii. 274, and φυσίωσις, iii. 384.
Φυσίωσις distinguished from φύσις, iii. 274, and φύσησις, iii. 275.
Piercing, the nature of Christ's, ii. 121 —126; the knowledge of this, the highest knowledge, ii. 122.
Pighius, Albert, owned that the schoolmen had obscured the doctrine of justification, v. 124.
Pilate, his question illustrates the way in which we seek God, i. 312; only an instrumental cause of Christ's death, ii. 125, 127, 151; acknowledged Christ's innocence, ii. 147.
Pilgrims, all Christians such, v. 377, 378, 380.
Pillar of salt, Lot's wife, why changed to, ii. 71.
Pillars of a land, what are they, ii. 4, seq.; how reestablished, ii. 4; counsel of man, and counsel of God, ii. 6; worship of God and execution of justice, ii. 7; God Himself, ii. 7; religion and justice, ii. 9, 10; they must be upheld by the prince, ii. 10; when one is neglected, the other will soon fail, ii. 12.
Pity naturally desired, ii. 139.
Plague, A, comes not by chance, v. 224; but by way of judgment, v. 225; thus much indicated by the Hebrew word for it, v. 225; its causes natural, v. 225, and supernatural, v. 226; inflicted by angels, v. 226; to be averted by prayer, v. 230, and by execution of judgment, v. 232; by public authority, v. 232; and by each man on himself, v. 233.
Planets, conjunction of, brings no good gifts to us, iii. 370.
Plato on the duality of man, i. 128.
Pleasure and Pride caused man's fall, ii. 165.
Pliny on the Star in the East, i. 255.
Plots averted by God's preventing goodness, iv. 112. See Gunpowder Plot.

Pœna damni and pœna sensus both suffered by Christ, ii. 143—146.
Ποιηταὶ and πρακτικοὶ distinguished, v. 195.
Poison, use of, approved of by the Jesuits, iv. 355.
Polycarp, S., observed Easter, ii. 425.
Poor, their relief a good end, ii. 42; they are forgotten amongst men's wastefulness, ii. 51; needless distinction between duties due to them and to Christ, ii. 53; Gospel addressed to them, iii. 290; especially to the poor in spirit, iii. 291; the strength of their cause is in God and their innocency, v. 18; public provision for them recommended, v. 43; two classes of, deserving and undeserving, the former to be relieved, the latter made to work, v. 43; well taken care of by foreigners in England, v. 43; the bankers with whom we may lay up our treasure, v. 46; helping them we do good to ourselves, v. 46, 47.
Poor, Christ manifested in them, v. 274, 278. (From Bishop Buckeridge's Funeral Sermon.)
Pope, wishes to claim emperors as his anointed, iv. 51, and to dispose of their kingdoms, iv. 51, if they were heretics, iv. 67, and when he judges it expedient, iv. 67; his power to make a book of Scripture authentic, iv. 314; dispenses with many of the commandments, v. 42; encouraged the English Romanists to put their livings to sale, v. 42.
Port-sale, iii. 149.
Postvorta and Antevorta, iv. 233, 235.
Pouring out of the Spirit, shows His Person, Procession, and Godhead, iii. 305; implies abundance, iii. 306; shows that the Spirit was sent, iii. 306; and that He may be withheld, iii. 306; implies also different degrees of his gifts, iii. 306; poured out through the Son, iii. 307; first on His nature, and through that on ours, iii. 307, 308; why said to be on all flesh, iii. 308—310; to run on from the day of Pentecost till the last day, iii. 315.
Power, all given from above, not below, iv. 52.
Praise, man's, a punishment, i. 400.
Πρακτικοὶ and ποιηταὶ distinguished, v. 195.
Prayer, of use in war, i. 328; of no avail without keeping from sin, i. 328; and preaching, no need to compare them together, iii. 22; useless without the Spirit, iii. 170; our tongue to God, iii. 311; the very end of preach-

ing, iii. 318; Satan would bring it into contempt, iii. 318; closely connected with salvation, iii. 320; presupposes faith, iii. 320; a part of righteousness, iii. 338, 339; and prophecy suit well together, iv. 6; abuses of the Church of Rome in, v. 68, 69; means of obtaining forgiveness, v. 95; and of appeasing God's anger, v. 230; goes up as incense, to remove the infection of sin, v. 230; of the priest, of greater efficacy, v. 231; grounded on our own insufficiency, v. 302, 310, 321, 332; the conduit of grace, v. 311, 327; means of coming to God, v. 321; its necessity, v. 323; should be earnest, v. 323, 329; enjoined on us, v. 323; its neglect a sin, v. 323; compared to incense, v. 324; promises attached to it, v. 326, 327; practised by God's saints, v. 326; comfort found in it, v. 327; a city of refuge, v. 327; all parts of our body to be used therein, v. 327; to be offered according to God's will, v. 328; denied if we ask for evil things, v. 328; to be offered with fervency and reverence, v. 329, 335; importunity needed therein, v. 330; God's threats if we neglect it, v. 331; power to pray given by the Spirit, v. 332; public and private benefits result from, v. 334; suggested by nature, v. 334, 335; to be offered with heart, understanding, and affections, v. 335; consists more in fervency than in fine words, v. 340; Christ and the saints patterns of, v. 343; it is a refuge and an offering, v. 344; a dignified pursuit, v. 345, 352; interruptions of, to be avoided, v. 345; an interpreter of our desires, v. 346, 351; a better pursuit than searching into curious questions, v. 347; a pledge of our charity, v. 350, 369; the effect of grace, v. 351; means of conversing with God, v. 352; needed because of our fears, or our wants, v. 353; a vent for our desires, v. 354; fixed hours to be appointed for, v. 354; specially necessary for God's ministers, v. 355; typified by incense, v. 355; public and private distinguished, v. 357; various kinds of, v. 357, 358; to be offered for persons of every class, v. 370, 371; a scourge of Satan, v. 424; a key to open and shut heaven, v. 424; hindered by sin, v. 425; means of obtaining forgiveness, v. 431.

Prayer, Form of, appointed by Moses, remained till S. John the Baptist's time, v. 348; who adopted another, v. 348; a better taught by Christ, v. 348; in answer to His disciples' request, v. 349.

Prayer, The Lord's, a vain imagination not to use it, v. 68; why used in all our services, v. 68; to be always used, v. 349, 360; is perfect, v. 349; teaches us that we should pray vocally as well as mentally, v. 349, 360; sure to be accepted, v. 349, 350; a compendium of our faith, v. 350, 369; its clauses considered, v. 351, *seq.;* contains an example of every kind of prayer, v. 359, 360, 369; to be used not only as a pattern, but in its actual words, v. 360; a most perfect form, v. 361; the order of the things asked for to be carefully noticed, v. 361, 381; teaches the duty of intercessory prayer, v. 370, 371; has seven petitions, v. 381; the first of them refers to God's glory, the last to our necessities, v. 381; it first teaches to ask for good, next for escaping evil, v. 391; the number of its petitions a disputed question, v. 449; the clauses which speak of not leading into temptation, and of deliverance from evil, not tautologous, v. 449, 450; the evil from which we pray to be delivered explained by the Greek Fathers to mean Satan, v. 451; doxology of, taken from the Old Testament, v. 458; begins and ends with an acknowledgment of God, v. 459; 'kingdom, power, and glory,' therein mentioned, represent the Trinity, v. 463; all its petitions found in substance in the Old Testament, v. 469.

Preaching, too much sought after, i. 299; the lighting of one torch by another, iii. 131; must be quickened by the Spirit, iii. 170; extempore, not approved of, iii. 281; liberty of, not sanctioned by the promise of the gift of prophecy to the Church, iii. 313, 315; the word of reconciliation, v. 94.

Precepts compared with examples, iv. 401.

Prerogative, our, as Christians, very great compared with all men besides, i. 2; of the last days above the first, i. 102; our, to be saints, given us by Christ, i. 109.

Presumption, when most likely to be indulged in, v. 514, and in what place, v. 515; the danger of, v. 521; too much stimulates our faith, v. 528; is bad divinity, v. 531; our way lies between it and desperation, v. 535.

Prevention better than deliverance, iv. 233, 267.

Pride healed by the Incarnation, i. 206;

loses Christ, i. 207; is prodigality's whetstone, a saying of S. Basil, ii. 93; v. 32; humbled, by falling into sin, iii. 174; an obstacle to receiving the Holy Ghost, iii. 196; spoils all the riches and virtues of the world, v. 9; comes of Satan, v. 9; the worm of riches, v. 11; makes a man despise his brethren, v. 13; outward signs of, v. 13, 14; exalts a man above his condition, v. 14, 15; makes him unwilling to receive reproof, v. 16; will be thrown down by God, v. 17; its root, confidence in riches, v. 18; a special cause of God's wrath, v. 227; succeeds, when every other temptation fails, v. 538.

Priests, office of, to purge, i. 116; Christ a, i. 24; Christ, the only true, i. 77; the counsel and direction of, not sought after as the Church directs, i. 450; beget again our souls, ii. 367; the words 'Receive ye the Holy Ghost,' &c. necessary for the consecration of, iii. 263; not the source of kingly power, iv. 281; succeeded to the seventy disciples, v. 64; to them committed the word of reconciliation, v. 94; prayers of, are of great efficacy, v. 231; should not only teach, but intercede for the people, v. 356; why termed the Lord's remembrancers, v. 356; divided into watches, among the Jews, for the purpose of continual prayer, v. 356.

Princes, a commendation of, ii. 5; from them peace and quietness, ii. 8; to be prayed for above all men, ii. 8; compared to stones, ii. 272; their tyranny towards their wealthy subjects, v. 23, 24. See also *Kings*.

Prison, there is one of the soul, as well as of the body, iii. 293.

Prison-irons, man's, are vanity and corruption, iii. 209.

Procession of the Son from the Father, i. 110.

Prodigality is excited by pride, ii. 93; v. 32; leads to selfishness, v. 32, 33.

Prometheus and *Epimetheus*, iv. 233.

Promises, God's, when fulfilled, are gospel, or good tidings, iii. 146; to be ever kept, v. 75.

Prophecies, the fulfilment of, a great stay to our faith, i. 18; can come from God only, i. 18; the chief of Christ, given in times of distress, i. 20, 238; the partial and detached predictions of Christ, i. 104; hang in suspense until fulfilled, i. 106; the most enduring witness, i. 255.

Prophecy of Isaiah to Ahaz, applied by the Jews to Hezekiah, i. 19; occasion of, i. 20; the most enduring witness, i. 255; the gift of the Spirit, iii. 304; compared to dew upon herbs, iii. 305; God's tongue to us, iii. 311; equivalent to preaching, iii. 312; makes not new predictions, interprets the old, iii. 312; as shown in S. Peter's case, iii. 313; not so 'poured on all flesh,' as to sanction liberty of preaching, iii. 313; gift of, not bestowed on all, iii. 314; those may prophecy who have the gift, iii. 314, 315; and in subjection to the Spirit, iii. 315; whether further gifts of prophecy will be conferred on the Church, iii. 315, 316; will not save a man, iii. 319; one of God's lights, iii. 372; suits well with prayer, iv. 16.

Prophets, in times past God spake by, i. 105; none in the Church now, iii. 233; when their actions are to be regarded as precedents, iv. 251.

Proverb, Greek, ii. 102.

——— Hebrew, 'we must leap into Gerizim, creep into Ebal,' iv. 9.

Proverbs, Solomon had special felicity in, ii. 3.

Providence, does not work by miracle, iv. 68; to be furthered by human foresight, iv. 68.

Psalm, the inscription of every, the key of, ii. 3.

——— lxviii. 18, applied to Christ by S. Paul, iii. 221; when first written and used, iii. 222.

——— lxxv., when written, ii. 3.

——— lxxvi., David's own prayer, iv. 319.

——— lxxvii., when written, ii. 16.

——— xcv., used in the early Church at the beginning of service, ii. 334.

——— cix., Psalm of imprecation, iv. 8; and against treachery, iv. 33.

——— cxviii., why read on Easter Day, ii. 271; originally meant of David, ii. 271.

——— cxlv., David's own song of praise, iv. 319.

Psalms, may all be resolved into two words, Hallelujah and Hosannah, iv. 225; the most comforting part of Scripture, v. 522; might lead to presumption, v. 527.

Punishment not always to be inflicted according to men's deserts, iv. 255.

Pur (the lot) compared with $\pi\hat{\upsilon}\rho$ (fire), iv. 388; meaning of the word in Hebrew, iv. 393.

Purim, feast of, why observed, iv. 204; when instituted, iv. 385, 386; by whose authority, iv. 401; how observed, iv. 403, 404.

Purposes, hell full of good, iv. 358.

Q.

Quartodecimans, their origin, ii. 415.
Questions, unprofitable and curious, to be avoided, v. 347.

R.

Rabbins considered the temple as a model of the whole world, ii. 348; explained the last days, the days of Christ, iii. 304.
Rabshakeh, why he spoke Hebrew, ii. 5.
Ragman roll, iii. 66.
Rainbow the close of the Deluge, ii. 17.
Rams-horn sounded at the Jubilee in remembrance of the ram caught in the thicket, iii. 299, 300.
Rantism (sprinkling), iii. 136.
Ravaillac, the murderer of Henry IV., tortured by red-hot pincers, iv. 71.
Readiness in good deeds valued by God, v. 39; helps in their performance, v. 39.
Reasons, inward and outward, ii. 46; one real, the other false, ii. 46.
Rebellion, sin of, i. 343; a sin against our baptism, iii. 255, 256; to be prevented by laws and human watchfulness, iv. 69; punished by God, iv. 70, 71.
Rebels, enemies to God, iv. 13, 14, 23; called sons of Belial, iv. 14, 23; enemies to mankind, iv. 15, 23; and to the Church, iv. 16, 17, 23; ever suffer punishment, iv. 18, 19, 33, 34, 70, 71; in various ways, iv. 34; justly cursed, iv. 23; plagued by God, iv. 93, 94; their evil ends, iv. 294.
Receiving, great, is little remembering, ii. 79.
Reconciliation the second degree of acceptance, iii. 298.
Red the colour of the passion, iii. 75; and also the colour of sin, iii. 75.
Red Sea a type of death, ii. 293, 294.
Redeemer, A, Job's belief in, ii. 258; must needs be a living person, ii. 258; both God, ii. 258, and man, ii. 259; of kin with the persons redeemed, ii. 259; therefore God Incarnate, ii. 259; represents the persons of the redeemed, ii. 261; will make a complete redemption both of body and soul, ii. 262.
Redemption, the price of, a high one, i. 58; the work of Christ, iii. 208; a buying back of what has been lost, iii. 208; His an entire redemption, iii. 208; how effected, iii. 209; on what day, iii. 209; when fully bestowed, iii. 209.

Reformers of the Church should reform themselves, ii. 43.
Regenerate, man, not to be inactive, v. 483; to go as he is led, v. 484; his course compared to that of a vessel, v. 484.
Regeneration, the laver of, cleanses us from original sin, i. 113; one of our three great blessings, ii. 365; produces hope, ii. 366; the result of God's mercy, ii. 370; a higher blessing than our natural birth, ii. 371; conferred by the sacrament of regeneration, ii. 372; implies previous loss, ii. 372; why needed, ii. 372; to what we are regenerate, ii. 372; our first resurrection, ii. 375; owing to Christ's resurrection, ii. 375; a supernatural gift, v. 307.
Rehoboam given as a ruler for a judgment on the people, ii. 20; drove his people, did not lead them, ii. 23.
Religion, the Christian, alone can satisfy the conscience, i. 182; one of the pillars of a land, ii. 9, 10; roots justice within, ii. 10; makes with justice an arch of government, ii. 10; not to be a passive thing, iii. 319; not to consist in set phrases, v. 38; *a religando,* v. 464; binds God and us together, v. 464; outward as well as inward, v. 554.
Remembrance, the duty of, ii. 64; God's ministers His remembrancers, ii. 64; Scripture frequently calls us to, ii. 64, 65; of two kinds, ii. 66; days of, enjoined in Scripture, iv. 204.
Remission of sins, continual need of, iii. 262; v. 425; proceeds from and by Christ through the Holy Ghost, iii. 265; both the Body of Christ and the Spirit operate towards it, iii. 279; the effect of Christ's death, v. 83; good tidings, v. 88; not granted to the angels which fell, v. 88; spoken of before retention, to show forth God's great mercy, v. 88, 89; power of remitting comes from God, v. 89; imparted to man, v. 90, 93; the ordinary act of the Church, v. 93; a Priest necessary for its conveyance, v. 93, 94; by what means remitted, v. 94; begins on earth, is carried on in heaven, v. 102; follows at once on absolution, v. 162.
Repentance, may be deferred too long, i. 315, 351; joy in, according to S. Augustine, i. 316, 319; death-bed repentance, i. 317; false, i. 318; war to be undertaken with, i. 322; spring a time for, i. 357, 432; complete, i. 359; the nature of, diversely set forth in Scripture, i. 360; should not be

turning from one sin to another, i. 363; gives up the occasion of sin, i. 364; accompanied with fasting, i. 365, 367, 393; when true, i. 365; best performed in retirement, i. 369; indignation and revenge pertain to, i. 371, 372; prayer, fasting, alms, exterior acts of, i. 381, 441, 442; topics of, i. 373; the four elements of, i. 386; the first commandment of the Gospel, i. 418; time required for, i. 431; is concerned with the body, i. 439; rules for, i. 441, 442; ours a 'pœnitentia pœnitenda,' i. 446; requires the counsel and direction of a priest, i. 450; a duty, in consequence of Christ's resurrection, ii. 399, 401; derives its virtue from it, ii. 402; is the soul's resurrection, ii. 402; delivers from death, ii. 401; vain imaginations respecting it, v. 58; needed in order to absolution, v. 98; its nature, v. 99, 100; consists of sorrow for past, and care against future sin, v. 442.

Repentance, in what sense ascribed to God, iii. 213, 214; and why, v. 221.

Reproach wounds deeply, ii. 124.

Reprobation, God's, not to be inquired into, v. 398.

Repropitiation the highest degree of acceptance, iii. 298.

Resistance, doctrine of modern Romanists on, iii. 255. See also *Romanists*.

Rest is inglorious, ii. 320.

Resurrection scoffed at by the Greeks, ii. 191; we have already risen with Christ, ii. 199; we must rise daily in spirit, ii. 199; from the dominion of sin, ii. 200; this a moral resurrection, ii. 202; from sin, harder than the resurrection of the body, ii. 203; ours twofold, ii. 206; illustrated by first-fruits, ii. 212, 214; by rising from sleep, ii. 213, 214; by sowing of seed, ii. 213, 214; what is the better resurrection, ii. 218; we shall then be like angels, ii. 231; our resurrection and Christ's closely bound together, ii. 261; the fruit of, to see God, ii. 261; will be of the same body, ii. 263; of the mind here, of the body hereafter, ii. 312; of the body the last regeneration, ii. 375; the great end of all things, ii. 381; the true Passover from death to life, ii. 381; compared to the springing of herbs, iii. 16; Easter the feast of, iii. 17; incomplete, unless followed by Ascension, iii. 46; of two kinds, to life and to death, iii. 46; Christ's, ascribed both to Himself and to the Father, iii. 89; a bringing back from a worse estate to a better, iii. 93; manifested in good works, iii. 99, 100; a transient act with permanent force, iii. 100; soul first raised from sin, body afterwards raised to life, iii. 101.

Retirement, the uses of, iii. 199.

Reubenites, by choosing Gilead, lost share in land of promise, ii. 90.

Revelation, different manners of, i. 104, 105; no new, to be looked for, i. 107; contempt of, i. 428.

Revenge one cause of rebellion, iv. 12; peculiar to the meanest natures, v. 436.

Reverence to be used in God's worship, ii. 333; used by the angels, ii. 338; neglect of, an injury to the Church, ii. 341; enjoined by Christ's words to Mary Magdalene, iii. 24, 28, *seq.*; due to Him from us now, iii. 33; too great better than too little, iii. 33; too much neglected, iii. 33; to be observed in prayer, v. 329, 363, 373; Scripture motives for, v. 329.

Reward, a Christian's, not the wages of a hireling, ii. 76.

Rheims, Council of. See *Council of Rheims*.

Rich, Christ gives them warning, ii. 80; may be found in Abraham's bosom, ii. 88; 1 Tim. vi. 17, called the rich man's Scripture, v. 4; the charge enjoined them, v. 4, 5; need a charge, v. 7; unwilling to hear it, v. 7; Timothy solemnly enjoined to give them one, v. 8; have the world at their will, v. 10; made much of by it, v. 11; make much of themselves, v. 11; their best support to be found in Scripture, v. 17; if proud, will be pulled down, v. 17; trust to their wealth when everything else fails, v. 19; 'rich of this world,' how explained, v. 20, 21; their posterity dwindles away, v. 24, 25; their misery at death, v. 26; their duty to do good to others, v. 31, 32; instances of such as did so, v. 34; more expected from them, v. 39.

Riches, their uncertainty, v. 9, 19, 20; prevail over other gifts of God, v. 10; rule in the seat of judgment, v. 10; Christ betrayed for the sake of, v. 11; prevail against learning and eloquence, v. 11; cause great danger of pride, v. 11, 12; confidence in, the root of pride, v. 18; not to be trusted in, v. 18, 19; much said against them in Scripture, v. 21; called the riches 'of this world,' because both gained and lost, and to be left here, v. 21; the dangers they are exposed to, v.

22; we must leave them if they do not leave us, v. 23; swept away by princes, or by war, v. 23, 24; sin committed in gaining them remains when they are gone, v. 26; their uncertainty a blessing, v. 26; we must do homage to God for them, v. 27; a vain idol to trust to, v. 27, 28; unable to remove any bodily suffering, v. 27, 28; come to us not by our own labour, but by God's blessing, v. 28; the true use of, v. 33; how much misused, v. 33, 34; riches of goodness compared with worldly wealth, v. 38; to be expended on the Church, v. 41, and on the poor, v. 43; to spend them on good works is indeed to store them up, v. 45; a heavenly exchange, v. 45; compared to seed, v. 47; stored up here will be wasted, v. 47; how to secure them, v. 49.

Righteousness, of the law, very different from that of Christ, i. 190; and peace not separable, i. 191, 192; what it consists in, iii. 38; man's natural, needs baptism, iii. 243; includes our duty to men, iv. 372; how distinguished from holiness, iv. 372, 373; not to be excused by attention to God's worship, iv. 379; not to be measured by human laws, iv. 379; does not overreach or extort, iv. 380; God delights to be called by this title, v. 104, 105; God's only worth remembering, v. 109; has salvation and peace for its fruits, v. 109; Christ is ours, not only our justifier, v. 112, 113; spoken of as wrought in us, or as imparted to us, v. 114; scriptural terms respecting it run in judicial phrase, v. 115; opposed to condemning, v. 116; whether our inherent righteousness can be accepted, v. 116, *seq.*; the saints of the Old Testament confessed its imperfection, v. 117; and so too the fathers and schoolmen, v. 118, *seq.*; opinions of Romish writers concerning inherent righteousness, v. 119.

Right hand, Christ's, Zebedee's son sought to sit at, ii. 317.

——— *God's*, a place of power, ii. 183; and of fulness of joy, ii. 184.

Rising up against, spoken of such as execute long-cherished malice, iv. 10; and of those who oppose lawful superiors, iv. 10.

Rod of government miraculous, ii. 20; of two kinds, ii. 28.

Romanists, modern, their rebellious doctrines, iii. 255; iv. 36, 57, 64, 67; make a conscience of them, iv. 65; boast of them, iv. 66; make rebellion an heroic act, iv. 69; promise it eternal rewards, iv. 69; their theory of the origin of kingly power, iv. 80; their opinions on treason alluded to, iv. 141, 142, 145, 146, 157, 160, 173, 188, 303, 305; accuse their opponents of negligence in well-doing, v. 35, 36.

Romans, first praised by S. Paul, afterwards fell back, ii. 63.

Rome, Council of. See *Council of Rome.*

Romulus, a shepherd, iii. 85.

Rulers set up for the good of mankind, iv. 15.

S.

Sabellius, his error concerning Christ's nature, i. 87; iii. 349.

Sacrament, of Lord's Supper, no public service complete without, i. 62; conduit-pipe of grace, i. 100; men become more like angels after receiving it, i. 214, 231; we are partakers of Christ's flesh and blood in it, i. 231; Christ's death set forth in it, ii. 121; therein Christ is in us, and we in Him, ii. 205; the application of Christ's sacrifice, ii. 301; iii. 102; neglect of, a cause of God's wrath, v. 228.

Sacraments, the two set forth in Christ's death, ii. 134; present what they represent, ii. 402; are *verba visibilia*, ii. 144; the number of, diversely stated, iii. 263; whether Holy Orders to be included in the number, iii. 263; strictly speaking, only two, iii. 348; grace in a sacrament is *gratum faciens*, not merely *gratis data* to confer an office, iii. 263; seals of the covenant, iii. 161, 219; and of God's acceptance, iii. 343; seven, in correspondence with the seven seals, iii. 219.

Sacrifice, in the Lord's Supper, i. 30, 82; the Christian's, threefold, i. 381; takes away sin by transferring it, ii. 297; the Eucharist a memorial, ii. 300; but one true, ii. 300; offered generally, applied specially by Sacraments, ii. 301; morning and evening, appointed under the law, v. 354.

——— Christ's the only true, v. 260; due only to God, v. 263; the Church offers herself as a, v. 263—265; of ourselves due to God, v. 266; of praise and of confession to be daily offered, v. 266, 267; alms a part of sacrifice, v. 267, 268, 280; also contrition and gratitude, v. 281. (*From Bishop Buckeridge's Funeral Sermon.*)

Sacrifices, in the Christian Church, applicatory of Christ's propitiation, v.

259; memorials of Christ, v. 260—262, 266. (*From Bp. Buckeridge's Funeral Sermon.*)
Sacrilege, to be avoided, i. 335; destroys, idolatry only pollutes a temple, ii. 351; prevalent, v. 42.
Sadducees were profane, ii. 305.
Saints, a cloud of witnesses, ii. 159; guides to us, followers of Christ, ii. 160; could not redeem others, as needing a Redeemer themselves, ii. 259; cannot challenge reward for their own merits, v. 121; their prayers benefit the whole body of the faithful, v. 339; long for the coming of Christ's kingdom, v. 394; do God's will in heaven, v. 408, 409.
Salem, as signifying peace, a fit tabernacle of the Holy Ghost, iii. 238.
Salt, a type of continuance, iii. 126.
Salvation, a ground of joy, iv. 106; a fruit of righteousness, v. 109; given by God, v. 238; of every kind, v. 239.
Samaritan, the good, a type of Christ, ii. 134, 142.
——— praised for returning to give glory to God, v. 460.
Samaritans, their ground of quarrel with the Jews, iv. 244; compared to ours with the Romanists, iv. 247; why inhospitable to Christ, iv. 246.
Sampson, why he held the two pillars, ii. 6; when placed between them, a type of Christ on the cross, ii. 329.
Samuel, in his old age ill requited, ii. 115; especially guided by God to choose David, iv. 80, 83; an example of intercessory prayer, v. 355.
Sanctification, God's gift, v. 389.
Sanctify, with God, means to make holy, with men, to account holy, v. 384; why applied to God's name, v. 385.
Sanders, Nicholas, in favour of destroying heretics, iv. 248; why sent into Ireland, iv. 256.
Sardica, Council of. See *Council of Sardica.*
Satan, always lying in wait, i. 401; by unhappy adages and wanton songs breathes infection and poison, ii. 3; v. 204; the spiritual Leviathan, ii. 401; led captive by Christ, iii. 228; detained Christ wrongfully in the grave, iii. 229; the arch-enemy, iv. 87, 335; as cruel as God is merciful, iv. 334, 335; condemns unthankfulness, v. 31; sets up vain imaginations for men to worship, v. 55; called Apollyon, and Abaddon, v. 239; busy in destruction, v. 239, 240, especially of kings, v. 240, 242; desires anarchy, v. 241; has become the tyrant of this world, v. 392; makes it rebel against God, v. 392; to be prayed against, v. 394; most malicious against those who are just delivered from his thraldom, v. 443; tempts us to our hurt, v. 443, 444, both by prosperity and adversity, v. 445; can go no further than God permits, v. 445; if he cannot tempt, will torment, v. 450, 451; a serpent and a lion, v. 452, 483, 494; his claws are all temporal calamities, v. 452; contrasted with Christ, v. 454; attacked our Lord as he had done our first parents, v. 480; means a defamer, v. 482; defames God to us, and us to God, v. 482, 483; has only such power as is given him, v. 484; always sets himself against good designs, v. 487; assaulted Christ as soon as baptized, v. 487, 488, 494; his temptations contrasted with God's, v. 494; tempts even in holiest places and times, v. 494; waits for the fittest time, v. 495; watches men's dispositions, v. 495; tempts through the means of grace, v. 496; suggested to Adam evil thoughts of God, v. 496; tempts to distrust, presumption, and idolatry, v. 497, 501, and to unlawful means of support, v. 498; endeavoured to overcome Christ by taunts, v. 499; would lead us to repine, v. 499; gives no comfort to his dupes, v. 500; wishes us to doubt our sonship to God, v. 502; to be repelled by Scripture texts, v. 503; his spite against Scripture, v. 504, 505; tempted the Israelites to idolatry, that Moses might break the tables of the law, v. 505; foiled in one temptation, tries another, v. 512, 513; has courage above his strength, v. 513; makes each defeat the means of a new temptation, v. 513; would lead either to distrust or to presumption, v. 514; makes choice of a new place for a new temptation, v. 514; why he led Christ to a pinnacle of the temple, v. 515; had power given him over Christ's body, v. 516, 517; wished to make it doubtful whether Christ were the Son of God, v. 518; a flatterer, v. 519; strives to quench faith, v. 519; puffs up, that he may cast down, v. 520; cannot ruin us unless we lend a helping hand, v. 520; quotes Scripture, v. 521, making it the savour of death, v. 522; misquotes it, v. 522, and perverts it, v. 526; importunate in his assaults, v. 536; varies them, v. 537; leads on from one to another, v. 537; why called Beelzebub, v. 538; why he carried Christ to a high moun-

tain, v. 539; uses craft and deceit, v. 539; lays bait for each one according to his special weakness, v. 542; tempted Christ with the kingdoms of the world, v. 543; demanded an exchange, v. 544; tempts by his instruments, v. 545; can buy men at a cheaper rate than with kingdoms, v. 546; when he gives he only barters, v. 547; to be withstood in various ways, v. 551; his promises false, v. 552.

Saul, his misgovernment, ii. 4; he and his sons slain, ii. 4; weakened the pillars of the land, ii. 11, 13; neglected religion, ii. 11, and justice, ii. 12; God took from him His Spirit, ii. 12, and sent on him a furious spirit, ii.12; weak towards the enemy, ii. 12; unjust in reward and punishment, ii. 12, 13; remained steadfast for two years, ii. 68; his enmity to David, iv. 27; without any reason, iv. 27; from envy, iv. 27, 28; was not to be killed, iv. 31, 34, 39, notwithstanding his tyranny, iv. 37; usurped the Priest's office, iv. 37, 38; he shed the Priests' blood, iv. 38, was possessed with an evil spirit, iv. 38; gained not the Holy Spirit by being anointed, iv. 58; a type of the destiny of all kings, iv. 155; David's enemy, iv. 158; corrupted by wealth, v. 12; his sin in choosing his own course, v. 229; fell from neglect of prayer, v. 323.

Saviour, joy in the name of, i. 73, 77; all have need to joy in the birth of, i. 74; sinners' need of, i. 74; many typical saviours, one perfect and complete, i. 75; concurrence of the Three Persons in, i. 77; no true, but the Lord, i. 79; the Divine nature implied in, i. 80.

Scarlet, why the colour of Doctors' and of Judges' robes, iii. 76; the principal colour in the Priests' garments, iii. 76; the colour of soldiers, iii. 76, 77.

Schoolmen, The, on the eternal generation of Christ, i. 164, 165; on seeking God for Himself, i. 313; their definition of mourning, i. 370; speak differently on the question of justification in their closets, and in their set discussions, v. 118; obscured the doctrine of justification, v. 124.

Scribes, no better for knowing where Christ was to be born, i. 260.

Scripture has four senses—1, literal; 2, analogical; 3, moral; 4, prophetical, iii. 222, 223; its profitableness in its several parts, v. 4; 1 Tim. vi. 17, called the rich man's Scripture, v. 4; to be interpreted according to the sense ever held in the Church, v. 57; the shield against Satan's fiery darts, v. 503; a storehouse of offensive or defensive armoury, v. 504; a charm against the serpent, v. 504; long kept from the people, v. 505; to be read with faith, v. 505, 525; the property of all God's children, v. 506; to be meditated on, v. 531.

Sealing, the work of the Holy Ghost, iii. 208, 211; a putting God's mark on us to show we are His, iii. 210; no redemption without it, iii. 211, 212; we should be willing and prepared for this sealing, iii. 216, 217; after sealing, we should not break the bond, iii. 217, or have another seal stamped over it, iii. 217; the Holy Ghost seals by sacraments, iii. 219.

Secrets, natural desire of man to pry into, i. 33.

Security is to be feared, ii. 72; of salvation, great danger in, v. 531.

——— (freedom from care), its dangers, v. 537.

Sedition, opposed both to God and the king, iv. 305; is explained to mean 'going aside,' iv. 306; meddlers with, censured, iv. 306, 307; how it can be meddled with, iv. 308.

Seed, the springing of, a type of the Resurrection, ii. 213, 214; riches compared to, v. 47.

Seleucia, Council of. See *Council of Seleucia.*

Self-deception the worst kind of deception, v. 200, 201; ends in eternal ruin, v. 201.

Self-love the cause of deceit, v. 173.

Sentences, like coins, those most valued which have most matter in fewest words, ii. 61; the shortest contain most matter, iv. 278.

Separation leads to sedition, iv. 306.

Sepulchre, our natural fear of, ii. 232. See *Grave.*

Sermons, Christ's, are law-lectures, i. 299; delusion in, i. 407, 421, 423; hearing of, has usurped too high a place, iv. 376, 377; all people admitted to hear them in the primitive Church, iv. 377; what irreverence now shown at, iv. 377; godliness consists not in hearing of them, v. 187, 202. See *Preaching.*

Sermon-warm, iii. 141.

Serpent, brazen, lifted up, ii. 120, so as to be seen, ii. 142; of use only to those who looked at it, ii. 128.

——— its head bruised at Christ's Ascension, iii. 229; poisonous breath

INDEX TO SERMONS, ETC.

of, infected our first parents, iii. 266; to be cured by the breath of Christ, iii. 266; cursed by God for tempting our first parents to rebel, iv. 13.

Servants under the Law, made children under the Gospel, iii. 258.

Servant, unmerciful, the parable of, v. 440.

Service, to God or to Satan, the condition of our life, iv. 372; Satan's, the worse of the two, iv. 372; God's, is in holiness and righteousness, iv. 372; consists in public worship, iv. 374, 376; not in hearing sermons, iv. 376; of what kind, out of the congregation, iv. 378; eye-service and heart-service distinguished, iv. 381; God's, should be continuous, iv. 381, 382; how rewarded, iv. 383; due to God only, v. 553; is the bowing of the soul, v. 555.

Sessions of our hearts a forerunner of the great sessions hereafter, iii. 334.

Seven, a perfect number, ii. 311; a sacred number, iv. 321.

Shallum, wasteful, ii. 41.

Sheba, Queen of, a type of the Three Kings, i. 261.

Shechem, men of, covetous, ii. 46.

Sheep, when there is a king, people are as sheep of the pasture; when no king, sheep for the slaughter, ii. 11; by nature, we are stray, ii. 22; a type of God's people, ii. 28, 29; docile, profitable, unable to guide themselves, ii. 28, 32; easily led astray, ii. 29, 32; in what their wisdom and strength consists, ii. 29; Christians are Christ's, iii. 86; all had gone astray, iii. 87; and were appointed to slaughter, iii. 87.

Shepherd, keeps the flock safe from without, quiet from within, ii. 9; a term applied to kings, iii. 85; specially to Christ, iii. 85; ventures much for the sheep, iii. 85, 86.

Shepherds, why first chosen to hear the news of the Nativity, i. 65.

Shields, five, against Satan's fiery darts, v. 503, 504.

Shiloh, gentle waters of, a type of the Spirit, iii. 268.

—— washing his clothes in the blood of the grape, a prophecy of Christ, iii. 72, 74.

Short-sighted, men are frequently so, iii. 165.

Sibyls had the word of prophecy by the Holy Spirit, iii. 207.

Sign, A, must be a thing contrary to the course of nature, i. 201; why refused to the Jews, ii. 386; why granted to Gideon and Hezekiah, ii. 386.

Signs, when offered by God, not to be refused, v. 530; but not needlessly to be sought, v. 533.

Simeon and *Levi* cursed and disinherited by their father, iv. 184, 185; how this curse fulfilled, iv. 195, 197; brethren in violence, iv. 187; their guilt in murdering innocent and guilty alike, iv. 192; the vengeance they took, beyond the offence, iv. 193; their anger implacable, iv. 194; their curse afterwards reversed, iv. 197, 198.

Simon Magus had the water of Baptism without the Spirit, iii. 355; his wicked fraternity with Judas Iscariot, iii. 395; wished to be a great one, v. 9; misused his wealth, v. 11; the first heretic, v. 56.

Simony prevalent, v. 42, 547, 548; encouraged by the Pope, v. 42.

Sin, whether considered external or internal, healed by the blood of Christ, i. 113; original, cleansed in regeneration, i. 113; actual, purged in the Holy Communion, i. 113; unseemly in time of war, i. 330, 331; a fall and an error, i. 342; of infirmity, ignorance, and rebellion, i. 343; conversion from, and contrition for, i. 359; should beget sorrow, i. 369; to be hated, not merely feared, ii. 8; human laws breed only fear of, ii. 8; our wounded Christ, ii. 126, 127; its bitterness could be cured only by Christ's bitter sufferings, ii. 129; the cause of God's wrath, ii. 149, 152; by justice deserved death, ii. 196; we should rise from its dominion, ii. 200; taken away by being transferred, ii. 297; the cause of our losing Christ, iii. 14; a true cause of sorrow, iii. 14; brake peace between God and man, iii. 87; made human nature disjointed, iii. 96; a grievance of our own spirit, iii. 204; more so of the Holy Spirit, iii. 204; men by nature sold under it, iii. 208; the guilt of, is in the heart, iii. 213; should be a grievous thing to us, iii. 214, 215; a leader under Satan, iii. 228; spoken of sometimes as a frost, sometimes as a mist, iii. 266, 269; should be not only feared, but hated, iii. 272; enslaves, darkens, and bruises the soul, iii. 292, 293; cries aloud for judgment, iii. 321; its guilt and taint both taken away by Christ, iii. 347; to take them away the object of every religion, iii. 347; it is not enough unless we have both its guilt and taint removed, iii. 350, 351; compared to imprisonment, v. 85, 86;

binding and loosing used with reference to this resemblance, v. 86; at first it is liberty, then bondage, v. 86; makes itself felt at the last, v. 87; if retained, it is because of our hardness, v. 89; by what means remitted, v. 94; none excepted from remission, v. 96, though not forgiven to all persons, v. 97, 98; must be let go by us, ere God will let it go to us, v. 101; the root of all misery, v. 110; the cause of God's wrath, v. 227; specially some sins, v. 227, 228; the corruption of the soul, v. 227; a disease cured by Christ, v. 227; why called our own 'invention,' v. 228; to have vengeance executed on it, v. 232, 233; consciousness of, a reason for prayer, v. 353; has set up a kingdom in this world, v. 392; an enemy to God's kingdom, v. 392; present sin to be prayed against, v. 394; and past also, v. 424; deserves future punishment, v. 424; opposed to God's kingdom, v. 425; separates between God and us, v. 425; hinders our prayers, v. 425; remission of, needed by all, v. 425, but granted to man only, v. 426; termed a debt, v. 426; a handwriting against us, v. 426; springs naturally from us, v. 427; is committed daily, v. 428; is manifold, v. 429; to be sorrowed for, v. 429; forgiven on condition of forgiving others, v. 430—434, 436, 437; must be forsaken, if we look for forgiveness, v. 441; consists in power, not only in guilt, v. 442; evil in itself, and in its effects, v. 449.

Sinner, A, may remit sin, though not absolved himself, iii. 277; to be prayed for, v. 371.

Sinners, blessings of the Resurrection extended to, ii. 223; after their recovery, frequently more earnest, ii. 224.

Sins, what specially prevalent in England in Andrewes' time, iv. 270, 271.

Sion, why her captivity spoken more of than that of Judah or Jerusalem, iv. 226; once favoured, afterwards afflicted, iv. 227; her joy in restoration, iv. 232.

Sirmium, Council of. See *Council of Sirmium.*

Sixtus V. approved of the murder of Henry III. of France, iv. 146.

Societies, public charitable, to be maintained, v. 40, 41; to misuse their revenues is a sin, v. 41.

Society, the origin of disorders in, iii. 379.

Sodom, vine of, ii. 62; spoken of in a spiritual sense, iii. 64.

Songs, by wanton, Satan breathes infection and poison, ii. 3; v. 204.

Solitude, an aid to repentance, i. 361, 369, 390, 453.

Solomon, had special felicity in Proverbs, ii. 3, iv. 204; named the pillars at the Temple gate, ii. 7; preferred wisdom to wealth, ii. 103; gifted with heavenly wisdom, iv. 299.

Son, 'Thou art My beloved Son,' how explained, iii. 257, 258.

Son of God, upon the word 'Son,' is grounded the term ὁμοούσιον, i. 108; used in a higher and lower sense, i. 109; procession of, from the personal essence of the Father, i. 110; by birth the heir of the Father, i. 111; as a Son, incapable of asking and receiving, i. 286; a Person, i. 294. See *Christ.*

Sons of God, we are, by our new birth, i. 23; there are diverse kinds of, i. 109, 292; by adoption not begotten, i. 291; angels so called, i. 292.

Sorrow wounds deeply, ii. 123; often needless, iii. 11.

Soul, the Eucharist the medicine of, i. 418; its value, ii. 111; more precious than aught else, ii. 193; the redemption of, without the body, is imperfect, ii. 162; desires to be clothed again with the same flesh, ii. 262; the garden of the Lord, iii. 16; Christ its gardener, iii. 16; should have a share in the use of riches, v. 33; its use in doing good to others, v. 33; famine of, worse than bodily famine, v. 419.

Speaking should follow knowledge, not precede it, iii. 137.

Speech, purity of, an evidence of the Spirit, iii. 358.

Speeches, good, may come from evil men, as Judas and Caiaphas, ii. 42, 43.

Spies sent to search the land, ii. 4.

Spirit, our own not to be followed, iii. 133, 275; nor that of the world, iii. 133, 275; this word opposed to flesh, letter, soul, &c., iii. 273, 274; the private spirit, and the spirit, distinguished from the Holy Spirit, iii. 275.

Spirits, different, suited to different times, iv. 252.

Spittle, The, Sermon preached at, v. 3, seq.; the pulpit was in the court of S. Mary's Hospital, v. 2; a description of it, v. 2.

Spotswood, Abp., his account of the Gowrie conspiracy, iv. 4, 5.

INDEX TO SERMONS, ETC. 451

Spring, a time for repentance, i. 357, 432; the resurrection of the year, ii. 192, 231; a type of Christ's resurrection, ii. 365, 376; an earnest of the future harvest, ii. 365.

Staff, of Beauty and of Bands, for the sake of order, iii. 387.

Stand, God is said to, as setting forth His presence, His attention, His perseverance, v. 213, 214.

Standing, the position of those in earnest, ii. 248, 249.

Stanley, Sir W., betrayed Deventer to the Spaniards, v. 10.

Stapleton, Thomas, acknowledged the imputation of Christ's righteousness, v. 119, 122.

Star, a threefold manifestation of, on the Nativity, i. 236; why anciently engraved on the sacramental vessels, i. 247.

State, endangered inwardly, v. 209; remedy for the danger, v. 210; and outwardly from enemies, v. 211.

Stone, why Job wished his words graven on, ii. 256, 257; Christ compared to a corner-stone, ii. 271, 274, 275.

Stones, witnesses to Christ's death, ii. 155, 173.

Strength, of a potsherd, what meant by, ii. 5; of Jacob and of Israel, how explained, ii. 6, 10; human, is changeable, like Jonah's gourd, iv. 107; our own insufficient, v. 301; comes from God, v. 301, 303, 304; this a ground for prayer, v. 302.

Study, one great present means of spiritual knowledge, iii. 287.

Suarez, Francis, maintained that confession should not be revealed in cases of treason, iv. 145; in favour of king-killing, iv. 160.

Submission, a token of God's true ministers, iii. 289.

Sudden emotions are startling, iii. 118.

Suffering, harder than doing, ii. 167.

Συμφέρον implies a general contribution of gifts to the general good, iii. 400.

Sun, witness to Christ's death, ii. 155, 173; is said to have danced at Christ's resurrection, iii. 78; changes in, compared with the stability of God, iii. 373, 374.

Συναντίληψις explained, iv. 87.

Superstition, has been used in most parts of worship, ii. 336; in driving it away, we must not drive away reverence, ii. 337; better than profaneness, ii. 337.

Swearing. See *Oaths*.

Sweat, Christ's, its wonderful nature, ii. 123, 144, 145.

Symbols, Evangelistic, visions of, in Ezekiel and the Revelation, i. 85.

T.

Tabernacle, of our Lord's flesh, i. 93; of God with men, i. 94; no continual dwelling, iii. 159; applied to Christ's sojourn on earth, iii. 159; various gifts contributed to erect it, iv. 38.

Tabitha, good to the poor, ii. 53.

Table, The Lord's, treated irreverently, iv. 375, 376.

Tables, The two, types of the two treasures of wisdom and knowledge, ii. 349; first broken, and then new hewn, types of Christ, ii. 349.

Tacitus on the character of the Jews, i. 13.

Talents, given by God to be employed to His glory, v. 427; by misusing them we incur a double debt, v. 427.

Talking, not to be put in the place of doing, v. 193, 194.

Talmud supposed to have been quoted by S. Paul, v. 61.

Tau, among the Hebrews, a sign of completion, ii. 76; the shape of the cross, why marked on us, ii. 165; marked on the forehead to show who are God's, iii. 210.

Teaching, implies both knowledge and hearers, iii. 137.

Tempest, God's wrath compared to, ii. 394; could not be stayed till Christ was cast forth, ii. 395.

Temple, The, made of fruit-bearing trees symbolically, i. 172; how long in building, ii. 345.

———— Christ's body compared to, ii. 345, 347—349; in its beginning and end, ii. 349; in details of its furniture, ii. 349; the Godhead dwelt in it bodily, ii. 348; never defiled by sin, ii. 348; every kind of sacrifice and offering made in it, ii. 350.

———— our bodies compared to, ii. 347; we should take care to keep them so, ii. 361.

Tempt, in what way God is said to, v. 443, 493; Satan tempts to our hurt, v. 443, 444; how God can be tempted, v. 528, *seq.*

Temptation is of two kinds, called δοκιμασία and πειρασμὸς, v. 443, 493; human and Satanical, v. 444; human results from weakness, v. 444; Satanical from malice, v. 444; inward and outward, v. 444, 494; outward of no force without inward, v. 445; can be overcome only by God, v. 445; comes by His permission, v. 445; what to be understood by being 'led into temptation,' v. 446; not being thrust into, and left in it, v. 485; how to escape it, v. 447; not the same with evil, v. 449; of two kinds, by enticement, and by violence, v. 483, 494; the different uses of, v. 485; no place free from, v. 488, 489, 516; ever hangs about us, v. 489; God's and Satan's contrasted, v. 493, 494; our Lord's three temptations include all kinds of temptation, v. 497; Satan fond of trying fresh ones, v. 513, 514; with change of place, v. 514; many sources of, v. 517.

Ten, a sacred number, iv. 321.

Teresh, one of Ahasuerus's chamberlains, iv. 134; his sin in seeking the king's life, iv. 135; the reason of his doing so, iv. 136; the strange way in which his treason was detected, iv. 138, 139.

Tertullian, on the language of philosophers respecting the Word, i. 88; on passionate addresses from God, i. 341; on fasting, i. 384, 385, 388, 390; how he explains 'grieving the Holy Spirit of God,' iii. 213; on the source of kingly power, iv. 53; on the number of the early Christians, iv. 355.

Testament, A, better than a covenant, iii. 90; confers gifts, not merely peace, iii. 91; is never broken, iii. 91, 92; made in Christ from everlasting, iii. 92; its virtue everlasting, iii. 92; no other to come after it, iii. 92; of no force, unless administered, iii. 169.

Testimony, as distinguished from the 'Law,' means the practice of the saints, iv. 401.

Thanksgiving, duty of, iv. 339, 340.

Θέλημα, used of God's will, without reference to the way in which we obey it, v. 405.

Theodobert, summoned the first Council of Auvergne, v. 162.

Theodoret, on the language of philosophers respecting the Word, i. 88; on the holy Eucharist as a sign of the hypostatical union, i. 281.

Theodoric, summoned a Council at Rome, v. 162.

Theodosius, summoned the Council of Aquileia, v. 161.

Theophania, the nativity of Christ so called by the Fathers, i. 198.

Theophilus Alexandrinus, on Lent, i. 392.

Theophylact tells us we must take our choice either with Mary Magdalene, or Judas, ii. 57.

Θεοφύλακτοι, a title assumed by kings, iv. 108.

Θεοστεφεῖς, a title applied to kings, iv. 114.

Theriacum, how compounded, ii. 71.

Thessalonica, Council of. See *Council of Thessalonica.*

Thomas, S., his doubt removed ours, ii. 190; addressed Christ with more reverence than did Mary Magdalene, iii. 30; was allowed to touch Christ, iii. 27, 28; as a cure for his unbelief, iii. 31.

Thoughts, evil, sweetened by prayer, v. 324.

Tidings, good, give a kind of resurrection, iii. 45.

Time, fulness of, i. 48, 268; illustration of advance of, i. 48; fulness of, the fulfilling of prophecies, i. 49.

Timothy, solemnly enjoined to give his charge to the rich, v. 8.

Tobias, his mode of fasting, i. 395.

Toledo, Council of. See *Council of Toledo.*

Tolet, Cardinal, on the meaning of the phrase God's 'good pleasure,' i. 218.

Tongue, both the best and the worst member, ii. 39; iii. 122; to be used in God's worship, ii. 337; its greatest glory to be the organ of the Holy Ghost, iii. 122; the instrument of taste, as well as of speech, iii. 161; the Holy Ghost wishes to put His seal upon it, iii. 215.

Tongues, sent from heaven at Pentecost to celebrate God's wonders, iii. 108; given to impart knowledge to others, iii. 121; given at Pentecost to show that the grace of the Holy Spirit was to be imparted to others, iii. 121; cloven tongues imply different languages, iii. 123, 137; God's cloven tongues preach the Gospel everywhere, Satan's cloven tongues preach discord everywhere, iii. 124; tongues of fire implied zeal, iii. 124, 137; their sitting on the disciples implied continuance, iii. 125; a sign that they were to speak to others of what God had done, iii. 137; divers, the curse of Babel, the blessing of Pentecost, iii. 139; gift of, has now ceased, iii. 139; the Holy Spirit came thereby, to teach us that we can taste Christ's graciousness, and drink of His Spirit, iii. 161; the gift of, at Pentecost, shows that our speech must be changed by the Holy Ghost, iii. 193; Satan sent his at Pentecost, in opposition to God's, iii. 302; they turned a mystery into a mockery, iii. 302; given both for prophecy and for prayer, iii. 319; at Pentecost, compared to lights, iii. 372.

Touch, (in the phrase, 'Touch not mine anointed,') to be understood of violence, virulent language, or the foot of pride, iv. 59—61; kings can be touched both in their persons and their states, iv. 61.

'*Touch me not*,' these words spoken to Mary Magdalene to beget reverence, iii. 24, 28, *seq.*; seemed to be a strange speech, iii. 25, 26; both considering the parties, iii. 25; and the reason, iii. 26; 'touch not' used at the beginning of the old, and the new creation, iii. 26; reasons for this prohibition given by S. Chrysostom, iii. 28, *seq.*; others allowed to touch Christ as a cure for their unbelief, iii. 31; God's secret counsels not to be touched, iii. 22; 'touch me not,' especially applies to reverent handling of Christ in the Holy Communion, iii. 34; these words explained by S. Gregory as implying haste, iii. 35, 39, 41; by S. Augustine as teaching the blessing of a truer and spiritual touch, iii. 36, 37, 39, 40; touching Christ should give place to teaching Him, iii. 45.

Tours, Council of. See *Council of Tours.*

Traitors, the miserable deaths of, iv. 33; v. 247, 248; come from Satan, iv. 87; saying respecting them, *Inter duos proditores diabolus est tertius*, iv. 133, 189; not to be registered as martyrs, iv. 146; imprecations against, iv. 180. See *Rebels.*

Transfiguration, Christ's, glory of, an infallible demonstration of God's presence, i. 95; an object of great joy, ii. 262; Christ manifested thereby as the Son of God in glory, iii. 260.

Transubstantiation irreconcilable with the Catholic argument against Eutyches, i. 282.

Treachery, affects both a man's soul and reputation, iv. 190.

Treason, condemned by the heathen, iv. 127; and both by law and theology, iv. 128; a capital offence, iv. 131; consists in purpose as well as in act, iv. 132; two accomplices required to it, iv. 133; inspired by Satan, iv. 133; how strangely detected, iv. 138, 139.

Treasures, of wealth or of knowledge, given for others' good, v. 35.

Tribur, Council of. See *Council of Tribur.*

Tribute, a giving back to the king what we owe him, v. 134; to be given cheerfully, v. 135; after Christ's example, iv. 138, 139.

Trinity, Holy, our thankfulness to, i. 62; taught in S. Luke, ii. 14; i. 216; the most perfect number of all, ii. 362; indicated in Christ's words, 'I will pray the Father,' &c., iii. 155, 188; each Person of, had His part in all God's great works, iii. 169; proved by the words of Baptism, iii. 187, 188; the Persons one in name, three in number, iii. 188; manifested at Christ's Baptism, iii. 188; the three Persons of, present at Christ's Baptism, iii. 242; which was a new creation, iii. 242; and also at the creation of the world, iii. 242; the commission for Baptism runs in their names, iii. 242; trinity of water, blood, and the Spirit, corresponding with the Trinity above, iii. 248; set forth in 1 Cor. xii. 4—7, iii. 380; manifested at the creation of the world, the Baptism of Christ, and the Baptism of the Church, iii. 380; bestows a trinity of gifts, administrations, and operations, iii. 380; the works of, except those that are personal, are never divided, iii. 381; neither of the Persons superfluous, iii. 383; represented by the words 'kingdom, power, and glory,' in the Lord's Prayer, v. 463.

Triumph, Christ's ascension compared to a, iii. 227, 231.

Trumpet, chosen by God for proclaiming the law, v. 147; and for the last doom, v. 147.

Trumpets, The two silver, of one piece, v. 143, 147; made by Moses, v. 144, 148; for calling the people together for war and in the congregation, v. 143—145; to be used by Moses as chief magistrate, v. 149; and by other chief magistrates after him, v. 149—151.

Trust, not to be placed in riches, but in God, v. 27, 33; nor in anything besides, because not our own, v. 29.

Truth, nothing without righteousness, i. 190, 191; our search after, too commonly no better than that of Pilate, i. 312; made known to those who live up to the light they have, iii. 329, 330; a means of keeping God near us, v. 219.

Turning of captivity as rivers in the south, how explained, iv. 234; turned by prevention or by deliverance, iv. 233, 235.

Types, numerous, of Christ, i. 105; of Christ as King and Priest, i. 297.

U.

Unanimity and uniformity, both needful, iii. 114.

Uncertainty of riches, v. 9, 19, 22; of man's life, v. 23; and of his prosperity, v. 23—25.

Unction, why the Holy Ghost so called,

iii. 285; needed for God's ministers, iii. 288.
Unity, acceptable to God, i. 270; not attained till Christ came, i. 273; taught by His being the Head of the Corner, ii. 280; a fit preparation for receiving the Holy Ghost, iii. 112, 113, 120, 129; is needful to bodily life, iii. 111; its restorer to the Church will gain a great blessing, iii. 113; unity of the Spirit is inward, bond of peace outward unity, iii. 114; a means of keeping God near us, v. 219.
Unthankfulness condemned by Satan, v. 31.
Usurpers reign not by God, iv. 287.
Usury, the devil's alchemy, v. 500.
Uz, signifies strength, iii. 65; the same as Edom, iii. 65; and so a type of death, iii. 65.
Uzzah, a warning not to go beyond one's calling, iii. 390.
Uzziah, a warning not to go beyond one's calling, iii. 390.

V.

Vagabonds to be made to work, v. 43.
Valentinian summoned the Council of Chalcedon, v. 160; and of Lampsacus, v. 161.
Valentinus, heresy of, i. 90; v. 56; that Christ's body was made in heaven, i. 140.
Varro, his sum of opinions on the chief good, i. 219.
Vegetius on the military oath, i. 94.
Velleity, iii. 218.
Vern, Council of. See Council of Vern.
Victory borne on the Roman standards, explains the phrase, ' O grave, where is thy victory?' iii. 66.
Violence, weapons of, not to be used by private men, iv. 187.
Virgil on the Star in the East, i. 142, 255.
Virgin, Jewish objection to the interpretation of Isaiah vii. 14, i. 137; the word 'Alma' properly so translated, i. 137.
Virtues called ἕξεις by the heathen, δωρήματα in Scripture, v. 312; to be distinguished from their shadows, v. 335.
Vossius, G. I., patronized by Andrewes, v. 292. (From Bishop Buckeridge's Funeral Sermon.)
Vow, a kind of prayer, v. 359.

W.

Walsingham, Sir Francis, patronized Andrewes, v. 290. (From Bp. Buckeridge's Funeral Sermon.)
Want, a motive to prayer, v. 353; a hindrance to spiritual progress, v. 414; a confession of, adds to God's glory, v. 416.
War, to be undertaken with repentance, i. 322, 329; may be lawful, i. 323, 324; the share priests have in, i. 326, 328; an act of corrective justice, i. 330.
Ward, Dr., Andrewes's schoolmaster, his gratitude to him, v. 289. (From Bishop Buckeridge's Funeral Sermon.)
Waste to be avoided in everything, ii. 40, 41; in time, in words, ii. 40; in buying, ii. 40; in spending, ii. 40; in giving, ii. 41; nothing is wasted which is given to Christ, ii. 50, 51; many kinds of, ii. 51.
Watchfulness, specially to be used when Satan is most busy, v. 491.
Water, that which came from the Lord's side, the fountain for sin, i. 113; a means and a type of purity, iii. 197; cleanses not the soul, save in virtue of Christ's blood, iii. 247; the element of destruction, now made the channel of grace, iii. 250; becomes the ark of our salvation, iii. 250; suited to remove stains, iii. 347; used by heathen in their lustrations, iii. 347; and by the Jews, iii. 347; cannot of itself cleanse the soul, iii. 347; Christ gave it its true power, iii. 347; of baptism, not without blood, iii. 352, 359; without the Spirit, a beggarly element, iii. 355.
Waters above the heavens, the graces of the Holy Spirit, iii. 249.
Watts, Dr., his scholarships at Pembroke Hall, v. 290. (From Bishop Buckeridge's Funeral Sermon.)
Way, Christ, as God, the end; as man, the way, i. 166.
Weakness of a land, cause of, ii. 4; gives enemies courage, ii. 5; men's natural, v. 302; its completeness, v. 303; in natural and in spiritual things, v. 305; this belonged to the Apostles, as well as to other men, v. 306.
Weariness, why ascribed to God, v. 220.
Whale, a type of destruction and death, ii. 400; and of Satan, ii. 401.
White, an Easter-day colour, iii. 9; token of the resurrection, iii. 9.
Whit-Sunday, the noblest of all feasts. iii. 108; specially dedicated to the

INDEX TO SERMONS, ETC. 455

Holy Ghost, iii. 130; in memory of His descent, iii. 130; the feast of love, iii. 147, 235, 238; connects the 'promise of the sending,' and the 'sending of the promise,' iii. 163; makes amends for the Ascension, iii. 164; a higher festival, iii. 168; the day of the Holy Ghost's sealing, iii. 218; the feast of Baptism, iii. 242; Baptism usually deferred to that time, iii. 242; the feast of the Holy Ghost, iii. 260; a *festum duplex*, iii. 299; feast of the Law and of the Spirit, iii. 352; a day for Baptism and Holy Communion, iii. 358; feast of tongues, iii. 378; Epiphany of the Holy Ghost, iii. 378.

Wickedness, son of, distinguished from an enemy, iv. 88; more malicious, iv. 88; more dangerous, iv. 88.

Widow, the poor, bound to serve Christ with her two mites, ii. 53.

Wilderness, combat between Christ and Satan a great sight beheld in, v. 480; a fit place for this contest, v. 488; no fit place for presumption, v. 514, 515, or for worldly pride, v. 539.

Will, a ready, accepted for obedience by Christ, iii. 152.

—— *of God,* secret and revealed, v. 397, 398; His revealed will is what we are concerned with, v. 397, 398; we must pray that it be accomplished in us, v. 398; His secret will is done in us, whether we will or no, v. 398; we may dissent from it, without doing wrong, v. 399; His revealed will to be submitted to, even when against our own, v. 399, 400; is perfect, v. 402; and full of goodness, v. 402; compared with man's, v. 402; we should earnestly pray that it may be done in us, v. 404; not to be done anyhow, but as in heaven, v. 405, *seq.;* two Greek words, θέλημα and εὐδοκία, used to describe it, v. 405; the latter implying cheerful obedience, v. 406; how done in the three heavens, v. 406—408; by thus doing it man made heavenly, v. 407; is obeyed in heaven both in accordance with, and against the nature of those who do it, v. 408, 409; men obey it reluctantly when against their own will, v. 409; can be obeyed here as readily, though not as perfectly, as in heaven, v. 410; to be obeyed in doing and in suffering, v. 411; without taking counsel whether we should do it, or no, v. 411.

—— *of man,* to be submitted to the will of God, v. 399—402; to be thought humbly of, v. 401; compared to a wild olive-tree, v. 401; inclined to evil, v. 401, 402; a desperate case, if we are given up to it, v. 401; compared with God's, v. 402.

Wind, a type of the Holy Ghost, iii. 117, 131; the same word used for wind, breath, and spirit, iii. 117; like the Spirit in its sudden operations, iii. 118; seemingly of little force, soon attains to great violence, iii. 118; on the day of Pentecost no ordinary wind, iii. 119, 120; and so a special type of the Spirit, iii. 120, 131; its substance unseen, its power manifest, like the Holy Spirit, iii. 204, 205.

Wine in the Holy Communion, a symbol of unity, iii. 239.

Winepress, twofold, trodden by Christ, of redemption and of vengeance, iii. 62, 70; we must take heed of the winepress of God's wrath, iii. 78.

Wise men, the fittest to find the wisdom of God, i. 235; their faith, i. 250; their bold confession of Jesus, i. 253; their promptitude, i. 257, 258; showed more faith than the Queen of Sheba, i. 261.

Witness, Holy Ghost a witness to Christ, iii. 353; all God's great works have one, iii. 353.

Witnesses, The Three, to Christ's work, iii. 354.

Wolf, type of inward enemies making ravage of souls, ii. 9.

Woman, by her came the first news of death, and of the resurrection, iii. 5.

Women, why Christ's resurrection first revealed to, ii. 223; more manly than men, ii. 223; their love, how shown, ii. 224; their several kinds of love, ii. 225—228; their earliness, ii. 227; yet would not break the law, ii. 227; contended against difficulties, ii. 228; their success, ii. 229; alarmed at the sight of the angel, ii. 231, 232; made the bearers of good tidings to the rest of the Apostles, ii. 235; fully recompensed for their labour, ii. 236.

—— the most passionate, and the most compassionate sex, iv. 322; more fretful than men, v. 436.

Word, The, i. 16; made flesh, i. 86, 90; not merely objective, effective, or preceptive, i. 87; His proceeding, i. 87; why so called, i. 88, 90, 293; the only-begotten of the Father, i. 88; all righteousness fulfilled by, i. 90; Creator, therefore Restorer, i. 90; made an infant, and so unable to speak, i. 92; more for Him 'to be made' than 'to make,' i. 91; dwelt visibly among us, i. 94; full of grace and truth, i. 97; we should make Him 'incarnate,' i. 99; present at the creation, iii. 242.

Word, The written, a means of receiving the Spirit, iii. 199; a great treasure of wisdom, v. 190, 191; its preaching a ground of joy, v. 191; to be heard and practised, v. 192, 193; doers of, have it incarnate within them, v. 195; a thing to be done, not merely listened to, v. 198, 199; as seed in the soil, should bear fruit, v. 199.

Word and Sacraments, no need to compare them together, iii. 22.

Words, good, compared to a tree with broad leaves and small fruit, v. 38.

Work, our own proper, distinguished from needless work, or other people's work, iii. 391.

Works of men rewarded by God's good will, i. 228; ability, authority, and diligence requisite for doing them, iii. 382, 383; to neglect doing them an offence to God, iii. 383; their goodness from God, their defect from ourselves, iii. 392, 393.

—— ascribed to God the Father, iii. 382.

—— good, valuable by God's putting a value on them, rather than by their own real worth, i. 452; the end of our creation and redemption, iii. 93, 94; God's will that we do them, iii. 94; faith perfected by them, iii. 94; we shall be disposed of according to them, iii. 94; spring from Christ's resurrection, iii. 94, 101; ours all imperfect, iii. 94, 95; are steps on our onward course, iii. 95; we must be fitted to do them, iii. 95, 96, 97; many hindrances to doing them, iii. 96, 97; all kinds of good works required, iii. 98; are God's work in us, and also our own, iii. 98; some more pleasing to God than others, iii. 98, 99. See also *Good works.*

World, is wandering in vanity, ii. 22; transitory, ii. 294; has a kind of passover, ii. 294; full of troubles, ii. 294; a troublesome place, ii. 319; no resting place, ii. 320; compared to a ship, ii. 394; like a sandy soil, cannot bear a firm foundation, v. 49; allures like Jael, v. 558.

World, heathen, needed the power of the Spirit to convert it, iii. 124.

Worms, Council of. See *Council of Worms.*

Worship, the end of, seeking and finding Christ, i. 260; the world's worship of Him, i. 260; three parts of, i. 262, 445; with the body, i. 262; due to God only, v. 553; shown in outward reverence, v. 554, 555.

Worthy, God makes men worthy, by counting them so, iii. 341; the best men own that they are not worthy, iii. 341.

Wrong, bearing it, a Christian duty, ii. 8; not doing it, a civil duty, ii. 8.

X.

Xerophagia, (Ξηροφαγία,) it nature, i. 395.

Y.

Year of the Lord, not a definite, but an indefinite time, iii. 298; why termed 'acceptable,' iii. 298, 299; acceptable to God Himself, iii. 299.

Z.

Zacchæus, his desire to see Christ was rewarded, i. 127.

Zacharias pronounced a blessing at Christ's birth, ii. 365.

Zechariah prophesied of Christ, ii. 119; as shown by S. John, ii. 119.

Zedekiah, his character at variance with the meaning of his name, v. 105, 106.

Zerubbabel, Christ the true, as freeing us from captivity to sin, i. 176.

INDEX

TO

BISHOP ANDREWES' MINOR WORKS,

CONTAINED IN THIS VOLUME.

A.

Adoration, twofold sense of, 16; not to be practised towards the Sacrament, 15—17.
Adultery, does not so dissolve the marriage bond, as to enable the parties to marry again, 106—110.
Africa, Council of. See *Council of Africa.*
Agapæ, an Apostolic institution, 26.
Alexander of Hales, what he understood by *suffragia,* 57.
Allen, William, Cardinal, quotes the Commentaries on S. Paul, as if written by S. Ambrose, 55, 72.
Altar, the word altar and table indiscriminately used by the Fathers, 20, 21; in accordance with Scripture, 21; may be either of wood or stone, 21.
Ambrose, S., a passage from him on the Invocation of Saints examined, 51; and on the efficacy of the Martyrs' blood to wash away sins, 51, 52; at what period of his life he wrote the treatise 'De Viduis,' 53, 54; Commentaries on the Epistles wrongly ascribed to him, 54, 55, 72; though quoted as his by many Divines, 55; Andrewes defends their genuineness, 55, 56; his tract on the death of Theodosius quoted, 59; says that God alone is to be invoked, 59; in his treatise on Prayer, makes no distinction between direct and relative prayers, 60; apostrophizes the water of Baptism, 63; on the duty of breaking wrong promises, 105.
Andrewes, Lancelot, his fragmentary reply to Cardinal Perron's 'Réplique à la Response du sérénissime Roy du Grande Bretagne,' 13—80; comments on Perron's authorities for the corporal presence, 13, 14; adoration of the Sacrament, 15—17; reservation of it, 17—19; Eucharistic sacrifice, 19, 20; use of altars, 20; worship of martyrs and relics, 21—23; traditions, 23, 24; prayers for dead, 24; Lent, 24; Christmas-day never being a fast, 24; Priests' marriage, 24; vows of celibacy, 25; mixed cup, 25; exorcism, 25; number of Sacraments, 25, 26; ceremonies used in Baptism, 26, 27; necessity of Baptism, 27; holy water, 27; the five orders of the ministry, 27—29; unbroken succession, 29; distinction of bishop and priest, 29; freewill, predestination, &c. 29, 30; several ceremonies of the Church, 30—34; sums up the points of agreement and difference, 34—36; reexamines the testimonies quoted by Bellarmine in favour of the Invocation of Saints, 39—80.
Andrewes, Lancelot, his answer to John Traske, 83—94.
——— his speech against the Countess of Shrewsbury, 97—105.
——— his treatise on second marriage after divorce, 106—110.
——— his Visitation Articles for the diocese of Winchester, A.D. 1610, 111—123; A.D. 1625, 125—140.
——— his notes on Book of Common Prayer, 141—158; the several transcripts of them noticed, 143, 144.
——— his form for consecrating Communion Plate, 159—163; an account of the MS. from which this form is taken, 159, 160.
——— his form of Induction, 164.

AND.—PERRON, ETC.   P P

Andrewes, Lancelot, his Manual for the Sick, 165—222; different editions of, noticed, 167.
——— his Private Devotions, 223—338; the different editions of, noticed, 225—227.
Angels not to be prayed to, 23, 72—74; decree of Council of Laodicea on this point, 23, 72—74; their worship (Col. ii. 18), how explained by Perron, 72, 73.
Apiarius, his appeal to Rome opposed by S. Augustine, 28, 29.
Apostrophe, An, not a serious invocation, 63.
Aquarii, or *Hydroparastatæ,* used water instead of wine at the Eucharist, 25.
Aquinas, S. Thomas, what he understood by *suffragia,* 57.
Athanasius, S., his argument that Christ is God, 68; whether he wrote the treatise 'De Sabbatis et Circumcisione,' 92, note ᵏ; this book referred to, 92, 94.
Augsburg Library, catalogue of, 43, 48.
Augustine, S., quoted by Perron to support the doctrine of Christ's presence in the Sacrament *sub speciebus,* 13, 14; maintained not a carnal presence, 14, 16, 17; nor the adoration of the Sacrament, 16, 17; understands eating Christ's body, not carnally, but spiritually, 17; on the sacrifice of Christ's death promised by the sacrifice of the Law, and commemorated in the sacrifice of the Eucharist, 20; maintained that the Martyrs were not worshipped, 20, note ʷ, 49, 50; mentions miracles wrought by the relics of S. Stephen, 22; how far he acknowledged the Pope's authority, 28; opposed the appeal of Apiarius, 28, 29; his opinion on freewill, and on the necessity of good works, 29, notes ᵘ, ˣ; and on presumption of our predestination, 30, note ᶻ; on S. Peter's vision, 87; held that the Law was dead and buried honourably, 87, note ᶜ; his argument against the Manichees, 90; on the duty of breaking wrong promises, 104.

B.

Bacon, Lord, his letter on Traske's case, 83, note ᵇ.
Baptism, what ceremonies of, retained by us, 26; necessary to salvation, as an ordinary means, 27; the three kinds of, 52; water of, greater than the blood of Martyrs, 53.
Baronius, on the date of some of the writings of S. Ambrose, 53, 54.
Basil, S., whether he were the author of the treatise 'De Spiritu Sancto,' 23; and of that 'De Fide,' 23; the latter question examined by Garnier, the Benedictine Editor, 23, note ʰ; the passage quoted from him by Perron, does not justify the use of paintings in churches, 32; his saying respecting the Fathers' polemical discourses, 68; rejected the Baptism of the Montanists, 94.
Believing and *believing in* distinguished, 70.
Bellarmine, Robert, Cardinal, quoted S. Chrysostom's lxvi. Homily to the People of Antioch, in favour of the Invocation of Saints, 40; though he admitted elsewhere that only xxi. of them were genuine, 40; said that the Fathers often spoke incautiously, 53, note ᵗ; especially S. Chrysostom, 62; quotes the Commentaries on the Epistles as if written by S. Ambrose, 55.
Bishop and *Priest,* the distinction between, 29.

C.

Candles, not retained by us in Baptism, 26.
Canons of the Apostles, forbade persons to put away their wives on pretence of religion, 25.
Carthage, Council of. See *Council of Carthage.*
Casaubon, Isaac, his arrival in England, 5; the correspondence between him and Card. Perron, 5; afterwards addressed a letter to Perron in King James's name, 5; the date of that letter ascertained, 5, note ᶜ; informed Bp. Andrewes that Card. Perron admitted to him that he had never prayed to the Saints, 76.
Ceremonies, retained or altered at the pleasure of the Church, 26; several Church ceremonies noticed, 30—34.
Chalcedon, Council of. See *Council of Chalcedon.*
Charity covereth a multitude of sins, how to be understood, 52.
Chemnitz, Martin, extracted prayers to Saints from Romish Books of Devotion, 76, note ᶻ; these quotations used by Andrewes, 76—80.
Chrism, an ancient ceremony in Baptism, yet not retained by us, 26.
Christ, how present in the Sacrament, 13; His flesh eaten spiritually, not

carnally, 17; prayed to in the Canon of the Mass, 50, 51; took away Jewish ordinances, 87; made an end of Sabbaths by His Sabbath in the grave, 91.
Chrysostom, S. John, enjoins reverence, not adoration of the Sacrament, 16; on the Eucharist offered for the dead, 20, notes ˣ, ᶻ; wrote only xxi. Homilies to the people of Antioch, 40; the lxvi. Homily wrongly quoted as his by Bellarmine, 40; the testimony in favour of the genuineness of only xxi. of those Homilies, 40; the genuineness of the Homilies on 2 Cor. wrongly questioned, 41; speaks in the passage quoted, only of the act of the Emperor, 43; does not himself enjoin Invocation of Saints, 43; said, by Bellarmine and others, to have spoken some things *per excessum*, 62.
Church, is visible, and has perpetual succession, 34.
Clement of Alexandria, his testimony to the observance of the Lord's Day, 93.
Codex Canonum Ecclesiæ Universæ, referred to, 90, note ᶜ; quoted in Council of Chalcedon, 90, 94.
Collyridians, condemned by Epiphanius for offering prayers to the Virgin Mary, 46, 47.
Communion under one kind, 19.
Consecration of water in Baptism retained by us, 26.
────── of Churches and of Church Plate, forms of preserved in Lambeth Library, 159, 160; Andrewes' own form of consecrating Church Plate, 160—163.
Cosin, Bishop, his transcript of Andrewes' notes on Common Prayer, 143, 144.
Council, A General, required the presence or sanction of the four chief Patriarchs, 29.
────── *of Africa*, opposed the appeal of Apiarius to Rome, 28.
────── *Carthage*, ordered prayers to be addressed to the Father only, 50; this Canon not observed by the Church of Rome, 50.
────── *second of Carthage*, forbade Priests' marriage, 24.
────── *of Chalcedon*, opposed S. Leo, 29; quoted the 'Codex Canonum Ecclesiæ Universæ,' 90, 94.
────── *Gangra*, held against Eustathius, 90; condemned distinction of meats, 90, 91.
────── *Laodicea*, forbade the worship of Angels, 23, 72, 73; its date, 94, note ᶠ; some of its Canons adopted by Council of Nice, 94; anathematized those who observe the Sabbath, 94.
Council of Neocæsarea, forbade Priests' marriage, 24.
────── *Nice*, on kneeling on Sundays, 26; adopted some of the Canons of Laodicea, 94.
────── *Saragossa*, forbade the reservation of the Sacrament, 18, 19.
────── *Toledo*, forbade the reservation of the Sacrament, 19.
────── *in Trullo*, allowed Priests' marriage, 24, 25.
Creatures, none unclean of themselves, 85, 88, 89.
Cross, the use of, retained by us in Baptism, 26, 32; rightly used by Christians when among the heathen, 33; not used by any one now, to the extent mentioned by Tertullian, 33; not to be adored, 33.
Cup, received by the laity in the time of S. Cyril of Jerusalem, 15.
Cyprian, S., calls the Eucharist both sacrament and a sacrifice, 19; cᵣ founded with S. Cyprian of Antⁱ by S. Gregory Nazianzen, 44, 45 testimony to the observance oᴀ ᴜne Lord's Day, 93.
Cyril, S., of Alexandria, denied that Christians worshipped the Martyrs, 67, 69.
────── *S., of Jerusalem*, on the reverential mode of receiving the Sacrament, 15; does not imply that the Sacrament was to be adored, 15; proves that the laity received the cup, 15; his Catechetical Lectures on the Mysteries, not spurious, 15, 48; on the offering of the Eucharist, 20, note ʸ; speaks of the Martyrs being mentioned only (not invoked) at the altar, 47, 49.

D.

David, his vow to kill Nabal rightly broken, 105.
Dionysius of Corinth, his testimony to the observance of the Lord's Day, 93.
Dispensations for marriages in Lent, Hooker's opinion respecting them, 24.
Drake, Richard, the original editor of Andrewes' Manual for Sick, 167; translated and published the first complete edition of the Private Devotions, 225; his history, 167.
Ducæus, Fronto, admitted only xxi. of S. Chrysostom's Homilies to the People of Antioch to be genuine, 40.

E.

Ephata, the use of this word not retained by us in Baptism, 26.
Epiphanius, S., on the practice of not fasting on the days between Easter and Whitsuntide, 26; condemns adoration of the Virgin Mary, 46, 47.
Erasmus, Desiderius, questioned the genuineness of S. Basil's treatise 'De Spiritu Sancto,' 23; wrongly questioned the genuineness of S. Chrysostom's Homilies on 2 Cor., 41; and those of S. Basil on the Holy Spirit, 41.
Eucharist, both a sacrament and a sacrifice, 19; as a sacrament, applies the sacrifice, 20; commemorates the sacrifice of Christ's death, 20; offered for the dead, absent, &c. 20.
Exorcisms, in Baptism, not retained by us, 26.

F.

Fasting, anciently not practised on the Fridays between Easter and Whitsuntide, 26.
Fathers, The, in their polemical discourses often overstrain their expressions, 68; Perron accuses them of concealment, 68, 69; and explains why they do not speak openly of praying to the Saints, 69.
Felix, S., miracles said to be worked by his relics, 22.
Freewill, held by us in S. Augustine's sense, 29.

G.

Gangra, Council of. See *Council of Gangra.*
Garetius quotes a passage from S. Chrysostom in favour of the Invocation of Saints, 42.
Garnier, the Benedictine Editor of S. Basil, examines the authorship of the treatise 'De Fide,' 23, note [h].
Gaudentius on the reverence due to relics, 51.
Good Works held by us as necessary to salvation, 29.
Gregory, S., Nazianzen, a passage from his Homily on S. Cyprian quoted by Bellarmine in favour of Invocation of Saints, 44; confuses the two Saint Cyprians, 44; the passage does not prove the Invocation of Saints to have been the general practice of the Church, 45; apostrophizes Easter, 63; doubted whether Constantius or Gorgonia could hear him when he apostrophized them, 64, 65; his testimony to the observance of the Lord's Day, 93.
Gregory, S., Nyssen, speaks both of the Altar and the Holy Table, 21; mentions that it was made of stone, 21; in apostrophizing Theodorus did not sanction the Invocation of Saints, 65.
——— *S., Thaumaturgus,* his canons quoted, 85.

H.

Habit, clerical, used by us, 30.
Herod, his vow should have been broken, 105.
Hilary, a deacon of the Romish Church, the real author of the Commentaries on the Epistles which used to be ascribed to S. Ambrose, 54, note [d], 56, 58.
Hœschelius, David, compiled the Catalogue of the Augsburg Library, 48, note [c].
Holydays observed by us, 30.
Holy water, the use of, not necessary in the Church, 27; miracles said to have been worked by, 27.
Hydroparastatæ. See *Aquarii.*

I.

Ignatius, S., his testimony to the observance of the Lord's Day, 93.
Incense, why used by the primitive Church, 33, 34.
Invocation, distinguished by Perron into direct and indirect, absolute and relative, sovereign and subaltern, in the mass and not in the mass, 50, 59, 66, 68, 75, 76.
——— *of Saints,* S. Chrysostom on 2 Cor. quoted in favour of, 39—42; though they may intercede, they must not be invoked, 44; S. Gregory Nazianzen quoted in favour of, 44 —47; mentioned, not invoked, at the altar, according to S. Cyril of Jerusalem, 48, 49; and S. Augustine, 49, 50; Perron's arguments in favour of this practice combatted, 57, *seq.*; modern instances of in the Church of Rome, 76—80.
Irenæus, S., his testimony to the observance of the Lord's Day, 93.
Isidore, S., of Seville, on the duty of breaking wrong promises, 104.

J.

Jackson, Hamlet, a disciple of John Traske, 83.
Jerome, S., against the worship of relics,

INDEX TO MINOR WORKS. 461

22; his controversy with Vigilantius, 22; how far he acknowledged the authority of the Pope, 28; admitted that he sometimes spoke rhetorically, 62; did not sanction the Invocation of Saints, 65, 66; Commentary on the Epistles not written by him, but by Pelagius, 72.

Judges, bound to investigate the truth of a case, 101; can demand an answer to their interrogatories, 101; on oath, 103.

Justin Martyr, S., his testimony to the observance of the Lord's Day, 93.

K.

Kneeling, anciently not practised on Sundays, or between Easter and Whitsuntide, 26.

L.

Laodicea, Council of. See *Council of Laodicea.*
Latria, due to God only, 19, note [u]; implies the divinity of the person worshipped, 46.
Lent not a season for marriage, 24.
Lights, why used in service by the primitive Church, 33, 34.
Lord's Day, The, the Christian day of rest, 92—94; testimonies to its observance, 92, 93.

M.

Μάγιστρος, the meaning of the word, 43.
Manichees held that there were two Gods, 85; and distinctions of meats, 90.
Marans, who they were, 85.
Marcellus, said to have destroyed the Temple of Jupiter by holy water, 27.
Marriage not to be celebrated in Lent, 24.
——— *of Priests*, Pius II. wished to allow it, 24, and some at the Council of Trent, 24; forbidden by decrees of provincial Councils, 24; allowed by the Council in Trullo, 24.
——— not entirely severed by adultery, 106—110.
Martyrs not to be worshipped, 21; their memories to be celebrated, 21; their relics to be reverenced, not worshipped, 22; on the power of their blood to wash away sins, 51, 52.
Mary, The Virgin, worshipped by the Collyridians, 46; not to be worshipped, 47; prayers addressed to her quoted from Romish Books of Devotion, 76—80.

Meats, distinction of clean and unclean no longer maintained, 85, 87—89; practice of the Christian Church respecting it, 89—91.
Mediator, one only, 58.
Midrash Tillim (the great Jewish Commentary on the Psalms), how it interprets Ps. cxlvi. 8; 86.
Moseley, Humphrey, his Preface to the first edition of Andrewes' Devotions, 225, 227.

N.

Neocæsarea, Council of. See *Council of Neocæsarea.*
Nice, Council of. See *Council of Nice.*
Novatian, his treatise 'De Cibis Judaicis,' quoted (as if written by Tertullian), 85, 89, 94.

O.

Oaths can be administered by judges, 103.
Optatus, S., speaks of altars as made of wood, 21.
Orders, The five, a question not worth disputing, 27; anointing not necessary in conferring, 30.
Origen, how his expression, 'the Saints pray for us *ultro*,' to be understood, 61, 62; denied that Christians worshipped the Martyrs, 67; says that the Saints pray for us, 71; his testimony to the observance of the Lord's Day, 93.

P.

Pagett, Ephraim, his Heresiography referred to, 83.
Paintings in churches not unlawful, 31, 32.
Parsons, Robert, under the name of Nicholas Doleman, urged the claims of Arabella Stuart to the crown of England, 102, note [u].
Paulinus speaks of miracles worked by the relics of S. Felix, 22; his verses on a font, 32, note [i].
Pax, as used by the Church of Rome, not the same as the kiss of peace in the ancient Church, 31.
Peace, kiss of, in ancient Church, not the same with the Pax in the Church of Rome, 31.
Pelagius wrote the Commentary on the Epistles, which passed under the name of S. Jerome, 72.
Perron, Jacques Davy, du, Cardinal, deputed Isaac Casaubon, in 1611, to open a communication between him-

self and King James, 5; a correspondence between him and Casaubon on the King's claim to the title of Catholic, 5; in which the King himself took part, 5, 6; resulting in the publication, in 1620, after his death, of his 'Réplique à la Response du sérénissime Roy de la Grande Bretagne,' 6; extracts from the 'Réplique,' to which an answer was given by Bishop Andrewes, 7—12; on the presence of Christ in the Sacrament *sub speciebus*, 13, 14; on the adoration of the Sacrament, 15—17; on the reservation of the Sacrament, 17; on the sacrifice of the altar, 19, 20; the use of altars, 20, 21; worship of martyrs and their relics, 21—23; traditions, 23, 34; prayers for the dead, 24; Lent, 24; Christmas-day, 24; priests' marriage, 24, 25; vows of celibacy, 25; the mixed cup, 25; five sacraments, 25, 26; ceremonies of baptism, 26, 27; necessity of baptism, 27; holy water, 27; the five orders, 27, 28; succession in the ministry, 29; distinction of bishop and priest, 29; freewill and predestination, 29, 30; service in unknown tongue, 30; certain ceremonies of the Church, 30—34; answers Bishop Andrewes' Reply to Bellarmine, on the Invocation of Saints, 39—80; distinguishes Invocation into direct and indirect, absolute and relative, sovereign and subaltern, in the mass and not in the mass, 50, 59, 66, 68, 75, 76; admits the Fathers do not make this distinction, 66, 67; distinguishes between speaking *with* and speaking *to* the Saints, 65, 66; says that the Fathers are often guilty of concealment, 68, 69; gives reasons for the Fathers not speaking openly of praying to the Saints, 69; how he explains the expression, 'worship of angels' (Col. i.), 72, 73; admitted to Casaubon he had never prayed to the Saints, 76.

Peter, S., the purport of his vision, 87.
—— *Lombard*, first defined the number of five Sacraments, 26, note ˣ; what he understood by *suffragia*, 57.

Poets, their language not to be quoted to prove doctrines, 60.

Pope, his precedence not *jure divino*, 28; his authority, how far acknowledged by SS. Jerome and Augustine, 28, 29.

Popular expressions no rules of doctrine, 62.

Possevine, Anthony, admitted that only twenty-one of S. Chrysostom's 'Homilies to the People of Antioch' were genuine, 40.

Prayer, The Book of Common, Andrewes' notes on, 141, 158.
—— *The Lord's*, a question raised in Scotland whether it might be addressed to Saints, 76.

Prayers for the dead an ancient practice, 24.

Predestination, danger of presuming on, 30; no man predestinated to do evil, 30.

Processions used by us in some cases, 31.

Prohibita quia mala distinguished from *mala quia prohibita*, 85.

Promises, wrong, not to be kept, 104, 105. See also *Vows*.

Prosper, S., on predestination, 30.

R.

Ralegh, Sir Walter, one object of his plot said to have been to place Arabella Stuart on the English throne, 102, note ᵘ.

Relics, true, to be reverenced, not worshipped, 22; sometimes had miraculous power, 22.

Reservation of the Sacrament practised in times of persecution, 18; and among hermits, 18; and for the sick, 18; forbidden by Councils of Saragossa and Toledo, 18, 19; this practice abused by Priscillianists, 19.

S.

Sabbath, not to be observed by Christians, 91; made an end of by Christ's Sabbath in the grave, 91; its observers anathematized, 94.

Sacrament not to be adored, 15—17; its symbols not changed in nature, 17; not necessarily to be reserved, 17—19.

Sacraments, the number of five first expressly defined by Peter Lombard, 26, note ˣ; the word Sacrament used by the Fathers in a lax sense, 26; a point not worth disputing, 26.

Sacrifice, The Eucharist a, 19; part of divine worship, 19; offered not to the Father alone, but to the whole Trinity, 50.
—— *of Christ's death*, available for both present, absent, living, and dead, 20; commemorated in the Eucharist, 20.

Saints, what to be understood by their praying for us *ultro*, 61, 62; prayers addressed to them directly, not relatively, in Breviaries, &c. 76—80. See *Invocation*.

INDEX TO MINOR WORKS. 463

Salt not used by us in Baptism, 26.
Saragossa, Council of. See *Council of Saragossa.*
Serapion had the sacrament sent him when sick, 19.
Service not to be said in a low voice, 31.
Seymour, Sir William, his secret marriage with Arabella Stuart, 97, note [a].
Shrewsbury, Mary, Countess of, her refusal to answer the Lords of the Council respecting the marriage of Arabella Stuart, 97, note [a]; her several imprisonments, 97, note [a]; Andrewes's speech against her, 97—105; her vow not to answer, 97, 98, 100, 101; against the ends of justice, 100.
Sixtus Sinensis, quotes the Commentaries on S. Paul as if written by S. Ambrose, 55; said that S. Chrysostom often spoke hyperbolically, 62; quotes Theodoret as denying that the Saints beheld Christ before the resurrection, 75.
Stephen, S., miracles said to be worked by his relics, 22.
Stuart, Arabella, her secret marriage with Sir William Seymour, 97, note [a]; her near connexion with the Crown, 102, note [u]; it is said to have been the intention of Sir Walter Ralegh's plot to place her on the throne, 102, note [u]; King James gave her permission to marry, 102, note [u].
Succession of ministers unbroken in the English Church, 29.
Suffragari and *suffragia,* the meaning of discussed, 57—59.

T.

Tertullian, his testimony to the observance of the Lord's Day, 93; wrote a book, 'De Sabbato Judaico,' now lost, 94; Novatian's treatise, 'De Cibis Judaicis,' quoted as if written by him, 85, 89, 94.
Theodoret denied any change in the substance of the Elements after consecration, 17; whether he wrote the books, 'De curandis Græcorum Affectibus,' 23, 70, 74; Rivet's opinion on the point, 74, note [u]; expressly states that Angels are not to be prayed to, 23, 72—74; denied that Christians worshipped the Martyrs, 69; whether he wrote the 'Religiosa Historia,' 74; his doctrine on the saints departed beholding the presence of Christ, 75.
Theodorus Daphnopates, whether more correctly called *Daphopatus,* 42; at what time he lived, 42, 43; not a schoolmaster, but an historian, 43; made selections from S. Chrysostom's Homilies, 43.
Theodosius, whether his conduct sanctioned the Invocation of Saints, 61.
Toledo, Council of. See *Council of Toledo.*
Torches used at burials, if by night, 31.
Traditions, S. Basil's opinion respecting them, 23.
Traske, John, his history, 83; a list of his works, 84; his Judaical opinions, 85; on distinction of meats, 85—91; on observance of the Sabbath, 91—94.
Trullo, Council in. See *Council in Trullo.*

V.

Velser, Mark, entrusted to Hœschelius the compilation of the Catalogue of the Augsburg Library, 48, note [c].
Vessels, sacred, used by us, 30; form for Consecrating, 159—163.
Vigilantius, his controversy with S. Jerome, 22, 23.
Vows, when made lawfully, 98; to be kept when lawful, 99; the proper matter of a vow, 99; a vow without proper matter is not binding, 103; a vow wrong in itself needs no dispensation, 103, 104; may be broken, 104, 105; Scripture instances of this, 105.
—— of *celibacy* to be kept if duly made, 25.

W.

Washing of the priest's hands, no point to be insisted on, 31.
Water, the mixture of it with wine in the Eucharist, a thing indifferent, 25.

Z.

Zuinglius, Huldrich, quoted S. Augustine as favouring the carnal presence, 13, 14; to avoid '*est*' in the Roman sense was all for *significat,* 14.

THE END.

www.ingramcontent.com/pod-product-compliance
Lightning Source LLC
Chambersburg PA
CBHW052013040526
R18239600001BA/R182396PG44108CBX00013BA/25